HACKERS IELTS 200%
Reading

KB132725

리딩 단어암기 MP3

교재에 수록된 어휘를 언제 어디서나 들으면서 완벽하게 학습할 수 있습니다.

이용방법

해커스인강 사이트(HackersIngang.com) 접속 ▶
상단 메뉴 [IELTS → MP3/자료 → 무료 MP3/자료] 클릭하여 이용하기

리딩 단어암기 MP3 바로 이용하기 ▶

IELTS 리딩/리스닝 실전문제

무료 제공되는 리딩/리스닝 실전문제를 풀고 복습하면서 실력을 키울 수 있습니다.

이용방법

고우해커스 사이트(goHackers.com) 접속 ▶
상단 메뉴 [IELTS → IELTS 리딩/리스닝 풀기] 클릭하여 이용하기

리딩 실전문제 바로 풀어보기 ▶

IELTS 라이팅/스피킹 첨삭 게시판

라이팅/스피킹 무료 첨삭 게시판을 통해 자신의 답안 및 답변을
첨삭받고 보완할 수 있습니다.

이용방법

고우해커스 사이트(goHackers.com) 접속 ▶
상단 메뉴 [IELTS → 라이팅 게시판 또는 스피킹 게시판] 클릭하여 이용하기

라이팅 첨삭 게시판 바로가기 ▶

HACKERS
IELTS Reading으로
목표 점수 달성!

HACKERS IELTS
Reading

ACADEMIC MODULE

해커스 어학연구소

HACKERS
IELTS
READING

goHackers.com

학습자료 제공·유학정보 공유

IELTS 최신 출제 경향을 반영한
『HACKERS IELTS Reading』을 내면서

───────────◯───────────

IELTS 시험은 더 넓은 세상을 향해 꿈을 펼치려는 학습자들이 거쳐 가는 관문으로서, 지금 이 순간에도 많은 학습자들이 IELTS 시험 대비에 소중한 시간과 노력을 투자하고 있습니다. <HACKERS IELTS>는 IELTS 학습자들에게 목표 달성을 위한 가장 올바른 방향을 제시하고자 『HACKERS IELTS Reading』을 출간하게 되었습니다.

유형별 학습을 통한 고득점 달성!

학습자들이 실제 시험에서 출제되는 문제를 유형별로 체계적으로 학습함으로써 보다 수준 높은 독해 실력을 쌓을 수 있도록 구성하였습니다. 또한, 다양한 문제에 대한 유형별 풀이 전략을 제공하였습니다.

최신 경향을 반영한 IELTS 실전 문제로 완벽한 실전 대비 가능!

IELTS 리딩의 최신 경향을 반영한 문제를 수록하였으며, 실제 시험과 동일한 구성의 Actual Test를 통해 실전에 철저히 대비할 수 있도록 하였습니다.

높은 목표 점수 달성을 위한 특별한 자료!

미국 영어와 영국 영어의 차이를 부록으로 구성하였으며, 각 챕터별 필수 어휘를 수록하고 무료 단어 암기 MP3를 제공하였습니다.

『HACKERS IELTS Reading』이 여러분의 IELTS 목표 점수 달성에 확실한 해결책이 되고 영어 실력 향상, 나아가 **여러분의 꿈을 향한 길**에 믿음직한 동반자가 되기를 소망합니다.

HACKERS IELTS READING

CONTENTS

goHackers.com 학습자료 제공·유학정보 공유

TOPIC LIST

다음의 TOPIC LIST는 교재에 수록된 지문을 주제별로 구분하여 목록으로 구성한 것이다.

교재에 수록된 모든 지문은 실제 IELTS Reading 시험의 주제별 출제 경향을 충실히 반영하여 구성되었다. 따라서 교재를 처음부터 끝까지 학습하면서 많이 출제되는 주제가 무엇인지, 자신이 취약한 주제가 무엇인지 파악할 수 있다. 특히 취약하다고 생각되는 주제들을 골라 다시 한 번 풀어보고, 해당 주제의 단어를 외워서 취약점을 보완한다.

Natural Science	Astronomy	Ch 6 HP 10	Ch 10 HP 3
	Biology	Ch 1 HP 5	Ch 2 HP 6
		Ch 3 HP 5	Ch 4 HP 2, 4, 6
		Ch 5 HP 4	Ch 6 HP 4, 6
		Ch 7 HP 1, 3, 7, HT	Ch 8 HP 1, 7, 10
		Ch 9 HP 2, 6	Ch 10 HP 2, 6, HT
		AT [2]	
	Chemistry	Ch 8 HP 2	
	Earth Science	DT [3]	Ch 1 HP 1
		Ch 4 HP 8	Ch 8 HP 3
		Ch 10 HP 8	
	Environment	Ch 2 HP 2	Ch 3 HP 3
		Ch 4 HP 7	Ch 5 HP 7
		Ch 6 HP 8	Ch 7 HP 10
		Ch 9 HT	
	Health	Ch 5 HP 8	Ch 8 HP 9
	Technology	Ch 1 HP 6	Ch 2 HP 3
		Ch 3 HP 9	Ch 4 HP 3, 10
		Ch 5 HT	Ch 9 HP 1, 10
		Ch 10 HP 4, 7	

Social Science	Business	Ch 4 HT	Ch 5 HP 3
		Ch 7 HP 4	Ch 9 HP 4
	Economics	DT [1]	Ch 2 HP 10
		Ch 6 HP 1	Ch 7 HP 2
		Ch 8 HP 4	
	Transportation	Ch 9 HP 3	
Humanities	Anthropology	Ch 1 HP 2, 8	Ch 2 HP 1, HT
		Ch 3 HP 4, 8	Ch 8 HP 6
		Ch 9 HP 8	Ch 10 HP 5
	Architecture	Ch 4 HP 1	Ch 6 HP 9
	Art	Ch 3 HP 6	
	Biography	Ch 2 HP 7	
	Education	DT [2]	Ch 5 HP 6
		Ch 8 HP 5	Ch 10 HP 10
	History	Ch 1 HP 4, 9	Ch 2 HP 4, 9
		Ch 3 HP 2	Ch 4 HP 5
		Ch 6 HP 2, 5, 7	Ch 7 HP 5
		Ch 8 HT	Ch 9 HP 9
		Ch 10 HP 1	AT [1]
	Language	Ch 3 HT	Ch 8 HP 8
	Linguistics	Ch 3 HP 1	Ch 5 HP 10
		Ch 6 HT	Ch 9 HP 5
	Literature	Ch 5 HP 5	Ch 7 HP 5
	Psychology	Ch 1 HP 3, 7, 10, HT	Ch 2 HP 5, 8
		Ch 3 HP 7, 10	Ch 4 HP 9
		Ch 5 HP 2, 9	Ch 6 HP 3
		Ch 7 HP 6, 8	Ch 9 HP 7
		Ch 10 HP 9	AT [3]
	Theatre	Ch 5 HP 1	

* DT: Diagnostic Test   HP: Hackers Practice   HT: Hackers Test   AT: Actual Test

HACKERS IELTS Reading으로
고득점이 가능한 이유!

01 전략적인 학습으로 아이엘츠 리딩 정복!

최신 출제 경향 완벽 반영 및 TOPIC LIST

이 책은 IELTS 리딩의 **최신 출제 경향**을 철저히 분석하여 모든 지문과 문제에 반영하였다. 또한, 교재에 수록된 모든 지문의 TOPIC을 목록으로 제공하여 학습자가 취약한 주제를 골라 공부하는 등 다양하게 활용할 수 있도록 하였다.

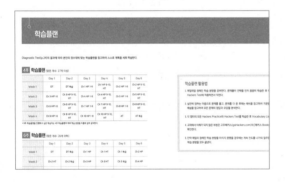

Diagnostic Test 및 4주/6주 학습플랜

실제 IELTS 리딩 시험의 구성 및 난이도와 유사하게 제작된 Diagnostic Test를 통해 학습자가 자신의 실력을 스스로 점검할 수 있도록 하였으며, 이에 따라 수준에 맞는 학습플랜을 활용하여 효과적으로 학습할 수 있도록 4주/6주 학습플랜을 제시하였다.

02 단계적인 학습으로 실력 다지기!

학습자가 단계별 학습을 통해 각 챕터의 문제 유형을 확실하게 체득할 수 있도록 구성하였다.

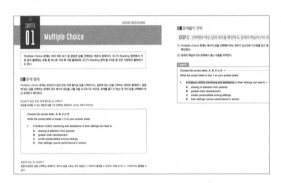

문제 형태 & 문제풀이 전략

문제에 대하여 간략히 소개하고 실제 시험에서는 어떤 형태로 출제되는지 제시하였다. 또한, 각 문제 유형마다 가장 효과적인 전략을 제공하고 적용 사례를 보여주어 실제 문제풀이에 쉽게 활용할 수 있다.

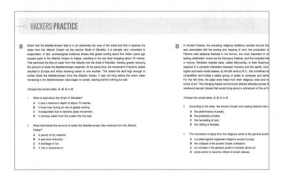

Hackers Practice & Hackers Test

앞서 배운 문제 유형과 문제풀이 전략을 실제 문제 유형과 유사한 다양한 길이의 연습 문제에 적용하여 풀어봄으로써 유형별 집중 학습이 가능하며, 실제 시험에 대한 적응력을 키울 수 있다.

Vocabulary List

각 챕터의 모든 지문으로부터 IELTS 필수 어휘를 선별하고 뜻을 함께 수록하여, 어휘 실력을 효율적으로 쌓을 수 있다.

Actual Test

실제 시험과 유사한 구성과 난이도로 제작된 문제를 제공하여, 실제 시험을 보기 전 자신의 실력을 측정하고, IELTS 리딩 학습을 효과적으로 마무리할 수 있다.

03 정확한 해석 및 해설과 정답의 단서로 실력 UP!

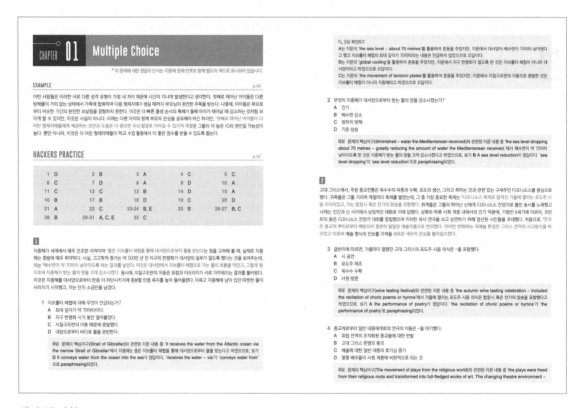

해석 및 어휘

교재에 수록된 모든 지문과 문제의 매끄러운 해석과 중요 어휘를 제공하여 학습자가 보다 정확하게 지문의 흐름을 이해하고 어휘 실력까지 함께 향상할 수 있도록 하였다.

정답의 단서 및 해설

교재에 수록된 모든 문제에 대한 정답의 단서를 상세한 해설과 함께 제공하여 문제에 대한 이해뿐만 아니라 문제 풀이 방법과 전략을 익힐 수 있도록 하였다.

04 해커스만의 다양한 학습 자료 제공!

단어암기 MP3

해커스인강 사이트(HackersIngang.com)에서 교재에 수록된 Vocabulary List의 어휘가 녹음된 무료 **단어암기 MP3**를 다운로드하여 학습 효과를 극대화할 수 있다.

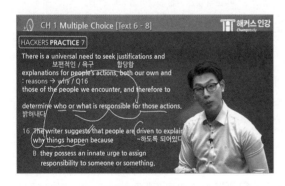

해커스인강(HackersIngang.com)

해커스인강 사이트에서는 **본 교재에 대한 유료 동영상 강의**를 수강할 수 있다. 스타 선생님의 노하우, 점수 공략 비법을 들으며 IELTS 리딩의 최신 경향 및 문제 유형별 전략에 대해 상세히 학습할 수 있다.

고우해커스(goHackers.com)

온라인 토론과 정보 공유의 장인 고우해커스 사이트에서 다른 학습자들과 함께 교재 내용에 대하여 서로 의견을 교류하고 문제를 **토론**할 수 있으며, 다양한 무료 학습자료와 IELTS 시험 및 유학에 대한 풍부한 정보도 얻고 IELTS 문제를 풀 수 있다.

IELTS 소개

■ IELTS란?

IELTS(International English Language Testing System)는 영어를 사용하는 곳에서 일을 하거나 공부를 하고 싶어 하는 사람들의 언어 능력을 측정하는 시험이다. Listening, Reading, Writing, Speaking 영역으로 구성되어 있으며 시험 시간은 약 2시간 55분이다. IELTS의 점수는 1.0부터 9.0까지의 Band라는 단위로 평가된다. 총점은 네 영역 점수의 평균 점수로 낸다.

시험은 두 가지 종류가 있는데, 대학교나 그 이상의 교육 기관으로의 유학 준비를 위한 Academic Module과 영국, 캐나다, 호주로의 이민, 취업, 직업 연수 등을 위한 General Training Module이 있다. Listening과 Speaking 영역의 경우 각 모듈별 문제가 같지만, Reading과 Writing 영역은 모듈별 시험 내용이 다르다.

■ IELTS 구성

시험 영역	출제 지문 및 문항 수	시험 시간	특징
Listening	4개 지문 출제 총 40문항 (지문당 10문항)	30분 (답안 작성 시간 10분 별도)	– 영국식, 호주식, 미국식 등의 발음이 출제 – 10분의 답안 작성 시간이 별도로 주어짐 – 객관식, 주관식, 빈칸 완성, 표 완성 등의 문제가 출제됨
Reading	3개 지문 출제 총 40문항 (지문당 13-14문항)	60분	– 길이가 길고 다양한 구조의 지문 출제 – 객관식, 주관식, 빈칸 완성, 표 완성 등의 문제가 출제됨
	* Academic Module은 저널, 신문기사 등과 같이 학술적인 내용의 지문 위주로 출제되며, General Training Module은 사용설명서, 잡지기사 등과 같이 일상생활과 관련된 지문 위주로 출제됩니다.		
Writing	Task 1: 1문항 Task 2: 1문항	60분	– Task 간의 시간 구분 없이 시험이 진행됨 – Task 1보다 Task 2의 배점이 높음
	* Academic Module의 Task 1은 그래프, 표 등 시각자료를 보고 요약문 쓰기가 과제로 출제되며, General Training Module의 Task 1은 부탁, 초대 등 주어진 목적에 맞게 편지 쓰기가 과제로 출제됩니다. Task 2는 에세이 쓰기 과제가 동일한 형식으로 출제됩니다.		
Speaking	3개 Part로 구성 Part 1: 10-15문항 Part 2: 1문항 Part 3: 4-6문항	11-14분	– 시험관과 1:1 인터뷰 형식으로 진행됨 – 모든 시험 내용이 녹음됨
약 2시간 55분			

▌IELTS 관련 제반 사항

실시일	· Paper-based IELTS는 매달 4회, Computer-delivered IELTS는 매주 최대 6회 시험이 있음
시험 장소	· Paper-based IELTS와 Computer-delivered IELTS는 영국 문화원 또는 IDP 주관 공식 지정 장소에서 치러짐
접수 방법	· Paper-based IELTS는 인터넷 또는 현장(IDP 공식 접수처) 접수 가능 · Computer-delivered IELTS는 인터넷 접수만 가능
시험 당일 준비물	· 신분 확인은 여권으로만 진행되므로 여권 필수 지참 (IDP 이외 경로로 시험을 접수한 경우, 여권 사본도 지참) · Paper-based IELTS로 등록한 경우, 필기구(연필/샤프, 지우개) 지참
성적 및 리포팅	· 성적 발표 소요 기간: 　- Paper-based IELTS는 응시일로부터 13일째 되는 날 　- Computer-delivered IELTS는 응시일로부터 1~2일 사이 · 성적표는 온라인으로 조회 가능하며, 방문 수령(휴일/공휴일 제외) 혹은 우편 수령 가능 · 재채점: 시험 응시일로부터 6주 이내에 4개 영역 중 원하는 영역에 대한 재채점 신청 가능 · IELTS One Skill Retake: Computer-delivered IELTS 응시일로부터 60일 이내에 4개 영역 중 한 영역만 　선택해 재시험 신청 가능 · 리포팅: 전자 성적표를 해외 기관에 보내는 것은 무료 · 성적표 재발급: 출력된 성적표는 시험일로부터 일부 기간만 재발급 가능하며, 일부 부수까지만 무료로 발급할 수 　있음 *재채점, IELTS One Skill Retake, 성적표 재발급에 대한 기한 및 비용 등과 같은 세부 규정은 시험 접수한 기관 홈페이지에서 　확인

▌시험장 Tips

· 입실 시 소지품을 모두 보관소에 맡긴다. 시험실에 들고 가는 필기구와 물병 등에 글씨가 쓰여 있는 경우 수거될 수 있다.
· 입실 전 본인 확인을 위한 사진 촬영과 지문 확인 시간이 있다.
· 감독관의 안내는 영어로 이루어진다.
· 필기 시험은 별도의 쉬는 시간 없이 이어서 진행된다. Paper-based IELTS와 Computer-delivered IELTS 시험 도중에
　화장실에 가야 할 경우 손을 들어 의사를 표시하면, 감독관의 동행하에 화장실을 갈 수 있다.

▓ IELTS Band Score

IELTS 시험은 Band Score로 수험자의 영어 실력을 평가한다. 각 Band Score에 대한 설명은 다음과 같다.

Band Score	숙련도	설명
9	Expert user	완전한 구사력을 갖추고 있고, 영어 사용이 적절하며, 정확하고, 유창하며 완벽한 이해를 보이는 경우
8	Very good user	약간의 부정확성과 부적절한 사용을 보이지만 완전한 구사력을 갖추고 있으며, 낯선 상황에서 잘못 이해할 수는 있으나 복잡하고 상세한 주장을 잘 다루는 경우
7	Good user	구사력을 갖추고 있으며 일부 상황에서 때때로 부정확성, 부적절한 사용, 착오를 보이지만, 전반적으로 복잡한 표현을 잘 다루고 상세한 주장을 이해하는 경우
6	Competent user	부정확성, 부적절한 사용, 착오를 보이지만, 효과적인 구사력을 갖추고 있으며 익숙한 상황에서 상당히 복잡한 표현을 이해하고 사용할 수 있는 경우
5	Modest user	부분적인 구사력을 갖추고 있으며 대부분의 상황에서 전반적인 의미를 이해하지만, 실수를 할 가능성이 높으며 자신의 분야에서는 기본적인 의사소통을 하는 경우
4	Limited user	기본적인 구사력이 익숙한 상황에만 한정되어 있고, 이해와 표현에 있어 자주 문제가 있으며 복잡한 표현을 할 수 없는 경우
3	Extremely limited user	매우 익숙한 상황에서 전반적인 의미만을 전달하고 이해하며, 의사소통에 있어 빈번한 실패를 겪는 경우
2	Intermittent user	영어를 이해하는 것을 매우 어려워하는 경우
1	Non-user	일부 단어를 제외하고 영어를 사용할 수 없는 경우
0	Did not attempt the test	시험 응시자가 문제를 풀지 않은 경우

■ IELTS Band Score 계산법

IELTS 점수는 각 영역에 대한 Band Score가 나오고, 모든 영역의 평균인 Overall 점수가 계산되어 나온다. IELTS 점수를 영어 실력 평가의 기준으로 적용하는 기관들은 각 영역의 개별 점수와 Overall 점수에 대한 다른 정책을 가지고 있으므로, IELTS를 준비하는 목적에 맞게 전략적으로 시험 대비를 해야 한다. 네 영역 중 자신 있는 영역에서 고득점을 받으면 상대적으로 취약한 영역의 점수를 보완할 수 있다는 장점이 있다. 하지만, 영역별 점수의 변동 폭이 크면 Overall 점수에도 영향이 있으므로 각 영역 중 한 영역만 대비해서는 고득점을 받기 어렵다.

아래는 Band Score 계산의 예이다. 네 영역 평균 점수의 소수점에 따라 반올림이 되어, Overall Band Score가 나온다.

	Listening	Reading	Writing	Speaking	네 영역 평균	Overall Band Score
응시자 A	5.5	5.5	4.0	6.0	5.25	5.5
응시자 B	5.0	4.5	5.0	5.0	4.875	5.0
응시자 C	7.5	7.5	6.5	7.0	7.125	7.0

IELTS Reading 소개 및 학습전략

IELTS Reading 영역에서는 다양한 문제 유형을 통해 독해 실력을 측정한다. 이는 주제와 세부사항을 파악하고, 논리적 주장을 이해하는 것 등을 포함한다.

Academic 모듈에서는 대개 책, 잡지, 저널, 신문 등에서 발췌된 다양한 종류의 지문이 출제된다. 학술적인 내용을 다룬 지문이 출제되기도 하지만, 문제에 답하기 위해 해당 지문에 관한 특별한 전문 지식이 필요하지는 않으며 문제를 푸는 데 필요한 모든 정보는 지문에서 찾을 수 있다. 그러나 짧은 시간 내에 긴 지문을 읽고 많은 문제를 풀어야 하므로 지문을 빨리 읽고 정확하게 이해하며 정리하는 능력이 요구된다.

■ IELTS Reading 구성

	문항 수	문항당 배점	시험 시간
지문 1	총 40문항 (지문당 13~14문항)	각 1점	60분
지문 2			
지문 3			

■ IELTS Reading 특이사항

· 매 시험 3지문 중 하나 이상은 저자의 주장을 포함한 논설문으로 출제된다.
· 책, 저널, 잡지, 신문 등 다양한 출처에서 지문이 발췌된다.
· 전문 용어가 등장할 경우 주석이 제공된다.
· 답안 작성 시간은 따로 제공되지 않는다.
· 답안지 상단에 응시하는 모듈(Academic 또는 General Training)을 체크한다.
· 주관식 답안의 경우 철자나 문법이 틀리면 오답 처리가 된다.

▦ IELTS Reading 문제 유형 소개

문제 유형	유형 소개
Multiple Choice	여러 개의 보기 중 알맞은 답을 선택하는 선다형 유형
True/False/Not Given	제시된 문장이 지문의 정보와 일치하는지를 판단하는 유형
Yes/No/Not Given	제시된 문장이 글쓴이의 견해와 일치하는지를 판단하는 유형
Note/Table/Flow-chart/ Diagram Completion	노트/표/순서도/다이어그램의 빈칸에 들어갈 답을 작성하는 주관식 유형
Sentence Completion	문장의 빈칸에 들어갈 답을 지문에서 찾아 적는 주관식 유형 또는 완성되지 않은 문장의 뒤에 들어갈 부분을 주어진 보기 리스트에서 골라 연결하는 선다형 유형
Summary Completion	요약문의 빈칸에 들어갈 답을 지문에서 찾아 적는 주관식 유형 또는 주어진 보기 리스트에서 알맞은 답을 고르는 선다형 유형
Matching Features	문제와 관련된 정보를 여러 개의 보기가 포함된 리스트에서 선택하는 선다형 유형
Matching Information	제시된 정보를 읽고 그 정보를 포함하는 지문의 단락을 선택하는 선다형 유형
Matching Headings	각 단락에 알맞은 제목을 주어진 보기 리스트에서 선택하는 선다형 유형
Short Answer	주어진 질문에 알맞은 답을 지문에서 찾아 적는 주관식 유형

▦ IELTS Reading 학습전략

1. 다양한 주제와 어조의 긴 글을 접한다.

   IELTS Reading 영역에 출제되는 지문들은 출처가 다양하다. 따라서 평소 여러 주제와 어조의 글들을 영어로 많이 읽어 두도록 한다. 영어 신문을 읽거나 잡지를 읽는 등 다양한 출처의 글에 익숙해지는 것이 좋다.

2. 어휘력을 기른다.

   어휘력이 풍부하면 글을 읽는 데 막힘이 없으므로, 평소에 교재에 수록된 어휘를 비롯해 다양한 어휘를 외워 두도록 한다. 어휘 암기 외에도 글에 사용된 어휘 중 익숙하지 않은 것은 주위 문맥을 이용하여 그 뜻을 추측해 보는 연습을 병행하는 것이 좋다.

3. 필요한 정보를 빠르게 찾는 연습을 한다.

   주요 내용만 빠르게 훑는 skimming으로 큰 주제를 신속히 파악하고, scanning을 통해 지문의 세부 사항을 찾는 연습은 독해에 있어 매우 중요하며, 문제 풀이 시간을 단축하는 데 많은 도움이 된다.

4. Paraphrasing 연습을 한다.

   시험에 출제되는 많은 문제들은 지문 속 내용이 paraphrasing된 경우이므로, 한 단어부터 시작해 한 문장, 한 단락 전체를 paraphrasing하는 연습을 해보되, 단순히 어휘만 동의어로 바꾸어 쓰는 것이 아니라 문장 구조까지 바꾸어서 표현해 본다.

SKIMMING & SCANNING

IELTS Reading 영역에서 출제되는 약 10가지의 서로 다른 문제 유형에 걸쳐, 알고 있으면 문제를 푸는 시간을 단축하는 데 도움이 되는 독해 방법을 소개한다. 바로 Skimming & Scanning으로, 모두 속독 방법에 속한다.

SKIMMING

Skimming은 글의 전반적인 개요를 알기 위한 속독 방법이다. Skimming을 함으로써 글이 어떻게 전개되는지 파악할 수 있기 때문에, 글의 주제·목적·제목 등을 묻는 문제를 풀 때 유용하다. Skimming은 글의 핵심 내용을 짧은 시간 안에 파악할 수 있게 하는 독해 방법이므로, 제한된 시간 안에 긴 글을 읽어야 할 때 특히 유용하게 쓰일 수 있다.

IELTS Reading 지문과 같은 긴 글을 Skimming할 때는 다음과 같은 사항을 숙지하여 두면 좋다.

· 제목과 부제는 글에 대한 가장 간단한 요약이므로, Skimming을 시작하기 전 먼저 읽어두면 글의 주제를 알기 쉽다.
· 지문의 첫 1~2 단락에는 글의 전반적인 주제가 소개되는 경우가 많으므로, 첫 1~2 단락을 읽으면 나머지 단락의 중심 내용을 이해하는 데 도움이 된다.
· 단락의 첫 부분에는 대개 중심 문장이 등장하므로, 각 단락의 첫 부분을 읽으면 그 단락의 중심 내용을 파악할 수 있다.
· 단어 하나 하나를 정확하게 이해하고 해석하려고 하기보다는, 글의 흐름을 이해하는 것에 중점을 두고 읽어야 시간을 단축할 수 있다.

SCANNING

Scanning은 글에 포함되어 있는 세부 사항을 찾아내기 위한 속독 방법이다. Scanning은 글의 주제나 목적보다는 특정한 세부 정보를 묻는 문제를 풀 때 유용하다. 따라서 Scanning을 할 때에는 글의 핵심 내용을 포함하고 있는 부분이더라도 문제와 관련이 없다면 생략하고 넘어갈 수도 있다.

IELTS Reading 지문과 같은 긴 글을 Scanning할 때는 다음과 같은 사항을 숙지하여 두면 좋다.

· 지문에서 어떤 정보를 찾아야 하는지 정확히 파악한다.
· 찾아야 하는 정보가 지문에서 어떤 형태로 등장할지 예상한다. 예를 들어, 특정 사람에 관한 정보는 그 사람의 성, 이름뿐 아니라 인칭대명사(He, She 등)로도 등장할 수 있다.
· Skimming을 통해 먼저 글의 전체적인 흐름을 파악해 두면 문제에서 묻는 정보를 찾아야 하는 범위가 줄어들기 때문에 시간을 단축할 수 있다.

SKIMMING & SCANNING 적용 예시

The Most Significant Theories of Social Change
Various theories which attempt to explain how societies develop.

Sociologists have argued over how social change occurs for centuries, with many suggesting that change is always economic in nature, whilst others claim that culture is more significant. The contemporary debate focuses on how societies become more or less wealthy, and how this influences change.

Economic theories of social change were particularly prevalent in the early years of the 20th century, and they tended to focus on the way in which different economic classes come into conflict. Theorists focused on how clashes between workers and managers over working conditions or pay could lead to more widespread changes in society.

However, perhaps the most influential idea of social change was put forward by the 19th century German philosopher Georg Wilhelm Friedrich Hegel. He suggested that two opposing forces will eventually come together in a new synthesis, which combines elements of both sides … (중략)

Skimming 적용 예시

*Choose the correct letter, **A**, **B**, **C** or **D**.*

1 The main topic discussed in the text is

  A how social change has been depicted by writers.

  B the impact of social change in particular societies.

  C the way in which theories of social change differ.

  D why academics reject the idea of social change.

> 지문의 주제를 묻는 문제이므로, Skimming을 통해 글의 주제를 파악한다. 지문의 제목과 부제를 통해 지문이 '사회가 발달한 방법에 관한 다양한 이론들'임을 알 수 있다. 첫 번째 단락에서 사회 변화의 원인으로 언급되는 두 가지를 언급한 뒤, 두 번째 단락과 세 번째 단락의 첫 문장에서 사회 변화에 대한 서로 다른 이론들을 소개하고 있으므로, 지문의 주제가 '사회 변화 이론들이 어떻게 서로 다른지'임을 알 수 있다. 따라서 보기 C the way in which theories of social change differ가 정답이다.

Scanning 적용 예시

*Choose **NO MORE THAN TWO WORDS** from the passage for the answer.*

2 When did the German philosopher Hegel write his theories of social change? 19th century

> 독일 철학자 Hegel이 이론을 제시한 시기를 묻는 문제이므로, Scanning을 통해 Hegel과 관련된 세부 정보를 확인한다. 'German philosopher Hegel'이 언급된 세 번째 단락의 내용 중 'the most influential idea of social change was put forward by the 19th century German philosopher Georg Wilhelm Friedrich Hegel'에서 가장 영향력 있는 사회 변화 이론은 19세기에 독일 철학자인 헤겔에 의해 제시되었다고 하였으므로, 19th century가 정답이다.

학습플랜

Diagnostic Test(p.24)의 결과에 따라 본인의 점수대에 맞는 학습플랜을 참고하여 스스로 계획을 세워 학습한다.

4주 학습플랜 (맞은 개수: 27개 이상)

	Day 1	Day 2	Day 3	Day 4	Day 5	Day 6
Week 1	DT	DT 복습	Ch 1 HP 1-8	Ch1 HP 9-10, HT	Ch 2 HP 1-8	Ch 2 HP 9-10, HT
Week 2	Ch 3 HP1-8	Ch 3 HP 9-10, HT	Ch 4 HP 1-8	Ch 4 HP 9-10, HT	Ch 5 HP 1-8	Ch 5 HP 9-10, HT
Week 3	Ch 6 HP1-8	Ch 6 HP 9-10, HT	Ch 7 HP 1-8	Ch 7 HP 9-10, HT	Ch 8 HP 1-8	Ch 8 HP 9-10, HT
Week 4	Ch 9 HP1-8	Ch 9 HP 9-10, HT	Ch 10 HP 1-8	Ch 10 HP 9-10, HT	AT	AT 복습

* 8주 학습플랜을 진행하고 싶은 학습자는 4주 학습플랜의 하루 학습 분량을 이틀에 걸쳐 공부한다.

6주 학습플랜 (맞은 개수: 26개 이하)

	Day 1	Day 2	Day 3	Day 4	Day 5	Day 6
Week 1	DT	DT 복습	Ch 1 HP	Ch 1 HT	Ch 1 복습	Ch 2 HP
Week 2	Ch 2 HT	Ch 2 복습	Ch 3 HP	Ch 3 HT	Ch 3 복습	Ch 4 HP
Week 3	Ch 4 HT	Ch 4 복습	Ch 5 HP	Ch 5 HT	Ch 5 복습	Ch 1-5 복습
Week 4	Ch 6 HP	Ch 6 HT	Ch 6 복습	Ch 7 HP	Ch 7 HT	Ch 7 복습
Week 5	Ch 8 HP	Ch 8 HT	Ch 8 복습	Ch 9 HP	Ch 9 HT	Ch 9 복습
Week 6	Ch 10 HP	Ch 10 HT	Ch 10 복습	Ch 6-10 복습	AT	AT 복습

* DT: Diagnostic Test   HP: Hackers Practice   HT: Hackers Test   AT: Actual Test

학습플랜 활용법

1. 매일매일 정해진 학습 분량을 공부한다. 문제풀이 전략을 먼저 꼼꼼히 학습한 후 이를 Hackers Practice와 Hackers Test에 적용하면서 익힌다.

2. 실전에 임하는 마음으로 문제를 풀고, 문제를 다 푼 후에는 해석을 참고하여 지문을 정독하고 정답의 단서와 해설을 참고하여 모든 문제의 정답과 오답을 분석한다.

3. 각 챕터의 모든 Hackers Practice와 Hackers Test를 학습한 후 Vocabulary List를 학습하여 마무리한다.

4. 교재에서 이해가 되지 않은 부분은 고우해커스(goHackers.com)의 [해커스 Books > 리딩 Q&A]를 이용하여 확인한다.

5. 만약 매일의 정해진 학습 분량을 마치지 못했을 경우에는 계속 진도를 나가되 일주일이 지나기 전에 해당 주의 학습 분량을 모두 끝낸다.

HACKERS
IELTS
READING

goHackers.com

학습자료 제공·유학정보 공유

DIAGNOSTIC TEST

* Answer sheet는 교재 마지막 페이지(p.299)에 수록되어 있습니다.

READING PASSAGE 1

*You should spend about 20 minutes on **Questions 1-13**, which are based on Reading Passage 1 on the following pages.*

Questions 1-6

Reading Passage 1 has seven paragraphs, **A-G**.

*Choose the correct heading for paragraphs **B-G** from the list of headings below.*

*Write the correct number, **i-ix**, in boxes 1-6 on your answer sheet.*

List of Headings
i   Implications of foreign investors avoiding regulations
ii   Government investment leads to jobs for locals
iii   The impact of tourism on real estate prices
iv   Competition presents challenges for local businesses
v   The problem of unequal income
vi   Non-economic consequences for communities
vii   Tourism as a fast way to grow the economy
viii   Widespread degradation of the environment
ix   Impact of neglecting the development of other industries

Example	Answer
Paragraph **A**	**vii**

1   Paragraph **B**

2   Paragraph **C**

3   Paragraph **D**

4   Paragraph **E**

5   Paragraph **F**

6   Paragraph **G**

Tourism Development: A Blessing or a Curse?

A   In developing countries, collectively referred to as the Global South, tourism is seen as a fast and effective means of economic development. This is especially true for countries that lack exportable natural resources, but possess plenty of natural attractions, such as beaches, mountains, lush forests, and jungles. As a means of maximising the economic benefits for their citizens, such countries are encouraged to capitalise on these attractions by promoting tourism and developing a suitable tourist infrastructure. Many countries are taking up this opportunity and there has been a noticeable tendency for developing nations to invest heavily in expanding their tourism industries.

B   In reality, however, tourism can cause extensive damage to the natural world. It can therefore bring more harm than good to the communities it is supposed to serve. Ecotourism, for example, is designed to take advantage of a locale's natural beauty to attract 'green' travellers, but ironically the environment is often sacrificed to accommodate them. Every year, hordes of tourists flock to St. Lucia to take in its gorgeous scenery, scuba dive among the coral reefs in its clear waters, and explore the rainforests of the island's interior. While well-managed scuba diving trips and excursions into the rainforest may not directly disturb the native wildlife and flora, the resorts built to accommodate eco-tourists have caused significant increases in beach erosion, and the demand for boating transport has resulted in the loss of mangrove swamps and increased pollution of the marine environment (Nagle, 1999).

C   Another problem is the income disparity that almost always occurs as a result of tourism in underdeveloped nations. It starts with governments investing heavily in infrastructure such as roads, airports, public transportation and the like. The money to fund these projects comes out of taxpayers' wallets, with the idea that the investment will create jobs and opportunities for the local population, but that is rarely the case. Contracts to build hotels, resorts, parks, and restaurants are often given to wealthy businesspeople who exploit local laborers in order to increase profit margins. Then, when the establishments open, the same pattern occurs with hired staff who work for wages barely above the minimum wage. Thus, the rich get richer while the increasing wealth gap forces the lower socioeconomic classes into deeper poverty.

D   Moreover, overseas investors make it impossible for small, local businesses to compete. International chains are the first in line to bid for spaces on beachfront property in almost every country of the world. They pay premium prices to secure their stronghold in developing tourist sectors. This has happened in Costa Rica, where foreign individuals or companies own 65 per cent of hotels in the country. Therefore, although tourism constitutes around 12.5 per cent of Costa Rica's GDP, local businesses have not benefited from this thriving industry.

E   These trends affect the private real estate market as well. Once a place becomes popular with foreigners, there's a rush to purchase vacation homes, dramatically increasing property values and displacing the native inhabitants. This is evident to anyone who has travelled along the coast of Spain or to any of the Greek islands. A San Francisco State University study on Belize revealed that as a result of tourism development, local prices have increased overall by around 8 per cent in the past decade alone. Some countries, such as Thailand, have made foreign direct ownership of property illegal, which has alleviated some of these effects. However, even with such rigid regulations, people still find a way to evade the laws by coordinating with Thai citizens or businesses to purchase property. In the end, an inflated real estate market is inevitable, as are increases in other basic costs such as food, water, clothing, and daily necessities.

F Regardless of who is making the profits, though, local populations become dependent on the influx of tourist cash, despite the hazards. In Gambia, for instance, 30 per cent of the workforce depends directly or indirectly on tourism, and in the Maldives, this figure is a striking 83 per cent. When a substantial quantity of available jobs revolves around tourism, countries often neglect developing other sectors that could decrease that dependency. While this may not seem problematic, it quickly becomes so when unforeseen events threaten the stability of a country and scare off tourists. This has happened to Thailand several times over the past decade, with both civil unrest and natural disasters resulting in recessions caused by dramatic decreases in tourism.

G Economics aside, there are also social consequences of high growth tourism for local communities; along with foreign influences can come unwelcome behaviour and activities. This can simply be undesirable habits or mannerisms that contradict local customs. But it can also be more serious, such as increases in drug use, alcohol abuse, and petty crime, all of which often accompany tourism. Even if locals don't participate directly in such misconduct, they are bound to be adversely affected by a rise in criminality, and will often report a decline in their sense of personal security and quality of life because of it. Thus, the development of a tourism industry can be a mixed blessing, bringing developing countries an influx of investment, visitors from around the world, and a variety of intractable problems. Governments in these countries must do their best to effectively regulate and manage tourism, so that the benefits can be widespread, and the negative effects can be avoided or minimised.

Questions 7 and 8

*Choose the correct letter, **A**, **B**, **C** or **D**.*

Write the correct letter in boxes 7 and 8 on your answer sheet.

7   One way that people have avoided strict regulations is by

    A   paying additional fees to government agencies.

    B   buying property with the help of local citizens.

    C   promising to invest in local infrastructure.

    D   guaranteeing good jobs to local residents.

8   When a large number of jobs are dependent on tourism, countries tend to

    A   invest heavily in other areas to create a balanced economy.

    B   grow concerned about the possibility of social instability.

    C   ignore the development of other sectors.

    D   increase the wages of citizens working in the tourist industry.

Questions 9-13

*Complete the summary using the list of words, **A-I**, below.*

*Write the correct letter, **A-I**, in boxes 9-13 on your answer sheet.*

Tourism for Economic Development

Tourism can be a fast and effective way for developing countries to expand their economies. Many of these countries are urged to take advantage of the **9** .... within their natural environment. However, it is unclear whether the development of tourism is the panacea that it is alleged to be; in certain cases the problems it causes for local **10** .... outweigh its benefits. Whilst developing the conditions for a local tourism industry is often funded by **11** ...., it is not necessarily the case that they will see any profits. It is **12** .... that hurry to buy coastal property, and they are willing to pay large amounts of money for a dominant position in the tourist industry. Moreover, influences from outside the country can also lead to behaviour that goes against the **13** .... of the local people.

A taxpayers	**B** infrastructure	**C** valuable materials
D customs	**E** international chains	**F** communities
G attractions	**H** industries	**I** uneven development

READING PASSAGE 2

*You should spend about 20 minutes on **Questions 14-26**, which are based on Reading Passage 2 below.*

Parental Involvement in Children's Education

At the most fundamental level, education is a human undertaking. It requires people and real human interaction. When we think of a child's education, the first people who come to mind are schoolteachers, and the importance of their role cannot be overstated. But what of the role of parents in children's education? At home, parental involvement can include everything from general encouragement to actively tutoring children. Furthermore, parents can also lend their support to schools in many ways, such as attending school functions, helping with school activities or serving as school governors or administrators. Does this parental involvement have a measurable effect on student outcomes? If so, what are the results of their involvement?

Extensive research has clearly demonstrated the positive benefit of parental involvement when it comes to academic achievement. Students of parents who engage directly with their children in the early years of childhood education show especially strong results (Cotton and Wikelund, 1989). In other words, the earlier parental involvement occurs, the more likely children are to have tremendous academic success. In the US, the National Head Start Impact Study collected detailed data on 5,000 children from kindergarten to 3rd grade. The Head Start programme provided comprehensive early childhood development services to low-income families, and actively encouraged parental involvement. The study collected student data measuring school readiness, language use and literacy, as well as cognition and general knowledge. Over the course of three years, the data definitively established a strong correlation between parental monitoring of school-related assignments, parental involvement in school activities, and academic performance. Though the long-term effectiveness of such programmes has been called into question, even critics such as psychologist Todd Wisley have noted that continued parental involvement is crucial for children's success.

Similarly, the connection between the extent of parental engagement and a child's attitude and behaviour in school was highlighted as early as 1973 when child development psychologist Walter Emmerlich posited that constructive parent interaction enhances their children's attitudes toward learning and gives them a more positive outlook on life. Since then, researchers have conducted in-depth analyses of such criteria as classroom behaviour, peer interactions, self-concept, motivation, and general socio-emotional functioning. Unlike academic achievement, however, in which parental help with studies and instruction was clearly the primary factor, there is no obvious form of involvement that stands out as contributing to improvements in attitude and behaviour. Thus, it seems that all forms of involvement contribute equally, and it is no surprise that schools which offer the greatest variety of opportunities for parental involvement see the most positive impact in this regard.

Even though parental involvement is widely encouraged both in school systems and in literature produced by education experts, it is not without controversy. Some educational professionals question whether it can go too far, and this sentiment is particularly common when it comes to parental involvement in school governance and administration. David Hart, the general secretary of the National Association of Head Teachers in the UK, has suggested that governing bodies in Britain are overloaded with parents, many of whom are unqualified for the job. Hart declared that parents were often too focused on the needs of their own children to think of the greater good when it came to governance. Nevertheless, polls consistently show that many parents would like to play a more active role in school affairs – whether it is through becoming a school governor or a member of a parental advisory committee or school improvement council.

In contrast, school administrators and teachers tend to support Hart's negative opinion of parents taking an active role; they continually demonstrate great reluctance to allow parents to get involved with goal setting, personnel decisions, assessment, and how to allocate funding. They point out that parents generally lack the training and capability to make decisions related to school administration and governance. Educational literature sometimes supports their view: some mainstream studies claim that parental involvement in school governance has no obvious correlation with increased academic achievement or improvements in student attitude and behaviour. Karen Reed Wikelund has pointed out that in half a dozen studies that addressed the link between parental involvement in school decision making, none could conclusively prove a causal relationship between it and student achievement. And Marylin Bruckman has argued that many early childhood educators have negative views of parental involvement in general, implying that some educators may have an adverse impact on family involvement.

Still, exceptions exist. In New Haven, Connecticut, the School Development Programme (SDP) started by James Comer of Yale University revealed that parents could provide meaningful contributions at all levels – whether it be at home, in the classroom, or school administration. He sought to 'change the ecology' of education by instituting a programme of electing parents to school planning and management teams, where they made substantial decisions along with teachers, the principal, and support staff. The SDP helped radically transform two of the worst-performing inner-city schools in Connecticut, and as many as 120 other inner-city schools have subsequently followed suit using his model. Comer's example proves that parents can play a constructive role within schools if an appropriate framework exists, which allows parents and teachers to work together constructively in getting the best for children.

Questions 14-17

Look at the following statements and the list of researchers below.

*Match each statement with the correct researcher, **A-E**.*

*Write the correct letter, **A-E**, in boxes 14-17 on your answer sheet.*

14 claimed that parents in administration tend to put the needs of their own children before others

15 proposed a connection between parental encouragement and children's views on education

16 argued that there was no evidence linking parental involvement in school decisions and student success

17 instituted a programme of parental participation in school decision making

List of Researchers
A   Karen Reed Wikelund
B   Walter Emmerlich
C   James Comer
D   Marylin Bruckman
E   David Hart

Questions 18-21

Complete the sentences below.

*Choose **NO MORE THAN TWO WORDS** from the passage for each answer.*

Write your answers in boxes 18-21 on your answer sheet.

18 Parents can support schools by becoming school .... and serving on administrative committees.

19 Early parental involvement increases the likelihood of great .... among children.

20 The most beneficial approach is for schools to provide diverse .... for parents to participate.

21 A decision school administrators do not want parents to get involved in is the allocation of ....

Do the following statements agree with the information given in Reading Passage 2?

In boxes 22-26 on your answer sheet, write

> **TRUE**　　　　*if the statement agrees with the information*
> **FALSE**　　　*if the statement contradicts the information*
> **NOT GIVEN**　*if there is no information on this*

22　Parental involvement tends to have more of an effect on older students than younger students.

23　Different types of parental involvement produce different results in attitude and behaviour.

24　Polls show that mothers are generally more likely to play a part in school affairs than fathers.

25　Research suggests that educators may have a negative effect on parental participation in schools.

26　The School Development Programme helped to revolutionise some urban schools.

READING PASSAGE 3

*You should spend about 20 minutes on **Questions 27-40**, which are based on Reading Passage 3 below.*

The Snowball Earth Hypothesis

Analysing the theory that Earth was once a giant ice-covered snowball

A debate has been raging among scientists about the plausibility of the 'snowball Earth' hypothesis, which posits that the Earth was once completely covered in ice and snow. If this theory is true, it could explain many geological mysteries, but some claim the planet could not have recovered from such a deep freeze.

Imagine an Earth entirely covered by ice, from the poles to the equator, where little to no life survives and temperatures are perpetually far below zero. That is the proposition of the 'snowball Earth' hypothesis. This is a contentious theory that suggests that the Earth was entirely frozen for at least one period in its history, and scientists are divided on how to interpret the geological record and the debate over the hypothesis is ongoing.

According to proponents of the theory this deep freeze occurred over 650 million years ago in at least one of three periods, the Neoproterozoic, the Palaeoproterozoic or the Karoo Ice Age. Scientists are however divided on both the geological evidence and the likelihood of Earth reviving, and fostering life, after such a period, as well as when exactly this could have taken place. Proponents nevertheless suggest that the theory explains some of the mysteries of the geological record.

The first geologist to put forward the idea of a snowball Earth was Douglas Mawson who discovered glacial sediments in southern Australia in the mid-20th century, which he took as evidence of global glaciation. However, this theory was superseded by the idea of continental drift, which more readily explained the existence of glaciers in Australia and other landmasses. The snowball Earth theory was revived in the 1960s by W. Brian Harland who suggested that glacial sediments in Greenland were actually deposited nearer to the tropics. According to Harland, the only thing that could account for these deposits was an extreme, worldwide ice age.

It was not until the 1990s that Joseph Kirschvink, a Professor of geobiology, coined the term 'snowball Earth' to describe this ice age. Kirschvink also proposed an ultra-greenhouse effect as a way in which the Earth may have escaped from this glacial condition. Kirschvink's ideas were taken up by Franklyn Van Houten, who stated that phosphorus deposits and banded iron formations proved that the Earth had once been ice-covered.

According to proponents of the snowball Earth hypothesis, there are several ways in which both the geological record and climate models support the theory. The most persuasive is perhaps the evidence of palaeomagnetism, a recent development in geology which can show when and where geological deposits were made, whilst taking into account continental drift. Through palaeomagnetism it has been possible to show that sediments of glacial origin were deposited near to the equator during the Neoproterozoic era. However scientists are sceptical of this conclusion due to other plausible explanations, such as the possibility that the Earth's magnetic field has shifted over time and the existence of an earlier magnetic pole near the equator which could account for these deposits.

The snowball Earth hypothesis has also been challenged on the grounds that glacial deposits could be accounted for by continents breaking up and causing a tectonic uplift, which would create extremely high plateaus where glaciers could potentially form. This theory of continental separation has been proposed by Nicholas Eyles, Professor of Geology at the University of Toronto, as the 'Zipper Rift hypothesis'. In this scenario, the separation of continents creates these high plateaus where glaciations occur, thus limiting the snowball effect to certain areas of the planet.

As Eyles' research suggests, one of the main points of contention of the snowball Earth debate is the extent to which this big freeze took hold across the planet. Many geologists and climate scientists claim that a 'hard snowball' effect, in which the planet is completely enveloped in ice sheets, would have obliterated life on Earth forever. They thus say that the most likely scenario was a partial freeze, in which some parts of the ocean remained free of ice.

The lack of a mass extinction event in the geological record proves that the snowball Earth was more temperate than some claim. They argue that carbon dioxide built up during the cold period, when vegetation was reduced and could not remove as much of it from the atmosphere. In turn, the carbon dioxide warmed the planet, leading to widespread thawing and release of water into the soil. Francis Macdonald, an Earth scientist at Harvard University, who has carried out research into volcanic rocks in Canada that suggested that the global glaciation did indeed occur, has suggested that in fact Earth wasn't 'just a white ball, but more of a mud ball' during this period.

This idea of a 'mud ball' rather than a snowball has gained many adherents among geologists. Richard Peltier of the University of Toronto says, 'The suggestion that the Earth was once entirely covered by ice – the continents by thick ice sheets and the oceans by thick sea ice – remains somewhat contentious'. Peltier created a climate model which suggests what actually occurred during the Neoproterozoic era was a 'negative feedback reaction', in which the Earth oscillated between

'glaciations and de-glaciations'.

Peltier's model demonstrated that despite deep glaciations across the planet, a large amount of water remained unfrozen in the tropical regions of the planet. This has been termed the 'slushball Earth' hypothesis, and it is supported by many who cite the survival of life during this period as evidence of a less extensive global freeze. If the slushball Earth hypothesis is true then a band of ice-free waters would have persisted around the equator; most experts now agree that this was the most probable situation.

The debate over the snowball Earth hypothesis seems to continue, although it is clear that some form of glaciation did occur. The idea of a completely frozen Earth nonetheless remains a thriving area of research, not only for geology but also for climate science. A recent study by Linda Sohl of Columbia University revealed how climate models using the snowball Earth theory can offer insight into future climate change, and the potential repercussions of catastrophic global climate shifts. As Sohl states, 'Studying snowball Earth glaciations can tell us just how bad it can get, in which case life as we know it would probably not survive'.

Do the following statements agree with the views of the writer in Reading Passage 3?

In boxes 27-31 on your answer sheet, write

> **YES**   *if the statement agrees with the views of the writer*
> **NO**   *if the statement contradicts the views of the writer*
> **NOT GIVEN**   *if it is impossible to say what the writer thinks about this*

27   Scientists agree the snowball Earth occurred in the Palaeoproterozoic era.

28   Climate models developed in the 20th century led to theories about paleomagnetism.

29   Some experts believe that if Earth had been totally enclosed in ice, life would have been permanently erased.

30   The 'slushball Earth' hypothesis shows how life evolved on Earth.

31   Linda Sohl showed that the snowball Earth model can teach us about climate change.

Questions 32–36

*Choose the correct letter, **A**, **B**, **C** or **D**.*

Write the correct letter in boxes 32-36 on your answer sheet.

32   In the first paragraph, the writer suggests that the 'snowball Earth' hypothesis

    A   has changed how geologists understand the formation of glaciers.

    B   is an experimental theory that has caused widespread confusion.

    C   has changed how scientists understand the origins of the planet.

    D   is a theory which has prompted extensive debate.

33   The writer says that scientists oppose the snowball Earth theory because

    A   it shows that climate change is not man-made.

    B   banded iron formations disprove it.

    C   there are other reasonable explanations.

    D   the theory of continental drift explains the evidence better.

34   The Zipper rift hypothesis suggests that

    A   continents moving apart created conditions for glaciers to appear.

    B   the snowball effect extended to every area of the planet.

    C   extremely high plateaus allowed life to survive during the snowball period.

    D   earthquakes caused the formation of glaciers.

35   What confirmed that the snowball Earth was warmer than some maintain?

    A   A new climate model developed at a university

    B   An absence of evidence for a mass extinction

    C   Carbon dioxide samples taken from sea ice

    D   Vegetation patterns in the geological record

36   The writer suggests that Richard Peltier's climate model proves

    A   the Earth was a mud ball rather than a snowball.

    B   the equator remained frozen throughout the snowball Earth period.

    C   life on Earth survived in spite of a negative feedback reaction.

    D   the water close to the tropics remained unfrozen.

Complete the summary below.

Choose **NO MORE THAN TWO WORDS** from the passage for each answer.

Write your answers in boxes 37-40 on your answer sheet.

The History of the Snowball Earth Theory

The snowball Earth hypothesis was first put forward by Douglas Mawson, who found 37 .... in southern Australia. This prompted him to theorise that the entire planet had at one point been covered in ice. However, 38 .... was proposed to explain existence of glaciers in Australia and other landmasses and Mawson's ideas were forgotten. W. Brian Harland brought the snowball Earth hypothesis back to prominence when he proposed that glaciers found in Greenland were originally deposited in the 39 .... due to a global freeze. This was reiterated by Joseph Kirschvink, who invented the term 'snowball Earth', and Franklyn Van Houten, whose discovery of phosphorus deposits and banded 40 .... formations provided evidence for the hypothesis.

정답·해석·해설 p.304

CHAPTER 01
Multiple Choice

Multiple choice 문제는 여러 개의 보기 중 알맞은 답을 선택하는 객관식 문제이다. IELTS Reading 영역에서 가장 많이 출제되는 유형 중 하나로 거의 매 시험 출제되며, IELTS Reading 영역 총 3지문 중 모든 지문에서 출제되기도 한다.

■ 문제 형태

Multiple choice 문제는 완성되지 않은 문장 뒤에 들어갈 답을 선택하거나, 질문에 맞는 답을 선택하는 형태로 출제된다. 질문에 맞는 답을 선택하는 문제의 경우 복수의 정답을 고를 것을 요구하기도 하므로, 문제를 풀기 전 항상 몇 개의 답을 선택해야 하는 문제인지 확인한다.

완성되지 않은 문장 뒤에 들어갈 답 선택하기
문장을 완성할 수 있는 알맞은 답을 1개 선택하는 문제이다. 보기는 4개가 주어진다.

---

*Choose the correct letter, **A**, **B**, **C** or **D**.*

Write the correct letter in boxes 1-3 on your answer sheet.

1   A firstborn child's mentoring and assistance of their siblings can lead to

    A   sharing of attention from parents.

    B   greater brain development.

    C   similar personalities among siblings.

    D   their siblings' poorer performance in school.

                     ⋮

질문에 맞는 답 선택하기
질문에 알맞은 답을 선택하는 문제이다. 복수의 답을 고르는 경우 정답은 2~5개까지 출제될 수 있으며, 이때 보기는 5~10개까지도 출제될 수 있다.

---

*Choose the correct letter, **A**, **B**, **C** or **D**.*

Write the correct letter in boxes 1-3 on your answer sheet.

1   What is said about The Land Bridge Theory?

    A   It ignores the earlier presence of the Clovis people.

    B   It originated in Spain during the 16th century.

    C   It is not supported by the archaeological record.

    D   It is rejected by the majority of modern experts.

                     ⋮

■ 문제풀이 전략

STEP 1   선택해야 하는 답의 개수를 확인하고, 문제의 핵심어구와 내용을 파악한다.

(1) Multiple choice 문제는 복수의 답을 선택해야 하는 경우가 있으므로 지시문을 읽고 몇 개의 답을 선택하는 문제인지 미리 확인한다.

(2) 문제의 핵심어구와 문제에서 묻는 내용을 파악한다.

EXAMPLE

*Choose the correct letter, **A**, **B**, **C** or **D**.* ●

Write the correct letter in box 1 on your answer sheet.

1   A firstborn child's mentoring and assistance of their siblings can lead to ●

    A   sharing of attention from parents.

    B   greater brain development.

    C   similar personalities among siblings.

    D   their siblings' poorer performance in school.

(1) 지시문을 읽고 한 개의 답을 고르는 문제임을 확인한다.

(2) 문제의 핵심어구인 A firstborn child's mentoring and assistance가 무엇으로 이어질 수 있는지를 묻고 있음을 파악한다.

지문을 scanning하여 문제의 핵심어구와 관련된 내용을 찾는다. 관련 내용이 언급된 주변에서 정답의 단서를 확인한다.

EXAMPLE

Some believe that these differing personality types occur because of differences in families over time. Firstborn children join families with few other distractions and they receive their parents' full attention until their next sibling arrives. Later, children do not get to experience a similar period of undivided attention from their parents. This may make it seem that the benefits of higher birth order decrease when a second child is born, but this is not true. While they must now share parental attention with another child, [1]the mentoring and assistance that firstborn children provide to their younger siblings can lead to more substantial development of the brain – likely the cause of their higher IQs. Furthermore, this helps younger siblings achieve better grades in academic coursework.

문제의 핵심어구인 **A firstborn child's mentoring and assistance**와 관련된 내용을 지문에서 찾는다. 관련 내용이 언급된 주변에서 'the mentoring and assistance that firstborn children provide to their younger siblings can lead to more substantial development of the brain'이라는 정답의 단서를 확인한다.

*Choose the correct letter, **A**, **B**, **C** or **D**.*

Write the correct letter in box 1 on your answer sheet.

1 A firstborn child's mentoring and assistance of their siblings can lead to

   A sharing of attention from parents.

   B greater brain development.

   C similar personalities among siblings.

   D their siblings' poorer performance in school.

지문 해석 p.316

✓ **TIPS**

Multiple choice 문제에서는 간혹 지문의 주제/목적/제목 등의 중심 내용을 묻는 문제가 출제되기도 한다. 중심 내용을 묻는 문제는 주로 아래와 같이 출제된다.

– **The main topic discussed in the text is ~** 지문에서 논의되는 주제는 ~이다.
– **What is the writer's (overall) purpose in Reading Passage 1?** Reading Passage 1에서 글쓴이의 (전반적인) 의도는 무엇인가?
– **What is the best title for Reading Passage 1?** Reading Passage 1에 가장 알맞은 제목은 무엇인가?

중심 내용을 묻는 문제의 경우, 지문을 읽으며 중심 내용을 나타내는 주제 문장을 찾는다. 주제 문장은 1~2 문단에 있는 경우도 있으나, 지문 전체를 skimming해야 알 수 있는 경우도 있다. *(skimming 기법은 p.18을 참고)

STEP 3 알맞은 보기를 선택한다.

각 보기를 읽고 정답의 단서가 바르게 paraphrasing된 보기를 정답으로 선택한다. 답안을 작성한 후에는 선택한 답을 답안지에 바르게 작성했는지 확인한다.

EXAMPLE

*Choose the correct letter, **A**, **B**, **C** or **D**.*

Write the correct letter in box 1 on your answer sheet.

1   A firstborn child's mentoring and assistance of their siblings can lead to

   A   sharing of attention from parents.

   B   greater brain development.

   C   similar personalities among siblings.

   D   their siblings' poorer performance in school.

---

1   지문 내용 중 'the mentoring and assistance that firstborn children provide to their younger siblings can lead to more substantial development of the brain'에서 첫째로 태어난 아이들이 더 어린 형제자매들에게 제공하는 조언과 도움은 더 중요한 두뇌 발달로 이어질 수 있다고 하였으므로, 보기 **B** greater brain development가 정답이다. 'more substantial development of the brain'이 'greater brain development'로 paraphrasing되었다.

🔍 오답 확인하기

지문의 단어 혹은 어구를 활용한 오답

A는 지문의 'parental attention'을 활용하여 혼동을 주었지만, 지문에서 첫째로 태어난 아이들의 조언과 도움이 부모로부터의 관심을 공유하는 것으로 이어진다는 내용은 언급하지 않았으므로 오답이다.

지문에 언급되지 않은 오답

C는 지문에 언급되지 않은 내용이므로 오답이다.

지문의 내용과 반대되는 오답

D는 지문 내용 중 'this helps younger siblings achieve better grades in academic coursework'에서 첫째로 태어난 아이들의 조언과 도움은 더 어린 형제자매들이 학교 수업 활동에서 더 좋은 점수를 받을 수 있도록 돕는다고 하였으므로, 지문의 내용과 반대되는 오답이다.

✅ TIPS

복수 정답을 고르는 문제의 경우, 정답은 각각 한 개의 문제로 취급된다. 그러므로 답안지에 답안을 작성할 때는 문제 한 칸에 한 개의 정답만 작성하도록 한다. 한 문제의 정답 칸에 여러 개의 답을 작성할 경우 오답 처리되므로 주의한다.

1 Given that the Mediterranean Sea is in an extremely dry area of the world and that it receives the water from the Atlantic Ocean via the narrow Strait of Gibraltar, it is actually very vulnerable to evaporation. In fact, archeological evidence shows that global cooling about five million years ago caused parts of the Atlantic Ocean to freeze, resulting in the sea level dropping about 70 metres. This stemmed the flow of water from the Atlantic into the Strait of Gibraltar, thereby greatly reducing the amount of water the Mediterranean received. At the same time, the movement of tectonic plates resulted in Europe and Africa drawing closer to one another. This raised the land high enough to further block the Mediterranean from the Atlantic Ocean. It was not long before the warm water remaining in the Mediterranean Sea began to vanish, leaving behind nothing but salt.

*Choose the correct letter, **A**, **B**, **C** or **D**.*

1 What is said about the Strait of Gibraltar?

   A It has a maximum depth of about 70 metres.

   B It froze over during an era of global cooling.

   C It evaporated due to tectonic plate movement.

   D It conveys water from the ocean into the sea.

2 What diminished the amount of water the Mediterranean Sea received from the Atlantic Ocean?

   A A period of dry weather

   B A sea level reduction

   C A blockage of ice

   D A rise in temperature

Mediterranean Sea phr. 지중해 via prep. ~을 통해 Strait of Gibraltar phr. 지브롤터 해협 vulnerable adj. 취약한, 연약한
evaporation n. 증발, 발산 archeological adj. 고고학적 stem v. 막다, 저지하다 tectonic plate phr. 지질구조판 vanish v. 사라지다

2 In Ancient Greece, the prevailing religious traditions centred around Dionysus, a saviour god who was associated with the sowing and reaping of corn, the production of grapes, and intoxication. Patrons held seasonal festivals in his honour, the most important of which was the autumn wine tasting celebration, known as the Dionysus Festival, and this included the recitation of choric poems or hymns. Revellers chanted odes, called dithyrambs, to their illustrious god while a priest would respond in a symbolic interaction between humans and the spirits. Due to its popularity within the higher and lower social classes, by the 6th century B.C., the Corinthian king established a dithyramb competition and invited a select group of poets to compose and perform these pseudo-dramas. For the first time, the plays were freed from their religious roots and transformed into full-fledged works of art. The changing theatre environment altered attitudes across Greece and thus triggered a newfound secular interest that would bring about a refinement of the art form.

*Choose the correct letter, **A**, **B**, **C** or **D**.*

3   According to the writer, the Ancient Greek wine tasting festival held each fall involved

   A   the performance of poetry.
   B   the production of wine.
   C   the harvesting of corn.
   D   the visiting of temples.

4   The movement of plays from the religious world to the general public caused

   A   a protest against organised religions across Europe.
   B   the collapse of the ancient Greek civilisation.
   C   an increase in the general public's curiosity about art.
   D   some actors to become critical of social classes.

---

intoxication n. 취하는 것, 도취 patron n. 평민을 보호하는 귀족 tasting n. 시음 choric adj. 합창의 hymn n. 찬가 reveller n. 취객, 술 마시고 흥청대는 사람
ode n. 송시 dithyramb n. 디오니소스 찬양가 illustrious adj. 뛰어난 priest n. 사제 Corinthian adj. 코린트의 pseudo adj. 유사한, 모조의
full-fledged adj. 충분히 발달된 secular adj. 세속적인 refinement n. 진보, 정제

3 With an estimated 440 million consumers worldwide now spending approximately $1.2 trillion a year on top-of-the-line products like watches, jewellery, clothing, handbags, and cars, the luxury goods retail market is steadily expanding. Yet, as a large portion of these consumers is not among the very wealthy, it has become clear that people are spending beyond their means. What then, is driving them to do so?

According to professors Niro Sivanathan and Nathan Petit, luxury items are indicators of success and thereby boost self-confidence. They have even conducted a survey that substantiates this idea. Participants in their study who had recently ended a relationship or missed out on a promotion, for instance, demonstrated much more of a desire to shop for high-end items as a means of consolation than those who were generally happy. The participants thought that purchasing luxury items would help them forget their failures and make them feel more successful. Retail therapy notwithstanding, many consumers simply believe that 'you get what you pay for' – that the most expensive items are of the highest quality and last the longest. For this reason, they are in high demand among shoppers. They feel that splurging on an item rather than buying a reasonably priced generic brand will result in significant savings on repair and replacement costs in the long run.

*Choose the correct letter, **A**, **B**, **C** or **D**.*

5   The main topic discussed in the text is

   A   worldwide production of luxury goods.

   B   the growth of a wealthy consumer class.

   C   factors influencing reckless spending.

   D   the role psychology plays in retail marketing.

6   Buying a luxury item instead of a similar, cheaper one can

   A   boost the economy.

   B   lead to people buying multiple luxury items.

   C   save money that would have been spent fixing it.

   D   increase demand for other affordable items.

---

top-of-the-line adj. 최고급품의 luxury goods phr. 사치품 retail market phr. 소매시장 indicator n. 지표 substantiate v. 입증하다
high-end adj. 고가의 consolation n. 위안 retail therapy phr. 쇼핑을 통한 기분 전환 splurge v. 돈을 펑펑 쓰다 generic adj. 상표가 없는

4 The history of mining in Nevada, nicknamed the 'Silver State', is so intertwined with the history of the state that, at certain points, the two cannot be separated. In fact, were it not for mining, Nevada would probably not have achieved statehood until decades later than it did. As it was, the Silver State bought its way into the Union with silver mined in the famous Comstock Lode. In the mid-1800s, the area that would become Nevada was mostly a highway for those heading to search for gold in California. In 1859, however, the discovery of massive silver deposits quickly made Virginia City the most famous of all western mining camps. The rapid influx of prospectors and settlers resulted in the organisation of the Nevada Territory just two years later.

In the east, the American Civil War was brewing. Lincoln, realising the area's great mineral wealth could help the Union, and needing another state to support his proposed anti-slavery amendment to the Constitution, encouraged the territory to seek admission to the Union. Even though Nevada boasted only about one-fifth of the 127,381 people required for statehood, with the motto 'Battle Born', it was admitted as the 36th state in 1864. Since then, mining's impact on Nevada's economy has remained immense, both in the influx of money it has brought in boom times and in the noticeable economic downturns during periods of low demand.

*Choose the correct letter, **A**, **B**, **C** or **D**.*

7   The writer mentions the Comstock Lode in order to illustrate

    A   the reason that miners began moving westward.

    B   a unique resource found in the region.

    C   one of the sources the state used for building infrastructure.

    D   the importance of mineral wealth in Nevada's statehood.

8   Lincoln encouraged the Nevada territory to join the union in order to

    A   gain additional support for his anti-slavery proposals.

    B   raise more tax revenues for the country.

    C   create a direct connection to the California gold mines.

    D   increase the population of the state.

9   According to the writer, since 1864 mining in Nevada

    A   has failed to generate money during economic downturns.

    B   has become the leading employment sector in the state.

    C   has had a diminished role in the state's economy.

    D   has continued to have a significant economic influence.

---

intertwine v. 밀접하게 연관시키다, 얽히다 statehood n. 주 지위 deposit n. 매장층 influx n. 유입 prospector n. 채광꾼 territory n. 준주, 지역
brew v. (~이) 일어나려 하다 mineral n. 광물 amendment n. 개정 the Constitution phr. 미국 헌법 admission n. 가입, 입회 immense adj. 막대한
noticeable adj. 현저한 downturn n. 침체

5 Some pet owners claim that, before an earthquake, their pets become restless and agitated, whine for no reason, or simply try to run away. This has led many people to believe that animals have an additional sense that warns them of these upcoming events. This, however, is not a new idea. In fact, the belief that animals can predict earthquakes appears as far back as the 4th century B.C., in the historical records of the Greek city of Helike. These records state that animals abandoned the city all at once just days before a major earthquake destroyed it, causing people to believe that the animals had been forewarned of the event. Given the existence of these types of anecdotal stories, one might begin to wonder if animals could possibly have a sixth sense that helps them predict seismic activity. Well, if we're to believe the U.S. Geological Survey – the agency charged with studying Earth – the answer is no. According to their studies, no credible evidence has been discovered to show that animals are able to predict earthquakes at all. But if this is correct, what explains the regular reports of strange behaviour before earthquakes? One theory is that animals simply have more highly effective senses than humans. With their superior hearing, dogs and cats – in addition to other animals – can perceive the infrasonic sounds produced by tectonic movement over long distances. However, without understanding what the sound is, they simply want to flee from it, causing them to act much differently than they normally would.

*Choose the correct letter, **A**, **B**, **C** or **D**.*

10   Why does the writer mention the ancient Greek town of Helike?

    A   To show how far back the theory stretches

    B   To suggest a flaw in a historical record

    C   To provide an example of a documented disaster

    D   To explain the source of a common idea

11   Why are studies that have been conducted by the U.S. Geological Survey mentioned?

    A   The writer wants to show that seismic activity is purely random.

    B   The writer wants to provide more information about animal senses.

    C   The writer wants to disprove a commonly held belief about animals.

    D   The writer wants to suggest that an ancient story was accurate.

12   What does the writer suggest about the animals and their response to infrasonic sound?

    A   They can detect it only from short distances.

    B   They do not hear it until after an earthquake begins.

    C   They want to run away despite not knowing what it is.

    D   They alert other animals about the pending danger.

---

restless adj. 가만히 있지 못하는 agitated adj. 불안해하는, 동요된 whine v. 낑낑거리다 abandon v. 떠나다, 버리다 forewarn v. 경고하다, 주의를 주다
anecdotal adj. 일화적인, 입증되지 않은 seismic adj. 지진의 U.S. Geological Survey phr. 미국 지질연구소 superior adj. 우월한
infrasonic adj. 초저주파의 tectonic adj. (지질) 구조상의

6 We often take air travel for granted today, but it is actually the result of centuries of experimentation. Since our earliest days, people have attempted to fly like the birds that they observed in the sky. These rudimentary attempts at flight included everything from jumping off ledges with simple feather-covered wings to elaborate flying machines like the one designed by Leonardo da Vinci. Unfortunately, none of these were ever able to overcome the inherent problem with flight – getting and keeping an object that is heavier than air aloft. This would remain the case until the mid-1800s, when George Cayley ascertained the fundamentals of aerodynamics. Using his newfound knowledge, Cayley was able to produce a rudderless glider that could lift a human 100 feet into the air. Cayley's work brought about even greater experimentation in aerodynamics. Amongst those whose interest was piqued were Orville and Wilbur Wright. These American brothers used a rudimentary air tunnel to perform tests on model wings. Using this device and Cayley's principles, the Wright brothers observed how winds affected planes and developed accurate mathematical formulas for flight. Eventually, they devised a way to change the wing configuration to control the plane's balance, in much the way that ailerons do today, and a rudder system, which allowed for lateral steering of the vessel. Their main problem was then figuring out a way to power the plane. Although steam engines of the day could've pushed the plane fast enough to provide lift, they were incredibly heavy. Luckily, the internal combustion engines developed for the burgeoning automobile industry were both powerful and light enough for the task. The Wright brothers attached one of these engines to a propeller on their aircraft and made the first controlled, self-propelled flight at Kittyhawk in 1903. This type of engine configuration became the standard in the aviation industry until the late 1930s, when the jet engine was developed.

*Choose the correct letter, **A**, **B**, **C** or **D**.*

13   Leonardo da Vinci's aircraft design was very complex, but

    A   it relied too heavily on the use of feathers.

    B   it weighed too much to become or remain airborne.

    C   it suffered several problems during its first flight.

    D   it did not have enough space to carry cargo.

14   The writer mentions that George Cayley

    A   invented the first powered aircraft.

    B   was inspired by da Vinci's work.

    C   worked with pilots like the Wright brothers.

    D   discovered the basics of aerodynamics.

15   Experiments by the Wright brothers allowed them to

    A   perform the calculations necessary for flight.

    B   develop an engine that could power aircraft and automobiles.

    C   invalidate some of the theories presented by Cayley.

    D   reduce the weight of steam-powered motors.

---

rudimentary adj. 가장 기본적인   ascertain v. 규명하다   rudderless adj. 방향타가 없는   configuration n. 배치   aileron n. 보조 날개
lateral adj. 측면의, 옆의   steering n. 조종   lift n. 양력(항공기가 비행할 때 밑에서 위로 작용하는 압력)   internal combustion engine phr. 내연기관
burgeon v. 급성장하다

7 Attribution Theory

There is a universal need to seek justifications and explanations for people's actions, both our own and those of the people we encounter, and therefore to determine who or what is responsible for those actions. Psychologists note that such an inherent need for explanation will often manifest itself as a tendency to attribute behaviour to either internal or external causes, depending on the circumstances. This tendency is known as attribution theory.

First proposed in 1958 by Austrian psychologist Fritz Heider, attribution theory presumes that all human behaviour is motivated by internal or external factors. In the latter case, situations are sometimes perceived as being beyond a person's control, meaning that individuals experience a diminished sense of responsibility. For instance, if an employee arrives to work late due to heavy traffic, the tendency is to project accountability outward. On the other hand, people tend to feel responsible when they can impact outcomes. Studying hard, training diligently, and doing one's best to be a good parent, for example, are viewed as stemming from personal motivations. In such cases, people describe their own efforts as the cause of their behaviours.

While it is easy to attribute unexpected events to external forces, the line between an internal and an external cause is often unclear. In a situation where a person is engaged in a heated argument and is behaving aggressively, an observer will likely think that person is prone to anger or mean-spiritedness. Such an attribution often happens without knowing how the argument arose in the first place, with the observer assuming the behaviour is due to the person's personality. This tendency for observers to focus on the internal reasons for behaviour, rather than the external, is known as 'correspondence bias'. In the same scenario, however, the person behaving aggressively may feel as if he or she has been the victim of some injustice and that such a reaction is therefore justified.

A similar tendency can be seen in the reactions people have to their own experiences. When individuals have positive experiences, like getting a promotion or achieving a goal, they are inclined to associate their own efforts with their success. In contrast, when people undergo negative experiences, the bias is inverted, and they are likely to ascribe disappointment to external factors. Rather than assigning failure to their faults or lack of ability, people magnify the factors outside their control. By casting responsibility outward, they are able to blame these external factors for their misfortunes and maintain the perception of themselves as victims.

Ultimately, it seems that offering internal and external reasons for our behaviours allows us to emphasise our positive aspects and boosts our self-esteem, while providing justification for our negative actions, which prevents us from feeling guilty. Only by understanding the role that ego and self-perception unconsciously play in attributing our successes and failures can we make changes to the way we act in any number of situations.

*Choose the correct letter, **A**, **B**, **C** or **D**.*

16 The writer suggests that people are driven to explain why things happen because

    A they feel as though it is possible to learn from past mistakes.

    B they possess an innate urge to assign responsibility to someone or something.

    C they are accountable to others for explaining why circumstances change.

    D they have a natural fear of things that are beyond their control.

17 According to the writer, individuals who feel they have no control of a situation

    A have a tendency to blame themselves for perceived failures.

    B believe they are less responsible for the outcome of an event.

    C are more likely to draw negative conclusions about people.

    D consider behaving poorly toward others to be justifiable.

18 The writer says that 'correspondence bias' occurs when people

    A fail to understand an individual's true personality.

    B interpret a person as a victim without justification.

    C attempt to change circumstances after reaching an outcome.

    D conclude that behaviour is determined by a person's personality.

19 The writer mentions that when people succeed, they tend to

    A magnify the extent of their accomplishments.

    B overlook the contribution of natural talent.

    C attribute their results to internal factors.

    D become less able to handle future disappointments.

---

attribution n. 귀인, 귀속　justification n. 정당한 이유　inherent adj. 선천적인, 내재적인　manifest v. 나타나다, 분명해지다　presume v. 추정하다
diminished adj. 감소된　accountability n. 책임, 의무　stem from phr. ~에서 기인하다　correspondence bias phr. 대응편향　invert v. 뒤집다, 도치시키다
ascribe v. ~을 탓하다　magnify v. 과장하다, 확대하다　self-esteem n. 자부심, 자존심　ego n. 자존심　self-perception n. 자아 인식

8 Population in Europe: The Great Transformation

Throughout the Late Middle Ages, Europe's population was declining due to poor harvests, war, and most significantly, the Black Death, a devastating strain of plague that spread throughout the continent. The constant threat of death from this pandemic created panic among the people, of the sort described by Giovanni Boccaccio in *The Decameron* in 1348. Reflecting how many Europeans felt at the time, Boccaccio created a fictional world where citizens ignored laws and lived every day as if it were their last. He was essentially attempting to depict the behaviour of people who believed the world was ending, which was not so far from what many may have thought at the time.

At its destructive peak in the 14th and 15th centuries it is estimated that the Black Death reduced Europe's population by between 30 to 60 per cent, but it did not end there. A resurgence of the plague occurred in the 17th century, and this – in conjunction with decades-long wars – resulted in millions of deaths. As a result, Europe's population increased only gradually from 1300 A.D. to 1800 A.D. This growth dramatically increased between 1800 and 1914, when the number of people in Europe surged from 188 million to 458 million.

Historians refer to this period as the 'Great Transformation', and credit major improvements in agricultural production, including the development of farming machinery and the cultivation of higher-yielding, more nutritious plants from the Americas, for this momentous population growth. With more nutritious food to eat, infants began surviving in far greater numbers than ever before, and the average life expectancy rose by about two decades. A further contribution to the declining mortality rate was an improved understanding of disease and infection.

However, the rapid increase in population was worrisome to some. In his 1798 paper, 'An Essay on the Principle of Population', economist Thomas Malthus suggested that Europe was becoming overcrowded. In a complete reversal from earlier writers who wrote about the chaos caused by Europe not being populated enough, Malthus emphasised that the number of births needed to be controlled. His paper gave rise to the popular concept of family planning and his views were used extensively by later proponents of the idea that giving birth should always be voluntary. In the 19th century women did begin limiting the number of children they had, and in a matter of decades, the fertility rate had decreased by 30 per cent.

In the 20th century, Europe's population was profoundly impacted by medical advances and improved nutrition to the extent that, with the exception of the period during the two world wars, longer lives became the norm. The birth rate continued to decline, and today, the population is experiencing negative growth for the first time in the modern era. This is expected to continue indefinitely, aided in part by such changes to legislation as the legalisation of abortion. In fact, the United Nations Population Division predicts that the population of Europe, measured at approximately 728 million in 2005, will dip below 665 million by 2050.

*Choose the correct letter, **A**, **B**, **C** or **D**.*

20 The writer mentions *The Decameron* because

    A   it was distinct from most writing of the time.

    B   it was the first piece of literature to emerge about the Black Plague.

    C   it emphasises the importance of population control.

    D   it illustrates the fear of Europeans in the early modern period.

21 What does the writer suggest about Thomas Malthus' essay?

    A   It inspired a population control movement.

    B   It directly contradicted popular opinion.

    C   It extensively promoted women's rights.

    D   It was first published in the 19th century.

22 The writer says that the European population in the 20th century

    A   reached its highest level during the first decade.

    B   was characterised by high birth rates.

    C   was affected by better medicine and nutrition.

    D   declined between the two world wars.

---

transformation n. 전환, 변화 the Black Death phr. 흑사병 devastating adj. 파괴적인, 황폐시키는 strain n. (동식물·질병 등의) 종류, 유형
plague n. 전염병 pandemic n. 전국적인 유행병 of the sort phr. 그와 같은, 그런 depict v. 묘사하다 in conjunction with phr. ~과 함께
surge v. 급증하다 momentous adj. 중대한 mortality rate phr. 사망률 proponent n. 지지자 fertility rate phr. 출산율 norm n. 일반적인 것, 표준
negative growth phr. 마이너스 성장 indefinitely adv. 무기한적으로 legislation n. 법률, 법령 legalisation n. 합법화

9   Unravelling African History

Although the history of Ancient Egypt and Roman North Africa is relatively well-documented, the dearth of primary sources related to sub-Saharan African antiquity is a major challenge for historians. This lack of information has led to considerable difficulty in developing an accurate picture of the varied societies that existed in this vast region prior to colonisation by Arab and European powers.

Though largely confined to certain areas, written materials do exist which offer insight into the political and social development of sub-Saharan Africa. These are often texts written by visitors who recorded their impressions for the benefit of their native society. Traders from Ancient Egypt, for example, often travelled south along the Nile to Nubia in northern Sudan and their trades were recorded in Egypt's hieroglyphic script. Following Islamic dominance of North Africa in the 8th century, official records in Arabic were kept about regions of sub-Saharan Africa. While many of these texts are polemic in tone and packed with religious themes, some are official documents containing information related to trade routes, agriculture and the extensive trans-Saharan slave trade which Arab rulers instituted during this period.

From the 15th century onwards written material in European languages about sub-Saharan Africa also began to appear in larger quantities. The earliest Europeans to arrive were explorers who aimed to take possession of the lands they were visiting. Conveying social and cultural information about indigenous peoples to European societies, they described local customs, ceremonies, and ways of life, often in stunning detail – but their accounts were marked by a pejorative attitude. European explorers, and the Christian missionaries who also began to visit sub-Saharan Africa during this period, viewed themselves as superior due in part to the natives' substandard weaponry and their ignorance of Christianity.

The lack of historical accounts from the viewpoint of indigenous societies is mostly because of the lack of a written form for many early African languages. Consequently, the extant historical information about sub-Saharan Africa has been gleaned largely from oral accounts passed down through the generations, often in the form of epic historical narratives. Since oral records are subject to differ somewhat each time a story is told, they are not considered to be as reliable as written sources.

Despite their pitfalls, oral records do have intrinsic value. Not only do they illuminate the culture of Africa and induce historians to look at the past from new angles, but they also present history in artistic and entertaining ways. Furthermore, some epics are filled with information that is accurately reflective of historical daily life. For instance, in the *Epic of Silamaka*, a tale from West Africa, listeners are told of shepherds in herding communities who were chosen to care for the king's flocks and how people wore shoes made of tanned ox hides, with one leather strap over the big toe and one over the heel. In short, while written sources and archaeological evidence provide a mere glimpse into the culture and history of sub-Saharan Africa, stories give us detailed clues about how people went about their everyday lives.

*Choose **TWO** letters, **A-E**.*

23-24 Which **TWO** effects of the Muslim dominance of North Africa are mentioned by the writer?

A Religiously themed literature was distributed.

B The trans-Saharan slave trade began.

C Documents in African languages were produced.

D Resources started being traded for agricultural goods.

E Official documents about sub-Saharan Africa were kept.

*Choose the correct letter, **A, B, C** or **D**.*

25 According to the writer, what was the goal of the first Europeans to arrive?

A The expansion of European culture

B The acquisition of land

C The education of indigenous peoples

D The spread of Christianity

*Choose **TWO** letters, **A-E**.*

26-27 Which **TWO** aspects are mentioned about orally transmitted historical accounts?

A They are reflective of archeological evidence.

B They include descriptive details of life in the past.

C They provide historians with new perspectives.

D They are prevalent among agricultural communities.

E They contain artistic and entertaining pictures.

---

unravel v. 끝까지 밝히다, 해명하다   dearth n. 부족, 결핍   primary source phr. (연구·조사 등의) 1차 자료   sub-Saharan adj. 사하라 사막 이남의
antiquity n. 유물   confine v. 국한시키다   hieroglyphic adj. 상형 문자의   polemic adj. 논쟁의, 논쟁을 좋아하는   pejorative adj. 경멸적인, 멸시적인
missionary n. (외국에 파견되는) 선교사   substandard adj. 수준 이하의, 열악한   weaponry n. 무기   extant adj. 현존하는   glean v. 수집하다, 얻다
epic adj. 방대한, 서사의   historical narrative phr. 사화, 역사서사   pitfall n. 위험, 곤란   intrinsic adj. 고유한, 본질적인   herding adj. 목축의
tanned adj. 무두질한, 햇볕에 탄   glimpse n. 짧은 경험

10 The Various Relationship Attachment Styles
Our ability to form strong emotional bonds as adults may be based on much more than we think.

How people feel when they are in relationships varies, and this variation is something that psychologists have long attempted to understand. In the 1960s and 1970s, developmental psychologist Mary Ainsworth found from her research into mothers and children that emotional attachment is established in infancy. She also speculated that attachment styles vary quite a bit among children, who all fall into one of several different attachment classifications.

The first is referred to as secure attachment and describes a relationship where a child feels safe with his or her caregivers. Secure attachments comprise an estimated 65 per cent of infants, and these attachments are formed by children who feel comfortable most of the time. Specifically, they feel at ease as long as their caregivers are around. They become upset when their caregivers leave but are content again when their caregivers return. Essentially, they form a secure attachment with their caregivers because all of their needs are consistently met.

Insecure attachments, such as anxious/avoidant attachment, also exist. According to Ainsworth, children with this level of attachment avoid or ignore their caregivers, show little emotion when they depart or return, and do not seek them out when distressed. Furthermore, infants with anxious/avoidant attachment act the same way with strangers as they do with their caretakers. Rather than facing rejection, these children mask their distress with apathy and direct attention away from their unfulfilled desire for closeness. This type of attachment, comprising about 15 per cent of infants, is common among children with caregivers who are unresponsive to their needs.

Affecting approximately the same percentage of infants is an insecure attachment called anxious/ambivalent attachment. With this level of attachment, children demonstrate both clinginess and resistance to their caregivers. For example, a child might become very distressed when the caregiver leaves and remain upset while alone with a stranger, but upon the caregivers' return, the child resists attention from him or her and thus remains upset. These children, who are nearly impossible to pacify, behave this way because their caregivers provide inconsistent levels of responsiveness to their needs.

It is simplistic to think that all children fall into one of three categories of behavior, which is why an unofficial category exists to classify children exhibiting mixed attachment styles. Called disorganised attachment, this classification is given to the small percentage of children whose temperamental response is inconsistent with how they are treated. This generally results from situations in which children have experienced several primary caregivers, such as with foster children.

Ultimately, attachment theory provides a clear explanation for why some people behave in ways that can leave their significant others frustrated, angry, or confused. We may not be able to do anything about the way we are treated as babies by those we depend on, but by understanding why we behave the way we do, it may be possible to make the changes necessary to form healthy relationships as an adult.

*Choose the correct letter, **A**, **B**, **C** or **D**.*

28 What is the writer's overall purpose in writing this article?

A To describe the innate ability of some infants to form strong bonds

B To explain the different forms of childhood attachment and its importance

C To stress the importance of setting a good example for children

D To suggest that attachment theory is based on common sense

*Choose **THREE** letters, **A-H**.*

29-31 Which **THREE** of the following statements are true of secure attachment?

A It is present in the majority of infants.

B It is rarely seen in very young children.

C It results in comfort in the presence of caregivers.

D It is characterised by little emotional expression.

E It creates temporary stress when caregivers leave.

F It occurs with both strangers and parents.

G It causes extreme attachment in 15 per cent of cases.

H It leads to confident independence in children.

*Choose the correct letter, **A**, **B**, **C** or **D**.*

32 What strategy do babies with anxious/avoidant attachment employ?

A They resist attempts to have their needs met.

B They seek out attention from strangers.

C They pretend that they do not care.

D They refuse to make eye contact.

정답·해석·해설 p.316

attachment style phr. 애착 유형 infancy n. 유아기 speculate v. 추측하다 secure attachment phr. 안정 애착 content adj. 만족해 하는
avoidant adj. 회피성의 distressed adj. 괴로워 하는 mask v. 감추다, 가리다 apathy n. 무관심 unresponsive adj. 반응이 없는
ambivalent adj. 양가적인, 반대 감정이 병존하는 clinginess n. 매달리는 것 pacify v. 달래다, 진정시키다 disorganised attachment phr. 불안정혼란애착
temperamental adj. 신경질적인

READING PASSAGE

*You should spend about 20 minutes on **Questions 1-13**, which are based on Reading Passage below.*

Infant Cognition: Acquired or Innate?

If infants are born with cognitive abilities, genetics may play a more significant role in development than environmental factors

Throughout history, psychologists have debated whether people are more strongly influenced by genetics (nature) or their environment (nurture). Because newborns are as close to 'nature' as a human can be, they have often been the object of study by experts attempting to better understand the origins of human cognition. According to Jean Piaget's famous theory of early human cognition, infants acquire intelligence only through the physical actions they perform with objects around them. To him, cognitive ability is not innate but is acquired over time through interaction with the phenomenal world. Newborns practise reflex behaviours and slowly gain control over them through repetition. Over the course of their first few months, they learn to perform actions over and over again, such as sucking their thumbs, which give them some sort of pleasure or satisfaction. In this stage, he maintained, they are still unable to fully anticipate or predict events. From around four to eight months, infants begin to use what Piaget called secondary circular reactions. These are secondary because they involve combining more than one process, e.g. shaking a rattle and hearing it make noise.

Through such actions, infants learn cause and effect and begin to realise that their own actions can create subsequent reactions. To Piaget, these were no more than conditioned responses to the connections between newly acquired actions and their effects on objects, and because these actions are undifferentiated, he believed that they were not goal-directed activities and, thus, they are not intentional. Therefore, only gradually do babies begin to realise that objects have an independent existence outside of their own perception. Piaget argued that infants have extremely limited cognitive ability until around nine months of age but reasoned that, by then, they have usually acquired the ability to recognise object permanence.

Piaget used object-hiding tasks to demonstrate this acquisition. For example, he would show babies an object and then hide it under a cloth or cup and analyse whether infants perceived that the object had disappeared or was merely hidden from view. Piaget based his conclusions on whether the infants responded by removing the cloth or cup to find the concealed item. If they did, he surmised that they had at least a limited apprehension of object permanence; however, he also suggested that this ability was immature and limited because if the object was moved to another location, the infant would still try to find it by removing the original item that obscured it. Nonetheless, according to Piaget, this stage represented the first truly intelligent behaviour in human cognitive development, and he believed it was the basis for all future problem solving.

Still, not everyone thought that Piaget's analysis was entirely correct. Canadian-born psychologist Renée Baillargeon's studies of cognitive development in infants challenged Piaget's beliefs. She pointed out the importance of conducting experiments and tests that are appropriate for the developmental level of infants, arguing that the limited motor skills of young infants may be responsible for their perceived lack of cognitive abilities. In other words, Baillargeon disagreed with Piaget and accused him of confusing motor skill limitations with cognitive limitations. To test this hypothesis, she focused her studies on visual tasks rather than manual tasks.

In one experiment, Baillargeon showed three-month-old infants a toy truck rolling down a track before getting obscured behind a screen, letting the infants focus on this process several times until they were habituated to it. Baillargeon then introduced a box which was positioned so that it looked like it would block the truck's journey down the track. However, when the truck was sent down again, it passed the box apparently unimpeded. Baillargeon discovered that infants would look for far longer at this unexpected event than they did at the normal progress of the truck before the box was placed on the track. Baillargeon concluded from this that they knew the truck should have been blocked, and were confused when it wasn't. She thus believed that they had an understanding of the properties of objects, including their permanence and their trajectory when in motion. This contradicted Piaget, who believed these abilities only developed at around nine to twelve months.

Her findings rest on the assumption – now widely accepted and supported by various studies – that infants focus longer on events that are novel or surprising, whereas events that are familiar to them capture their attention for a shorter period. This presumption has come to be known as the violation of expectation (VOE) paradigm. She reasoned that, to the infant, the novel event was surprising and even 'impossible'. According to Baillargeon, this means that very young children have the capacity to distinguish between events that are possible and not possible, suggesting that they have far more inborn cognitive ability than Piaget thought.

Yet to say that infants can conceive of objects in the physical world in the same way that adults do does not mean that they always reason in the same manner as adults. Therefore, the innate 'pre-wiring' of the human brain must continue to develop through childhood and adolescence. In this sense, it goes without saying that experience, or nurture, remains a crucial factor in human cognitive development. Still, the experiments of Baillargeon and other child development psychologists built upon the work of Piaget and reenergised the field in much the same way that Noam Chomsky's studies of language acquisition revolutionised linguistics.

Questions 1-8

*Choose the correct letter, **A**, **B**, **C** or **D**.*

1   According to Piaget, infants gain knowledge solely through

    A   observing the world around them.

    B   interacting with things close to them.

    C   learning to repeat actions.

    D   interacting with other people.

2   Why did Piaget believe infants have some understanding of object permanence?

    A   They had no difficulty determining what was hiding an object.

    B   They recognised when an object was moved to a different location.

    C   They were not deceived when an object was replaced with another.

    D   They uncovered the object that had been hidden.

3   According to Baillargeon, it is important to carry out experiments that are

    A   easily repeatable and objective.

    B   focused on innate rather than acquired skills.

    C   suitable for infants' stage of development.

    D   undertaken with infants of varying ages.

4   What was Baillargeon's criticism of Piaget?

    A   His assumptions were founded on insufficient research.

    B   His research was not backed by experimental evidence.

    C   He put too much emphasis on visual tasks in his studies.

    D   He mistook a lack of motor skills with a lack of cognitive ones.

5   In the experiment involving a truck, Baillargeon

    A   showed infants the same process numerous times.

    B   moved a screen in front of the infants.

    C   observed infants playing with a toy truck.

    D   tested the motor functions of infants.

6   In the last paragraph, the writer suggests that infants' ability to conceive of objects

    A   reveals how the human brain develops through childhood.

    B   shows they can reason at the same level of adults.

    C   demonstrates that their cognitive ability is not innate.

    D   does not mean they are able to reason like adults.

7 The writer refers to Noam Chomsky to compare

    A the value of linguistic research with psychological research.

    B Baillargeon with someone else who made a major academic contribution.

    C Baillargeon's work with that of another child development psychologist.

    D the differences between the distinct academic goals.

8 What is the writer's overall purpose in writing this article?

    A To show that infant development relies on both nature and nurture

    B To prove that cognitive abilities develop before birth

    C To explain how cognitive abilities affect infant development

    D To prove that nature is more important than nurture in development

Questions 9-11

Complete the sentences below.

*Choose **ONE WORD ONLY** from the passage for each answer.*

9 Recently born babies will try to master their movement through ....

10 Infants only gradually understand the independent existence of ....

11 In the experiment, Baillargeon positioned a .... which appeared to obstruct the vehicle.

Questions 12 and 13

*Choose **TWO** letters, **A-E**.*

12-13 On what points do Baillargeon and Piaget disagree?

    A the importance of education in cognitive development

    B the age that infants become aware of object permanence

    C how infants learn to distinguish between objects

    D the extent to which infant cognition is inborn

    E when infant cognition equals to that of adults

정답·해석·해설 p.328

VOCABULARY LIST

Chapter 01에서 선별한 다음의 어휘들을 음성파일을 들으며 암기한 후 퀴즈로 확인해보세요.

*해커스 동영상강의 포털 해커스 인강(HackersIngang.com)에서 단어암기 MP3를 무료로 다운로드할 수 있습니다.

- [ ] **via** prep. ~을 통해
- [ ] **vulnerable** adj. 취약한, 연약한
- [ ] **evaporation** n. 증발, 발산
- [ ] **archeological** adj. 고고학적
- [ ] **stem** v. 막다, 저지하다
- [ ] **vanish** v. 사라지다
- [ ] **illustrious** adj. 뛰어난
- [ ] **priest** n. 사제
- [ ] **secular** adj. 세속적인
- [ ] **refinement** n. 진보, 정제
- [ ] **substantiate** v. 입증하다
- [ ] **high-end** adj. 고가의
- [ ] **consolation** n. 위안
- [ ] **splurge** v. 돈을 펑펑 쓰다
- [ ] **intertwine** v. 밀접하게 연관시키다, 얽히다
- [ ] **statehood** n. 주 지위
- [ ] **deposit** n. 매장층
- [ ] **influx** n. 유입
- [ ] **territory** n. 준주, 지역
- [ ] **brew** v. (~이) 일어나려 하다
- [ ] **mineral** n. 광물
- [ ] **amendment** n. 개정
- [ ] **admission** n. 가입, 입회
- [ ] **immense** adj. 막대한
- [ ] **noticeable** adj. 현저한
- [ ] **downturn** n. 침체

- [ ] **restless** adj. 가만히 있지 못하는
- [ ] **agitated** adj. 불안해하는, 동요된
- [ ] **abandon** v. 떠나다, 버리다
- [ ] **forewarn** v. 경고하다, 주의를 주다
- [ ] **anecdotal** adj. 일화적인, 입증되지 않은
- [ ] **seismic** adj. 지진의
- [ ] **superior** adj. 우월한
- [ ] **rudimentary** adj. 가장 기본적인
- [ ] **ascertain** v. 규명하다
- [ ] **lateral** adj. 측면의, 옆의
- [ ] **burgeon** v. 급성장하다
- [ ] **justification** n. 정당한 이유
- [ ] **inherent** adj. 선천적인, 내재적인
- [ ] **manifest** v. 나타나다, 분명해지다
- [ ] **presume** v. 추정하다
- [ ] **diminished** adj. 감소된
- [ ] **accountability** n. 책임, 의무
- [ ] **stem from** phr. ~에서 기인하다
- [ ] **invert** v. 뒤집다, 도치시키다
- [ ] **ascribe** v. ~을 탓하다
- [ ] **magnify** v. 과장하다, 확대하다
- [ ] **self-esteem** n. 자부심, 자존심
- [ ] **ego** n. 자부심
- [ ] **transformation** n. 전환, 변화
- [ ] **the Black Death** phr. 흑사병
- [ ] **devastating** adj. 파괴적인, 황폐시키는

Quiz

각 단어의 알맞은 뜻을 찾아 연결하시오.

01 immense	ⓐ 개정	06 rudimentary	ⓐ 급성장하다
02 influx	ⓑ 현저한	07 superior	ⓑ 무기
03 secular	ⓒ 막대한	08 invert	ⓒ 가장 기본적인
04 amendment	ⓓ 위안	09 burgeon	ⓓ 감소된
05 consolation	ⓔ 유입	10 diminished	ⓔ 우월한
	ⓕ 세속적인		ⓕ 뒤집다, 도치시키다

ⓓ 01 ⓔ 02 ⓕ 03 ⓐ 04 ⓓ 05 ⓒ 06 ⓔ 07 ⓕ 08 ⓐ 09 ⓓ 10

- ☐ strain n. (동식물 · 질병 등의) 종류, 유형
- ☐ plague n. 전염병
- ☐ pandemic n. 전국적인 유행병
- ☐ depict v. 묘사하다
- ☐ in conjunction with phr. ~과 함께
- ☐ surge v. 급증하다
- ☐ momentous adj. 중대한
- ☐ mortality rate phr. 사망률
- ☐ proponent n. 지지자
- ☐ fertility rate phr. 출산율
- ☐ norm n. 일반적인 것, 표준
- ☐ indefinitely adv. 무기한적으로
- ☐ legislation n. 법률, 법령
- ☐ legalisation n. 합법화
- ☐ unravel v. 끝까지 밝히다, 해명하다
- ☐ dearth n. 부족, 결핍
- ☐ primary source phr. (연구 · 조사 등의) 1차 자료
- ☐ antiquity n. 유물
- ☐ confine v. 국한시키다
- ☐ hieroglyphic adj. 상형 문자의
- ☐ pejorative adj. 경멸적인, 멸시적인
- ☐ substandard adj. 수준 이하의, 열악한
- ☐ weaponry n. 무기
- ☐ extant adj. 현존하는
- ☐ pitfall n. 위험, 곤란
- ☐ intrinsic adj. 고유한, 본질적인

- ☐ infancy n. 유아기
- ☐ speculate v. 추측하다
- ☐ content adj. 만족해 하는
- ☐ avoidant adj. 회피성의
- ☐ distressed adj. 괴로워 하는
- ☐ mask v. 감추다, 가리다
- ☐ apathy n. 무관심
- ☐ unresponsive adj. 반응이 없는
- ☐ ambivalent adj. 양가적인, 반대 감정이 병존하는
- ☐ pacify v. 달래다, 진정시키다
- ☐ temperamental adj. 신경질적인
- ☐ cognition n. 인지
- ☐ genetics n. 유전적 특징, 유전학
- ☐ phenomenal adj. 인지할 수 있는, 감각적인
- ☐ subsequent adj. 그 다음의
- ☐ undifferentiated adj. 구분되지 않는, 획일적인
- ☐ goal-directed adj. 목표 지향적인
- ☐ surmise v. 추정하다, 추측하다
- ☐ obscure v. 가리다, 덮다
- ☐ motor skill phr. 운동 기능
- ☐ habituate v. 익숙하게 하다, ~을 길들이다
- ☐ unimpeded adj. 방해받지 않는, 가로막는 것이 없는
- ☐ property n. 속성, 특성
- ☐ presumption n. 가정, 추정
- ☐ violation n. 위반, 방해
- ☐ paradigm n. 전형, 예

Quiz

각 단어의 알맞은 뜻을 찾아 연결하시오.

01 confine   ⓐ 유물
02 norm   ⓑ 국한시키다
03 antiquity   ⓒ 지지자
04 depict   ⓓ 상형 문자의
05 proponent   ⓔ 일반적인 것, 표준
                    ⓕ 묘사하다

06 content   ⓐ 무관심
07 property   ⓑ 신경질적인
08 apathy   ⓒ 만족해 하는
09 speculate   ⓓ 그 다음의
10 subsequent   ⓔ 추측하다
                    ⓕ 속성, 특성

CHAPTER 02 T/F/NG (True / False / Not Given)

T/F/NG 문제는 제시된 문장이 지문의 정보와 일치하는지, 일치하지 않는지, 혹은 알 수 없는지를 판단하는 문제이다.
IELTS Reading 영역에서 가장 많이 출제되는 유형 중 하나로, 거의 매 시험 출제되고 있다.

■■ 문제 형태

T/F/NG 문제는 제시된 문장이 지문의 정보와 일치한다면 True, 일치하지 않는다면 False, 알 수 없다면 Not given을 적는 형태로 출제된다.

Do the following statements agree with the information given in Reading Passage 1?

In boxes 1-3 on your answer sheet, write

> **TRUE**   *if the statement agrees with the information*
> **FALSE**   *if the statement contradicts the information*
> **NOT GIVEN**   *if there is no information on this*

1   Firstborn children have higher IQ scores than second children.

2   The role of birth order requires further study.

3   Last-born children are not as socially outgoing as their older siblings.

STEP 1 문제의 핵심어구와 내용을 파악한다.

T/F/NG 문제를 풀기 위해서는 먼저 문제의 핵심어구와 핵심 내용을 파악한다.

EXAMPLE

Do the following statements agree with the information given in Reading Passage?

In boxes 1-3 on your answer sheet, write

> **TRUE**   *if the statement agrees with the information*
> **FALSE**   *if the statement contradicts the information*
> **NOT GIVEN** *if there is no information on this*

1   Firstborn children have higher IQ scores than second children. ●

2   The role of birth order requires further study. ●

3   Last-born children are not as socially outgoing as their older siblings. ●

문제의 핵심어구인 Firstborn children이 둘째 아이들보다 높은 IQ 점수를 가지고 있다는 내용을 파악한다.

문제의 핵심어구인 The role of birth order가 추후 연구를 필요로 한다는 내용을 파악한다.

문제의 핵심어구인 Last-born children이 더 나이가 많은 형제자매들만큼 사회적으로 외향적이지 않다는 내용을 파악한다.

☑ **TIPS**

T/F/NG 문제는 여러 개의 문제가 한 번에 출제되므로, 제시된 모든 문제의 핵심어구를 미리 파악해두기보다는 한 문제씩 핵심어구를 파악하여 답을 쓰고 다음 문제로 넘어가는 것이 좋다.

지문을 scanning하여 문제의 핵심어구와 관련된 내용을 찾는다. 관련 내용이 언급된 주변에서 정답의 단서를 확인한다.

EXAMPLE

According to social psychologist Robert Zajonc, firstborn children tend to be measurably more intelligent. In fact, studies by Norwegian researchers have shown that [1]firstborn children score three points higher on the IQ scale than second children. This type of gap was also found, to a lesser extent, between the second and third child.

However, [2]intelligence is not the only difference attributed to birth order. Firstborn children also tend to do better in school, receive better pay in adulthood, and bear more familial responsibilities. [3]Last-born children, on the other hand, are more likely to be humorous, less disciplined, less risk averse, and more sociable than their older siblings.

Do the following statements agree with the information given in Reading Passage?

In boxes 1-3 on your answer sheet, write

TRUE	*if the statement agrees with the information*
FALSE	*if the statement contradicts the information*
NOT GIVEN	*if there is no information on this*

1 Firstborn children have higher IQ scores than second children.

2 The role of birth order requires further study.

3 Last-born children are not as socially outgoing as their older siblings.

지문 해석 p.333

1번 문제의 핵심어구인 Firstborn children과 관련된 내용을 지문에서 찾는다. 관련 내용이 언급된 주변에서 'firstborn children score three points higher on the IQ scale than second children'이라는 정답의 단서를 확인한다.

2번 문제의 핵심어구인 The role of birth order와 관련된 내용을 지문에서 찾는다. 관련 내용이 언급된 주변에 정답의 단서가 등장하지 않음을 확인한다.

3번 문제의 핵심어구인 Last-born children과 관련된 내용을 지문에서 찾는다. 관련 내용이 언급된 주변에서 'Last-born children ~ more sociable than their older siblings'라는 정답의 단서를 확인한다.

✓ TIPS

T/F/NG 문제는 보통 지문의 내용이 전개되는 순서대로 출제되므로, 정답의 단서도 지문에서 순서대로 등장한다. 예를 들어 2번 문제의 정답의 단서는 1번 문제의 정답의 단서보다 이후에 등장할 가능성이 높다. 그러므로 정답의 단서를 찾지 못한 문제가 있다면, 이전 문제의 정답의 단서와 다음 문제의 정답의 단서 사이를 살펴보도록 한다.

정답의 단서와 제시된 문제의 내용이 서로 일치하는지 판단하여 답을 적는다.

EXAMPLE

Do the following statements agree with the information given in Reading Passage?

In boxes 1-3 on your answer sheet, write

TRUE   *if the statement agrees with the information*
FALSE   *if the statement contradicts the information*
NOT GIVEN *if there is no information on this*

1   Firstborn children have higher IQ scores than second children. True

2   The role of birth order requires further study. Not given

3   Last-born children are not as socially outgoing as their older siblings. False

1 문제의 핵심어구(Firstborn children)와 관련된 지문 내용 중 'firstborn children score three points higher on the IQ scale than second children'에서 첫째로 태어난 아이들은 둘째 아이들보다 IQ 등급에서 3점을 더 기록한다고 하였으므로, 주어진 문장은 지문의 내용과 일치한다. 따라서 정답은 **True**이다.

2 문제의 핵심어구(The role of birth order)와 관련된 지문 내용 중 'intelligence is not the only difference attributed to birth order'에서 지능이 출생 순서가 원인인 유일한 차이점이 아니라고는 하였지만, 주어진 문장의 내용은 확인할 수 없다. 따라서 정답은 **Not given**이다.

3 문제의 핵심어구(Last-born children)와 관련된 지문 내용 중 'Last-born children ~ more sociable than their older siblings.'에서 막내로 태어난 아이들은 나이가 많은 형제자매들보다 더 외향적이라고 하였으므로, 주어진 문장은 지문의 내용과 일치하지 않는다. 따라서 정답은 **False**이다.

⊘ TIPS

False와 Not given 구별하기

- False: 지문에서 등장한 단어 혹은 어구를 포함하며, 지문에서 언급된 내용과 완전히 반대되는 내용이 제시된다.
  ex) 지문 그 그림은 17세기에 유명했던 그림이다.
  문제 그 그림은 17세기에 전혀 알려지지 않았다.
  → 지문에서 17세기에 유명했던 그림이라고 했는데, 17세기에 전혀 알려지지 않았다는 반대 내용을 언급하였으므로 정답은 False이다.

- Not given: 지문에서 등장한 단어 혹은 어구를 포함하지만, 문제의 중심 내용은 지문에서 언급되지 않는다.
  ex) 지문 그 그림은 17세기에 유명했던 그림이다.
  문제 그 그림은 17세기에 가장 유명했기 때문에 현재까지 보존된 것이다.
  → 지문에서 그림이 17세기에 가장 유명했다고만 했지, 현재까지 보존되었는지의 여부에 대한 언급은 하지 않았으므로 정답은 Not given이다.

1 The Pueblo Indians were a major cultural influence in the United States' Four Corners region for over one thousand years. Initially, the civilisation was based in individual homesteads in the Colorado Plateau's highlands, where its members farmed and developed various handicrafts, such as pottery and blankets. However, during the 11th and 12th centuries the Pueblo moved into the neighbouring canyons and built the massive multifamily dwellings from which their names are derived. Archaeologist Kristen Kuckelman believes this occurred after persistent droughts made farming on plateau lands impossible. She believes that the region's inhabitants moved into the valleys because they were less impacted by the droughts. After they migrated, they had to learn how to produce food more effectively on less land, so they implemented a system of agricultural cooperation that eventually led to specialism. Once they settled in the canyons, the civilisation became increasingly more communal in order to maximise the returns on its labour.

Do the following statements agree with the information given in the passage?

Write

TRUE	*if the statement agrees with the information*
FALSE	*if the statement contradicts the information*
NOT GIVEN	*if there is no information on this*

1 The Pueblo got their names from their style of housing.

2 The Pueblo people moved into neighbouring communities with more farmland.

---

homestead n. 농가, 주택 plateau n. 고원 handicraft n. 수공예품 canyon n. 협곡 dwelling n. 주거지, 주택 persistent adj. 끊임없이 지속되는
communal adj. 공동 사회의, 공동체의 maximise v. 극대화하다 return n. 수익

2   We now know that trees and other vegetation play an invaluable role in reducing air pollution in cities. Not so long ago, in the early 1980s, chemists discovered that trees produce emissions. This prompted the then U.S. President Ronald Reagan to falsely declare, 'Trees cause more pollution than automobiles do.' This, of course, caused people to speculate that trees were harmful, despite the facts that the words 'emission' and 'pollution' are not synonymous and that the president's remark was not accurate. While it is true that trees and plants, like all living things, emit chemical substances as byproducts of their metabolisms, these emissions are not a threat, but instead include the oxygen we breathe and the various chemical compounds that give flowers and shrubs their fresh and fragrant scents. It is only in the presence of significant amounts of man-made pollution, like that caused by the emissions of automobiles, that plants and trees release volatile organic hydrocarbons. But when they do, they can become participants in the formation of such ground-level ozone pollution as photochemical smog.

Do the following statements agree with the information given in the passage?

Write

TRUE	*if the statement agrees with the information*
FALSE	*if the statement contradicts the information*
NOT GIVEN	*if there is no information on this*

3   A politician in the 1980s incorrectly blamed plants for air pollution.

4   Plants contribute to photochemical smog as much as automobiles.

---

emission n. 배출물 declare v. 공표하다 speculate v. 추측하다, 짐작하다 synonymous adj. 동의어의 byproduct n. 부산물 metabolism n. 신진 대사 shrub n. 관목 volatile adj. 휘발성의 hydrocarbon n. 탄화수소 photochemical adj. 광화학의

3 Industrialisation and corporate growth in the late 19th century created an environment in which business correspondence increased monumentally, calling for a way to transcribe messages more quickly and legibly than handwritten script. The first device capable of fulfilling this need was the Sholes and Glidden typewriter. However, before it would become a commercial success, certain issues needed to be remedied. For instance, the type bars in their earliest typewriters moved very sluggishly, and the keys and other components tended to jam often. To fix this problem, Sholes – the designer – rearranged the layout of the keyboard so that the letters in subsequent versions of his machine no longer appeared in alphabetical order. Instead, he placed the keys with the intention that the most commonly used letter combinations in the English language, like ST and TH, would be spread far apart from one another. This modification caused a dramatic decline in mechanical jams and typing errors because the new arrangement increased the time it took for users to locate letters. Thereby it ensured that each key had enough time to fall back into its position before the next one was struck. These seemingly small changes were key to making typewriters a useful transcription and correspondence device.

Do the following statements agree with the information given in the passage?

Write

TRUE	*if the statement agrees with the information*
FALSE	*if the statement contradicts the information*
NOT GIVEN	*if there is no information on this*

5 Industrialisation created a need for a writing method that produced more readable text.

6 The type bars on early typewriters had to be replaced often.

7 The redesign made locating letters more time-consuming.

---

correspondence n. 서신 monumentally adv. 엄청나게 call for phr. ~을 필요로 하게 하다 transcribe v. 기록하다 remedy v. 개선하다, 교정하다
sluggishly adv. 느리게 subsequent adj. 다음의, 이후의 modification n. 변경, 수정 seemingly adv. 겉보기에는 transcription n. 표기, 인쇄

4 While writing utensils have been around since antiquity, the pencil as we know it today only came into existence after the discovery of a large graphite deposit in the 1560s. According to the story, some English shepherds came across an unknown black substance stuck to the roots of a fallen tree, and handling it, found that it left behind a dark mark. Initially, they used it to draw brands on their livestock so that they could more easily differentiate whose sheep was whose, but they soon realised that the graphite, which they called 'black lead', could very easily be formed into sticks and used to write and draw. With string or twigs wrapped around it to reduce its brittleness, a stick of graphite not only required the user to apply less pressure than the metal alloy styluses then in use, but it also produced far darker lines. In addition, it was possible to erase graphite marks using a bit of soft bread and to draw on top of them with ink – neither of which could be done with lead or charcoal. It was not long before people began gluing bits of graphite into grooves cut into strips of wood, thereby creating the much sturdier wooden pencil we are now familiar with.

Do the following statements agree with the information given in the passage?

Write

TRUE	*if the statement agrees with the information*
FALSE	*if the statement contradicts the information*
NOT GIVEN	*if there is no information on this*

8 Writing with graphite sticks required more pressure than other writing tools.

9 Users could not see graphite marks after they had been inked over.

utensil n. 도구 antiquity n. 고대 come into existence phr. 나타나다, 생기다 graphite deposit phr. 흑연 매장층 brand n. 낙인
black lead phr. 석묵, 흑연 brittleness n. 깨지기 쉬움, 불안정함 alloy n. 합금 stylus n. 철필 groove n. 홈 sturdy adj. 튼튼한, 견고한

5 The ability to make a good impression on people is important to many of us as humans are inherently social creatures driven by a desire to connect with others. However, it can sometimes be difficult to interpret exactly what other people think of us. It would be easy if they all simply saw us the way we try to appear. Unfortunately, everyone we encounter views the world through his or her own unique lens, and people tend to not be very direct about how they feel about others unless in the privacy of their own trusted social circles. It is for this reason that, in order to determine how other people view us, it is sometimes necessary to rely on our metaperceptions.

A metaperception is how a person views others' perceptions of him or herself. Metaperceptions are usually fairly accurate in individuals who have a strong sense of self because these sorts of people are easily able to pick up on how others respond to their words or actions. This enables them to know whether they are liked or not. Individuals with a good sense of who they are tend to have no problems adjusting their behaviours to better suit the situation – if, that is, being liked is their end goal. People with a weak sense of self, on the other hand, are often wrong about how others see them. This is because they often lack self-confidence in the first place and therefore have numerous personal biases. They might, for example, not really like themselves for any number of reasons and therefore think that everyone else hates them, too, when this is not necessarily the case. Conversely, others might believe that they are witty and fun to be around when the reality is that they are rude and burdensome. Unfortunately for people like these, social exclusion and all the negative consequences associated with it sometimes occur as a result.

Do the following statements agree with the information given in the passage?

Write

TRUE	*if the statement agrees with the information*
FALSE	*if the statement contradicts the information*
NOT GIVEN	*if there is no information on this*

10 People are generally honest about how they perceive others.

11 Those with a strong sense of self usually know how others see them.

12 Individuals with weak self-perception fail when they try to adjust their behaviours.

---

inherently adv. 선천적으로 metaperception n. 상위 인지 sense of self phr. 자의식 pick up phr. 알아차리다, 알게 되다 adjust v. 조정하다
bias n. 편견 conversely adv. 반대로, 역으로 witty adj. 재치 있는 burdensome adj. 부담이 되는, 성가신 exclusion n. 배제, 제외

6 Animals use a wide range of signals to communicate with one another. In addition to the auditory cues like barking and meowing that everyone thinks of when considering animal signals, we know that they also utilise chemical, visual, and tactile signals. Using these varied signalling systems or combinations of them, some species have developed highly advanced methods of transferring information to one another. One great example of this was discovered in honeybees by animal behaviourist Karl von Frisch. Dr von Frisch was the first to interpret the round and waggle dances that foraging honeybees perform when they return to the hive. From his research, he found that these were a form of signalling for the bees. Using dances, the bees could communicate the distance and location of sources of high quality pollen. He also noted that by performing the dance in close contact, the bees could also signal the type of food through their scents.

Signalling, however, is not used only for food gathering. Many animals use various means to signal their ownership of a territory and its boundaries. Perhaps the most common is scent marking. In this system, animals mark their territories by rubbing on items or urinating and defecating within their territories to warn other animals. This can also lead to a visual signal to other animals. Brown bears, for instance, rub their scent into trees and often leave behind tufts of hair in the bark. These clumps of hair can signal that the bear was there even after the scent has dissipated.

The great amount of information that animals can communicate using signals raises another important question: Does signalling constitute a language? Noted 19th-century naturalist Charles Darwin conducted basic research into this topic for his book *Descent of Man* (1871). In it, Darwin discussed similarities between animals' auditory signals and human communication. Although he ultimately felt that language distinguished humans from lesser animals, he could not help but notice that baby birds are taught to signal by their parents and that some gibbons utilise musical sounds for courtship and competition with rivals, much like humans.

Do the following statements agree with the information given in the passage?

Write

TRUE	*if the statement agrees with the information*
FALSE	*if the statement contradicts the information*
NOT GIVEN	*if there is no information on this*

13 Sounds are one of many communication mechanisms used by animals.

14 Scent marking conveys less information about territories than other forms of animal signalling.

15 Similarities between animal signalling and human communication caused Darwin to believe it was a basic language.

---

auditory adj. 청각의 tactile adj. 촉각을 이용한 waggle dance phr. (꿀벌의) 8자 춤 forage v. 먹이를 찾다 pollen n. 꽃가루 defecate v. 대변을 보다
tuft n. 뭉치, 다발 clump n. 무더기, 덤불 dissipate v. 흩어져 사라지다 constitute v. ~이 되는 것으로 여겨지다, ~이 되다 naturalist n. 동식물학자
gibbon n. 긴팔원숭이 courtship n. 구애

7 Charles Ives

Born in 1874, modernist composer Charles Ives studied music as a child and served as a church organist during his youth. Influenced by his father, who was a bandleader in the army, he went on to compose religious choral pieces at Yale University. Yet despite his talent and penchant for music, Ives was a businessman for most of his life.

Ives joined the insurance agency Charles H. Raymond & Co. in 1899 but left to found an insurance business of his own with one of his colleagues, Julian Myrick, in 1907. Ives quickly earned a reputation among his peers for being a shrewd businessman who was adept at making money. However, believing that insurance was, first and foremost, a means of benefiting the public, he upheld the humanitarian ideals of the industry and had no involvement in the corruption scandals prevalent within it during his time. When he retired in 1930, Ives and Myrick's firm was the largest of its kind in America.

Ives' business success so overshadowed his musical endeavours that some of his friends were entirely unaware that he was a composer. Publishing pieces at his own expense and having them performed in obscure places by little-known musicians, Ives kept his distance from the mainstream musical community. His doing so gave him the confidence to experiment, borrowing elements from a variety of musical genres. For instance, he integrated the popular music and religious choral pieces of his teenage and college years with European concert music. It was his creativity and ability to mix genres that ultimately brought him renown among music critics.

The work that best epitomises his talent for synthesis is Piano Sonata No. 2, more commonly known as Concord Sonata. The piece was inspired by the American transcendentalist writers of the 19th century, who were active in the vicinity of Concord, Massachusetts. One of the central tenets of transcendentalism was that personal intuition, rather than society and its various institutions, opened the gateway to imagination. Utilising quotations from Beethoven, excerpts from popular and religious music, and sounds from everyday life, such as trains, Ives attempted to capture this spirit in his sonata. Public performances of the work also included an experimental dimension: before each of the four movements, Ives read from the works of the authors that inspired them – Emerson, Hawthorne, the Alcott family, and Thoreau. The sonata had a triumphant premiere in 1938 – more than 20 years after it had been completed – and news of his work soon spread.

9 years later, in 1947, Ives rose to the very forefront of classical music when he was awarded the Pulitzer Prize for Symphony No. 3. Despite gaining this acknowledgement for his musical contribution during his lifetime, he did not live to see many of his works performed live, and Ives' fame among the public was mostly posthumous. Today, Ives is regarded as a pioneer in American musical history, and his reputation continues to grow. In the last 15 years of the 20th century alone, at least twenty books were released about his life and work.

Do the following statements agree with the information given in the passage?

Write

TRUE	*if the statement agrees with the information*
FALSE	*if the statement contradicts the information*
NOT GIVEN	*if there is no information on this*

16 Corruption was widespread among insurance firms during Charles Ives's time.

17 The mainstream musical community was strictly against experimentation.

18 Ives did not use popular and religious music in his sonata.

19 Charles Ives received no recognition for his work until after he had passed away.

---

choral adj. 합창의 penchant n. 애호 shrewd adj. 영리한, 통찰력이 있는 be adept at phr. ~에 능숙하다 uphold v. 유지하다
humanitarian adj. 인도주의적인 ideal n. 이상 overshadow v. 무색하게 만들다, 그늘을 드리우다 obscure adj. 외진, 잘 알려져 있지 않은
integrate v. 통합하다 epitomise v. 전형적으로 보여주다 synthesis n. 통합, 합성 transcendentalist n. 초월주의자 in the vicinity of phr. ~의 부근에
tenet n. 교리, 주의 triumphant adj. 성공적인 premiere n. 초연 posthumous adj. 사후의

8 The Hazards of Multitasking

We live in a fast-paced world, and many people these days seem to feel as though it is necessary to complete as many tasks as possible at the same time in order to keep up. Multitasking, as this behaviour is known, may provide some with the sense that they are making efficient use of their time, but this is far from the truth. What is more, juggling more than one can handle can have detrimental effects on a person's physical health and mental well-being.

Contrary to popular belief, the human brain is ill-equipped to process multiple forms of information simultaneously – so ill-equipped that what we believe to be multitasking may not even be possible. When people attempt to engage in multiple activities at once, what their brains are actually doing is frantically switching between tasks. Rather than giving their undivided attention to a single activity, people engaged in multitasking are able to focus on each thing they are trying to do for only a few seconds at a time. Repeatedly moving between tasks is, unsurprisingly, exhausting and makes it extremely difficult to filter information and recall it afterwards. Ultimately, multitasking is counterproductive in that it slows us down. Seeing one task through to completion before beginning another one is far more efficient, as the time it takes the brain to jump back and forth and refocus on an activity it was previously engaged in is time wasted.

If that wasn't bad enough, multitasking can lead to poor health. When the brain, the control system for the body's nervous system, attempts to conduct multiple tasks at the same time, it almost always releases stress hormones and adrenaline. When this happens, the adrenaline provides a temporary energy boost, often resulting in the body accomplishing what it has been tasked to do, however inefficiently that may be. At the same time, though, the release of stress hormones causes blood pressure to rise, which most people know can be dangerous because it makes the heart work harder. While being stressed from time to time is to be expected, experiencing it all the time, as an increasing number of us do, can make us sick. In fact, the chronically stressed not only experience headaches, digestion problems, and a general sense of unease on a regular basis, but they are also vulnerable to exhaustion, depression, and viruses, and are more likely to develop potentially fatal conditions, such as heart disease. All in all, while multitasking may seem like the only way to cope in a world full of stimuli, its potential to damage both our health and productivity is reason enough to avoid it.

Do the following statements agree with the information given in the passage?

Write

TRUE	*if the statement agrees with the information*
FALSE	*if the statement contradicts the information*
NOT GIVEN	*if there is no information on this*

20   The brain can focus on several things at once for extended periods of time.

21   Switching between tasks makes it hard to remember information.

22   The boost that adrenaline provides helps increase a person's overall efficiency.

23   People who experience stress from time to time are the most likely to develop serious conditions.

---

fast-paced adj. 빠른 속도로 돌아가는   juggle v. (두 가지 이상의 일을 동시에) 곡예하듯 하다   detrimental adj. 해로운   simultaneously adv. 동시에
frantically adv. 정신없이, 극도로 흥분하여   filter v. 거르다, 여과하다   counterproductive adj. 역효과를 낳는
see through phr. (포기하지 않고) ~을 끝까지 해내다   back and forth phr. 왔다 갔다   chronically adv. 만성적으로   unease n. 불안(감), 우려
all in all phr. 대체로

9 Books in the Middle Ages

The story of how the written word emerged from the shadows of the medieval period

At the beginning of the European Middle Ages, books were extremely rare. Those that existed were produced entirely by hand and were very expensive, meaning that other than the Catholic Church, which produced them, only the wealthy ever saw them, let alone owned them. Furthermore, education was only available to the clergy and the most affluent members of society. This meant that the vast majority of the population spent their lives labouring in fields, remaining completely illiterate, with everything they knew about history and mythology limited to the spoken-word stories and songs delivered to them by the bards, minstrels, and poets of the day. Society functioned in this manner for hundreds of years during this period until the printed book was introduced, marking a turning point in European society and changing how information was passed onto future generations.

The main reason so few books existed had to do with the fact that making one was an arduous process that took years to complete. Animal hides had to be cured to produce pages, and then ink had to be made by mixing pigments derived from various sources. This was followed by preparing quills with which to write and ruling lines on each page to guide where the script would be placed. Only once all these preparations had been completed could a scribe actually write the book, which involved transcribing every word by hand. Afterwards, illustrations could be added, the pages could be decorated with borders made of gold, silver, and copper leaf, and everything would be bound together. Essentially, the labor intensiveness involved in finishing a single copy of a book meant that very few were ever made and that only the elite could buy one.

Without a doubt, it was the Catholic Church that maintained control over most books during the Middle Ages. Some monasteries even made it their mission to keep libraries full of the literary, scientific, and philosophical works of the ancient Greeks and Romans, preserving them through the ages. The ability of monasteries to have so much information yet keep such a tight rein on it was due to the fact that the Church was the most important facet of society at the time, above even the nobility, and that clergy members were among the few people capable of scribing and illustrating. Tasks like these were in such high demand among people wanting copies of the Bible that by the 14th century, certain monasteries were set aside for the sole purpose of producing them.

In 1445, a man by the name of Johann Gutenberg forever changed the lives of people in Europe, and eventually the entire world, with his invention of the printing press. Gutenberg's press could produce books quickly and cheaply, which resulted in two major changes in European society. The first was that papal authorities were no longer able to control literature and information; not only could books be printed outside of monasteries, but they were also available at such low prices that even the common man could purchase them. The second was that written works found their way to the general public. This incited more people to learn to read and write, which increased literacy rates considerably.

Do the following statements agree with the information given in the passage?

Write

TRUE	*if the statement agrees with the information*
FALSE	*if the statement contradicts the information*
NOT GIVEN	*if there is no information on this*

24   Oral accounts provided historical knowledge during the Early Middle Ages.

25   A special technique used in monasteries kept books preserved.

26   The power of the Catholic Church was equal to that of the nobility.

27   The printing press loosened the control the Church had over information.

---

let alone phr. ~은 고사하고   clergy n. 성직자들   affluent adj. 부유한   bard n. 음유 시인   minstrel n. 음악가, 음유 시인   arduous adj. 고된, 몹시 힘든
hide n. 가죽   cure v. 보존 처리하다   pigment n. 안료   quill n. 깃펜   scribe n. 서기   transcribe v. 기록하다   border n. 테두리, 가장자리
monastery n. 수도원   keep a tight rein on phr. ~을 엄격히 통제하다   facet n. 일면   set aside phr. 확보하다, 챙겨두다   papal adj. 교황의
incite v. 고무시키다, 자극하다   literacy rate phr. 식자율(국민 중 글을 아는 사람들의 비율)

Europe's Commercial Revolution

The social and economic effects of international trade and colonisation

Europeans were introduced to spices, silks, and other goods from the Middle East during the Crusades, a series of holy wars aimed at driving Muslims from the region. Over the course of nearly two hundred years of war, many Middle Eastern products had become highly sought after, so when the Crusades finally came to an end in 1291, trade between Europe and the Middle East did not. Business between the two regions was carried out freely until 1453, when Constantinople was conquered. This made land routes inaccessible, motivating Europeans to find new ways of reaching the Middle East, and by extension, Asia. These developments, combined with the rise of England, Portugal, and Spain as European powers, ushered in an age during which lucrative trade networks were established and new lands were colonised.

Christopher Columbus's 1492 voyage to the New World and Vasco da Gama's circumnavigation of Africa six years later were among Europe's first successes. Not long after, colonies were set up in the Americas, and trade routes connecting Europe to the rest of the world were established. In addition to spices and silks from the Middle East and Asia, Europeans began to import raw materials from Africa and the Americas to use in the production of goods that would be sold both domestically and abroad. Known as the Commercial Revolution, this period of European economic expansion between the 16th and 18th centuries had wide-reaching consequences.

One of the most immediate effects was inflation. Prior to the Commercial Revolution, much of Europe's gold and silver had been used to trade in the Middle East. With gold and silver mines exhausted and little money remaining in circulation, a downward trend in prices occurred. However, gold and silver began to pour into Europe once precious metals were discovered in the New World. Spain alone imported more than 180 tonnes of gold and more than 16,000 tonnes of silver from its colonies between 1500 and 1650, and as this new money entered circulation, prices rose dramatically. Inflation was further compounded by a rising demand for goods from a population recovering from the Black Death.

The Commercial Revolution also impacted society profoundly. The currency surplus was beneficial for labourers, who could demand higher wages, but it also meant that it was costlier for the nobility to hire them. As a result, many members of the aristocracy had to sell off properties piecemeal to maintain their lifestyles. The buyers were not other members of the nobility but newly wealthy merchants, many of whom fenced off the land, breaking with the tradition of the aristocracy permitting the peasants to cultivate it. With no fields to tend, farmers moved to cities and ultimately became the new urban workforce.

Although trade during the Commercial Revolution was highly profitable, war, weather, and piracy could cause major losses. Consequently, organisations called joint-stock companies were established to mitigate these hazards. Considered the forerunners of modern corporations, these businesses were privately owned companies that sold stock to investors for a share of the profits. The money earned from selling shares was used to fund projects and acquire trade goods. And although there was still a chance that shipments would be destroyed, stolen, or lost, given the fact that there were generally numerous investors, the risk borne by the company and each stockholder was minimal.

Do the following statements agree with the information given in the passage?

Write

TRUE	*if the statement agrees with the information*
FALSE	*if the statement contradicts the information*
NOT GIVEN	*if there is no information on this*

28 Trade between the Middle East and Europe stopped when the Crusades ended.

29 Spain imported more gold and silver from the Americas than any other European state.

30 The aristocracy once allowed poor farmers to use their land for agricultural purposes.

31 Joint-stock companies minimised financial risk because multiple people invested money in them.

정답·해석·해설 p.333

colonisation n. 식민지화 spice n. 향신료, 양념 the Crusades phr. 십자군 전쟁 sought after phr. 인기 있는, 수요가 많은 lucrative adj. 수익성이 좋은
circumnavigation n. (세계) 일주 raw material phr. 원자재 domestically adv. 국내에서 downward trend phr. 하락세 precious metal phr. 귀금속
the Black Death phr. 흑사병 surplus n. 과잉 piecemeal adv. 조금씩, 조각조각으로 tend v. 돌보다 joint-stock company phr. 주식 회사

READING PASSAGE

*You should spend about 20 minutes on **Questions 1-13**, which are based on Reading Passage below.*

The Impact of Global Urbanisation: The Costs and Benefits

Urbanisation, which can refer to either the process by which rural communities grow into cities or the migration of people from rural to urban areas, has its roots in ancient human history. Historians widely agree that urbanisation first occurred in ancient Mesopotamia, beginning with the first true city of Uruk around 4500 B.C., and then continuing with the establishment of Ur around 3800 B.C.

But this phenomenon is usually associated more with modern times. In Europe, a much broader and more extensive urbanisation occurred in the 19th century as a result of the Industrial Revolution. In England, the urban population increased from 17 per cent in 1801 to an astonishing 72 per cent in 1891, primarily congregating in the cities of London, Manchester, Newcastle, and Birmingham, where factories offered promising jobs to impoverished peasants traditionally dependent on subsistence agriculture. Life in the cities, with its abundant work, entertainment, and social services, seemed like a far more promising alternative to the toil of farm life.

And that lure has continued. In 2008, the world's urban population exceeded its rural population for the first time. But contemporary instances of urbanisation are not relegated to industrialised countries, as was the case prior to the 1950s. Since then, urbanisation has primarily occurred in less developed regions, and it is estimated that by 2030 virtually all developing regions will have more people living in urban environments than in rural areas. There are several reasons for this. One is the lack of resources in rural areas to accommodate an ever-expanding global population. The second is the lure of employment opportunities that people associate with cities. The third is the desire for higher quality health care and education than what most rural communities are able to provide.

However, it's important to keep in mind that while this shift in demographics promises many opportunities, it's not without its challenges. Often, the job market cannot keep up with the pace of urban growth. This means that many of the poor who migrate to cities will find themselves relocated without improving their economic situations. And without the family and community support that is often present in people's hometowns, urban migrants can find themselves even worse off than they were back home. This in part explains the prevalence of urban slums in our cities today.

Another disturbing aspect of modern urbanisation is the high rate of certain types of crime that plagues many major cities. Decker, Sichor, and O'Brien (1982) conducted a detailed study of how population density affects crime and found that there is a direct correlation between urbanisation and crimes such as robbery and larceny with face-to-face contact. They also discovered that vehicle theft occurred at a much higher rate in urban areas than in rural areas – a finding that is surprising because per capita car ownership is considerably less in cities than in less populated areas, which tend to be car dependent and without public transportation. The problem of crime in urban areas is particularly dire in times of social unrest, such as during the politically volatile years of the late 1960s in the United States, and law enforcement agencies are searching for answers about how to tackle the rampant crime in American cities. Despite increases in the number of law enforcement officers patrolling Chicago's streets, the total number of murders there has risen dramatically in recent years.

But perhaps most pressing on the minds of both city inhabitants and city planners is how to best feed these massive numbers of people. Although the past century has seen dramatic advances in agricultural efficiency and productivity, hundreds of thousands of city dwellers continue to suffer from undernutrition. This issue is not directly related to agricultural production itself, which is more than capable of meeting world demand;

rather, it is a combination of lack of access to foodstuffs – e.g. due to poverty – and the growing propensity to substitute whole foods with packaged and processed foods (de Haen, 2003), which has been blamed for the epidemic of obesity and its health-related problems in many cities.

Moreover, with cities' greater dependence on supermarkets, the economics of food logistics promotes fewer agricultural sources, as it is far more cost effective for retailers to streamline their supply chains. This has led to a much heavier reliance on imported goods – a trend that has resulted in the elimination of many small local farms. One solution being tried out in numerous cities in North America and Europe is the transplantation of rural farms to urban gardens and greenhouses. This allows for locally grown produce, which might be attractive to many consumers. Some large-scale urban farming initiatives are already underway and thus far have shown promising results.

Questions 1-9

Do the following statements agree with the information given in Reading Passage?

Write

TRUE	*if the statement agrees with the information*
FALSE	*if the statement contradicts the information*
NOT GIVEN	*if there is no information on this*

1   England's 19th century urban population boom was focused on four cities.

2   An increase in urban migration has led to severe housing shortages in cities.

3   Many migrants do not see any improvement in their economic circumstances.

4   A lack of family support in cities can lead people to crime.

5   Social instability causes an increase in criminal activity in cities.

6   Increasing the presence of Chicago police decreased the murder rate.

7   Poverty causes people to restrict their diet since they are unable to afford fresh vegetables.

8   The availability of factory produced foods is causing obesity to decline.

9   Urban farms have the potential to make local produce more appealing.

*Choose the correct letter, **A**, **B**, **C** or **D**.*

10   In the second paragraph, the writer makes a point that

    A   the failure of agriculture forced people to move to cities.

    B   urbanisation allowed for new industrial practices.

    C   industrialisation can have a beneficial effect on urban life.

    D   urbanisation is widely considered a modern trend.

11   According to the writer, a greater dependence on supermarkets

    A   resulted in the closure of many small grocers in urban areas.

    B   led to stiff opposition from advocates of urban agriculture.

    C   caused the development of more diverse supply chains.

    D   brought about a stronger need for goods from other countries.

Questions 12 and 13

Complete the sentences below.

*Choose **NO MORE THAN TWO WORDS** from the passage for each answer.*

12   In the last 60 years, urbanisation has mainly happened in less .... than in wealthy countries.

13   A crime that occurs far more in cities than in rural areas is .... theft.

정답·해석·해설 p.342

VOCABULARY LIST

Chapter 02에서 선별한 다음의 어휘들을 음성파일을 들으며 암기한 후 퀴즈로 확인해보세요.

*해커스 동영상강의 포털 해커스 인강(HackersIngang.com)에서 단어암기 MP3를 무료로 다운로드할 수 있습니다.

- ☐ persistent adj. 끊임없이 지속되는
- ☐ communal adj. 공동 사회의, 공동체의
- ☐ maximise v. 극대화하다
- ☐ return n. 수익
- ☐ emission n. 배출물
- ☐ declare v. 공표하다
- ☐ synonymous adj. 동의어의
- ☐ byproduct n. 부산물
- ☐ metabolism n. 신진 대사
- ☐ correspondence n. 서신
- ☐ monumentally adv. 엄청나게
- ☐ call for phr. ~을 필요로 하게 하다
- ☐ transcribe v. 기록하다
- ☐ remedy v. 개선하다
- ☐ sluggishly adv. 느리게
- ☐ modification n. 변경, 수정
- ☐ seemingly adv. 겉보기에는
- ☐ transcription n. 표기, 인쇄
- ☐ utensil n. 도구
- ☐ come into existence phr. 나타나다, 생기다
- ☐ alloy n. 합금
- ☐ sturdy adj. 튼튼한, 견고한
- ☐ inherently adv. 선천적으로
- ☐ sense of self phr. 자의식
- ☐ pick up phr. 알아차리다, 알게 되다
- ☐ adjust v. 조정하다

- ☐ bias n. 편견
- ☐ conversely adv. 반대로, 역으로
- ☐ witty adj. 재치 있는
- ☐ burdensome adj. 부담이 되는, 성가신
- ☐ exclusion n. 배제, 제외
- ☐ auditory adj. 청각의
- ☐ dissipate v. 흩어져 사라지다
- ☐ constitute v. ~이 되는 것으로 여겨지다, ~이 되다
- ☐ courtship n. 구애
- ☐ be adept at phr. ~에 능숙하다
- ☐ uphold v. 유지하다
- ☐ humanitarian adj. 인도주의적인
- ☐ ideal n. 이상
- ☐ overshadow v. 무색하게 만들다, 그늘을 드리우다
- ☐ integrate v. 통합하다
- ☐ synthesis n. 통합, 합성
- ☐ in the vicinity of phr. ~의 부근에
- ☐ triumphant adj. 성공적인
- ☐ premiere n. 초연
- ☐ posthumous adj. 사후의
- ☐ fast-paced adj. 빠른 속도로 돌아가는
- ☐ detrimental adj. 해로운
- ☐ simultaneously adv. 동시에
- ☐ frantically adv. 정신없이, 극도로 흥분하여
- ☐ filter v. 거르다, 여과하다
- ☐ counterproductive adj. 역효과를 낳는

Quiz

각 단어의 알맞은 뜻을 찾아 연결하시오.

01 communal	ⓐ 부담이 되는, 성가신	
02 call for	ⓑ ~을 필요로 하게 하다	
03 synonymous	ⓒ 부산물	
04 byproduct	ⓓ 공동 사회의, 공동체의	
05 monumentally	ⓔ 엄청나게	
	ⓕ 동의어의	

06 detrimental	ⓐ 통합하다
07 be adept at	ⓑ 배제, 제외
08 integrate	ⓒ ~에 능숙하다
09 posthumous	ⓓ 해로운
10 exclusion	ⓔ 구애
	ⓕ 사후의

ⓓ 01 ⓑ 02 ⓕ 03 ⓒ 04 ⓔ 05 ⓓ 06 ⓒ 07 ⓐ 08 ⓕ 09 ⓑ 10

- ☐ see through phr. (포기하지 않고) ~을 끝까지 해내다
- ☐ back and forth phr. 왔다 갔다
- ☐ chronically adv. 만성적으로
- ☐ unease n. 불안(감), 우려
- ☐ all in all phr. 대체로
- ☐ let alone phr. ~은 고사하고
- ☐ clergy n. 성직자들
- ☐ affluent adj. 부유한
- ☐ arduous adj. 고된, 몹시 힘든
- ☐ cure v. 보존 처리하다
- ☐ pigment n. 안료
- ☐ scribe n. 서기
- ☐ border n. 테두리, 가장자리
- ☐ monastery n. 수도원
- ☐ keep a tight rein on phr. ~을 엄격히 통제하다
- ☐ facet n. 일면
- ☐ set aside phr. 확보하다, 챙겨두다
- ☐ incite v. 고무시키다, 자극하다
- ☐ literacy rate phr. 식자율(국민 중 글을 아는 사람들의 비율)
- ☐ spice n. 향신료, 양념
- ☐ the Crusades phr. 십자군 전쟁
- ☐ lucrative adj. 수익성이 좋은
- ☐ raw material phr. 원자재
- ☐ domestically adv. 국내에서
- ☐ downward trend phr. 하락세
- ☐ precious metal phr. 귀금속
- ☐ surplus n. 과잉
- ☐ piecemeal adv. 조금씩, 조각조각으로
- ☐ tend v. 돌보다
- ☐ urbanisation n. 도시화
- ☐ cost and benefit phr. 비용과 편익
- ☐ migration n. 이주, 이동
- ☐ congregate v. 모이다
- ☐ impoverished adj. 빈곤한
- ☐ peasant n. 소작농
- ☐ toil n. 노역, 고역
- ☐ lure n. 매력, 유혹
- ☐ contemporary adj. 현대의, 동시대의
- ☐ relegate v. (어떤 종류 · 등급 등에) 분류하다, 소속시키다
- ☐ demographics n. 인구 통계
- ☐ prevalence n. 만연, 유행
- ☐ slum n. 빈민가, 슬럼
- ☐ dire adj. 심각한, 엄청난
- ☐ unrest n. 불안, 불만
- ☐ tackle v. (문제 등을) 다루다
- ☐ rampant adj. 만연하는
- ☐ patrol v. 순찰을 돌다
- ☐ undernutrition n. 영양 결핍
- ☐ propensity n. 경향
- ☐ substitute v. 대체하다
- ☐ epidemic n. 급속한 확산, 유행
- ☐ produce n. 농산물

Quiz

각 단어의 알맞은 뜻을 찾아 연결하시오.

01 affluent	ⓐ 만성적으로
02 set aside	ⓑ 일면
03 lucrative	ⓒ 확보하다, 챙겨두다
04 facet	ⓓ 고무시키다, 자극하다
05 chronically	ⓔ 부유한
	ⓕ 수익성이 좋은

06 tackle	ⓐ 현대의, 동시대의
07 contemporary	ⓑ 만연한
08 rampant	ⓒ 빈곤한
09 surplus	ⓓ 매력, 유혹
10 impoverished	ⓔ 과잉
	ⓕ (문제 등을) 다루다

01 ⓔ 02 ⓒ 03 ⓕ 04 ⓑ 05 ⓐ 06 ⓕ 07 ⓐ 08 ⓑ 09 ⓔ 10 ⓒ

CHAPTER 03
Y/N/NG (Yes / No / Not Given)

Y/N/NG 문제는 제시된 문장이 지문에 나타난 작가의 견해와 일치하는지, 일치하지 않는지, 혹은 알 수 없는지를 판단하는 문제이다. Y/N/NG 문제는 지문의 정보가 아닌 작가의 견해와 일치하는지를 묻는다는 점에서 T/F/NG 문제와 구분된다. IELTS Reading 영역에서 가장 많이 출제되는 유형 중 하나로, 거의 매 시험 출제되고 있다.

■ 문제 형태

Y/N/NG 문제는 제시된 문장이 지문에 나타난 작가의 견해와 일치한다면 Yes, 일치하지 않는다면 No, 알 수 없다면 Not given을 적는 형태로 출제된다.

Do the following statements agree with the claims of the writer in Reading Passage 1?

In boxes 1-3 on your answer sheet, write

 YES   *if the statement agrees with the claims of the writer*
 NO   *if the statement contradicts the claims of the writer*
 NOT GIVEN *if it is impossible to say what the writer thinks about this*

1 A second child of the opposite gender is less influenced by the firstborn.

2 Children born around the same time usually get along well.

3 Personality traits are clearly determined by the birth order effect.

■ 문제풀이 전략

Y/N/NG 문제를 풀기 위해서는 먼저 문제의 핵심어구와 핵심 내용을 파악한다.

EXAMPLE

Do the following statements agree with the claims of the writer in Reading Passage?

In boxes 1-3 on your answer sheet, write

> **YES**   *if the statement agrees with the claims of the writer*
> **NO**   *if the statement contradicts the claims of the writer*
> **NOT GIVEN** *if it is impossible to say what the writer thinks about this*

1   A second child of the opposite gender is less influenced by the firstborn.

2   Children born around the same time usually get along well.

3   Personality traits are clearly determined by the birth order effect.

문제의 핵심어구인 A second child of the opposite gender가 첫째로 태어난 아이들에게 영향을 덜 받는다는 내용을 파악한다.

문제의 핵심어구인 Children born around the same time이 대개 잘 어울려 지낸다는 내용을 파악한다.

문제의 핵심어구인 Personality traits가 출생 순서의 영향에 의해 명확히 결정된다는 내용을 파악한다.

✓ TIPS

Y/N/NG 문제는 여러 개의 문제가 한 번에 출제되므로, 제시된 모든 문제의 핵심어구를 미리 파악해두기보다는 한 문제씩 핵심어구를 파악하여 답을 쓰고 다음 문제로 넘어가는 것이 좋다.

지문을 scanning하여 문제의 핵심어구와 관련된 내용을 찾는다. 관련 내용이 언급된 주변에서 정답의 단서를 확인한다.

EXAMPLE

A number of other factors have also been identified that can throw off the birth order effect. One of the most important of these is gender. Dr Alan Stewart of the University of Georgia noted that [1]when another child of the opposite gender follows the firstborn, the second child is not as affected by the first and often acts like a firstborn child itself. The span of time between births can also skew the birth order effect. [2]Children born within relatively short time periods can take on opposite roles. Taking these and other factors – such as overall temperament, physical size differences, and uniqueness – into account, [3]the birth order effect does not seem incredibly reliable for determining personality traits. In fact, a report shows that only 15 per cent of men and 23 per cent of women have personalities that match their birth order.

1번 문제의 핵심어구인 A second child of the opposite gender와 관련된 내용을 지문에서 찾는다. 관련 내용이 언급된 주변에서 'when another child of the opposite gender follows the firstborn, the second child is not as affected by the first'라는 정답의 단서를 확인한다.

2번 문제의 핵심어구인 Children born around the same time과 관련된 내용을 지문에서 찾는다. 관련 내용이 언급된 주변에 정답의 단서가 등장하지 않음을 확인한다.

3번 문제의 핵심어구인 Personality traits와 관련된 내용을 지문에서 찾는다. 관련 내용이 언급된 주변에서 'the birth order effect does not seem incredibly reliable for determining personality traits'라는 정답의 단서를 확인한다.

Do the following statements agree with the claims of the writer in Reading Passage?

In boxes 1-3 on your answer sheet, write

> **YES**   *if the statement agrees with the claims of the writer*
> **NO**   *if the statement contradicts the claims of the writer*
> **NOT GIVEN**   *if it is impossible to say what the writer thinks about this*

1   A second child of the opposite gender is less influenced by the firstborn.

2   Children born around the same time usually get along well.

3   Personality traits are clearly determined by the birth order effect.

지문 해석 p.346

✓ **TIPS**

Y/N/NG 문제는 보통 지문의 내용이 전개되는 순서대로 출제되므로, 정답의 단서도 지문에서 순서대로 등장한다. 예를 들어 2번 문제의 정답의 단서는 1번 문제의 정답의 단서보다 이후에 등장할 가능성이 높다. 그러므로 정답의 단서를 찾지 못한 문제가 있다면, 이전 문제의 정답의 단서와 다음 문제의 정답의 단서 사이를 살펴보도록 한다.

STEP 3 정답의 단서와 문제의 일치 여부를 판단한다.

정답의 단서와 제시된 문제의 내용이 서로 일치하는지 판단하여 답을 적는다.

EXAMPLE

Do the following statements agree with the claims of the writer in Reading Passage?

In boxes 1-3 on your answer sheet, write

YES	*if the statement agrees with the claims of the writer*
NO	*if the statement contradicts the claims of the writer*
NOT GIVEN	*if it is impossible to say what the writer thinks about this*

1   A second child of the opposite gender is less influenced by the firstborn. Yes

2   Children born around the same time usually get along well. Not given

3   Personality traits are clearly determined by the birth order effect. No

---

1   문제의 핵심어구(A second child of the opposite gender)와 관련된 지문 내용 중 'when another child of the opposite gender follows the firstborn, the second child is not as affected by the first'에서 반대 성별의 다른 아이가 첫째 아이를 따라 태어나면 둘째 아이는 첫째 아이에게 그렇게 많은 영향을 받지는 않는다고 하였으므로, 주어진 문장은 글쓴이의 견해와 일치함을 알 수 있다. 따라서 정답은 **Yes**이다. 'not as affected'가 'less influenced'로 paraphrasing되었다.

2   문제의 핵심어구(Children born around the same time)와 관련된 지문 내용 중 'Children born within relatively short time periods can take on opposite roles.'에서 비교적 더 적은 기간 차이로 태어난 아이들이 정반대의 역할을 맡을 수 있다고는 하였지만, 주어진 문장의 내용은 확인할 수 없다. 따라서 정답은 **Not given**이다.

3   문제의 핵심어구(Personality traits)와 관련된 지문 내용 중 'the birth order effect does not seem incredibly reliable for determining personality traits'에서 출생 순서의 영향은 성격 유형을 결정하는 데 매우 믿을 만한 것처럼 보이지는 않는다고 하였으므로, 주어진 문장은 글쓴이의 견해와 일치하지 않음을 알 수 있다. 따라서 정답은 **No**이다.

✅ TIPS

No와 Not given 구별하기

· No: 지문에서 등장한 단어 혹은 어구를 포함하며, 지문에서 언급된 내용과 완전히 반대되는 내용이 제시된다.

　ex) **지문**　언어가 없이, 인류는 자연 생태계와 비교할 수 없는 힘을 얻지 못했을 것이다.
　　　문제　인류는 언어 없이도 그들의 현재의 지위를 획득할 수 있었을 것이다.
　　　→ 문장에서 인류는 언어 없이 힘을 얻지 못했을 것이라고 했는데, 인류는 언어 없이도 지위를 획득할 수 있었을 것이라는 반대 내용을 언급하였으므로 작가의 견해와 일치하지 않는다. 따라서 정답은 No이다.

· Not given: 지문에서 등장한 단어 혹은 어구를 포함하지만, 문제의 중심 내용은 지문에서 언급되지 않는다.

　ex) **지문**　언어가 없이, 인류는 자연 생태계와 비교할 수 없는 힘을 얻지 못했을 것이다.
　　　문제　인류는 자연 생태계를 파괴함으로써 스스로 힘을 잃었다.
　　　→ 문장에서 언어가 없이 인류는 자연 생태계와 비교할 수 없는 힘을 얻지 못했을 것이라고 했지, 인류가 자연 생태계를 파괴함으로써 힘을 잃었는지 여부는 언급하지 않았으므로, 작가의 견해가 어떤지 알 수 없다. 따라서 정답은 Not given이다.

1 Some linguists believe that language comprehension is a learned skill and that adults will, therefore, be able to understand even unfamiliar language better than children. This theory rests on the idea that over time we develop the ability to understand both verbal and non-verbal clues when communicating. Since this is a learning process, it seems only logical that children would be less skilled at discerning meaning from context. However, this is unlikely to be true. In fact, recent studies by linguists at Germany's Bielefeld University have shown that although children do not accurately anticipate visual clues while listening to stories, they are able to rapidly interpret visual clues to assist with their overall language comprehension. This does not mean that their skills will not improve over time, but it does show that determining context from non-auditory clues is a basic element of language comprehension.

Do the following statements agree with the claims of the writer in the passage?

Write

YES	*if the statement agrees with the claims of the writer*
NO	*if the statement contradicts the claims of the writer*
NOT GIVEN	*if it is impossible to say what the writer thinks about this*

1 Children are not able to determine meaning from context.

2 Understanding unspoken signals is a fundamental aspect of human language.

---

comprehension n. 이해(력) learned adj. 학습된, 후천적인 rest on phr. ~에 기초하다 logical adj. 타당한, 사리에 맞는 discern v. 파악하다, 알아차리다 interpret v. 이해하다, 해석하다 non-auditory adj. 비청각의

2 When first introduced, coins were known as 'commodity money'. This means that the actual coin had an inherent monetary value because of the materials of which it was made. In the earliest coins from Anatolia – what is now Turkey – and ancient Greece, this was a natural alloy of gold and silver called electrum. By the 7th century, coins had begun to be manufactured from pure gold and silver in the Middle East. However, this eventually changed and coins began to be made of cheaper metals that had no intrinsic value. These types of coins were referred to as 'fiat currency' because the government single-handedly set and guaranteed their values. While this may seem illogical, it actually had several benefits. Perhaps the most obvious of these is that the value of the currency remained more stable, since it did not fluctuate with the price of the precious metals. Further, it conserved these valuable resources. The reason that gold and silver were valuable was because of their scarcity, so using them for minting coins reduced the world's supply of them. Finally, coins in the fiat system were less prone to manipulation, since their constituent metals were not all that valuable. For instance, when coins were made of gold or silver, people sometimes clipped off pieces of the coin and kept the valuable metals.

Do the following statements agree with the views of the writer in the passage?

Write

YES	*if the statement agrees with the views of the writer*
NO	*if the statement contradicts the views of the writer*
NOT GIVEN	*if it is impossible to say what the writer thinks about this*

3 Coins originally had no value of their own due to the materials they were made of.

4 Precious metals are now too rare to be currency.

---

commodity money phr. 상품 화폐   inherent adj. 고유한, 내재적인   alloy n. 합금   electrum n. 호박금(고대 그리스에서 화폐로 쓴 호박색의 금은 합금)
intrinsic adj. 고유한, 본질적인   fiat currency phr. 신용 화폐   single-handedly adv. 단독으로   fluctuate with phr. ~에 따라 변화하다
scarcity n. 희귀함, 부족   mint v. (화폐를) 주조하다   manipulation n. 속임수, 조작   constituent adj. ~을 이루는, ~을 구성하는
clip v. (금화·은화의) 가장자리를 깎아내다

3 Today, about 30 per cent of the Earth's surface is covered by forestland. However, deforestation is dramatically reducing this percentage each year. Currently, human activity claims more than 13.7 million hectares of forestland annually – an area approximately equal to that of Greece. While it may be assumed that we are cutting down trees to meet our timber needs, the bigger culprit is actually agriculture. Earth's growing population has increased our need for agricultural products and farmers have begun clear-cutting forestland to convert it into farmland where they can plant crops.

This is especially true in countries such as Brazil and Indonesia, where large areas of forestland have been cleared for farmland for cash crops such as soybeans and oil palms. The intense farming methods used for these crops further compound the problem. Continuous crop production depletes the soil of its nutrients so that it can no longer support the biodiversity it once could, making it nearly impossible to return it to forestland in the future. This continued disappearance of the forests will have a major impact on our environment. Trees play an important role in removing carbon dioxide from the air and in returning water to the atmosphere. If the forests are allowed to further deteriorate, it could disrupt the life cycle of plants and animals, and even eliminate entire ecosystems. To avoid this outcome, we must find a way to conserve our forestlands and replace the trees that we remove each year.

Do the following statements agree with the claims of the writer in the passage?

Write

YES	*if the statement agrees with the claims of the writer*
NO	*if the statement contradicts the claims of the writer*
NOT GIVEN	*if it is impossible to say what the writer thinks about this*

5 Timber is the most common reason for cutting down trees.

6 Clear-cutting forests threatens to destroy ecological systems.

---

deforestation n. 삼림 파괴 claim v. 빼앗다, 앗아 가다 culprit n. (문제의) 원인(이 되는 것) clear-cut v. (숲의 한 구역을) 개벌(삭베기)하다
convert v. 개조하다, 전환시키다 cash crop phr. 환금 작물 oil palm phr. 기름 야자 compound v. 악화시키다, 더 심각하게 만들다
biodiversity n. 생물의 다양성 deteriorate v. 악화되다, 저하되다

4 Over the course of time, members of the genus Homo have undergone a great deal of evolutionary change to morph into anatomically modern humans – members of the Homo sapiens species that have the physical features of modern humans. Today, it is commonly believed by the scientific community that earlier species of Homo sapiens evolved in eastern Africa around 200,000 years ago. In fact, the earliest anatomically modern human fossils were discovered there dating to about 195,000 years ago. Members of this species gradually migrated out of their African homeland and by 60,000 years ago one group had settled in Eurasia and the Middle East. This brought them in contact with another early human species that had previously left Africa, the Neanderthals. Some scientists believe that this interaction brought about violent clashes between the two groups, which eventually led to the extinction of the Neanderthals.

However, separate evolution is probably a more likely explanation for their disappearance. Despite their shared heritage, these two groups of early humans had evolved quite differently, both physically and intellectually. In their time in more northerly climates, the Neanderthals had become broader, stronger, and more acclimated to cold than the early anatomically modern humans. In other words, they would have physically dominated the newly arrived Homo sapiens. However, differences in brain structure seemed to have had a bigger impact on the two species. Paleoanthropologist Chris Stringer says that Homo sapiens had larger frontal lobes, the area of the brain that produces abstract, creative thoughts, than Neanderthals. This would have allowed them to develop more efficient methods of hunting and gathering, as well as food processing techniques that saved energy. These more advanced skills would have given them enough of an advantage over the Neanderthals to prevail in the long term, and that appears to be what has happened.

Do the following statements agree with the views of the writer in the passage?

Write

> **YES**   *if the statement agrees with the views of the writer*
> **NO**   *if the statement contradicts the views of the writer*
> **NOT GIVEN**   *if it is impossible to say what the writer thinks about this*

7   Modern humans migrated to Africa from the Middle East.

8   Homo sapiens are intellectually superior to their evolutionary ancestors.

9   The Neanderthals were less skilled than Homo sapiens.

Homo n. 사람, 인간 genus n. 속(과와 종의 중간) undergo v. 겪다, 받다 morph v. 변하다, 바뀌다 anatomically adv. 해부학상, 해부학적으로
clash n. 충돌, 격돌 acclimated adj. 익숙해진, 순응한 dominate v. 우세하다, 지배하다 paleoanthropologist n. 고인류학자
frontal lobe phr. (대뇌의) 전두엽 abstract adj. 추상적인 prevail v. 우세하다, 이기다

5 Phenetics is the systematic classification of organisms based on their morphological, or structural, similarities. Although, on its surface, phenetics seems to be a valid classification method, there are some problems with it. Perhaps the most important of these is that phenetic classifications sometimes show inaccurate evolutionary relationships between species. Palaeontologists have discovered that phenetic classifications can indicate relationships where they do not actually exist. This most likely occurs when species that seem similar are not closely related, but are actually at similar evolutionary levels. This inaccuracy can cause pheneticists to separate an organism from its evolutionary group, because it has a unique evolutionary adaptation. It can also lead to erroneously showing relationships between organisms with similar primitive traits. The classification of dinosaurs is a good example of these problems. We now know that birds from the Mesozoic era and some dinosaurs from the Jurassic and Cretaceous periods have very similar skeletal structures, indicating that they share an evolutionary link. However, dinosaurs are generally lumped in with lizards and alligators – species that they are more distantly related to – as reptiles. One of the reasons for this is the presence of a unique evolutionary adaptation in birds, feathers. Since we did not traditionally believe that dinosaurs had feathers, pheneticists inaccurately classified them based on other physical features. All of this shows the most inherent problem with phenetic classification: it is entirely done through the subjective observations of the pheneticist. Since there is no hierarchical classification in morphological similarity, researchers must make the ultimate decision based on their subjective observations.

Do the following statements agree with the claims of the writer in the passage?

Write

YES	*if the statement agrees with the claims of the writer*
NO	*if the statement contradicts the claims of the writer*
NOT GIVEN	*if it is impossible to say what the writer thinks about this*

10 Phenetics is currently the most trusted method of studying evolution.

11 Dinosaurs should be classified as both reptiles and birds.

12 Researchers can come to different conclusions about the same evidence.

---

phenetics n. 표현학 classification n. 분류 organism n. 생물(체), 유기체 valid adj. 타당한 morphological adj. 형태학상의
palaeontologist n. 고생물학자 pheneticist n. 표현학자 adaptation n. 적응 primitive adj. 초기의, 원시의 Mesozoic era phr. 중생대
Jurassic period phr. 쥐라기 Cretaceous period phr. 백악기 skeletal structure phr. 골격 구조 lump v. 일괄하여 다루다 subjective adj. 주관적인
hierarchical adj. 계층에 따른

6 Today, one in three seniors is suffering from one form of dementia or another. To deal with this debilitating health problem, many patients and their families are turning to alternative treatments. One of these is music therapy. At its core, music therapy works as a traditional therapy with the addition of singing, playing, or listening to music.

While this type of treatment will not cure cases of dementia, it can help patients recall memories and ease the anxiety they often feel. Neurologist Oliver Sacks believes that this occurs because listening to music evokes emotions that stimulate memories and increase cognitive ability. One of the main reasons for this is that music plays a large role in every stage of our lives. While we may not consciously think about it, we often associate music with certain activities and events. By playing music that was important at one point in the patient's life, long forgotten memories may be recalled. This could occur when playing music that was popular during a certain time period or music that was played for a special event, like a jazz song heard in a movie or a song at a patient's wedding. Music therapy can also help patients remain independent longer. By pairing music with everyday activities, patients can learn to associate the music and its patterns with the activity. This can help them recall the activity much longer.

Perhaps the most interesting discovery about music therapy is that it even works with non-verbal, late-stage patients who have lost the ability to control their emotions. These patients have very different needs than others, because they are not able to express themselves. This may cause them to feel trapped and frustrated. Oftentimes, this can lead to agitation and disruptive behaviour. By introducing music therapy activities, such as singing, dancing, or rhythm playing, the patients' attention can be redirected and they may be able to find a way to express themselves through music, which will calm them. Surprisingly, these effects take place almost immediately and continue after the music therapy session has ended. Studies by music therapist and researcher Dr Linda A. Gerdner have shown that they can be seen for at least one hour after the therapy session.

Do the following statements agree with the views of the writer in the passage?

Write

YES	*if the statement agrees with the views of the writer*
NO	*if the statement contradicts the views of the writer*
NOT GIVEN	*if it is impossible to say what the writer thinks about this*

13　Music therapy is incapable of curing dementia.

14　Listening to music can increase brain activity in patients.

15　Jazz music is particularly effective at helping patients remember the past.

16　Patients who cannot speak do not benefit from music therapy.

---

senior n. 고령자　dementia n. 치매　debilitating adj. 심신을 쇠약하게 하는　alternative adj. 대체의, 대안의　neurologist n. 신경학자
cognitive adj. 인지의　agitation n. 불안, 동요　disruptive adj. 분열성의　redirect v. ~의 방향을 바꾸다

7 The Emergence of Writing

In order to understand the origins of writing, it is necessary to debunk a couple of once-popular theories about language and culture. First, languages are not descended from a single prototype, as many scholars have suggested. That view largely derived from a Biblical interpretation of the origin of language and held that writing systems emerged in ancient Mesopotamia, and then spread and evolved throughout the rest of the world. Further, 19th century sociologists who applied the biological theory of evolution to language development viewed writing as not only having a common ancestor but also exhibiting an evolutionary hierarchy, which placed alphabetical scripts above ideographic or syllabic writing systems. In the context of the linguistic history of the ancient world, that perspective presented European and Near Eastern cultures as more highly evolved than those of Asia, Africa, and Mesoamerica. Nothing could be further from the truth given that empires rich in cultural splendour, complete with magnificent architecture, art, laws, and infrastructure, were built by civilisations with non-alphabetic scripts.

Scholars now agree that the advent of writing seems to coincide with the transition from nomadic lifestyles to more permanent agrarian ones – because people were growing food and tending to livestock, it became necessary to develop ways of keeping track of inventory and property. It is also agreed that different forms of writing developed not only in the Fertile Crescent, but also within the ancient societies of Asia and Mesoamerica and that none of these civilisations had any contact with one another during this time. Of these geographical areas, it is most likely that the earliest writing occurred in the Fertile Crescent territory of Sumer, possibly as early as 8000 B.C. The ancient Sumerians originally used tokens, such as small clay triangles, spheres, and cones, to symbolise sheep, measures of grain, jars of oil, and other goods. Basically, the shape of the token carried the meaning of the word that was being represented. Eventually, the Sumerians began pressing the tokens into soft clay tablets, much as one would use stamps, to transcribe their dealings. Much later, around 3100 B.C., the Sumerians invented numerals, separating the symbol for an object from the number of an object, suggesting that writing and mathematics could have evolved together. Archeological excavations at Uruk, once the largest city of the ancient world, show that the Sumerian script gradually advanced from pictographs to ideographic writing, meaning that some symbols represented concepts rather than just the symbol itself. At that point, writing was already developing into a tool that went beyond simply transmitting information; it was becoming a means of communicating ideas, sharing knowledge, and recording history.

Do the following statements agree with the views of the writer in the passage?

Write

> **YES**   *if the statement agrees with the views of the writer*
> **NO**   *if the statement contradicts the views of the writer*
> **NOT GIVEN**   *if it is impossible to say what the writer thinks about this*

17   The Bible's account of the origin of language is accurate.

18   Cultures with alphabets were no more advanced than others.

19   Asian writing systems were less technical than Middle Eastern ones.

20   In Sumer, mathematics developed separately from writing.

---

debunk v. (생각, 믿음 등이) 틀렸음을 밝히다 **descend** v. (언어가) ~에서 유래하다 **prototype** n. 원형 **hierarchy** n. 계층 구조, 계급
ideographic adj. 표의 문자의 **syllabic** adj. 음절의 **Mesoamerica** n. 중앙아메리카 **splendour** n. 탁월함, 현저함 **advent** n. 출현, 도래
nomadic adj. 유목의, 방랑의 **agrarian** adj. 농업의 **sphere** n. 구(체) **pictograph** n. 상형 문자

8 Nature or Nurture: Which One Shapes Us More?

Two main topics direct the study of human emotion: nature and nurture. Biological determinists believe emotion is determined by nature and that it develops intrinsically. According to this view, a person's genes affect how an individual behaves and changes over time. Meanwhile, social determinists believe emotion is shaped by nurture, meaning that environment plays the main role in emotional development. To them, variables such as parenting, poverty, education, and exposure to violence can impact a child's emotional state permanently. So, which plays a greater role?

The primary point made by social determinists is that substantial differences can and do occur in the psychological and behavioural patterns of growing children that can only be explained by experiential factors. The assumption that someone is born a certain way, they argue, offers an immediate defence for unwarranted behaviour and severs human responsibility from human action. It is reasonable to accept that a child's home environment, the opportunities he or she is given, and how the child is raised factor into the sort of adult that child grows up to be to some degree. However, the view of social determinists implies that the underlying character of a child will change if his or her environmental circumstances do, which is not always the case. Ultimately, findings suggest that when it comes to the fundamental traits that dictate our emotional responses to any number of environmental situations, genes take centre stage.

Evidence for the biological approach can be found in the shared emotional reactions of people growing up in different cultures. For their 1976 work *Unmasking the Face*, neuropsychologists Paul Ekman and Wallace Friesen undertook an extensive cross-cultural study of facial expressions. Ekman and Friesen interviewed isolated tribes in Papua New Guinea and showed them photographs of people from other parts of the world. The psychologists discovered that not only could the participants clearly identify facial expressions with particular emotions but they could also describe situations in which the expressions may arise. This led the authors to conclude that six basic human emotions (anger, disgust, fear, happiness, sadness, surprise), as well as the physical expression of those emotions, are universal among people no matter which environment they grow up in.

Recent evidence from the study of twins has also suggested that nature plays a greater role in impacting our emotional development than nurture. In a study at Edinburgh University led by Professor Timothy Bates, more than 800 sets of fraternal and identical twins were asked a series of questions in order to assess their personality traits. In the end, it was found that identical twins, who share the exact same genetic information, are more than twice as likely to possess the same personality traits as fraternal twins, whose genetic information is not shared. Given that each set of siblings shared the same home environment and parents, the researchers concluded that DNA had a more substantial impact on how people behaved than environmental factors. Further substantiating this idea are the numerous studies on children adopted into homes with other siblings. Most indicate that, even if the child is an infant when he or she is adopted, the family's effect on his or her personality is often practically negligible.

Do the following statements agree with the claims of the writer in the passage?

Write

YES	*if the statement agrees with the claims of the writer*
NO	*if the statement contradicts the claims of the writer*
NOT GIVEN	*if it is impossible to say what the writer thinks about this*

21   Certain aspects of one's environment affect how one grows up.

22   An unfamiliar environment will not always change a child's character.

23   Emotional expressions remain the same as a child grows up.

24   Family interactions will cause great changes in a child's personality.

determinist n. 결정론자 variable n. 변수 parenting n. 육아 experiential adj. 경험에 의한, 경험상의 unwarranted adj. 부적절한, 부당한
sever v. 분리하다, 단절하다 factor into phr. ~을 요인으로 포함하다 underlying adj. 근본적인 dictate v. ~을 좌우하다, ~에 영향을 주다
neuropsychologist n. 신경심리학자 cross-cultural study phr. 비교 문화 연구 fraternal twins phr. 이란성 쌍둥이 substantiate v. 입증하다
negligible adj. 무시해도 될 정도의

9   Harnessing the Immense Power of the Tides

Increasing demographic pressures and environmental concerns about climate change have been the impetus for global research into feasible alternative energy sources. Being clean, abundant, and renewable, water power is an obvious resource to turn to. However, building large-scale hydroelectric dams, as has been done in the past, is no longer an ideal solution as the hydropower facilities currently in use are known to cause a number of devastating ecological and social issues. But all hope is not lost for water power as research is now focused on harnessing the incredible power of the tides to generate clean energy with minimal repercussions.

In fact, the fundamental technology is already available, as is evident in the tidal power plants being operated today. A good example is France's La Rance, the first tidal power plant in the world. La Rance is a barrage, which means that it is essentially a very large dam built across an estuary. Rather than storing water until it is needed as hydroelectric facilities do, water at La Rance flows through the dam and is collected in a basin whenever the tide comes in. Then, as soon as the tide goes out, the water in the basin is released and passes through turbines in order to generate electricity. While the dam at La Rance still poses a possible threat to the local ecosystem, electricity production by this means is extraordinarily reliable. Given that tidal forces are generated by gravity and the ongoing movements of the Earth – forces that are unlikely to change – it is possible to accurately predict the rise and fall of tides and by extension, when electricity can be produced.

Recognising that tides have incredible potential that may never be realised unless the environmental impact of such technology can be reduced, engineers are now working to develop hydroelectric technologies without using dams. One solution they have come up with is to install turbines on the sea floor relatively close to the shore in order to exploit underwater tidal currents. To produce energy, the underwater turbines would spin as the surf rose and fell, sending electricity through a cable to an onshore power station. This method is very promising as evidence suggests that it would result in limited environmental harm. For example, this technology would not create the damage to aquatic organisms that is frequently caused by dams. Furthermore, because tidal farms would be located underwater, they would not be an eyesore or cause a noise disturbance – both common complaints about wind farms.

It is true that the initial costs of constructing the appropriate infrastructure for a tidal farm would be high. However, research suggests that the maintenance and the replacement of equipment would be required infrequently, making it worthwhile in the long run to invest in this extremely efficient energy source. Ultimately, while there is no way of knowing what the future of tidal power will be, one thing is clear: the ocean, our most abundant and inexhaustible resource, has tremendous potential.

Do the following statements agree with the claims of the writer in the passage?

Write

YES	*if the statement agrees with the claims of the writer*
NO	*if the statement contradicts the claims of the writer*
NOT GIVEN	*if it is impossible to say what the writer thinks about this*

25 Hydroelectric dams can cause serious environmental problems.

26 Scientists predict tidal power will be more effective than wind as a means of producing energy.

27 The cost of maintenance makes tidal power inefficient.

---

harness v. (동력원 등으로) 이용하다   impetus n. 자극, 추동력   feasible adj. 실현 가능한   hydroelectric dam phr. 수력 발전 댐   repercussion n. 영향   barrage n. 보, 댐   estuary n. (큰 강의) 하구, 어귀   basin n. (큰 강의) 유역   exploit v. 이용하다, 활용하다   eyesore n. 보기 흉한 것, 눈에 거슬리는 것   inexhaustible adj. 무궁무진한, 고갈될 줄 모르는

⑩ Introverts and Extroverts: Explaining Different Personalities
The Science Behind a Fundamental Concept in Human Personality Theory

In his 1923 book *Psychological Types*, analytical psychologist Carl Jung identified two types of person: the introvert and the extrovert. The former was described as a shy, sensitive, socially anxious being while the latter was portrayed as a gregarious sort who enjoyed spending most of his or her time in the company of others. Although Jung's early classification of the two personality types was generally accurate and has stood the test of time, the underlying reasons for introversion and extroversion were never scientifically analysed. It was not until recently that modern psychological researchers began presenting more nuanced and factual interpretations of the extroversion-introversion spectrum.

Contemporary researchers have found that the brains of extroverts actually release a significant amount of dopamine, the neurotransmitter that controls the brain's pleasure centre, during social interaction. Consequently, an extrovert's brain activity noticeably increases when he or she is smiled at, for instance. And because they are rewarded for social engagement, extroverts feel compelled to seek it out by constantly displaying attractive behaviour, such as smiling, cracking jokes, and being friendly. Essentially, we now know that what were once considered the characteristics of extroverts are, in reality, the tools that extroverted people use to obtain the chemical rewards they want to receive.

These tools may seem like a positive thing on the surface, but they are not without fault. A high investment in time and energy is required to gain social rewards, leaving little energy for less socially oriented tasks. Some studies have even shown that extroverts are more likely than introverts to be injured from physical activities because extroversion is correlated with a higher tendency to explore one's environment. Others indicate that extroverts are poor financial planners since they are far more willing than their introvert counterparts to spend impulsively, especially if it will produce a social reward.

So, given that introverted people are on the opposite side of the spectrum from extroverts, does that mean they experience no social rewards and therefore have no desire to interact with others? No, but because the reward value from social experiences is markedly less for introverts, it is understandable why they often have no compulsion to seek other people out. Science has yet to find a satisfactory explanation for why their social rewards are few, but some experts believe human evolution has something to do with it. One theory postulates that having a complex social life drove the evolution of intelligence, creativity, language, and even consciousness among our early ancestors, who essentially had to be extroverted in order to survive. The emergence of introverts was only made possible once survival was no longer dependent upon gaining the attention and assistance of others, and spending more time on intellectual pursuits was an option.

Although introverts do not experience a significant release of dopamine in social situations, the opposite is true when they pour their energies into intellectual and imaginative projects. It's no surprise, then, that many of the world's geniuses and great inventors have been introverts. It takes significant time in solitude to work through complex mathematical, scientific, or philosophical puzzles, after all. So while extroverts may have played a substantial role in the evolution of our species up until now, the contributions of introverts are certainly not to be overlooked.

Do the following statements agree with the claims of the writer in the passage?

Write

> **YES**　　　　if the statement agrees with the claims of the writer
> **NO**　　　　if the statement contradicts the claims of the writer
> **NOT GIVEN**　if it is impossible to say what the writer thinks about this

28　The original categorisation of introverts and extroverts has changed significantly.

29　Jung's fellow psychologists never challenged his theories on introversion and extroversion.

30　Extroverts sometimes engage in careless behaviour.

31　Introverts are generally better at analytical thinking than extroverts.

CH 03
Y/N/NG (Yes / No / Not Given)　HACKERS **IELTS** READING

정답·해석·해설 p.346

---

introvert n. 내향적인 사람　extrovert n. 외향적인 사람　gregarious adj. 사교적인, 남과 어울리기 좋아하는
stand the test of time phr. 오랜 세월에도 불구하고 건재하다　introversion n. 내향성　extroversion n. 외향성　neurotransmitter n. 신경 전달 물질
pleasure centre phr. 쾌락 중추　crack a joke phr. 농담하다　oriented adj. ~을 지향하는　correlate with phr. ~과 관련 있다
financial planner phr. 금융설계사　impulsively adv. 충동적으로　markedly adv. 현저히, 두드러지게　compulsion n. 충동, 강요
postulate v. 가정하다, ~라고 주장하다　pursuit n. 활동, 일

READING PASSAGE

*You should spend about 20 minutes on **Questions 1-13**, which are based on Reading Passage below.*

The Fifth Language Skill

Culture is often left out of language courses, but some claim that it is the most important aspect of picking up a new language

Language learners and instructors know that four skills are needed to be able to communicate in any language: speaking, listening, reading and writing. This 'communicative approach' to language has long been the primary basis of second language learning environments. In this approach, some information about culture may be provided to language learners, but the overwhelming emphasis is on the four skills and basic, mostly literal, communication. Of late, however, more emphasis is being placed on the fifth language skill of cultural communication, as more and more experts are stressing the importance of assimilating the culture associated with a language. In fact, this 'intercultural approach' is now considered so essential that it cannot be avoided if learners hope to gain true command of any language.

The intercultural approach to language learning first attracted the attention of language experts after the publication of Louise Damen's *Culture Learning: The Fifth Dimension in the Language Classroom*. In it, she outlined the need for both intercultural awareness and intercultural skill development, and put both of these aims under the umbrella term 'pragmatic ethnography.' The implication of Damen's intercultural approach is that native language skills and competence in the target language are insufficient for instruction and that educators must function more like experienced cultural guides who are trained observers and capable of facilitating effective intercultural communication.

In the cultural context of second language learning, a useful heuristic paradigm is a four-stage model of language acquisition that separates understanding into four levels: tourist, survivor, immigrant, and citizen (Acton and Walker de Felix, 1995). Under this model, it is impossible for any person to acquire a citizen level of communicative competence if they do not have a thorough understanding of the myriad cultural aspects of language, and such an achievement is likely only for highly motivated students who are both willing to acculturate and are from a culture that is not extreme in its 'social distance' from the culture of the target language (Schumann, 1978).

Thus, it goes without saying that the 'big four' language skills alone are not always enough for a foreign speaker to fully master a second language or gain acceptance among a community of native speakers. Without cultural sensitivity and awareness, and a careful reflection of his or her own values, norms, and attitudes, a person's linguistic ability alone may not prevent the perception that they are an 'outsider'. To achieve status of an 'insider', he or she must learn to not only recognise and accept cultural differences but also to appreciate and value them.

But what culture should be taught in classrooms? For simplicity and convenience, researchers refer to 'Big C' and 'little c' culture to distinguish the more formal elements of a culture from those that are encountered in less formal, everyday situations. Big C culture corresponds to the social, political, and economic institutions of a given society as well as the great historical figures that contributed to the artistic, literary, and scientific achievements of that society (National Standards in Foreign Language Education Project, 1996), while little c culture represents the sum of patterns of behaviour that members of a given culture consider necessary for daily life, including clothing, housing, food, transportation, etc.

Another way to look at it is that the former represents the 'elite' culture of high society, whereas the latter corresponds to the interests and activities of ordinary people. This does not mean there is no overlap at all, however, because even though citizens spend their time with mundane tasks like greeting people, working, or shopping, they are nonetheless interested in bigger issues, such as social stratification and economic policy, which directly impact their lives. It is generally the case that little c culture is the most absent in language curricula and the most difficult to include due to its continually changing nature.

Yet a problematic issue exists with the epithet 'fifth skill' itself, which suggests that culture is an 'added on' element to language learning rather than a fundamental one. Kramsch (1993) claims that culture is always in the background, right from day one, ready to unsettle the good language learners when they expect it least, making evident the limitations of their hard-won communicative competence, challenging their ability to make sense of the world around them. This axiomatic approach to culture as an integral and inescapable part of communication underscores the importance of, and the challenges inherent in, language teaching.

Therefore, some educators think that culture should be viewed as the first, rather than the fifth, skill (Tomlinson 1999). Although this primacy of culture is a noble goal, it is nonetheless hopeful thinking to assume that it can be easily prioritised in a curriculum or that teachers are generally capable of carrying it out. The language curriculum is already full as it is, and language teachers typically have very limited instruction time with any given student or group of students. Many educators are not trained to handle this burden and, thus, in-service training and faculty development would be necessary to put culture at the centre of the language curriculum. The bottom line is that any 'fifth skill' time in the classroom will need to be supplemented by an enormously greater number of hours spent by the student immersing himself or herself in the culture of the target language 'in the real world'.

Questions 1-9

Do the following statements agree with the claims of the writer in Reading Passage?

Write

> **YES**   *if the statement agrees with the claims of the writer*
> **NO**   *if the statement contradicts the claims of the writer*
> **NOT GIVEN** *if it is impossible to say what the writer thinks about this*

1 The communicative approach has ignored the cultural component of language.

2 Under the four-stage model, a person can be fluent without cultural knowledge.

3 Learning the four language skills is not sufficient for fluent communication.

4 The categorisation of Big C and little c culture differs in countries around the world.

5 Big C and little c culture are not unconnected although they represent different ideas.

6 Language students should be more interested in political issues.

7 Big C culture is the hardest to include in curricula.

8 Labelling culture a 'fifth skill' implies that it is less important for education.

9 Prioritising culture in a language course is not always possible.

Questions 10 and 11

*Choose the correct letter, **A**, **B**, **C** or **D**.*

10   Louise Damen's view of intercultural approach implies that

    A   intercultural communication is absent in most language programmes.

    B   most native language speakers are incapable of teaching their own culture.

    C   culture and language are equally important but should be taught separately.

    D   language teachers must have expertise beyond the language itself.

11   According to the writer, what is necessary for making culture a priority in the classroom?

    A   a smaller student-to-teacher ratio

    B   longer working hours for teachers

    C   additional training for educators

    D   development of new teaching materials

Questions 12 and 13

Complete the sentences below.

*Choose **NO MORE THAN TWO WORDS** from the passage for each answer.*

12   Students from a similar culture to that of the .... have the best chance to succeed.

13   A second language speaker can not appear to be an insider based solely on ....

정답·해석·해설 p.355

VOCABULARY LIST

Chapter 03에서 선별한 다음의 어휘들을 음성파일을 들으며 암기한 후 퀴즈로 확인해보세요.

*해커스 동영상강의 포털 해커스 인강(HackersIngang.com)에서 단어암기 MP3를 무료로 다운로드할 수 있습니다.

- □ comprehension n. 이해(력)
- □ learned adj. 학습된, 후천적인
- □ rest on phr. ~에 기초하다
- □ logical adj. 타당한, 사리에 맞는
- □ discern v. 파악하다, 알아차리다
- □ interpret v. 이해하다, 해석하다
- □ non-auditory adj. 비청각의
- □ single-handedly adv. 단독으로
- □ fluctuate with phr. ~에 따라 변화하다
- □ scarcity n. 희귀함, 부족
- □ mint v. (화폐를) 주조하다
- □ manipulation n. 속임수, 조작
- □ constituent adj. ~을 이루는, ~을 구성하는
- □ deforestation n. 삼림 파괴
- □ claim v. 빼앗다, 앗아 가다
- □ culprit n. (문제의) 원인(이 되는 것)
- □ clear-cut v. (숲의 한 구역을) 개벌(삭벌)하다
- □ convert v. 개조하다, 전환시키다
- □ compound v. 악화시키다, 더 심각하게 만들다
- □ biodiversity n. 생물의 다양성
- □ deteriorate v. 악화되다, 저하되다
- □ undergo v. 겪다, 받다
- □ morph v. 변하다, 바뀌다
- □ anatomically adv. 해부학상, 해부학적으로
- □ clash n. 충돌, 격돌
- □ acclimated adj. 익숙해진, 순응한

- □ dominate v. 우세하다, 지배하다
- □ paleoanthropologist n. 고인류학자
- □ abstract adj. 추상적인
- □ prevail v. 우세하다, 이기다
- □ phenetics n. 표현학
- □ classification n. 분류
- □ organism n. 생물(체), 유기체
- □ valid adj. 타당한
- □ pheneticist n. 표현학자
- □ adaptation n. 적응
- □ primitive adj. 초기의, 원시의
- □ lump v. 일괄하여 다루다
- □ subjective adj. 주관적인
- □ hierarchical adj. 계층에 따른
- □ senior n. 고령자
- □ dementia n. 치매
- □ debilitating adj. 심신을 쇠약하게 하는
- □ alternative adj. 대체의, 대안의
- □ cognitive adj. 인지의
- □ agitation n. 불안, 동요
- □ disruptive adj. 분열성의
- □ redirect v. ~의 방향을 바꾸다
- □ debunk v. (생각, 믿음 등이) 틀렸음을 밝히다
- □ descend v. (언어가) ~에서 유래하다
- □ prototype n. 원형
- □ hierarchy n. 계층 구조, 계급

Quiz

각 단어의 알맞은 뜻을 찾아 연결하시오.

01 clash	ⓐ 생물의 다양성	06 agitation	ⓐ 주관적인
02 logical	ⓑ 악화시키다, 더 심각하게 만들다	07 subjective	ⓑ 추상적인
03 interpret	ⓒ 겪다, 받다	08 primitive	ⓒ 계층 구조, 계급
04 compound	ⓓ 충돌, 격돌	09 abstract	ⓓ 원형
05 undergo	ⓔ 이해하다, 해석하다	10 hierarchy	ⓔ 불안, 동요
	ⓕ 타당한, 사리에 맞는		ⓕ 초기의, 원시의

ⓒ 01 ⓕ 02 ⓔ 03 ⓑ 04 ⓒ 05 ⓔ 06 ⓐ 07 ⓕ 08 ⓑ 09 ⓒ 10

☐ ideographic adj. 표의 문자의

☐ syllabic adj. 음절의

☐ splendour n. 탁월함, 현저함

☐ advent n. 출현, 도래

☐ nomadic adj. 유목의, 방랑의

☐ agrarian adj. 농업의

☐ determinist n. 결정론자

☐ variable n. 변수

☐ parenting n. 육아

☐ experiential adj. 경험에 의한, 경험상의

☐ unwarranted adj. 부적절한, 부당한

☐ sever v. 분리하다, 단절하다

☐ factor into phr. ~을 요인으로 포함하다

☐ underlying adj. 근본적인

☐ dictate v. ~을 좌우하다, ~에 영향을 주다

☐ fraternal twins phr. 이란성 쌍둥이

☐ negligible adj. 무시해도 될 정도의

☐ harness v. (동력원 등으로) 이용하다

☐ impetus n. 자극, 추동력

☐ feasible adj. 실현 가능한

☐ hydroelectric dam phr. 수력 발전 댐

☐ repercussion n. 영향

☐ exploit v. 이용하다, 활용하다

☐ eyesore n. 보기 흉한 것, 눈에 거슬리는 것

☐ inexhaustible adj. 무궁무진한, 고갈될 줄 모르는

☐ introvert n. 내향적인 사람

☐ extrovert n. 외향적인 사람

☐ gregarious adj. 사교적인, 남과 어울리기 좋아하는

☐ stand the test of time phr. 오랜 세월에도 불구하고 건재하다

☐ neurotransmitter n. 신경 전달 물질

☐ pleasure centre phr. 쾌락 중추

☐ oriented adj. ~을 지향하는

☐ correlate with phr. ~과 관련 있다

☐ impulsively adv. 충동적으로

☐ markedly adv. 현저히, 두드러지게

☐ compulsion n. 충동, 강요

☐ postulate v. 가정하다, ~이라고 주장하다

☐ pursuit n. 활동, 일

☐ assimilate v. 완전히 이해하다, 동화되다

☐ intercultural adj. 상호문화적, 문화 간의

☐ command n. 구사력

☐ umbrella term phr. 포괄적 용어

☐ heuristic adj. 학습을 돕는

☐ myriad adj. 무수한

☐ acculturate v. 다른 문화에 성공적으로 동화되다

☐ correspond v. 해당하다, 부합하다

☐ mundane adj. 일상적인

☐ stratification n. 계층화

☐ epithet n. 통칭, 별칭

☐ primacy n. 제1위, 최고

☐ prioritise v. 우선순위를 결정하다

☐ immerse v. 몰두시키다, 열중시키다

Quiz

각 단어의 알맞은 뜻을 찾아 연결하시오.

01 variable   ⓐ 영향
02 advent   ⓑ 근본적인
03 repercussion   ⓒ 변수
04 impetus   ⓓ 실현 가능한
05 underlying   ⓔ 자극, 추동력
                     ⓕ 출현, 도래

06 stratification   ⓐ 일상적인
07 compulsion   ⓑ 충동적으로
08 markedly   ⓒ 계층화
09 mundane   ⓓ 활동, 일
10 impulsively   ⓔ 현저히, 두드러지게
                     ⓕ 충동, 강요

ⓑ 01 ⓒ 02 ⓕ 03 ⓐ 04 ⓔ 05 ⓑ 06 ⓒ 07 ⓕ 08 ⓔ 09 ⓐ 10 ⓑ

CHAPTER 04
Note/Table/Flow-chart/Diagram Completion

Note/Table/Flow-chart/Diagram completion 문제는 지문의 정보를 사용하여 제시된 노트/표/순서도/다이어그램의 빈칸을 채워 완성하는 문제이다. 매 시험 출제되지는 않지만 자주 출제되고 있다.

■ 문제 형태

Note/Table/Flow-chart/Diagram completion 문제는 제시된 노트/표/순서도/다이어그램의 빈칸에 들어갈 답을 지문에서 찾아 적는 주관식 형태로 출제되며, 간혹 보기와 함께 객관식으로도 출제된다. 주관식으로 출제되는 경우에는 몇 단어 혹은 숫자로 답을 작성해야 하는지 반드시 확인한다.

Note completion

노트는 지문의 내용을 간략하게 요약하여 정리한 형태로, 하나의 큰 제목과 여러 개의 소제목이 있는 형태가 자주 출제된다.

Complete the notes below.

*Choose **ONE WORD ONLY** from the passage for each answer.*

Write your answers in boxes 1-2 on your answer sheet.

Controversy over the Birth Order Effect

According to some scientists:

- It is very difficult to find an average **1** .... to study.
- This is because of socio-economic, ethnic and religious **2** ....

Table completion

표는 지문의 내용을 항목에 따라 분류하여 정리한 형태로, 주로 주관식으로 출제되지만 간혹 보기 리스트가 함께 주어지기도 한다.

Complete the table below.

*Choose **ONE WORD AND/OR A NUMBER** from the passage for each answer.*

Write your answers in boxes 1-4 on your answer sheet.

Types of Radiation

Type	Composition	Rays
Alpha	two protons and neutrons identical to a **1** .... nucleus	cannot pass through a **2** .... of paper
Gamma	photons with a **3** .... of more than 1019 Hz	can be stopped by a **4** .... of material

---

Flow-chart completion

순서도는 지문에 등장한 특정 순서·절차 등을 요약하여 정리한 형태로, 주로 위에서 아래로 흐르는 형태로 출제된다.

Complete the flow-chart below.

Choose **ONE WORD ONLY** from the passage for each answer.

Write your answers in boxes 1-5 on your answer sheet.

Method of excavation to determine presence
of dinosaur fossils and results

Step 1

71 Multiple sites were excavated to a depth of three metres and

all **1** .... were gathered for sorting and analysis.

Step 2

The dinosaur remains were sorted according to species as well as by size and

2 ....

Result: Intact bones were placed in a **3** .... arrangement and set aside.

Bone fragments, teeth and eggshells were carefully washed and put through screens.

Step 3

Bones determined to be from the same individuals were assembled, and several

4 .... skeletons were found.

Result: The remains from these skeletons were transported for **5** .... in the

museum of natural history.

Step 4

Fossils were quantified and catalogued and the information was entered in a searchable

database.

Diagram completion

다이어그램은 주로 건축물·기기·자연물 등의 구조 혹은 작동 과정을 그림으로 나타낸 형태로, 특정 부위의 명칭을 적거나 그에 대한 설명을 완성하는 형태로 출제된다.

Label the diagram below.

*Choose **NO MORE THAN TWO WORDS** from the passage for each answer.*

Write your answers in boxes 1-3 on your answer sheet.

A Truss Bridge

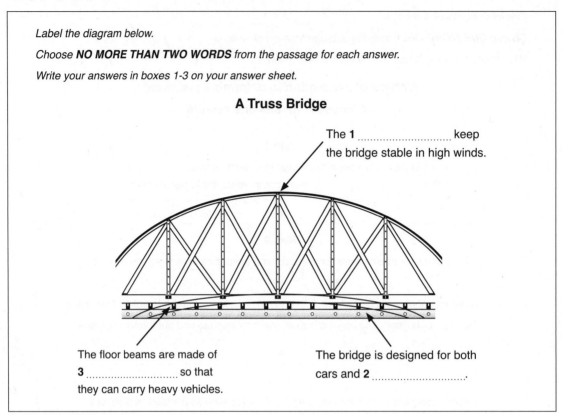

The **1** .... keep the bridge stable in high winds.

The floor beams are made of **3** .... so that they can carry heavy vehicles.

The bridge is designed for both cars and **2** ....

■ 문제풀이 전략

STEP 1 답안 작성 조건을 확인하고, 문제의 핵심어구와 내용을 파악한다.

(1) 지시문을 읽고 지문에서 몇 단어 혹은 숫자의 답을 찾아야 하는지 확인한다.

(2) 제시된 노트/표/순서도/다이어그램의 핵심 내용을 파악한다.
- 제목 확인하기: 제목이 주어진 경우, 제목을 미리 읽어 지문에서 어떤 내용을 찾아야 하는지 확인한다. 노트의 경우 소제목을 확인한다.
- 첫 행과 첫 열의 정보 확인하기: 표의 경우 첫 행과 첫 열의 정보를 통해 지문의 내용이 표에 어떤 식으로 정리되어 있는지 확인한다.

(3) 문제의 핵심어구와 빈칸 주변 내용을 통해 빈칸에 어떤 내용이 들어가야 하는지 파악한다. 이때, 빈칸 앞뒤를 확인하여 문법에 맞는 품사 등을 예상한다.

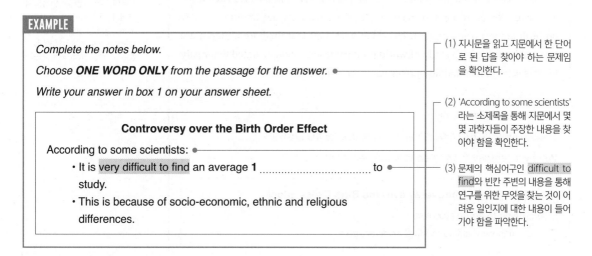

EXAMPLE

Complete the notes below.

Choose **ONE WORD ONLY** from the passage for the answer. ●

Write your answer in box 1 on your answer sheet.

Controversy over the Birth Order Effect

According to some scientists: ●
- It is very difficult to find an average 1 .... to ● study.
- This is because of socio-economic, ethnic and religious differences.

(1) 지시문을 읽고 지문에서 한 단어로 된 답을 찾아야 하는 문제임을 확인한다.

(2) 'According to some scientists'라는 소제목을 통해 지문에서 몇몇 과학자들이 주장한 내용을 찾아야 함을 확인한다.

(3) 문제의 핵심어구인 difficult to find와 빈칸 주변의 내용을 통해 연구를 위한 무엇을 찾는 것이 어려운 일인지에 대한 내용이 들어가야 함을 파악한다.

✅ TIPS

- **ONE WORD ONLY**: 한 단어로만 답안을 작성한다.
  ex) images (O), clear images (×)

- **ONE WORD AND/OR A NUMBER**: 한 단어 / 한 단어와 숫자 하나 / 숫자 하나로 답안을 작성한다.
  ex) images (O), 2 images (O), 2 (O), 2nd (O), 2 clear images (×)

- **NO MORE THAN TWO WORDS**: 두 단어 이내로 답안을 작성한다.
  ex) images (O), clear images (O), 2 clear images (×)

- **NO MORE THAN TWO WORDS AND/OR A NUMBER**: 두 단어 이내 / 숫자 하나 / 한 단어와 숫자 하나 / 두 단어와 숫자 하나로 답안을 작성한다.
  ex) images (O), clear images (O), 2 (O), 2nd (O), 2 images (O), 2 clear images (O)

(1) 지문을 scanning하여 노트/표/순서도/다이어그램의 제목이나 소제목 등을 통해 확인한 내용이 언급된 부분을 찾는다.

(2) 문제의 핵심어구가 그대로 언급되거나 paraphrasing된 부분을 찾아 정답의 단서를 확인한다.

EXAMPLE

Despite the years of research into the birth order effect and the many family anecdotes that would seem to support it, it is not universally accepted. Some scientists reject the validity of the studies that have 'proven' the effect. [1]They point out that it is nearly impossible to identify a standard family to use in research. Because of socio-economic, ethnic, religious and other differences, it is impossible to find one family that can provide relevant data for such tests. Moreover, there are far too many cases that contradict the traditional view on birth order. For example, it has often been said that firstborn children are 'natural leaders', but a study of world political leaders demonstrated that many leaders were in fact middle-born or last-born people (Hudson, 1990).

(1) 'Some scientists'를 통해 앞에서 파악한 소제목과 관련된 내용이 언급된 주변임을 확인한다.

(2) 문제의 핵심어구인 difficult to find와 관련된 내용을 지문에서 찾는다. 관련 내용이 언급된 주변에서 'They point out that it is nearly impossible to identify a standard family to use in research.'라는 정답의 단서를 확인한다.

Complete the notes below.

*Choose **ONE WORD ONLY** from the passage for the answer.*

Write your answer in box 1 on your answer sheet.

Controversy over the Birth Order Effect

According to some scientists:
- It is very difficult to find an average **1** .... to study.
- This is because of socio-economic, ethnic and religious differences.

지문 해석 p.360

✓ TIPS

다이어그램의 경우 문제에 문장이 주어지지 않고 빈칸만 주어지는 경우가 있다. 이런 경우 지문에서 정답의 단서를 찾을 핵심어구가 없으므로, 제목을 읽고 지문에서 관련 내용이 언급된 곳을 찾아 주변을 모두 꼼꼼히 읽어가며 정답을 찾는다. 빈칸만 주어지는 경우 정답은 주로 다이어그램의 각 부분에 맞는 명칭으로 출제되므로, 특정 부분을 가리키는 고유명사 혹은 명사 위주로 정답을 찾는다.

(1) 정답의 단서에서 문맥상 빈칸에 들어가기에 알맞은 단어를 찾는다. 이때 앞에서 예측한 품사에 맞는 단어 위주로 찾는다.

(2) 찾은 단어를 답안 작성 조건에 맞게 작성한다. 답안을 작성한 후에는 빈칸의 앞뒤를 살펴 완성된 문장에 문법적으로 틀린 부분이 없는지 확인한다. 문법적으로 틀린 문장이 된다면 오답 처리되므로, 이를 반드시 확인해야 한다.

EXAMPLE

Despite the years of research into the birth order effect and the many family anecdotes that would seem to support it, it is not universally accepted. Some scientists reject the validity of the studies that have 'proven' the effect. [1]They point out that it is nearly impossible to identify a standard family to use in research. Because of socio-economic, ethnic, religious and other differences, it is impossible to find one family that can provide relevant data for such tests. Moreover, there are far too many cases that contradict the traditional view on birth order. For example, it has often been said that firstborn children are 'natural leaders', but a study of world political leaders demonstrated that many leaders were in fact middle-born or last-born people (Hudson, 1990).

(1) '과학자들은 연구에 활용할 표준 가족을 찾는 것은 거의 불가능하다고 지적한다'라는 정답의 단서에서 'family'가 답이 될 수 있음을 확인한다.

Complete the notes below.

*Choose **ONE WORD ONLY** from the passage for the answer.*

Write your answer in box 1 on your answer sheet.

(2) 답안 작성 조건에 맞게 한 단어인 family를 정답으로 작성한다.

Controversy over the Birth Order Effect

According to some scientists:
- It is very difficult to find an average **1** ......family...... to study.
- This is because of socio-economic, ethnic and religious differences.

✅ **TIPS**

노트/표/순서도/다이어그램 주관식 문제의 정답은 주로 명사로 출제되지만, 간혹 동사 혹은 형용사로 출제되는 경우도 있다. 동사로 출제된 경우, 반드시 시제와 단·복수를 잘 확인하도록 한다. 객관식으로 출제된 경우, 선택한 답을 답안지에 바르게 작성했는지 반드시 확인한다.

CH 04

Note/Table/Flow-chart/Diagram Completion HACKERS **IELTS** READING

1 When studying historical buildings, one can see a clear progression in construction materials. Before the medieval period, timber was the most widely used building material in Europe, but it came to be replaced by stone in most major structures. Even the use of metals was limited in structural architecture before the industrial age. At that time, metal was mainly used for bridges and greenhouses due to its limited aesthetic appeal. However, the public perception of manmade materials changed and technological progress brought down metalwork's cost, leading to it being used more. The first metal commonly used in architecture was cast iron, which could be formed into decorative shapes like stone. Architects even began using cast iron to construct building frames. Unfortunately, this particular metal has a low tensile strength and several of these buildings collapsed. To address this problem, builders turned to wrought iron and eventually to steel. As public opinion about manmade materials continued to change in the 19th century, the use of concrete became acceptable. The combination of steel and concrete was incredibly strong and allowed for the construction of taller buildings – thoroughly changing urban landscapes. Construction of the tallest building in the world, Dubai's Burj Khalifa, used 4,000 tonnes of steel in combination with 330,000 cubic metres of concrete and 55,000 tonnes of reinforcing steel rebar.

Complete the notes below.

Choose **ONE WORD AND/OR A NUMBER** *from the passage for each answer.*

History of Architectural Materials

– Most pre-medieval buildings in Europe used **1** .... for construction.
– Stone construction became popular in the medieval period.
– Manmade materials were not widely used before the industrial age.
– Building the world's highest skyscraper utilised 330,000 cubic metres of concrete and
  2 .... of steel.

---

progression n. 발전, 진보 timber n. 목재 aesthetic adj. 심미적인 perception n. 인식 metalwork n. 금속 가공 cast iron phr. 주철
decorative adj. 장식의 frame n. 골조 tensile strength phr. 장력 wrought iron phr. 연철 steel n. 강철 rebar n. 철근 landscape n. 풍경, 경치

CH
04

Note/Table/Flow-chart/Diagram Completion HACKERS **IELTS** READING

2 If you have ever been snorkelling or diving along a tropical coral reef, then you have probably heard regular crunching sounds while underwater. These are made when the colourful parrotfish remove algae from the reef's surface by biting and scraping it with their parrot-like beaks. The lifecycle of these fascinating fish begins when they travel into the open sea to discharge their eggs, where they hatch. Following this their early life is spent as larvae in the ocean's plankton population. They then move to the mangroves as juveniles and then to a reef where they will both hide from predators and clean the reef. Interestingly, throughout these stages of development, all parrotfish are drably coloured females. This is because parrotfish are sequential hermaphrodites, meaning they change gender as they age. When they enter the terminal phase of their lives, the young female parrotfish morph into more colourful males. These males then collect a harem of younger female parrotfish and spawn to produce yet another all-female group of larval parrotfish. A further interesting aspect of the parrotfish is its importance in the reef's survival. According to researchers at the International Union for Conservation of Nature, without the cleaning activities of the parrotfish, the reefs would soon be overrun with algae and die.

Complete the flow-chart below.

*Choose **ONE WORD ONLY** from the passage for each answer.*

Parrotfish Lifecycle

Spawning
Adult parrotfish move into the open ocean to release their eggs.

Initial Stage
Parrotfish enter the ocean's plankton fields as 3 ....

Juvenile Stage
Juvenile parrotfish spend time in the 4 .... before moving to the reefs.

Terminal Stage
Adult male parrotfish live on the reef with a group of females.

---

parrotfish n. 비늘돔 algae n. 조류 larvae n. 유충 mangrove n. 맹그로브 (강가나 늪지에서 뿌리가 지면 밖으로 나오게 자라는 열대 나무)
juvenile n. 청소년 drably adv. 담갈색으로 sequential hermaphrodite phr. 인접적 자웅동체 morph v. 바뀌다 harem n. 암컷의 무리
spawn v. 산란하다 larval adj. 유충의 International Union for Conservation of Nature phr. 세계자연보전연맹 overrun v. 들끓다

3 Zimbabwe's Eastgate Centre should be the model for modern midrise commercial architecture. It was constructed without mechanical air conditioning, resulting in savings of approximately 3 million pounds for the complex's owners. Surprisingly, the building is never uncomfortably hot or cold. This is because the architect utilised the process of biomimicry when designing it. Biomimicry involves humans studying a natural process and imitating it to solve a complex human problem. In this case, the designer, Mick Pearce, was inspired by termite mounds. These wood-eating pests build large mounds that can reach 25 metres in height. However, most termites do not inhabit the upper part of the mounds, but they live in a gallery at the base of it. The tall structure above is essentially a large chimney. It contains a central shaft that moves warmer air upward. This warm air then exits through holes near the mound's top. Radial vents at the base intensify this action by capturing the wind and cooling the air at the base of the mound, creating a convection cycle in the structure. After understanding this process, Pearce designed the Eastgate Centre's buildings as a series of rooms around a central shaft. Each room has ducts into the shaft and to the exterior resulting in heat dissipation as in the termite mound. Fans that pull air into the central shaft, producing continuous airflow, assist this system. Through this system, the offices in the Eastgate Centre have a stable internal temperature of approximately 23°C regardless of the external temperature.

Label the diagram below.

*Choose **ONE WORD** from the passage for each answer.*

Termite Mound Layout

air holes

central shaft

the 5 ....

radial

6 ....

---

midrise adj. 중층의 biomimicry n. 생체 모방(생물체의 특성, 구조 및 원리를 산업 전반에 적용시키는 것) imitate v. 모방하다 termite n. 흰개미
mound n. 언덕 pest n. 해충 gallery n. 좁고 긴 방, 복도 shaft n. 통로 radial adj. 방사의 convection n. 대류 duct n. 배관 dissipation n. 방출

4 Prairie ecosystems are characterised by even terrain or gently sloping rolling hills, and by a predominance of herbaceous plant life. Trees, shrubs, and other woody plants are virtually absent in prairies, and there is very little shelter from the solar radiation and harsh breezes. Prairies generally receive a moderate amount of yearly precipitation, but summers are occasionally marked by severe drought. Consequently, for plants to thrive in the prairie ecosystem, they must endure seasonally dry conditions. Among the herbaceous plants suited for life in these ecosystems are prairie grasses, which have several adaptive mechanisms for survival.

Leaves of prairie grasses vary in width, but most are long, thin blades. On the epidermal layer of the leaves are small holes, called stomata, which can be opened to let in carbon dioxide and release oxygen, or closed to retain moisture. Because carbon dioxide is essential for plant photosynthesis, the stomata must remain wide for gas exchange; however, air spaces within the leaf are full of water vapour, which evaporates unless the pores remain closed and presents a challenge during dry conditions. To overcome the problem, prairie grasses have evolved to distinguish between day and night. In the daytime, the grasses keep their stomata shut to minimise moisture loss. The plants then expand the pores in the evening when the air is cooler for respiration.

Complete the notes below.

*Choose **NO MORE THAN TWO WORDS** from the passage for each answer.*

How Prairie Grasses Survive

Harsh prairie conditions

- Flat land with a few small hills
- A limited amount of protection from **7** .... and high winds
- Some rainfall every year, but summer months bring drought

Prairie grasses' evolutionary adaptation

- Stomata:
  – Tiny holes on the **8** .... of the leaves
- Open to allow carbon dioxide in and oxygen out, or closed to preserve moisture
- The stomata remain closed during the **9** .... to decrease loss of water
- The plant pores are opened in the cooler nighttime air

---

prairie n. 초원 even adj. 평평한 terrain n. 지대 sloping adj. 경사진 rolling adj. 굽이치는, 구릉으로 된 predominance n. 지배, 우위
solar radiation phr. 태양 복사열 moderate adj. 적당한, 온건한 adaptive mechanism phr. 적응기전 herbaceous adj. 초본의 blade n. 잎
epidermal adj. 상피의 stomata n. 기공 pore n. 구멍 respiration n. 호흡

5 Around 2000 B.C., a new invention emerged that changed warfare during the period, the horse-drawn chariot. These light carriages provided cavalry archers with a flat platform from which to attack their enemies. Prior to this time armies that wished to proceed rapidly rode on horseback, but this was cumbersome because saddles and stirrups had not been invented. This made it difficult to steer, hold on to the horse and fire at the same time. Chariots made this much easier. At their most basic, chariots were wheeled platforms drawn behind one or more horses. Perhaps the most famous of these fighting vehicles were used by the ancient Egyptians. Although they did not invent the chariot, the Egyptians adapted them to improve their usefulness. One of the biggest changes was lightening the overall weight of the chariot by utilising newly invented spoked wheels rather than the traditional disk wheel. This made it easier for the horses to pull the chariots faster. However, speed was not the only benefit of the changes implemented by the Egyptians. They also made them much easier to control through the use of the yoke saddle and basic design changes. The yoke saddle was a saddle-like pad that sat on the horses' backs with leather pieces across the horse's chests and bellies to prevent slippage and increase control. The riders' platform, which was connected to the yoke saddle by a long wooden rod, was also redesigned. By moving the rider closer to the chariot's axle, it became more stable for the riders, making it easier to aim and fire at their enemies. Finally, the Egyptians covered the axle with metal to prevent friction against the chariot's platform. This not only improved the vehicle's movement, but it also reduced damage to the vehicle, making them more reliable. Unfortunately, none of these improvements corrected other problems inherent with the chariot's design, and by 1500 B.C. cavalry troops on horseback had replaced them in most military settings. However, they did remain in use as racing vehicles for hundreds of years to come.

Label the diagram below.

*Choose **ONE WORD ONLY** from the passage for each answer.*

The Ancient Chariot

To reduce weight,
10 ....
wheels were used instead of traditional disk wheels.

The 11 ....
was covered with metal to stop it from rubbing against the platform.

---

warfare n. 전투, 전쟁 chariot n. 전차 carriage n. 마차 cavalry archer phr. 기마 궁사 platform n. 단, 연단 cumbersome adj. 번거로운
saddle n. 안장 stirrup n. (말 안장 양쪽에 달린) 등자 steer v. 몰다, 조종하다 adapt v. 개조하다, 적응시키다 spoke v. (바퀴에) 살을 달다
yoke n. 굴레, 멍에 pad n. (말의) 안장 받침 slippage n. 미끄러짐 rod n. 막대 axle n. 차축 friction n. 마찰 inherent adj. 내재된 troop n. 부대, 군대

6 Every year, millions of birds participate in annual migrations – moving from one area to another when weather changes make it difficult to find food or when they must seek out potential mates. Some of these journeys are rather simple and merely involve moving to a nearby area, but others can cover more than 10,000 kilometres. To travel such a great distance, birds must possess a strong ability to navigate. Today, it is believed that birds have three methods of navigation: piloting, orientation, and true navigation. Piloting is the easiest of these to understand, because it is how we most often find our way. Put simply, they move from one recognisable visual landmark to the next. Much like we know to turn left after a certain feature when coming home from the supermarket, birds know to follow landmarks, like a river that runs north and south, until they get to the next feature, like a lake. However, this can lead to a problem. When the bird looks at the river, which way should it head? To answer this question, birds may use the second method, orientation, which entails using clues to figure out direction. Over the course of the last 50 years, scientists have observed birds using the sun and stars as compasses to check their direction. Some have even been shown to be able to sense and use Earth's magnetic field to orient themselves. The final method is true navigation, which requires the bird to determine its final destination and find a way to it from their current location. For scientists, this is the most fascinating aspect of avian navigation, because it cannot be explained as simply as the other two. At its most basic, true navigation is the way that birds compensate for problems with the other two systems. For instance, if a bird only knew to fly due south or to only follow one particular geological feature it would be highly susceptible to getting lost. If a storm pushed the bird far west, then flying south would not necessarily get it to the correct destination. Also, what's a bird to do if a landmark has been destroyed since the last migration? While the mechanism used for true navigation remains undiscovered, some researchers, such as Professor Thomas Collett, believe that the birds possess a 'cognitive map'. They believe that birds can use this map, along with the cues they gather from piloting and orienting and their internal clocks, to find their way.

Complete the table below.

*Choose **ONE WORD AND/OR A NUMBER** from the passage for each answer.*

Methods of Avian Navigation

Piloting	Orientation	True Navigation
Birds look for 12 .... which they recognise to navigate by, much like humans do when performing daily errands.	It was discovered within the last 13 .... that birds use cues such as the location of the sun or stars.	Birds set a course between the current location and the ultimate 14 ....

---

migration n. 이동, 이주 navigate v. 항해하다 piloting n. 조종 orientation n. 방위 측정, 방향 landmark n. 지형지물 feature n. 지형, 지세
entail v. 수반하다 magnetic field phr. 자기장 orient v. 자신의 위치를 알다 avian adj. 조류의 compensate v. 보완하다, 보상하다
due adv. 정확히 (북/남/동/서) 쪽으로 susceptible to phr. ~하기 쉽다, ~에 영향을 받기 쉽다

7 Wind Power

Wind power has been used by humans for almost two millennia, usually in the form of windmills which ground grain or pumped water. Horizontal windmills were first introduced in ancient Persia before spreading throughout the Middle East and then being exported to Central Asia, China and India. The vertical windmills which are typical in European agriculture began to be used in the Middle Ages, initially in England, northern France and Flanders. At its peak in 1850, it is thought that there were around 200,000 windmills across Europe, but this number rapidly declined as the Industrial Revolution took hold.

Now wind power is making a dramatic comeback in the form of renewable energy, and the distinctive sight of fields full of towering wind turbines is becoming common throughout the developed world. Wind power is a plentiful source of power, which does not produce gas emissions and uses little land. Although they require significant investment for construction, wind farms are far less costly to run than other energy sources, and their effect on the environment is limited. Denmark currently generates 40 per cent of its electrical power from wind and over 80 other countries around the world are using wind power to generate electricity. There is particularly substantial investment in wind energy in China, which already has the largest wind farm in the world, located in western Gansu province.

Wind power works by very simply using the kinetic energy generated by wind to power generators which produce electricity. Each wind turbine consists of a tower made from tubular steel, on top of which sits a rotor, formed of blades and a hub, and a nacelle, within which sits the gear box and generator. As the wind flows towards the wind turbine, it propels the blades, a process optimised by a pitch system which adjusts the rotor so that it picks up the optimal amount of wind. This is supplemented by a yaw drive inside the tower, which turns the nacelle to keep the blades facing directly into the wind. An anemometre on the back of the turbine collects wind speed and direction data so that the yaw drive and pitch system can adjust the turbine accordingly. The wind should not be too powerful, as this could damage the blades so the wind turbine's computer system makes sure that high winds are avoided. In case of an emergency the rotors are also connected to a brake, which can shut them down at any time.

The blades are connected to a low-speed shaft, so when the wind pushes the blades around this shaft also begins to spin. This in turn makes the cogs in the gear box spin, which transfers the rotation of the low-speed shaft onto a high-speed shaft, thus increasing the rotational speed to the rate required to generate energy. The spinning of the high-speed shaft then powers a 60-cycle AC generator, converting the energy into electricity which travels down the tower and into a power station where it is converted to the correct voltage to be used in homes, workplaces and factories.

Label the diagram below.

*Choose **NO MORE THAN TWO WORDS** from the passage for each answer.*

How a Wind Turbine Works

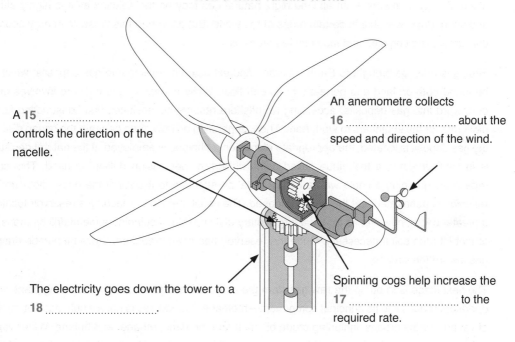

A **15** .... controls the direction of the nacelle.

An anemometre collects **16** .... about the speed and direction of the wind.

The electricity goes down the tower to a **18** ....

Spinning cogs help increase the **17** .... to the required rate.

---

windmill n. 풍차   renewable energy phr. 신재생 에너지   substantial adj. 상당한   kinetic adj. 운동의   tubular adj. 튜브형의, 관으로 된
rotor n. 회전 날개   hub n. 축   nacelle n. 엔진실   gear box phr. 변속기   propel v. 추진하다, 나아가게 하다   optimise v. 최적화하다   pitch n. 상하 요동
optimal adj. 최적의   supplement v. 보충하다   drive n. 전동 장치   anemometre n. 풍속계   accordingly adv. 알맞게, 적절히   shaft n. 기둥   cog n. 톱니
AC generator phr. 교류 발전기   voltage n. 전압

8 Natural Gas: From the Ground to Your Home

Given the recent decline in the demand for oil and the move away from coal toward cleaner-burning energy sources, natural gas is expected to dominate fossil fuel production in the coming years. With global energy demands at an all-time high, natural gas may be the solution as it is highly efficient and abundantly available in certain areas of the world. But delivering this versatile energy source to consumers is a complex and multifaceted process.

First, gas must be brought to Earth's surface and extracted by drilling into gas deposits, which can be found both on land and beneath the ocean floor. While extracting gas onshore involves drilling downward into gas deposits, accessing an offshore reserve necessitates first constructing floating platforms for the engineers to work from. Then, depending on how deep beneath the ocean's surface the gas deposit is located, the appropriate extraction technique is employed. If the natural gas supply is in shallow water, a technique called cable drilling, or percussion drilling, is used. This entails repeatedly dropping a cable with a heavy metal bit attached to it against the ocean floor until the reservoir is penetrated and the gas is released. The usual method of reaching a reservoir located at a greater depth, however, is to use a large rotary drill capable of spinning a metal drill bit thousands of feet into the soil if necessary. Once the reservoir has been breached, powerful pumps draw the gas toward the surface.

The next stage is to pump the raw gas from the extraction site to a nearby processing plant, where operators reduce it to its principal component – methane. Natural gas is not a single gas but made up of various hydrocarbons, including crude oil, methane, propane, ethane, and butane. Water vapour, helium, nitrogen, and carbon dioxide are also sometimes present. The process of isolating methane and disposing of the other parts involves multiple steps, which can make the overall cost of natural gas production quite high. However, some byproducts, like propane, crude oil, and butane, all have value of their own and can be sold to offset the expenses of those various steps.

After processing, the gas must be transported to its intended customer market through a vast underground pipeline system that can pump the resource from one place to another. In most cases, the gas is moved great distances, crossing state, provincial, and even international borders, to its eventual point of use. Metering stations are built along the length of the pipeline to allow the gas to be measured and monitored, while valves can be found every ten kilometres or so. These valves can be opened or closed to control the flow of gas through the pipeline so that, in the event that maintenance needs arise, the gas can be stopped to provide safe access to crews entering the interior of the pipe. The final step of the procedure is to deflect the gas into distribution lines, which convey it to local sources where it is used for, among other things, heating and electricity and as a power source for automobiles.

Complete the flow-chart below.

Choose **NO MORE THAN TWO WORDS** *from the passage for each answer.*

The Process of Extracting and Refining Natural Gas

If gas reserves are beneath the water's surface, **19** .... are built.
Outcome: Engineers have a place to work from.

⬇

Engineers either drop a heavy metal bit onto the bottom of the ocean over and over, or they drill a hole in the soil in cases where the **20** .... of the gas reservoir is much greater.
Outcome: Natural gas is released and can be brought to the **21** ....
using pumps.

⬇

The gas is transported to a processing plant.
Outcome: Methane is separated from the **22** .... and other elements that might be present.

⬇

Byproducts of natural gas are sold.
Outcome: The money can help pay for the various **23** .... involved in isolating methane.

---

all-time high phr. 사상 최고치 **abundantly** adv. 풍부하게 **versatile** adj. 다용도의 **multifaceted** adj. 다면적인 **onshore** adv. 내륙에서
offshore adj. 앞바다 해저에 있는 **reserve** n. 매장량 **drilling** n. 시추 **bit** n. 비트 (다양한 물체에 구멍을 뚫기 위해 사용되는 도구) **reservoir** n. 매장층
breach v. 구멍을 뚫다 **reduce** v. 환원시키다 **hydrocarbon** n. 탄화 수소 **crude oil** phr. 원유 **nitrogen** n. 질소 **offset** v. 상쇄하다 **metering** n. 계량
deflect v. 방향을 바꾸다

9 Do Placebos Have a Place in Medicine?

A placebo is an imitation medicine that doctors sometimes administer to patients. Although they contain no pharmacological substances, patients who are given placebos are often convinced that these sugar pills possess the power to alleviate their symptoms or even cure them of their illnesses. What is most remarkable is that sometimes, they do. This baffling psychological and medical phenomenon is known as the placebo effect.

Some medical practitioners believe that the apparent efficacy of placebos lies in the simple act of writing a prescription. Essentially, it is thought that patients assume their ailments can be overcome if it is possible to prescribe medications for them. This view is substantiated by studies indicating that a large percentage of those seeking medical treatment suffer from disorders that the body is capable of healing itself. However, patients strongly think otherwise, and this attitude makes them attribute getting better, when they eventually do, solely to the medication they were prescribed. This, coupled with the trust they have in their doctor's ability to treat them, is what some say accounts for the positive performance of placebos.

Nevertheless, most experts strongly oppose medicating patients with placebos, suggesting the practice violates the doctor-patient relationship. Medical ethics standards maintain that trust is paramount and that doctors should be honest. However, some physicians are tempted to provide misinformation or gloss over the truth because they believe doing so is in the patient's best interests. For instance, a doctor may choose to present patients with a more optimistic picture of possible outcomes in order to convince them to undergo treatments they might otherwise reject. It is the hope that comes from believing it is still possible to be cured that can make all the difference in the end.

Further studies report of some patients learning they have been given placebos instead of actual drugs. In many cases, this causes patients to lose faith in their doctors, resulting in exacerbated symptoms and their health taking a turn for the worse. Due to the possibility of malpractice suits, the use of placebos in clinical practice has become increasingly uncommon. These days, placebos are almost exclusively administered in research situations where the subjects are informed that they may or may not receive a placebo and told about all potential risks in advance. In addition, policies are implemented to ensure that informed consent is observed, thus aligning standards for medical research and practice with the need for further investigation into the so-called placebo effect.

Complete the notes below.

*Choose **ONE WORD ONLY** from the passage for each answer.*

The Placebo Effect

How placebos work

- Some professionals think that a placebo's effectiveness could be due to a doctor making a 24 ....
- Research shows that many patients asking for medicine will heal without it.
- A patient's 25 .... makes them think any improvement they feel is due to medicine.

The opinion of doctors

- Most 26 .... are against giving patients placebos.
- The honesty of doctors is considered ethically important.
- Doctors sometimes think it's in the patient's best 27 .... not to tell the truth.
- The health of patients who find out they've been given placebos can become 28 ....

Current usage

- Today, placebos are mostly used for 29 ....

---

placebo n. (유효 성분이 없는) 위약   administer v. 투여하다, (치료를) 해주다   pharmacological adj. 약물학적의   alleviate v. 완화하다
baffling adj. 이해할 수 없는   placebo effect phr. 플라시보 효과 (위약 투여를 통한 심리 효과로 실제 호전이 되는 일)   efficacy n. 효험   ailment n. 질병
substantiate v. 입증하다   medicate v. 약을 투여하다   paramount adj. 가장 중요한   gloss over phr. ~에 대해 얼버무리다   exacerbate v. 악화시키다
malpractice suit phr. 의료 과실에 대한 소송   informed consent phr. 고지에 입각한 (수술 환자 등의) 동의

10 Urban Farming

Over the course of the last century, farming was transformed from a small-scale, subsistence-based activity to an industrialised global enterprise. However, the industry is currently under extreme strain from a lack of arable land. Furthermore, studies have shown that people will increasingly abandon farming in favour of more reliable work in cities. This will put added pressure on an already stretched global food supply. Societies must create innovative new ways of ensuring that their residents' fundamental need for sustenance continues to be met.

One trend that city planners around the world are embracing to address concerns about the growing lack of agricultural land is urban farming, which utilises infrastructure found in cities, such as buildings, vacant lots, and backyards to grow crops. One benefit of this practice is that fewer resources are used to transport food as growers and buyers are provided with fast access to agricultural yields. Also, because many urban farming projects use hydroponics, a method of growing plants in nutrient-enriched water, soil – which is increasingly facing mineral degradation due to harmful farming practices – is conserved. Finally, urban agriculture solves the problem of sometimes losing crops to extreme weather as city structures make it easier to cultivate plants in a strictly controlled environment.

An exemplary model of urban agriculture is a farm located beneath Pasona headquarters in Tokyo, Japan, where more than 200 plant species grow in a 43,000-square-foot space. The plants are grown using both hydroponic and soil-based farming methods, and an intelligent climate control system monitors humidity, temperature, and breeze. Because the farm at Pasona is located underground and has no direct sunlight, which plants need to survive, artificial lighting sustains the crops planted there. On the other side of the globe, in New York City, people are turning to rooftop greenhouse farming. One such operation, called BrightFarms, boasts automated sensors to activate lights, fans, shade curtains, and heat blankets. It also has tanks to catch and store rainwater. Selling nearly 500 pounds of produce each day to local supermarkets and restaurants, BrightFarms is able to avoid the expense of investing in delivery vehicles while keeping its carbon footprint to a minimum.

It is important to note that despite the success urban agriculture has so far experienced in places like Tokyo and New York, there remain significant obstacles to overcome. One challenge lies in supplying farms with adequate amounts of uncontaminated soil as soil in and around urban areas often contains high amounts of lead, which is poisonous to humans. Not using soil at all and relying instead on hydroponic systems is not yet an option everywhere since reliable and safe freshwater sources are scarce in many parts of the world, especially with global climate change negatively affecting precipitation rates. However, new developments, such as the ability to remove salt from ocean water for safe use in hydroponic systems and the creation of methods to treat contaminated soil, may help to resolve these issues one day soon.

Complete the table below.

*Choose **NO MORE THAN TWO WORDS** from the passage for each answer.*

Problem	Solution
More people will give up farming and move to cities.	Societies need to start developing new ways of feeding their people.
There is a lack of land on which to grow agricultural crops.	Grow plants using urban 30 ....
Crops are sometimes lost because of the 31	Take care of plants in a 32 .... environment.
The farm beneath Pasona headquarters gets no 33	Use artificial lighting to keep the plants alive.
Buying and using delivery vehicles is an additional cost.	Sell products to 34 .... clients.
There has been a negative effect on 35 .... due to climate change.	Remove the salt from seawater so it is safe to use on crops.

정답·해석·해설 p.360

subsistence n. 생계, 생존 strain n. 부담, 압박 stretch v. 부담을 주다 sustenance n. 생계, 생활 hydroponics n. 수경 재배 degradation n. 저하
cultivate v. 재배하다, 가꾸다 exemplary adj. 본보기가 되는, 모범적인 turn to phr. 전향하다 rooftop n. 옥상 produce n. 농작물
carbon footprint phr. 탄소 발자국 (온실 효과를 유발하는 이산화탄소의 배출량) uncontaminated adj. 오염되지 않은 precipitation n. 강수

READING PASSAGE

*You should spend about 20 minutes on **Questions 1-14**, which are based on Reading Passage below.*

Ford vs. GM: A Rivalry of Automobile Giants

The modern auto industry had its origin in the United States, where two automobile giants, Ford Motor Company and General Motors, became the major players in one of the greatest corporate rivalries in economic history. Henry Ford's Ford Motor Company started out quickly and enjoyed an early monopoly in car making. It became the dominant leader in production, economies of scale, and enjoyed widespread dealer networks. But before long, General Motors grew to become a formidable force in its own right. In the early 1910s, the two companies combined for more than half of the world automobile industry and were operating some of the largest factory complexes on earth. Despite their common ground in production and scale, the two firms nonetheless had significant differences in their business models and strategies.

For Ford, its enormous investment in production facilities was singular in focus as it was entirely dedicated to the manufacture of a single model, the famous Model T. The company's standardised design targeted mass markets and allowed them to keep production costs down to make a universal automobile for the 'common man'. Although this strategy proved excellent in the short term, it turned out to be extremely costly in the long term. When increased competition and lagging popularity for the Model T made it necessary for Ford to alter its product in the late 1920s, the facilities were not sufficiently equipped. Virtually every piece of equipment had to be torn down and rebuilt or replaced to facilitate the production of a different model. What's worse, Ford did not alter his manufacturing strategy. He merely replicated it to produce a new model, the Model A, to replace the Model T. In short, while Ford excelled at being an entrepreneur, he developed a reputation for being unwilling to adapt to changing market realities.

General Motors had a very different experience in the early 20th century. Although GM was second in market share in 1920, its total unit sales were less than 25 per cent of Ford's. Yet GM had an advantage that seemingly was outside the scope of the rival's founder: GM executives understood oligopolistic competition. The company's first CEO, William Durant, set out to create a large automobile company by gaining control of numerous small companies which produced either automobiles or auto parts. Durant understood that the auto market was changeable. Thus, GM created factories that made use of standardised and interchangeable parts, such as the chassis, but which allowed for the production of various body styles and car sizes. The company also introduced luxury brands to appeal to a different sector of the population who desired, and could afford, something more unique and with more class. Finally, in a major marketing breakthrough, GM introduced annual model changes, and this annual product variety was influential in convincing customers to upgrade to new models even if their older cars were still fully functional.

Durant's successor, Alfred P. Sloan, built upon the original model and put in place procedures that conveyed detailed financial and performance information from all divisions to ensure that the entire operation could maximise returns on investment. He also sought to emphasise the use of interchangeable parts across models in addition to investing resources into discovering consumer trends and market conditions. This included the collecting of all manner of consumer-demand information, such as seasonal and long-term variations in demand, buyer income levels, commodity price trends, etc., so that they could develop predictive indicators of economic trends in light of past business cycles. This plan proved effective, and it meant GM would gradually overtake Ford in the following years, allowing it to maintain a dominant position in the rivalry for half a century.

However, in the 70s and 80s, the market share held by General Motors began to erode in the face of foreign competition – from the Japanese in the budget lines and the Germans in the luxury lines – and this, in combination with GM's antagonism toward growing concerns about safety and environmental quality, gave Ford the opportunity to come back to prominence by the 1990s. Between 1975 and 2000, GM's market share plummeted from 55 to 27 per cent. Ford, though its market share did not catch up completely, fared better overall despite also experiencing challenges and setbacks. In the early 1980s, it suffered 3.3 billion dollars in losses before making a comeback mid-decade. It began to significantly cut production costs, and its new introduction for 1985, the aerodynamic Taurus, was very well received in the market. These changes, in combination with adapting to growing concerns about safety and the environment, allowed the company to remain successful.

Then came the devastating automotive industry downturn following the financial crisis of 2008, which further complicated the plight of the two industry giants. In the years leading up to the crisis, Ford had made sound decisions that helped it avoid bankruptcy. For example, Ford had eliminated one of its largest vehicles, the Excursion, in anticipation of dwindling demand for gas-guzzling SUVs. They replaced its production with more production of medium-sized vehicles, which were more marketable as gas prices soared. GM did not have such foresight and continued to rely heavily on the production of trucks and SUVs. They also had amassed financial liabilities on par with the entire national debt of Mexico. Consequently, even laying off up to 21,000 workers and getting rid of three of its brands – keeping only Buick, Cadillac, GMC, and Chevrolet intact – could not keep it from declaring bankruptcy, which it did in June of 2009. There is no doubt that were it not for the enormous, and infamous, government bailout, General Motors would have ceased to exist.

Questions 1-6

Complete the table below.

*Choose **ONE WORD AND/OR A NUMBER** from the passage for each answer.*

Company	Original Strategy	Achievements	Failures
Ford	totally dedicated to making just one 1	began rapidly and boasted a 2 .... in the automobile industry	once had to rebuild or replace all 3 ....
General Motors	capable of producing a range of car sizes and body 4	held a 5 .... position in the rivalry for 50 years	laid off as many as 6 .... before declaring bankruptcy

Questions 7-14

Do the following statements agree with the views of the writer in Reading Passage?

Write

    YES   *if the statement agrees with the views of the writer*

    NO   *if the statement contradicts the views of the writer*

    NOT GIVEN   *if it is impossible to say what the writer thinks about this*

7   GM and Ford differed greatly in their business planning.

8   Ford's use of a universal design saved money in the long term.

9   Ford changed his manufacturing plan to produce the Model A.

10   GM leaders had an understanding about competition that Henry Ford lacked.

11   Durant attempted to gain control of a company owned by Ford.

12   The yearly model changes introduced by GM were highly successful.

13   GM's investment in gathering consumer information ultimately was ineffective.

14   The 1985 Taurus had the most attractive design of any Ford vehicle.

정답·해석·해설 p.371

VOCABULARY LIST

Chapter 04에서 선별한 다음의 어휘들을 음성파일을 들으며 암기한 후 퀴즈로 확인해보세요.

*해커스 동영상강의 포털 해커스 인강(HackersIngang.com)에서 단어암기 MP3를 무료로 다운로드할 수 있습니다.

- ☐ progression n. 발전, 진보
- ☐ timber n. 목재
- ☐ aesthetic adj. 심미적인
- ☐ perception n. 인식
- ☐ decorative adj. 장식의
- ☐ frame n. 골조
- ☐ tensile strength phr. 장력
- ☐ steel n. 강철
- ☐ landscape n. 풍경, 경치
- ☐ larva n. 유충
- ☐ overrun v. 들끓다
- ☐ midrise adj. 중층의
- ☐ imitate v. 모방하다
- ☐ mound n. 언덕
- ☐ pest n. 해충
- ☐ radial adj. 방사의
- ☐ convection n. 대류
- ☐ dissipation n. 방출
- ☐ even adj. 평평한
- ☐ terrain n. 지대
- ☐ sloping adj. 경사진
- ☐ predominance n. 지배, 우위
- ☐ moderate adj. 적당한, 온건한
- ☐ respiration n. 호흡
- ☐ warfare n. 전투, 전쟁
- ☐ platform n. 단, 연단

- ☐ cumbersome adj. 번거로운
- ☐ steer v. 몰다, 조종하다
- ☐ friction n. 마찰
- ☐ troop n. 부대, 군대
- ☐ navigate v. 항해하다
- ☐ piloting n. 조종
- ☐ orientation n. 방위 측정, 방향
- ☐ landmark n. 지형지물
- ☐ feature n. 지형, 지세
- ☐ entail v. 수반하다
- ☐ magnetic field phr. 자기장
- ☐ orient v. 자신의 위치를 알다
- ☐ compensate v. 보완하다, 보상하다
- ☐ susceptible to phr. ~하기 쉽다, ~에 영향을 받기 쉽다
- ☐ windmill n. 풍차
- ☐ renewable energy phr. 신재생 에너지
- ☐ substantial adj. 상당한
- ☐ kinetic adj. 운동의
- ☐ propel v. 추진하다, 나아가게 하다
- ☐ optimise v. 최적화하다
- ☐ optimal adj. 최적의
- ☐ anemometre n. 풍속계
- ☐ accordingly adv. 알맞게, 적절히
- ☐ voltage n. 전압
- ☐ all-time high phr. 사상 최고치
- ☐ abundantly adv. 풍부하게

Quiz

각 단어의 알맞은 뜻을 찾아 연결하시오.

01 predominance   ⓐ 평평한
02 imitate   ⓑ 지배, 우위
03 moderate   ⓒ 인식
04 progression   ⓓ 적당한, 온건한
05 perception   ⓔ 발전, 진보
       ⓕ 모방하다

06 substantial   ⓐ 보완하다, 보상하다
07 friction   ⓑ 수반하다
08 compensate   ⓒ 상당한
09 susceptible to   ⓓ 마찰
10 entail   ⓔ ~에 영향을 받기 쉽다
       ⓕ 조종

ⓑ 10 ⓔ 09 ⓐ 08 ⓓ 07 ⓒ 06 ⓒ 05 ⓔ 04 ⓓ 03 ⓕ 02 ⓑ 01

CH 04

- [ ] versatile adj. 다용도의
- [ ] multifaceted adj. 다면적인
- [ ] onshore adv. 내륙에서
- [ ] reserve n. 매장량
- [ ] reservoir n. 매장층
- [ ] breach v. 구멍을 뚫다
- [ ] offset v. 상쇄하다
- [ ] metering n. 계량
- [ ] deflect v. 방향을 바꾸다
- [ ] administer v. 투여하다, (치료를) 해주다
- [ ] pharmacological adj. 약물학적의
- [ ] alleviate v. 완화하다
- [ ] baffling adj. 이해할 수 없는
- [ ] efficacy n. 효험
- [ ] ailment n. 질병
- [ ] medicate v. 약을 투여하다
- [ ] paramount adj. 가장 중요한
- [ ] exacerbate v. 악화시키다
- [ ] subsistence n. 생계, 생존
- [ ] stretch v. 부담을 주다
- [ ] sustenance n. 생계, 생활
- [ ] degradation n. 저하
- [ ] exemplary adj. 본보기가 되는, 모범적인
- [ ] turn to phr. 전향하다
- [ ] rooftop n. 옥상
- [ ] uncontaminated adj. 오염되지 않은

- [ ] precipitation n. 강수
- [ ] giant n. 거대 조직
- [ ] monopoly n. 독점
- [ ] scale n. 규모
- [ ] in one's own right phr. 스스로
- [ ] ground n. 기반
- [ ] standardised adj. 표준화된
- [ ] mass n. 대중
- [ ] lagging adj. 뒤쳐지는
- [ ] replicate v. 복제하다
- [ ] excel v. 뛰어나다
- [ ] entrepreneur n. 기업가
- [ ] successor n. 계승자
- [ ] variation n. 변동
- [ ] erode v. 약화되다
- [ ] antagonism n. 적대감
- [ ] prominence n. 우위
- [ ] plummet v. 급락하다
- [ ] setback n. 차질
- [ ] plight n. 역경
- [ ] bankruptcy n. 부도
- [ ] dwindle v. 줄어들다
- [ ] foresight n. 통찰력
- [ ] amass v. 축적하다
- [ ] liability n. 채무
- [ ] on par phr. ~과 동등한

Quiz

각 단어의 알맞은 뜻을 찾아 연결하시오.

01 degradation	ⓐ 질병	06 erode	ⓐ 대중
02 alleviate	ⓑ 가장 중요한	07 dwindle	ⓑ 우위
03 paramount	ⓒ 상쇄하다	08 scale	ⓒ 약화되다
04 offset	ⓓ 완화하다	09 replicate	ⓓ 줄어들다
05 ailment	ⓔ 저하	10 mass	ⓔ 복제하다
	ⓕ 방향을 바꾸다		ⓕ 규모

ⓐ 01 ⓒ 02 ⓑ 03 ⓒ 04 ⓐ 05 ⓒ 06 ⓓ 07 ⓕ 08 ⓔ 09 ⓐ 10

CHAPTER 05

Sentence Completion

Sentence completion 문제는 지문의 내용과 일치하도록 문장을 완성하는 문제이다. IELTS Reading 영역에서 간혹 출제되고 있다.

■■ 문제 형태

Sentence completion 문제는 완성되지 않은 문장의 뒤에 들어갈 내용을 보기 리스트에서 선택하거나, 지문에서 단어를 찾아 그대로 적는 주관식 형태로 출제된다. 주관식으로 출제되는 경우에는 몇 단어 혹은 숫자로 답을 작성해야 하는지 반드시 확인한다.

보기 리스트에서 알맞은 답 선택하기
주어진 보기 리스트에서 문장을 완성할 수 있는 알맞은 보기를 선택하는 문제이다.

---

*Complete each sentence with the correct ending, **A-G**, below.*

*Write the correct letter, **A-G**, in boxes 1-2 on your answer sheet.*

1   Last-born children are likely to

2   First-born children learn how to

> **A**   make outrageous statements about family members.
> **B**   use jokes to avoid disputing with their family.
> ⋮
> **G**   develop more serious personalities than other people.

빈칸에 알맞은 답을 지문에서 찾아 적기
문장이 빈칸에 들어갈 알맞은 단어를 지문에서 찾아 적는 문제이다.

Complete the sentences below.

*Choose **ONE WORD ONLY** from the passage for each answer.*

Write your answers in boxes 1-2 on your answer sheet.

1   Last-born children make .... about family members.

2   First-born children learn how to develop more serious .... than other people.

■ 문제풀이 전략

STEP 1 문제의 핵심어구와 내용을 파악한다.

Sentence completion 문제를 풀기 위해서는 먼저 문제의 핵심어구와 핵심 내용을 파악한다.

EXAMPLE

*Complete the sentence with the correct ending, **A-D**, below.*

*Write the correct letter, **A-D**, in box 1 on your answer sheet.*

1 Last-born children are likely to ●———————————————

      A make outrageous statements about family members.

      B use jokes to avoid disputing with their family.

      C assume the responsibilities of their older siblings.

      D develop more serious personalities than other people.

> 문제의 핵심어구인 Last-born children이 어떤 경향이 있는지를 묻고 있음을 파악한다.

✔ TIPS

1. Sentence completion 문제는 보통 여러 개의 문제가 한 번에 출제되므로, 모든 문제의 핵심어구를 한꺼번에 파악하기보다는 한 문제씩 핵심어구를 파악하여 답을 쓰고 다음 문제로 넘어가는 것이 좋다.

2. Sentence completion 문제에서 보기 리스트가 주어지는 경우에는 보기가 문제보다 더 많이 제공되므로, 정답으로 쓰이지 않는 보기들이 존재한다. 그러므로 보기를 미리 다 읽을 필요가 없다. 보기는 정답을 찾을 때 한 번만 읽어 시간을 효율적으로 사용한다.

지문을 scanning하여 문제의 핵심어구와 관련된 내용을 찾는다. 관련 내용이 언급된 주변에서 정답의 단서를 확인한다.

EXAMPLE

For siblings born later, their personalities may be highly influenced by their order of birth. Since they are unlikely to benefit from a familial system that is clearly more advantageous to their older siblings, they must find a way to equalise the playing field. One way that this happens is through [1]the use of humour, which last-born children often rely upon to keep from getting in trouble or arguing with other family members. This can lead to funnier or more outrageous personalities amongst last-born children. Firstborn children, on the other hand, tend to be more responsible and mature even at a young age, since they are expected to provide guidance to their younger siblings.

문제의 핵심어구인 Last-born children과 관련된 내용을 지문에서 찾는다. 관련 내용이 언급된 주변에서 'the use of humour, which last-born children often rely upon to keep from getting in trouble or arguing with other family members'라는 정답의 단서를 확인한다.

*Complete the sentence with the correct ending, **A-D**, below.*

*Write the correct letter, **A-D**, in box 1 on your answer sheet.*

1 Last-born children are likely to

> **A** make outrageous statements about family members.
> **B** use jokes to avoid disputing with their family.
> **C** assume the responsibilities of their older siblings.
> **D** develop more serious personalities than other people.

지문 해석 p.375

☑ **TIPS**

Sentence completion 문제는 보통 지문의 내용이 전개되는 순서대로 출제되므로, 정답의 단서도 지문에서 순서대로 등장한다. 예를 들어 2번 문제의 정답의 단서는 1번 문제의 정답의 단서보다 이후에 등장할 가능성이 높다. 그러므로 정답의 단서를 찾지 못한 문제가 있다면, 이전 문제의 정답의 단서와 다음 문제의 정답의 단서 사이를 살펴보도록 한다.

(1) 각 보기를 읽고 정답의 단서가 바르게 paraphrasing된 보기를 정답으로 선택한다.

(2) 선택한 보기를 문제에 넣었을 때 문장이 지문의 내용과 일치하는지 확인한다.

EXAMPLE

For siblings born later, their personalities may be highly influenced by their order of birth. Since they are unlikely to benefit from a familial system that is clearly more advantageous to their older siblings, they must find a way to equalise the playing field. One way that this happens is through [1]the use of humour, which last-born children often rely upon to keep from getting in trouble or arguing with other family members. This can lead to funnier or more outrageous personalities amongst last-born children. Firstborn children, on the other hand, tend to be more responsible and mature even at a young age, since they are expected to provide guidance to their younger siblings.

*Complete the sentence with the correct ending, **A-D**, below.*

*Write the correct letter, **A-D**, in box 1 on your answer sheet.*

1 Last-born children are likely to use jokes to avoid disputing with their family. B

> **A** make outrageous statements about family members.
> **B** use jokes to avoid disputing with their family.
> **C** assume the responsibilities of their older siblings.
> **D** develop more serious personalities than other people.

(1) 정답의 단서에서 'use of humor, which last-born children ~ rely upon to keep from ~ arguing with other family members'가 'use jokes to avoid disputing with their family'로 paraphrasing되었음을 확인한다.

(2) 보기 B를 문제에 넣었을 때, 막내로 태어난 아이들이 가족들과 언쟁하는 것을 피하기 위해 농담을 활용한다는 내용이 지문의 내용과 일치함을 확인한다.

⊘ TIPS

Sentence completion 주관식 문제의 정답은 주로 명사로 출제되지만 간혹 동사, 형용사, 혹은 부사로 출제되는 경우도 있다. 그러므로 주관식으로 출제되는 경우 빈칸에 들어갈 단어의 품사를 반드시 확인한다. 명사로 출제된 경우 단·복수를, 동사로 출제된 경우 시제와 단·복수를 잘 확인한다.

1 A statue of Shakespeare, the world's most renowned playwright, stands in Leicester Square in London's West End. Rather appropriately, too, as the West End is a major attraction, boasting about 40 venues that show some of the highest quality theatre in the world. The area – also known as Theatreland – has a rich history, with many of the theatres dating back to the Victorian and Edwardian periods. These historic buildings now coexist with contemporary shops and offices in what is now one of London's busiest districts. The oldest of these West End theatres is Theatre Royal Drury Lane which opened in 1663, although it has been rebuilt several times due to fire. West End theatres continue to put on an array of shows including contemporary productions, revivals of classics, and, most famously, musicals. The latter draw the most viewers, and have been known to run for decades. This is the case with the *Les Misérables* and *The Phantom of the Opera*, which both opened in the mid-1980s and are among the highest grossing of all West End productions.

*Complete each sentence with the correct ending, **A-E**, below.*

1   A lot of the theatres in the West End

2   The most popular West End plays

A	are set to be modernised soon.
B	have been running for decades.
C	do not show contemporary productions.
D	are located alongside modern structures.
E	are revivals of classics.

---

playwright n. 극작가 venue n. 장소 coexist v. 공존하다 contemporary adj. 최신식의, 현대의 revival n. 재공연, 부활 gross v. 수익을 올리다

2 While pet owners have long believed that their animal companions display feelings such as empathy, jealousy, and guilt, scientists have historically said that this was impossible. They held that only humans felt emotions and that our recognition of them in other species was due to anthropomorphism, or the attribution of human traits to animals. However, recent research has shown that this may not actually be true. By utilising testing methods usually used on non-verbal infants, researchers Christine Harris and Caroline Prouvost of the University of California, San Diego found that dogs displayed jealous behaviours when their owners showed affection to other dogs. The discovery of demonstrable jealousy in another social species indicates that emotions are not likely a strictly human trait. Historical anthropologists like Laurel Braitman and Elizabeth Marshall Thomas take this further. They suggest that emotions have evolutionary value and that when we see a human emotion in animals, we may be recognising a common feature acquired long ago in our shared past.

*Complete each sentence with the correct ending, **A-E**, below.*

3   Scientists traditionally felt that animals

4   Dogs showing envy proves that emotions

A	communicate thoughts to other animals.
B	lack the emotions.
C	are present in more than one species.
D	separate feelings from emotions.
E	share an emotional bond with humans.

---

companion n. 반려, 동행 empathy n. 공감 anthropomorphism n. 인격화 attribution n. 귀속 trait n. 특성 demonstrable adj. 입증할 수 있는
value n. 의의, 가치

3 While companies were established to produce a product or perform a service for a profit, there is a general consensus that they should give back to the community as well. Many corporate owners and managers share this belief and feel that they have a responsibility to improve conditions for the disadvantaged. Some of these, such as Toms Shoes, were actually established with this in mind. Since its foundation, Toms has given one pair of shoes to a person in need for every pair sold. To date, this has resulted in the donation of more than 50 million pairs of shoes. The cosmetics company NuSkin is another example of a socially responsible company. They set up an initiative called *Nourish the Children*, which allows customers to donate healthy meals to impoverished children when making a purchase. These types of programmes are praiseworthy for their impact on poverty, but they also help the bottom line of companies who undertake them. By advertising these types of socially responsible programmes, companies boost profits. This is because the programmes make customers who are concerned about social issues feel that they are doing good in the world by patronising the company. Overall, these types of corporate programmes have a positive impact on everyone involved and should be an example for other companies to follow.

*Complete each sentence with the correct ending, **A-G**, below.*

5 Some corporate leaders think that it is important to

6 Corporate giving programmes can

7 Many consumers feel better when they

> **A** make companies more successful.
> **B** provide free items during economic depressions.
> **C** distribute profits to employees.
> **D** advertise changes in company policies.
> **E** support businesses with charitable programmes.
> **F** reduce the impact of customer purchases.
> **G** make better conditions for people in need.

---

consensus n. 합의, 의견 일치 the disadvantaged phr. 사회적 약자들, 사회적으로 혜택을 받지 못하는 사람들 initiative n. (새로운 중요) 기획, 계획
impoverished adj. 빈곤한 bottom line phr. 순익, 최종 결산 undertake v. 착수하다 patronise v. 애용하다, 후원하다

4 Found in Southeast Asia and Australia, weaver ants are most notable for their ability to construct nests from living leaves located high in the treetops. Like most ant varieties, a weaver ant's life revolves around providing for its queen. In fact, it is to serve her that they build their nests in the first place. It all starts with a queen founding a colony by laying a clutch of eggs on a leaf and raising the larvae until they become mature workers. In order to increase the size of the colony, the queen must lay more eggs, but this will require additional living space for the already mature ants. Thus, a nest must be built – a task that requires significant collaboration. First, a single ant reaches toward a distant leaf. Unable to get to it alone, the other ants hold onto the first ant, forming a chain until the leaf is finally grasped. Once they have it, they pull as one until both leaves have been drawn together. Keeping the leaves in place, they wait for other workers to arrive carrying larvae, which are capable of producing silk. The larvae are prompted to release the silk from their salivary glands, and the worker ants dab the sticky substance from one leaf to another, essentially binding them. Ultimately, the process is repeated until a nest large enough to accommodate the colony's growing population has been constructed, and the cycle is likewise repeated each time the queen lays more eggs.

Complete the sentences below.

*Choose **ONE WORD ONLY** from the passage for each answer.*

8   A .... establishes a colony by laying eggs and raising young.

9   The ants connect to form a .... in order to collect leaves.

10   The .... of larvae sticks to the leaves of a nest.

---

weaver ant phr. 베짜기개미   revolve around phr. ~을 중심으로 돌아가다   clutch n. 배, 무리   larvae n. 유충   collaboration n. 협력
reach v. 뻗다, 내밀다   prompt v. 유도하다   salivary gland phr. 침샘   dab v. 바르다   bind v. 묶다   accommodate v. 수용하다

5 *Cinderella*, *Snow White*, and *Sleeping Beauty* are all considered animated classics, but all three are actually based on stories published by two German writers commonly known as the Brothers Grimm. Although Jacob and Wilhelm Grimm are often referred to as the authors of these fairy tales, they did not actually come up with the stories themselves. The stories had been passed down through the oral tradition from one generation to the next in Germany and the surrounding regions long before the Brothers Grimm. However, the brothers, seeing that the stories were at risk of being lost, started documenting them. In order to do this, they interviewed friends, relatives, storytellers and aristocrats to learn the stories of the culture. After they had collected the stories, the Brothers Grimm set about putting them to paper. During the writing and editing processes, they combined differing versions of the same tales and edited them to impart a stylistic consistency and to improve the basic plots, thereby making them their own. When it was finally published, their book *Nursery and Household Tales* was a blockbuster. It went on to be reprinted repeatedly and eventually had its title altered to *Grimm's Fairy Tales*. Even though this is still the name we use for the book, the stories it contained were not exactly the same as the ones that we know today. Most of the brothers' original stories had more adult themes, as they had not been written for children. Over time, the stories were edited to make them more appropriate for younger audiences and became staples of childhood libraries worldwide. In fact, their works have been translated into more than 100 languages.

Complete the sentences below.

Choose **NO MORE THAN TWO WORDS** *from the passage for each answer.*

11   The stories the brothers used were handed down by the ....

12   The brothers put together many different .... of the same story.

13   The book *Nursery and Household Tales'* original .... was changed after its first publication.

14   The .... in the brother's works show that they were not for young readers.

---

oral tradition phr. 구전 document v. (상세한 내용을) 기록하다 aristocrat n. 귀족 impart v. (특정한 특성을) 부여하다 stylistic adj. 문체(양식)의
consistency n. 일관성 blockbuster n. 베스트셀러, 히트작 staple n. 주요 품목, 주성분

6 Education is one of the most important issues addressed by societies. It provides people with the basic skills required to survive in the world, but it also allows them to make societal contributions. In fact, former American first lady Eleanor Roosevelt claimed that education was essential to good citizenship. Unfortunately, in large multi-cultural societies like the United States, educating the populace can be difficult. This, according to Dr M. S. Rosenberg, is due to distinct cultural approaches to education. For instance, the parents of Asian-American students sometimes encourage them to sit quietly, listen intently, and avoid eye contact with their teachers, as these were the educational values of their cultures. This stands in stark contrast to the importance of classroom discussion and eye contact instilled in most European and American students. This problem can be magnified by the differing ways that cultures view the role of the teacher in the classroom. European or American parents often see the teacher as a participant in educating their children with whom they work. Many Hispanic cultures, on the other hand, regard teachers as experts and defer to them on nearly all aspects of educational decision-making. Unfortunately, not understanding these cultural differences can have a major negative impact on students. Teachers who have been trained in the European and American style of education may see the active participation of students of that culture as superior to that of others. They may also see the involvement of European or American parents as a sign of greater concern for their children's educations. However, they could simply be misunderstanding cultural norms. In order to avoid these kinds of problems and to more effectively teach in a multicultural setting, teachers are trained to recognise cultural differences and to adapt their lessons and evaluation styles to reflect them. In other words, they attempt to implement uniform education standards which allow for cultural diversity.

Complete the sentences below.

*Choose **NO MORE THAN THREE WORDS** from the passage for each answer.*

15 Education provides essential knowledge and the opportunity to make ....

16 Failing to understand .... may have a significant negative effect on students.

17 Teachers are trying to put in place .... which respect different backgrounds.

citizenship n. 시민의 자질, 시민권 populace n. 대중들 in stark contrast to phr. ~와 아주 대조적인 instil v. 주입하다, 불어넣다
defer to phr. ~의 의견에 따르다 norm n. 규범, 표준 implement v. 시행하다 allow for phr. ~을 고려하다, 참작하다

7 Environmental Conservation Through Urban Density

The first image that comes to mind when considering environmental sustainability is usually not a densely packed urban landscape. However, since *Compact City: A Plan for a Liveable Urban Environment* was released in 1974 by authors George Dantzig and Thomas Saaty, most urban planners agree that the most effective way to keep the planet green is to pack as many people as possible into compact cities. The most important reason to contain people in cities, they say, is to decrease sprawl, the expansion of urban areas into surrounding land. Not only does the infringement of human populations into undeveloped areas destroy arable soil and ecosystems, but it also creates suburbs that are energy inefficient and automobile dependent. Building cities upward rather than outward is the best way to avoid this.

If everyone lived in cities, the need for automobiles would be greatly reduced, which would minimise the pollution they cause and conserve the fossil fuels they require to operate. Studies show that people who live in densely populated cities, like New York, are 40 per cent less likely to own cars and use far less gasoline because public transit is readily available and walking or cycling is often an option. The fact that driving in cities has become increasingly difficult also contributes to people giving it up. With parking restrictions and expensive toll fees to contend with, not to mention the glut of other vehicles that, sadly, remain on the road, many city dwellers simply choose not to drive when there are far more attractive transportation alternatives available.

But the environmental sustainability of cities has to do with more than just transportation: it's also about housing. The vast majority of people in high-density cities live in apartment buildings, which are the most energy-efficient residential structures in the world. The shared walls of apartment buildings mean that less heat is lost and thus, less fuel is used to generate it. In addition, because apartments are usually smaller than, say, a typical single-family home in the suburbs, far less electricity is consumed per household – as much as 50 per cent less than in sparsely populated areas, actually. It's thus no surprise that the carbon footprint of most high-density city inhabitants is around 30 per cent smaller than the global average.

Ultimately, while being shoulder-to-shoulder with millions of other people may seem unpleasant, it is the best way to handle our ever-growing population while preserving the resources that subsequent generations will need to survive. The cities that exist today are far from perfect, but that just means that there is still a lot that can be done – from replacing diesel fleets with hybrid and electric ones to updating archaic, inefficient infrastructure – to make urban communities not only more sustainable but also nicer places to live.

Complete the sentences below.

*Choose **ONE WORD ONLY** from the passage for each answer.*

18   The primary reason for containing people in cities is to limit ....

19   A major decrease in the need for cars would reduce .... and save fossil fuels.

20   Due to their smaller size, urban apartments use less .... than suburban homes.

21   Living in densely populated cities is the best way to protect resources for future ....

---

density n. 밀도, 농도   sustainability n. 지속 가능성   pack v. 가득 채우다   compact adj. 꽉 찬, 빽빽한   sprawl n. 도시 스프롤 현상 (도시 개발이 확산되는 현상)   infringement n. 침해   arable adj. 경작할 수 있는   contend with phr. ~과 씨름하다   glut n. 공급 과잉, 과도한 양   sparsely adv. 드문드문   carbon footprint phr. 탄소 발자국 (이산화탄소의 배출량)   fleet n. (기관 소유의 비행기·버스·택시 등의) 무리   archaic adj. 낡은

8 Gene Therapy

A revolutionary treatment

Millions of dollars are spent on medical research each year, and although new techniques are being developed and important discoveries are being made at an unprecedented rate, the cures for a number of life-threatening diseases, like cancer and AIDS, continue to elude scientists. But there may be hope in the form of a treatment known as gene therapy, which involves using genetic material to manipulate a patient's cells. The idea was first proposed in 1972 by Theodore Friedmann and Richard Roblin in *Gene Therapy for Human Genetic Disease?* This article cited US physician Stanfield Roger's early notion that healthy DNA could be used to replace defective DNA in people with genetic disorders. Building off Roger's idea, Friedmann and Roblin suggested ways in which healthy DNA could be used to fix, replace, or supplement a faulty gene to make it function properly. Researchers quickly latched onto this innovative new concept, and the first gene therapy case was approved in the United States in September of 1990.

Although gene therapy has successfully cured patients with diseases such as leukaemia, haemophilia, and Parkinson's disease in the years since then, it is not without its problems. The most difficult part of administering healthy DNA to a patient is getting the unhealthy cell to accept it. While techniques that involve directly injecting the healthy DNA into the recipient cell have shown some success, the more commonly employed method is through the use of a vector – a DNA molecule that serves as a vehicle to carry foreign genetic material into another cell.

Viruses are the most commonly used vectors because they naturally invade cells. When they are used, some of the virus's DNA is removed and replaced with the therapeutic DNA, but the virus's structural sequence stays intact and serves as the 'backbone' of the vector. This tricks the patient's cells into allowing it to enter, but it does not always work as hoped. This is due to the fact that there is always the chance the patient's immune system will kick in and fight off the virus, killing the therapeutic gene at the same time. This process can produce an inflammatory response within the patient, and in certain cases, lead to organ failure.

Alternatively, the viral vector could potentially cause disease once inside the patient and even target more cells than it is supposed to, including ones that are healthy. Because of these risks, gene therapy is still considered experimental and the only way to receive it is through participation in a clinical trial. Doctors still have a long way to go before they understand all the potential effects gene therapy can have on a person's body, so research is likely to continue until further breakthroughs are made and both the Food and Drug Administration and the National Institutes of Health deem the treatment safe enough to enter mainstream medical practice.

*Complete each sentence with the correct ending, **A-G**, below.*

22 When a virus is used as a vector, its structure

23 When an immune system fights viruses, it also

24 Due to certain dangers, gene therapy

A	destroys any genetic material that is meant to cure disease.
B	manages to cure a life-threatening disease.
C	accepts the healthy DNA that is added.
D	retains its basic form.
E	remains experimental for now.
F	invades the cells of the patient.
G	removes the diseased elements.

gene therapy phr. 유전자 치료 unprecedented adj. 전례 없는 elude v. ~에게 발견되지 않다 genetic material phr. 유전 형질 manipulate v. 조작하다 supplement v. 보완하다 leukaemia n. 백혈병 haemophilia n. 혈우병 administer v. (음식·약 따위를) 주다, (약을) 투여하다 vector n. (질병의) 매개체 molecule n. 분자 sequence n. 순서 kick in phr. (기능을) 발휘하다, 효과가 나타나기 시작하다 inflammatory adj. 염증의 organ failure phr. 장기부전 clinical trial phr. 임상 시험

9 The Psychology of Emotion

Since they encompass such a wide spectrum of human behaviour, emotions have always been a central site of psychological study. One of the first figures to introduce a theory of emotion was the Greek philosopher Aristotle, who thought that they were connected to appetites. This idea held sway for centuries, until Charles Darwin formulated an evolutionary concept of emotions. Darwin suggested that emotions had evolved through natural selection and therefore must have a purpose. However, his ideas were supplanted as the field of psychology became more prominent.

A highly influential theory of how emotions work was developed independently by two scholars, William James and Carl Lange, in the late 19th century. This theory, which has come to be known as the James-Lange theory, suggested that physiological arousal leads to the experience of emotion. This was a reversal of the conventional conception that emotion was primarily mental in character. In James and Lange's conception, the body was the source of the emotional response. James suggested that the sense organs are the first part of the body to experience the stimulus of an outside object, and that the information from these is then passed to the brain.

As the James-Lange theory became the dominant conceptualisation of emotion in the early 20th century, it inspired criticism from other researchers. One critical response came from the Harvard physiologist Walter Bradford Cannon and his student Philip Bard in the 1920s. Cannon and Bard believed that emotional responses were the result of cognitive reactions within the hypothalamic structures of the brain, with the thalamic region being the centre of emotional response. According to Cannon and Bard, the physical responses to emotion could be considered separate from the mental responses, and did not always precede them.

While the James-Lange theory foregrounded the body, and the Cannon-Bard theory prioritised the brain, the two-factor theory of emotion offered a more balanced approach. This theory – put forward by Stanley Schachter and Jerome E. Singer in the 1960s – suggested that emotional reactions are based on two factors: physical arousal and mental labelling. Therefore, when a person experiences an emotion, they initially feel some form of physiological arousal, and then they search their environment for things they can use to label this as an emotion. This can occasionally result in misattribution, as when someone feels the physical symptoms of anxiety, but believes them to be related to romantic arousal. With no clear consensus emerging within psychological circles, it seems that the debate over whether it is in the mind or the body that emotions are formed is set to continue.

Complete the sentences below.

*Choose **NO MORE THAN TWO WORDS** from the passage for each answer.*

25   The James-Lange theory countered the traditional idea of emotion as a .... experience.

26   James believed that the .... experience a stimulus before the brain does.

27   The signs of .... can sometimes be confused with romantic sensations.

---

hold sway phr. 지배하다   **formulate** v. 만들어 내다, 표현하다   **natural selection** phr. 자연 도태   **supplant** v. 대체하다   **arousal** n. 자극, 흥분
reversal n. 반전   **conceptualisation** n. 개념적인 해석   **hypothalamic** adj. 시상하부의   **thalamic** adj. 시상의
foreground v. 특히 중시하다, 최전면에 내세우다   **misattribution** n. 오귀인   **circles** n. 집단

10   Speaking Pidgin

It has long been said that 'necessity is the mother of invention', and nowhere is this sentiment more applicable in the context of linguistics than it is for pidgin languages. Found throughout Africa, the Caribbean, Hawaii, and parts of Southeast Asia, pidgin languages are simple dialects that evolve when two or more groups must communicate for a prolonged period of time but their members do not share a common tongue.

Historically, pidgins arose due to the colonial encroachment of European powers into the New World during the 17th and 18th centuries. As the British, French, Portuguese, Spanish, and Dutch colonised various areas of the Americas, it was inevitable that they would come into contact with native peoples with whom they were unable to communicate verbally. Initially, they may have used a few hand gestures to get their point across, but people are innately inclined to language acquisition and eventually, words were learned and used to facilitate activities like bartering.

The slave trade, which saw millions of Africans exported to plantations in the Americas, is especially responsible for the further development of pidgin tongues. As a great many dialects were spoken throughout Africa and because people were seized from various parts of the continent, new slaves were often able to understand neither their captors nor their fellow slaves. In order to communicate at all, they were forced to adapt, picking up a word from one language here and a word from another language there. Eventually, through this method, conveying the most basic information became possible and people began to rely on this unstructured dialect as the language they used most.

While pidgins vary from group to group, they do share certain features. According to 19th century American folklorist Charles Leland, all pidgin languages sound similar to how a very young child might communicate. Specifically, the pronunciation of words is generally only approximated and the parts of speech are highly flexible, often being modified spontaneously. He also found that speakers of pidgin languages tend to ignore the conventions of language. For instance, rather than incorporating function words, like pronouns and prepositions, into their speech, they rely almost exclusively on content words. Essentially, speakers of pidgin languages, having a superficial knowledge of the most indispensable words and no regard for grammar, are able to convey their main ideas but not much more.

Of course, pidgin languages do not often last long. Generally, within a few decades, as children are born into the families of pidgin speakers, one group will have learned the language of the other or both groups will have learned a new common language. Sometimes, the necessity of speaking pidgin is removed when one group leaves an area. For instance, during the French occupation of Vietnam, many Vietnamese learned to communicate with their imperialist rulers in a pidgin French. When Vietnam declared its independence in 1954 and the French left, there was no longer a need for this dialect, so people mostly returned to speaking their primary languages. In the rare instances when pidgin does survive, meaning that children of the next generation adopt it as their mother tongue, it invariably evolves to become increasingly standardised and structured, with a fully developed vocabulary and system of grammar. Ultimately, it becomes a form of colloquial speech known as a creole.

*Complete each sentence with the correct ending, **A-G**, below.*

28 To communicate with natives, Europeans first may have relied on

29 Slaves combined words from various dialects to allow for

30 According to Charles Leland, pidgin speakers do not stick to

31 Pidgin French in Vietnam is mentioned to exemplify

A	the process of providing structure to a pidgin language.
B	the use of body language.
C	a dialect that eventually became unnecessary.
D	the passing on of pidgin to the next generation.
E	communication with people in the Americas.
F	the enduring impact of colonialism on oppressed peoples.
G	the standards that generally shape verbal expression.

정답·해석·해설 p.375

pidgin n. 피진어(어떤 언어의 제한된 어휘들이 토착 언어 어휘들과 결합되어 만들어진 단순한 형태의 혼성어) **encroachment** n. 침략 **bartering** n. 물물 교환
plantation n. 대규모 농장 **seize** v. 붙잡다 **folklorist** n. 민속학자 **approximated** adj. 거의 정확한 **part of speech** phr. 품사
spontaneously adv. 즉흥적으로, 자발적으로 **superficial** adj. 얇은, 깊이 없는 **indispensable** adj. 필수적인 **colloquial** adj. 구어의, 일상 대화의
creole n. 크레올어(유럽의 언어와 서인도 제도 노예들이 사용하던 아프리카어의 혼성어로 모국어로 사용되는 언어)

READING PASSAGE

You should spend about 20 minutes on **Questions 1-14**, which are based on Reading Passage below.

3D Printers and Human Tissue

Is 3D printing the future of medicine?

Although the technology for 3D printers has been around since the 1980s, it hasn't been so long that 3D printers became widely available commercially. The practice of producing three-dimensional solid objects of almost any shape from a digital model has since taken off exponentially, with virtually every sector of the economy eager to find ways to apply this technological breakthrough. While most people expect that 3D printing would be useful in fields such as architecture, construction, industrial design, and aerospace, few consider the implications of this technology for biotechnology and medical research. But, in fact, the ability to create live human tissue, and potentially even whole organs, is what has the medical community so excited.

For the last 20 years, medical researchers have been experimenting with ways to use the technology to create three-dimensional biological structures for medical purposes. To understand how this is possible, it's important to grasp how 3D printing works. The first step is to create a 3D image of the desired item using a computer-aided design software programme. The programme then slices the digital object into hundreds or even thousands of horizontal layers that become the blueprint for the printing stage. The actual printing is achieved using an additive process, in which the printer lays down successive layers of liquid, powder, paper or other material, from the bottom up to build the model from a series of cross sections. It then combines these layers to produce the final shape.

As soon as this technology came out, medical researchers thought, why not layer living cells just as with any other material, and thereby engineer biological structures such as tissue? Since the mid-2000s, biotech firms have taken up this question. In only a few years, they achieved significant success in producing human tissues that preserve cell function and viability. The types of human tissue that have thus far been successfully produced include bits of lung and heart muscles, as well as valves, and even a human ear. Experiments transplanting these tissues into laboratory animals have produced overwhelmingly positive results. Surgeons have also been able to implant some of this bioprinted* tissue – including

---

*bioprint: to 3D print a biological structure (a tissue, an organ, etc.) using a bioprinter

skin and muscle – into human patients.

While these advances are encouraging, the ultimate goal remains printing internal organs for humans in need of a transplant. Developing complex organs is a major challenge, especially in regard to creating one that has enough oxygen to survive until it can integrate with the body. One recent breakthrough at Harvard University's Jennifer Lewis lab has brought this closer to reality by creating the first 3D printed kidney tissues. Researchers at the lab came up with an innovative bioprinting process that allows them to print both the complex structures from which the kidney tissue is made, and the vascular systems which are necessary to keep the tissue alive. Using this system they were able to create a proximal tubule, a fundamental part of the kidney and the element responsible for filtering blood. The Jennifer Lewis team hopes to be able to manufacture a kidney in its entirety in a matter of years. Since around 10 per cent of the world's population suffers from chronic kidney disease, with many relying on machines to survive until they get a transplant, this could be a life-changing medical advance for millions of people. Scientists now believe that other 3D printed organs could also be available in less than a decade.

Aside from organ replacement, bioprinted tissue can also be used for medical research and drug development. For example, scientists have found that bioprinted slivers of the liver, although extremely tiny, respond to drugs in ways that are very similar to the full-grown human liver. This has allowed researchers to test the toxicity of new drugs before approving expensive clinical trials with patients. The potential to save billions of dollars in clinical research each year has caught the attention of investors. There are other possibilities on the horizon as well. Several laboratories are currently developing bioprinters that could apply skin cells directly onto wounds. Working in conjunction with a laser, the printer would scan the size and depth of an injury and then produce a topological 3D map of the wound that would be used to determine how much material to deposit on the wound site. The same technology could be used to close wounds of the elderly or people with diabetes, whose bodies don't heal well. It could even eventually be a solution to simple surgeries such as stitches for large cuts. With all the ways that the bioprinting of tissues could be useful, it's no wonder that it's taking the medical community by storm.

Complete each sentence with the correct ending, **A-G**, below.

1   Medical researchers have been conducting tests to

2   The eventual goal of bioprinting technology is to

3   A difficult task is making organs with sufficient oxygen until they can

4   Harvard researchers developed a process for creating structures that can

5   A laser and printer could possibly scan an injury and then

---

A   make medical equipment.

B   keep tissues alive.

C   perform surgery unassisted.

D   provide organs for transplants in humans.

E   make 3D biological structures for use in medicine.

F   fuse with the body.

G   create a 3D map of the wound.

Complete the sentences below.

*Choose **NO MORE THAN TWO WORDS** from the passage for each answer.*

6   In recent years, the practice of creating various 3D objects based on a .... has exploded.

7   Before printing, a computer programme makes a blueprint by cutting a 3D image into numerous ....

8   In a short time, biotech firms made human tissues that maintained the .... and viability of cells.

9   A team at Harvard aims to produce a complete .... in the near future.

10   Researchers can now test the .... of drugs prior to human trials.

Do the following statements agree with the information given in Reading Passage?

Write

TRUE	*if the statement agrees with the information*
FALSE	*if the statement contradicts the information*
NOT GIVEN	*if there is no information on this*

11   Most people understand the usefulness of 3D printing for medical research.

12   Tests of bioprinted tissue in animals have shown promising results.

13   Using 3D printed organs could reduce the cost of transplantation within 10 years.

14   Drugs affect small bioprinted pieces of liver as they do a whole liver.

정답·해석·해설 p.385

VOCABULARY LIST

Chapter 05에서 선별한 다음의 어휘들을 음성파일을 들으며 암기한 후 퀴즈로 확인해보세요.

*해커스 동영상강의 포털 해커스 인강(HackersIngang.com)에서 단어암기 MP3를 무료로 다운로드할 수 있습니다.

- [ ] playwright n. 극작가
- [ ] venue n. 장소
- [ ] coexist v. 공존하다
- [ ] contemporary adj. 최신식의, 현대의
- [ ] revival n. 재공연, 부활
- [ ] gross v. 수익을 올리다
- [ ] companion n. 반려, 동행
- [ ] empathy n. 공감
- [ ] attribution n. 귀속
- [ ] anthropomorphism n. 인격화
- [ ] trait n. 특성
- [ ] demonstrable adj. 입증할 수 있는
- [ ] value n. 의의, 가치
- [ ] consensus n. 합의, 의견 일치
- [ ] the disadvantaged phr. 사회적 약자들
- [ ] initiative n. (새로운 중요) 기획, 계획
- [ ] praiseworthy adj. 칭찬할 만한
- [ ] bottom line phr. 순익, 최종 결산
- [ ] undertake v. 착수하다
- [ ] patronise v. 애용하다, 후원하다
- [ ] revolve around phr. ~을 중심으로 돌아가다
- [ ] clutch n. 배, 무리
- [ ] collaboration n. 협력
- [ ] reach v. 뻗다, 내밀다
- [ ] prompt v. 유도하다
- [ ] dab v. 바르다

- [ ] bind v. 묶다
- [ ] accommodate v. 수용하다
- [ ] oral tradition phr. 구전
- [ ] document v. (상세한 내용을) 기록하다
- [ ] aristocrat n. 귀족
- [ ] impart v. (특정한 특성을) 부여하다
- [ ] consistency n. 일관성
- [ ] stylistic adj. 문체(양식)의
- [ ] blockbuster n. 베스트셀러, 히트작
- [ ] staple n. 주요 품목, 주성분
- [ ] citizenship n. 시민의 자질, 시민권
- [ ] populace n. 대중들
- [ ] instil v. 주입하다, 불어넣다
- [ ] defer to phr. ~의 의견에 따르다
- [ ] implement v. 시행하다
- [ ] allow for phr. ~을 고려하다, 참작하다
- [ ] density n. 밀도, 농도
- [ ] sustainability n. 지속 가능성
- [ ] pack v. 가득 채우다
- [ ] compact adj. 꽉 찬, 빽빽한
- [ ] infringement n. 침해
- [ ] arable adj. 경작할 수 있는
- [ ] contend with phr. ~과 씨름하다
- [ ] sparsely adv. 드문드문
- [ ] fleet n. (기관 소유의 비행기 · 버스 · 택시 등의) 무리
- [ ] archaic adj. 낡은

Quiz

각 단어의 알맞은 뜻을 찾아 연결하시오.

01 trait	ⓐ 애용하다	06 implement	ⓐ 일관성
02 prompt	ⓑ 협력	07 accommodate	ⓑ 꽉 찬, 빽빽한
03 patronise	ⓒ 착수하다	08 compact	ⓒ 시행하다
04 empathy	ⓓ 특성	09 archaic	ⓓ 지속 가능성
05 undertake	ⓔ 공감	10 consistency	ⓔ 수용하다
	ⓕ 유도하다		ⓕ 낡은

ⓓ 01 ⓕ 02 ⓐ 03 ⓔ 04 ⓒ 05 ⓒ 06 ⓔ 07 ⓑ 08 ⓕ 09 ⓐ 10

□ unprecedented adj. 전례 없는

□ elude v. ~에게 발견되지 않다

□ genetic material phr. 유전 형질

□ manipulate v. 조작하다

□ supplement v. 보완하다

□ administer v. (음식 · 약 따위를) 주다, (약을) 투여하다

□ vector n. (질병의) 매개체

□ molecule n. 분자

□ sequence n. 순서

□ kick in phr. (기능을) 발휘하다, 효과가 나타나기 시작하다

□ inflammatory adj. 염증의

□ organ failure phr. 장기부전

□ clinical trial phr. 임상 시험

□ hold sway phr. 지배하다

□ formulate v. 만들어 내다, 표현하다

□ natural selection phr. 자연 도태

□ supplant v. 대체하다

□ arousal n. 자극, 흥분

□ reversal n. 반전

□ conceptualisation n. 개념적인 해석

□ hypothalamic adj. 시상하부의

□ thalamic adj. 시상의

□ foreground v. 특히 중시하다, 최전면에 내세우다

□ misattribution n. 오귀인

□ circles n. 집단

□ encroachment n. 침략

□ bartering n. 물물 교환

□ plantation n. 대규모 농장

□ seize v. 붙잡다

□ folklorist n. 민속학자

□ approximated adj. 거의 정확한

□ part of speech phr. 품사

□ spontaneously adv. 즉흥적으로, 자발적으로

□ superficial adj. 얕은, 깊이 없는

□ indispensable adj. 필수적인

□ colloquial adj. 구어의, 일상 대화의

□ tissue n. 조직

□ solid adj. 입체의

□ exponentially adv. 기하급수적으로

□ horizontal adj. 수평의

□ blueprint n. 설계도, 청사진

□ cross section phr. 횡단면, 단면도

□ viability n. 생존 능력

□ valve n. 판막

□ transplant v. 이식하다

□ kidney n. 신장

□ vascular system phr. 혈관계

□ sliver n. (깨지거나 잘라낸) 조각

□ toxicity n. 독성

□ on the horizon phr. 곧 일어날 듯한

□ topological adj. 위상의

□ diabetes n. 당뇨

Quiz

각 단어의 알맞은 뜻을 찾아 연결하시오.

01 manipulate	ⓐ 보완하다
02 inflammatory	ⓑ 분자
03 sequence	ⓒ 조작하다
04 molecule	ⓓ 전례없다
05 supplement	ⓔ 순서
	ⓕ 염증의

06 seize	ⓐ 수평의
07 superficial	ⓑ 필수적인
08 horizontal	ⓒ 독성
09 indispensable	ⓓ 붙잡다
10 toxicity	ⓔ 조직
	ⓕ 얕은, 깊이 없는

01 ⓒ 02 ⓕ 03 ⓔ 04 ⓑ 05 ⓐ 06 ⓓ 07 ⓕ 08 ⓐ 09 ⓑ 10 ⓒ

Summary Completion

Summary completion 문제는 지문의 내용과 일치하도록 요약문을 완성하는 문제이다. IELTS Reading 영역에서 가장 많이 출제되는 유형 중 하나로 거의 매 시험 출제되고 있다.

■ 문제 형태

Summary completion 문제는 주로 주어진 보기 리스트에서 알맞은 단어를 선택하거나, 지문에서 단어를 찾아 그대로 적는 주관식 형태로 출제된다. 주관식으로 출제되는 경우에는 몇 단어 혹은 숫자로 답을 작성해야 하는지 반드시 확인한다.

보기 리스트에서 알맞은 답 선택하기
주어진 보기 리스트에서 요약문을 완성할 수 있는 알맞은 보기를 선택하는 문제이다.

---

*Complete the summary using the list of words, **A-H**, below.*

*Write the correct letter, **A-H**, in boxes 1-2 on your answer sheet.*

Llamas in the Incan Empire

Llamas disappeared from North America during the last ice age. But in South America, they were domesticated. Llamas became important for delivering **1** .... and building materials. Although they were not very fast, they made it much easier to carry things for long **2** ....

A shipments	**B** travellers	**C** food products	**D** other animals
E natural resources	**F** villagers	**G** distances	**H** depths

---

빈칸에 알맞은 답을 지문에서 찾아 적기
요약문의 빈칸에 들어갈 알맞은 단어를 지문에서 찾아 적는 문제이다.

Complete the summary below.

*Choose **ONE WORD ONLY** from the passage for each answer.*

Write your answers in boxes 1-2 on your answer sheet.

The Hibernation of Black Bears

Like some other mammals, black bears hibernate during winter to avoid the extreme cold, and this allows them to remain **1** .... for months. During the hibernation period, the **2** .... of black bears slows considerably, allowing them to conserve energy.

■ 문제풀이 전략

> **STEP 1** 요약문의 핵심 내용을 확인하고, 문제의 핵심어구와 내용을 파악한다.

(1) 요약문의 제목과 내용을 빠르게 확인하여 무엇에 대한 요약문인지 파악한다.

(2) 문제의 핵심어구와 핵심 내용을 파악한다.

EXAMPLE

*Complete the summary using the list of words, **A-E**, below.*

*Write the correct letter, **A-E**, in box 1 on your answer sheet.*

Llamas in the Incan Empire ●

Llamas disappeared from North America during the last ice age. But in South America, they were domesticated. Llamas became important for delivering ●
1 .... and building materials. Although they were not very fast, they made it much easier to carry things for long distances.

A shipments	**B** travellers	**C** food products
D other animals	**E** villagers	

─ (1) 제목과 내용을 확인하여 잉카 제 국에서의 라마 활용에 대한 요약 문임을 파악한다.

─ (2) 문제의 핵심어구인 Llamas ~ important for delivering을 통해 라마가 무엇을 운송하는 데 있어 중요해졌는지를 묻고 있음 을 파악한다.

✅ TIPS

요약문의 제목이 주어지지 않는 경우, 요약문 전체를 빠르게 훑어 전반적인 내용을 파악한다.

지문을 scanning하여 문제의 핵심어구와 관련된 내용을 찾는다. 관련 내용이 언급된 주변에서 정답의 단서를 확인한다.

EXAMPLE

The camel-like llama once inhabited North America, but disappeared during the last ice age. However, it survived in South America, where the Incas used it for various purposes. They domesticated the llama as early as 6,000 years ago and developed close ties with the animal. By 600 A.D., ¹the animals had become essential as beasts of burden for farmers and villagers to transport food products and construction materials. A large male animal could carry approximately 30 kilograms of cargo 20 kilometres in a day. Though the pace was not great, their trainability made them more suited to the task than any other animals. The llamas greatly alleviated the burden of carrying or hauling materials across significant distances by hand.

문제의 핵심어구인 Llamas ~ important for delivering과 관련된 내용을 지문에서 찾는다. 관련 내용이 언급된 주변에서 'the animals had become essential as beasts of burden ~ to transport food products'라는 정답의 단서를 확인한다.

*Complete the summary using the list of words, **A-E**, below.*

*Write the correct letter, **A-E**, in box 1 on your answer sheet.*

Llamas in the Incan Empire

Llamas disappeared from North America during the last ice age. But in South America, they were domesticated. Llamas became important for delivering

1 .... and building materials. Although they were not very fast, they made it much easier to carry things for long distances.

A shipments	**B** travellers	**C** food products
D other animals	**E** villagers	

지문 해석 p.389

(1) 정답의 단서의 내용을 바르게 나타낼 수 있는 보기를 정답으로 선택한다.

(2) 선택한 보기를 문장의 빈칸에 넣었을 때 문장이 지문의 내용과 일치하는지 확인한다.

EXAMPLE

The camel-like llama once inhabited North America, but disappeared during the last ice age. However, it survived in South America, where the Incas used it for various purposes. They domesticated the llama as early as 6,000 years ago and developed close ties with the animal. By 600 A.D., [1]the animals had become essential as beasts of burden for farmers and villagers to transport food products and construction materials. A large male animal could carry approximately 30 kilograms of cargo 20 kilometres in a day. Though the pace was not great, their trainability made them more suited to the task than any other animals. The llamas greatly alleviated the burden of carrying or hauling materials across significant distances by hand.

(1) '라마가 농부들과 주민들에게 식료품을 운송하는 짐 운반용 동물로서 중요해졌다'는 정답의 단서에서 'food products'가 답이 될 수 있음을 확인한다.

*Complete the summary using the list of words, **A-E**, below.*

*Write the correct letter, **A-E**, in box 1 on your answer sheet.*

Llamas in the Incan Empire

Llamas disappeared from North America during the last ice age. But in South America, they were domesticated. Llamas became important for delivering **1** ....food products.... and building materials. Although they were not very fast, they made it much easier to carry things for long distances.

(2) 보기 C를 문제에 넣었을 때, 문장이 지문의 내용과 일치함을 확인한다.

A shipments	B travellers	C food products
D other animals	E villagers	

⊘ TIPS

Summary completion 문제의 보기들은 간혹 지문에서 사용된 단어가 그대로 나오지 않고 비슷한 의미의 다른 단어로 출제되기도 하므로, 보기를 주의 깊게 읽는다.

HACKERS **PRACTICE**

1 In 1879, the Canadian government enacted the National Policy, an economic programme that sought to safeguard Canadian manufacturers and promote settlement of Canada's western frontier. A primary goal of the programme's leading advocate, Prime Minister John Macdonald, was to decrease Canada's reliance on imported products. To achieve this, he instituted a high tariff on all manufactured goods that were imported. He argued that the tariff would lead to a higher standard of living and greater employment security for Canadians, and it did for those in the manufacturing sectors of the East, where Canada immediately experienced increased production and profits.

However the ambition of western settlement was slow to be realised. Despite aggressive immigration campaigns, which tried to lure farmers from abroad with free or cheap land, Canada witnessed a decline in immigration in the 1880s. According to economist Ken Norrie, this shows that the influence of the National Policy on settlement of the West was mediocre. In fact, external factors, such as the development of improved agricultural techniques, and favourable economic conditions globally, were largely responsible. The price of wheat, for instance, quadrupled between 1891 and 1921, and this brought profit-seeking agriculturists to Canada's fruitful wheat-growing regions in droves.

Complete the summary below.

*Choose **ONE WORD ONLY** from the passage for each answer.*

The National Policy was designed to protect the manufacturing industry and encourage economic growth and western settlement. By using a high tariff, the prime minister increased living standards and job **1** .... in the eastern part of the country. But the goal of western settlement did not happen quickly. Actually, the National Policy had a modest effect on this. Better **2** .... in agriculture and a good world economy were of greater importance.

---

enact v. 제정하다   National Policy phr. 내셔널폴리시(1879년 캐나다가 채택한 보호관세정책의 별칭)   economic programme phr. 경제 계획
safeguard v. 보호하다   frontier n. 국경 지역   advocate n. 지지자   prime minister phr. 수상   institute v. (제도, 정책 등을) 도입하다   tariff n. 관세
standard of living phr. 생활 수준   sector n. 분야   mediocre adj. 썩 좋지는 않은, 평범한   favourable adj. 순조로운, 좋은
quadruple v. 네 배가 되다, 네 배로 만들다   agriculturist n. 농업 종사자, 농업 전문가   fruitful adj. 비옥한, 생산적인   in droves phr. 떼지어

2   Although attaching studs and spikes to clothing is today associated with the punk and metal subcultures of the 1980s, the practice is nothing new. In fact, studs and spikes have been around for as long as it has been necessary to protect oneself and exude a spirit of aggression. The medieval brigandine, for instance, was a form of armour that consisted of steel plates on top of fabric, and the plates were riveted there by fasteners that resembled the studs used in contemporary fashions. But apart from keeping the steel plates attached, they also helped absorb the shock from heavy blunt weapons and made it more difficult for blades to pierce through. The same idea was applied to the protective clothing put on animals. Hunting dogs, notably, were often put in spiked collars when their ancient Roman owners took them out to capture dangerous game, like lions and bears. This way, if a dog were to get bitten on the neck, the spikes would protect it and likely injure the more savage beast in the process. And because it was quite obvious that the only individuals who wore studded or spiked garments in the first place were warriors, intimidation was one of the reasons as well; people automatically stayed away from anyone in such clothing. Essentially, while studs and spikes may not serve many practical applications today, they live on as a symbol of ferocity and as a warning to others to keep their distance.

Complete the summary below.

*Choose **ONE WORD ONLY** from the passage for each answer.*

History of Studs

Studs and spikes have been used throughout history for protection. On the type of medieval armour known as the brigandine they fastened steel plates to **3** ...., keeping people safe from injury. They were also used for intimidation; people in spiked or studded clothes were known to be dangerous because they were **4** ...., so others avoided them.

---

stud n. 금속 단추 **spike** n. 징, 못 **subculture** n. 하위문화 **practice** n. 관행 **exude** v. 드러내다, 스며 나오게 하다 **medieval** adj. 중세의
brigandine n. 미늘 갑옷 **armour** n. 갑옷 **rivet** v. 고정시키다 **absorb** v. 흡수하다 **blunt** adj. 뭉툭한 **collar** n. (개 등의 목에 거는) 목걸이
game n. 사냥감 **savage** adj. 사나운, 맹렬한 **warrior** n. 전사 **intimidation** n. 위협, 협박 **live on** phr. 존속하다, 계속 살다 **ferocity** n. 포악성

3 It may be tempting to put on a false face or stretch the truth at times, but it turns out that even the most convincing among us may be incapable of pulling off an act of deception that leaves no one in doubt. This is because muscles in the human face react involuntarily to emotions. The scowls, smirks, and frowns that can betray how a liar truly feels may only flash across his or her face for a brief moment – so brief, in fact, that research psychologist Paul Ekman called these emotional displays 'micro expressions' – but they do occur, and they are detectable. According to Ekman, there are seven universal micro expressions: disgust, anger, fear, sadness, happiness, surprise, and contempt. When we feel any of these emotions, they are beyond our control for at least one twentieth of a second. Videotaping a person who is providing a false statement and then going through the tape frame by frame can reveal these expressions, even in people who seem very genuine in person. Of course, this may not always be an option. In such cases, keeping an eye out for hand gestures that obscure the face is advisable. People who move their hands toward their eyes or their mouths – the most expressive parts of the face – may be trying to avoid being caught in the split second that micro expressions occur.

Complete the summary below.

*Choose **NO MORE THAN TWO WORDS** from the passage for each answer.*

Due to the automatic reactions of our facial 5 .... when we experience certain emotions, the perfect lie may not be possible. These reactions, which are called micro expressions, can be revealed by analysing the individual frames of a videotape of someone who is giving a 6 .... In cases where this is not possible, it is a good idea to watch for hand 7 .... that hide the face.

---

false face phr. 가면 stretch v. (진실 등을) 과장하다, 왜곡하다 turn out phr. ~으로 보이다, ~인 것으로 밝혀지다 pull off phr. (~을) 해내다
deception n. 사기, 속임 involuntarily adv. 무의식중에 scowl n. 노려봄, 쏘아봄 smirk n. 능글맞은 웃음, 뽐내는 웃음 betray v. 드러내다, 무심코 노출하다
flash across phr. 확 나타나다, 퍼뜩 떠오르다 micro expression phr. (숨기고 있는 감정을 드러내는) 미세 표정 disgust n. 혐오(감) contempt n. 경멸, 멸시
genuine adj. 진실된 keep an eye out phr. 지켜보다, 살펴보다 obscure v. 가리다

4 The bluegill is one of the most popular gaming fish in North America and is frequently found in freshwater lakes and ponds. This relatively small fish has been the subject of intense study by wildlife biologists for its unusual mating habits. While similar to other fish in that the male cares for the offspring, the bluegill is unique in that some males use deception and mimicry to inseminate eggs meant for a different, larger male. Around 20 per cent of bluegill males attempt to enter the mating process through trickery before they are fully grown. These fish, known as cuckolds or sneakers, will seek out a large parental male, hide in the weeds adjacent to the male's grounds, and wait for a school of female fish to pass over. Once a female chooses a partner, she will tilt her body and release roughly 30 eggs. Normally, the resident male would shower these eggs with his seed, but before he has a chance to reach them, the diminutive cuckold will leave his safety zone and dart into the nest of the larger male to inseminate the eggs himself, quickly returning to his point of origin without being caught.

With this tactic, the cuckold can fertilise as many of the eggs as possible before they settle into the hole, and then use his undersized body to escape undetected. This technique is only available to younger bluegills, however, since the size of adult bluegills precludes the agility required for this operation. Nonetheless, older cuckolds do adopt another method to achieve their goals. An adult cuckold is still smaller than most male bluegills and can easily be mistaken for a female. As they age, the cuckold will acquire a set of shaded areas and stripes on its body that is similar to that on females, which completely disguises them from other males and allows them to easily slip into schools of female fish unnoticed. In this fashion, they wait until a nearby female decides to release her eggs before swooping down and inseminating them. If a good selection is fertilised, then the cuckold has accomplished his reproductive duties.

*Complete the summary using the list of words, **A-G**, below.*

Techniques of Bluegill Cuckolds

Bluegill cuckolds cheat their way into fertilising eggs that are not meant for them. They do this by hiding near another male's **8** .... and darting into it at just the right moment. Because a cuckold has a much smaller **9** .... than most males, it can easily get out of danger quickly. Older cuckolds have another method. They are still not as big as most males, so they swim with female bluegills and wait for one to release its eggs. These cuckolds can avoid being noticed because they take on a **10** .... that looks like the one on females.

A hole	**B** colour	**C** nest	**D** pattern
E seed	**F** tail	**G** body	

---

offspring n. (동식물의) 새끼 **deception** n. 속임수 **mimicry** n. 모방 **inseminate** v. 수정시키다 **trickery** n. 속임수 **adjacent to** phr. 근처의, 인접한 **school** n. 떼, 무리 **diminutive** adj. 작은 **dart** v. 쏜살같이 돌진하다 **tactic** n. 전략 **fertilise** v. 수정시키다 **preclude** v. 불가능하게 하다 **agility** n. 민첩성 **swoop** v. 급강하하다 **reproductive** adj. 생식의, 번식의

5 Whilst often considered a modern invention, zoos are actually embedded in a history of animal captivity that spans back thousands of years. A discovery during excavations near Hierakonpolis, Egypt, uncovered the remnants of hippos, elephants, baboons and wildcats buried in the city's cemetery. Dating back to around 3500 B.C., the remnants point to the existence of a menagerie, a private collection of animals kept by the wealthiest members of society to demonstrate power, to intimidate enemies, to entertain rulers and their guests, and even to hunt. Menageries remained popular in Egypt and elsewhere for quite some time. Queen Hatshepsut of Egypt, who ruled around 1500 B.C., kept a menagerie of animals acquired during expeditions to Punt, in present-day Somalia. Around the same time in China, Emperor Wen Wang founded the Garden of Intelligence, which included a huge collection of animals kept on a 1,500-acre property.

Menageries were also a central part of the Aztec culture of central Mexico between the 14th and 16th centuries. When Spanish explorer Hernán Cortés reached the New World in 1520, he wrote about his discovery of a massive collection of animals at Tenochtitlan, the capital of Aztec ruler Montezuma. More than 300 people were assigned to the care of the extensive royal menagerie, reputed to be the largest assortment of animals in history. The complex in which the animals were housed was impressive enough in its own right, with two main houses, a botanical garden and an aquarium. Unfortunately, the facilities and the animals kept within them were subsequently destroyed by the Spanish during an attack. Zoos began to replace menageries in Europe during the 18th century, when the Age of Enlightenment ushered in a new belief in science and reason, which extended to the field of biology. Therefore zoos were created to facilitate the scientific observation of animals in something similar to their natural habitat. They were open to the public, for a fee, to ensure they had the necessary funding. The first of these modern zoos was the Tiergarten Schonbrunn, opened in Vienna, Austria in 1752, inaugurating a new age of zoology and consigning the menagerie to ancient history.

*Complete the summary using the list of words, **A-G**, below.*

From Menageries to Zoos

An archaeological dig in the Egyptian city of Hierakonpolis revealed the **11** .... of many species of animal, which had been buried within the city's cemetery thousands of years ago. This was evidence of a menagerie, a private collection of exotic creatures. The **12** .... would use such a collection to show their authority and scare enemies.

Zoos as we know them today began to appear during the 18th century, when the Enlightenment spread an interest in science throughout Europe, which included **13** .... These zoos tried to create something like a natural **14** .... for their animals, so that they could be studied.

A environment	**B** army	**C** garden	**D** biology
E elite	**F** remains	**G** architecture	

---

embed v. ~을 깊이 새겨 두다 captivity n. 감금 excavation n. 발굴 작업 uncover v. 보여주다, 폭로하다 menagerie n. 동물 사육소, (관람용의) 동물들
expedition n. 원정 reputed adj. ~이라고 알려진 usher in phr. ~을 시작되게 하다 inaugurate v. 막을 열다, 개시하다 consign v. 두다, 맡기다

6

There are thirteen species of otter, all of which are associated with water, such as rivers, or in the case of the sea otter, coastal areas of the sea. Otters can be distinguished by their elongated body, their stubby arms and legs, and their webbed feet, which allow them to traverse the water with considerable dexterity. They also have the ability to hold their breath underwater for long periods of time, and some otters have been observed staying under the surface for up to five minutes. They can also be distinguished by their fur, which is very dense and has unfortunately made them the target of humans throughout history. The sea otter, which lives in coastal regions of the northern Pacific Ocean, has the thickest fur of any animal. Historically, this made it one of the most lucrative species for hunters and led to a sharp drop in the worldwide population of sea otters, which is only now starting to abate. As the value of its fur increased, demand for this 'soft gold', as it was called, also grew and brought about a period called the 'Great Hunt'. During this period, which lasted from approximately 1741 to 1911, hunters from Russia and other regions ravaged wild sea otter populations with great intensity.

The hunting of sea otters only started to decline when the disappearance of large populations made commercial hunting no longer possible. Eventually an international accord was signed in 1911 that imposed a ban on the hunting of sea otters. By that point, it was estimated that only around two thousand sea otters remained in the wild, and most experts believed the species would eventually become extinct. However, conservation efforts during the 20th century contributed to a substantial growth in the sea otter population, and their return to the habitats of the Pacific coast from which they had almost completely disappeared. Nonetheless, sea otters are still considered an endangered species, and are threatened by fishing, disease, and pollution, as well as poaching. Sea otters may represent one of the great success stories of marine conservation, but their recovery is still at risk by human activity, and maintaining that success requires renewed vigilance.

*Complete the summary using the list of words, **A-H**, below.*

Saving the Otter

Renowned for the ability to hold its breath for lengthy spells underwater, the otter has unfortunately been the target of hunters because of its **15** .... fur. Along with their fur, these otters are notable for having short arms and **16** .... bodies.

The **17** .... otter population was hunted intensely during the 18th century, a period when their fur was one of the most profitable commodities in the world. However, a ban was instituted in the early 20th century and populations have recovered, in a rare example of a successful **18** .... conservation effort.

A glossy	B strong	C local	D thick
E marine	F global	G long	H wild

---

otter n. 수달 elongated adj. 가늘고 긴 stubby adj. 짤막한 traverse v. 가로지르다 dexterity n. 민첩성, 재주 lucrative adj. 수익성이 좋은 abate v. 완화되다 bring about phr. 초래하다 ravage v. 파괴하다, 약탈하다 accord n. 협약 impose a ban on phr. ~을 금지하다 substantial adj. 상당한 poaching n. 밀렵, 침범 vigilance n. 경각심, 경계

7   How Steam Power Drove the Industrial Revolution

Prior to the industrialisation and urbanisation that fuelled spectacular growth in Britain's economy over the course of the 19th century, most work was performed by manual labour and animals, heat was provided by the burning of organic materials, and energy needs were satisfied by watermills. While waterpower offered abundant and cheap energy, its geographical constraints made it inconvenient. The steam engine, however, faced no such limitations. It would not be long before it became the icon of the Industrial Revolution and the driving force behind the fundamental changes that all of Western civilisation would ultimately undergo.

As commercial enterprises began to equip themselves with steam-driven machines, the manufacturing industry was transformed. Textile machines running on steam power, for example, could spin multiple threads with the turn of a single wheel and coordinate precise movements using levers, cams, and gears. The mining industry also benefitted because, for these machines to effectively produce mechanical power, water had to be heated in a boiler, which required a cheap and reliable fuel source – coal.

In transport, high horsepower steam engines gave life to ships and locomotives, greatly improving their reliability, precision, and speed. Consequently, urban industrialists were able to deliver tons of finished products to previously unreachable areas in relatively little time, while raw materials from distant British colonies zoomed into the massive and more cost-effective factories that had replaced smaller production plants. These mega factories, although initially built on the outskirts of residential areas, expanded into cities as more than half of the English population, lured by the job opportunities manufacturers were offering, moved away from the countryside. Adjusting to life in cities would prompt eye-opening lifestyle shifts for the majority of British people.

Among these is that people learned to read, with the literacy rate skyrocketing. Books had previously been a rare and tightly-controlled resource because they were quite time-consuming and expensive to produce, but millions of pages of text could be churned out in a single day thanks to the efficiency of these new machines. With printing presses and literacy, new forms of thought in the fields of politics, philosophy, and science began to spread among the people.

Ultimately, the age of the steam engine had drawn to a close by the end of the 19th century, when it was replaced by a new form of power called electricity. Although electricity is a vital part of contemporary existence, it is questionable whether it ever would have been possible without the technological breakthrough – and the social, intellectual, and cultural advances it spurred – that was the steam engine.

Complete the summary below.

*Choose **ONE WORD ONLY** from the passage for each answer.*

Urbanisation and the Steam Engine

The steam engine allowed manufacturers to bring resources from all around the world into their **19** .... At first, they were built on the edges of populated areas, but it wasn't long before they began opening in **20** .... People began leaving rural jobs to pursue the new opportunities factory work offered. This led to many changes in the **21** .... of most of the British population.

---

manual labour phr. 육체 노동 organic material phr. 유기 물질 abundant adj. 풍부한 constraint n. 제한, 제약 steam engine phr. 증기 기관
driving force phr. 원동력 textile n. 직물, 옷감 cam n. 캠(바퀴의 회전 운동을 왕복 운동으로 바꾸는 장치) horsepower n. 마력 locomotive n. 기관차
outskirt n. 변두리 eye-opening adj. 놀랄 만한, 경이로운 literacy rate phr. 식자율, 국민 중 글을 아는 사람들의 비율 skyrocket v. 치솟다
churn out phr. 대량 생산하다 contemporary adj. 현대의, 동시대의 spur v. ~의 원동력이 되다, 자극하다

8   Our Vanishing Rainforests

Found primarily in Latin America but also existing in areas of Asia and Africa, the world's rainforests are under siege, losing between 46 and 58 thousand square miles every year. These areas of the world are indispensible, not just to the flora and fauna that live there, but also to the Earth itself. This is due to the fact that vegetation keeps pollution levels at bay by absorbing the massive amounts of carbon dioxide humans continually pump into the atmosphere through the burning of fossil fuels. Because trees from the planet's rainforests are disappearing at an alarming rate, they are less able to perform this vital ecological service, thereby speeding up climate change – and making the global implications associated with it an inevitable reality.

The factors driving the widespread devastation of the world's rainforests through deforestation are numerous but all are related to industrial development and population growth. One way rainforest resources are exploited is through unsustainable commercial logging practices. Loggers are only permitted to cut down trees that are fully grown, and are supposed to avoid causing excess damage when doing so. However, massive trees cannot help but tear down numerous other forms of vegetation in the process of collapsing. Cutting down trees also creates holes in the canopy. These holes, which take hundreds of years to revive naturally, will likely remain permanently unfilled as the heavy machinery used to penetrate the forests causes irreversible harm to the soil. Meanwhile, higher global demand for meat products has led to the burning down of vast areas of forests in order to grow soybeans, which is an ingredient for livestock feed. This saps nutrients from the soil, making it only a matter of time before crop yields decrease and more areas are cleared.

Also causing soil erosion and, by extension, the loss of trees are mining and oil projects. The extraction of gold from the Amazon, for instance, requires high concentrations of mercury, which leaks into the soil and renders it barren. Likewise, since the discovery of oil reserves in the region, there have been a number of oil spills. It is well known that oil contamination changes the properties of earth, meaning that it is unlikely for anything to grow back in affected areas. Moreover, for activities like mining and oil extraction to be possible at all, trees must be cut down to construct roads; it is estimated that for every 40 metres of road that is built, developers sacrifice 600 square kilometres of rainforest. Making matters worse, roads open the rainforests up to illegal loggers, settlers, and land speculators, whose activities also tend to result in large areas of vegetation being removed.

Unfortunately, the nations where rainforests are found are often faced with more immediate problems than preserving trees, like mounting debt and poverty. Receiving financial assistance from wealthy countries does help, but it is somewhat of a 'band-aid' solution. Only by collectively acknowledging that the future of the planet is of utmost importance can we begin to save what remains of the rainforests.

*Complete the summary using the list of words, **A-I**, below.*

The Causes of Deforestation

One of the reasons that deforestation persists is that logging is 22 ...., when it is carried out commercially. Logging companies are only allowed to remove 23 .... trees. However this has a knock-on effect on surrounding 24 ...., which can be damaged as trees collapse.

A further threat to the rainforests is the mining of precious metals or fossil fuels, which can have negative effects on the surrounding soil, for example when harmful chemicals are used to mine gold. Similarly, the 25 .... of soil can be completely transformed by contamination from oil spills.

A illegal	**B** plants	**C** qualities
D mature	**E** unsustainable	**F** balance
G common	**H** concentration	**I** earth

---

under siege phr. 포위당한 indispensible adj. 없어서는 안 되는, 필수의 flora n. 식물군 fauna n. 동물군 vegetation n. 초목 implication n. 영향
logging n. 벌목 practice n. 관행, 관습 logger n. 벌목꾼 canopy n. 우거진 숲의 지붕, 덮개 irreversible adj. 되돌릴 수 없는 sap v. 서서히 빼앗다
by extension phr. 더 나아가 concentration n. 농도, 집중 mercury n. 수은 render v. ~하게 하다 barren adj. (토지가) 메마른, 불모의
peculator n. 투기꾼 mounting adj. 증가하는 collectively adv. 공동으로, 집단으로

9 Shaping America: The Erie Canal

The Erie Canal, which connects the Great Lakes to the Atlantic Ocean via New York's Hudson River, was one of the most influential public works projects of its time. First opened in 1825 after eight years of construction, it is credited with dramatically increasing trade, turning New York into a thriving international port, and spurring westward expansion.

The states surrounding the Great Lakes are home to a wealth of natural resources, which were extremely difficult for colonists living on America's eastern coast to access in the early 19th century. Likewise, the European goods available in cities like New York were practically unheard of in the nation's interior. As a railway had not yet been established, the only way of moving supplies back and forth was by horse-drawn wagons – vehicles with a limited capacity for trade goods. In addition, most journeys lasted weeks due to poor road conditions, not to mention the barrier created by the Appalachian Mountains, and cost a significant amount of money given the time and labour each trip entailed. However, once the Erie Canal opened, ships were able to haul up to 50 tonnes of freight from point to point in a matter of days. Because they could carry so much, the quantity of goods that was transported skyrocketed, and the price of certain commodities decreased by as much as 95 per cent. It wasn't long before hundreds of boats were coming in and out of New York City on a daily basis, making it the busiest port in America.

With so many goods entering New York City, it made sense for the state to start shipping commodities down along the East Coast, to the West Indies, and across the Atlantic Ocean to Europe. Doing so was very profitable, but the revenue didn't stop there; shipment tolls were collected on each of the many arriving freights, allowing the state to quickly fill its coffers. Among other things, the money was used to pay off the seven million dollars that had been used to construct the canal, to help fund government operations in Washington, and to market popular sites along the canal route, like Niagara Falls. Consequently, New York quickly became a top destination for both American and international tourists, with thousands taking advantage of the canal to flock into New York each year.

New York's ever-growing prosperity, coupled with the fact that travelling there was no longer difficult, saw the population increase from 124,000 to nearly 800,000 within the first few years of the canal's use. While a great many people moved to New York City, some disembarked at other stops along the canal route, where a number of boom towns had been established. This helped to populate areas of New York like Rochester and Buffalo. Furthermore, because the canal went west beyond the Appalachian Mountains, it encouraged people to venture further, to the states surrounding the Great Lakes: Michigan, Ohio, Indiana, and Illinois. Many of those who settled in these areas were new European immigrants who had been lured to America by the availability of inexpensive arable farmland. Within a matter of decades, this area had established itself as the heart of America's agricultural industry – the breadbasket supplying wheat to the nation.

Complete the summary below.

*Choose **NO MORE THAN TWO WORDS** from the passage for each answer.*

Life Before the Erie Canal

There were many **26** .... in the Great Lakes region. However, the only way to transport them to colonists in New York was through the use of **27** .... These journeys took a long time and were very difficult. The main **28** .... was the Appalachian Mountains, and crossing them was both time-consuming and expensive. Because of the difficulty in reaching the Great Lakes area, communities there were not able to purchase the foreign goods which could be found on the coast. After the canal was built, **29** .... were able to carry a great amount of cargo to their destinations in a very short time.

the Great Lakes phr. 미국과 캐나다 국경의 오대호 canal n. 운하 spur v. ~의 원동력이 되다, 자극하다 interior n. 내륙, 내부 entail v. 수반하다
haul v. 운반하다, 차로 나르다 freight n. 화물 skyrocket v. 급증하다 commodity n. 상품, 물품 on a daily basis phr. 매일 revenue n. 세입, 수익
toll n. 요금 coffer n. 금고 disembark v. (배에서) 내리다 boom town phr. 신흥 도시 venture v. (모험하듯) 가다 breadbasket n. 곡창 지대

10   Dark Matter

A Curious Observation

The existence of invisible matter in the universe was first suggested by Dutch astronomer Jan Hendrik Oort in 1932 when he observed that the stars at the outer edge of the galaxy were moving much faster than they should be given the weak gravitational pull at the ends of galaxies. Oort believed that their speed was being influenced by a material with intense gravitational force, which he called 'dark matter' because it could not be seen. Substantiating this discovery a year later was Swiss astronomer Fritz Zwicky who, after a similar observation, maintained that hidden masses lay among invisible ones. However, neither claim was accepted by the scientific community because it was unheard of for a substance with mass to be invisible.

An Invisible Web

By the 1950s, technology had progressed enough to confirm that outlying stars actually have the same velocity as the stars at the center of a galaxy. Scientists surmised that galaxies must contain significant amounts of dark matter for this to be possible, so they set about learning as much as they could about the elusive material. Aided by computer-generated models, they speculated that filaments of dark matter comprising up to 85 per cent of the universe's total mass formed a web and that woven into this web was all the visible matter of the universe. Some have compared dark matter to connective tissue in that its apparent function is to bind the various components of the universe together. In other words, without it, galaxies would simply break apart and float away.

Theories on the Composition of Dark Matter

But just what is dark matter made of? Many cosmologists believe that it may be composed of a subatomic particle that has not yet been identified. Meanwhile, some astronomers consider massive compact halo objects, or MACHOs, a possibility. MACHOs are believed to reside in the halos of galaxies but defy detection because of their low luminosities. Other astronomers think that WIMPs, or weakly interacting massive particles, are strong candidates. WIMPs are hypothetical at this point but are a popular choice because scientists believe that they formed shortly after the Big Bang. Being massive, slow-moving, and incapable of emitting light, it is theorised that these particles clumped together to form the structure of the universe. Unsurprisingly, attempts to prove their existence have been determined, and state-of-the-art technologies, such as the Large Hadron Collider, are currently being used to try to produce them.

Mapping Dark Matter

Although there remains a lack of solid evidence, support for the theory of dark matter has grown extensively. It is now the consensus among scientists that it does exist and that, despite its inability to produce light, it can be detected. This is due to the fact that it causes light from galaxies to distort, creating luminous optical illusions. Scientists observing these phenomena measure the displacement of light to determine the approximate location of the dark matter. They then chart these positions on maps. While scientists engaged in the search for dark matter often come up empty-handed, they remain optimistic and driven by discoveries like one made by a team in Munich, Germany in which it was possible to detect and map dark matter in a cluster of galaxies about 2.7 billion light years away.

*Complete the summary using the list of words, **A-H**, below.*

What is Dark Matter?

There are several theories about what comprises dark matter. Some say it is made up of an undiscovered **30** ...., while others think that dense halo objects are more likely candidates. WIMPs are yet another possibility. This is because their **31** .... may have begun immediately following the Big Bang. The **32** .... of these particles is something that scientists are currently trying to prove using the Large Hadron Collider. Scientists now believe that even though dark matter produces no **33** ...., it will be possible to detect it somehow. They are studying dark matter's impact on the light emitted by galaxies to judge its **34** .... and chart it on a map.

A light	**B** force	**C** formation
D velocity	**E** presence	**F** position
G particle	**H** illusion	

정답·해석·해설 p.389

dark matter phr. 암흑 물질(우주에 존재하는 물질 중 아무런 빛을 내지 않는 물질) substantiate v. 입증하다 mass n. 질량, 덩어리 velocity n. 속도
elusive adj. 찾기 힘든, 알기 어려운 filament n. 가는 실 weave v. 엮다 connective tissue phr. 결합 조직 cosmologist n. 우주론자
subatomic particle phr. 아원자 입자(원자보다 더 작은 입자) halo n. 광륜, 헤일로(은하계를 둘러싸고 있는 비열적 전파를 발하는 원형의 영역) luminosity n. 광명
theorise v. 이론을 제시하다 clump together phr. 함께 모이다, 무리를 짓다 Large Hadron Collider phr. 강입자충돌기 consensus n. 일치된 의견
distort v. 일그러지다 optical illusion phr. 착시 chart v. 기록하다, 지도로 만들다

READING PASSAGE

*You should spend about 20 minutes on **Questions 1-13**, which are based on Reading Passage below.*

The Speech Chain

An overview of the process through which communication is possible

It is possible to argue that the complexity and versatility of human language systems is what distinguishes us from other animals. Language is however a recent phenomenon in evolutionary terms, having arisen only over the last 200,000 years, and it is one that is grounded in basic biology. This biological basis is largely cognitive; studies of primates show no significant difference between them and humans in their anatomical capacity for speech. It is our cognitive capacity for language, working in conjunction with our physical apparatus for speaking and listening, that therefore distinguishes humanity.

The neurophysiological process for speaking and understanding is complex and requires multiple organs working in conjunction with our cognitive capacity. This process has been labelled the 'speech chain' and understanding how it works requires a combination of linguistics, cognitive science, biology and pragmatics, the study of how language is used to communicate. The speech chain describes the process by which a piece of speech is transmitted from the speaker to the listener, breaking it down into multiple stages which reveal the complex interplay of physical and cognitive processes involved.

The speech chain is useful for researchers who want to understand how the feedback between the brain, sensory nerves and sound waves, as well as the vocal cords and ear, can influence meaning and either enable or disrupt full understanding. Speech science, the experimental study of communication, focuses on the moment when language is a physical rather than mental process. Researchers involved in this field thus study the speech chain to determine how acoustic sounds relate to articulation and how speech sounds can vary in styles and emotions.

The speech chain itself describes the process which occurs when a message travels from the mind of a speaker to the mind of a listener. The process can be broken down into several stages, each of which occurs in a different part of either the speaker's or listener's head. It also occurs on a succession of levels which reflect the complex coordination of linguistic and biological processes that are incorporated into the chain. These levels include the linguistic level, the physiological level and the acoustic level, and an utterance must use all three to be successfully communicated.

The first step of the speech chain is the encoding of the message as a linguistic concept, which occurs in the brain. In this step the message must be put into a linguistic form and the pronunciation elements must be programmed correctly so that it is coherent. Following this encoding the appropriate instructions of the brain will travel along the motor nerves in the form of impulses before they reach the vocal organs, which include the lungs, vocal cords, tongue and lips. These will then enact the process of speech by collectively creating a sound wave; this noise generating part of the chain is also known as an aeroacoustic process.

The sound waves travel through the air, toward the listener, where they are picked up by their ears' hearing mechanisms and are translated into nerve impulses which travel towards their brain. Here they are decoded to establish meaning. The brain activity during this moment reveals recognition of the speaker's statement and the interpretation of these auditory sensations as pronunciation and meaning – if the message is understood. This establishes a connection between the speaker's brain and the listener's brain, which is the ultimate aim of the speech chain and is what enables communication.

There is one more step in the chain, which is the simultaneous transmission of sound waves to the speaker's ears from his or her vocal organs. This creates a feedback link which allows the speaker to check the coherence or accuracy of their own statement. This is fundamental to the process of communication since it allows the speaker to compare the quality of their expression with what they intended and make adjustments based on this feedback. The disruption to this feedback loop caused by deafness can have significant detrimental effects on the ability to speak coherently.

Overall this speech chain reveals the basis for speech and establishes a framework for the study of communication. Researchers continue to delve into how exactly the brain encodes meaning, and how the vocal organs are capable of creating sound waves, as well as the effect of feedback on the speech process. It is worth noting that whilst this process describes the cognitive and auditory basis for communication, there is also a very important visual element; facial gestures and bodily motions play a key part in the production of meaning. It is also worth remembering that the process illustrated in the speech chain happens almost instantaneously, or at least at the speed of sound, a fact that underlines the staggering complexity and capability of the human body.

CH 06

Summary Completion HACKERS **IELTS** READING

Complete the summary using the list of words **A-I**, below.

Researching the Speech Chain

Experts can utilise the speech chain to learn about feedback between the brain and other auditory factors. This feedback can be supportive of or disruptive to complete **1** .... They can also gain knowledge about the relationship of acoustic sounds to **2** .... The various stages of the speech chain happen on different levels that indicate the complicated **3** .... of different processes. The final **4** .... of the speech chain is to establish a connection between the brain of a speaker and listener. An additional phase involves the **5** .... of sound between the speaker's vocal cords and ears. Feedback then lets the speaker make sure that his or her **6** .... meets the intended quality. Overall, the speech chain is a fundamental aspect of biology which has allowed humankind to develop as a social, communicative species. It is this chain that is behind the foundation of speech, and it sets up the **7** .... for communication research.

A framework	**B** coordination	**C** sensation
D transmission	**E** aim	**F** expression
G articulation	**H** perception	**I** understanding

Questions 8-10

Complete each sentence with the correct ending, **A-G**, below.

8   The human differs from other primates because it

9   The breaking down of speech into stages

10   The visual component in the production of meaning

A	depends heavily on communicative feedback.
B	uses only the sensory nerves when communicating.
C	utilises a unique anatomical set of speech organs.
D	shows the interaction of cognitive and physical processes.
E	includes body movements and facial expressions.
F	has more than just a physical capacity for speech.
G	translates verbal signs into visual symbols.

Questions 11-13

Label the diagram.

*Choose **NO MORE THAN TWO WORDS** from the passage for each answer.*

The Speech Chain

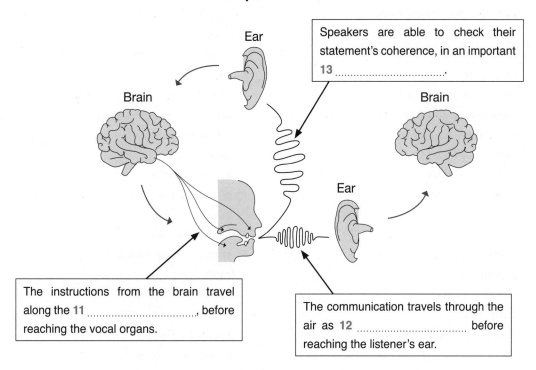

Ear

Speakers are able to check their statement's coherence, in an important **13** ....

Brain

Brain

The instructions from the brain travel along the **11** ...., before reaching the vocal organs.

Ear

The communication travels through the air as **12** .... before reaching the listener's ear.

정답·해석·해설 p.400

VOCABULARY LIST

Chapter 06에서 선별한 다음의 어휘들을 음성파일을 들으며 암기한 후 퀴즈로 확인해보세요.

*해커스 동영상강의 포털 해커스 인강(HackersIngang.com)에서 단어암기 MP3를 무료로 다운로드할 수 있습니다.

☐ institute v. (제도 · 정책 등을) 도입하다	☐ contempt n. 경멸, 멸시
☐ safeguard v. 보호하다	☐ genuine adj. 진실된
☐ advocate n. 지지자	☐ offspring n. (동식물의) 새끼
☐ tariff n. 관세	☐ mimicry n. 모방
☐ sector n. 분야	☐ trickery n. 속임수
☐ mediocre adj. 썩 좋지는 않은, 평범한	☐ adjacent to phr. 근처의, 인접한
☐ favourable adj. 순조로운, 좋은	☐ diminutive adj. 작은
☐ fruitful adj. 비옥한 생산적인	☐ tactic n. 전략
☐ in droves phr. 떼지어	☐ fertilise v. 수정시키다
☐ subculture n. 하위 문화	☐ preclude v. 불가능하게 하다
☐ practice n. 관행	☐ agility n. 민첩성
☐ exude v. 드러내다, 스며 나오게 하다	☐ reproductive adj. 생식의, 번식의
☐ medieval adj. 중세의	☐ embed v. ~을 깊이 새겨 두다
☐ armour n. 갑옷	☐ captivity n. 감금
☐ absorb v. 흡수하다	☐ excavation n. 발굴 작업
☐ blunt adj. 뭉툭한	☐ uncover v. 보여주다, 폭로하다
☐ savage adj. 사나운, 맹렬한	☐ expedition n. 원정
☐ warrior n. 전사	☐ reputed adj. ~이라고 알려진
☐ intimidation n. 위협, 협박	☐ usher in phr. ~을 시작되게 하다
☐ live on phr. 존속하다, 계속 살다	☐ inaugurate v. 막을 열다, 개시하다
☐ ferocity n. 포악성	☐ consign v. 두다, 맡기다
☐ turn out phr. ~으로 보이다, ~인 것으로 밝혀지다	☐ traverse v. 가로지르다
☐ deception n. 사기, 속임	☐ dexterity n. 민첩성, 재주
☐ involuntarily adv. 무의식중에	☐ abate v. 완화하다
☐ betray v. 드러내다, 무심코 노출하다	☐ bring about phr. 초래하다
☐ disgust n. 혐오(감)	☐ ravage v. 파괴하다, 약탈하다

Quiz

각 단어의 알맞은 뜻을 찾아 연결하시오.

01 intimidation	ⓐ 무의식중에	06 traverse	ⓐ 전략
02 sector	ⓑ 흡수하다	07 bring about	ⓑ 진실된
03 involuntarily	ⓒ 분야	08 genuine	ⓒ 작은
04 practice	ⓓ 위협, 협박	09 abate	ⓓ 가로지르다
05 absorb	ⓔ 포악성	10 tactic	ⓔ 완화하다
	ⓕ 관행		ⓕ 초래하다

ⓐ 01 ⓒ 02 ⓐ 03 ⓕ 04 ⓑ 05 ⓓ 06 ⓕ 07 ⓑ 08 ⓔ 09 ⓐ 10

☐ accord n. 협약

☐ impose a ban on phr. ~을 금지하다

☐ poaching n. 밀렵, 침범

☐ vigilance n. 경각심, 경계

☐ manual labour phr. 육체 노동

☐ abundant adj. 풍부한

☐ constraint n. 제한, 제약

☐ steam engine phr. 증기 기관

☐ driving force phr. 원동력

☐ textile n. 직물, 옷감

☐ horsepower n. 마력

☐ locomotive n. 기관차

☐ outskirt n. 변두리

☐ eye-opening adj. 놀랄 만한, 경이로운

☐ under siege phr. 포위당한

☐ flora n. 식물군

☐ fauna n. 동물군

☐ vegetation n. 초목

☐ implication n. 영향

☐ logging n. 벌목

☐ irreversible adj. 되돌릴 수 없는

☐ sap v. 서서히 빼앗다

☐ by extension phr. 더 나아가

☐ concentration n. 농도, 집중

☐ render v. ~하게 하다

☐ barren adj. (토지가) 메마른, 불모의

☐ mounting adj. 증가하는

☐ collectively adv. 공동으로, 집단으로

☐ canal n. 운하

☐ spur v. ~의 원동력이 되다, 자극하다

☐ interior n. 내륙, 내부

☐ haul v. 운반하다, 차로 나르다

☐ freight n. 화물

☐ skyrocket v. 급증하다

☐ commodity n. 상품, 물품

☐ on a daily basis phr. 매일

☐ revenue n. 세입, 수익

☐ toll n. 요금

☐ disembark v. (배에서) 내리다

☐ venture v. (모험하듯) 가다

☐ velocity n. 속도

☐ elusive adj. 찾기 힘든, 알기 어려운

☐ luminosity n. 광명

☐ theorise v. 이론을 제시하다

☐ distort v. 일그러지다

☐ chart v. 기록하다, 지도로 만들다

☐ interplay n. 상호 작용

☐ articulation n. 발화, 발음

☐ style n. 어조, 방식

☐ utterance n. 발성, 말

☐ coherent adj. 일관성 있는, 분명히 말할 수 있는

☐ impulse n. 자극

Quiz

각 단어의 알맞은 뜻을 찾아 연결하시오.

01 outskirt	ⓐ 풍부한	06 revenue	ⓐ 일그러지다
02 irreversible	ⓑ 협약	07 skyrocket	ⓑ 공동으로, 집단으로
03 accord	ⓒ 영향	08 impulse	ⓒ 속도
04 vigilance	ⓓ 되돌릴 수 없는	09 collectively	ⓓ 급증하다
05 implication	ⓔ 경각심, 경계	10 distort	ⓔ 세입, 수익
	ⓕ 변두리		ⓕ 자극

ⓐ 01 ⓓ 02 ⓑ 03 ⓔ 04 ⓒ 05 | ⓔ 06 ⓓ 07 ⓕ 08 ⓑ 09 ⓐ 10

CHAPTER

07 | Matching Features

Matching features 문제는 각각의 문제와 관련된 정보를 보기 리스트에서 고르는 객관식 문제이다. 매 시험 출제되지는 않지만 자주 출제되고 있다.

문제 형태

Matching features 문제는 각각의 문제와 관련된 알맞은 정보를 보기 리스트에서 고르는 형태로 출제된다. 이때 리스트에는 주로 학자, 연구원 등의 이름이 주어지며, 문제에는 리스트에 등장한 학자나 연구원의 의견이 언급된다.

Look at the following statements (Questions 1-3) and the list of researchers below.

*Match each statement with the correct researcher, **A-E**.*

*Write the correct letter, **A-E**, in boxes 1-3 on your answer sheet.*

** **NB** You may use any letter more than once.*

1 Approaching decisions with discipline leads to better results.

2 Intuitive decisions are usually made in an instant.

3 There is a greater need for gender equality in the field of anthropology.

List of Researchers

A Tom Gilovich
B Lyndsay Swinton
C Robin M. Hogarth
D David Price
E William Caudell

---

*리스트의 보기 개수와 문제의 개수는 항상 일치하지는 않는다. 이런 경우 정답으로 사용되지 않거나 한 번 이상 정답으로 사용되는 보기가 있을 수 있다. 한 번 이상 정답으로 사용되는 보기가 있는 경우에는 **NB** You may use any letter more than once라는 지시문이 주어진다.

문제풀이 전략

STEP 1 지시문을 확인하고, 문제의 핵심어구와 내용을 파악한다.

(1) 지시문을 읽고 문제에서 요구하는 것을 파악한다.

(2) 문제의 핵심어구와 핵심 내용을 파악한다.

EXAMPLE

Look at the following statement (Question 1) and the list of researchers below.

*Match the statement with the correct researcher, **A**, **B** or **C**.*

*Write the correct letter, **A**, **B** or **C**, in box 1 on your answer sheet.*

1 Approaching decisions with discipline leads to better results.

> **List of Researchers**
>
> **A** Tom Gilovich
> **B** Lyndsay Swinton
> **C** Robin M. Hogarth

(1) 지시문을 읽고 문제에 언급된 내용과 관련된 과학자를 고르는 문제임을 파악한다.

(2) 문제를 읽고 핵심어구인 Approaching decisions with discipline이 더 나은 결과로 이어진다는 내용을 파악한다.

지문을 scanning하여 문제의 핵심어구와 관련된 내용을 찾는다. 관련 내용이 언급된 주변에서 정답의 단서를 확인한다.

EXAMPLE

According to psychologist Tom Gilovich, decisions based on intuition are typically made instantaneously, and these decisions are not always well informed or products of rational thought. One of the easiest ways to see the problems with intuitive decision-making is to look at the way that people act during game play. Even though everyone understands that most games are based purely on luck, players often make wagers based on irrational feelings.

Management consultant [1]Lyndsay Swinton points out that rational deliberative decision making, on the other hand, allows decisions to be approached with discipline so that more appropriate outcomes can be secured. This occurs because the deliberative decision-making process requires considering the larger ramifications of a decision rather than just how it feels at the moment. In the end, it yields more appropriate choices with fewer negative repercussions.

문제의 핵심어구인 Approaching decisions with dischipline과 관련된 내용을 지문에서 찾는다. 관련 내용이 언급된 주변에서 'rational deliberative decision making ~ allows decisions to be approached with discipline so that more appropriate outcomes can be secured'라는 정답의 단서를 확인한다.

Look at the following statement (Question 1) and the list of researchers below.

*Match the statement with the correct researcher, **A**, **B** or **C**.*

*Write the correct letter, **A**, **B** or **C**, in box 1 on your answer sheet.*

1 Approaching decisions with discipline leads to better results.

List of Researchers

A Tom Gilovich

B Lyndsay Swinton

C Robin M. Hogarth

지문 해석 p.404

정답의 단서에 언급된 올바른 학자의 이름을 보기 리스트에서 찾아 답을 적는다.

EXAMPLE

According to psychologist Tom Gilovich, decisions based on intuition are typically made instantaneously, and these decisions are not always well informed or products of rational thought. One of the easiest ways to see the problems with intuitive decision-making is to look at the way that people act during game play. Even though everyone understands that most games are based purely on luck, players often make wagers based on irrational feelings.

Management consultant [1]Lyndsay Swinton points out that rational deliberative decision making, on the other hand, allows decisions to be approached with discipline so that more appropriate outcomes can be secured. This occurs because the deliberative decision-making process requires considering the larger ramifications of a decision rather than just how it feels at the moment. In the end, it yields more appropriate choices with fewer negative repercussions.

Look at the following statement (Question 1) and the list of researchers below.

*Match the statement with the correct researcher, **A**, **B** or **C**.*

*Write the correct letter, **A**, **B** or **C**, in box 1 on your answer sheet.*

1 Approaching decisions with discipline leads to better results. B

지문에서 Lyndsay Swinton이 이성적이고 의도적인 의사 결정은 더 적절한 결과가 보장될 수 있도록 결정이 규율에 의해 접근되게 한다고 주장한 내용과 일치하므로, 정답은 B이다. 'more appropriate outcomes'가 'better results'로 paraphrasing되었다.

List of Researchers

A Tom Gilovich
B Lyndsay Swinton
C Robin M. Hogarth

HACKERS **PRACTICE**

1 Although known primarily for their honey production, bees are actually more important to human well-being as pollinators of the staple crops that make up our diet. In fact, the American Environmental Protection Agency claims that pollinators are responsible for nearly one in every three bites of food you eat. If this is true, then the fact that honeybee numbers are dwindling should be a major cause of concern, not only for their survival but for ours. A study carried out by Nicholas Calderone, associate professor of entomology at Cornell University, showed that crops pollinated by honeybees and other insects contributed 29 billion dollars of annual farm income in the United States, revealing the extent of their importance both agriculturally and economically. This point was emphasised by Vera Lucia Imperatriz-Fonseca, senior professor at the University of São Paulo, who stated in a United Nations report that pollinator's health is directly linked to our own well-being. In fact, a study by Professor Simon Potts in the UK revealed how a massive decline in honeybee colonies has made agriculture reliant upon pollination by wild bee species, many of which are also under threat.

Look at the following statements (Questions 1-2) and the list of researchers below.

*Match each statement with the correct researcher, **A**, **B** or **C**.*

1   The welfare of creatures that pollinate crops, such as bees, has a direct connection to human health.

2   Agriculture has become dependent on a certain kind of bee for pollination.

List of Researchers

A   Simon Potts
B   Vera Lucia Imperatriz-Fonseca
C   Nicholas Calderone

---

pollinator n. 꽃가루 매개자   staple adj. 주요한, 주된   Environmental Protection Agency phr. 환경보호국   dwindle v. 줄어들다   entomology n. 곤충학
colony n. 군집, 집단   pollination n. 수분

2 Despite being less than 250 years old, the United States has become one of the world's economic powerhouses. Although the country's location, vast size, and abundant natural resources played a large role in its success, these would have had little impact without advances in the transportation industry. Until around 1800, the country relied mainly on water-based transportation, such as ships and boats for its cargo needs. Since the country was rather small and most early cities were on the East Coast, early Americans could easily trade with one another and with their European trading partners using this form of transportation. However, as the 19th century got underway, the Louisiana Purchase doubled the size of the nation and it eventually reached the West Coast. This resulted in vast interior areas that were not accessible by boat and therefore ended the water-based transportation era. The problem was solved by the construction of the transcontinental rail system, which brought the country into the land-based transportation era. The new railways allowed large-scale shipping of large items from one coast to the other for the first time. Later, after the invention of the automobile, highways mirrored this transcontinental system and people could easily drive across the country on their own. These land-based systems dominated transportation in America until the mid to late-1900s. The following period saw the simultaneous rise of air travel and information technology. As the air-based transportation era began, people could travel or send parcels across the country in a matter of hours rather than days or weeks, and transferring information became instantaneous.

Classify the following statements as referring to

A	Air-based transportation era
B	Land-based transportation era
C	Water-based transportation era

3   The speed of the postal service was reduced to less than a day.

4   A new form of travel emerged at the same time as a new technology.

5   A new system provided a way of travelling alone across the country.

6   The location of cities on one coast made trade easy.

---

powerhouse n. 강국 abundant adj. 풍부한 cargo n. 화물 interior adj. 내륙의, 내부의 transcontinental adj. 대륙 횡단의 shipping n. 운송, 선적
mirror v. 모방하다 simultaneous adj. 동시의 instantaneous adj. 즉각적인

CH
07

Matching Features HACKERS **IELTS** READING

3 Sleep is a necessity for all animals which, according to some scientists, could reveal something about our shared evolutionary ancestry. Because of its universality, many early sleep researchers felt that it must have begun very early in animal evolution. However, this view is contested by some scientists, such as Jerry Siegel of the University of California, who suggests that the need for sleep could have developed in each species separately. 'It could be more of a case of convergent evolution', he states, suggesting that sleep is 'an adaption to an animal's environment' rather than a trait inherited from a common evolutionary ancestor. Siegel's theory is backed up by the massive variation in sleep patterns across different species, from possums that can sleep for up to 18 hours a day, to birds that take hundreds of short naps every day. He has also discovered that dolphins, which are renowned for their ability to put one side of their brain to sleep at a time, have another unique sleep pattern. After an adult dolphin gives birth, neither she nor her offspring will sleep for an extended period of time. This practice, the opposite of what occurs in land mammals, suggests that animals adapt their own system of sleep, rather than inherit a universal one. Nonetheless many scientists still hope to find an overarching theory for why all animals need sleep. Paul Shaw, a researcher at Washington University in St. Louis, claims that because 'sleep is costly' in terms of vulnerability to ambush from other animals, there must be an underlying evolutionary reason for its universality. Shaw cites sleep research pioneer Alan Rechtschaffen, who stated, 'If sleep doesn't serve an absolutely vital function, it is the biggest mistake evolution ever made.'

Look at the following findings (Questions 7-8) and the list of scientists below.

*Match each finding with the correct scientist, **A**, **B** or **C**.*

7   Animals developed unique sleep habits to match their specific surroundings, rather than inheriting a general trait.

8   The importance of sleep is evident when we consider how a sleeping animal is much more open to attack from a predator.

List of Scientists
A   Alan Rechtschaffen
B   Paul Shaw
C   Jerry Siegel

---

universality n. 보편성 contest v. 이의를 제기하다 convergent adj. 융합의 variation n. 차이, 변형 possum n. 주머니쥐 overarching adj. 중요한
vulnerability n. 취약(성) ambush n. 매복 공격 underlying adj. (겉으로 잘 드러나지 않지만) 근본적인

4 In nature, most animals avoid eating things that have a bitter taste. This occurs, according to Oxford researcher J. Zhang, because bitterness often indicates toxicity. Therefore, animals can prolong their lives by avoiding bitter foods. Using this knowledge, some manufacturers have begun using bitter flavours to act as an animal repellent. In fact, researcher A. L. Riley showed in his research that applying bitter compounds to objects could train birds to avoid them. Interestingly, humans seem to have lost the aversion to bitterness that other animals display. This can be seen through our use of bitter flavours in commercial food production. Food manufacturers have developed 'bittering agents' specifically to add this flavour to certain foods.

A good example of the use of these bittering agents occurs in the brewing of beer. The hops that brewers add to their product are meant to impart a bitter flavour to balance the sweetness of the sugars that ferment in the malt. This is also the reason that caffeine is added to colas. When its caffeine is removed, cola is simply cloying fizzy water and must be balanced with another bittering agent. One of these is liquid 'bitters' made from aromatic herbs and other plant materials. These commercially available liquids are now widely used in food and cocktail preparation, but they once had a very different use. They were seen as health tonics. This was exactly the case with the popular 'bitters' produced by the House of Angostura. Dr Johann Gottlieb Benjamin Siegert developed the concoction to ease seasickness and marketed the product to sailors. Over time, his product came to be used to cut the sweetness of drinks such as lemonade or the Sazerac cocktail.

Look at the following statements (Questions 9-11) and the list of people below.

*Match each statement with the correct person, **A**, **B** or **C**.*

9 developed a product to relieve a medical condition

10 explained why animals avoid food with a certain taste

11 conducted research into using bitter items to train animals

List of People
A Zhang
B Riley
C Siegert

---

prolong v. 연장하다 repellent n. 퇴치제 compound n. 화합물 aversion n. 반감, 혐오감 agent n. (특정 효과·목적을 위해 쓰이는) 물질 brew v. 양조하다
hop n. 홉 impart v. 첨가하다, 덧붙이다 ferment v. 발효하다 malt n. 맥아 cloying adj. 질릴 정도의 fizzy adj. 탄산이 많은, 거품이 나는 tonic n. 강장제
concoction n. 혼합물 ease v. 완화하다 seasickness n. 뱃멀미

5 The region between the Tigris and Euphrates rivers in the Middle East is known to have been inhabited by primitive people for hundreds or even thousands of years before the development of a settled population. This area, which was named the 'Fertile Crescent' by early 19th-century archaeologist James Breasted for its fertility, provided a bounty of products from its soil, rivers, and wildlife that allowed these early inhabitants to feed themselves and their families. Eventually, this brought about the first active production of food and, in turn, the first true settled civilisations. Over time, the ability of these civilisations to produce food with regularity led to an increase in the number of people in the area and, around 4500 B.C., something interesting happened. The people built a large, densely populated permanent settlement called Uruk, which we now know as the first city.

The new city of Uruk had a large temple, homes, and other buildings created entirely with sun-dried bricks. This, according to historian Stephen Bertman, was due to the lack of timber and stone commonly used in construction elsewhere. We know that the use of these bricks allowed them to create large structures with columns, arches, and fortifying walls for the first time, but it doesn't explain why such a settlement was developed. In traditional retellings such as the *Epic of Gilgamesh*, the leader of the civilisation ordered the building of the city and its fortifications. However, research by anthropologist Jason Ur calls this into question. According to Dr Ur's research, early urbanisation likely occurred organically, not because of a political ruler. He showed that different civilisations from the area settled around a central mound. These clusters allowed the different civilisations to live near one another, but kept the appropriate social distance. As time passed, they came together to form an interconnected city with one leader.

Look at the following statements (Questions 12-14) and the list of researchers below.

*Match each statement with the correct researcher, **A**, **B** or **C**.*

12   He determined the reason that an early society used sun-dried bricks.

13   He revealed that the growth of the first cities happened naturally.

14   He coined a term to represent the agricultural strength of a region.

List of Researchers
A   James Breasted
B   Stephen Bertman
C   Jason Ur

---

crescent n. 초승달 (모양) a bounty of phr. 풍부한 bring about phr. 발생시키다, 야기하다 temple n. 사원 column n. 기둥 retelling n. 개작된 이야기
fortification n. 요새 call into question phr. 이의를 제기하다 mound n. 언덕 cluster n. 무리, 집단 come together phr. 합쳐지다

6 Many parents complain that their children are no longer the same people they once were. During their preadolescent stage, these children were generally docile and amenable. They were very loving and attached to their parents who probably had no trouble interacting with them. At this point, many parents believe that they have a strong bond with their children that will never weaken. Unfortunately for them, this stage only lasts until about the ages of 10-13. As children enter adolescence, they undergo changes that can make them quite difficult to deal with. This period of increased conflict with parents, rapid mood changes, and increasingly risky behaviour caused early psychologist G. S. Hall to refer to this early teenage period as the 'storm and stress' stage.

One reason for the undesirable behaviours associated with this teenage stage is the rapid change that the body goes through at this time. The adolescent's body is maturing rapidly and it may appear that they are adults acting with childish impulsivity and emotional instability. This can frustrate parents, but is simply a sign that the frontal lobes of the brain, the areas that control these behaviours, are not yet fully developed. In fact, Donald Stuss has found that the frontal lobes sometimes do not fully mature until the early to mid-twenties. In addition to these physical changes, the adolescent's social interactions are undergoing major changes as well. Most adolescents will become distant from their parents and focus on external relationships as they prepare to enter society as an adult on their own. This distance is more pronounced now than when it was proposed in the 1950s. Today, a more interconnected world has dramatically increased the number of social relationships we develop outside the family. Adolescents now must figure out who they are while living in larger cities and interacting with more people both in real world situations and through online interactions and social media. This can lead to greater identity confusion than in the past and may increase the stress of parents dealing with the 'storm and stress' stage in their adolescents.

Classify the following statements as referring to

A	Preadolescence
B	Teenage period

15 Family relations are less important than socialising with others.

16 A deep connection exists between children and parents.

17 There are more unsafe activities.

---

preadolescent adj. 사춘기 이전의 docile adj. 유순한 amenable adj. 순종적인, 말을 잘 듣는 undergo v. 겪다 impulsivity n. 충동
instability n. 불안, 불안정 frontal lobe phr. 전두엽 pronounce v. 두드러지게 나타나다

7 Does Yawning Have a Function?

Theories for why we yawn date back more than 2,000 years to the time of Hippocrates, who considered yawning to be the respiratory system's way of removing 'bad air' from the lungs. Centuries later, scientists claimed that yawning indicated a lack of oxygen to the brain. Today, we know that neither of these theories has strong scientific merit, prompting contemporary researchers to carry on trying to unravel the mystery of one of our most common biological reflexes.

Robert Provine, a neuroscientist at the University of Maryland, points to the obvious, noting that people tend to yawn most when they are bored, hungry, and fatigued. Because all of these states can easily lead to the inability to focus on whatever task is at hand, he believes that yawning is our bodies' way of alerting us that we need to perk up. When this theory was tested, it was found that subjects did in fact tend to engage in some sort of physical activity directly after yawning, suggesting that the subjects' yawns led to their getting up and seeking out stimulation. Essentially, Provine contends that yawning occurs due to an absence of stimuli and is simply how our bodies try to regain focus.

Then again, so many things seem to cause people to yawn that it is hardly satisfying to simply blame a lack of stimulation. One situation many of us are probably familiar with is being unable to control ourselves from yawning after seeing someone else yawn. A team of researchers from the University of Leeds headed by Catriona Morrison believe that this has to do with our inclination to show empathy for other people. In other words, if someone yawns in exhaustion, and others in the room follow suit, it is likely because they identify with and feel sympathy for the original yawner. This claim is substantiated by studies demonstrating that yawning is most contagious among members of the same family or social group and lowest among those with autism and psychopathy, conditions associated with the inability to empathise.

Meanwhile, evolutionary psychologist Gordon Gallup of the University of Albany builds on both Provine's and Morrison's theories with his hypothesis that yawning developed as a way to alert group members to potential threats. Agreeing that yawning is followed by a feeling of improved attentiveness and that it is contagious, he believes that early humans capitalised on these effects to quickly convey the message to others that it was necessary to be on guard against attacks. Essentially, if everyone was yawning and feeling more alert because of it, the likelihood of falling prey to a predator was far lower.

Look at the following statements (Questions 18-20) and the list of researchers below.

*Match each statement with the correct researcher, **A**, **B** or **C**.*

18 Yawning may be linked to the ability to experience the same emotions as the people around us.

19 The contagiousness of yawning helped to promote alertness among members of a group.

20 Yawning results from lack of stimuli and is an attempt by our bodies to refocus.

List of Researchers

A Gordon Gallup

B Robert Provine

C Catriona Morrison

---

date back phr. (~로) 거슬러 올라가다   respiratory system phr. 호흡기관   unravel v. 풀다, 해명하다   reflex n. 반사 작용(운동)   fatigued adj. 피로한
at hand phr. 눈앞에 있는, 가까이에 있는   perk up phr. 기운을 차리다   empathy n. 공감   follow suit phr. 따라 하다   autism n. 자폐
attentiveness n. 경각심, 조심성   capitalise v. ~을 활용하다

8　The Importance of Gesture

Gesture is a vital and often overlooked element of communication. It can be either a supplement to spoken language or an autonomous language system in its own right. Cognitive scientist Philip Lieberman has suggested that gesture is actually the oldest form of language and that it originated in the pre-linguistic stage of human evolution. Lieberman has carried out research into the use of gesture by both primates and infants to support his theory. Lieberman contends that language was formed from non-verbal gestures, rather than gesture emerging from language, and that our current use of gesture stems from pre-linguistic communication.

As Natasha Abner, Kensy Cooperrider and Susan Goldin-Meadow state in their article 'Gesture for Linguists: A Handy Primer', gestures can be broadly split into two categories, communicative and informative. The former includes intentionally produced communicative gestures which are consciously used in addition to verbal communication, either to provide emphasis or through modifying the literal meaning. Informative communication, on the other hand, refers to passive or involuntary gestures that are not necessarily part of a communicative act, but can nevertheless alter the meaning of such an act. Adam Kendon, co-editor of the journal *Gesture* and a global authority on the subject, has developed a categorisation system for differentiating various gestures. These include 'gesticulation', a gesture which mirrors accompanying speech, 'speech-framed gestures', which replace part of a sentence, 'emblems', conventionalised signs like the 'OK' symbol made by touching the index finger and thumb, which occur outside verbal communication, and 'signs', gestures with lexical meaning in a system of sign language. Kendon cites the longstanding interest in gesture in Western culture as evidence of its importance to communication. This interest was evident during the Classical era when gesture was considered a crucial part of effective rhetoric, as the Roman philosopher and politician Cicero emphasised in his work *De Oratore*. It is also apparent in the unique gestural systems of religions from Catholicism to Buddhism, through which adherents can communicate a variety of complex meanings.

The contemporary academic interest in gesture derives from both its roots in humankind's pre-linguistic stage, which suggests that gesture is a universal form of communication, and the recent interest in close psychological reading of face-to-face communication, from which it is possible to garner numerous non-verbal gestural cues. The complexity of gesture as a system of individual communication is evident in the range of gesture variants that can express different meanings. Geneviève Calbris suggests that gesture variants reveal how 'gesture is not a word illustrator but represents an underlying thought that is formulated and expressed during the course of an utterance'. This is apparent in Calbris's analysis of gestures related to time, which can express complex and varied meanings about duration without the use of verbal communication. According to Calbris, these wide-ranging gestural variants reveal the complexity of this system of communication, which can both accentuate and alter the meaning of verbal communications.

Look at the following statements (Questions 21-25) and the list of people below.

*Match each statement with the correct person, **A-E**.*

NB *You may use any letter more than once.*

21   suggested that gesture stood for an idea lying beneath words

22   created an approach to distinguish different types of gestures

23   carried out analysis of how gestures can say many different things about time

24   established the theory that gesture preceded language

25   conducted research into the use of gestures by apes

List of People

A   Adam Kendon
B   Geneviève Calbris
C   Philip Lieberman
D   Natasha Abner
E   Susan Goldin-Meadow

---

overlook v. 간과하다 supplement n. 보완, 보충 autonomous adj. 자율적인, 자주적인 primate n. 영장류 contend v. 주장하다
consciously adv. 의식적으로 modify v. 변형하다, 수정하다 literal adj. 문자 그대로의 passive adj. 수동적인 alter v. 바꾸다 mirror v. 반영하다
accompanying adj. 수반되는 emblem n. 상징 lexical adj. 어휘적인, 어휘의 longstanding adj. 오랜 세월 동안의 rhetoric n. 수사
adherent n. 신자, 지지자 garner v. 수집하다, 모으다 accentuate v. 강조하다

9 Is the Detective Novel a Literary Genre?

When Edgar Allen Poe introduced C. Auguste Dupin in the 1841 novel *The Murders in the Rue Morgue*, the word 'detective' was unheard-of. However, the idea of an intelligent amateur out-sleuthing the police intrigued many writers, who began creating crime fiction of their own. Yet, given the predictability of the plots and characters in these early tales, readers began to question whether the detective novel was even a genre at all.

These days, it is undeniable that crime fiction is far more complex than before. Mystery writer Simon Brett makes the point that crime in modern-day stories is no longer seen as black or white and that detectives are rarely portrayed as morally infallible anymore. He also refutes claims that detective stories follow a formula as cases are not always neatly resolved by the end, which shows that plotlines can be hard to predict. So what makes a crime fiction novel? At the very least, it is the fact that there is a mystery in every one.

But mystery novelist Nicholas Blincoe believes that the similarities in detective stories extend further, making the genre easily identifiable; every story has a crime and its solution (or non-solution), a community where the crime has been committed, and central characters. These characteristics are necessary to define the genre but do not, argues Blincoe, limit it, suggesting that writers have a degree of freedom in many facets of their work. According to him, crime fiction 'has produced the widest variety of archetypes and the most inventive improvisations in plot or character'.

That mainstream writers are known to incorporate elements of the crime fiction style into their work adds weight to the idea that the genre is distinctive. According to the detective novelist Phyllis Dorothy James, sometimes detective story plots are found weaved into the much broader plots of other genres of fiction. She cites the example of John le Carré's 1974 novel *Tinker, Tailor, Soldier, Spy*. In this story, which is technically an espionage novel, the main character emerges from retirement to take a case that happens to involve a common theme in crime fiction – a race against time to identify a wrongdoer.

According to crime fiction aficionado George Demko, another characteristic that sets crime fiction apart is how the setting is used. Specifically, detective mysteries often take place in a real place and time, and this has a significant impact on the case. He discusses this in an essay, providing the example of how widespread corruption was usually emphasised in crime novels set in Mexico during the 1940s. By explaining that the perpetrator's surroundings were part of the reason the crime was committed, readers were left to ponder whether society as a whole shared responsibility for the terrible actions of an individual.

Perhaps the simplest argument for detective fiction deserving its own genre is that people from all walks of life read it. That it is both engaging and suspenseful is certainly a draw for many devoted fans, but maybe the popularity of crime fiction goes far deeper, playing on people's innate desire to know the truth. The modernist poet T. S. Eliot, himself a great fan of detective novels, believed their appeal lay in the mathematical beauty of their mysteries. Ultimately, by presenting mysteries that only the best can solve, whodunits appeal to our inner natures.

Look at the following statements (Questions 26-29) and the list of people below.

*Match each statement with the correct person, **A-E**.*

26 Narratives that are characteristic of detective stories can sometimes be found in other types of fiction.

27 Detective stories must follow certain rules but writers are free to be creative in all other aspects.

28 That detective stories are not always solved in the end proves that they can be unpredictable.

29 The writers' use of an actual social or historical period as a setting distinguishes crime fiction as a genre.

List of People
A Simon Brett
B Phyllis Dorothy James
C George Demko
D Nicholas Blincoe
E T. S. Eliot

---

detective n. 탐정, 형사 sleuth v. 추적하다 black or white phr. 이분법적인 infallible adj. 잘못이 전혀 없는, 절대 옳은 refute v. 반박하다
formula n. 공식 plotline n. 줄거리 archetype n. 전형 facet n. 측면, 양상 improvisation n. 즉흥 요소, 즉석에서 만든 것 espionage n. 간첩
wrongdoer n. 범법자 aficionado n. 마니아 perpetrator n. 범죄자 ponder v. 생각하다, 숙고하다 walks of life phr. 계층, 직업
suspenseful adj. 긴장감이 넘치는 draw n. 마음을 끄는 요소 whodunit n. 추리 소설

10   Climate Change and Human Conflict

For as long as academics have been researching climate change, it has been theorised that a change in weather will result in lack of rain and soil degradation. While many of us think immediately of the ecological repercussions, fewer of us realise that the loss of arable land and the ensuing poor crop yields will likely lead to higher rates of poverty, political instability, famine, war, and ultimately death for a large percentage of humanity.

It is, of course, beyond the power of researchers to alter a region's climate to determine whether this will in fact come to pass. However, by studying the existing documentation on weather disturbances and their link to human conflicts throughout history, researchers can draw some conclusions and speculate about what might happen in the future. A team headed by Solomon Hsiang of the University of California at Berkeley has perhaps come as close as possible to predicting how climate change will affect human behaviour.

According to their research, extreme weather does show a strong correlation with a rise in human conflict. Specifically, the frequency of interpersonal and intergroup violence rose by 4 and 14 per cent, respectively, for each standard deviation change in climate toward warmer temperatures or more extreme rainfall. Dr Hsiang's conclusion is startling. He argues that because locations throughout the inhabited world are expected to warm significantly by 2050, this climate change will result in an increase in human conflicts in the next 30 years.

Are there recent situations that bear out Dr Hsiang's conclusions? Sadly, yes. Darfur is perhaps the best example. In 2007, Achim Steiner, executive director of the United Nations Environment Programme, published a research report calling Darfur 'the first climate change war'. The nation has experienced a 30 per cent drop in precipitation in the last 40 years, and in the early 2000s, a lack of rainfall in the northern part of the country caused agricultural production to drop sharply. With no food or water to sustain them, more than two million people migrated to refugee camps in the south, where tensions began to mount, and conflict eventually broke out in 2003. It is estimated that as many as 500,000 civilians died, and this does not include those who perished from starvation.

Other academics, such as agricultural economist Marshall Burke of the University of California contend that Darfur is hardly the first climate change war. He points to sub-Saharan Africa as having a history of civil wars due to warmer temperatures. Somalia, for instance, has been at war now for over two decades. And some academics, such as University of South Carolina professor Edward Carr, have criticised Dr Hsiang's study. Carr emphasised that focusing solely on climate as a conflict cause is both reductive and dangerous, suggesting that it might disproportionately influence policy decisions in unproductive or even problematic directions.

According to Dr Carl Schleussner of the Potsdam Institute for Climate Impact Research, 'Devastating climate-related natural disasters have a disruptive potential that seems to play out in ethnically fractionalised societies in a particularly tragic way'. Essentially, because the entire country is faced with famine due to climate change and there is no clear majority group, peoples' allegiances lie with their respective clans. And because each clan has the same goal – gain more land to enable survival – violent disputes among groups have been unavoidable.

Look at the following findings (Questions 30-34) and the list of researchers below.

*Match each finding with the correct researcher, **A-E**.*

30 Rates of human conflict will increase significantly in the next few decades.

31 Darfur is the first location where conflict has erupted due to climate change.

32 Other wars in Africa before the one in Darfur occurred due to increases in temperature.

33 Conflicts related to climate change are more likely to occur in countries with multiple ethnicities.

34 Concentrating on one cause for conflicts could have problematic consequences for policy makers.

List of Researchers

A Marshall Burke
B Solomon Hsiang
C Achim Steiner
D Carl Schleussner
E Edward Carr

정답·해석·해설 p.404

---

academics n. 학계, 학자 degradation n. 악화 repercussion n. 반향 arable adj. 경작 가능한 famine n. 기근 intergroup adj. 집단 간의
respectively adv. 각각 standard deviation phr. 표준편차 bear out phr. 지지하다, 옳음을 증명하다 mount v. 고조되다, (서서히) 증가하다
perish v. 사망하다 starvation n. 기아, 굶주림 reductive adj. 환원주의적인 fractionalise v. 분열하다, 분해하다 clan n. 집단, 무리 dispute n. 분쟁

READING PASSAGE

*You should spend about 20 minutes on **Questions 1-13**, which are based on Reading Passage below.*

ARE PLANTS INTELLIGENT?

In the 1973 book *The Secret Life of Plants*, Peter Tompkins and Christopher Bird reported that plants had feelings, could read human emotions and thoughts, and had a predilection for classical music. Their assertions generated an uproar among members of the scientific community, with many arguing that thinking and feeling require the presence of a brain and that nothing in a plant, internally or externally, even remotely resembles one. However, members of the reading public who believed that their plants thrived when dealt with affectionately were quick to give their support. Although much of the evidence in the Tompkins-Bird book has since been discredited, numerous articles and studies claiming that plants are more than insentient organisms have since been published.

A well-known experiment conducted by Monica Gagliano's team at the University of Western Australia and reported in the journal *Oecologia* is worth mentioning. For the test, the scientists selected the mimosa plant, which reactively folds its leaves as a natural protective adaptation when the plant perceives danger. They came up with an apparatus with a vertical rail, which potted mimosa plants could slide down before landing on a foam base, and then subjected a large number of plants to the shock of being dropped from a height of about 15 centimetres. The plants were not damaged in any way since the pots fell only a short distance onto a soft surface, but the shock was considerable enough to cause the plants' leaves to close. But Gagliano's team was testing for intelligence, so they were seeking more than a knee-jerk reaction from the plants; they wanted to determine if the plants would be able to recall their experience and even learn from it.

To test their hypothesis, they dropped the plants 60 times at intervals of a few seconds, with each series of 60 drops being repeated a total of seven times. The team observed that toward the end of the day, the plants' leaves stopped closing. This indicated that they had 'adjusted' to their experience and no longer perceived falling to be a threat. The plants were then left undisturbed for nearly a week before being again subjected to the test. This time, some of the mimosa plants did not fold their leaves at all in response to the drop, while others stopped closing their leaves after only a couple of drops. Gagliano reasoned that the plants had a recollection of what had happened in the prior experiment, and postulated they had something akin to memory. Gagliano's research, which was heavily publicised, was criticised for conflating 'learning' with 'adapting'. Fred Sack, a botanist at the University of British Columbia, suggested that the distinction was very clear; plants evolve, animals learn.

Another study putting forward the idea that plants can 'think' focused on the way trees are able to organise themselves. Suzanne Simard, a forest ecologist at the University of British Columbia, discovered how trees in a forest arrange themselves in widely distributed networks in a manner that allows the trees to share resources and protect fellow trees. They injected the trees with a radioactive carbon and followed the flow of nutrients and chemical signals through the community with a Geiger counter. A diagram they made of these movements showed that the oldest trees served as hubs and had as many as 47 connections to other trees. The diagram, they said, looked like an airline route map. Through the networks, the trees may share information about gravity, moisture, light, pressure, volume, gases, salts, microbes and potential danger, and plants receiving the information may change the direction of their growth, restrain their growth, or pass on warnings to other plants.

Still, sceptics of plant intelligence find ammunition in the bizarre pseudoscientific experiments that abound, such as the one done on a carrot tied down to an examining table by the respected botanist and biologist Sir Jagandish Chandra Bose. Bose, after noting that a machine connected to the carrot registered 'twitches, starts and tremors', concluded, 'Thus can science reveal the feelings of even so stolid a vegetable as the carrot.' Even more provocative was the work of Cleve Backster, a former CIA operative turned lie detector instructor, who connected a polygraph machine to a leaf of the houseplant in his office. Backster found out that when he deliberately thought about setting the plant on fire, the machine registered a surge of activity. This led him to the conclusion that not only can plants think, but they can also read minds. In another experiment, he recruited five volunteers and instructed one of them to root up, stomp on, and destroy one of two plants in a room. Later, Backster allowed the volunteers to enter, one by one, and claimed that polygraph metre 'went wild' when the perpetrator entered the room, leading him to declare that the surviving plant had identified the killer.

Regardless of whether plants are insightful or merely responding to environmental stimuli in a more primitive manner, the experimental evidence supports the idea that plants, like animals, are capable of habituation. But does this mean plants have brains? Words such as *feel*, *perceive*, *learn*, and *remember* are typically used for creatures with brains, and supporters must show that a brain, along with its neurons and synapses, is not necessary for knowledge. Stefano Mancuso, a leading figure in the field of 'plant neurobiology', states that 'if you are a plant, having a brain is not an advantage', and therefore we should stop thinking in terms of brain responses when it comes to plant intelligence. Thus, adherents like Mancuso continue to conduct research in hopes of one day conclusively proving that other ways of processing stimuli and information, such as with special cells and cell networks, and electrical or chemical signals, are indeed clear indicators of some form of intelligence among plants.

Questions 1-6

Look at the following statements (Questions 1-6) and the list of researchers below.

Match each statement with the correct researcher, **A-E**.

NB You may use any letter more than once.

1   Plant adaptation should not be confused with learning.

2   Trees position themselves to promote sharing and protection.

3   Plants can identify someone who had done a violent act.

4   Plants' recall of events in a previous experiment suggests some form of memory.

5   It is misleading to think of plant intelligence in terms of brains.

6   Plants can understand people's thoughts.

List of Researchers

A   Suzanne Simard
B   Cleve Backster
C   Stefano Mancuso
D   Monica Gagliano
E   Fred Sack

Complete the summary using the list of words, **A-I**, below.

Testing for Intelligence in Plants

Monica Gagliano's team set out to test the intelligence of plants through their responses to danger. They chose the mimosa plant because it has developed an **7** .... through which it counters threats by folding its leaves. The team tested this by pushing the plants down a **8** .... The fall was not harmful, but the plants did fold their leaves when they were dropped.

However, Gagliano's team was focused on the question of intelligence, and did not want to simply test the plant's immediate **9** .... This exercise was therefore repeated to see if the plants would recollect their **10** .... and understand that it was not harmful. Eventually the plant's leaves stopped closing, allowing Gagliano to conclude that the plants had learned that this was not a danger.

A stairs	**B** injury	**C** memory
D adaptation	**E** reaction	**F** adoption
G foam	**H** experience	**I** rail

Questions 11-13

Do the following statements agree with the information given in Reading Passage?

Write

TRUE	if the statement agrees with the information
FALSE	if the statement contradicts the information
NOT GIVEN	if there is no information on this

11 The claims of Tompkins and Bird caused controversy among scientists.

12 Some readers who owned plants agreed with the ideas in the Tompkins-Bird book.

13 When connected to a polygraph machine, plants gave no response to a given stimulus.

정답·해석·해설 p.416

VOCABULARY LIST

Chapter 07에서 선별한 다음의 어휘들을 음성파일을 들으며 암기한 후 퀴즈로 확인해보세요.

*해커스 동영상강의 포털 해커스 인강(HackersIngang.com)에서 단어암기 MP3를 무료로 다운로드할 수 있습니다.

- [ ] **powerhouse** n. 강국
- [ ] **cargo** n. 화물
- [ ] **shipping** n. 운송, 선적
- [ ] **mirror** v. 모방하다
- [ ] **simultaneous** adj. 동시의
- [ ] **instantaneous** adj. 즉각적인
- [ ] **universality** n. 보편성
- [ ] **contest** v. 이의를 제기하다
- [ ] **convergent** adj. 융합의
- [ ] **overarching** adj. 중요한
- [ ] **vulnerability** n. 취약(성)
- [ ] **ambush** n. 매복 공격
- [ ] **prolong** v. 연장하다
- [ ] **repellent** n. 퇴치제
- [ ] **aversion** n. 반감, 혐오감
- [ ] **ferment** v. 발효하다
- [ ] **tonic** n. 강장제
- [ ] **concoction** n. 혼합물
- [ ] **ease** v. 완화하다
- [ ] **seasickness** n. 뱃멀미
- [ ] **crescent** n. 초승달 (모양)
- [ ] **a bounty of** phr. 풍부한
- [ ] **temple** n. 사원
- [ ] **column** n. 기둥
- [ ] **retelling** n. 개작된 이야기
- [ ] **fortification** n. 요새

- [ ] **call into question** phr. 이의를 제기하다
- [ ] **cluster** n. 무리, 집단
- [ ] **come together** phr. 합쳐지다
- [ ] **preadolescent** adj. 사춘기 이전의
- [ ] **docile** adj. 유순한
- [ ] **amenable** adj. 순종적인, 말을 잘 듣는
- [ ] **impulsivity** n. 충동
- [ ] **instability** n. 불안, 불안정
- [ ] **pronounce** v. 두드러지게 나타나다
- [ ] **date back** phr. (~로) 거슬러 올라가다
- [ ] **respiratory system** phr. 호흡기관
- [ ] **reflex** n. 반사 작용(운동)
- [ ] **fatigued** adj. 피로한
- [ ] **at hand** phr. 눈앞에 있는, 가까이에 있는
- [ ] **perk up** phr. 기운을 차리다
- [ ] **follow suit** phr. 따라 하다
- [ ] **autism** n. 자폐
- [ ] **attentiveness** n. 경각심, 조심성
- [ ] **capitalise** v. ~을 활용하다
- [ ] **overlook** v. 간과하다
- [ ] **autonomous** adj. 자율적인, 자주적인
- [ ] **primate** n. 영장류
- [ ] **contend** v. 주장하다
- [ ] **consciously** adv. 의식적으로
- [ ] **modify** v. 변형하다, 수정하다
- [ ] **literal** adj. 문자 그대로의

Quiz

각 단어의 알맞은 뜻을 찾아 연결하시오.

01 ease	ⓐ 동시의	06 pronounce	ⓐ 의식적으로
02 aversion	ⓑ 모방하다	07 follow suit	ⓑ 주장하다
03 mirror	ⓒ 연장하다	08 cluster	ⓒ 두드러지게 나타나다
04 simultaneous	ⓓ 완화하다	09 contend	ⓓ 따라 하다
05 prolong	ⓔ 요새	10 consciously	ⓔ 무리, 집단
	ⓕ 반감, 혐오감		ⓕ 간과하다

ⓐ 01 ⓕ 02 ⓑ 03 ⓐ 04 ⓒ 05 ⓒ 06 ⓓ 07 ⓔ 08 ⓑ 09 ⓐ 10

☐ passive adj. 수동적인

☐ alter v. 바꾸다

☐ accompanying adj. 수반되는

☐ emblem n. 상징

☐ lexical adj. 어휘적인, 어휘의

☐ longstanding adj. 오랜 세월 동안의

☐ rhetoric n. 수사

☐ adherent n. 신자, 지지자

☐ garner v. 수집하다, 모으다

☐ accentuate v. 강조하다

☐ detective n. 탐정, 형사

☐ black or white phr. 이분법적인

☐ infallible adj. 잘못이 전혀 없는, 절대 옳은

☐ refute v. 반박하다

☐ formula n. 공식

☐ plotline n. 줄거리

☐ archetype n. 전형

☐ improvisation n. 즉흥 요소, 즉석에서 만든 것

☐ wrongdoer n. 범법자

☐ perpetrator n. 범죄자

☐ ponder v. 생각하다, 숙고하다

☐ walks of life phr. 계층, 직업

☐ suspenseful adj. 긴장감이 넘치는

☐ draw n. 마음을 끄는 요소

☐ academics n. 학계, 학자

☐ famine n. 기근

☐ intergroup adj. 집단 간의

☐ respectively adv. 각각

☐ bear out phr. 지지하다, 옳음을 증명하다

☐ mount v. 고조되다, (서서히) 증가하다

☐ perish v. 사망하다

☐ starvation n. 기아, 굶주림

☐ reductive adj. 환원주의적인

☐ fractionalise v. 분열하다, 분해하다

☐ clan n. 집단, 무리

☐ dispute n. 분쟁

☐ uproar n. 엄청난 논란, 대소동

☐ discredit v. 신용하지 않다

☐ interval n. 간격

☐ akin adj. ~과 유사한

☐ conflate v. 혼합하다, 융합하다

☐ sceptic n. 회의론자

☐ ammunition n. 공격 수단, 탄약

☐ bizarre adj. 이상한, 별난

☐ abound v. 많이 있다, 풍부하다

☐ twitch n. 경련

☐ start n. 놀라움, 움찔함

☐ tremor n. 떨림

☐ provocative adj. 도발적인, 화나게 하는

☐ root up phr. 뿌리째 뽑다

☐ stomp on phr. 짓밟다

☐ habituation n. 습관화

Quiz

각 단어의 알맞은 뜻을 찾아 연결하시오.

01 accentuate   ⓐ 반박하다
02 passive   ⓑ 바꾸다
03 alter   ⓒ 기근
04 academics   ⓓ 수동적인
05 refute   ⓔ 강조하다
     ⓕ 학계, 학자

06 interval   ⓐ 이상한, 별난
07 provocative   ⓑ 각각
08 dispute   ⓒ 신용하지 않다
09 discredit   ⓓ 분쟁
10 respectively   ⓔ 간격
     ⓕ 도발적인, 화나게 하는

ⓑ 01   ⓓ 02   ⓑ 03   ⓕ 04   ⓐ 05   ⓔ 06   ⓕ 07   ⓓ 08   ⓒ 09   ⓑ 10

CHAPTER
08   Matching Information

Matching information 문제는 제시된 정보를 읽고 그 정보를 포함하는 단락을 고르는 문제이다. 매 시험 출제되지
는 않지만 자주 출제되고 있다.

■■ 문제 형태

Matching information 문제는 주어진 지문에서 문제에 제시된 내용을 포함하고 있는 단락을 찾아, 해당 단락의 알파벳을 적는
형태로 출제된다. 문제에는 어떤 사실에 대한 언급, 설명, 예시 등 지문의 특정 부분에 포함된 정보가 무엇인지 서술한 내용이 제
시된다. 지문에는 간혹 하나 이상의 단락이 함께 묶여 하나의 알파벳으로 표시되기도 한다.

Reading Passage 1 has nine paragraphs, **A-I**.

Which paragraph contains the following information?

*Write the correct letter, **A-I**, in boxes 1-3 on your answer sheet.*

* **NB** *You may use any letter more than once.*

1   a reason that unusual sharks are increasing

2   an explanation for why sharks have drastically decreased in number

3   mention of why inbreeding is rare in sharks

---

*문제의 개수와 단락의 개수는 항상 일치하지는 않는다. 이런 경우 정답으로 사용되지 않거나 한 번 이상 정답으로 사용되는 단락이 있을 수 있다.
한 번 이상 정답으로 사용되는 보기가 있는 경우에는 **NB** *You may use any letter more than once*라는 지시문이 주어진다.

STEP 1 문제의 핵심 내용을 확인하고, 핵심어구를 파악한다.

(1) 문제를 읽고 지문에서 찾아야 하는 정보의 내용을 파악한다.

(2) 문제의 핵심어구를 파악한다.

EXAMPLE

Reading Passage has nine paragraphs, **A-I**.

Which paragraph contains the following information?

*Write the correct letter, **A-I**, in box 1 on your answer sheet.*

1   a reason that unusual sharks are increasing ●————

(1) 비정상적인 상어가 증가하는 이유를 지문에서 찾아야 함을 파악한다.

(2) 문제에서 unusual sharks라는 핵심어구를 파악한다.

지문을 scanning하여 문제의 핵심어구와 관련된 내용을 찾는다. 관련 내용이 언급된 주변에서 문제의 핵심 내용에 관한 정보가 등장하는지 확인한다.

EXAMPLE

A Although mutated animals are not unheard of in nature, the number of two-headed sharks discovered recently is much higher than expected – at least five have been found in the last ten years. In addition, researcher Valentin Sans-Coma has even found one in an egg-laying shark species for the first time ever. These discoveries have left scientists puzzled.

B Because they are still relatively rare, it is difficult to pinpoint one definitive cause of the mutation. However, [1]one unique explanation blames the increasing number of mutated sharks on overfishing. According to marine scientist Nicolas Ehemann, human fishing activity has led to a dramatic decrease in the number of sharks in the ocean, and therefore a smaller gene pool. He contends that this has led to more inbreeding resulting in more genetic abnormalities.

문제의 핵심어구인 unusual sharks 와 관련된 내용을 지문에서 찾는다. 관련 내용이 언급된 주변인 'one unique explanation blames the increasing number of mutated sharks on overfishing'에서 증가하고 있는 돌연변이 상어 수에 관한 정보가 등장함을 확인한다.

⋮

Reading Passage has nine paragraphs, **A-I**.

Which paragraph contains the following information?

*Write the correct letter, **A-I**, in box 1 on your answer sheet.*

1   a reason that unusual sharks are increasing

지문 해석 p.420

관련 내용이 언급된 주변에서 정답의 단서가 등장하는 것이 맞는지 확인한 뒤, 올바른 단락을 정답으로 적는다.

EXAMPLE

A Although mutated animals are not unheard of in nature, the number of two-headed sharks discovered recently is much higher than expected – at least five have been found in the last ten years. In addition, researcher Valentin Sans-Coma has even found one in an egg-laying shark species for the first time ever. These discoveries have left scientists puzzled.

B Because they are still relatively rare, it is difficult to pinpoint one definitive cause of the mutation. However, [1]one unique explanation blames the increasing number of mutated sharks on overfishing. According to marine scientist Nicolas Ehemann, human fishing activity has led to a dramatic decrease in the number of sharks in the ocean, and therefore a smaller gene pool. He contends that this has led to more inbreeding resulting in more genetic abnormalities.

> 돌연변이 상어가 증가하는 이유가 남획 때문이라는 정답의 단서를 확인한다.

⋮

Reading Passage has nine paragraphs, **A-I**.

Which paragraph contains the following information?

*Write the correct letter, **A-I**, in box 1 on your answer sheet.*

1 a reason that unusual sharks are increasing **B**

> 단락 B에서 비정상적인 상어가 증가하는 이유를 언급하고 있으므로, 정답은 B이다. 'mutated sharks'가 'unusual sharks'로 paraphrasing 되었다.

1

A Today, there are more than 350 extant species of parrots. These intelligent birds come in a variety of sizes and vibrant colours. While they are prized as pets around the world for their ability to mimic speech, they are not always as beloved in their native lands.

B One good example of this is Australia, which is home to the sulphur-crested cockatoo, a large parrot with vivid yellow feathers on its head. These birds move in large flocks and have become a nuisance to local inhabitants. Not only do their chatter and pre-dawn calls disturb humans, but they are also very destructive. Local farmers and homeowners often complain that they are decimating crops and destroying timber used in homebuilding by chewing on it. They are also expanding their territory, which displaces other native bird species.

C To address these problems, sulphur-crested cockatoos have been declared a pest species in some areas. This prevents them from being imported into new areas and puts regulations on their ownership. In some regions, there are also regular culls to keep the populations in check and to prevent them from damaging the local ecosystem. While these policies may have an impact, it is unclear whether they will resolve the issue.

The reading passage has three paragraphs, **A-C**.

Which paragraph contains the following information?

1 a reference to a banning a bird species from certain areas

2 details of how parrots impact humans in terms of noise

---

extant adj. 현존하는 vibrant adj. 선명한, 강렬한 mimic v. 따라 하다 sulphur-crested cockatoo phr. 큰유황앵무 nuisance n. 골칫거리
chatter n. 재잘거림 decimate v. 훼손하다, 대량으로 죽이다 displace v. 쫓아내다 pest n. 유해 동물 cull n. (노쇠한 가축 등을) 추려내기, 추려서 죽이는 것

2　**A**　German alchemist Hennig Brandt made an important discovery in the mid-1600s. By evaporating urine and heating the resulting residue, he distilled a new vapour, which he thought to be the Philosopher's Stone – a substance with which he could turn base metals into gold. Unfortunately for Brandt, the Philosopher's Stone was just a myth and what he had actually discovered was one form of the element phosphorus.

　　B　Through later experimentation, scientists made additional discoveries about the different forms of Brandt's mineral. For instance, in its purest state, white phosphorous, the mineral is so combustible that it will burst into flames if it comes into contact with air, so it must be kept underwater. Also, it can only be handled with tools, as it is toxic and can cause severe burns. These properties may make white phosphorous seem useless, but they actually make it important in one field – munitions. Several incendiary weapons have been developed using this form of the element.

　　C　For most other uses, white phosphorous must be converted into the more stable red form by heating. The red phosphorous will not spontaneously ignite like the white form, but it is not without its dangers, such as producing toxic vapours when heated. Nonetheless, its use is quite common. We can see this in our own homes. The red material on the head of matches is a form of red phosphorous. Red phosphorous can also be ground into a powder and used as a fertiliser.

The reading passage has three paragraphs, **A-C**.

Which paragraph contains the following information?

3　　a description of the dangers of combining a chemical with air

4　　a reference to the agricultural uses of a form of phosphorus

CH 08

Matching Information　HACKERS **IELTS** READING

---

residue n. 잔여물　distill v. 증류하다　vapour n. 기화 물질, 증기　base metal phr. 비금속　phosphorus n. 인
combustible adj. 가연성이 있는, 불이 붙기 쉬운　munition n. 군수품　incendiary adj. 방화의　spontaneously adv. 저절로, 자발적으로
ignite v. 불이 붙다, 점화하다

3 **A** Carbon is found all around us today – in the air, the earth, and in all living things – but it is neither created nor destroyed. This is due to a process called the carbon cycle. About 99 per cent of Earth's carbon is trapped in the rocks of its crust, but through this process, it is slowly released into the atmosphere. Plants can then take in the carbon, as carbon dioxide, for photosynthesis and pass it along to animals when it is consumed. Eventually, as these animals die and their bodies decompose, the carbon is returned to the soil.

B An often-overlooked aspect of the carbon cycle is that oceans are a highly significant factor in determining the level of carbon in the atmosphere. Our oceans act as large carbon sinks, or storage units. This occurs because carbon dioxide enters the ocean from the atmosphere, undergoes a chemical reaction, and becomes trapped there. Unfortunately, since the Industrial Revolution, the burning of fossil fuels has greatly increased the amount of carbon dioxide we release into the atmosphere, while the oceans' ability to take in more carbon dioxide has remained the same. This is resulting in a build-up of carbon dioxide in the atmosphere and leading to higher global temperatures.

C The increased carbon dioxide levels in the oceans since the Industrial Revolution are also leading to problems for marine life. The chemical reactions that occur as carbon dioxide is dissolved into the seawater lowers the pH level of water at the surface. This acidification slows the growth of microscopic marine life such as plankton and coral. These tiny organisms form the base of the marine food web, so the acidification can have a negative impact on the entire system. And, since we also rely on the marine food web, our food supply is threatened as well.

The reading passage has three paragraphs, **A-C**.

Which paragraph contains the following information?

5   a reason why one process can influence a whole system

6   the role of oceans in the carbon-cycle

7   how carbon gets put back into the earth

---

crust n. 지각 photosynthesis n. 광합성 decompose v. 분해되다, 부패되다 often-overlooked adj. 자주 간과되는
carbon sink phr. 이산화탄소 흡수계(지구 온난화를 줄이는 데 도움이 되는 넓은 삼림 지대) build-up n. 축적, 증가 dissolve v. 용해하다
pH level phr. 피에이치 수치 acidification n. 산성화 microscopic adj. 미세한

4 **A** With today's aging population, the debate over seniors in the workforce has begun to heat up. Some people believe that their prolonged place in the workforce can be harmful to society. Others think senior employment can have positive consequences for social cohesion and economic growth.

B Those who oppose employing seniors past the current age of retirement generally cite the argument that an aging workforce is less productive, as health issues and a lack of technical abilities limit the capacity of the elderly to do certain jobs. Although this may be the case with the very elderly, in the United States the current generation of over 60s is highly educated and relatively healthy, particularly in comparison to previous generations.

C Others complain that it is too difficult to train seniors. They say, 'you can't teach an old dog new tricks'. However, this too is a misleading argument. Seniors have a wealth of experience which, with the right management, can be highly effective in the proper context. Many already have applicable skills that can be useful in the job market and are well-versed in the activities of the business world, eliminating the need for training altogether.

D One argument against senior employment that does have some validity is the fact that they reduce the number of jobs available in the market place. For every job that a senior is given, one job is unavailable for a younger person. While this is true, the jobs seniors and younger people generally look for are quite different. Instead of taking a job, they're usually filling a job that no one else wants, so it is clear that there is little reason to avoid hiring seniors. In fact, it will likely have a positive impact on both the senior and the employer. It will also reduce the need for seniors to rely upon social security programs or pensions, thereby saving money for the entire society.

The reading passage has four paragraphs, **A-D**.

Which paragraph contains the following information?

NB You may use any letter more than once.

8   a claim about possible benefits to employers and workers

9   a reason why training may not be needed

10   one effect of senior employment on welfare

---

workforce n. 노동 인구 prolonged adj. 장기적인, 오래 계속되는 social cohesion phr. 사회적 결속력 cite v. 인용하다 misleading adj. 오해의 소지가 있는 proper adj. 적절한 context n. 상황, 배경 applicable adj. 적절한, 들어맞는 well-versed adj. 조예가 깊은, 정통한 eliminate v. 제거하다, 없애다 validity n. 타당성 pension n. 연금

A As every teacher knows, the ability of any group of students of the same age usually does not vary tremendously. Occasionally however, a student will be so talented that he or she is dramatically out of step with his or her classmates across many subjects, and this can have a disruptive effect on both the student's progress and that of the class. In these situations the obvious strategy is to allow such a student to advance a year. However, this is not necessarily the best practice, and some advocate for challenging gifted students within their year group. The debate over what is the best approach is known as 'acceleration vs. enrichment' among education professionals.

B Acceleration to a higher year, whilst superficially the simplest solution in terms of handling gifted students, can in fact hold them back as they will inevitably miss out on skills that they would have learned in a given year. The students in question can also suffer from intense pressure on account of acceleration, as they struggle to acclimatise to a new peer group and set of expectations. The separation from their social group, and the emotional support it offers, is also a major concern.

C Enrichment on the other hand, can be more difficult to put in place, as this involves providing opportunities for students to stretch themselves within their original class. Teachers are therefore expected to generate an enrichment programme that will match the strengths and skills of the gifted students, and allow them to take on advanced work while maintaining a connection with their peer group so that they can continue to engage socially with other students of the same age.

D Studies have shown that the most effective strategy for dealing with talented students is to combine a measure of acceleration in certain subjects with enrichment in others. This necessitates a programme which is tailored for the student in question, and will play to his or her strengths and weaknesses. In actual fact, the fundamental problem with dealing with talented students in many countries, including the UK, is not which approach to choose out of acceleration and enrichment but that neither is available, and students are forced to learn in what educational researcher Maureen Marron calls a rigid 'lock-step manner' with their age group.

The reading passage has four paragraphs, **A-D**.

Which paragraph contains the following information?

11 a reference to the effect gifted students can have on their classmates

12 a mention of a shortage of options for talented students

13 how teachers can help talented students succeed within their peer group

---

disruptive adj. 지장을 주는, 파괴적인 advocate v. 지지하다, 옹호하다 acceleration n. 월반, 특별 진급 enrichment n. 심화학습
superficially adv. 표면적으로 inevitably adv. 불가피하게 in question phr. 논의가 되고 있는, 문제의 acclimatise v. 적응하다, 익숙해지다
put in place phr. 시행하다 tailor v. 맞추다, 맞게 하다 lock-step adj. 융통성이 없는

A The indigenous communities of the United States' Pacific Northwest practised a ceremonial distribution of property, known as the potlatch, to rid themselves of spiritual burdens brought about by ownership of material objects. These communal events usually centred on a large feast to reflect the bounty of the hunting season. These feasts featured large amounts of salmon or seal meat, along with other foods, and were usually attended by community elders, faith healers, and visitors from great distances. In honour of these respected guests, the hosts served the meals on special hand-carved and painted platters that were much more ornate than those used for everyday situations.

B The potlatch was also celebrated with song and dance. These activities were meant to honour relatives, celebrate relationships and give thanks for abundant harvests. Since the dances were each performed by individual families, they also provided them with the opportunity to display their unique heritage. In addition, some of the singers and dancers wore masks depicting supernatural beings throughout the potlatch. These were meant to honour the beings that had bestowed the song and dance upon the particular family.

C However, perhaps the most important aspect of the potlatch was gift giving. This act not only showed generosity, but also allowed the tribe members to relinquish material possessions. By doing this, they could repay debts, show appreciation for help, and ensure continued relationships. All of these activities reinforced the communal values of the society. The tribe members would, therefore, trade canoes, blankets, and other items. If they happened to be too big to move or too valuable, they were simply destroyed.

D Despite the great cultural importance of these events, the European governments of the American colonies did not appreciate them. In order to force the tribe members to assimilate into their new societies, the governments banned the practice. This didn't, of course, eradicate the ceremonies. They were simply performed in secret until the ban was lifted in the mid-1900s.

The reading passage has four paragraphs, **A-D**.

Which paragraph contains the following information?

NB You may use any letter more than once.

14   how indigenous people handled restrictions on their customs

15   an example of a way of celebrating the hunting season's yield

16   a mention of visitors travelling from far away

---

indigenous adj. 토착의   communal adj. 공동의   bounty n. 풍부함, 포상금   faith healer phr. 기도 치료사   ornate adj. 화려하게 장식된
depict v. 묘사하다, 그리다   supernatural adj. 초자연적인   bestow v. 부여하다, 수여하다   relinquish v. 내주다, 포기하다
appreciate v. 인정하다, 가치를 알다   assimilate v. 동화하다   eradicate v. 근절시키다, 뿌리째 뽑다

7   Disappearing Lions

A   Lions, which once roamed large expanses of Europe, began to dwindle in number during the end of the last ice age when climate change altered the landscape. Formerly, vast steppes – flat grassland areas – covered the continent, making it easy for lions to spot and capture their prey. But as the environment grew warmer and tall forests grew, other animals became far more difficult to hunt. With food harder to come by, it was impossible for lions to sustain their former numbers.

B   There were, however, occasional sightings of lions in southern Europe during historic times. According to ancient Greek historian Herodotus, the big cats could be found between the Achelos and Nestos rivers. As this is a relatively small geographical area, the species was probably already on its way to disappearing from the region at this time, with its demise no doubt hastened by the Greeks' love of sport hunting and the Romans' demand for beasts to fight in their arenas.

C   As for Africa, lions survived in significant numbers until the 19th century, when they began to vanish due to human population growth. Because machinery allowed people to access the wilderness, human contact with lions increased dramatically and so did the number of lions that were shot or poisoned with chemical pesticides. In fact, the lion population decreased by about 95 per cent in less than 200 years. Of the approximately 30,000 currently left on the continent, nearly all are in sub-Sahara and many face habitat repurposing, conflicts with farmers, and loss of prey due to the trade in bushmeat among humans. Given that the human population of this region is expected to double by the year 2050, the future for lions looks bleak.

D   The situation for lions in Asia is even worse. The sole surviving Asiatic lion population now lives in India's Gir National Park. Despite their protected status, the few hundred that live there are in severe danger because they are highly inbred, being descendants of only about a dozen lions. This makes them genetically weak and vulnerable to disease; if a contagious illness were to spread, many of the lions would perish, and their numbers might fall to unrecoverable levels.

E   With Asiatic lions being officially critically endangered and their African counterparts earning a recent endangered species listing by the U.S. Fish and Wildlife Service, it is clear that conservationist groups want to protect the big cats from extinction. While their efforts are to be admired, the reality is that the future of lions and the potential reversal of the patterns leading to their demise thus far will depend on a commitment to lions' protection on an international level.

The reading passage has five paragraphs, **A-E**.

Which paragraph contains the following information?

NB *You may use any letter more than once.*

17 a mention of when lion numbers began to fall in Africa

18 a reference to the use of lions for human entertainment purposes

19 an example of something which might wipe out one type of lion

20 the reason for the loss of lions' food supply today

---

roam v. 거닐다, 배회하다 **expanse** n. 넓게 트인 지역, 광활한 장소 **dwindle** v. 줄어들다 **alter** v. 바꾸다 **steppe** n. (특히 유럽 동남부·시베리아의) 스텝 지대
come by phr. 구하다, 얻다 **sighting** n. 목격 **big cat** phr. (사자·호랑이 등과 같은) 대형 고양이과 동물 **demise** n. 종말, 죽음 **hasten** v. 앞당기다, 재촉하다
repurpose v. 용도를 변경하다 **bushmeat** n. (음식 재료로 쓰는) 야생 동물 고기 **bleak** adj. 암울한, 절망적인 **inbred** adj. (동식물이) 근친 교배한
descendant n. 자손, 후예 **genetically** adv. 유전적으로 **perish** v. 죽다 **Fish and Wildlife Service** phr. 어류 및 야생동물관리국 **reversal** n. 전환, 반전
commitment n. 약속, 헌신

8 Language and Dialect

A   If two speakers can understand each other despite using different expressions, slang, and accents, do they speak the same language? That's a question that has long plagued sociolinguists, who struggle to define exactly what differentiates a language from a dialect, a regionally specific type of speaking that is related to a more formally recognised one. There are, of course, several views on how one is distinguished from the other and how language varieties are related.

B   Some linguists believe historical origins are significant, viewing any speech form that is derived from an older variety of communication as being a dialect. By this notion, modern Romance languages, such as French and Italian, would be dialects deriving from Latin. But this view is somewhat flawed as although these languages may have come from the same tongue, they are now quite far removed from each other and are not necessarily mutually comprehensible. In other words, Italian speakers and French speakers may not be able to understand one another as their respective vernaculars bear little resemblance. Likewise, they would not find it beneficial to consult the same linguistic authority to solve a language usage issue. This means that though the Romance languages were initially dialects of Latin that shared various similarities, they have evolved over time – due to the migration of various groups throughout Europe – and are now considered separate official languages rather than dialects.

C   Meanwhile, a more pertinent way of designating a type of speech as a language is to see whether it is officially recognised, which means it is used in official government correspondence, has its own grammar, and is taught in schools. But does this 'official' recognition truly distinguish between languages and dialects? The fact is that some recognised languages seem quite a bit like dialects given their undeniable similarities to languages used in geographically distant locations. But when distinct languages do happen to share almost the same vocabulary and grammar, with only a few exceptions that mostly appear in slang and idiomatic expressions, they are said to be 'standard forms' rather than regionally specific dialects.

D   One language for which this is true is English, for which there are various standard forms, including British, American, Canadian, and Australian. Vocabulary, speech patterns, and even spelling vary among each of these languages. For instance, Canadians say, 'I have a new car', while the British say, 'I've got a new car'. Meanwhile, the speech of an Australian is extremely different from that of an American – even though each would understand the other. As the various forms of English used throughout the world are in fact traced back to British English, which itself has Germanic roots, wouldn't all forms of English be dialects given that all Anglophones can more or less understand one another? It seems not. Since they are recognised by the governments of their respective countries and have their own standardised writing systems, the status of each is elevated to that of 'language.'

E   Ultimately, attempting to find a satisfying distinction for language and dialect is a challenge as they both enable communication, which is universal. The languages and dialects we use today will change over time, as all forms of speech before them have, and some will fall out of use while others will be adopted by large portions of the population. For now, it may just be best to agree that if two people hailing from different areas of this world of more than 7,000 languages can understand each other reasonably well, they can communicate just fine.

The reading passage has five paragraphs, **A-E**.

Which paragraph contains the following information?

NB *You may use any letter more than once.*

21   an example of a modern language with various forms

22   a statement about the potential future of languages and dialects

23   an explanation of how a language developed into various languages

24   how history could help define a dialect

9   Antibiotic Resistance on the Rise

A   A legacy of decades of overuse, antibiotic resistance is spreading across the globe and has been recognised by professionals as one of the most dangerous threats to global health and development. Antibiotic resistance arises when bacteria mutate and become impervious to the effects of antibiotics, either through genetic mutation or through a gradual build-up of resistance. The bacteria that emerge are extremely difficult to treat, and in some cases no medicines exist to counter them. This is becoming such a pressing problem that the World Health Organisation has described it as 'one of the biggest threats to global health', and has introduced a global action plan in an attempt to counter it.

B   Antibiotic resistance emerged because of decades of misuse due to the widespread availability and a lack of education about the capabilities of these drugs. This was exacerbated by the unregulated sale of antibiotic drugs over the counter, without a doctor's prescription. It is estimated that around half of antibiotic use is unnecessary. For example, many people take antibiotics for the common cold even though they have no impact on viruses. The overuse of antibiotics causes the development of stronger bacteria, as antibiotics kill off all the weak bacteria, allowing the stronger strains to multiply and develop immunity to the drugs that are designed to treat them.

C   These strains of bacteria are known as multidrug resistant, or superbugs, and are a major health risk throughout the world. It is estimated that millions die every year from these drug resistant bacteria, and the number of infections that are untreatable is growing. A few common bacterial infections, including pneumonia, E. coli, and gonorrhea, are now developing immunity to antibiotics and researchers are struggling to find alternative treatments. It has been predicted that, if uncontrolled, antibiotic resistant bacteria will kill up to 300 million people by 2050.

D   It is not just misuse in humans that contributes to antibiotic resistance but also excessive prescription for animals. It is estimated that 80 per cent of antibiotics sold in the United States are given to animals, and they are generally not given to sick animals. Indeed, it is often standard practice in large farms to mix antibiotics with general feed to improve the animals' health and well-being. As with humans, this acts as a catalyst for the development of drug resistant bacteria, which can spread into food products and infect humans.

E   The fight against antibiotic resistance is a global health priority, and research laboratories around the world are working on solutions to the issue. Developing new types of antibiotics is no longer a feasible option, as the drug resistant strains of bacteria are appearing at such a rate that countering them directly with new antibiotics is impossible. However, there has been a recent breakthrough that could be significant; scientists have discovered a molecule that reverses antibiotic resistance in multiple strains of bacteria. This could allow doctors to use medicines that are currently thought to be useless. This molecule has yet to be tested on humans, so it is still at an early stage of development. It may nonetheless be the best hope against this increasing global health threat.

The reading passage has five paragraphs, **A-E**.

Which paragraph contains the following information?

25　an account of how food could be infected with drug resistant bacteria

26　a mention of the purchase of medicine without consulting a doctor

27　a reference to a possible new treatment

28　a statement about the number of people whose lives might be at risk

29　an account of how a global body has responded to this issue

---

antibiotic resistance　phr. (세균의) 항생 물질에 대한 내성　overuse　n. 남용　mutate　v. 변형되다　impervious　adj. 영향받지 않는　build-up　n. 증가, 축적
counter　v. 대응하다　pressing　adj. 긴급한, 절박한　exacerbate　v. 악화시키다　over the counter　phr. 처방전 없이 (살 수 있는)　prescription　n. 처방전
strain　n. 변종, 변형　immunity　n. 면역력　superbug　n. 슈퍼버그(항생제로 쉽게 제거되지 않는 박테리아)　pneumonia　n. 폐렴　E. coli　phr. 대장균
gonorrhea　n. 임질　standard practice　phr. 흔한 일, 보통 사례　catalyst　n. 촉매(제), 자극　feasible　adj. 실현 가능한, 있음직한　molecule　n. 분자

10   The Survival of Coral Reefs

A   In the tropical and subtropical regions of three major oceans – the Pacific, Atlantic and Indian – there is an abundance of coral reefs of varying sizes. They lie no deeper than 200 feet below the ocean surface, for corals require sufficient sunlight, clear water, the presence of zooxanthellae or algae, and a temperature range of 17 to 34 degrees Celsius in order to thrive. Due to these specific ecological requirements, coral reefs are mostly found in areas where shallow submarine platforms occur in the Earth's southern hemisphere.

B   When the required conditions are met, corals can grow into massive structures. Living organisms, particularly the coral polyp, secrete calcium carbonate to create the hard exoskeleton of the coral. In time, coral colonies form a reef, a highly interconnected ecosystem of great diversity. As a reef grows, a complex system of mutual cooperation and symbiosis develops among many of the organisms that inhabit the corals. It is not an overstatement to say that corals are critical for the survival of numerous marine organisms. In fact, many describe coral reefs as the 'rainforests of the seas', and like rainforests, if destroyed, the organisms that depend on them either become endangered or are eliminated.

C   In the past few decades, scientists have discovered that corals are also important to humans in many ways. They not only provide a crucial ecosystem for ocean life, but they also remove carbon dioxide from the air and shelter land from ocean storms. Moreover, coral reefs attract tourists, providing employment valued at around 375 billion dollars annually. Despite the value of corals to humanity and their importance in maintaining the health of the oceans, they are increasingly at risk of destruction from human activity.

D   Research studies indicate that the primary dangers to coral reefs are all related to human activity. When ocean waters become too warm, for example, due to global warming, corals expel the zooxanthellae living in their tissues. This causes the corals to turn white in colour, a phenomenon known as coral bleaching. Although the coral is not dead at this point, its health is in serious jeopardy. The use of pesticides and fertilisers, chemical pollution, sedimentation, deforestation, and oil slicks, have also all taken a toll on the corals.

E   These threats are increasing from year to year, and this is having dramatic consequences for the health of the corals. A study concluded that about 70 per cent of the world's coral reefs were either being threatened or destroyed by human activity. Although some reefs have the potential for recovery, about 20 per cent have no hope of revival. Jamaica's reefs have been hit the hardest, and about 95 per cent of them have now been completely destroyed.

F   A report on Australia's Great Barrier Reef concluded that a decline in water quality was causing deterioration in the health of the reef. In response, the Australian government has made a great effort to protect the reef, with the result that its ecosystem is more likely to survive than reefs located in other areas. It remains to be seen whether politicians around the world have the will, or the means, to follow suit and halt the decline of coral reefs before it is too late.

The reading passage has six paragraphs, **A-F**.

Which paragraph contains the following information?

30 an example of a country where coral reefs have experienced widespread damage

31 a description of the relationship which develops among creatures who inhabit coral reefs

32 a reference to a successful conservation effort

33 a mention of a change in coral appearance

34 details of the conditions corals need to flourish

정답·해석·해설 p.420

coral reef phr. 산호초 subtropical adj. 아열대의 zooxanthellae n. 황록공생조류 algae n. 조류 submarine adj. 해저의, 해양의
platform n. 대지, 높은 지대 coral polyp phr. 산호충 secrete v. 분비하다 calcium carbonate phr. 탄산칼슘 exoskeleton n. 외골격
symbiosis n. 공생 inhabit v. 서식하다 shelter v. 보호하다 expel v. 방출하다 tissue n. (세포들로 이뤄진) 조직 bleaching n. 탈색
in jeopardy phr. 위기에 처한 sedimentation n. 퇴적 작용 oil slick phr. 유막, 기름띠 take a toll on phr. ~에 큰 피해를 주다
have consequences for phr. ~에 대해 영향을 미치다 revival n. 재생 follow suit phr. ~을 따르다 halt v. 중단시키다, 멈추다

READING PASSAGE

*You should spend about 20 minutes on **Questions 1-14**, which are based on Reading Passage below.*

Keeping Time: Clockmaking in Britain, Switzerland, and America

A Timepieces of various sorts have been in circulation since ancient times, but the history of the clock industry in the modern sense begins in the 18th century. Prior to then, clocks and watches were largely confined to the realms of wealthy hobbyists, and were only used to tell time in a crude way, but changes in transportation brought on by the Industrial Revolution made timekeeping a necessity and helped cement time consciousness in the minds of the masses.

B In design, production, and trade, Britain was the frontrunner in the modern clock industry. The British penchant for producing clocks known for their accuracy and portability was perfectly suited for the needs of a growing, mobile population, and the early development of the railroad in Britain provided a catalyst for its market hegemony in the first half of the 19th century. Because the safe and predictable operation of railways was highly dependent upon keeping track of time, clocks were posted at intervals throughout the railway system to allow engineers to synchronise their chronometers, and telegraph services would periodically wire times to stations throughout the railway system so that clocks could be continually adjusted for accuracy.

C While this helped prevent accidents and allowed railway companies to keep tighter schedules, it also helped travellers to anticipate arrivals, departures, and connections with greater precision. These developments underpinned a burgeoning awareness of the importance of time throughout society, prompting those with sufficient means to purchase pocket watches. Thus, train travel increased the demand for timepieces and bolstered the overall clock industry in the United Kingdom.

D However, there were drawbacks to the British system that would be exploited by competitors. Namely, the British market was solely devoted to handmade clocks, and avaricious craftsmen who profited from their esoteric skills viewed mechanisation as a threat and actively lobbied against the use of machinery to craft 'fake clocks'. As a result, British timepieces remained extremely costly to produce. But while the British were antagonistic toward mechanisation, this was not the case in Switzerland, where companies began to experiment with the automated manufacture of individual components, such as plates and wheels. By using machines to fashion some parts, Swiss timepieces could be fabricated more quickly and cheaply than British timepieces.

E But the Swiss did not submit to the allure of fully mechanised production. Instead, they adopted a flexible system whereby machines were used in the first stage of production to create semi-finished products, and highly skilled artisans were responsible for the final touches. This approach afforded the best of both worlds, as Swiss timepieces could be produced efficiently without sacrificing the diversity and quality of hand craftsmanship. State-of-the-art machinery and an expert and adaptable workforce allowed Swiss companies to respond quickly to fluctuations in market demand and consumer preferences, and Swiss timepieces, especially watches, gradually became synonymous with 'top quality' in the minds of buyers. Watches under the moniker 'Swiss made' fetched handsome prices in jewellers and other high-end shops both at home and abroad, and ultimately the Swiss overtook the British as the recognised industry leader and held that position for many years. Many Swiss-made timepieces ended up in US markets, where American clockmakers focused on quantity at the expense of quality.

F Although the United States lacked the sheer numbers of skilled craftsmen of their European counterparts, American artisans paved the way for inexpensive timepieces through perfecting the art of mass production. By 1815, Eli Terry, an engineer in Connecticut, was using water-powered mills to fabricate completely uniform and interchangeable parts that were ready to be assembled without any manipulation or fine tuning by skilled labourers. Consequently, his clocks could be produced quickly by apprentices without the need for journeymen. Understanding the commercial value of his undertakings, Terry attempted to safeguard his methods with patents, but his legal actions did not hold back the tide of competitors for long. Other companies followed suit and by the late 1800s, Americans were producing timepieces quickly and cheaply on a massive scale. In 1899, the Ingersoll Watch Company's 'Yankee' pocket watch sold for one dollar, and these dollar watches were coming off the assembly line on the order of eight thousand per day.

G The fact that the Americans could produce timepieces virtually anyone could afford had its advantages. American clocks and watches flooded the world market, eventually overtaking Swiss brands not only in sales but also in revenue. Between 1945 and 1970, the Swiss share of the global watch market plummeted from 80 to 42 per cent, and by 1970, two US watch companies, Timex and Bulova, ranked first in worldwide sales and total revenues, respectively.

CH 08

Matching Information   HACKERS **IELTS** READING

Questions 1-8

Reading passage has seven paragraphs, **A-G**.

Which paragraph contains the following information?

NB *You may use any letter more than once.*

1   contrasts between British and Swiss attitudes toward mechanisation

2   a reference to watches being restricted to one segment of society

3   mention of how an individual tried to legally protect his production process

4   examples of benefits that timekeeping provided for rail travellers

5   a description of changes in global market shares among watch companies

6   reasons why certain watches were recognised for their craftsmanship

7   a statement of how American mass production laid the foundation for cheaper timepieces

8   how timekeeping was maintained on early railway networks

Questions 9-14

Complete the notes below.

*Choose **NO MORE THAN TWO WORDS** from the passage for each answer.*

A Tale of Three Countries: The Clock Industry in England, Switzerland, and the United States

• British clocks were renowned for their 9 .... as well as their accuracy.

• British craftsmen saw 10 .... as a danger to their industry.

• Swiss watches were partly machine built but 11 .... supplied the final touches.

• Swiss watches were costly and could be found in high-end shops and 12 ....

• In America, 13 .... were used to make regular parts that were interchangeable.

• Eli Terry did not require journeymen, as his clocks were rapidly put together by 14 ....

정답·해석·해설 p.430

VOCABULARY LIST

Chapter 08에서 선별한 다음의 어휘들을 음성파일을 들으며 암기한 후 퀴즈로 확인해보세요.

*해커스 동영상강의 포털 해커스 인강(HackersIngang.com)에서 단어암기 MP3를 무료로 다운로드할 수 있습니다.

- [ ] **vibrant** adj. 선명한, 강렬한
- [ ] **mimic** v. 따라 하다
- [ ] **nuisance** n. 골칫거리
- [ ] **decimate** v. 훼손하다, 대량으로 죽이다
- [ ] **displace** v. 쫓아내다
- [ ] **residue** n. 잔여물
- [ ] **distill** v. 증류하다
- [ ] **vapour** n. 기화 물질, 증기
- [ ] **base metal** phr. 비금속
- [ ] **combustible** adj. 가연성이 있는, 불이 붙기 쉬운
- [ ] **ignite** v. 불이 붙다, 점화하다
- [ ] **crust** n. 지각
- [ ] **photosynthesis** n. 광합성
- [ ] **decompose** v. 분해되다, 부패되다
- [ ] **often-overlooked** adj. 자주 간과되는
- [ ] **build-up** n. 축적, 증가
- [ ] **dissolve** v. 용해하다
- [ ] **acidification** n. 산성화
- [ ] **workforce** n. 노동 인구
- [ ] **prolonged** adj. 장기적인, 오래 계속되는
- [ ] **social cohesion** phr. 사회적 결속력
- [ ] **cite** v. 인용하다
- [ ] **proper** adj. 적절한
- [ ] **context** n. 상황, 배경
- [ ] **applicable** adj. 적절한, 들어맞는
- [ ] **eliminate** v. 제거하다, 없애다

- [ ] **validity** n. 타당성
- [ ] **pension** n. 연금
- [ ] **superficially** adv. 표면적으로
- [ ] **inevitably** adv. 불가피하게
- [ ] **in question** phr. 논의가 되고 있는, 문제의
- [ ] **put in place** phr. 시행하다
- [ ] **tailor** v. 맞추다, 맞게 하다
- [ ] **indigenous** adj. 토착의
- [ ] **bounty** n. 풍부함, 포상금
- [ ] **ornate** adj. 화려하게 장식된
- [ ] **supernatural** adj. 초자연적인
- [ ] **bestow** v. 부여하다, 수여하다
- [ ] **relinquish** v. 내주다, 포기하다
- [ ] **appreciate** v. 인정하다, 가치를 알다
- [ ] **eradicate** v. 근절시키다, 뿌리째 뽑다
- [ ] **roam** v. 거닐다, 배회하다
- [ ] **expanse** n. 넓게 트인 지역, 광활한 장소
- [ ] **come by** phr. 구하다, 얻다
- [ ] **sighting** n. 목격
- [ ] **demise** n. 종말, 죽음
- [ ] **hasten** v. 앞당기다, 재촉하다
- [ ] **repurpose** v. 용도를 변경하다
- [ ] **bleak** adj. 암울한, 절망적인
- [ ] **inbred** adj. (동식물을) 근친 교배한
- [ ] **descendant** n. 자손, 후예
- [ ] **genetically** adv. 유전적으로

Quiz

각 단어의 알맞은 뜻을 찾아 연결하시오.

01 build-up		ⓐ 제거하다, 없애다
02 context		ⓑ 잔여물
03 proper		ⓒ 축적, 증가
04 residue		ⓓ 상황, 배경
05 eliminate		ⓔ 쫓아내다
		ⓕ 적절한

06 inevitably		ⓐ 초자연적인
07 bleak		ⓑ 불가피하게
08 appreciate		ⓒ 토착의
09 relinquish		ⓓ 암울한, 절망적인
10 indigenous		ⓔ 인정하다, 가치를 알다
		ⓕ 내주다, 포기하다

ⓒ 01 ⓓ 02 ⓕ 03 ⓑ 04 ⓐ 05 ⓑ 06 ⓓ 07 ⓔ 08 ⓕ 09 ⓒ 10

□ reversal n. 전환, 반전

□ commitment n. 약속, 헌신

□ dialect n. 방언, 사투리

□ slang n. 속어, 은어

□ sociolinguist n. 사회언어학자

□ flawed adj. 결함이 있는

□ mutually adv. 서로, 상호간에

□ comprehensible adj. 이해할 수 있는

□ resemblance n. 유사성

□ pertinent adj. 적절한, 관련 있는

□ designate v. 지정하다

□ idiomatic adj. 관용적인

□ elevate v. 승격시키다

□ fall out of use phr. 쓰이지 않게 되다, 필요 없게 되다

□ hail from phr. ~의 출신이다

□ overuse n. 남용

□ mutate v. 변형되다

□ impervious adj. 영향받지 않는

□ counter v. 대응하다

□ pressing adj. 긴급한, 절박한

□ over the counter phr. 처방전 없이 (살 수 있는)

□ prescription n. 처방전

□ immunity n. 면역력

□ pneumonia n. 폐렴

□ standard practice phr. 흔한 일, 보통 사례

□ catalyst n. 촉매(제), 자극

□ coral reef phr. 산호초

□ secrete v. 분비하다

□ expel v. 방출하다

□ bleaching n. 탈색

□ in jeopardy phr. 위기에 처한

□ sedimentation n. 퇴적 작용

□ take a toll on phr. ~에 큰 피해를 주다

□ halt v. 중단시키다, 멈추다

□ timepiece n. 시계

□ in circulation phr. 유통되는

□ realm n. 영역, 범위

□ crude adj. 대강의; 거친

□ cement v. 굳게 하다, 접합하다

□ portability n. 휴대성

□ synchronise v. (시간을) 맞추다

□ underpin v. 토대가 되다

□ burgeoning adj. 급증하는

□ bolster v. 강화시키다, 북돋다

□ namely adv. 다시 말해, 즉

□ craftsman n. 장인, 공예가

□ lobby against phr. 반대 활동을 펼치다

□ fashion v. 만들다

□ artisan n. 장인, 공예가

□ fetch v. 팔리다, 가져오다

□ fabricate v. 제작하다, 날조하다

□ undertaking n. 사업, 일

Quiz

각 단어의 알맞은 뜻을 찾아 연결하시오.

01 counter	ⓐ 결함이 있는
02 commitment	ⓑ 긴급한, 절박한
03 flawed	ⓒ 지정하다
04 designate	ⓓ 대응하다
05 pressing	ⓔ 약속, 헌신
	ⓕ 처방전

06 realm	ⓐ 휴대성
07 bolster	ⓑ 중단시키다, 멈추다
08 fashion	ⓒ 영역, 범위
09 halt	ⓓ 만들다
10 portability	ⓔ 강화시키다, 북돋다
	ⓕ 사업, 일

ⓐ 01 ⓔ 02 ⓐ 03 ⓒ 04 ⓑ 05 ⓒ 06 ⓔ 07 ⓓ 08 ⓑ 09 ⓐ 10

CHAPTER 09 Matching Headings

Matching headings 문제는 주어진 제목의 리스트에서 지문의 각 단락에 알맞은 제목을 고르는 문제이다. IELTS Reading 영역에서 가장 많이 출제되는 유형 중 하나로, 거의 매 시험 출제되고 있다.

■ 문제 형태

Matching headings 문제는 주어진 제목의 리스트에서 지문의 각 단락에 알맞은 제목을 골라 해당 제목의 로마자를 적는 형태로 출제된다. 이때 문제와 리스트는 지문보다 앞에 주어지며, 1~2개 정도의 정답을 참고할 수 있는 예시를 함께 보여주기도 한다. 지문에는 간혹 하나 이상의 단락이 함께 묶여 하나의 알파벳으로 표시되기도 한다.

Reading Passage 1 has five paragraphs, **A-E**.

*Choose the correct heading for paragraphs **B-E** from the list of headings below.*

*Write the correct number, **i-v**, in boxes 1-4 on your answer sheet.*

List of Headings

i   The excellent source of leather llamas provided to the Incas
ii Llamas as essential resources to the Incan people
iii Incan society's heavy dependence on the textile industry
iv The early domestication of the llama by the Incas
v   Various ways Incan travellers used llamas

Example	*Answer*
Paragraph **A**	ii

1   Paragraph **B**

2   Paragraph **C**

3   Paragraph **D**

4   Paragraph **E**

■ 문제풀이 전략

STEP 1	지문을 단락별로 읽어 내려가며 각 단락의 중심 내용을 파악한다.

Matching headings 문제를 풀기 위해서는 지문을 단락별로 skimming하여 중심 내용을 파악해야 한다. 중심 문장은 주로 단락의 앞부분 혹은 뒷부분에 주어지므로, 각 단락의 앞부분과 뒷부분을 주의 깊게 읽고 중심 내용을 파악한다. 단락에 중심 문장이 뚜렷하게 드러나 있지 않은 경우, 단락 전체를 읽고 중심 내용을 파악한다.

EXAMPLE

A The llama was an indispensable constituent of Incan society. The only large animals ever domesticated in ancient America, llamas provided the Incas with food and materials for textiles. A single adult male yielded 100 kilograms of meat, which could be dried for storage. Lightweight and nutritious, dried llama meat was a staple of Incan soldiers and travellers. The animals' hides were transformed into leather for weather-resistant garments. The soles of the Incan sandal, for instance, were made from llama leather. In addition, the fur was turned into cloth, which was used for the clothes worn by common people.

⋮

단락을 읽고 '라마는 잉카 사회의 필수적인 요소였다'라는 중심 문장을 파악한다.

지문 해석 p.434

✅ TIPS

Matching headings 문제를 풀 때는 읽어야 할 단락이 많으므로, 한꺼번에 모든 단락의 중심 문장을 찾아두려고 하기보다는 한 단락의 중심 문장을 찾아 문제를 푼 뒤 다음 단락으로 넘어가는 식으로 푸는 것이 좋다.

주어진 제목 리스트를 읽고, 중심 문장을 paraphrasing했거나 바르게 요약한 보기를 찾는다. 중심 문장이 없는 경우 단락 전체의 내용을 바르게 요약한 보기를 찾는다.

EXAMPLE

Reading Passage has five paragraphs, **A-E**.

Choose the correct heading for the paragraph from the list of headings below.

*Write the correct number, **i-v**, in box 1 on your answer sheet.*

> **List of Headings**
>
> i The excellent source of leather llamas provided to the Incas
> ii Llamas as essential resources to the Incan people ●————
> iii Incan society's heavy dependence on the textile industry
> iv The early domestication of the llama by the Incas
> v Various ways Incan travellers used llamas

중심 문장 'The llama was an indispensable constituent of Incan society.'에서 'indispensable constituent'가 'essential resources'로 paraphrasing되었음을 확인한다.

1 Paragraph **A**

A ¹The llama was an indispensable constituent of Incan society. The only large animals ever domesticated in ancient America, llamas provided the Incas with food and materials for textiles. A single adult male yielded 100 kilograms of meat, which could be dried for storage. Lightweight and nutritious, dried llama meat was a staple of Incan soldiers and travellers. The animals' hides were transformed into leather for weather-resistant garments. The soles of the Incan sandal, for instance, were made from llama leather. In addition, the fur was turned into cloth, which was used for the clothes worn by common people.

⋮

단락 전체의 내용을 잘 반영한 보기인지 확인한다.

Reading Passage has five paragraphs, **A-E**.

Choose the correct heading for the paragraph from the list of headings below.

*Write the correct number, **i-v**, in box 1 on your answer sheet.*

List of Headings
i   The excellent source of leather llamas provided to the Incas
ii   Llamas as essential resources to the Incan people
iii Incan society's heavy dependence on the textile industry
iv   The early domestication of the llama by the Incas
v   Various ways Incan travellers used llamas

1   Paragraph **A** ii

A ¹The llama was an indispensable constituent of Incan society. The only large animals ever domesticated in ancient America, llamas provided the Incas with food and materials for textiles. A single adult male yielded 100 kilograms of meat, which could be dried for storage. Lightweight and nutritious, dried llama meat was a staple of Incan soldiers and travellers. The animals' hides were transformed into leather for weather-resistant garments. The soles of the Incan sandal, for instance, were made from llama leather. In addition, the fur was turned into cloth, which was used for the clothes worn by common people.

⋮

중심 문장과 라마 고기가 군인과 여행자들의 주식이었으며 의복과 신발을 위해 가죽과 털을 사용했다는 단락 전체 내용을 통해 ii Llamas as essential resources to the Incan people이 정답임을 확인한다.

1 *Choose the correct heading for each paragraph from the list of headings below.*

List of Headings

i Opposing views on microfibres

ii The need to expand the uses of microfibres

iii The development of a new manmade material

iv The future applications of a new product

---

1 Paragraph **A**

2 Paragraph **B**

A In the 20th century, a pioneer in Japan made a technological breakthrough in the production of soft, and extremely thin, synthetic fibres. These microfibres are finer than a silk thread, or one hundred times thinner than a human hair. Industrialist Miyoshi Okamoto first produced these fibres by squeezing two kinds of plastic threads, polyester and nylon, through a small pipe and heating them so that they weave together. Subsequently, microfibre technology took hold in the United States and Sweden, where refinements continued to be made, expanding its potential uses. Today, a wide variety of materials, including rayon and acrylic, have been used to produce microfibres, which are used in a tremendous number of practical applications, such as apparel, cleaning cloths, and vehicle upholstery.

B However, this synthetic technology has also become the source of tremendous controversy. On the one hand, many people have praised its virtues. For example, cleaning cloths weaved from these fibres can absorb up to seven times their weight in liquid, and most do not even require cleaning chemicals. Animal rights activists have even embraced it for limiting dependence on silk and wool. On the other hand, some people believe that microfibres are damaging our environment and should be banned. This is because the fine fibres are entering our water systems in great quantities. In fact, nearly 16 per cent of the plastic recovered from Lake Michigan was in the form of these petroleum-based plastic filaments.

---

microfibre n. 극세사 **pioneer** n. 선구자, 개척자 **synthetic** adj. 합성한, 인조의 **fine** adj. 가는 **weave** v. 엮이다, 엮다 **take hold** v. 장악하다
refinement n. 개선 **apparel** n. 의류 **upholstery** n. 커버, 덮개 **virtue** n. 장점, 가치 **embrace** v. 수용하다 **filament** n. 섬유, 가는 실

2 *Choose the correct heading for sections A and B from the list of headings below.*

List of Headings

i	Differing views on why ancient megafauna died out
ii	Why marsupials are so abundant in Australia
iii	How marsupials avoided extinction
iv	Why Australian mammals are unique

---

3   Section **A**

4   Section **B**

A   A special feature of the mammals of Australia is that they all happen to be marsupials. A total of 159 Australian marsupial species are currently identified, an overwhelming number that is unique in the world. Another distinctive characteristic is that the mammalian megafauna of Australia tend to be smaller than other large mammals around the world. Commonly, the term *megafauna* refers to animals that weigh over 100 kilograms. But because Australian mammals are smaller, biologists have amended that threshold to include the Australian fauna that have a body mass of 45 kilos or greater.

B   However, this diminutive size has not always been the case. The fossil record shows that megafauna in Australia once thrived, but the largest animals died out around 45,000 years ago. For years, the leading theory was that humans killed off the megafauna by overhunting. This hypothesis is accepted by professor Gifford Miller, who participated in a study of sediment core samples. His team focused on the presence of a fungus spore in the dung of large herbivores, and found that the spores were abundant before plummeting in the few thousand years leading up to the extinctions. Because the region also shows signs of human habitation by 50,000 years ago, the researchers inferred a causal relationship between human settlement and loss of megafauna.

More recent arguments blame climate change. Larisa DeSantis of Vanderbilt University claims that climate change led to the demise of megafauna. She and her team studied changing patterns in fossil teeth of large herbivores. By comparing the isotopes stored in the tooth enamel, they deduced the average temperature in the environment as the teeth were formed. She therefore could determine that their diets began to shift suddenly as climate changed prior to their extinction, suggesting that the much drier climate left them without appropriate food.

---

megafauna n. 거대동물 marsupial n. 유대목 동물(캥거루·코알라처럼 육아낭에 새끼를 넣어 가지고 다니는 동물) threshold n. 기준(점), 문턱
fauna n. 동물군, 동물구계 sediment core phr. 침전물 중심부 fungus spore phr. 균류 포자 isotope n. 동위 원소 deduce v. 추론하다, 연역하다

3 *Choose the correct heading for each paragraph from the list of headings below.*

List of Headings

i   Reasons for the rise in automobile sales

ii Changes in automobile use in the United States

iii The history of transportation in America

iv Problems with car ownership

v   Seeking solutions for a transportation problem

vi The impact of the automobile on America

5   Paragraph **A**

6   Paragraph **B**

7   Paragraph **C**

A During American history, perhaps nothing has had such an immense influence on the American lifestyle than the growth of personal car ownership. The automobile allowed Americans to easily travel across their immense nation and came to symbolise freedom. Car ownership became a rite of passage and as more and more Americans bought them, this caused a great shift in demographics in the country. With their increased mobility, Americans were able to move out of the cities and into the suburbs. For many, owning a suburban home with a yard and white picket fence came to symbolise the 'American Dream'.

B However, some do not see the automobile as a great symbol of freedom. In fact, they consider our reliance upon automobiles to be a burden. For most people, the ever-increasing prices of automobiles make them large investments. Further, fuel, insurance, and maintenance costs can make them even more unaffordable. While this may seem like an individual problem, it has had a major negative impact on society as a whole. When the previously mentioned suburban flight drained cities of middle and upper class citizens who could afford private transportation, the overall income levels of the cities dropped. This led to a decline in tax revenue and caused widespread urban decay.

C Interestingly, with more than 250 million cars currently on the roads of America, some believe that the country has reached what professor Phil Goodwin refers to as 'peak car'. This basically means that Americans are travelling less by car than they were before. One of the most commonly cited reasons for this is that people are moving back into the cities. With this reurbanisation, citizens have increased access to affordable public transportation. After comparing the costs of purchasing and maintaining a car to this public transportation, many Americans have begun to forego car ownership altogether.

---

immense adj. 거대한 symbolise v. 상징하다 rite of passage phr. 통과 의례 demographics n. 인구 통계 mobility n. 기동(력), 움직이기 쉬움
drain v. 유출시키다, 고갈시키다 income level phr. 소득 수준 tax revenue phr. 세입 decay n. 쇠퇴 forego v. 포기하다

4 *Choose the correct heading for each paragraph from the list of headings below.*

List of Headings

i   Current views about a style of business administration

ii The need to develop new management styles

iii Conditions required to succeed in business management

iv The contribution of the Industrial Revolution to business

v   The development of a new scheme for workplace organisation

vi An explanation of early labour movements

---

8   Paragraph **A**

9   Paragraph **B**

10 Paragraph **C**

A   The Industrial Revolution caused a great shift in manufacturing from the late 18th to early 19th centuries. During this time, manufacturing moved from small home-based enterprises to large factories with many employees working with machines. Unfortunately, this change was not accompanied by a shift in management styles to maximise the new systems' efficiency. It was soon clear that mismanagement was resulting in financial losses that reduced the benefits of the increased output. Therefore, there was a pressing need for a new way of management.

B   One of the first people to address this problem was American engineer Frederick Winslow Taylor, whose experiments brought about a new way to direct the workforce – 'scientific management'. This new management style sought to organise companies in a more efficient and rational way. Through his work, Taylor identified several problems with management styles of the time. The lack of knowledge of the entire production process was the most basic of these. By giving managers more knowledge, Taylor felt they could better understand all aspects of the business and identify the inefficiencies of some manufacturing processes. He also thought the basic role of supervisors was incorrect. He preferred a white-collar managerial style, in which supervisors controlled employees' roles, methods, and time. Further, he developed formulas to determine peak employee efficiency by studying tasks and calculating the most efficient means of doing them. This included determining the ideal size of a shovelful of dirt and the speed at which employees should move when pushing a wheelbarrow.

C   Taylor's work led to a micromanaged hierarchy of power, but contemporary opinions do not suggest that this was a positive outcome. They claim that Taylor's management style leads to dehumanised and dissatisfied workers. And they also point out that it was exactly these feelings that led to workers movements in the early 1900s and brought about the first labour unions.

---

administration n. 관리, 행정 scheme n. 계획, 제도 workforce n. 노동 인구, 노동자 rational adj. 합리적인 supervisor n. 관리자, 감독
white-collar adj. 사무직의 wheelbarrow n. 손수레 micromanaged adj. 세부 사항까지 통제되는 hierarchy n. 체계, 계층
dehumanise v. 인간성을 말살시키다

5 *Choose the correct heading for each paragraph from the list of headings below.*

List of Headings

i   Explanation of unique aspects of human language

ii   A description of less common language development theories

iii   Various theories based on one idea of language origin

iv   Difficulty in determining the birth of language

v   Discovery of physical evidence of early human communication

vi   Methods used to communicate with non-verbal species

---

11   Paragraph **A**

12   Paragraph **B**

13   Paragraph **C**

A   Researchers have tried to understand the origin of human language for millennia. However, this job is quite difficult as there is little physical evidence to be studied. Because of this, linguists must use modern languages, theories of language acquisition, and studies of language systems to infer information about how, when, and why human linguistic communication began. Using these techniques, two main theories have been developed. These are continuity theory, which states that language evolved from previous forms of communication and appeared gradually over time, and discontinuity theory, according to which human language is a unique form of communication and probably appeared suddenly.

B   Continuity theories are often divided into vocal, gestural, and social origin theories. Under vocal theory, language originated from primates mimicking natural sounds and using them to identify objects. Gestural theories, on the other hand, posit that as humans became bipedal they developed a form of sign language, but over time this was replaced by sounds. Although both theories have their merits, many sociolinguists believe that language developed as a survival mechanism along with societal complexity. By spreading information about other society members, early humans could form alliances and identify friends and foes.

C   Conversely, the relatively fewer discontinuity theories point to a sudden development of language. This is most commonly seen to be the result of divine intervention. Many traditional stories explain how language was given to humans by gods or other supernatural deities. However, other proponents of a genetic discontinuity theory have come to believe that humans have an innate capacity for language. This, according to Noam Chomsky, means that language likely appeared instantly due to an evolutionary mutation. Many linguists originally dismissed this theory, but mounting evidence of the relationships between languages is increasing its popularity.

---

physical adj. 물리적인   acquisition n. 습득   vocal adj. 발성의   primate n. 영장류   mimic v. 흉내 내다   posit v. 가정하다   bipedal adj. 두 발로 걷는
alliance n. 동맹   foe n. 적   divine adj. 신의   supernatural adj. 초자연적인   deity n. 신적 존재   proponent n. 지지자   mutation n. (형태·구조상의) 변화
dismiss v. (고려할 가치가 없다고) 묵살하다   mounting adj. 증가하는

6 *Choose the correct heading for each paragraph from the list of headings below.*

List of Headings

i   The effect of geographic location on an animal group
ii The impact of climate change on the tuatara
iii Evidence of the reproduction of a species
iv The consequences of human intervention
v   Two keys that have led to the tuatara's survival
vi Explanations for a low reproductive rate

---

14   Paragraph **A**

15   Paragraph **B**

16   Paragraph **C**

17   Paragraph **D**

A   Recently, researchers from the University of Otago made a surprising discovery. They found the remains of eggs from the tuatara on New Zealand's South Island. This was important because tuatara had not reproduced on either of New Zealand's two main islands in over a century. The new discovery has conservationists excited because it shows that efforts to reintroduce breeding populations on the mainland have been successful.

B   These small reptiles have a crest of triangular skin folds down their backs and can grow to approximately 75 centimetres. They are the only living species of the order Rhynchocephalia, which flourished over 200 million years ago. This may be attributable to living on remote islands with no large predators. These islands have large seabird populations that produce guano, which attracts the parasites that the tuataras eat. Both of these factors allowed them to flourish for hundreds of millions of years.

C   Unfortunately, human activity greatly affected the tuatara populations. This is because non-native animals, such as rats, that ate the tuataras' eggs were introduced when humans arrived on the islands. This devastated the population due to their low reproductive rate. It is estimated that around 25 per cent of the tuatara died due to these rats.

D   Surprisingly, climate change also has a strong influence on the numbers of the tuatara. Tuatara gender, like that of some other reptiles, is dependent upon nest temperature. When nests are 21°C or below, the hatchlings will be female but even a 1° increase in temperature will produce males. Rising temperatures are now reducing the likelihood of new hatchlings being female. Because of this, researchers must find innovative conservation techniques to save this ancient species.

---

tuatara n. 큰도마뱀 reproduce v. 번식하다 breeding n. 번식 crest n. 볏, 갈기 skin fold phr. 피부주름 order Rhynchocephalia phr. 훼두목
guano n. 조분석(바닷새의 배설물) parasite n. 기생충 hatchling n. (갓) 부화한 새끼

7 *Choose the correct heading for each paragraph from the list of headings below.*

List of Headings

i   Various types of care for PTSD patients

ii   Some symptoms of PTSD

iii   The difficulty of detecting PTSD

iv   The meaning and origin of the term PTSD

v   The effect on families

vi   Why meditation helps PTSD

vii   Causes of trauma that can lead to PTSD

---

18   Paragraph **A**

19   Paragraph **B**

20   Paragraph **C**

21   Paragraph **D**

Post-Traumatic Stress Disorder

A Post-traumatic stress disorder is a clinical mental illness that was first observed in war veterans. The condition results from trauma that is either life threatening, the cause of a serious injury, or something that the affected person responded to with intense fear, helplessness or horror. In the 1970s, in the aftermath of the Vietnam War, a behavioural pattern was observable in many of the returning American soldiers. They were emotionally distant, irritable, had trouble sleeping and were prone to severe fits of anger. Anti-Vietnam War activists advocating the troubled veterans coined the term 'post-Vietnam Syndrome' to describe their array of severe psychological symptoms.

B The type of trauma that leads to PTSD is almost always unexpected, and leaves the person involved feeling powerless to stop the traumatic event. Situations that are likely to result in such trauma are varied. Accidents, serious crimes, combat experience, and the sudden death of loved ones can all lead to PTSD. However, not everyone who experiences trauma develops PTSD, and researchers are still trying to figure out why some people are more susceptible to this condition.

C Symptoms of PTSD can include persistent memories or nightmares about a traumatic event, dissociation from the surrounding world, avoidance of anything related to the trauma and increased anxiety or 'hyper arousal'. People with PTSD are constantly on guard for danger even when there is no indication of threat in their immediate environment. This heightened state of anxiety or irritability has other consequences as well, such as being prone to outbursts of anger or violent aggression, having difficulties concentrating, and having trouble sleeping.

D Contrary to common belief, PTSD is a treatable disorder, and there is a range of treatments available to PTSD sufferers. Once a patient is diagnosed with PTSD, they are almost always put on some form of anti-anxiety or anti-depressant medication, which will often be used in conjunction with some form of therapy. The most effective therapeutic models for PTSD sufferers are exposure therapy, eye movement desensitisation and reprocessing (EMDR), and cognitive-behavioural therapy (CBT). As the name suggests, exposure therapy involves exposing the patient to their trauma in a safe environment so that they can become desensitised. EMDR combines exposure therapy with guided eye movements that help individuals process traumatic memories. CBT, on the other hand, teaches patients skills such as relaxation and mindfulness techniques that help them deal with their memories of trauma more effectively. Although these treatments can be highly effective, many victims of PTSD will experience painful relapses during the course of their lives; ensuring the long-term availability of care and support is thus of paramount importance.

CH 09

Matching Headings HACKERS **IELTS** READING

---

post-traumatic stress disorder phr. 외상 후 스트레스 장애   war veteran phr. 참전 용사   aftermath n. 여파   irritable adj. 짜증을 잘 내는, 화가 난
prone adj. ~하는 경향이 있는   advocate v. 변호하다   susceptible adj. 쉽게 영향을 받는, 감염되기 쉬운   dissociation n. 분리, 분열   anxiety n. 불안(감)
hyper arousal phr. 과다각성   on guard phr. 경계하는   heighten v. 고조시키다   irritability n. 과민성   outburst n. 표출, 분출
desensitise v. 둔감하게 하다   mindfulness technique phr. 명상 기법   relapse n. (병의) 재발   paramount adj. 다른 무엇보다 중요한

8 *Choose the correct heading for each paragraph from the list of headings below.*

List of Headings

i   Evidence that eye makeup can attract a partner
ii   Eye makeup for beauty rather than celebration
iii   Eye makeup in Egyptian hieroglyphics
iv   The use of eye makeup in Greece to keep evil away
v   The development of mascara
vi   A superstition and its connection to the origins of eye makeup
vii   Changes in the types of pigments used for cosmetics
viii   Cosmetics from the theatre to mainstream society

---

22   Paragraph **A**

23   Paragraph **B**

24   Paragraph **C**

25   Paragraph **D**

The Folkloric Roots of Eye Makeup

A The 'evil eye' is an element of many folklore traditions throughout the world, and while the exact nature of its meaning varies from one culture to another, it is generally thought to represent the sin of covetousness, or jealousy. According to many legends, a person who is envious can unintentionally harm another by gazing at him or her with desire. Archaeologists believe that this superstition is tied to the origins of eye makeup as protection. In Ancient Egypt, for example, protective measures against the evil eye involved painting the eyes with kohl, a mixture of soot and minerals. The typical blend included some combination of copper, ash, lead, and ocher, a yellow-brown pigment derived from iron oxide.

B In Ancient Greece, the use of cosmetics around the eye developed independently in the first century B.C. as a form of apotropaic magic, a ritual observance that was intended to ward off evil. Both men and women lined their eyes with lampblack – a black pigment produced by burning oil in shallow pans – and occasionally darkened their eyebrows as a superstition. Archaeologists in Greece have uncovered black-figured drinking vessels painted with apotropaic eyes, which they believe were drawn to protect the user from poison. Therefore, the Egyptians were not the only civilisation to develop this kind of protective response to threats.

C The use of cosmetics was so common around the Mediterranean that they found their way into other facets of society, initially as a theatrical device, and later as fashion. On stage, for example, actors employed masks to symbolise typical characters, and these were painted to intensify the desired features. This was due, in part, to the necessity of making the face visible to a large audience, but at the same time, it was a means to move away from realist facial appearances and convey a sense of the fantastic. Eventually the custom of wearing eye makeup directly on the face in the theatre was echoed by some members of high society, particularly during social gatherings. In addition, the range of pigmentation and types of cosmetics grew, and colorful paint, glitter, and sheen began to increasingly adorn the eyes of performers and the general public alike.

D In modern times, applying eye makeup has become a mundane daily ritual across the globe for many women, most of whom wear it to highlight beauty, rather than for any celebratory reason. Modern cosmetics such as eye shadow and mascara are now part of the massive global cosmetics industry and are used as means of highlighting the eyes for everyday occasions worldwide. In many societies, the use of eye makeup among men is also increasingly common, a phenomenon which revives its ancient unisex roots, albeit for cosmetic rather than superstitious reasons. Eye makeup is thus more popular than ever in the contemporary world, extending across both class and gender boundaries in its use.

---

hieroglyphic n. 상형문자 superstition n. 미신 folklore n. 민속, 전통 문화 covetousness n. 탐욕
kohl n. 콜(특히 동양 일부 국가에서 여성들이 화장용으로 눈가에 바르는 검은 가루) soot n. 검댕, 그을음 derive from phr. ~에서 나오다, 파생하다
iron oxide phr. 산화철 apotropaic adj. 액막이의 observance n. 의식 ward off phr. 막다, 피하다 lampblack n. 유연(검은 물감) pigment n. 색소
black-figured adj. (고대 그리스의) 흑회식의(그리스 도기에서 제작 기법의 하나) facet n. 측면, 양상 echo v. 되풀이하다, 반복하다 sheen n. 광택
adorn v. 돋보이게 하다, 꾸미다 mundane adj. 일상적인

9 *Choose the correct heading for each paragraph from the list of headings below.*

List of Headings

i   The development of universal voting rights

ii   America emerging from Britain's influence

iii Focusing on regional government

iv An undemocratic electoral system

v   The end of the British Empire

vi The development of British monarchy

vii Corruption in American democracy

viii The royal roots of British democracy

26   Paragraph **A**

27   Paragraph **B**

28   Paragraph **C**

29   Paragraph **D**

Democracy in Britain and America

A Waves of people from diverse ethnic backgrounds have migrated to North America since Europeans first arrived on the continent. In the colonial period, however, it was the British who dominated immigration to America and they brought with them the political and legal values of their homeland. As the colonies evolved and America began its struggle for independence, differences emerged because of the geography of the land and the makeup of society, as well as the desire of the Founding Fathers to introduce a new form of democracy. These differences would define how American democracy evolved separately from its former colonial rulers. America's unique system of representation was partly inspired by the British model, but was stripped of its aristocratic and royal roots in favour of a more local emphasis.

B Britain's model of representative government has its origins in the practice of medieval English kings, who enlisted the advice of a small group of confidants concerning their 'subjects' wishes'. British monarchs recognised the role of consultation in garnering support from the people, and in turn, their obeisance. The parliamentary system that subsequently developed was composed of an upper and lower house, the House of Lords and House of Commons, respectively. The House of Lords was founded as a hereditary body for the clergy and nobility, and the House of Commons was comprised of elected members from administrative districts.

C Even though the British parliamentary system had two separate houses claiming to represent the interests of the respective classes, elections were far from democratic. General elections were based on rigid constituencies, a system resulting in an electorate made up of a minute portion of the population. Consequently, politically influential self-governing townships whose populations had dissipated could elect two members of parliament, the same number as cities with large populations. Some of these electoral districts with disproportionate representation had fewer than ten voters. A related issue was the fact that these districts could effectively be controlled by a single wealthy aristocrat. Bribery was often rampant, and hopeful representatives would bestow gifts or proffer promises upon patrons for votes, or simply buy the borough outright. These practices created a voting process that resembled pre-ordained consensus rather than democracy.

D The situation differed dramatically across the Atlantic: the manner in which the legislative assemblies arose in the colonies was not governed by the influence of a social hierarchy, but rather, the particular needs of regional and local communities. Since colonial charters allowed, but did not require, representative government, the assemblies of individual colonies developed under conditions of relative heterogeneity. The legislative bodies thus arose not to address the concerns of an entire country, but those of separate aggregates of people, emphasising plurality and diversity in a way that set the stage for American democracy as we know it today.

---

electoral adj. 선거의 monarchy n. 군주제 makeup n. 구조, 구성 Founding Fathers phr. 미국 헌법 제정자들 aristocratic adj. 귀족의
enlist v. (~의 협력을) 얻다 confidant n. 믿을 만한 사람, 친구 consultation n. 자문, 상의 garner v. 얻다 obeisance n. 복종, 존경
parliamentary adj. 의회의 composed of phr. ~으로 구성된 house n. 의회, 의사당 House of Lords phr. 상원 House of Commons phr. 하원
hereditary adj. 세습의, 대물림의 administrative district phr. 행정 구역 constituency n. 선거구 self-governing township phr. 자치구
dissipate v. 흩어지다 electoral district phr. 선거구 bestow v. 주다, 수여하다 proffer v. 제의하다, 제시하다 borough n. 자치구
pre-ordained adj. 이미 내정된 legislative assembly phr. 입법 의회 charter n. 헌장 heterogeneity n. 이질성 aggregate n. 집단
plurality n. 다수

10 *Choose the correct heading for each paragraph from the list of headings below.*

List of Headings

i   Countries implementing universal incomes

ii   How technology has changed culture

iii   The revolution of digital communications

iv   The origins of mechanisation

v   Necessary skills for the digital economy

vi   The prospects for alleviating unemployment

vii   Pros and cons of digitisation

viii   The damaging impact of automation

ix   Transformation of trade by computerisation

30   Paragraph **A**

31   Paragraph **B**

32   Paragraph **C**

33   Paragraph **D**

34   Paragraph **E**

Technology and the Workforce

A   The technological transformation of the workplace, in industry, the service sector and traditionally white-collar jobs, threatens to have a largely negative impact on global employment as more and more jobs are automated. Automation is not only inevitable, it is already happening in many industries, and politicians and economists around the world are considering whether it will be at all possible to mitigate its negative effects, the most pressing of which is the possibility of mass unemployment. The threat of robots taking over people's jobs was once the theme of science fiction, but for many people it will become a reality within the next decade.

B   This shift towards mechanisation can be traced back to the Industrial Revolution, the precursor to the digital age, which initiated a symbiotic relationship between technology and humanity that has now extended into every area of daily life. The Industrial Revolution ushered in the replacement of hand-production methods with machine-based processes. In general, these innovations had a positive effect on the economies of industrialised nations, which experienced sustained growth for an unprecedented period of time. However, in the mid-20th century the widespread shift to mass production techniques made many unskilled factory jobs obsolete, starting a trend that continues today.

C   In the 1970s, the advent of the personal computer marked the beginning of the 'Digital Age', and in the developed world there was a transition to a high-tech economy based on computerisation. Not only manufacturing, but services and communications were made far more efficient and convenient than ever before. While a lot of people enjoyed this unprecedented convenience, technological innovation also disrupted many service sector jobs; typists, switchboard operators, and production-line jobs have largely disappeared, and many of the skilled jobs that were once a middle-class domain are now also threatened by automation.

D   This is a trend that is set to increase dramatically over the next ten years. Employability in the modern age will be very much contingent on technical ability, whether in terms of programming or other computer-related skills. Many prominent tech figures have already come forward to suggest that people should 're-skill' by learning how to write computer code or create algorithms, and there is already a lot of emphasis on teaching those skills to young people. However, it remains to be seen whether there will be enough coding jobs to replace the massive amount of jobs which will be lost to automation, especially since computers are able to do many coding jobs themselves.

E   One solution that has been suggested as a means of mitigating mass unemployment is to introduce a universal basic income, in which all citizens of a country receive an unconditional sum of money every month. This radical idea has gained many supporters among economists, but it is doubtful whether politicians have the will to put in place such a drastic measure. The issue of how to fund such a pay out, particularly since tax revenues will drop with the lower employment rate, is a complicated one. However, as more and more people find themselves out of work because of automation, governments around the world will have no choice but to act.

정답·해석·해설 p.434

---

alleviate v. 완화하다 automation n. 자동화 mitigate v. 완화하다 precursor n. 전조, 선두자 symbiotic adj. 공생의, 공생하는
obsolete adj. 쓸모없게 된, 구식의 switchboard operator phr. 전화 교환원 employability n. 취직 능력 contingent adj. ~에 의존하는

READING PASSAGE

*You should spend about 20 minutes on **Questions 1-13**, which are based on Reading Passage on the following pages.*

Questions 1-6

Reading Passage has six paragraphs, **A-F**.

Choose the correct heading for each paragraph from the list of headings below.

List of Headings

i	Research into forest fragmentation and possible solutions
ii	Deforestation in certain areas of the world
iii	The history of land use patterns and their impact on forests
iv	A study of forest fragmentation's destruction of native animals
v	The scale of deforestation seen from space
vi	An explanation of how deforestation began
vii	Forest fragmentation's impact on entire ecosystems
viii	Loss of intact forests and the need to address deforestation

1   Paragraph **A**

2   Paragraph **B**

3   Paragraph **C**

4   Paragraph **D**

5   Paragraph **E**

6   Paragraph **F**

Forest Fragmentation: A Growing Concern

When forests become fragmented, the consequences for the local ecosystem are usually dire

A Deforestation has been occurring at an increasing rate in recent years, and this trend is alarming to ecologists due to its potentially devastating effect on ecosystems. The full extent of this deforestation has become obvious because of research conducted by a team led by Matthew Hansen, a remote sensing scientist, who reviewed more than 600,000 global satellite photographs produced by the US Geological Survey. The team estimated that approximately 2.3 million km² of land was deforested worldwide during a 13-year period. The researchers also produced the world's first high-resolution maps that show clearly where trees are growing and disappearing, and these maps showed some obvious patterns.

B For example, the data demonstrated that the vast majority of deforestation happened in subtropical and tropical areas, though the exact locations changed periodically. It was recently reported that, almost half of all humid tropical forest loss around the world occurred in Brazil alone. Alarmingly, a whopping 90 per cent of the forest cover in the Amazon has been cleared for crops, grazing, and urban development. Yet rates of deforestation in Brazil began to slow in recent years due to regulations and the activities of environmentalists, and Indonesia has now overtaken Brazil as the country with the highest rate of deforestation. The data also revealed that trees are disappearing more rapidly in lowland areas than on sloped terrain, as these areas are more accessible and more suitable for logging and development. Moreover, the study found that only in areas where the human population is scant do researchers find a continuous spread of virtually untouched forest.

C Continuous or intact forest is defined as an unbroken expanse of forest ecosystem at least 500 square kilometres in size, with little or no sign of human activity. Such ecosystems are capable of supporting a broad range of animal and plant species. They also play a crucial role in storing carbon, which aids in the control of global warming, and help to regulate the water cycle. Today, only 23.5 per cent of existing forest on Earth is intact; this is a mere 8.8 per cent of total land area. Recently, it was estimated that over the course of just over a decade, the world's intact forest was reduced by more than 7 per cent, whilst only 12 per cent of these forests were protected. Furthermore, the most recent rate was triple what it was 10 years earlier. The rapid vanishing of these intact forests demonstrates the dire necessity of confronting the issue of deforestation.

D Yet in places of intense human activity, most of the forest cover is characterised by discontinuity. This is because only isolated sections, or fragments, remain when trees are cleared for other purposes. This consequence of deforestation is known as forest fragmentation, and it has repercussions that can dramatically impact the sustainability of the whole ecosystems. When the majority of trees are cut down, this leaves isolated patches of wooded land bound by completely different habitats, such as grassland. In the absence of trees, the earth becomes windswept and exposed to the elements. Laid bare to sunlight, these areas experience a rise in temperatures. These new conditions are devastating to herbaceous woodland plants, which cannot survive in these harsh conditions. Forest birds are left without a proper habitat for nesting, and predatory mammals that depend on dense forests no longer have cover to conceal their presence while hunting prey. These animals must leave and travel in search of a suitable habitat or they will perish. What was a vast expanse of forest becomes a patchwork that is not conducive to species that depend on the dense canopy and undergrowth of the inner forest.

E   This negative effect on animals was witnessed by researchers observing native species in Thailand where a hydroelectric reservoir was constructed. Scientists from the University of California in San Diego began studying a dozen small native mammal species – composed of mice, rats, and tree shrews – in 1990 after the dam project flooded a national park, leaving approximately 90 forested islands in the newly made lake. Within 25 years, virtually all of the animals had disappeared, which was two to three times faster than the researchers had expected. 'It was like ecological Armageddon', said graduate student Luke Wilson. The fragmented forests simply lacked the resources to support the animals. It can thus be seen that fragmented forests result in a drastic reduction in native biodiversity.

F   At present, studies on forest fragmentation focus on patterns of existing forest cover, how these patterns have been changing, and what effect these patterns have on the biodiversity of the forest ecosystem. However, some experts recommend an analysis of the forces driving fragmentation and a re-evaluation of how human activity might be altered to benefit industry and nature. One proposal, based on analysis of teak plantations in Benin, is to plant commercially valuable trees in planned corridors between areas of isolated natural forest. This would provide wood production and carry out the ecological function of helping to connect fragmented forest environments.

Questions 7-13

Do the following statements agree with the information given in Reading Passage?

Write

TRUE	*if the statement agrees with the information*
FALSE	*if the statement contradicts the information*
NOT GIVEN	*if there is no information on this*

7   Over two million square kilometres of forest was lost in just over a decade.

8   The Amazon has maintained around 90 per cent of its forest cover despite deforestation.

9   Flat land is experiencing more rapid deforestation than areas with hills.

10   Less than 10 per cent of the Earth's ground is covered by intact forest.

11   Deforestation harms forest wildlife but benefits species fit for grassland.

12   Herbaceous plants do well in the additional sunlight when trees are cut.

13   Recently, Benin has begun policies to protect forest ecosystems.

정답·해석·해설 p.446

VOCABULARY LIST

Chapter 09에서 선별한 다음의 어휘들을 음성파일을 들으며 암기한 후 퀴즈로 확인해보세요.

*해커스 동영상강의 포털 해커스 인강(HackersIngang.com)에서 단어암기 MP3를 무료로 다운로드할 수 있습니다.

- [ ] microfibre   n. 극세사
- [ ] pioneer   n. 선구자, 개척자
- [ ] synthetic   adj. 합성한, 인조의
- [ ] fine   adj. 가는
- [ ] apparel   n. 의류
- [ ] virtue   n. 장점, 가치
- [ ] embrace   v. 수용하다
- [ ] filament   n. 섬유, 가는 실
- [ ] megafauna   n. 거대동물
- [ ] threshold   n. 기준(점), 문턱
- [ ] rite of passage   phr. 통과 의례
- [ ] mobility   n. 기동(력), 움직이기 쉬움
- [ ] drain   v. 유출시키다, 고갈시키다
- [ ] income level   phr. 소득 수준
- [ ] tax revenue   phr. 세입
- [ ] decay   n. 쇠퇴
- [ ] forego   v. 포기하다
- [ ] scheme   n. 계획, 제도
- [ ] rational   adj. 합리적인
- [ ] supervisor   n. 관리자, 감독
- [ ] white-collar   adj. 사무직의
- [ ] micromanaged   adj. 세부 사항까지 통제되는
- [ ] dehumanise   v. 인간성을 말살시키다
- [ ] physical   adj. 물리적인
- [ ] acquisition   n. 습득
- [ ] vocal   adj. 발성의

- [ ] posit   v. 가정하다
- [ ] bipedal   adj. 두 발로 걷는
- [ ] alliance   n. 동맹
- [ ] foe   n. 적
- [ ] divine   adj. 신의
- [ ] deity   n. 신적 존재
- [ ] mutation   n. (형태·구조 상의) 변화
- [ ] dismiss   v. (고려할 가치가 없다고) 묵살하다
- [ ] reproduce   v. 번식하다
- [ ] breeding   n. 번식
- [ ] crest   n. 볏, 갈기
- [ ] parasite   n. 기생충
- [ ] hatchling   n. (갓) 부화한 새끼
- [ ] war veteran   phr. 참전 용사
- [ ] aftermath   n. 여파
- [ ] irritable   adj. 짜증을 잘 내는, 화가 난
- [ ] susceptible   adj. 쉽게 영향을 받는, 감염되기 쉬운
- [ ] dissociation   n. 분리, 분열
- [ ] anxiety   n. 불안(감)
- [ ] hyper arousal   phr. 과다각성
- [ ] on guard   phr. 경계하는
- [ ] heighten   v. 고조시키다
- [ ] irritability   n. 과민성
- [ ] outburst   n. 표출, 분출
- [ ] desensitise   v. 둔감하게 하다
- [ ] relapse   n. (병의) 재발

Quiz

각 단어의 알맞은 뜻을 찾아 연결하시오.

01 synthetic	ⓐ 수용하다	06 posit	ⓐ 기생충
02 pioneer	ⓑ 쇠퇴	07 anxiety	ⓑ 동맹
03 embrace	ⓒ 합성한, 모조의	08 alliance	ⓒ 두 발로 걷는
04 forego	ⓓ 포기하다	09 bipedal	ⓓ 가정하다
05 decay	ⓔ 세입	10 parasite	ⓔ 여파
	ⓕ 선구자, 개척자		ⓕ 불안(감)

ⓐ 10 ⓒ 60 ⓑ 80 ⓕ 70 ⓓ 90 ⓑ 50 ⓓ 40 ⓐ 30 ⓕ 20 ⓒ 10

☐ superstition n. 미신

☐ folklore n. 민속, 전통 문화

☐ covetousness n. 탐욕

☐ derive from phr. ~에서 나오다, 파생하다

☐ observance n. 의식

☐ ward off phr. 막다, 피하다

☐ echo v. 되풀이하다, 반복하다

☐ sheen n. 광택

☐ adorn v. 돋보이게 하다, 꾸미다

☐ electoral adj. 선거의

☐ monarchy n. 군주제

☐ makeup n. 구조, 구성

☐ aristocratic adj. 귀족의

☐ enlist v. (~의 협력을) 얻다

☐ confidant n. 믿을 만한 사람, 친구

☐ consultation n. 자문, 상의

☐ obeisance n. 복종, 존경

☐ parliamentary adj. 의회의

☐ composed of phr. ~으로 구성된

☐ house n. 의회, 의사당

☐ hereditary adj. 세습의, 대물림의

☐ administrative district phr. 행정 구역

☐ electoral district phr. 선거구

☐ proffer v. 제의하다, 제시하다

☐ pre-ordained adj. 이미 내정된

☐ heterogeneity n. 이질성

☐ aggregate n. 집단

☐ plurality n. 다수

☐ automation n. 자동화

☐ mitigate v. 완화하다

☐ precursor n. 전조, 선두자

☐ symbiotic adj. 공생의, 공생하는

☐ obsolete adj. 쓸모없게 된, 구식의

☐ employability n. 취직 능력

☐ contingent adj. ~에 의존하는

☐ fragmentation n. 붕괴, 분열

☐ remote sensing phr. 원격 탐사

☐ high-resolution adj. 고해상도의

☐ whopping adj. 막대한

☐ grazing n. 방목지

☐ overtake v. 넘어서다, 능가하다

☐ scant adj. 거의 없는

☐ intact adj. 무손상의, 온전한

☐ windswept adj. 강한 바람에 노출되어 있는

☐ herbaceous adj. 초본의

☐ elements n. 폭풍우, 악천후

☐ predatory adj. 포식의

☐ prey n. 먹이

☐ perish v. 죽다

☐ patchwork n. 잡동사니, 긁어 모은 것

☐ conducive adj. 도움이 되는

☐ undergrowth n. 관목

Quiz

각 단어의 알맞은 뜻을 찾아 연결하시오.

01 adorn	ⓐ 구조, 구성	06 contingent	ⓐ 자동화
02 proffer	ⓑ 군주제	07 prey	ⓑ 거의 없는
03 obeisance	ⓒ 탐욕	08 scant	ⓒ 집단
04 makeup	ⓓ 돋보이게 하다, 꾸미다	09 automation	ⓓ 완화하다
05 monarchy	ⓔ 제의하다, 제시하다	10 mitigate	ⓔ ~에 의존하는
	ⓕ 복종, 존경		ⓕ 먹이

01 ⓓ 02 ⓔ 03 ⓕ 04 ⓐ 05 ⓑ 06 ⓔ 07 ⓕ 08 ⓑ 09 ⓐ 10 ⓓ

CHAPTER 10

Short Answer

Short answer 문제는 지문의 단어를 사용하여 제시된 질문에 알맞은 답을 적는 주관식 문제이다. IELTS Reading 영역에서 간혹 출제되고 있다.

■ 문제 형태

Short answer 문제는 주로 What/Which/How/Who 등의 의문사를 사용한 질문이나, What/Which + 명사구 형태의 질문에 알맞은 답을 작성하는 형태로 출제된다. 문제를 풀기 전 항상 몇 단어 혹은 숫자로 답을 작성해야 하는지 확인한다.

Answer the questions below.

*Choose **ONE WORD ONLY** from the passage for each answer.*

Write your answers in boxes 1-3 on your answer sheet.

1　What type of new problem has arisen for the elderly?

2　Who would benefit from increasing elderly employment?

3　Which skill do elderly people typically possess?

■ 문제풀이 전략

STEP 1 답안 작성 조건을 확인하고, 문제의 핵심어구와 내용을 파악한다.

(1) 지시문을 읽고 지문에서 몇 단어 혹은 숫자의 답을 찾아야 하는지 확인한다.

(2) 문제의 핵심어구와 문제에서 묻는 내용을 파악한다.

EXAMPLE

Answer the question below.

Choose ***ONE WORD ONLY*** *from the passage for the answer.* ●━━━━━━┓

Write your answer in box 1 on your answer sheet.

1　　What type of new problem has arisen for the elderly? ●━━━

(1) 지시문을 읽고 지문에서 한 단어로 된 답을 찾아야 하는 문제임을 확인한다.

(2) 문제의 핵심어구인 new problem ~ for the elderly를 통해 '고령 인구에게 생긴 새로운 문제'에 대해 묻고 있음을 파악한다.

✅ TIPS

Short answer 문제는 여러 개의 문제가 한 번에 출제되므로, 제시된 모든 문제의 핵심어구를 미리 파악해두기보다는 한 문제씩 핵심어구를 파악하여 답을 쓰고 다음 문제로 넘어가는 것이 좋다.

지문을 scanning하여 문제의 핵심어구와 관련된 내용을 찾는다. 관련 내용이 언급된 주변에서 정답의 단서를 확인한다.

EXAMPLE

The United Nations Population Prospects report showed that average worldwide life expectancy has reached 70 years and more than 80 years in some developed nations. Not only are people living longer, but they're also enjoying better health into their old age. While this is great news, [1]it has brought about a new problem for the senior citizens – unemployment. Traditionally, people retired at a certain age and left the workforce permanently. Now, however, people may need to continue working in order to fund a longer retirement period due to increased life spans. Unfortunately, it can be difficult for these older people to find jobs. Employers may worry that they will require more training and sick leave, or that they will be less productive.

문제의 핵심어구인 new problem ~ for the elderly와 관련된 내용을 지문에서 찾는다. 관련 내용이 언급된 주변에서 정답의 단서를 확인한다.

Answer the question below.

*Choose **ONE WORD ONLY** from the passage for the answer.*

Write your answer in box 1 on your answer sheet.

1　What type of new problem has arisen for the elderly?

지문 해석 p.450

✅ **TIPS**

Short answer 문제는 지문의 내용이 전개되는 순서대로 출제되므로, 정답의 단서도 지문에서 순서대로 등장한다. 예를 들어 2번 문제의 정답의 단서는 1번 문제의 정답의 단서보다 이후에 등장할 가능성이 높다. 그러므로 정답의 단서를 찾지 못한 문제가 있다면, 이전 문제의 정답의 단서와 다음 문제의 정답의 단서 사이를 살펴보도록 한다.

(1) 정답의 단서에서 답이 될 수 있는 단어를 찾는다. 이때 문제의 의문사구에 맞는 단어 위주로 찾는다.

(2) 찾은 단어를 답안 작성 조건에 맞게 작성한다. 답안을 작성한 후에는 질문의 의문사에 알맞은 답을 적었는지 반드시 확인한다.

EXAMPLE

The United Nations Population Prospects report showed that average worldwide life expectancy has reached 70 years and more than 80 years in some developed nations. Not only are people living longer, but they're also enjoying better health into their old age. While this is great news, [1]it has brought about a new problem for the senior citizens – unemployment. Traditionally, people retired at a certain age and left the workforce permanently. Now, however, people may need to continue working in order to fund a longer retirement period due to increased life spans. Unfortunately, it can be difficult for these older people to find jobs. Employers may worry that they will require more training and sick leave, or that they will be less productive.

Answer the question below.

*Choose **ONE WORD ONLY** from the passage for the answer.*

Write your answer in box 1 on your answer sheet.

1   What type of new problem has arisen for the elderly? unemployment

(1) '늘어난 수명과 더 나은 건강이 고령 인구에게 실업이라는 새로운 문제를 가져왔다'라는 정답의 단서에서 'unemployment'가 답이 될 수 있음을 확인한다.

(2) 답안 작성 조건에 맞게 한 단어인 unemployment를 정답으로 작성한다.

1 The mural, a type of artwork that involves applying paint directly to a wall, was the earliest kind of painting. Murals could not be detached, but later, the technique of painting on panels was developed. Panel paintings were done on thin strips of wood that were later put together. This production process also made it possible to quickly take them apart later. Quick disassembly was a feature which made these paintings highly portable. In the 14th century, painters began painting on fabric canvas, which was easy to work with and transport as it was lightweight. The surface of canvas held paint much better than wood did and was not prone to warping and cracking. However, the woven fabric affected the surface of paintings in a way that Renaissance artists disliked. They wanted to attain a glossy finish, and therefore went to great lengths to smooth the texture of the painting so that it had a similar feel to a photograph.

Answer the questions below.

*Choose **NO MORE THAN TWO WORDS** from the passage for each answer.*

1 What characteristic made panel paintings easy to move?

2 What texture did Renaissance artists want to achieve?

---

mural n. 벽화 detach v. 분리하다, 떼다 disassembly n. 해체, 분리 portable adj. 휴대하기 쉬운 lightweight adj. 가벼운
prone to phr. ~의 경향이 있는 warp v. 휘다, 틀어지다 glossy adj. 반들반들한, 윤이 나는 finish n. 마감 칠 (상태), 마무리 칠
go to great lengths to phr. ~하려고 무엇이든 하다 feel n. 질감

2 Animals have an internal mechanism that responds rhythmically to environmental cycles. A cycle can operate according to many different time frames, but the most obvious among them are those related to lunar phases, seasonal patterns, and the 24-hour cycle. The mechanism, called a biological clock, functions to make an animal aware of upcoming environmental events and to regulate when it sleeps, mates, and feeds. The kind of biological clock an organism has generally depends on its genetics rather than on external stimuli. Creatures such as crabs innately regulate their behaviours according to the rise and fall of the tides. Meanwhile, in areas of the world where there are dramatic changes in the length of the day and night as the weather gets colder, most animals are influenced by seasonal patterns. For instance, a brown bear's biological clock will perceive that the days are getting shorter as winter approaches and respond by eating large quantities of food before entering a state of hibernation.

Answer the questions below.

Choose **ONE WORD ONLY** *from the passage for each answer.*

3　What commonly determines the sort of biological clock animals have?

4　What causes some sea creatures to act differently according to its height?

---

internal adj. 체내의, 내부의　mechanism n. 기제, 방법　time frame phr. 기간, 시간　mate v. 짝짓기를 하다　genetics n. 유전적 특징, 유전학
brown bear phr. 불곰　hibernation n. 동면, 겨울잠

3 In the early 1900s, astronomers noticed that an unknown object's gravity was affecting the orbits of Neptune and Uranus. They tentatively named whatever was responsible 'Planet X' and began their search for it. One of the scientists involved was Percival Lowell, and it was he that, through tireless calculations and observations, ultimately identified the area of the sky where this elusive celestial body would be found. When he died in 1916, other astronomers carried on his work; one of them, Clyde Tombaugh, systematically took photographs of various areas of the sky every few days and then analysed them using a machine called a blink comparator. This machine works by rapidly alternating from one image to the next, allowing users to find differences between any two photographs. He believed this technique would allow him to see if objects in the sky changed position. Finally, in 1930, he noticed a moving speck of light where Planet X had been predicted to be. Telescopic analysis over the ensuing months identified the object's orbit and confirmed its presence. Planet X was subsequently named Pluto, and it remained our solar system's ninth planet until it was recognised to be a dwarf planet.

Answer the questions below.

Choose **NO MORE THAN TWO WORDS** *from the passage for each answer.*

5   What device did Clyde Tombaugh study his photos with?

6   What kind of planet was Pluto later identified as?

---

orbit n. 궤도 Neptune n. 해왕성 Uranus n. 천왕성 tentatively adv. 잠정적으로 tireless adj. 끊임없는 elusive adj. 찾기 힘든 celestial adj. 천체의
carry on phr. ~을 계속하다 blink comparator phr. 블링크 콤퍼레이터(똑같은 것을 찍은 두 사진의 미소한 차이를 알아내는 광학 기기)
alternate v. 교차하다, 엇갈리다 speck n. 입자, 작은 조각 telescopic adj. 망원경의 ensuing adj. 뒤이은, 다음의 dwarf planet phr. 왜소행성

4 In the simplest terms, a drone is an unmanned, remote-controlled aircraft. The idea of using drones originated in the 1850s, during Austria's war against Italy. During this conflict, drones appeared in the form of balloons filled with bombs. But now that they are available to the general public, people are finding extremely innovative uses for them that not only make everyday tasks easier but also improve society as a whole. Because they are equipped with the highly efficient architecture of a smart phone, they are able to capture videos, take pictures, and use their GPS capacities to transmit data wirelessly. Adding all of these features, in addition to their ability to fly makes it possible to monitor forest fires, flash floods, and traffic flow, optimise agricultural production, and keep international borders secure. It is also possible to equip drones with other machinery to broaden their capabilities. For example, hospitals have successfully attached containers to drones tasked with transporting medicine and supplies to difficult-to-access areas. Meanwhile, some drones are outfitted with thermal sensors. The uses for drones of this type are myriad but as of now, they are proving invaluable to parks and wildlife management authorities. Because they are able to pick up signs of life as sensitive as a heartbeat, drones help keep endangered species safe by locating poachers who enter protected areas.

With technology improving on a daily basis, the future possibilities for drones seems limitless, but it is optimistic to expect that they will only be used for good. It is therefore vital that the Federal Aviation Administration (FAA) closely implement new legislation governing drones. This includes the prohibition of their use in heavily populated or secure areas and the requirement that registration of each drone be completed after purchase.

Answer the questions below.

*Choose **ONE WORD ONLY** from the passage for each answer.*

7   What did the first drones resemble?

8   What do drones help find in order to protect animals?

---

unmanned adj. 무인의   flash flood phr. 갑작스런 홍수   optimise v. 최적화하다, 최고로 활용하다   outfit v. (특정 목적에 필요한 복장·장비를) 갖추어 주다
thermal sensor phr. 열 감지기   myriad adj. 무수히 많은, 막대한   as of now phr. 현재로서는   poacher n. 밀렵꾼   optimistic adj. 낙관적인
Federal Aviation Administration phr. 미국연방항공국

5 The cocoa bean had enormous significance to the Aztec people. Unlike the chocolate we make with it today, it was mostly combined with chilli peppers or vanilla and used to make a spicy beverage during the time of the Aztecs. However, this was no dessert. Historical chronicles have noted that the beverage, often drunk at the end of a banquet and served with tobacco, could be incredibly intoxicating. This has caused some scholars to speculate that the drink was mixed with wine or that its contents underwent fermentation in order to turn it into alcohol. Perhaps it was this effect that made it valuable enough to be regarded as an acceptable form of currency. But it more likely had to do with the fact that the Aztecs believed that the cocoa tree was a bridge connecting heaven and Earth and that consuming cocoa beans instilled one with divine wisdom. For this reason, drinks made of cocoa were often included in ritual sacrifices to the gods, used to celebrate special occasions, and mostly limited to members of the upper echelons of society. But there was one problem. Cocoa would not grow at the Aztec court of Tenochtitlan, where the climate was too cool and dry. Luckily for the Aztecs, it could be acquired in conquered states. Under Aztec rule, these states were required to pay a tax in the form of goods and labour, called a tribute. When it came time to collect resources from these areas, cocoa beans were undoubtedly a top priority.

Answer the questions below.

*Choose **NO MORE THAN TWO WORDS** from the passage for each answer.*

9   What was often provided with a spicy drink at the end of a formal meal in Aztec culture?

10   What did the Aztecs believe could be gained by eating cocoa?

11   Which section of Aztec society were cocoa drinks associated with?

---

chronicle n. 기록, 연대기 intoxicating adj. 취하게 만드는 speculate v. 추측하다, 짐작하다 fermentation n. 발효 (작용) instill v. 서서히 주입시키다
divine adj. 신성한 echelon n. 계급, 계층 tribute n. 조공, 공물 top priority phr. 최우선 순위

6 In early spring, frogs emerge from hibernation and make their way to aquatic breeding grounds. The males are the first to arrive and begin croaking out mating calls to announce their presence to females, who select mates based on the length of their songs. Their calls also serve as a warning to other males, with the hope of discouraging potential competitors from encroaching on their space. Successful males engage with females in an embrace known as an amplexus, the goal of which is for females to release eggs into shallow, still water and for males to simultaneously fertilise them with their sperm. These eggs, of which there can be thousands, are covered with a thick, nutrient-rich jelly that swells in the water. As the parents typically abandon the eggs at this point, this substance serves as a means of protection for the fragile embryos. As the embryos grow, they turn into tadpoles and, if they are lucky, they emerge from their soft encasements; a large percentage, up to 95 per cent, of frog eggs fail to hatch due to either predation or environmental damage, such as a sudden hard freeze or drought. During the early part of their lives, tadpoles have a diet that is made up primarily of algae. They must eat voraciously at this time as they require a great deal of energy to complete their metamorphosis. Like fish, tadpoles have gills that allow them to breathe underwater and tails that enable them to swim. However, within a few weeks, skin starts to grow over their gills, which eventually disappear, with lungs developing in their place. After about 6 to 9 weeks, the tadpoles start eating insects and less vegetation. Their arms and legs begin to form at this point, too, and their tails become increasingly smaller before eventually being completely absorbed by their growing bodies. They then resemble miniature adults and can leave the water. Depending on how much food is available, a frog will be fully grown between 12 and 16 weeks of age and ready to mate, beginning the whole cycle once again.

Answer the questions below.

Choose **ONE WORD ONLY** *from the passage for each answer.*

12 What aspect of the male frog's call determines whether it will find a mate?

13 What is the main type of food eaten by a tadpole in its early life?

14 What do lungs replace as tadpoles become frogs?

---

breeding ground phr. 번식지 encroach v. 침해하다 embrace n. 짝짓기, 포옹
amplexus n. 포접(개구리처럼 암수가 몸을 밀착시켜 낳은 알에 즉시 정액을 뿌리는 행위) fertilise v. 수정시키다 sperm n. 정자 swell v. 부풀다, 부어 오르다
embryo n. 배아 tadpole n. 올챙이 encasement n. 포장 algae n. 조류 voraciously adv. 왕성하게, 게걸스럽게 metamorphosis n. 변태, 변형
gill n. 아가미

7 What is GPS?

GPS, or Global Positioning System, is a navigation and tracking system used for determining one's precise location and providing a highly accurate time reference almost anywhere on Earth. Designed and controlled by the United States Department of Defense, it was originally intended for military use, but today it is commonly used in a wide variety of civilian devices such as automobile navigation systems.

It is divided into three segments: space, control, and user. The space segment comprises the network of GPS satellites, which circle the Earth twice a day in a very precise orbit and transmit signal information. Powered by solar energy, they are equipped with backup batteries to keep them running in the event of a solar eclipse. Small rocket boosters on each satellite keep them flying on the correct path.

The control segment consists of ground stations around the world that are responsible for monitoring the flight paths of the GPS satellites, synchronising the satellites' onboard atomic clocks and collecting and uploading data for transmission by the satellites. These ground stations utilise an automated process to measure the orbit of the satellites to ensure they are precise enough to transmit accurate GPS data. If the orbit of a satellite veers off course, the ground stations mark it 'unhealthy', which means it cannot be used until it corrects its orbit, at which point it will be marked 'healthy' again.

The user segment is comprised of GPS receivers, which are devices that can determine a user's exact location by using distance measurements from multiple satellites. A GPS receiver must be locked on to the signal of at least three satellites to calculate a two-dimensional position – showing latitude and longitude – and to track movement. With four or more satellites in view, the receiver can determine a user's three-dimensional position – latitude, longitude, and altitude. Once the user's position has been determined, a GPS unit can calculate other information, such as speed, bearing, and distance travelled.

Although GPS is now widely known as a tool for personal navigation, its applications are far more widespread. They include the fields of international trade, agriculture, disaster relief, tectonics, robotics, and many more. Militaries around the world also use GPS for navigation and reconnaissance, but since the technology is owned and operated by the United States, they can deny use to other countries, as occurred in the 1999 Kargil War between India and Pakistan. The most prevalent use is perhaps in mobiles phones, where GPS is used not only for geo-location, but also for clock synchronisation and emergency calls.

Answer the questions below.

*Choose **ONE WORD ONLY** from the passage for each answer.*

15   What type of energy powers GPS satellites?

16   What are satellites labelled if they are considered to be on an incorrect path around the Earth?

17   What capability does GPS offer armies in addition to navigation?

---

civilian adj. 민간의   segment n. 부분   transmit v. 전송하다   backup adj. 예비의, 대체의   solar eclipse phr. 일식   rocket booster phr. 추진 로켓
ground station phr. (우주선의) 지상 관제소   synchronise v. 일치시키다   atomic clock phr. 원자 시계   veer off course phr. 항로를 이탈하다
latitude n. 위도   longitude n. 경도   altitude n. 고도   bearing n. 방위   disaster relief phr. 재난 구호   tectonics n. 구조 지질학
reconnaissance n. (군사적인 목적의) 정찰   synchronisation n. 동기화, 시계를 맞추기

8 Hydrothermal Vents

Prior to the 1970s, scientists assumed that no life could possibly survive the harsh environment of the ocean floor, the principle reason being lack of sunlight, which plant life requires for photosynthesis. Serious attempts to study the ocean floor did begin in the late 19th century, but researchers were faced with several challenges, primarily the fact that the vessels they travelled in were not equipped to withstand the extreme pressure at that depth. These excursions were very dangerous, as some vessels were unable to return to the ocean surface once submerged. A solution to these problems came in the 1970s, however, with the introduction of submersibles: vehicles designed to withstand the extreme conditions of the deep ocean. With this new technology researchers have discovered vast ecosystems, the existence of which is possible because of hydrothermal vents, which cause seawater to converge with magma flowing within the Earth's core.

Hydrothermal vents exist in many of the world's oceans, and are typically found in the gaps between tectonic plates. When these tectonic plates spread apart, magma rises and cools to form new crust. As the oceanic crust stretches, it thins and large cracks appear in these chains. These cracks have created the ideal conditions for ocean water to penetrate into the depths of the Earth's crust.

Once the water travels deep into the crust it comes into contact with magma and reaches extremely high temperatures. As pressure in the crust builds, the seawater warms and then rises to the ocean floor, dissolving minerals in the Earth's crust along the way. Before the water spurts forth from the vents, its temperature can reach as high as 400 degrees Celsius, although it ends up cooling down relatively quickly as it combines with the freezing temperatures of the ocean. As the hot and cold waters meet, minerals suspended in the hot water solidify and drop onto the ocean floor as they emerge from the vent. This causes an accumulation of minerals around the vent, which results in large formations known as chimneys.

The presence of minerals around the vents on the ocean floor allows the surrounding areas to sustain ecosystems flourishing with life. Bacteria convert the minerals into energy, thus providing nutrients to the surrounding species. Scientists are fascinated by the process of converting minerals into energy in this way, known as chemosynthesis, because it is one of the few instances where energy is developed without sunlight. They are also interested in this process because one of the chief minerals converted into energy in these vents is hydrogen sulphide, a mineral highly toxic to most plant-based life. Scientists researching hydrothermal vents have speculated that this toxic mineral could shed some light on the origins of life on Earth, as it may reveal how organisms survived millions of years ago without much oxygen.

Answer the questions below.

*Choose **NO MORE THAN TWO WORDS** from the passage for each answer.*

18   What technology allowed scientists to overcome the challenges of deep sea exploration?

19   Which geological features are hydrothermal vents usually found in between?

20   What term is used to describe the large structures which develop near hydrothermal vents?

---

hydrothermal vent phr. 열수 분출공   **ocean floor** phr. 해저, 대양저   **excursion** n. 여행   **submersible** n. 잠수함   **converge** v. ~을 만나게 하다, 모이다
gap n. 갈라진 틈   **tectonic plate** phr. 지질 구조판   **crust** n. (지질) 지각   **penetrate** v. 관통하다   **dissolve** v. 용해시키다, 녹다
spurt from phr. ~에서 뿜어져 나오다   **suspend** v. 떠 있게 하다   **solidify** v. 굳어지다   **accumulation** n. 퇴적, 축적   **chimney** n. 분화구
chemosynthesis n. 화학 합성   **hydrogen sulphide** phr. 황화수소   **speculate** v. 추측하다, 짐작하다   **shed light on** phr. 밝히다, 해명하다

9 The Tragedy of Dementia

Statistics reveal that approximately 35.6 million people worldwide are living with dementia, a brain disorder that results in the progressive loss of cognitive ability and, eventually, death. As the risk of developing the condition doubles every half decade after the age of 65, society is growing increasingly concerned about how we will care for our rapidly aging population.

Dementia causes the brain's neurons to deteriorate over time, so those who have it experience difficulty learning, reasoning, speaking, recalling past experiences, and controlling their emotional reactions. It is even very common for those with dementia to be unable to recognise their family members. While this can obviously be an upsetting experience for a son, daughter, or spouse, the inability to place a familiar face is most demoralising and frustrating for the dementia sufferer. It is therefore unsurprising that severe anxiety goes hand in hand with dementia and that this accompanying condition often exacerbates the disorder by causing fits of psychosis and aggression.

Because dementia victims lose the ability to make sense of their thoughts and feelings, their behaviour becomes unpredictable. They may experience what are known as 'catastrophic reactions', which involve sudden emotional shifts to tears or anger upon finding themselves in situations they cannot handle. To prevent them from wandering off aimlessly, attempting to drive a vehicle, or forgetting to eat, they will usually require full-time care and supervision. This becomes a necessity for people in the final stages of dementia, when they may also lose the ability to control their movements or even digest food due to muscle deterioration. Frail and out of touch with reality, dementia patients become very susceptible to illness at this point and often succumb to accidents or common colds.

The burden of dementia sufferers on their family and caretakers is quite severe. The emotional toll of slowly losing a family member or spouse notwithstanding, caretakers commonly experience burnout from trying to cope with the confusion, irrationality, and sometimes abusive behaviour of their loved ones. The financial fallout can be equally as devastating given the amount of time and resources required to provide care to dementia sufferer. Hiring a full-time nurse to administer home-based care or arranging for the patient to be moved to an assisted-living facility or nursing home is a major expense which a large portion of the population simply cannot afford.

It is clear that we are not yet equipped to handle the challenges of dementia. In addition to developing more health and social services for sufferers and their families, governments are strongly encouraged to increase the public's awareness of the condition. This way, people will be more conscious of the symptoms as they get older and know when it is time to seek help. With an early diagnosis, symptoms can be controlled from the beginning, which can greatly prolong life. Early diagnoses also give patients the opportunity to plan for their own long-term treatment and to settle their affairs. Until a cure is found for this terrible affliction, resources that improve patients' day-to-day lives and help them live out their final days with dignity are vital.

Answer the questions below.

*Choose **NO MORE THAN TWO WORDS AND/OR A NUMBER** from the passage for each answer.*

21   After what age does the chance of developing dementia double every five years?

22   Which separate condition can make the symptoms of dementia worse?

23   What causes problems with motion and food digestion in the final stages of dementia?

---

dementia n. 치매 deteriorate v. ~을 악화시키다, 나쁘게 하다 place v. (누구인지를) 알아보다, 생각해 내다 demoralising adj. 혼란시키는
go hand in hand phr. 관련되다 exacerbate v. 악화시키다 fit n. 발작 psychosis n. 정신병 catastrophic reaction phr. 파국반응
deterioration n. 퇴화 frail adj. 허약한 susceptible adj. 감염되기 쉬운 succumb to phr. (병 따위로) 쓰러지다, ~에 굴복하다 toll n. 희생, 대가
burnout n. 극도의 피로, 연료 소진 fallout n. 악영향 administer v. 실행하다 prolong v. 연장시키다 affliction n. 고통

10 Early Childhood Education and Sign Language

The ability to communicate with others is essential to the emotional development and well-being of any individual, which is why sign language is an invaluable tool for the deaf and hard of hearing. It is also becoming increasingly apparent that learning sign language offers individuals who can hear, in particular very young children, numerous benefits as well.

At its most basic level, teaching sign language to children instills in them an awareness of and sensitivity to deaf people. However, it also allows them to acquire a second language, which is beneficial as it is widely accepted that bilingualism improves cognitive ability. It seems that this is especially the case with sign language since toddlers and babies, who are limited in their oral capacity, have a strong response to motion. As every educator and parent knows, when actions are put to a song or story, children tend to repeat the movements over and over. By developing muscle memory in this way, they are better able to retain the words because they associate them with specific motions.

This response is related to the theory of multiple intelligences, which suggests that people learn, remember, and understand in a variety of different ways – linguistic, logical-mathematical, bodily-kinaesthetic, musical, visual, interpersonal, and intrapersonal. According to the developer of this theory, Harvard University Professor of Cognition and Education Howard Gardner, most educational curricula are based on the linguistic model, and this holds less verbally intelligent students back. When all the various intelligences are engaged, children are given more of a chance at success and a more well-rounded education. It has been found that teaching sign language to children who can hear is an excellent way to apply many of the intelligences.

For instance, by using their hands when they speak or sing – either by signing or tracing words onto a child's palm – educators can cater to linguistic and musical learners as well as bodily-kinaesthetic and visual learners. This is because students can listen to the words being spoken or sung in addition to feeling them on their skin or seeing them signed. Likewise, signing can help logical-mathematical learners because it is full of patterns that can make grammar easier for these types of learners to grasp. Interpersonal and intrapersonal learners, meanwhile, can respectively practice signing with other children and on their own.

But perhaps just as significant as making very young children better learners is that signing provides them with an easy way of expressing their basic wants and needs in a way that adults can understand. Cassie Hulse, the director of professional development at Thread, an early education resources centre in Alaska, states that 'Children are using the signs regularly, and it is very rewarding and exciting to see them effectively communicate with us. One of the benefits is that the children in our childcare centre have less frustration because they can 'tell us' what they want'. This is equally true for children with conditions like autism who may be able to speak but find conveying their thoughts and feelings a challenge.

Ultimately, there is nothing to lose and everything to gain by teaching a child sign language. From encouraging them to learn, to empowering them to communicate, signing gives children a step up in life.

Answer the questions below.

*Choose **NO MORE THAN TWO WORDS** from the passage for each answer.*

24 What do children build up through the repetition of motions?

25 Which educational model can prevent some students from succeeding?

26 Which disorder inhibits children's ability to translate their emotions into speech?

정답·해석·해설 p.450

---

sign language phr. 수화 **instill** v. 서서히 주입시키다 **bilingualism** n. 2개 국어를 말하는 능력 **toddler** n. 유아 **retain** v. 잊지 않고 있다, 마음에 간직하다
logical-mathematical adj. 논리-수학적인 **bodily-kinaesthetic** adj. 신체-운동 감각의 **interpersonal** adj. 대인적 **intrapersonal** adj. 개인적
well-rounded adj. 균형이 잡힌, 다재다능한 **cater** v. 만족시키다, 제공하다 **autism** n. 자폐증 **empower** v. ~할 수 있도록 하다, 권한을 주다

READING PASSAGE

*You should spend about 20 minutes on **Questions 1-13**, which are based on Reading Passage below.*

The Bittern in the UK: Reason for Hope in the Face of Concern

A   In modern times, an enormous number of species have disappeared from the planet permanently. Similarly, many species have become locally rare or absent, and these cases are also of concern for conservationists. One example is the Eurasian bittern, a bird species in the heron family with an extremely broad distribution throughout much of Europe, Asia, and parts of Africa. Though abundant worldwide, it has struggled in some places, such as the United Kingdom, where its numbers have plummeted over the past two centuries. This is particularly true of non-migrating breeding pairs as seasonal winter visitors are a regular occurrence in parts of Great Britain. In the UK, the bittern became extinct by the late 1880s before reappearing in 1911. Subsequently its population gradually increased until the 1960s, when it once again began to decline dramatically. By the early 1990s, the bittern was on the verge of vanishing in the UK for the second time in as many centuries, with as few as 11 males remaining.

B   Hunting was probably the greatest threat to the bittern in the early 1800s, as the birds were easy targets for Scottish nobles who practised falconry, and they were widely valued among the population at large for their highly palatable meat. But the bittern's demise in the second half of the 19th century, and the more recent decline encompassing the period from the 1960s to the 1990s, was due to environmental mismanagement. Much of this was a result of human-induced habitat loss or destruction, primarily through the draining of wetlands for agricultural purposes. Eurasian bitterns require freshwater wetlands, and in the UK these birds are particularly associated with beds of reed; indeed, these reed marshes are the lifeblood of this vulnerable species. It is estimated that as much as 40 per cent of this habitat was lost between 1945 and 1990 due to human development.

C   However, some of the loss of habitat was due to the drying up of wetlands because of the encroachment of plants and trees. Interestingly, this was also due to human behavioral patterns. Historically in Great Britain, reeds were cut, dried, and bundled for use in the thatching industry, which supplied the traditional thatched roofs that can still be seen in some English towns. But in modern times, changes in building patterns led to the decline of this practice, which had traditionally maintained the reed monoculture that bitterns seem to favour. Thus, leaving the wetlands to nature ironically contributed to the bittern's demise.

D   A continual challenge is that the largest remaining marshes of this type are in the eastern coastal areas of England, where they are susceptible to occasional but recurring infiltration by saltwater. Though these reed marshes support bittern populations, they are too at risk of natural tidal influences to be relied on exclusively. In addition, the diet of these birds is based heavily on two fish, eels and rudd, which are also frequent visitors to reed beds. This dependence is particularly true in the breeding season, as studies of regurgitated food indicate that the diet of bittern chicks is almost exclusively made up of these fish.

E   The answer to the problem, then, is the creation of completely new wetlands suitable for bittern occupation, which must be done in conjunction with the extension of existing ones, and this challenge has recently been taken on by conservationists. At Avalon Marshes, environmental projects have been conducted to reclaim traditional marshland that had been altered by development on many occasions throughout history. This undertaking has resulted in new small, landscape-scale reed beds, and whilst they are insufficient to maintain a huge bittern population on their own, they significantly add to the strength of the overall bittern population in England. This effort was essentially a wetland reclamation project after minerals and peat had been extracted for commercial purposes. Similarly, agencies such as the Royal Society for the Protection of Birds (RSPB) have mobilised 'to create new wetlands on a previously unimaginable scale'.

F   Environmentalists have determined that upwards of 1 million hectares are suitable for the creation of new reed beds, and they've found an ally in the resurgence of the thatching industry. A space of 10 hectares can sustain one reed cutter for a whole season, and considering that every 1000 additional hectares can support 50 more bitterns, the only thing standing in the way of a successful bittern revival is the collective will of government agencies, private industry, and landowners.

G   Due to conservation efforts, the population of bitterns began to rise after 1997, and while the future of the bittern in Great Britain is uncertain, it is potentially bright based on recent trends. Though counts are imprecise – the birds are extremely secretive and difficult to observe, so numbers must be inferred from the calls ('booms') of males – detailed studies reveal promising results. A comprehensive assessment of nearly 400 sites determined that a minimum of 600 bitterns were present in Great Britain in the winter of 2009-2010. Of these, researchers estimated that approximately two-thirds were winter immigrants, leaving perhaps 200 or so year-round residents. Recently, a subsequent partial survey by the RSPB indicated that there were at least 132 resident males, and in an example of localised population growth, Avalon Marshes reported that their population of bitterns had grown considerably over the past few seasons.

Questions 1-6

Answer the questions below.

Choose **NO MORE THAN TWO WORDS AND/OR A NUMBER** from the passage for each answer.

1   How many bitterns remained in Britain in the early 1990s?

2   Who was mentioned in relation to the hunting of bitterns?

3   What kinds of roofs were traditionally used on houses in Great Britain?

4   What sometimes flows onto the reed marshes in the east of England?

5   How much land is needed to support a reed cutter for a season?

6   Which local area saw an increase in the bittern population?

Questions 7-11

Reading Passage has seven paragraphs, **A-G**.

Which paragraph contains the following information?

7   a reference to the prior extinction of bitterns in the United Kingdom

8   how a wetland was rescued after their commercial use

9   a description of the amount of land that is suitable for creating new reeds

10   a statement about wetlands being drained to support agriculture

11   the way a decline in reed cutting negatively affected the bittern population

Questions 12 and 13

Choose **TWO** correct letters, **A-E**.

12-13   Which **TWO** characteristics of the fish that bitterns rely on for food are mentioned?

    A   They are usually found in tidal areas.

    B   They are far more numerous than in the past.

    C   They often spend time in reed beds.

    D   They are especially important in the breeding season.

    E   They are in danger of becoming extinct soon.

정답·해석·해설 p.458

VOCABULARY LIST

Chapter 10에서 선별한 다음의 어휘들을 음성파일을 들으며 암기한 후 퀴즈로 확인해보세요.

*해커스 동영상강의 포털 해커스 인강(HackersIngang.com)에서 단어암기 MP3를 무료로 다운로드할 수 있습니다.

☐ mural n. 벽화
☐ detach v. 분리하다, 떼다
☐ disassembly n. 해체, 분리
☐ portable adj. 휴대하기 쉬운
☐ lightweight adj. 가벼운
☐ warp v. 휘다, 틀어지다
☐ glossy adj. 반들반들한, 윤이 나는
☐ finish n. 마감 칠 (상태), 마무리 칠
☐ feel n. 질감
☐ go to great lengths to phr. ~하려고 무엇이든 하다
☐ internal adj. 체내의, 내부의
☐ mechanism n. 기제, 방법
☐ time frame phr. 기간, 시간
☐ mate v. 짝짓기를 하다
☐ hibernation n. 동면, 겨울잠
☐ orbit n. 궤도
☐ Neptune n. 해왕성
☐ Uranus n. 천왕성
☐ tentatively adv. 잠정적으로
☐ tireless adj. 끊임없는
☐ celestial adj. 천체의
☐ carry on phr. ~을 계속하다
☐ alternate v. 교차하다, 엇갈리다
☐ speck n. 입자, 작은 조각
☐ telescopic adj. 망원경의
☐ ensuing adj. 뒤이은, 다음의

☐ dwarf planet phr. 왜소행성
☐ unmanned adj. 무인의
☐ flash flood phr. 갑작스런 홍수
☐ outfit v. (특정 목적에 필요한 복장·장비를) 갖추어 주다
☐ thermal sensor phr. 열 감지기
☐ as of now phr. 현재로서는
☐ poacher n. 밀렵꾼
☐ optimistic adj. 낙관적인
☐ chronicle n. 기록, 연대기
☐ intoxicating adj. 취하게 만드는
☐ fermentation n. 발효 (작용)
☐ echelon n. 계급, 계층
☐ tribute n. 조공, 공물
☐ top priority phr. 최우선 순위
☐ breeding ground phr. 번식지
☐ encroach v. 침해하다
☐ sperm n. 정자
☐ swell v. 부풀다, 부어 오르다
☐ embryo n. 배아
☐ tadpole n. 올챙이
☐ encasement n. 포장
☐ voraciously adv. 왕성하게, 게걸스럽게
☐ metamorphosis n. 변태, 변형
☐ gill n. 아가미
☐ civilian adj. 민간의
☐ segment n. 부분

Quiz

각 단어의 알맞은 뜻을 찾아 연결하시오.

01 mechanism   ⓐ 기제, 방법
02 disassembly   ⓑ ~을 계속하다
03 alternate   ⓒ 해체, 분리
04 internal   ⓓ 끊임없는
05 carry on   ⓔ 교차하다, 엇갈리다
                    ⓕ 체내의, 내부의

06 optimistic   ⓐ 계급, 계층
07 swell   ⓑ 부풀다, 부어 오르다
08 segment   ⓒ 최우선 순위
09 echelon   ⓓ 번식지
10 top priority   ⓔ 부분
                    ⓕ 낙관적인

ⓒ 01 ⓐ 02 ⓒ 03 ⓔ 04 ⓕ 05 ⓑ 06 ⓕ 07 ⓑ 08 ⓔ 09 ⓐ 10 ⓒ

- ☐ transmit v. 전송하다
- ☐ backup adj. 예비의, 대체의
- ☐ solar eclipse phr. 일식
- ☐ rocket booster phr. 추진 로켓
- ☐ ground station phr. (우주선의) 지상 관제소
- ☐ atomic clock phr. 원자 시계
- ☐ veer off course phr. 항로를 이탈하다
- ☐ latitude n. 위도
- ☐ longitude n. 경도
- ☐ altitude n. 고도
- ☐ bearing n. 방위
- ☐ disaster relief phr. 재난 구호
- ☐ tectonics n. 구조 지질학
- ☐ reconnaissance n. (군사적인 목적의) 정찰
- ☐ synchronisation n. 동기화, 시계를 맞추기
- ☐ ocean floor phr. 해저, 대양저
- ☐ excursion n. 여행
- ☐ submersible n. 잠수함
- ☐ converge v. ~을 만나게 하다, 모이다
- ☐ gap n. 갈라진 틈
- ☐ penetrate v. 관통하다
- ☐ spurt from phr. ~에서 뿜어져 나오다
- ☐ suspend v. 떠 있게 하다
- ☐ solidify v. 굳어지다
- ☐ accumulation n. 퇴적, 축적
- ☐ chimney n. 분화구

- ☐ chemosynthesis n. 화학 합성
- ☐ shed light on phr. 밝히다, 해명하다
- ☐ place v. (누구인지를) 알아보다, 생각해 내다
- ☐ demoralising adj. 혼란시키는
- ☐ go hand in hand phr. 관련되다
- ☐ fit n. 발작
- ☐ deterioration n. 퇴화
- ☐ frail adj. 허약한
- ☐ succumb to phr. (병 따위로) 쓰러지다, ~에 굴복하다
- ☐ burnout n. 극도의 피로, 연료 소진
- ☐ fallout n. 악영향
- ☐ affliction n. 고통
- ☐ sign language phr. 수화
- ☐ bilingualism n. 2개 국어를 말하는 능력
- ☐ toddler n. 유아
- ☐ retain v. 잊지 않고 있다, 마음에 간직하다
- ☐ well-rounded adj. 균형이 잡힌, 다재다능한
- ☐ cater v. 만족시키다, 제공하다
- ☐ empower v. ~할 수 있도록 하다, 권한을 주다
- ☐ palatable adj. 맛있는, 맛좋은
- ☐ encompass v. 포함하다, 아우르다
- ☐ infiltration n. 침투
- ☐ regurgitate v. 역류시키다
- ☐ reclamation n. 재생 (이용), 개간
- ☐ mobilise v. 동원되다, 조직되다
- ☐ resurgence n. 부활, 재기

Quiz

각 단어의 알맞은 뜻을 찾아 연결하시오.

01 converge	ⓐ 민간의
02 transmit	ⓑ 퇴적, 축적
03 accumulation	ⓒ 예비의, 대체의
04 penetrate	ⓓ 전송하다
05 backup	ⓔ ~을 만나게 하다, 모이다
	ⓕ 관통하다

06 affliction	ⓐ 포함하다, 아우르다
07 resurgence	ⓑ 침투
08 encompass	ⓒ 고통
09 frail	ⓓ 동원되다, 조직되다
10 mobilise	ⓔ 허약한
	ⓕ 부활, 재기

ⓓ 01 ⓔ 02 ⓑ 03 ⓕ 04 ⓒ 05 ⓒ 06 ⓕ 07 ⓐ 08 ⓔ 09 ⓓ 10

HACKERS
IELTS
READING

goHackers.com

학습자료 제공·유학정보 공유

ACTUAL
TEST

* Answer sheet는 교재 마지막 페이지(p.299)에 수록되어 있습니다.

READING PASSAGE 1

*You should spend about 20 minutes on **Questions 1-13**, which are based on Reading Passage 1 below.*

The Cloud of Promise: The 2008 Olympic Torch and Relay

Prior to the 2006 Winter Olympics in Turin, Italy, Lenovo, an international China-based computer company, signed up to be an Olympic sponsor in the 2006 Games as well as the 2008 Summer Olympics in Beijing, China. Moreover, it won the bid to design the Olympic torch for 2008. The company's design, 'Cloud of Promise', upstaged the designs of over 300 competitors. The 'Cloud of Promise' sought to wed modern technological design with elements from traditional Chinese aesthetics and culture. The design mimicked the form of a traditional Chinese scroll, which signified the invention of paper – one of the four great inventions of ancient China – as well as the color red, an auspicious colour in China, and swirling 'lucky clouds' that visually evoked the thought of the Olympic rings.

Yet it was not merely something pretty to look at. The cutting-edge technology used to create the torch was part graphic design and part rocket science. Fashioned from polished, lightweight aluminum-magnesium alloy, the torch came in at 72 cm in height and only 985 grams. The international team of designers sought to create a torch that was 'attractive to those who see it, and light for those who carry it'. Also contributing to the item's wieldable quality was the presence of a thin rubber-based varnish on the handle to facilitate grip and ease of handling.

For the internal portion of the torch, Lenovo turned to the China Aerospace Science and Industry Group. Indeed, both the private and state-sponsored technological acumen of China were on full display. Of crucial importance was the requirement that the flame remain lit for the entire duration of the torch's long journey, including during a widely publicised side trip in which athletes lugged a modified replica to the summit of the Himalayan mountain range. Inside the handle of the Olympic torch was a small canister of pure liquid propane, which was presumably chosen over the conventional precedent of using mixed gases due to propane's strong resistance to cold. When the ignition switch was turned on, it created a sudden drop in pressure, causing the gas to vaporise and flow through tiny holes at the top of the torch, fueling the 'never-ending' Olympic flame.

The designers also came up with a pressure-stabilisation system and a heat-recovery device that provided further security against the flame's extinguishment, and had the foresight to include a special oxidiser in the replica to supply the necessary oxygen for propane to combust in environmental conditions of low oxygen, such as on Mt. Everest, where this flame would have to withstand extremely low air pressure, frigid temperatures, and high winds. All in all, the Olympic torch was rumored to be able to withstand temperatures of minus 40 degrees Celsius, rains of five centimetres per hour, and winds of 65 kilometres per hour, and the rigorous preparation paid off on 8 May when a team of mountaineers scaled the summit of the world's most famous mountain on live television to be seen across the globe. This side trip was conducted separately from the main relay, which at the time was occurring on the Chinese mainland.

Of course, the carriers of the torch were the people selected to bear it in the prestigious Olympic torch relay, and 21,800 participants got the opportunity to run with the torch in the main relay. The relay was the longest in Olympic history, starting in March of 2008 in Olympia, Greece and ending in August in Beijing, China with the lighting of the cauldron in the opening ceremonies. The torchbearers traversed a route of 137,000 kilometres involving 6 continents, 21 countries and 113 Chinese cities, and was thus a true world tour. Although the relay was unprecedented in scale, its magnificence was at times overshadowed by unusual and unfortunate circumstances. For instance, the planned June trip through the province of Sichuan was postponed until August due to the devastating 7.9 magnitude earthquake that happened there in May of 2008.

In addition, the relay endured widespread political demonstrations and protests by activists demanding that China change its position on Tibet and condemning its controversial human rights record in general. As a result, the torch relay was unusually costly in terms of security: in London, nearly 2,000 law enforcement officers were employed to confront thousands of protestors, who were trying to extinguish the Olympic flame and encourage sponsors to boycott the relay and the Olympic games, which cost £750,000. And in France, over 3,000 motorcycle police accompanied the torch and torch bearers as they travelled through Paris. In a sense, the emotional and symbolic effects of the torch representing goodwill and the Olympic image were muted by the controversy and surrounding security presence, which inhibited the torch's public accessibility. The 'Journey of Harmony' around the world had not been so harmonious after all, and the international press pounced on the opportunity to make disparaging statements about the relay, using such headlines as 'a Tour de Farce' or 'Torch's Journey Descends into Chaos'.

In the end, however, the torch found its proper place, arriving in Beijing on 6 August and being paraded around the capital for three days. The final relay was conducted by seven famous Chinese athletes, each taking their turn in getting the torch to the stadium, where it was then turned over to six-time Olympic gymnastics medallist, Ning Li. In a dramatic finale, the relay ended with Li being lifted in the air by cables as if he had taken flight, and he 'flew' a complete lap around the stadium before finally reaching and lighting the cauldron in a dazzling and triumphant display.

Questions 1-7

Do the following statements agree with the information given in Reading Passage 1?

In boxes 1-7 on your answer sheet, write

TRUE   *if the statement agrees with the information*
FALSE   *if the statement contradicts the information*
NOT GIVEN   *if there is no information on this*

1   The design and technology that went into the torch were solely developed by Lenovo.

2   Lenovo's 2008 torch required a different type of propane when it was taken to the Himalayas.

3   Turning the torch's ignition switch on resulted in an instantaneous decrease in pressure.

4   Although the 2008 torch relay was a momentous undertaking, it was not the longest in history.

5   The security cost for the London portion of the relay was highest along the entire route.

6   In Paris, the public's access to the torch was high due to a smaller security presence.

7   Some media outlets made negative comments about the torch relay.

Answer the questions below.

*Choose **ONE WORD ONLY** from the passage for each answer.*

Write your answers in boxes 8-13 on your answer sheet.

8   Which traditional Chinese motif was the physical design of the Olympic torch largely based on?

9   What was added to the exterior of the torch to make it easier to carry?

10   What did athletes carry when they went to the top of the Himalayas?

11   Which part of the torch allowed the flame to withstand the harsh conditions on Mt. Everest?

12   What natural disaster was mentioned as a disruption to the schedule of the torch relay?

13   What allowed the final athlete in the relay to appear suspended above the stadium?

READING PASSAGE 2

*You should spend about 20 minutes on **Questions 14-26**, which are based on Reading Passage 2 below.*

The Scent of Bygone Days: Is Smell Uniquely Intertwined with Memory?

A   There is a popular and widely circulated claim that odours are the strongest cues to memory. This adage has been promulgated in scientific as well as popular publications. Take Diane Ackerman's 1990 declarations that 'Perfume is liquid memory' and 'Smells detonate softly in our memory like poignant land mines' as examples, and the role of the olfactory sense in emotion and memory comes vividly to life in literary allusion and allegory.

B   Through smell, we are instantaneously taken back to an intact simulated excerpt from our past. In 1991, Trygg Engen wrote that smell generates episodic memory, providing a richly detailed autobiographical episode borne totally complete in a single memory unit. He contrasted this to semantic memory, which relies on words, categories, indexing, and the like. In his view, smell may be the most primal of the senses and a product of a primitive world prior to language. But is scent really such a powerful cue for reminiscences as received wisdom would suggest?

C   The phenomenon of smell-induced recollection has been studied in experiments, with mixed results. David Rubin and his colleagues at Duke University sought to investigate the assumption that an actual scent, rather than the idea of a scent, had a special function in memory. In 1984, they recruited forty student participants and assigned them randomly to either be presented with an odour or written words representing the odour. They utilised what they thought would be familiar smells, particularly ones that might provoke an early memory; these included Johnson & Johnson's baby powder, plasters, soap, peanut butter, etc.

D   Then participants were asked to describe any memories awakened by the scents or descriptions and respond to questions like 'How clear or vivid was the memory?' or 'How did you feel emotionally at the time of the memory?' In a second experiment, the researchers used a similar method but added photographs representative of an odour in addition to the actual scent and written words. The team made some surprising discoveries, such as that a memory triggered by an actual scent was likely to have never been thought of before, or thought of less often, and odour might often evoke a more pleasing or emotional memory than pictures or words.

E   Subsequent experiments have shed additional light on the issue. In 2000, British psychologist John Downes of the University of Liverpool discovered that the connection between an actual scent and a memory seems to be tied to age. He gathered subjects in their late 60s and early 70s, presented them with olfactory cues or verbal cues (smell-related words), and asked them to describe a related autobiographical experience that came to mind. Their analysis revealed that the actual odours triggered memories from a much younger age than the verbal cues. The former tended to revive recollections from age 6 to 10, whereas the latter generally evoked memories from between 11 and 25 years of age. This suggests both that smell is a crucial factor in providing a backdrop of contextual details for childhood experiences and that it is indeed closely tied to episodic memory because semantic abilities are still limited in late childhood and continue to form well into adolescence.

F Another interesting experiment was described in a 1999 article in the *British Journal of Psychology*. The author, John Aggleton of Cardiff University, employed a double-cueing methodology in an ingenious manner: he sought to test the relationship between odour and memory outside the laboratory, so he visited the Jorvik Viking Centre, a museum in York, where an exhibition had piped 'Viking odours' into the exhibit area for a multisensory effect. Aggleton wanted to know if these odours would aid repeat visitors in remembering details of the exhibit years later. He gave three groups of returning museum goers questionnaires in various conditions – in the presence of the same original 'Viking odours', a control odour, and no odour. He then repeated the test but with changed conditions for each group. Only the group that took the second test in the presence of 'Viking odours' improved their performance on the questionnaire. Thus, Aggleton concluded that odours 'can provide strong contextual cues that aid in the recall of information originally presented in the presence of those odours'.

G Still, the vast majority of experts agree that the notion of smell being the 'best' cue to memory is largely unfounded because there is no proof that an odour-evoked memory is more accurate than that of any of the other stimuli. However, there does seem to be a consensus that odour-related memories are more emotional in essence. According to Rachel Hertz's article in *The Oxford Handbook of Social Neuroscience*, when an odour evokes a memory, this first creates emotional sensations, 'After which the event which initially brought about the emotion emerges. In other words, the experiential order of odour-evoked memory appears to follow the temporal sequence of the neurological pathways that are involved.' This order progresses from the sensory-perceptual, to the limbic-emotional and then on to higher cognitive structures. Hertz claims that the 'bottom-up versus top-down temporal unfolding of odour-evoked memory may distinguish it from other memory experiences'.

H Thus, the strong association between olfaction and emotional recollection likely has an evolutionary basis as it has undoubtedly played a key role in human survival. Anatomically, olfactory centres are in close proximity to the most basic portions of the brain, which are directly responsible for emotional experience and memory. Only two synapses separate the olfactory nerve from the amygdala, a set of neurons responsible for emotion, emotional behaviour, and motivation. In evolutionary terms, this integrative emotional centre – indeed, the entire limbic system – arose from the olfactory area of the brain. Considering this, some researchers, such as Michael Jawer, have suggested that without a sense of smell, we may have never evolved to have emotions at all.

Questions 14-19

Reading Passage 2 has eight paragraphs, **A-H**.

Which paragraph contains the following information?

*Write the correct letter, **A-H**, in boxes 14-19 on your answer sheet.*

14   the use of photos to signify smells

15   examples of well-known scents

16   a reference to the use of smell in metaphor

17   a mention of how feelings arise from memories

18   a description of a study conducted in a real-life setting

19   how different cues evoke the memories of different age periods

Questions 20-23

Complete the notes below.

*Choose **ONE WORD ONLY** for each answer.*

Write your answers in boxes 20-23 on your answer sheet.

Smell and Memory

– Smells may be the most powerful **20** .... in bringing up memory

Types of memory

– Trygg Engen: smells can offer an entire **21** .... of someone's life in one memory
– Smell might be the most primitive of the senses

Evoking childhood memories

– John Downes: smells set off memories of childhood more than statements
– Smell gives background information for **22** .... from youth

Order of smell memory

– Rachel Hertz: smell related memories progress from sense/perception, limbic/emotional to advanced

  23 .... structures
– Smell has a strong basis in evolution

Questions 24-26

Do the following statements agree with the information given in Reading Passage 2?

In boxes 24-26 on your answer sheet, write

TRUE   *if the statement agrees with the information*
FALSE   *if the statement contradicts the information*
NOT GIVEN   *if there is no information on this*

24   Photographs bring up more moving memories than smells.

25   Odour is more effective than taste for memory.

26   The better accuracy of smell for remembering is not proven.

Group Behaviour

Most people consider themselves autonomous individuals who make their own decisions. However, studies have shown that conformity is a natural human impulse, and people will go to astonishing lengths just to fit in.

In sociology, the similarity with which members of a group behave is known as group behaviour, and a peculiar aspect of people in groups is that they tend to conform to the beliefs, opinions, and behaviours of the other members. At times, people may even engage in conduct that conflicts with their personal moral and ethical code. Some violate these conventional codes because they perceive membership as too valuable to compromise. In such cases, their conscience may become disturbed, but they tend to go along with the group anyway. Many studies have explored or attempted to explain this phenomenon.

A series of tests conducted by Solomon Asch, an American Gestalt psychologist, examined the willingness of a group member to conform to the viewpoint of fellow members even if the members' viewpoint was incorrect. In each test, he put people in groups of seven at a table and showed them two cards – one with a single line and one with three lines of varying lengths. The participants were then asked which of the three lines on the second card was the same length as the single line on the first card. However, there was a catch. In each experiment, only one out of the seven subjects was 'real'; the others had been coached to respond to questions in a certain way. Specifically, they were told to purposely answer some questions incorrectly to pressure the real student to conform. Asch discovered that more than half of the real subjects went along with the incorrect answer at least once.

But is this really a simple matter of peer pressure or fear of going against the mainstream? Neurologist Gregory Berns sought a physiological explanation and conducted an experiment with MRI scanners to determine which parts of the brain were 'activated' when a person accepted a decision that was in conformation with the group, even when they felt it was incorrect. He reasoned that if peer pressure was responsible, he would see changes in activity in the forebrain, which is involved in monitoring conflicts. But what Berns discovered was that when people follow a group's opinion, the posterior areas of the brain were stimulated. This indicated that a change in spatial perception had occurred, and led Berns to conclude that the incorrect responses the false respondents had provided literally altered the perception of the true participants. Thus, he challenged the notion that the participants in the Asch experiment were merely giving in to peer pressure. In fact, they were actually seeing the length of the lines differently from how they would have if no false responses were given.

Social psychologist Stanley Milgram went even further in his experiments at Yale University in the early 1960s. The Milgram experiments were groundbreaking in that they were the first extensive ones carried out that focused on extreme obedience to authority and its potentially destructive repercussions. Milgram told the subjects that they were participating in a study about learning and memory and then assigned them to be 'teachers', with the stated goal of determining the role of punishment in learning. However, what Milgram actually wanted to do was find out the extremes to which people would go to punish others when instructed to do so. In the experiment Milgram designed, the subjects were instructed to punish the 'learners', who in fact were actors, by giving them an electric shock each time they failed to offer the correct answer. His experiments demonstrated that even when the actors screamed in agony for the test to stop, the majority of 'teachers' continued to administer the shocks at the request of the experimenter.

An even more ominous experiment conducted by a high school teacher in Palo Alto, California underscores the dangers of conforming. History teacher Ron Jones was teaching his class about totalitarianism when he was interrupted by a question asking how the citizens of any nation could be convinced to accept living under a dictatorship. This gave him an idea. The next week, he began lecturing on the positive qualities of discipline and instituted new rules, under the name 'Third Wave', which mandated that students answer questions succinctly, in three words or less. He also introduced slogans like 'Strength through discipline; strength through community' and had the students stand and recite the new mottos. Furthermore, he introduced a Third Wave salute and membership cards, and suggested that members report others who were breaking rules. He was astounded when

they willingly did so.

On the fourth day of the experiment, Jones told the students that Third Wave was based on an actual political movement in history and that he would reveal the leader of the movement the next day, and he did this by showing a film which featured Adolf Hitler and footage of the German labour camps during World War II. The students were stunned, and some were in tears. Jones pointed out to them that out of regard for the group's objectives, they had failed to examine their own convictions and the principles on which the group was founded. The name 'Third Wave' had not been accidental. Indeed, a new Third Reich had nearly been born.

Experiments aside, it goes without saying that in any society, group members must conform to some degree for cooperation and sound decision making. Yet the dangers of rigid conformity must be avoided, or it can result in 'groupthink', creating excessive loyalty to an idea, cause, action, or decision at the expense of critical thinking. So, then, in any group, deviance in some form is necessary to guarantee that the ramifications of a proposition are explored from every possible angle. Still, deviance in its extreme form can lead to stalemates, arguments, or even anarchy. Thus, it is imperative that constructive forms of criticism be encouraged while destructive criticism is regarded with the utmost vigilance.

Complete each sentence with the correct ending, **A-G**, below.

Write the correct answer, **A-G**, in boxes 27-31 on your answer sheet.

27 When membership of a group is considered so desirable, people

28 According to Berns, the false responses

29 In Milgram's experiment, subjects were told to

30 The Third Wave experiment required that students must

31 Strict compliance should be avoided because it can

A	have changed the participant's actual perception.
B	respond to questions with concise answers.
C	go against the accepted code.
D	prove that conformity influences behaviour.
E	get in the way of critical thinking.
F	have an impact on group decisions.
G	impose punishment at false responses.

Questions 32-35

Do the following statements agree with the views of the writer in Reading Passage 3?

In boxes 32-35 on your answer sheet, write

YES	if the statement agrees with the views of the writer
NO	if the statement contradicts the views of the writer
NOT GIVEN	if it is impossible to say what the writer thinks about this

32 Asch found that only a few of the real participants chose incorrect answers.

33 Milgram intended to test how much punishment a person would inflict on another when told to.

34 Any form of deviance will ensure that an idea is effective enough to realise.

35 Criticism which is not beneficial must be viewed with the greatest caution.

Questions 36-40

*Choose the correct letter, **A**, **B**, **C** or **D**.*

Write the correct letter in boxes 36-40 on your answer sheet.

36 What was Solomon Asch trying to find out?

    A   what type of people conform to a group consensus

    B   how people reacted to the correct choice

    C   whether people could identify a group's incorrect viewpoint

    D   whether people would conform to a wrong opinion

37 The false participants in Asch's study were there to

    A   challenge the answers of real participants.

    B   agree with the answers of other members of the group.

    C   pressure the real participant to conform by giving wrong answers.

    D   ask the other participants to conform.

38 When conducting his experiment, Gregory Berns found that

    A   accepting group decisions created activity in the posterior regions of the brain.

    B   the participants were the same as those who were used in Asch's experiments.

    C   physiological explanations had been largely ignored by previous researchers.

    D   the front area of the brain is responsible for people's tendency to conform.

39 According to the writer, Milgram's experiments were innovative because

    A   they investigated the relationship between learning and punishment.

    B   they emphasised the possible negative consequences of accepting authority.

    C   they were the first to make use of electric shock on unsuspecting participants.

    D   they were sceptical of the role that memory plays in overall student learning.

40 The teacher who conducted the Third Wave experiment was shocked when students

    A   came up with punishment for violation.

    B   strongly opposed the rules.

    C   organised a group to resist him.

    D   told on classmates who didn't follow the rules.

정답·해석·해설 p.462

HACKERS
IELTS
READING

goHackers.com

학습자료 제공·유학정보 공유

미국 영어와
영국 영어의 차이

IELTS Reading 영역에서는 영국식 어휘와 철자가 등장한다. 그동안 미국식 영어에 많이 노출되어 있던 한국 학습자들에게 영국식 영어는 낯설게 느껴질 수 있으므로, 기본적인 어휘와 철자의 차이를 숙지하여 두는 것이 좋다.

미국 영어와 영국 영어의 어휘와 철자 차이

IELTS Reading 영역에서는 영국 영어의 어휘와 철자가 지문과 문제에 출제된다. 미국 영어와 영국 영어에서 사용하는 어휘와 철자가 서로 다른 경우는 많지 않지만, 시험에 자주 등장하므로 꼭 알아두도록 한다.

어휘 차이

미국 영어와 영국 영어에서 사용되는 어휘가 다른 경우도 있다. 같은 어휘이지만 다른 의미로 쓰이는 경우도 있다.

1 동일한 뜻, 다른 어휘

	미국	영국
1층, 2층	first floor, second floor	ground floor, first floor
대중 교통	public transportation	public transport
고속도로	highway; freeway	motorway
공립학교	public school	state school
주택 단지	housing development	housing estate
대학교 1학년	freshman	first-year student
대학교 2학년	sophomore	second-year student
대학교 3학년	junior	third-year student
대학교 4학년	senior	fourth-year student
변호사	attorney/lawyer	barrister/solicitor
영화관	theater	cinema
왕복 여행	round trip	return trip
우편	mail	post
우편번호	zip code	postal code
일정표	schedule	timetable
주차장	parking lot	car park
줄을 서다	stand in line	queue
지폐	bill	note
지하철	subway	tube/underground
초등학교	elementary school	primary school
화물차	truck	lorry
휘발유	gas/gasoline	petrol
휴가	vacation	holiday

2 동일한 어휘, 다른 뜻

	미국	영국
football	미식 축구	축구
homely	잘나지 못한	가정적인
merchant	소매 상인	도매상, 무역상
pavement	포장도로	보도
pocketbook	핸드백	수첩
public school	공립학교	사립 중등학교
subway	지하철	지하도
vest	조끼	속옷

철자 차이

미국 영어와 영국 영어에서 사용되는 어휘와 의미는 같지만, 철자가 조금씩 다른 경우가 있다.

차이	의미	미국	영국
-ck/-k & -que	수표	check	cheque
	체크무늬	checker	chequer
-er & -re	영화관	theater	theatre
	중심	center	centre
-ll & -l	달성하다	fulfill	fulfil
	입학, 등록	enrollment	enrolment
-og & -ogue	독백	monolog	monologue
	목록	catalog	catalogue
-or & -our	색	color	colour
	행동	behavior	behaviour
-se & -ce	방어	defense	defence
	허가	license	licence
-ze & -se	인식하다	recognize	recognise
	준비하다	organize	organise
기타	계획표	program	programme
	쟁기	plow	plough

goHackers.com

학습자료 제공·유학정보 공유

IELTS READING DIAGNOSTIC TEST ANSWER SHEET

Test Date (Shade ONE box for the day, ONE box for the month and ONE box for the year)

Day: 01 02 03 04 05 06 07 08 09 10 11 12 13 14 15 16 17 18 19 20 21 22 23 24 25 26 27 28 29 30 31

Month: 01 02 03 04 05 06 07 08 09 10 11 12   **Year** (last 2 digits): 17 18 19 20 21 22 23 24 25

Reading	Reading Reading Reading Reading Reading Reading		Reading	Reading Reading Reading Reading Reading Reading
1		21		
2		22		
3		23		
4		24		
5		25		
6		26		
7		27		
8		28		
9		29		
10		30		
11		31		
12		32		
13		33		
14		34		
15		35		
16		36		
17		37		
18		38		
19		39		
20		40		

Reading Total	

IELTS READING ACTUAL TEST ANSWER SHEET

Test Date (Shade ONE box for the day, ONE box for the month and ONE box for the year)

Day: 01 02 03 04 05 06 07 08 09 10 11 12 13 14 15 16 17 18 19 20 21 22 23 24 25 26 27 28 29 30 31

Month: 01 02 03 04 05 06 07 08 09 10 11 12   **Year** (last 2 digits): 17 18 19 20 21 22 23 24 25

Reading	Reading	Reading	Reading	Reading	Reading	Reading

1		21	
2		22	
3		23	
4		24	
5		25	
6		26	
7		27	
8		28	
9		29	
10		30	
11		31	
12		32	
13		33	
14		34	
15		35	
16		36	
17		37	
18		38	
19		39	
20		40	

Reading Total	

아이엘츠 유형별 공략으로 Overall 고득점 달성!

HACKERS IELTS Reading

초판 17쇄 발행 2025년 1월 13일

초판 1쇄 발행 2017년 5월 29일

지은이	해커스 어학연구소
펴낸곳	(주)해커스 어학연구소
펴낸이	해커스 어학연구소 출판팀

주소	서울특별시 서초구 강남대로61길 23 (주)해커스 어학연구소
고객센터	02-537-5000
교재 관련 문의	publishing@hackers.com
동영상강의	HackersIngang.com

ISBN	978-89-6542-229-7 (13740)
Serial Number	01-17-01

외국어인강 1위,
해커스인강(HackersIngang.com)

㉮ 해커스인강

1. IELTS 리딩 **단어암기 MP3**
2. 내 답안을 고득점 에세이로 만드는 **IELTS 라이팅 1:1 첨삭**
3. 해커스 스타강사의 **IELTS 인강**

전세계 유학정보의 중심,
고우해커스(goHackers.com)

㉮ 고우해커스

1. **IELTS 라이팅/스피킹 무료 첨삭 게시판**
2. **IELTS 리딩/리스닝 실전문제** 등 다양한 IELTS 무료 학습 콘텐츠
3. **IELTS Q&A 게시판** 및 영국유학 Q&A 게시판

너는 오르고, 나는 오르지 않았던 이유
너만 알았던 그 비법!

goHackers.com

HACKERS IELTS Reading

ACADEMIC MODULE

IELTS 인강 · 리딩 단어암기 MP3
해커스인강 HackersIngang.com

IELTS 리딩/리스닝 무료 실전문제 · IELTS 라이팅/스피킹 무료 첨삭 게시판
고우해커스 goHackers.com

해커스 어학연구소

HACKERS IELTS

Reading

ACADEMIC MODULE

정답 · 해석 · 해설

해커스 어학연구소

HACKERS
IELTS
READING

goHackers.com

학습자료 제공·유학정보 공유

CONTENTS

*각 문제에 대한 정답의 단서는 지문에 문제 번호와 함께 별도의 색으로 표시되어 있습니다.

1	viii	2	v	3	iv	4	iii
5	ix	6	vi	7	B	8	C
9	G	10	F	11	A	12	E
13	D	14	E	15	B	16	A
17	C	18	governors	19	academic success	20	opportunities
21	funding	22	False	23	False	24	Not given
25	True	26	True	27	No	28	Not given
29	Yes	30	Not given	31	Yes	32	D
33	C	34	A	35	B	36	D
37	glacial sediments	38	continental drift	39	tropics	40	iron

READING PASSAGE 1

[1-6]

제목 리스트

i   규제를 회피하는 해외 투자자들의 영향
ii 정부의 투자는 지역 주민의 일자리로 이어진다
iii 부동산 가격에 대한 관광업의 영향
iv 경쟁은 현지 사업체들에게 난제가 된다
v   불평등한 소득의 문제
vi 지역 사회에 대한 비경제적 결과
vii 경제를 성장시키는 신속한 방법으로서의 관광업
viii 널리 퍼진 환경 악화
ix 다른 산업의 개발을 방치하는 것의 영향

1 단락 B

2 단락 C

3 단락 D

4 단락 E

5 단락 F

6 단락 G

관광 개발: 축복인가 저주인가?

A   한데 묶여 제3세계라고 불리는 개발도상국들에서, 관광업은 빠르고 효율적인 경제 발전의 수단으로 여겨진다. 이는 수출할 만한 천연자원은 부족하지만, 해변, 산맥, 우거진 산림, 그리고 밀림과 같은 자연 관광 명소를 많이 보유하고 있는 나라들에 특히 해당한다. 시민들을 위한 경제 수익을 극대화하는 수단으로써, ⁹그러한 나라들은 관광업을 홍보하고 적합한 관광 기반 시설을 구축하여 이런

관광 명소들을 활용하도록 장려된다. 많은 국가들이 이 기회를 받아들이고 있으며 개발도상국들이 관광 산업을 확장하는 데 크게 투자하는 현저한 경향이 있어왔다.

B 그러나, 현실에서는, [1]관광업은 자연계에 광범위한 피해를 야기할 수 있다. [10]그러므로 그것은 기여해야 할 사회에 이익보다 더 많은 피해를 가져올 수 있다. 예를 들어, 생태 관광은, '환경 친화적인' 여행객들을 끌어들이기 위해 그 장소의 자연의 아름다움을 활용하도록 구상되었지만, 얄궂게도 그들의 편의를 도모하기 위해 자연은 종종 희생된다. 매년, 수많은 관광객들이 화려한 경관을 보고, 깨끗한 물속 산호초 가운데서 스쿠버 다이빙을 하고, 섬 내륙의 열대 우림을 탐험하기 위해 세인트루시아 섬으로 모여든다. 관리가 잘 되는 스쿠버 다이빙 여행과 열대 우림 여행은 토종 야생동물과 식물군을 직접적으로 침해하지는 않을 수도 있겠지만, 생태 관광객을 수용하기 위해 건설된 리조트는 해안 침식의 상당한 증가를 야기했고, 보트 운송업의 수요는 맹그로브 늪지의 상실과 해양 환경 오염의 증가를 야기했다 (Nagle, 1999).

C [2]또 다른 문제는 후진국들에서 거의 언제나 관광업의 결과로 나타나는 소득 격차이다. 이는 정부가 도로, 공항, 대중교통 등의 공공 기반 시설에 대량으로 투자하면서 시작된다. [11]이런 계획 사업에 투자할 자금은, 이 투자가 지역 인구를 위한 일자리와 기회를 창출할 것이라는 믿음에서 납세자들의 지갑으로부터 나오지만, 그렇게 되는 일은 거의 없다. 호텔, 리조트, 공원, 그리고 식당을 건설하는 계약은 흔히 이윤을 증대시키기 위해 현지 노동자들을 착취하는 부유한 기업가들에게 주어진다. 그 후, 시설이 개방되면, 최저 임금을 간신히 넘기는 임금을 받고 근무하는 고용된 직원들에게도 같은 일이 발생한다. 그러므로, 증가하는 빈부 격차가 더 낮은 사회경제적 계층들을 더 심한 가난으로 몰아세우는 동안 부유한 사람들은 더 부유해진다.

D 게다가, [3]해외 투자자들은 소규모의 현지 기업들이 경쟁하는 것을 불가능하게 만든다. [12]국제적인 체인들은 세계의 거의 모든 국가에서 해안 부지 공간을 위한 입찰의 가장 우선순위에 있다. 그들은 발달하는 관광 구역들에서 거점을 확보하기 위해 아주 높은 비용을 지불한다. 이런 일이 코스타리카에서 발생했는데, 그곳에서는 외국인이나 외국 기업이 나라에 있는 호텔의 65퍼센트를 소유한다. 그러므로, 관광업이 코스타리카 국내 총생산의 12.5퍼센트를 구성하고 있음에도 불구하고, 현지 사업체들은 이 번창하는 산업으로부터 이익을 얻지 못했다.

E 이런 추세는 민간 부동산 시장에도 영향을 미친다. [4]한 장소가 일단 외국인들에게 유명해지면, 별장을 구매하기 위한 수요가 급증하는데, 이는 극적으로 부동산 가치를 상승시키며 본래의 주민들을 쫓아낸다. 이는 스페인 연안이나 그리스 섬 중 어느 곳이라도 여행해본 사람에게는 명백할 것이다. 벨리즈에 관한 샌프란시스코 주립 대학의 연구는 관광 개발의 결과로, 지난 10년 동안에만 현지 시세가 전반적으로 약 8퍼센트 증가했음을 보여주었다. 태국과 같은 일부 국가들에서는, 외국인의 직접적인 부동산 소유를 불법화했는데, 이는 이런 영향을 어느 정도 완화했다. 하지만, 이런 엄격한 규정에도 불구하고, [7]사람들은 여전히 부동산을 구매하기 위해 태국 시민이나 기업과 협력하여 법을 교묘히 피할 방법을 찾아낸다. 결국에는, 음식, 물, 의류, 그리고 생필품과 같은 다른 기본 비용의 인상이 그러하듯, 가격이 폭등한 부동산 시장이 불가피해진다.

F 하지만 누가 수익을 얻고 있는지와는 관계없이, 위험에도 불구하고 현지 인구는 관광객 화폐의 유입에 의존하게 된다. 예를 들어, 감비아에서는, 노동인구의 30퍼센트가 직접적으로 혹은 간접적으로 관광업에 의존하며, 몰디브에서, 이 수치는 놀랄 만한 83퍼센트이다. [8]상당한 양의 가능한 일자리가 관광업을 중심으로 돌아갈 때, 국가들은 종종 이 의존도를 감소시킬 수 있는 다른 분야의 개발을 방치한다. 이것이 문제가 되는 것처럼 보이지 않을 수도 있지만, 예상치 못한 사건이 국가의 안정을 위협하고 관광객들을 불안하게 하면 금세 문제가 드러난다. 이는 사회 불안과 자연 재해가 관광의 극적인 감소로 인한 불황을 야기한 태국에서 지난 10년 동안 수 차례 발생해왔다.

G [6]경제적 측면 외에도, 고성장 관광업의 지역 사회에 대한 사회적 영향 또한 존재한다. [13]외국의 영향과 더불어 반갑지 않은 행동 방식과 활동이 나타날 수 있다. 이는 달갑지 않은 관습이나 지역 풍속과 상반되는 버릇일 뿐일 수도 있다. 하지만 약물 사용, 알코올 남용, 경범죄의 증가와 같이 이는 또한 더 심각한 것일 수도 있는데, 모두 관광에 종종 수반되는 것들이다. 지역 주민들이 직접적으로 이런 위법 행위에 관여하지 않더라도, 범죄 행위의 증가로 인해 악영향을 받을 수밖에 없으며, 그 때문에 종종 개인 신변의 안전과 삶의 질이 감소했다는 느낌을 받았다고 이야기할 것이다. 그러므로, 관광 산업의 개발은 개발도상국에 투자와, 세계의 방문객들, 그리고 다루기 힘든 다양한 문제들의 유입을 야기하는 좋기도 하고 나쁘기도 한 것이 될 수 있다. 이런 국가들의 정부는 이익은 널리 퍼지고, 부정적인 영향은 피하거나 최소화될 수 있도록 효율적으로 관광업을 규제하고 운영하기 위해 최선을 다해야 한다.

어휘   Global South phr. 제3세계   exportable adj. 수출할 만한   lush adj. 우거진, 무성한   capitalise v. 활용하다   locale n. 장소, 현장   green adj. 환경 친화적인   accommodate v. ~의 편의를 도모하다, 수용하다   hordes of phr. 수많은   flora n. 식물군   erosion n. 침식, 부식   swamp n. 늪지, 습지   disparity n. 격차   first in line phr. 우선순위에 있는   premium adj. 아주 높은, 고급의   stronghold n. 거점, 본거지   constitute v. ~을 구성하다   displace v. 쫓아내다   revolve around phr. ~을 중심으로 돌아가다   unrest n. 불안   mannerism n. 버릇, 특징   petty crime phr. 경범죄   mixed blessing phr. 좋기도 하고 나쁘기도 한 것   intractable adj. 다루기 힘든

1 해설 단락 B의 중심 문장 'tourism can cause extensive damage to the natural world'에서 관광업은 자연계에 광범위한 피해를 야기할 수 있다고 하였으므로, 보기 **viii** Widespread degradation of the environment가 정답이다. 'extensive damage'가 'Widespread degradation'으로 paraphrasing되었다.

2 해설 단락 C의 중심 문장 'Another problem is the income disparity'에서 또 다른 문제는 소득 격차라고 하였으므로, 보기 **v** The problem of unequal income이 정답이다. 'income disparity'가 'unequal income'으로 paraphrasing되었다.

3 해설 단락 D의 중심 문장 'overseas investors make it impossible for small, local businesses to compete'에서 해외 투자자들은 소규모의 현지 기업들이 경쟁하는 것을 불가능하게 만든다고 하였으므로, 보기 **iv** Competition presents challenges for local businesses가 정답이다. 'overseas investors make it impossible ~ to compete'가 'Competition presents challenges'로 paraphrasing되었다.

4 해설 단락 E의 중심 문장 'Once a place becomes popular with foreigners, there's a rush to purchase vacation homes, dramatically increasing property values'에서 한 장소가 일단 외국인들에게 유명해지면 별장을 구매하기 위한 수요가 급증하며 이는 극적으로 부동산 가치를 상승시킨다고 하였으므로, 보기 **iii** The impact of tourism on real estate prices가 정답이다.

5 해설 이 단락에는 중심 문장이 없으므로, 단락 전체를 읽고 중심 내용을 파악한다. 단락 F는 관광업에 의존하여 다른 산업을 방치하는 것에 대해 주로 언급하고 있다. 따라서 이를 '다른 산업의 개발을 방치하는 것의 영향'으로 요약한 보기 **ix** Impact of neglecting the development of other industries가 정답이다.

6 해설 단락 G의 중심 문장 'Economics aside, there are also social consequences of high growth tourism for local communities'에서 경제적 측면 외에도 고성장 관광업의 지역 사회에 대한 사회적 영향 또한 존재한다고 하였으므로, 보기 **vi** Non-economic consequences for communities가 정답이다. 'social'이 'Non-economic'으로 paraphrasing되었다.

7 사람들이 엄격한 규제를 피한 방법 중 하나는 −이다.
  A 정부 기관에 추가 비용을 지불하는 것
  B 현지 시민의 도움으로 부동산을 구매하는 것
  C 현지 사회 기반 시설에 투자하기로 약속하는 것
  D 현지 주민을 위한 좋은 일자리를 보장하는 것

  해설 문제의 핵심어구(avoided strict regulations)와 관련된 지문 내용 중 'people still find a way to evade the laws by coordinating with Thai citizens or businesses to purchase property'에서 사람들은 여전히 부동산을 구매하기 위해 태국 시민이나 기업과 협력하여 법을 교묘히 피할 방법을 찾아낸다고 하였으므로, 보기 **B** buying property with the help of local citizens가 정답이다. 'coordinating with Thai citizens'가 'with the help of local citizens'로 paraphrasing되었다.

8 많은 양의 일자리가 관광업에 의존할 때, 국가들은 −하는 경향이 있다.
  A 균형 잡힌 경제를 창출하기 위해 다른 영역에 크게 투자한다
  B 사회 불안의 가능성에 대해 우려하게 된다
  C 다른 분야의 개발을 돌보지 않는다
  D 관광 산업 분야에서 일하는 시민들의 임금을 인상한다

  해설 문제의 핵심어구(a large number of jobs are dependent on tourism)와 관련된 지문 내용 중 'When a substantial quantity of available jobs revolves around tourism, countries often neglect developing other sectors'에서 상당한 양의 가능한 일자리가 관광업을 중심으로 돌아갈 때 국가들은 종종 다른 분야의 개발을 방치한다고 하였으므로, 보기 **C** ignore the development of other sectors가 정답이다. 'a substantial quantity of ~ jobs revolves around'가 'a large number of jobs are dependent'로, 'neglect developing'이 'ignore the development'로 paraphrasing되었다.

[9-13]

경제 발전을 위한 관광업

관광업은 개발도상국들이 경제를 성장시키는 빠르고 효율적인 수단이 될 수 있다. 이러한 많은 국가들은 자연 환경에 있는 9 ....을 활용하도록 장려된다. 하지만, 관광 개발이 주장되는 만큼 만병통치약인지는 명확하지 않다. 어떤 경우에 관광 개발이 현지 10 ....에 야기하는 문제들은 이익보다 더 크다. 현지 관광 산업을 위한 환경을 구축하는 것의 자금은 흔히 11 ....에 의해 제공되지만, 그들이 항상 이윤을 얻는 것은 아니다. 해안의 부지를 구매하려고 서두르는 것은 12 ....이며, 그들은 관광 산업에서의 우위를 위해 기꺼이 많은 돈을 지불한다. 게다가, 국가 밖으로부터의 영향들은 또한 현지 사람들의 13 ....에 반하는 행동으로 이어질 수 있다.

A	납세자	B	사회 기반 시설	C	값비싼 원료
D	풍습	E	국제적인 체인	F	사회
G	관광 명소	H	산업	I	불균형 개발

---

9 해설 문제의 핵심어구(urged to take advantage of)와 관련된 지문 내용 중 'such countries are encouraged to capitalise on these attractions'에서 그러한 나라들은 이런 관광 명소들을 활용하도록 장려된다고 하였으므로, 보기 **G** attractions가 정답이다. 'encouraged to capitalise on'이 'urged to take advantage of'로 paraphrasing되었다.

10 해설 문제 핵심어구(problems it causes ~ outweigh its benefits)와 관련된 지문 내용 중 'It can therefore bring more harm than good to the communities'에서 그러므로 그것은 사회에 이익보다 더 많은 피해를 가져올 수 있다고 하였으므로, 보기 **F** communities가 정답이다. 'bring more harm than good'이 'outweigh its benefits'로 paraphrasing되었다.

11 해설 문제의 핵심어구(local tourism industry ~ funded by)와 관련된 지문 내용 중 'The money to fund these projects comes out of taxpayers' wallets'에서 이런 계획 사업에 투자할 자금은 납세자들의 지갑으로부터 나온다고 하였으므로, 보기 **A** taxpayers가 정답이다. 'money to fund ~ comes out of'가 'funded by'로 paraphrasing되었다.

12 해설 문제의 핵심어구(hurry to buy coastal property)와 관련된 지문 내용 중 'International chains are the first in line to bid for spaces on beachfront property'에서 국제적인 체인들은 해안 부지 공간을 위한 입찰의 가장 우선순위에 있다고 하였으므로, 보기 **E** international chains가 정답이다. 'the first in line to bid for ~ beachfront property'가 'hurry to buy coastal property'로 paraphrasing되었다.

13 해설 문제의 핵심어구(influences from outside the country)와 관련된 지문 내용 중 'along with foreign influences can come unwelcome behaviour and activities. This can simply be undesirable habits or mannerisms that contradict local customs.'에서 외국의 영향과 더불어 반갑지 않은 행동 방식과 활동이 나타날 수 있고, 이는 달갑지 않은 관습이나 지역 풍습과 상반되는 버릇일 뿐일 수도 있다고 하였으므로, 보기 **D** customs가 정답이다. 'habits or mannerisms that contradict local customs'가 'behaviour that goes against the customs of the local people'로 paraphrasing되었다.

READING PASSAGE 2

아이들의 교육에 대한 부모의 관여

가장 근본적인 차원에서, 교육은 인간의 일이다. 이것은 사람과 진정한 인간 상호 작용을 필요로 한다. 우리가 아이들의 교육에 대해 생각할 때, 제일 처음으로 떠오르는 것은 교사이고, 교사들의 역할의 중요성은 아무리 강조해도 지나치지 않다. 하지만 아이들의 교육에서 부모의 역할은 무엇인가? 가정에서, 부모의 관여는 전반적인 지지부터 적극적으로 자녀를 가르치는 것까지 모든 것을 포함할 수 있다. 게다가, [18]부모는 또한 학교 행사에 참석하는 것, 교내 활동을 돕는 것 또는 학교 운영 위원이나 관리자로 일하는 것과 같이 다양한 방식으로 학교에 도움을 제공할 수 있다. 이러한 부모의 관여가 학생의 성과에 중요한 영향을 미치는가? 만약 그렇다면, 그 관여의 결과는 무엇인가?

광범위한 연구는 학습 성취도와 관련해서 부모의 관여가 미치는 긍정적인 이익을 분명히 증명했다. [22]아동 교육의 초기에 자녀와 직접적으로 관계를 맺은 부모 밑에서 자란 학생들은 특히 더 확실한 결과를 보인다 (Cotton and Wikelund, 1989). 다시 말해서, [19]부모의 관여가 더 빨리 나타날수록, 자녀가 학업에서 큰 성공을 거둘 가능성이 더 높다. 미국에서, 국내 영세민층 미취학 자녀 교육 영향 연구는 유치원에서 3학년까지 5천명의 아이들에 대한 상세한 자료를 수집했다. 영세민층 미취학 자녀 교육 프로그램은 저소득 가정에게 종합적인 유아기 발달 서비스를 제공했으며, 부모의 관여를 적극적으로 장려했다. 이 연구는 인지 능력과 일반 상식뿐 아니라 학생들의 학습 준비도, 언어 사용 그리고 글을 읽고 쓸 줄 아는 능력을 측정하는 자료를 수집했다. 3년 동안, 자료는 학교 관련 과제에 대한 부모의 검사, 교내 활동에 대한 부모의 관여와 학업 성취도 사이의 강한 연관성을 규명했다. 이런 프로그램들의 장기적인 영향에 대해서는 의문이 제기되었지만, 심리학자 Todd Wisley와 같은 비평가들조차도 부모의 지속적인 관여가 자녀의 성공에 중요하다고 언급했다.

유사하게, 부모의 개입 정도와 학교에서의 자녀의 태도 및 행동 양식 간의 연관성은 [15]아동 발달심리학자 Walter Emmerlich가 적극적인 부모의 상호 작용이 학습에 대한 자녀의 태도를 향상시키며 삶에 대해 더 긍정적인 관점을 제공한다고 가정했던 1973년에 이미 강조되었다. 그 이후로, 연구자들은 수업 태도, 또래 상호 작용, 자아 개념, 동기, 그리고 전반적인 사회정서적 기능과 같은 기준들에 대한 심층 분석을 시행했다. 하지만, 학습과 가르침에 대한 부모의 도움이 명백하게 주요 요인이었던 학업 성취도와는 다르게, [23]태도와 행동 양식의 개선에 기여하는 눈에 띄는 관여의 형태는 나타나지 않는다. 그러므로, 모든 형태의 관여가 균일하게 기여하는 것으로 보이며, 이와 관련해서 [20]부모의 관여를 위한 가장 다양한 기회를 제공하는 학교들이 가장 긍정적인 영향을 경험한다는 것은 전혀 놀랍지 않다.

학교 제도와 교육 전문가들에 의해 쓰인 논문 모두에서 부모의 관여가 널리 장려되긴 하지만, 논란이 없는 것은 아니다. 일부 교육 전문가들은 그것이 도를 넘지는 않을지 의문을 제기하며, 이런 의견은 학교 운영과 행정에 대한 부모의 관여에 있어 특히 흔하다. 영국 전국 교장협의회의 사무총장 David Hart는, 영국의 이사회들은 지나치게 많은 부모들로 이루어져 있는데, 그중 다수는 그 직무에 부적당하다고 시사했다. [14]Hart는 운영과 관련하여 부모들이 종종 더 중요한 이익을 생각하기에는 자신들의 자녀에게 필요한 것에 과도하게 중점을 두고 있었다고 말했다. 그럼에도 불구하고, [24]여론 조사들은 많은 부모들이 학교 운영 위원이 되는 것을 통해서든 혹은 부모 자문 위원회나 학교 개선 이사회의 일원이 되는 것을 통해서든 학교의 일에 있어 더 적극적인 역할을 맡고 싶어함을 지속적으로 보여준다.

대조적으로, 학교 관리자들과 교사들은 부모가 적극적인 역할을 맡는 것에 대한 Hart의 부정적인 의견을 지지하는 경향이 있다. [21]그들은 부모가 목표 설정, 인사 결정, 평가, 그리고 어떻게 자금을 할당할지에 관여하는 것에 대해 지속적으로 강한 저항을 보여주고 있다. 그들은 부모들이 일반적으로 학교 행정과 운영에 관한 결정을 하기에는 훈련과 능력이 부족하다는 것을 지적한다. 교육 관련 논문들은 가끔 그들의 관점을 지지한다. 일부 주류 연구들은 학교 행정에 대한 부모의 관여가 높아진 학업 성취도 또는 학생의 태도 및 행동 양식의 개선과 명확한 연관성이 없다고 주장한다. [16]Karen Reed Wikelund는 학교의 의사결정에 있어 부모 관여의 관련성을 다룬 6개의 연구에서, 어느 것도 부모의 관여와 학생 성취도의 인과 관계를 확정적으로 증명할 수 없었음을 지적했다. 또한 Marylin Bruckman은 많은 유아 교사들이 일반적으로 부모의 관여에 대해 부정적인 시각을 가지고 있다고 주장했는데, 이는 [25]일부 교사들이 가족의 개입에 부정적인 영향을 미치고 있을 수도 있음을 시사한다.

그러나, 예외는 있다. 예일 대학의 James Comer에 의해 시작된 코네티컷 주 뉴헤이븐에 있는 School Development Programme (SDP)은 집에서든, 교실에서든, 혹은 학교 행정에서든 부모들이 모든 단계에서 의미 있는 기여를 할 수 있다는 것을 밝혀냈다. [17]그는 학교 계획 및 운영 단체에 부모들을 선출하는 프로그램을 도입함으로써 교육의 '생태학을 변경하는' 것을 시도했는데, 여기서 부모들은 교사들, 교장, 그리고 직원들과 함께 중요한 결정들을 내렸다. [26]SDP는 코네티컷 주의 도심에 있는 가장 성과가 나쁜 학교 두 곳이 근본적으로 변하도록 도왔고, 도심에 위치한 학교들 중 무려 120곳이 그의 방식을 사용하여 그 뒤를 따랐다. Comer의 사례는 적절한 체제가 있다면 부모가 학교에서 건설적인 역할을 수행할 수 있다는 것을 증명하는데, 이는 부모와 교사가 자녀에게 가장 좋은 것을 위해 함께 적극적으로 일할 수 있도록 한다.

어휘   **undertaking** n. (중요한·힘든) 일 **function** n. 행사, 의식 **governor** n. 운영 위원 **administrator** n. 관리자
           measurable adj. 중요한, 주목할 만한 **academic achievement** phr. 학습 성취도 **head start** phr. 영세민층 미취학 자녀 교육

comprehensive adj. 종합적인 cognition n. 인지 call into question phr. ~에 의문을 제기하다 constructive adj. 적극적인, 건설적인
literature n. 논문, 연구 보고서 sentiment n. 의견, 감정 general secretary phr. 사무총장 advisory committee phr. 자문위원회
allocate v. 할당하다 conclusively adv. 확정적으로 causal adj. 인과 관계의 adverse adj. 부정적인, 불리한
radically adv. 근본적으로, 철저히 follow suit phr. 따라 하다, 선례를 따르다 framework n. 체제

[14-17]

14 운영을 하는 부모들은 자녀의 필요를 다른 사람들보다 먼저 생각하는 경향이 있다고 주장했다

15 부모의 격려와 교육에 대한 아이들의 견해 사이의 연관성을 제시했다

16 학교 결정에 관한 부모의 관여를 학생의 성공과 관련짓는 증거가 없다고 주장했다

17 학교 의사결정에 부모의 참여 프로그램을 도입했다

연구원 리스트

A Karen Reed Wikelund
B Walter Emmerlich
C James Comer
D Marylin Bruckman
E David Hart

14 해설 문제의 핵심어구(put the needs of their own children before others)와 관련된 지문 내용 중 'Hart declared that parents were often too focused on the needs of their own children to think of the greater good'에서 Hart 는 부모들이 종종 더 중요한 이익을 생각하기에는 자신들의 자녀에게 필요한 것에 과도하게 중점을 두고 있었다고 말했다고 하였으므로, 보기 **E** David Hart가 정답이다. 'focused on'이 'put ~ before'로 paraphrasing되었다.

15 해설 문제의 핵심어구(parental encouragement and children's views on education)와 관련된 지문 내용 중 'child development psychologist Walter Emmerlich posited that constructive parent interaction enhances their children's attitudes toward learning'에서 아동 발달심리학자 Walter Emmerlich가 적극적인 부모의 상호 작용이 학습에 대한 자녀의 태도를 향상시킨다고 가정했다고 하였으므로, 보기 **B** Walter Emmerlich가 정답이다. 'parent interaction'이 'parental encouragement'로, 'attitudes toward learning'이 'views on education'으로 paraphrasing되었다.

16 해설 문제의 핵심어구(parental involvement in school decisions and student success)와 관련된 지문 내용 중 'Karen Reed Wikelund has pointed out that in half a dozen studies that addressed the link between parental involvement in school decision making, none could conclusively prove a causal relationship between it and student achievement.'에서 Karen Reed Wikelund는 학교의 의사결정에 있어 부모 관여의 관련성을 다룬 6개의 연구에서 어느 것도 부모의 관여와 학생 성취도의 인과 관계를 확정적으로 증명할 수 없었음을 지적했다고 하였으므로, 보기 **A** Karen Reed Wikelund가 정답이다. 'none could conclusively prove'가 'there was no evidence'로 paraphrasing되었다.

17 해설 문제의 핵심어구(programme of parental participation)와 관련된 지문 내용 중 'He sought to 'change the ecology' of education by instituting a programme of electing parents to school planning and management teams, where they made substantial decisions'에서 James Comer는 학교 계획 및 운영 단체에 부모들을 선출하는 프로그램을 도입함으로써 교육의 '생태학을 변경하는' 것을 시도했는데 여기서 부모들은 중요한 결정들을 내렸다고 하였으므로, 보기 **C** James Comer가 정답이다. 'electing parents'가 'parental participation'으로 paraphrasing되었다.

[18-21]

18 부모들은 학교의 ....이 되고 운영 위원회에서 일함으로써 학교를 지지할 수 있다.

19 초기의 부모 관여는 자녀의 큰 ....의 가능성을 증가시킨다.

20 가장 이로운 접근은 학교가 부모들이 참여할 수 있는 다양한 ....을 제공하는 것이다.

21 학교 관리자들이 부모들이 관여하는 것을 원하지 않는 한 가지 결정은 ....의 할당이다.

18 해설 문제의 핵심어구(and serving on administrative committees)와 관련된 지문 내용 중 'parents can also lend their support to schools in many ways, such as ~ serving as school governors or administrators'에서 부모는 또한 학교 운영 위원이나 관리자로 일하는 것과 같이 다양한 방식으로 학교에 그들의 도움을 제공할 수 있다고 하였으므로, **governors**가 정답이다. 'serving as ~ administrators'가 'serving on administrative committees'로 paraphrasing되었다.

19 해설 문제의 핵심어구(Early parental involvement)와 관련된 지문 내용 중 'the earlier parental involvement occurs, the more likely children are to have tremendous academic success'에서 부모의 관여가 더 빨리 나타날수록 자녀가 학업에서 큰 성공을 거둘 가능성이 더 높다고 하였으므로, 'tremendous academic success'가 답이 될 수 있다. 지시문에서 두 단어 이내로 답을 작성하라고 하였으므로, **academic success**가 정답이다.

20 해설 문제의 핵심어구(most beneficial approach ~ provide diverse)와 관련된 지문 내용 중 'schools which offer the greatest variety of opportunities for parental involvement see the most positive impact'에서 부모의 관여를 위한 가장 다양한 기회를 제공하는 학교들이 가장 긍정적인 영향을 경험한다고 하였으므로, **opportunities**가 정답이다. 'offer the greatest variety of opportunities for parental involvement'가 'provide diverse opportunities for parents to participate'로 paraphrasing되었다.

21 해설 문제의 핵심어구(do not want parents to get involved in is the allocation)와 관련된 지문 내용 중 'they continually demonstrate great reluctance to allow parents to get involved with ~ how to allocate funding.'에서 학교 관리자들과 교사들은 부모가 어떻게 자금을 할당할지에 관여하는 것에 대해 지속적으로 강한 저항을 보여주고 있다고 하였으므로, **funding**이 정답이다. 'demonstrate great reluctance to allow parents to get involved with'가 'do not want parents to get involved in'으로 paraphrasing되었다.

[22-26]

22 부모의 관여는 더 어린 학생들보다 나이가 더 많은 학생들에게 더 많은 영향을 미치는 경향이 있다.

23 서로 다른 유형의 부모의 관여는 태도와 행동 양식에 다른 결과를 야기한다.

24 여론 조사들은 어머니들이 일반적으로 아버지들보다 학교 일에 있어 역할을 맡을 가능성이 더 크다는 것을 보여준다.

25 연구 결과는 교사들이 학교에서 부모의 참여에 대해 부정적인 영향을 미칠 수도 있다고 제시한다.

26 School Development Programme은 몇몇 도시 학교들을 근본적으로 바꾸는 것을 도왔다.

22 해설 문제의 핵심어구(Parental involvement ~ more of an effect on older students)와 관련된 지문 내용 중 'Students of parents who engage directly with their children in the early years of childhood education show especially strong results'에서 아동 교육의 초기에 자녀와 직접적으로 관계를 맺은 부모 밑에서 자란 학생들은 특히 더 확실한 결과를 보인다고 하였으므로, 주어진 문장은 지문의 내용과 일치하지 않음을 알 수 있다. 따라서 정답은 **False**이다.

23 해설 문제의 핵심어구(different results in attitude and behaviour)와 관련된 지문 내용 중 'there is no obvious form of involvement that stands out as contributing to improvements in attitude and behaviour'에서 태도와 행동 양식의 개선에 기여하는 눈에 띄는 관여의 형태는 나타나지 않는다고 하였으므로, 주어진 문장은 지문의 내용과 일치하지 않음을 알 수 있다. 따라서 정답은 **False**이다.

24 해설 문제의 핵심어구(Polls)와 관련된 지문 내용 중 'polls consistently show that many parents would like to play a more active role in school affairs'에서 여론 조사들은 많은 부모들이 학교의 일에 있어 더 적극적인 역할을 맡고 싶어함을 지속적으로 보여준다고는 하였지만, 주어진 문장의 내용은 확인할 수 없다. 따라서 정답은 **Not given**이다.

25

해설 문제의 핵심어구(educators may have a negative effect on parental participation)와 관련된 지문 내용 중 'some educators may have an adverse impact on family involvement'에서 일부 교사들이 가족의 개입에 부정적인 영향을 미치고 있을 수도 있다고 하였으므로, 주어진 문장은 지문의 내용과 일치함을 알 수 있다. 따라서 정답은 **True**이다. 'adverse impact'가 'negative effect'로, 'family involvement'가 'parental participation'으로 paraphrasing되었다.

26

해설 문제의 핵심어구(The School Development Programme)와 관련된 지문 내용 중 'The SDP helped radically transform two of the worst-performing inner-city schools'에서 SDP는 도심에 있는 가장 성과가 나쁜 학교 두 곳이 근본적으로 변하도록 도왔다고 하였으므로, 주어진 문장은 지문의 내용과 일치함을 알 수 있다. 따라서 정답은 **True**이다. 'radically transform ~ inner-city schools'가 'revolutionise some urban schools'로 paraphrasing되었다.

READING PASSAGE 3

눈덩이 지구 가설
지구가 한때 얼음으로 덮인 거대한 눈덩이였다는 이론 분석하기

[32]과학자들 사이에서 '눈덩이 지구' 가설의 타당성에 대한 논쟁은 맹렬히 계속되어 왔는데, 이 이론은 지구가 한때 얼음과 눈으로 완전히 뒤덮여 있었을 것이라고 가정한다. 만약 이 이론이 사실이라면 많은 지질학적 불가사의들을 설명할 수 있을 것이지만, 일부는 지구가 그런 극심한 빙결로부터 회복할 수 없었을 것이라고 주장한다.

지구가 극에서 적도까지 완전히 얼음으로 덮여, 거의 혹은 전혀 생명체가 살 수 없으며 기온이 일 년 내내 0도보다 훨씬 낮다고 상상해 보라. 그것이 '눈덩이 지구' 가설의 명제이다. 이것은 지구가 적어도 역사의 한 시대 동안 완전히 얼어 있었다고 주장하는 논쟁이 많이 벌어지는 이론이고, 과학자들은 지질학적 기록을 어떻게 해석할지에 대해 의견이 나뉘고 있으며 이 가설에 대한 논쟁은 계속되고 있다.

이 이론의 지지자들에 따르면 [27]이 극심한 빙결은 6억 5천 년 전에 신원생대, 구원생대 혹은 카루 빙하 시대의 세 시대 중 적어도 한 시대에서 발생했다. 하지만 과학자들은 이것이 정확히 언제 일어났을 것인지에 대해서뿐만 아니라 지질학적 증거와 지구가 그러한 시기 이후 되살아나고, 생명을 육성했을 가능성에 대해서도 의견이 나뉜다. 그럼에도 불구하고 지지자들은 이 이론이 지질학적 기록의 몇 가지 불가사의를 설명한다고 주장한다.

[37]처음으로 눈덩이 지구에 대한 의견을 내세운 지질학자는 20세기 중반에 호주 남부에서 빙하 퇴적물을 발견했던 Douglas Mawson이었는데, 그는 이 빙하 퇴적물을 전 지구적 빙결의 증거로 들었다. 하지만, [38]이 이론은 대륙 이동설에 의해 대체되었는데, 이는 더 쉽게 호주와 다른 대륙들에 있는 빙하의 존재를 설명했다. [39]눈덩이 지구 이론은 1960년대에 그린란드의 빙하 퇴적물이 사실 열대 지방에 더 가까운 곳에서 퇴적되었다고 주장했던 W. Brian Harland에 의해 부활했다. Harland에 따르면, 이런 퇴적물을 설명할 수 있는 유일한 것은 극심한, 세계적인 빙하기였다.

1990년대가 되어서야 지구생물학 교수인 Joseph Kirschvink가 이 빙하기를 묘사하기 위해 '눈덩이 지구'라는 용어를 만들었다. Kirschvink는 또한 지구가 이 빙하 환경에서 벗어났을 방법으로 극온실 효과를 제시했다. Kirschvink의 의견은 [40]Franklyn Van Houten에 의해 받아들여졌는데, 그는 인 퇴적물과 호상철광층이 지구가 한때 얼음으로 뒤덮여 있었음을 증명한다고 말했다.

눈덩이 지구 가설의 지지자들에 따르면, [28]지질학적 기록과 기후 모형 모두가 이 이론을 뒷받침하는 몇 가지 경우가 있다. 가장 설득력 있는 것은 아마도 고자기학의 증거인데, 이는 대륙 이동을 고려하면서도 언제 어디서 지질학적 퇴적물이 만들어졌는지를 보여줄 수 있는 지질학에서의 최근의 발전이다. 고자기학을 통해 신원생대 동안 빙하기 기원의 퇴적물이 적도 근처에서 퇴적되었음을 밝히는 것이 가능했다. 하지만 [33]과학자들은 지구의 자기장이 시간이 지나며 변했을 가능성과 이러한 퇴적물들의 원인이 될 수 있는 적도 근처 초기 전극의 존재와 같은 다른 그럴 듯한 설명들 때문에 이 결론에 대해 회의적이다.

눈덩이 지구 가설은 또한 빙하 퇴적물이 대륙이 갈라져 지각의 융기를 야기한 것에 의해 설명될 수 있다는 이유로 이의가 제기되기도 했는데, 이는 아마 빙하가 형성될 수 있을 만큼 매우 높은 대지를 형성했을 것이었다. 이 대륙 분리 이론은 토론토 대학의 지질학 교수인 Nicholas Eyles에 의해 'Zipper Rift 가설'이라는 이름으로 제안되었다. [34]이 시나리오에서는, 대륙의 분리가 빙결이 일어나는 이러한 높은 지대를 만들고, 그렇게 함으로써 눈덩이 효과를 지구의 특정 지역에 한정한다.

Eyles의 연구가 보여주듯이, 눈덩이 지구 논쟁의 주요 쟁점 중 하나는 지구 전반에 걸쳐 일어난 이 거대한 빙결의 규모이다. [29]많은 지질학자들과 기상 과학자들은 지구가 완전히 대륙 빙하에 싸인 '딱딱한 눈덩이' 효과는, 지구에서 생명체를 영영 사라지게 했을 것이라고 주장한다. 그러므로 그들은 바다의 일부는 얼지 않은 채로 남았던 부분적인 빙결이 가장 유력한 시나리오라고 말한다.

³⁵지질학 기록에 대멸종 사건이 없다는 것은 일부가 주장하는 것보다 눈덩이 지구가 더 온건했음을 증명한다. 그들은 빙하기 동안에 이산화탄소가 축적되었다고 주장하는데, 이때 초목은 줄어들었고 대기로부터 이산화탄소를 그다지 제거할 수 없었다. 결국, 이산화탄소가 지구를 따뜻하게 했는데, 이는 광범위한 융해와 토양으로의 물의 방출로 이어졌다. 전 지구적인 빙결이 실제로 발생했다는 것을 암시한 캐나다의 화산암에 대한 연구를 진행했던 하버드 대학의 지구과학자인 Francis Macdonald는, 이 시기에 지구가 '단순한 흰 눈덩이보다는, 진흙 공에 더 가까웠다'고 주장했다.

눈덩이라기보다는 '진흙 공'이라는 이런 발상은 지질학자들 사이에서 많은 지지자를 얻었다. 토론토 대학의 Richard Peltier는, "대륙은 두꺼운 대륙 빙하로 바다는 두꺼운 해빙으로 지구가 한때 완전히 얼음으로 뒤덮여 있었다는 주장은 여전히 다소 논쟁의 여지가 있다."고 말한다. Peltier는 신원생대에 실제로 일어났던 일은 '음성 피드백 반응'임을 보여주는 기후 모형을 만들었는데, 이는 지구가 '빙하기와 해빙기'를 왔다 갔다 했다는 것을 보여준다.

³⁶Peltier의 모형은 지구 전체에 걸친 극심한 빙결에도 불구하고, 지구의 열대 지역에서는 많은 양의 물이 얼지 않은 상태로 남아있었다는 것을 증명했다. ³⁰이는 '슬러시볼 지구' 가설이라고 명명되었으며, 이 시기 동안의 생명체의 생존을 더 작은 규모의 전 지구적 빙결에 대한 증거로 인용하는 많은 사람에게 지지를 받는다. 만약 슬러시볼 지구 가설이 사실이라면 얼지 않은 물의 띠가 적도 근처에 존속했을 것이다. 대부분의 전문가들이 현재 이것이 가장 개연성 있는 상황이라는 데 동의한다.

어떤 형태의 빙결이 실제로 발생했다는 것이 명백하긴 하지만, 눈덩이 지구 가설에 관한 논쟁은 지속될 것으로 보인다. 그럼에도 불구하고 완전히 얼어붙은 지구는 지질학뿐만 아니라 기후 과학에서도 여전히 성행하고 있는 연구 분야이다. ³¹컬럼비아 대학의 린다 솔에 의한 최근 연구는 눈덩이 지구 이론을 이용한 기후 모형이 어떻게 미래의 기후 변화와, 비극적인 전 세계적 기후 변동이 미칠 잠재적 영향에 대한 통찰을 제공해줄 수 있는지를 보여주었다. 솔이 말하듯, "눈덩이 지구 빙결을 연구하는 것은 우리에게 상황이 얼마나 나빠질 수 있는지를 알려주는데, 그런 상황에서는 아마 우리가 생명체라고 알고 있는 것은 살아남지 못할 것이다".

어휘 **snowball Earth** phr. 눈덩이 지구 **hypothesis** n. 가설 **rage** v. 맹렬히 계속되다 **plausibility** n. 타당성 **posit** v. 가정하다, 설치하다
pole n. (지구의) 극 **equator** n. (지구의) 적도 **perpetually** adv. 일 년 내내, 끊임 없이 **proposition** n. 명제, 문제
contentious adj. 논쟁이 많이 벌어지는, 이론이 분분한 **proponent** n. 지지자 **Neoproterozoic** n. 신원생대
Palaeoproterozoic n. 구원생대 **foster** v. 육성하다 **sediment** n. 퇴적물, 침전물 **glaciation** n. 빙결, 빙하 작용 **deposit** v. 퇴적시키다
coin v. (신어를) 만들어 내다 **phosphorus** n. 인(비금속 원소) **banded iron formation** phr. 호상철광층
palaeomagnetism n. 고자기학(암석의 잔류 자기를 측정하여 지질 시대의 지구 자기장의 강도와 방향을 연구하는 학문)
continental drift phr. 대륙 이동설 **sceptical** adj. 회의적인 **plausible** adj. 그럴 듯한, 타당한 것 같은 **plateau** n. 대지, 고원
obliterate v. 사라지게 하다, 없애다 **temperate** adj. 온건한 **adherent** n. 지지자 **oscillate** v. 왔다 갔다 하다 **repercussion** n. 영향
catastrophic adj. 비극적인, 파멸의

[27-31]

27 과학자들은 눈덩이 지구가 구원생대에 발생했다는 것에 동의한다.

28 20세기에 개발된 기후 모형들은 고자기학에 대한 이론으로 이어졌다.

29 몇몇 전문가들은 지구가 얼음으로 완전히 둘러싸여 있었다면, 생명은 영구적으로 소멸되었을 것이라고 믿는다.

30 '슬러시볼 지구' 가설은 지구에서 생명체가 어떻게 진화했는지 보여준다.

31 린다 솔은 눈덩이 지구 모형이 우리에게 기후 변화에 대해 알려줄 수 있다는 것을 보여주었다.

27 해설 문제의 핵심어구(occurred in the Palaeoproterozoic era)와 관련된 지문 내용 중 'this deep freeze occurred ~ in at least one of three periods, the Neoproterozoic, the Palaeoproterozoic or the Karoo Ice Age'에서 이 극심한 빙결은 신원생대, 구원생대 혹은 카루 빙하 시대의 세 시대 중 적어도 한 시대에서 발생했다고 하였으므로, 주어진 문장은 글쓴이의 견해와 일치하지 않음을 알 수 있다. 따라서 정답은 **No**이다.

28 해설 문제의 핵심어구(paleomagnetism)와 관련된 지문 내용 중 'there are several ways in which both the geological record and climate models support the theory. The most persuasive is perhaps the evidence of palaeomagnetism'에서 지질학적 기록과 기후 모형 모두가 이 이론을 뒷받침하는 몇 가지 경우 중 가장 설득력 있는 것은 아마도 고자기학의 증거일 것이라고는 하였지만, 주어진 문장의 내용은 확인할 수 없다. 따라서 정답은 **Not given**이다.

29 해설 문제의 핵심어구(life ~ permanently erased)와 관련된 지문 내용 중 'Many geologists and climate scientists claim that a 'hard snowball' effect, in which the planet is completely enveloped in ice sheets, would have obliterated life on Earth forever.'에서 많은 지질학자들과 기상 과학자들은 지구가 완전히 대륙 빙하에 싸인 '딱딱한 눈덩이' 효과는 지구에서 생명체를 영영 사라지게 했을 것이라고 주장한다고 하였으므로, 주어진 문장은 글쓴이의 견해와 일치함을 알 수 있다. 따라서 정답은 **Yes**이다. 'planet ~ completely enveloped in ice sheets'가 'Earth ~ totally enclosed in ice'로, 'obliterated life on Earth forever'가 'life would have been permanently erased'로 paraphrasing되었다.

30 해설 문제의 핵심어구('slushball Earth' hypothesis)와 관련된 지문 내용 중 'This has been termed the 'slushball Earth' hypothesis, and it is supported by many who cite the survival of life during this period as evidence of a less extensive global freeze.'에서 이는 '슬러시볼 지구' 가설이라고 명명되었으며 이 시기 동안의 생명체의 생존을 더 작은 규모의 전 지구적 빙결에 대한 증거로 인용하는 많은 사람에게 지지를 받는다고는 하였지만, 주어진 문장의 내용은 확인할 수 없다. 따라서 정답은 **Not given**이다.

31 해설 문제의 핵심어구(the snowball Earth model ~ teach us about climate change)와 관련된 지문의 내용 'A recent study by Linda Sohl ~ revealed how climate models using the snowball Earth theory can offer insight into future climate change'에서 린다 솔에 의한 최근 연구는 눈덩이 지구 이론을 이용한 기후 모형이 어떻게 미래의 기후 변화에 대한 통찰을 제공해줄 수 있는지를 보여주었다고 하였으므로, 주어진 문장은 글쓴이의 견해와 일치함을 알 수 있다. 따라서 정답은 **Yes**이다. 'offer insight into ~ climate change'가 'teach us about climate change'로 paraphrasing되었다.

[32-36]

32 첫 번째 단락에서, 글쓴이는 '눈덩이 지구' 이론이 -하다고 제시한다.
  A 지질학자들이 빙하 형성을 이해하는 방식을 바꾸었다
  B 광범위한 혼란을 야기한 실험적인 이론이다
  C 과학자들이 지구의 기원을 이해하는 방식을 바꾸었다
  D 광범위한 논쟁을 불러일으킨 이론이다

  해설 문제의 핵심어구('snowball Earth' hypothesis)와 관련된 첫 번째 단락의 내용 중 'A debate has been raging among scientists about the plausibility of the 'snowball Earth' hypothesis'에서 과학자들 사이에서 '눈덩이 지구' 가설의 타당성에 대한 논쟁은 맹렬히 계속되어 왔다고 하였으므로, 보기 **D** is a theory which has prompted extensive debate가 정답이다. 'A debate has been raging'이 'prompted extensive debate'로 paraphrasing되었다.

33 글쓴이는 -하기 때문에 과학자들이 눈덩이 지구 이론에 반대한다고 말한다.
  A 기후 변화가 인간에 의한 것이 아님을 보여주기 때문에
  B 호상철광층이 그것이 틀렸음을 입증하기 때문에
  C 다른 타당한 설명들이 있기 때문에
  D 대륙 이동설이 증거를 더 잘 설명하기 때문에

  해설 문제의 핵심어구(scientists oppose the snowball Earth theory)와 관련된 지문 내용 중 'scientists are sceptical of this conclusion due to other plausible explanations'에서 과학자들은 다른 그럴 듯한 설명들 때문에 이 결론에 대해 회의적이라고 하였으므로, 보기 **C** there are other reasonable explanations가 정답이다. 'sceptical of this conclusion' 이 'scientists oppose'로, 'other plausible explanations'가 'other reasonable explanations'로 paraphrasing되었다.

  🔍 오답 확인하기
  B는 지문의 'banded iron formations proved that the Earth had once been ice-covered'에서 호상철광층이 지구가 한 때 얼음으로 뒤덮여 있었음을 증명한다고 하였으므로 지문의 내용과 반대되는 오답이다.

34 Zipper rift 가설은 -라고 제시한다.
   A   서로 멀어지는 대륙이 빙하가 발생할 수 있는 환경을 만들었다
   B   눈덩이 효과는 지구의 모든 지역으로 확대되었다
   C   극도로 높은 대지가 눈덩이 시기 동안 생명체가 생존할 수 있게 했다
   D   지진이 빙하의 형성을 야기했다

> 해설 문제의 핵심어구(Zipper rift hypothesis)와 관련된 지문 내용 중 'In this scenario, the separation of continents creates these high plateaus where glaciations occur'에서 이 시나리오에서는 대륙의 분리가 빙결이 일어나는 이러한 높은 지대를 만든다고 하였으므로, 보기 **A** continents moving apart created conditions for glaciers to appear가 정답이다. 'high plateaus where glaciations occur'가 'conditions for glaciers to appear'로 paraphrasing되었다.
>
> 🔍 오답 확인하기
> **B**는 지문 내용 중 'limiting the snowball effect to certain areas of the planet'에서 Zipper rift 가설에서는 눈덩이 효과를 지구의 특정 지역에 한정한다고 하였으므로 지문의 내용과 반대되는 오답이다.

35 무엇이 일부가 주장하는 것보다 눈덩이 지구가 더 따뜻했다는 것을 확인했는가?
   A   대학에서 개발된 새로운 기후 모형
   B   대멸종에 대한 증거 부재
   C   해빙에서 채취한 이산화탄소 견본
   D   지질학적 기록에 있는 초목의 패턴

> 해설 문제의 핵심어구(the snowball Earth was warmer)와 관련된 지문의 내용 'The lack of a mass extinction event in the geological record proves that the snowball Earth was more temperate than some claim.'에서 지질학 기록에 대멸종 사건이 없다는 것은 일부가 주장하는 것보다 눈덩이 지구가 좀 더 온건했음을 증명한다고 하였으므로, 보기 **B** An absence of evidence for a mass extinction이 정답이다.

36 글쓴이는 Richard Peltier의 기후 모형이 -을 증명한다고 말한다.
   A   지구가 눈덩이라기보다는 진흙 공이었다
   B   눈덩이 지구 시기 동안 적도는 얼어있었다
   C   음성 피드백 반응에도 불구하고 지구에 생명체가 생존했다
   D   열대 지방 근처의 물은 얼지 않은 채로 남아 있었다

> 해설 문제의 핵심어구(Richard Peltier's climate model)와 관련된 지문 내용 중 'Peltier's model demonstrated that ~ a large amount of water remained unfrozen in the tropical regions of the planet.'에서 Peltier의 모형은 지구의 열대 지역에서는 많은 양의 물이 얼지 않은 상태로 남아있었다는 것을 증명했다고 하였으므로, 보기 **D** the water close to the tropics remained unfrozen이 정답이다. 'a large amount of water remained unfrozen in the tropical regions'가 'water close to the tropics remained unfrozen'으로 paraphrasing되었다.
>
> 🔍 오답 확인하기
> **B**는 'a large amount of water remained unfrozen in the tropical regions'에서 지구의 열대 지역에서 많은 양의 물이 얼지 않은 상태로 남아있었다고 하였으므로 지문의 내용과 반대되는 오답이다.

눈덩이 지구 이론의 역사

눈덩이 지구 가설은 Douglas Mawson에 의해 처음으로 제시되었는데, 그는 호주 남부에서 37 ....을 발견했다. 이것은 그로 하여금 지구 전체가 어느 한 시점에 빙하로 뒤덮여 있었을 것이라는 이론을 제시하도록 했다. 하지만, 38 ....이 호주와 다른 대륙들에 있는 빙하의 존재를 설명하기 위해 제안되었고 Mawson의 견해는 잊혀졌다. W. Brian Harland는 그린란드에서 발견되는 빙하가 전 지구적인 빙결로 인해 원래는 39 ....에서 퇴적되었다고 제안하면서 눈덩이 지구 가설의 명성을 다시 상기시켰다. 이는 '눈덩이 지구'라는 용어를 만든 Joseph Kirschvink와, 그의 인 퇴적물과 호상 40 ....층에 대한 발견이 이 가설에 대한 증거를 제공했던 Franklyn Van Houten에 의해 재조명되었다.

---

37 해설 문제의 핵심어구(Douglas Mawson ~ found in southern Australia)와 관련된 지문 내용 중 'The first geologist to put forward the idea of a snowball Earth was Douglas Mawson who discovered glacial sediments in southern Australia'에서 처음으로 눈덩이 지구에 대한 의견을 내세운 지질학자는 호주 남부에서 빙하 퇴적물을 발견했던 Douglas Mawson이었다고 하였으므로, **glacial sediments**가 정답이다.

38 해설 문제의 핵심어구(existence of glaciers in Australia and other landmasses)와 관련된 지문 내용 중 'this theory was superseded by the idea of continental drift, which more readily explained the existence of glaciers in Australia and other landmasses'에서 이 이론은 대륙 이동설에 의해 대체되었는데 이는 더 쉽게 호주와 다른 대륙들에 있는 빙하의 존재를 설명했다고 하였으므로, **continental drift**가 정답이다. 'this theory was superseded'가 'Mawson's ideas were forgotten'으로 paraphrasing되었다.

39 해설 문제의 핵심어구(W. Brian Harland brought ~ back to prominence)와 관련된 지문 내용 중 'The snowball Earth theory was revived in the 1960s by W. Brian Harland who suggested that glacial sediments in Greenland were actually deposited nearer to the tropics.'에서 눈덩이 지구 이론은 1960년대에 그린란드의 빙하 퇴적물이 사실 열대 지방에 더 가까운 곳에서 퇴적되었다고 주장했던 W. Brian Harland에 의해 부활했다고 하였으므로, **tropics**가 정답이다. 'was revived'가 'brought ~ back to prominence'로 paraphrasing되었다.

40 해설 문제의 핵심어구(Franklyn Van Houten, whose discovery of phosphorus deposits)와 관련된 지문 내용 중 'Franklyn Van Houten, who stated that phosphorus deposits and banded iron formations proved that the Earth had once been ice-covered'에서 Franklyn Van Houten은 인 퇴적물과 호상철광층이 지구가 한때 얼음으로 뒤덮여 있었음을 증명한다고 말했다고 하였으므로, **iron**이 정답이다.

* 각 문제에 대한 정답의 단서는 지문에 문제 번호와 함께 별도의 색으로 표시되어 있습니다.

EXAMPLE

p.40

어떤 사람들은 이러한 서로 다른 성격 유형이 가정 내 차이 때문에 시간이 지나며 발생한다고 생각한다. 첫째로 태어난 아이들은 다른 방해물이 거의 없는 상태에서 가족에 합류하며 다음 형제자매가 생길 때까지 부모님의 완전한 주목을 받는다. 나중에, 아이들은 부모로부터 비슷한 기간의 완전한 보살핌을 경험하지 못한다. 이것은 더 빠른 출생 순서의 특혜가 둘째 아이가 태어날 때 감소하는 것처럼 보이게 할 수 있지만, 이것은 사실이 아니다. 이제는 다른 아이와 함께 부모의 관심을 공유해야 하긴 하지만, ¹첫째로 태어난 아이들이 더 어린 형제자매들에게 제공하는 조언과 도움은 더 중요한 두뇌 발달로 이어질 수 있으며 이것은 그들의 더 높은 IQ의 원인일 가능성이 높다. 뿐만 아니라, 이것은 더 어린 형제자매들이 학교 수업 활동에서 더 좋은 점수를 받을 수 있도록 돕는다.

HACKERS PRACTICE

p.42

1 D	2 B	3 A	4 C	5 C
6 C	7 D	8 A	9 D	10 A
11 C	12 C	13 B	14 D	15 A
16 B	17 B	18 D	19 C	20 D
21 A	22 C	23-24 B, E	25 B	26-27 B, C
28 B	29-31 A, C, E	32 C		

1

지중해가 세계에서 매우 건조한 지역이며 ¹좁은 지브롤터 해협을 통해 대서양으로부터 물을 받는다는 점을 고려해 볼 때, 실제로 지중해는 증발에 매우 취약하다. 사실, 고고학적 증거는 약 500만 년 전 지구의 한랭화가 대서양의 일부가 얼도록 했다는 것을 보여주는데, 이는 ²해수면이 약 70미터 낮아지도록 하는 결과를 낳았다. 이것은 대서양에서 지브롤터 해협으로 가는 물의 흐름을 막았고, 그렇게 함으로써 지중해가 받는 물의 양을 크게 감소시켰다. 동시에, 지질구조판의 이동은 유럽과 아프리카가 서로 가까워지는 결과를 불러왔다. 이것은 지중해를 대서양으로부터 한층 더 차단시키기에 충분할 만큼 육지를 높이 들어올렸다. 이윽고 지중해에 남아 있던 따뜻한 물이 사라지기 시작했고, 이는 단지 소금만을 남겼다.

1 지브롤터 해협에 대해 무엇이 언급되는가?
 A 최대 깊이가 약 70미터이다.
 B 지구 한랭화 시기 동안 얼어붙었다.
 C 지질구조판의 이동 때문에 증발했다.
 D 대양으로부터 바다로 물을 운반한다.

> 해설 문제의 핵심어구(Strait of Gibraltar)와 관련된 지문 내용 중 'it receives the water from the Atlantic ocean via the narrow Strait of Gibraltar'에서 지중해는 좁은 지브롤터 해협을 통해 대서양으로부터 물을 받는다고 하였으므로, 보기 D It conveys water from the ocean into the sea가 정답이다. 'receives the water ~ via'가 'conveys water from'으로 paraphrasing되었다.

A는 지문의 'the sea level ~ about 70 metres'를 활용하여 혼동을 주었지만, 지문에서 대서양의 해수면이 70미터 낮아졌다고 했고 지브롤터 해협의 최대 깊이가 70미터라는 내용은 언급하지 않았으므로 오답이다.
B는 지문의 'global cooling'을 활용하여 혼동을 주었지만, 지문에서 지구 한랭화가 얼도록 한 것은 지브롤터 해협이 아니라 대서양이라고 하였으므로 오답이다.
C는 지문의 'the movement of tectonic plates'를 활용하여 혼동을 주었지만, 지문에서 지질구조판의 이동으로 증발한 것은 지브롤터 해협이 아니라 지중해라고 하였으므로 오답이다.

2 무엇이 지중해가 대서양으로부터 받는 물의 양을 감소시켰는가?
   A 건기
   B 해수면 감소
   C 빙하의 방해
   D 기온 상승

해설 문제의 핵심어구(diminished ~ water the Mediterranean received)와 관련된 지문 내용 중 'the sea level dropping about 70 metres ~ greatly reducing the amount of water the Mediterranean received.'에서 해수면이 약 70미터 낮아지도록 한 것은 지중해가 받는 물의 양을 크게 감소시켰다고 하였으므로, 보기 B A sea level reduction이 정답이다. 'sea level dropping'이 'sea level reduction'으로 paraphrasing되었다.

2

고대 그리스에서, 주된 종교전통은 옥수수의 파종과 수확, 포도의 생산, 그리고 취하는 것과 관련 있는 구세주인 디오니소스를 중심으로 했다. 귀족들은 그를 기리며 계절마다 축제를 벌였는데, 그 중 가장 중요한 축제는 ³디오니소스 축제로 알려진 가을에 열리는 포도주 시음 의식이었고, 이는 합창시 혹은 찬가의 암송을 포함했다. 취객들은 그들의 뛰어난 신에게 디오니소스 찬양가로 불린 송시를 노래했고 사제는 인간과 신 사이에서 상징적인 대화로 이에 답했다. 상류와 하류 사회 계층 내에서의 인기 덕분에, 기원전 6세기에 이르러, 코린트의 왕은 디오니소스 찬양가 대회를 창립했으며 이러한 유사 연극을 쓰고 상연하기 위해 엄선된 시인들을 초대했다. 처음으로, ⁴연극은 종교적 뿌리로부터 해방되어 충분히 발달된 예술작품으로 변모했다. 이러한 변화하는 극예술 환경은 그리스 전역의 사고방식을 바꾸었고 이로써 예술 형식의 진보를 가져올 새로운 세속적 관심을 불러일으켰다.

3 글쓴이에 따르면, 가을마다 열렸던 고대 그리스의 포도주 시음 의식은 -을 포함했다.
   A 시 공연
   B 포도주 제조
   C 옥수수 수확
   D 사원 방문

해설 문제의 핵심어구(wine tasting festival)와 관련된 지문 내용 중 'the autumn wine tasting celebration ~ included the recitation of choric poems or hymns'에서 가을에 열리는 포도주 시음 의식은 합창시 혹은 찬가의 암송을 포함했다고 하였으므로, 보기 A the performance of poetry가 정답이다. 'the recitation of choric poems or hymns'가 'the performance of poetry'로 paraphrasing되었다.

4 종교계로부터 일반 대중에게로의 연극의 이동은 -을 야기했다.
   A 유럽 전역의 조직화된 종교들에 대한 반발
   B 고대 그리스 문명의 붕괴
   C 예술에 대한 일반 대중의 호기심 증가
   D 몇몇 배우들이 사회 계층에 비판적으로 되는 것

해설 문제의 핵심어구(The movement of plays from the religious world)와 관련된 지문 내용 중 'the plays were freed from their religious roots and transformed into full-fledged works of art. The changing theatre environment ~

triggered a newfound secular interest'에서 연극은 종교적 뿌리로부터 해방되어 충분히 발달된 예술작품으로 변모했으며 이러한 변화하는 극예술 환경이 새로운 세속적 관심을 불러일으켰다고 하였으므로, 보기 **C** an increase in the general public's curiosity about art가 정답이다. 'a newfound secular interest'가 'an increase in the general public's curiosity'로 paraphrasing되었다.

3

전 세계적으로 현재 4억 4천만 명으로 추산되는 소비자들이 1년에 거의 1조 2천억 달러를 시계, 보석류, 의류, 핸드백, 그리고 자가용과 같은 최고급품에 소비함에 따라, 사치품 소매시장은 꾸준히 확대되고 있다. 그러나, 이러한 소비자들의 대부분은 매우 부유한 층에 속하지는 않기 때문에, 사람들이 그들의 수입 이상을 쓴다는 것은 명백해졌다. [5]그렇다면, 무엇이 소비자들을 그렇게 하도록 부추기는 것일까?

Niro Sivanathan 교수와 Nathan Petit 교수에 따르면, [5]사치품들은 성공의 지표이며 그러므로 자신감을 끌어올린다. 그들은 이러한 견해를 입증하는 설문조사를 실시하기도 했다. 예를 들어, 최근에 연인과 헤어졌거나 승진을 놓친 연구 참가자들은, 일반적으로 행복한 사람들보다 위안의 수단으로 고가품을 사고 싶어 하는 훨씬 더 많은 욕구를 보였다. 참가자들은 사치품을 구입하는 것이 실패를 잊고 더 성공했다고 느끼도록 도울 것이라고 생각했다. 쇼핑을 통한 기분 전환에도 불구하고, [5]많은 소비자들은 단순히 '지불한 만큼 얻는다', 즉 가장 비싼 물품이 가장 고품질이고 가장 오래 갈 것이라고 생각한다. 이러한 이유로, 그것들은 쇼핑객들 사이에 수요가 크다. 그들은 [6]상표가 없는 적정한 가격의 물품을 구매하는 것보다는 물건에 돈을 펑펑 쓰는 것이 궁극적으로는 수리와 교체에 있어 상당한 비용 절감을 가져올 것이라고 믿는다.

5 지문에서 논의되는 주제는 –이다.
  A 사치품들의 전 세계적인 제조
  B 부유한 소비층의 성장
  C 무모한 소비에 영향을 미치는 요인
  D 소매시장에 있어 심리학이 수행하는 역할

> **해설** 이 지문에는 주제 문장이 없으므로 지문 전체를 읽고 주제를 파악한다. 첫 번째 단락의 마지막 문장 'What then, is driving them to do so?'에서 무엇이 소비자들을 그렇게 하도록 부추기는 것인지 질문을 던진 뒤, 'luxury items are indicators of success and thereby boost self-confidence'와 'many consumers simply believe ~ the most expensive items are of the highest quality and last the longest'에서 사치품들은 성공의 지표이며 그러므로 자신감을 끌어올린다는 것과 많은 소비자들이 가장 비싼 물품이 가장 고품질이고 가장 오래 갈 것이라고 생각한다는 것 두 가지를 요인으로 언급하고 있으므로, 보기 **C** factors influencing reckless spending이 정답이다.

6 유사하고 더 저렴한 것을 사는 대신 사치품을 사는 것은 –할 수 있다.
  A 경기를 부양한다
  B 사람들이 많은 사치품을 구매하도록 야기한다
  C 수리하는 데 소비되었을 비용을 절약한다
  D 가격이 알맞은 다른 물품들에 대한 수요를 증가시킨다

> **해설** 문제의 핵심어구(luxury item instead of a similar, cheaper one)와 관련된 지문 내용 중 'splurging on an item rather than buying a reasonably priced generic brand will result in significant savings on repair and replacement costs'에서 상표가 없는 적정한 가격의 물품을 구매하는 것보다는 물건에 돈을 펑펑 쓰는 것이 수리와 교체에 있어 상당한 비용 절감을 가져올 것이라고 하였으므로, 보기 **C** save money that would have been spent fixing it이 정답이다. 'result in ~ savings on repair and replacement costs'가 'save money that would have been spent fixing it'으로 paraphrasing되었다.

'은의 주'라는 별명이 붙은 네바다 주 광산업의 역사는 그 주의 역사와 너무나도 밀접하게 연관되어 있어, 특정 시기들에서, 그 두 가지는 분리될 수 없을 정도이다. 사실, [7]광산업이 아니었다면, 아마도 실제로 주 지위를 획득한 시기의 수십 년 후에도 네바다 주는 주 지위를 획득할 수 없었을 것이다. 당시 으레 그러했듯이, 은의 주는 유명한 캄스톡 광맥에서 캐낸 은을 써서 연방으로 편입했다. 1800년대 중반에, 이후 네바다 주가 된 그 지역은 주로 캘리포니아 주로 금을 찾으러 가는 사람들을 위한 고속도로였다. 그러나, 1859년에, 대규모 은 매장층의 발견은 금세 버지니아시티를 서부 지역의 모든 채광소 중 가장 유명한 곳으로 만들었다. 채광꾼들과 정착민들의 급격한 유입은 불과 2년 만에 네바다 준주의 조직화로 이어졌다.

동부에서는, 미국 남부 전쟁이 일어나려 하고 있었다. [8]그 지역의 풍부한 광물 자원이 연방에 도움이 될 것임을 깨달은데다, 그가 제안한 노예 제도를 폐지하는 미국 헌법 개정을 지지해줄 또 다른 주가 필요했던 링컨은, 그 지역이 연방으로의 가입을 모색하도록 원조했다. 비록 네바다 주는 주 지위에 필요한 127,381명 인구의 5분의 1 정도밖에 되지 않았지만, '전쟁으로 인해 태어난 주'라는 표어와 함께, 1864년에 36번째 주로 인정되었다. [9]그 이후로, 호황 시기에 들어온 돈의 유입과 수요가 적은 시기 동안의 현저한 경제 침체 모두에 있어 광산업은 계속해서 네바다 주의 경제에 막대한 영향을 미쳤다.

7 글쓴이는 -을 설명하기 위해 캄스톡 광맥을 언급한다.
  A 채광꾼들이 서쪽으로 이동하기 시작한 이유
  B 그 지역에서 발견되는 고유의 자원
  C 사회 기반 시설을 건축하는 데 그 주가 사용한 자원들 중 하나
  D 네바다 주의 주 지위에 있어 풍부한 광물의 중요성

  해설 문제의 핵심어구(Comstock Lode)와 관련된 지문 내용 중 'were it not for mining, Nevada would probably not have achieved statehood ~. As it was, the Silver State bought its way into the Union with silver mined in the famous Comstock Lode.'에서 광산업이 아니었다면 네바다 주는 주 지위를 획득할 수 없었을 것이며, 당시 으레 그러했듯이 은의 주는 유명한 캄스톡 광맥에서 캐낸 은을 써서 연방으로 편입했다고 하였으므로, 글쓴이가 네바다 주의 주 지위에 있어 풍부한 광물의 중요성을 설명하기 위해 캄스톡 광맥을 언급했음을 알 수 있다. 따라서 보기 D the importance of mineral wealth in Nevada's statehood가 정답이다.

8 링컨은 -하기 위해 네바다 지역이 연방에 합류하도록 원조했다.
  A 그의 반노예제 제의에 대한 추가적인 지지를 얻기 위해
  B 국가를 위한 세입을 더 많이 거두기 위해
  C 캘리포니아 주 금광과 직접적인 연결로를 설립하기 위해
  D 주의 인구를 증가시키기 위해

  해설 문제의 핵심어구(Lincoln)와 관련된 지문 내용 중 'Lincoln, ~ needing another state to support his proposed anti-slavery amendment to the Constitution, encouraged the territory to seek admission to the Union.'에서 그가 제안한 노예 제도를 폐지하는 미국 헌법 개정을 지지해줄 또 다른 주가 필요했던 링컨은 그 지역이 연방으로의 가입을 모색하도록 원조했다고 하였으므로, 보기 A gain additional support for his anti-slavery proposals가 정답이다. 'another state to support'가 'additional support'로 paraphrasing되었다.

9 글쓴이에 따르면, 1864년 이후 네바다 주에서의 광산업은
  A 경제 침체기 동안 자금을 마련하는 것에 실패했다.
  B 주에서 주요 고용 분야가 되었다.
  C 주 경제에서 역할이 감소했다.
  D 계속해서 상당한 경제적 영향을 미쳤다.

  해설 문제의 핵심어구(since 1864 mining in Nevada)와 관련된 지문 내용 중 'Since then, mining's impact on Nevada's economy has remained immense'에서 그 이후로 광산업은 계속해서 네바다 주의 경제에 막대한 영향을 미쳤다고 하였으므로, 보기 D has continued to have a significant economic influence가 정답이다. 'impact on ~ economy'가 'economic influence'로 paraphrasing되었다.

5

몇몇 애완동물 주인들은, 지진 전에, 애완동물들이 가만히 있지 못하고 불안해하며, 아무 이유 없이 낑낑거리거나, 혹은 그저 도망치려고 한다고 주장한다. 이것은 많은 사람들이 동물들에게 이런 다가오는 사건들에 대해 경고하는 특별한 감각이 있다고 믿게 했다. [10]그러나, 이것은 새로운 생각은 아니다. 사실, 동물들이 지진을 예측할 수 있다는 믿음은 기원전 4세기까지 거슬러 올라간, 그리스의 도시 헬리케의 역사적 기록에 등장한다. 이 기록들은 거대한 지진이 그곳을 파괴하기 바로 며칠 전에 동물들이 갑자기 도시를 떠났다고 명시하는데, 이는 사람들이 동물들이 그 사고에 대해 경고를 받았다고 믿게 만들었다. 이러한 종류의 일화가 있다는 점을 고려해볼 때, 누군가는 동물들이 지진 활동을 예측하도록 도와주는 육감을 가지고 있을지를 궁금해하기 시작할지도 모른다. 자, 만약 우리가 지구를 연구하는 일을 맡고 있는 기관인 미국 지질연구소를 믿는다면 대답은 '아니다'이다. [11]그들의 연구에 따르면, 동물들이 지진을 예측할 수 있다는 것을 보여주는 어떤 믿을 만한 증거도 발견되지 않았다. 하지만 이것이 옳다면, 지진 전의 이상한 행동들에 대한 정기적인 보고들은 무엇이 설명할 것인가? 한 가지 이론은 동물들이 단지 인간보다 훨씬 더 효과적인 감각을 가지고 있다는 것이다. 우월한 청력으로, 다른 동물뿐 아니라 개와 고양이는 먼 거리에 있는 지질 구조상의 움직임에 의해 만들어진 초저주파 소리를 감지할 수 있다. 그러나, [12]그 소리가 무엇인지 이해하지 못한 채로, 그들은 그저 그것으로부터 도망치고 싶어 하는데, 이는 그들이 보통 행동하는 것과 매우 다르게 행동하도록 한다.

10 글쓴이는 왜 고대 그리스의 도시 헬리케를 언급하는가?

A 이론이 얼마나 멀리까지 거슬러 올라가는지 보여주기 위해
B 역사적 기록의 오류를 암시하기 위해
C 문서로 기록된 재난의 예시를 제공하기 위해
D 통념의 근원을 설명하기 위해

해설 문제의 핵심어구(Helike)와 관련된 지문 내용 중 'This ~ is not a new idea.'와 'the belief ~ appears as far back as the 4th century B.C., in the historical records of the Greek city of Helike'에서 이것은 새로운 생각이 아니라고 하며 그 믿음은 기원전 4세기까지 거슬러 올라간 그리스의 도시 헬리케의 역사적 기록에 등장한다고 하였으므로, 글쓴이가 이론이 얼마나 멀리까지 거슬러 올라가는지 보여주기 위해 고대 그리스의 도시 헬리케를 언급했음을 알 수 있다. 따라서 보기 **A To show how far back the theory stretches**가 정답이다.

11 미국 지질연구소에 의해 진행된 연구는 왜 언급되는가?

A 글쓴이는 지진 활동이 순전히 무작위적이라는 것을 보여주고 싶어 한다.
B 글쓴이는 동물의 감각에 대해 더 많은 정보를 제공하고 싶어 한다.
C 글쓴이는 동물에 대해 흔히 가지는 믿음이 틀렸음을 입증하고 싶어 한다.
D 글쓴이는 고대의 이야기가 정확하다는 것을 암시하고 싶어 한다.

해설 문제의 핵심어구(U.S. Geological Survey)와 관련된 지문 내용 중 'According to their studies, no credible evidence has been discovered to show that animals are able to predict earthquakes at all.'에서 미국 지질연구소의 연구에 따르면 동물들이 지진을 예측할 수 있다는 것을 보여주는 어떤 믿을 만한 증거도 발견되지 않았다고 하였으므로, 글쓴이가 동물에 대해 사람들이 흔히 가지는 믿음이 틀렸음을 입증하고 싶어 함을 알 수 있다. 따라서 보기 **C The writer wants to disprove a commonly held belief about animals**가 정답이다.

12 글쓴이는 동물들과 초저주파 소리에 대한 그들의 반응에 대해 무엇을 암시하는가?

A 짧은 거리에서만 감지할 수 있다.
B 지진이 시작되고 난 이후까지 그것을 듣지 못한다.
C 그것이 무엇인지 알지 못함에도 불구하고 도망가고 싶어 한다.
D 임박한 위험에 대해 다른 동물들에게 알린다.

해설 문제의 핵심어구(response to infrasonic sound)와 관련된 지문 내용 중 'without understanding what the sound is, they simply want to flee from it'에서 초저주파 소리가 무엇인지 이해하지 못한 채로 그들은 그저 그것으로부터 도망치고 싶어한다고 하였으므로, 보기 C They want to run away despite not knowing what it is가 정답이다. 'flee from'이 'run away'로 paraphrasing되었다.

6

우리는 오늘날 비행기 여행을 종종 당연하게 여기지만, 그것은 실제로 수 세기에 걸친 실험의 결과이다. 인류 초기부터, 사람들은 하늘에서 관찰한 새처럼 나는 것을 시도해왔다. 비행에 대한 이러한 가장 기본적인 시도들은 단순히 깃털로 덮인 날개를 달고 절벽에서 튀어나온 바위에서 뛰어내리는 것에서부터 [13]레오나르도 다빈치에 의해 설계되었던 것과 같은 정교한 비행 기계까지 모든 것을 포함했다. 유감스럽게도, 이들 중 어떤 것도 공기보다 무거운 물건을 하늘 높이 띄우고 유지하는 비행의 본질적인 문제를 극복하지 못했다. 이것은 [14]조지 케일리가 항공역학의 기본 원칙을 규명했던 1800년대 중반까지 여전히 마찬가지였다. 새로 발견된 지식을 활용하여, 케일리는 사람을 공중으로 100피트 들어올릴 수 있는 방향타가 없는 글라이더를 제작할 수 있었다. 케일리의 성과는 항공역학에서 더 대단한 실험을 가져왔다. 흥미를 느낀 사람들 중에는 오빌 라이트와 윌버 라이트 형제가 있었다. 이 미국인 형제는 모형 날개에 대한 시험을 수행하기 위해 가장 기본적인 공기 터널을 사용했다. 이 장치와 케일리의 원리를 활용하여, [15]라이트 형제는 바람이 어떻게 비행기에 영향을 주는지 관찰했으며 비행을 위한 정확한 수학 공식을 개발했다. 마침내, 그들은 비행기의 균형을 제어하기 위해 오늘날의 보조 날개가 하는 것과 같이 날개 배치를 바꾸기 위한 방법과, 선체의 측면 조종을 가능하게 한 방향타 시스템을 고안해냈다. 그 다음 그들의 주요 문제는 비행기에 동력을 공급하는 방법을 찾아내는 것이었다. 당시 증기 기관이 양력을 제공할 수 있을 정도로 비행기를 충분히 빠르게 밀 수 있긴 했지만, 그것들은 엄청나게 무거웠다. 다행히도, 급성장하는 자동차 산업을 위해 개발된 내연기관이 그 작업을 위해 충분할 만큼 강력하고 가벼웠다. 라이트 형제는 이 엔진들 중 하나를 항공기 프로펠러에 달고 1903년 키티호크에서 제어되며, 자력으로 추진하는 첫 번째 비행기를 만들었다. 이러한 엔진 배치 유형은 제트 엔진이 개발되었던 1930년대 후반까지 항공 산업에서 표준이 되었다.

13 레오나르도 다빈치의 항공기 설계는 매우 복잡했으나,
  A 깃털의 사용에 너무 크게 의존했다.
  B 하늘로 띄워지거나 떠 있기에는 너무 무거웠다.
  C 첫 비행에서 몇 가지 문제를 겪었다.
  D 화물을 실을 수 있는 충분한 공간이 없었다.

해설 문제의 핵심어구(Leonardo da Vinci's aircraft design)와 관련된 지문 내용 중 'elaborate flying machines like the one designed by Leonardo da Vinci ~ were ever able to overcome the inherent problem with flight – getting and keeping an object that is heavier than air aloft.'에서 레오나르도 다빈치에 의해 설계되었던 것과 같은 정교한 비행 기계는 공기보다 무거운 물건을 하늘 높이 띄우고 유지하는 비행의 본질적인 문제를 극복하지 못했다고 하였으므로, 보기 B it weighed too much to become or remain airborne이 정답이다. 'getting and keeping an object ~ aloft'가 'become or remain airborne'으로 paraphrasing되었다.

14 글쓴이는 조지 케일리가 –했다고 언급한다.
  A 동력이 공급되는 첫 번째 비행기를 발명했다
  B 다빈치의 작품에 영감을 받았다
  C 라이트 형제와 같은 조종사들과 작업했다
  D 항공역학의 근본 원리를 발견했다

해설 문제의 핵심어구(George Cayley)와 관련된 지문 내용 중 'George Cayley ascertained the fundamentals of aerodynamics'에서 조지 케일리가 항공역학의 기본 원칙을 규명했다고 하였으므로, 보기 D discovered the basics of aerodynamics가 정답이다. 'ascertained the fundamentals'가 'discovered the basics'로 paraphrasing되었다.

15 라이트 형제의 실험은 그들이 –하는 것을 가능하게 했다.
  A 비행에 필요한 계산을 하는 것
  B 비행기와 자동차에 동력을 공급할 수 있는 엔진을 개발하는 것

C 케일리에 의해 제시된 몇몇 이론들이 틀렸음을 입증하는 것
D 증기 기관 모터의 무게를 줄이는 것

해설 문제의 핵심어구(Experiments by the Wright brothers)와 관련된 지문 내용 중 'the Wright brothers ~ developed accurate mathematical formulas for flight'에서 라이트 형제가 비행을 위한 정확한 수학 공식을 개발했다고 하였으므로, 보기 A perform the calculations necessary for flight가 정답이다. 'developed ~ mathematical formulas'가 'perform the calculations'로 paraphrasing되었다.

🔍 오답 확인하기
B는 지문의 'Their main problem was then figuring out a way to power the plane.'을 활용하여 혼동을 주었지만, 라이트 형제가 비행기와 자동차에 동력을 공급할 수 있는 엔진을 개발한 것이 아니라 자동차 산업을 위해 개발된 내연기관을 항공기 프로펠러에 달았다고 하였으므로 오답이다.

7

귀인이론

[16]우리 자신과 우리가 마주치는 사람들 모두의 행동에 대한 정당한 이유와 설명을 찾고, 그 결과 누가 또는 무엇이 그러한 행동들에 책임이 있는지를 찾고자 하는 보편적인 욕구가 있다. 심리학자들은 설명에 대한 그런 선천적인 욕구가 상황에 따라 종종 행동을 내적 또는 외적 요인의 책임이라고 생각하는 경향으로 나타날 것이라는 데 주목한다. 이러한 경향은 귀인이론으로 알려져 있다.

오스트리아의 심리학자 Fritz Heider에 의해 1958년에 처음으로 제안된 귀인이론은, 모든 인간 행동이 내적 또는 외적 요인에 의해 동기가 부여된다고 추정한다. 후자의 경우에서, [17]상황은 때때로 사람의 통제 너머에 있다고 인식되는데, 이는 개인이 감소된 책임감을 경험한다는 것을 의미한다. 예를 들어, 한 직원이 교통 체증 때문에 직장에 늦게 도착한다면, 그 경향은 책임을 외부로 투사하는 것이다. 반면에, 사람들은 결과에 영향을 줄 수 있을 때 책임을 느끼는 경향이 있다. 예를 들어, 좋은 부모가 되기 위해 열심히 공부하고, 부지런히 훈련하고, 최선을 다하는 것은 개인적인 동기에서 기인하는 것으로 여겨진다. 이런 경우에, 사람들은 자신들의 노력을 행동의 원인으로 설명한다.

예상치 못한 일을 외적인 힘 때문이라고 생각하는 것은 쉽지만, 내적 요인과 외적 요인 사이의 경계는 종종 분명하지 않다. 한 사람이 격한 언쟁에 참여하며 공격적으로 행동하고 있는 상황에서, 관찰자는 그 사람이 쉽게 분노하거나 속이 좁다고 생각하기 쉽다. 이런 귀인은 종종 논쟁이 처음에 어떻게 일어났는지에 대해 알지 못한 채로, [18]관찰자가 그 행동을 그 사람의 성격에 의한 것이라고 추정하며 발생한다. [18]관찰자들이 행동의 외적 요인보다 내적 요인에 주목하는 이러한 경향은, '대응편향'으로 알려져 있다. 그러나, 마찬가지로, 공격적으로 행동하는 사람은 그 또는 그녀가 어떤 부당함의 피해자이며 그러므로 그러한 반응이 정당화된다고 느낄 수 있다.

비슷한 경향이 사람들이 그들 자신의 경험에 보이는 반응에서 발견될 수 있다. [19]승진을 하거나 목표를 이루는 것과 같이 개인이 긍정적인 경험을 할 때, 그들은 자신의 노력을 성공과 연관 짓는 경향이 있다. 반대로, 사람들이 부정적인 경험을 할 때, 편향은 뒤집히고, 그들은 실망을 외적 요인 탓으로 돌릴 가능성이 있다. 실패를 그들의 잘못이나 능력 부족 탓으로 돌리기보다는, 사람들은 통제 밖의 요인을 과장한다. 책임을 외부로 던짐으로써, 그들은 불행에 대해 이 외적 요인들을 탓할 수 있고 그들 자신이 피해자라는 인식을 유지할 수 있다.

결국, 우리의 행동에 대해 내적 요인과 외적 요인을 제공하는 것은 우리가 죄책감을 느끼지 못하도록 부정적인 행동에 대한 정당한 이유를 주는 것과 동시에, 우리의 긍정적인 측면을 강조할 수 있게 해주고 자부심을 북돋아주는 것처럼 보인다. 자부심과 자아 인식이 우리의 성공과 실패의 원인을 돌리는 데 있어 무의식적으로 수행하는 역할을 이해해야만 많은 상황에서 우리가 행동하는 방식에 대해 변화를 일으킬 수 있다.

16 글쓴이는 사람들이 ~하기 때문에 왜 어떤 일들이 일어나는지 설명하고자 한다고 제시한다.
A 과거의 실수로부터 배우는 것이 가능한 것처럼 느끼기 때문에
B 누군가 혹은 어떤 것에 책임을 지우려는 내적인 욕구를 가지고 있기 때문에
C 다른 사람들에게 왜 상황이 변화하는지를 설명할 책임이 있기 때문에
D 자신의 통제 너머에 있는 일들에 대해 선천적인 두려움을 가지고 있기 때문에

해설 문제의 핵심어구(driven to explain why)와 관련된 지문 내용 중 'There is a universal need to seek justifications and explanations for people's actions ~ and therefore to determine who or what is responsible for those actions.'에서 사람들의 행동에 대한 정당한 이유와 설명을 찾고 그 결과 누가 또는 무엇이 그러한 행동들에 책임이 있는지를 찾고자 하는 보편적인 욕구가 있다고 하였으므로, 보기 **B** they possess an innate urge to assign responsibility to someone or something이 정답이다. 'a universal need ~ to determine who or what is responsible'이 'an innate urge to assign responsibility to someone or something'으로 paraphrasing되었다.

17 글쓴이에 따르면, 어떤 상황을 통제할 수 없다고 느끼는 사람들은
   A 인지한 실패에 대해 자기 자신을 탓하는 경향이 있다.
   B 사건의 결과에 대해 자신들의 책임이 덜 있다고 생각한다.
   C 사람들에 대해 부정적인 결론을 이끌어낼 가능성이 더 크다.
   D 다른 사람들에게 좋지 못하게 행동하는 것이 정당화될 수 있다고 생각한다.

   해설 문제의 핵심어구(have no control of a situation)와 관련된 지문 내용 중 'situations are sometimes perceived as being beyond a person's control, meaning that individuals experience a diminished sense of responsibility'에서 상황은 때때로 사람의 통제 너머에 있다고 인식되는데 이는 개인이 감소된 책임감을 경험한다는 것을 의미한다고 하였으므로, 보기 **B** believe they are less responsible for the outcome of an event가 정답이다. 'beyond a person's control'이 'have no control'로, 'experience a diminished sense of responsibility'가 'believe they are less responsible for'로 paraphrasing되었다.

   🔍 오답 확인하기
   A는 지문 내용 중 'individuals experience a diminished sense of responsibility'에서 통제 너머에 있는 상황에서 개인은 감소된 책임감을 경험한다고 하였으므로 지문의 내용과 반대되는 오답이다.

18 글쓴이는 '대응편향'이 사람들이 -할 때 발생한다고 말한다.
   A 개인의 진정한 성격을 이해하지 못할 때
   B 정당한 이유 없이 개인을 피해자라고 해석할 때
   C 결론에 도달한 뒤 상황을 바꾸려고 시도할 때
   D 행동이 개인의 성격에 의해 결정된다고 결론지을 때

   해설 문제의 핵심어구(correspondence bias)와 관련된 지문 내용 중 'the observer assuming the behaviour is due to the person's personality. This tendency ~ to focus on the internal reasons ~ is known as 'correspondence bias'.'에서 관찰자가 그 행동을 그 사람의 성격에 의한 것이라고 추정하며 내적 요인에 주목하는 이러한 경향은 '대응편향'으로 알려져 있다고 하였으므로, 보기 **D** conclude that behaviour is determined by a person's personality가 정답이다. 'assuming the behaviour is due to'가 'conclude that behaviour is determined by'로 paraphrasing되었다.

19 글쓴이는 사람들이 성공할 때, 그들이 -하는 경향이 있다고 언급한다.
   A 성취의 정도를 과장한다
   B 타고난 재능의 기여를 간과한다
   C 결실을 내적 요인의 덕으로 돌린다
   D 미래의 실망감을 다스리는 것이 덜 가능해진다

   해설 문제의 핵심어구(when people succeed)와 관련된 지문 내용 중 'When individuals have positive experiences ~ they are inclined to associate their own efforts with their success.'에서 개인이 긍정적인 경험을 할 때 그들은 자신의 노력을 성공과 연관 짓는 경향이 있다고 하였으므로, 보기 **C** attribute their results to internal factors가 정답이다. 'individuals have positive experiences'가 'people succeed'로, 'associate their own efforts with their success'가 'attribute their results to internal factors'로 paraphrasing되었다.

유럽의 인구: 거대한 전환

후기 중세 시대 내내, 유럽의 인구는 흉작, 전쟁, 그리고 가장 중요하게, 대륙 전역에 걸쳐 퍼졌던 파괴적인 전염병 종류인 흑사병 때문에 줄어들고 있었다. [20]이 전국적인 유행병으로부터의 끊임없는 죽음의 위협은 사람들 사이에 극심한 공포를 불러일으켰는데, 그와 같은 공포는 1348년 지오바니 보카치오에 의해 '데카메론'에서 서술된 것과 같은 것이었다. 그 당시 많은 유럽인들이 어떻게 느꼈는지를 반영하여, 보카치오는 시민들이 법을 무시하고 매일이 마지막 날인 것처럼 살아가는 허구의 세계를 창조했다. 그는 근본적으로 세계가 끝나가고 있다고 믿었던 사람들의 행동을 묘사하려고 시도했는데, 이것은 그 당시 많은 사람들이 생각할 수도 있었던 것과 크게 다르지 않았다.

14세기와 15세기에 파괴적인 절정에 이르렀을 때 흑사병은 유럽의 인구를 30퍼센트에서 60퍼센트 사이로 감소시켰다고 추산되었으나, 거기서 끝나지 않았다. 17세기에 전염병은 재발했고, 이것은 수십 년 간의 전쟁과 함께 수백만 명의 죽음을 초래했다. 결과적으로, 유럽의 인구는 서기 1300년부터 1800년까지 그저 서서히 증가했다. 이러한 성장은 1800년과 1914년 사이에 극적으로 증가했는데, 이때 유럽의 인구 수는 1억 8천 8백만에서 4억 5천 8백만으로 급증했다.

역사학자들은 이 시기를 '거대한 전환'이라고 부르며, 이 중대한 인구 성장을 농기계 발전과 아메리카에서 온 수확량이 더 높고 더 영양가 있는 농작물의 경작을 포함하여 농업 생산에서의 주요 개선 사항들의 덕분으로 돌린다. 더 영양가 높은 음식을 먹을 수 있게 되어, 그 어느 때보다도 훨씬 더 많은 수의 유아들이 살아남기 시작했고, 20년 가까이 평균 기대 수명이 증가했다. 사망률을 낮추는 데 한층 더한 기여는 질병과 감염에 대한 향상된 이해였다.

그러나, 인구의 빠른 증가는 누군가에게는 걱정되는 일이었다. 1798년 논문 '인구론'에서, 경제학자 토머스 맬서스는 유럽이 인구 과잉이 되고 있다고 시사했다. 유럽에 충분한 인구가 거주하지 않아 야기된 혼돈에 대해 쓴 초기 저자들과 완전히 반대로, 맬서스는 신생아 수가 제한되어야 한다고 강조했다. [21]그의 논문은 가족 계획이라는 대중적인 개념이 생기게 했고 그의 견해는 출산을 하는 것이 항상 자발적이어야 한다는 개념의 후기 지지자들에 의해 널리 사용되었다. 19세기에 여성은 실제로 그들이 가지는 아이의 수를 제한하기 시작했고, 몇 십 년 만에, 출산율은 30퍼센트 감소했다.

[22]20세기에, 유럽의 인구는 의학 발전과 그리고 두 번의 세계 대전 동안의 기간을 제외하고, 장수가 일반적인 것이 될 정도로 개선된 영양에 의해 깊은 영향을 받았다. 출생률은 계속해서 감소했고, 오늘날, 인구는 현대에 처음으로 마이너스 성장을 경험하고 있다. 이것은 부분적으로는 낙태의 합법화와 같은 법률 변화의 도움으로 무기한적으로 계속될 것으로 예상된다. 사실, UN 인구분과위원회는 2005년에 7억 2천 8백만 정도로 측정된 유럽의 인구가 2050년까지 6억 6천 5백만 이하로 내려갈 것으로 예상한다.

20 글쓴이는 '데카메론'을 –하기 때문에 언급한다.

   A   그 당시 대부분의 글들과 완전히 달랐기 때문에

   B   흑사병에 대해 등장한 첫 번째 문학 작품이었기 때문에

   C   인구 억제의 중요성을 강조하기 때문에

   D   근대 초기 유럽인들의 공포를 분명히 보여주기 때문에

> 해설 문제의 핵심어구(*The Decameron*)와 관련된 지문 내용 중 'The constant threat of death from this pandemic created panic among the people, of the sort described ~ in *The Decameron*'에서 이 전국적인 유행병으로부터의 끊임없는 죽음의 위협은 사람들 사이에 극심한 공포를 불러일으켰는데 그와 같은 공포는 '데카메론'에서 서술된 것과 같은 것이었다고 하였으므로, 글쓴이가 '데카메론'이 근대 초기 유럽인들의 공포를 분명히 보여주고 있기 때문에 언급했음을 알 수 있다. 따라서 보기 **D** it illustrates the fear of Europeans in the early modern period가 정답이다.

21 글쓴이는 토머스 맬서스의 논문에 대해 무엇을 암시하는가?

   A   인구 억제 운동에 영감을 주었다.

   B   대중적인 견해를 직접적으로 부정했다.

   C   여성의 권리를 광범위하게 촉진시켰다.

   D   19세기에 처음으로 발행되었다.

해설 문제의 핵심어구(Thomas Malthus' essay)와 관련된 지문 내용 중 'His paper gave rise to the popular concept of family planning ~ women did begin limiting the number of children they had'에서 그의 논문은 가족 계획이라는 대중적인 개념이 생기게 했으며 여성들이 실제로 그들이 가지는 아이의 수를 제한하기 시작했다고 하였으므로, 보기 **A It inspired a population control movement**가 정답이다.

Q 오답 확인하기
B는 지문 내용 중 'gave rise to the popular concept of family planning'에서 가족 계획이라는 대중적인 개념이 생기게 했다고 하였으므로 지문의 내용과 반대되는 오답이다.
C는 지문의 'women did begin limiting the number of children they had'를 활용하여 혼동을 주었지만, 지문에서 토머스 맬서스의 논문이 여성의 권리를 광범위하게 촉진시켰다는 내용은 언급하지 않았으므로 오답이다.
D는 지문 내용 중 'In his 1798 paper'에서 그의 1798년 논문, 즉 18세기 논문이라고 하였으므로 오답이다.

22 글쓴이는 20세기 유럽의 인구는 -했다고 말한다.
A 첫 10년 동안 최고 수준에 이르렀다
B 높은 출생률로 특징지어졌다
C 향상된 의술과 영양에 의해 영향을 받았다
D 두 세계 대전 기간 사이에 감소했다

해설 문제의 핵심어구(European population in the 20th century)와 관련된 지문 내용 중 'In the 20th century, Europe's population was profoundly impacted by medical advances and improved nutrition'에서 20세기에 유럽의 인구는 의학 발전과 개선된 영양에 의해 깊은 영향을 받았다고 하였으므로, 보기 **C was affected by better medicine and nutrition**이 정답이다. 'medical advances and improved nutrition'이 'better medicine and nutrition'으로 paraphrasing되었다.

9

아프리카의 역사를 밝히는 것

고대 이집트와 로마의 북아프리카의 역사는 비교적 잘 기록되어 있지만, 사하라 사막 이남 아프리카의 유물과 관련된 1차 자료의 부족은 역사가들에게 큰 어려움이다. 이러한 정보의 부족은 아랍과 유럽 열강에 의한 식민지화 이전에 이 거대한 지역에 존재했던 다양한 사회의 정확한 모습을 밝히는 데 있어 상당한 어려움으로 이어져왔다.

주로 특정 지역에 국한되어 있긴 하지만, 사하라 사막 이남 아프리카의 정치적 그리고 사회적 발전에 대한 통찰력을 제공하는 기록물들이 존재하기는 한다. 이것들은 종종 모국의 사회를 위해 그들의 인상을 기록했던 방문자들에 의해 쓰인 문서들이다. 예를 들어, 고대 이집트에서 온 상인들은, 종종 나일강을 따라서 북수단에 있는 누비아까지 남쪽으로 여행했고 그들의 거래는 이집트의 상형 문자로 기록되었다. ²³8세기 이슬람의 북아프리카 지배를 뒤이어, 아랍어로 쓰인 사하라 사막 이남 아프리카 지역에 대한 공식 기록들이 보관되었다. 이 문서들 중 많은 것들이 논쟁적 어조이고 종교적 주제로 가득하긴 하지만, 일부는 교역로와 농업, 그리고 ²⁴이 시기 동안 아랍 지도자들이 시작했던 대규모의 사하라 종단 노예 무역에 관련된 정보를 담고 있는 공식 문서이다.

15세기 이래로 계속해서 사하라 사막 이남 아프리카에 대해 유럽 언어로 쓰인 기록물 또한 대량으로 나타나기 시작했다. ²⁵가장 먼저 도착했던 유럽인들은 방문하고 있던 땅을 손에 넣는 것을 목표로 했던 탐험가들이었다. 유럽 사회에 토착민들에 대한 사회적 그리고 문화적 정보를 전달하면서, 그들은 종종 놀랄 만큼 자세하게 현지 풍습, 의식, 그리고 생활 방식에 대해 묘사했으나 그들의 이야기는 경멸적인 태도로 특징지어졌다. 유럽의 탐험가들과, 이 시기 동안 마찬가지로 사하라 사막 이남 아프리카를 방문하기 시작했던 기독교 선교사들은, 부분적으로는 토착민들의 수준 이하의 무기와 기독교에 대한 무지 때문에 그들 자신을 우월하게 여겼다.

토착 사회 관점에서의 역사적 설명의 부족은 주로 많은 초기 아프리카 언어의 문자 형태의 부재 때문이다. 그 결과, 사하라 사막 이남 아프리카에 대한 현존하는 역사적 정보는 종종 방대한 사회의 형태로 세대를 거쳐 전해져 내려온 구전 이야기로부터 주로 수집되어 왔다. 구전 기록은 이야기할 때마다 다소 달라질 수밖에 없기 때문에, 그것들은 글로 된 자료만큼 믿을 만하다고 여겨지지는 않는다.

위험에도 불구하고, 구전 기록은 실제로 고유한 가치가 있다. ²⁶그것들은 아프리카의 문화를 설명하고 역사학자들에게 새로운 각도에서 과거를 보도록 할 뿐만 아니라, 역사를 예술적이고 재미있는 방식으로 제시한다. 더욱이, ²⁷몇몇 서사시는 역사상의 일상 생활을 정확히 반영하는 정보로 가득하다. 예를 들어, 서아프리카의 이야기인 'Epic of Silamaka'에서, 청자들은 왕의 무리를 돌보기 위해 선택된 목축 공동체의 양치기와 사람들이 어떻게 가죽 끈이 엄지발가락과 뒤꿈치 위에 있는 무두질한 소가죽으로 만든 신발을 신었는지에 대해 듣는다. 요약하면, 글로 된 자료들과 고고학적 증거는 사하라 사막 남부 아프리카의 문화와 역사에 대해 그저 짧은 경험만을 제공하는 반면, 이야기는 우리에게 사람들이 일상 생활을 계속했던 방법에 대한 상세한 실마리를 제공한다.

23-24 북아프리카에 대한 이슬람 지배의 어떤 **두 가지** 영향이 글쓴이에 의해 언급되는가?

A 종교적인 주제의 문학 작품이 배포되었다.

B 사하라 종단 노예 무역이 시작되었다.

C 아프리카 언어로 된 문서들이 제작되었다.

D 자원이 농업 제품과 교환되기 시작했다.

E 사하라 사막 이남에 대한 공식 문서들이 보관되었다.

> **해설** 문제의 핵심어구(Muslim dominance of North Africa)와 관련된 지문 내용 중 'Following Islamic dominance of North Africa in the 8th century, official records in Arabic were kept about regions of sub-Saharan Africa.'와 'the extensive trans-Saharan slave trade which Arab rulers instituted during this period'에서 8세기 이슬람의 북아프리카 지배를 뒤이어 아랍어로 쓰인 사하라 사막 이남 아프리카 지역에 대한 공식 기록들이 보관되었으며, 이 시기 동안 아랍 지도자들이 대규모의 사하라 종단 노예 무역을 시작했다고 하였으므로, 보기 **B** The trans-Saharan slave trade began과 보기 **E** Official documents about sub-Saharan Africa were kept가 정답이다.

25 글쓴이에 따르면, 처음 도착한 유럽인들의 목표는 무엇이었는가?

A 유럽 문화의 확장

B 토지 획득

C 토착민 교육

D 기독교 전파

> **해설** 문제의 핵심어구(first Europeans to arrive)와 관련된 지문 내용 중 'The earliest Europeans to arrive were explorers who aimed to take possession of the lands they were visiting.'에서 가장 먼저 도착했던 유럽인들은 방문하고 있던 땅을 손에 넣는 것을 목표로 했던 탐험가들이었다고 하였으므로, 보기 **B** The acquisition of land가 정답이다. 'take possession of the lands'가 'acquisition of land'로 paraphrasing되었다.

26-27 구전되는 역사적 이야기들에 대해 어떤 **두 가지** 측면이 언급되는가?

A 고고학적 증거를 반영한다.

B 과거의 삶에 대한 사실에 근거한 세부 사항들을 포함한다.

C 역사학자들에게 새로운 관점을 제공한다.

D 농업 공동체 사이에 널리 퍼져 있다.

E 예술적이고 재미있는 그림들을 포함한다.

> **해설** 문제의 핵심어구(orally transmitted historical accounts)와 관련된 지문 내용 중 'Not only do they ~ induce historians to look at the past from new angles'와 'some epics are filled with information that is accurately reflective of historical daily life'에서 구전 기록은 역사학자들에게 새로운 각도에서 과거를 보도록 할 뿐만 아니라, 몇몇 서사시는 역사상의 일상 생활을 정확히 반영하는 정보로 가득하다고 하였으므로, 보기 **B** They include descriptive details of life in the past와 보기 **C** They provide historians with new perspectives가 정답이다. 'induce historians to look at the past from new angles'가 'provide historians with new perspectives'로, 'information ~ accurately reflective of historical daily life'가 'descriptive details of life in the past'로 paraphrasing되었다.

10

다양한 관계 애착 유형
성인으로서 강한 정서적 유대를 형성하는 우리의 능력은 우리가 생각하는 것보다 더 많은 것에 기반할지도 모른다.

관계 속에서 사람들이 어떻게 느끼는지는 서로 다르며, 이 차이는 심리학자들이 오랫동안 이해하려고 시도해왔던 것이다. 1960년대와 1970년대에, 발달심리학자 Mary Ainsworth는 어머니와 아이들에 대한 연구에서 정서적 애착이 유아기 때 정해진다는 것을 알아냈다. 그녀는 또한 애착 형태가 아이들 사이에서 상당히 다르다고 추측했는데, 이 아이들은 모두 몇 개의 서로 다른 애착 분류 중 하나로 나뉜다.

첫 번째는 안정 애착이라고 불리며 아이가 자신을 돌보는 사람과 있을 때 안전하다고 느끼는 관계를 설명한다. [29]안정 애착은 유아의 약 65퍼센트를 구성하고, 이 애착은 대부분의 경우에 편하다고 느끼는 아이들에 의해 형성된다. 특히, [30]그들은 돌보는 사람이 주위에 있는 한 마음이 편안하다고 느낀다. [31]그들은 돌보는 사람이 떠나면 당황하지만 돌보는 사람이 돌아오면 다시 만족해한다. 근본적으로, 그들의 모든 욕구가 끊임없이 충족되기 때문에 그들은 돌보는 사람과 안정 애착을 형성한다.

불안/회피성 애착과 같은 불안정 애착도 존재한다. Ainsworth에 따르면, 이 애착 단계에 있는 아이들은 돌보는 사람을 피하거나 무시하고, 그들이 떠나거나 돌아왔을 때 거의 감정을 보여주지 않으며, 괴로울 때 그들을 찾지 않는다. 더욱이, 불안/회피성 애착을 갖고 있는 유아들은 낯선 사람과 있을 때 돌보는 사람과 있을 때 행동하는 것처럼 행동한다. 거절을 대면하기보다는, [32]이 아이들은 무관심으로 괴로움을 감추고 친밀함에 대한 충족되지 않은 욕구로부터 주의를 돌린다. 이러한 애착 유형은, 유아의 15퍼센트를 이루고 있는데, 그들의 요구에 대해 반응이 없는 돌보는 사람과 있는 아이들 사이에서 흔하다.

거의 같은 비율의 유아들에게 영향을 미치는 것은 불안/양가적 애착이라고 불리는 불안정 애착이다. 이 애착 단계에 있는 아이들은, 돌보는 사람에게 매달리는 것과 저항하는 것 둘 다를 보여준다. 예를 들어, 아이는 돌보는 사람이 떠났을 때 매우 괴로워하고 낯선 사람과 혼자 있는 동안 마음이 상한 상태로 남아있을 수도 있지만, 돌보는 사람이 돌아오면, 아이는 그 혹은 그녀의 관심에 저항하고 따라서 여전히 마음이 상한 상태로 있다. 달래기가 거의 불가능한 이러한 아이들은, 돌보는 사람이 그들의 요구에 대해 일관성 없는 수준의 반응을 주기 때문에 이런 방식으로 행동한다.

모든 아이들이 이 세 가지 행동 분류 중 하나로 나뉠 것이라고 생각하는 것은 지나치게 단순화한 것인데, 이는 혼합된 애착 유형을 보여주는 아이들을 분류하기 위해 비공식적인 분류가 존재하는 이유이다. 불안정혼란애착이라고 불리는 이 분류는, 신경질적인 반응이 그들이 어떻게 대우받는지와 부합하지 않는 적은 비율의 아이들에게 해당한다. 이것은 일반적으로 위탁 아동들처럼 아이들이 여러 명의 주요 돌보는 사람들을 겪는 상황에 기인한다.

궁극적으로, 애착 이론은 왜 일부 사람들이 그들에게 중요한 다른 사람들이 좌절하고, 분노하고, 혹은 혼란스러워하게 할 수 있는 방식으로 행동하는지에 대한 명백한 설명을 제공한다. 우리는 아기였을 때 우리가 의지했던 사람들에게 대우받았던 방식에 대해 어떤 것도 할 수 없을지도 모르지만, 왜 우리가 하고 있는 방식으로 행동하는지를 이해함으로써, 성인으로서 건강한 관계를 형성하는 데 필요한 변화를 일으키는 것이 가능할지도 모른다.

28 이 기사를 쓴 글쓴이의 전반적인 목적은 무엇인가?
   A 강한 유대를 형성하는 몇몇 유아의 내재된 능력을 설명하기 위해
   B 유아기 애착의 다양한 형태와 중요성을 설명하기 위해
   C 아이들에게 좋은 모범을 보이는 것의 중요성을 강조하기 위해
   D 애착 이론이 상식에 기반한다는 것을 제안하기 위해

> 해설 이 지문에는 목적을 나타내는 문장이 없으므로 지문 전체를 읽고 목적을 파악한다. 지문에서 Mary Ainsworth의 이론에 따른 여러 유아기 애착의 형태에 대해 설명한 뒤 유아기에 형성하는 애착 형태가 성인이 되어 인간 관계를 맺는 방식에 미치는 영향에 대해 이야기하고 있으므로, 지문의 목적은 유아기 애착의 다양한 형태와 중요성을 설명하기 위함임을 알 수 있다. 따라서 **B To explain the different forms of childhood attachment and its importance**가 정답이다.

29-31 다음 진술 중 어느 **세 가지** 진술이 안정 애착에 대해 옳게 설명하는가?
   A 가장 많은 수의 유아들에게서 나타난다.
   B 아주 어린 아이들에게서는 거의 찾아볼 수 없다.
   C 돌보는 사람이 있을 때 편안함을 가져온다.
   D 감정 표현이 거의 없는 것으로 특징지어진다.
   E 돌보는 사람이 떠나면 일시적인 스트레스를 유발한다.
   F 낯선 사람과 있을 때와 부모와 있을 때 모두 발생한다.
   G 15퍼센트의 경우에 극단적인 애착을 초래한다.
   H 아이들의 자신감 있는 독립으로 이어진다.

해설 문제의 핵심어구(secure attachment)와 관련된 지문 내용 중 'Secure attachments comprise an estimated 65 per cent of infants'와 'they feel at ease as long as their caregivers are around. They become upset when their caregivers leave'에서 안정 애착은 유아의 약 65퍼센트를 구성하고, 돌보는 사람이 주위에 있는 한 마음이 편안하다고 느끼며, 돌보는 사람이 떠나면 당황한다고 하였으므로, 보기 **A** It is present in the majority of infants, 보기 **C** It results in comfort in the presence of caregivers, 보기 **E** It creates temporary stress when caregivers leave가 정답이다.

🔍 오답 확인하기
D는 지문의 'show little emotion'을 활용하여 혼동을 주었지만, 감정 표현이 거의 없는 것으로 특징지어지는 것은 안정 애착이 아니라 불안정 애착이라고 하였으므로 오답이다.

32 불안/회피성 애착을 가진 아기들은 어떤 전략을 이용하는가?
  A 그들의 욕구를 충족시키려는 시도에 저항한다.
  B 낯선 사람으로부터의 관심을 추구한다.
  C 신경 쓰지 않는 척한다.
  D 눈을 마주치는 것을 거부한다.

해설 문제의 핵심어구(anxious/avoidant attachment)와 관련된 지문 내용 중 'these children mask their distress with apathy'에서 이 아이들은 무관심으로 괴로움을 감춘다고 하였으므로, 보기 **C** They pretend that they do not care가 정답이다. 'mask ~ with apathy'가 'pretend that they do not care'로 paraphrasing되었다.

🔍 오답 확인하기
B는 지문의 'infants with anxious/avoidant attachment act the same way with strangers'를 활용하여 혼동을 주었지 만, 불안/회피성 애착을 가진 아기들이 낯선 사람으로부터의 관심을 추구하는 것이 아니라 낯선 사람과 있을 때 돌보는 사람과 있 을 때 행동하는 것처럼 행동한다고 하였으므로 오답이다.

HACKERS TEST
p.56

1 B	2 D	3 C	4 D	5 A
6 D	7 B	8 A	9 repetition	10 objects
11 box	12-13 B, D			

영아 인지: 습득된 것인가 아니면 타고난 것인가?
영아들이 인지 능력을 갖고 태어난다면, 유전적 특징은 환경적 요소보다 발달에 있어 더 중요한 역할을 할 수도 있다

[8]역사를 통틀어, 심리학자들은 사람이 유전적 특징(본성)에 의해 더 크게 영향을 받는지 아니면 환경(양육)에 의해 더 크게 영향을 받는 지에 대해 논쟁해왔다. 신생아들은 사람이 할 수 있는 한 가장 '본성'에 가깝기 때문에, 인간 인지의 기원에 대해 더 잘 이해하고자 하는 전문가들에 의해 종종 연구 대상이 되어 왔다. [1]Jean Piaget의 유명한 초기 인간 인지 이론에 따르면, 영아들은 주위에 있는 대상을 가 지고 행하는 물리적 행동을 통해서만 지식을 습득한다. 그에게, 인지 능력은 타고난 것이 아니라 인지할 수 있는 세계와의 상호 작용을 통해 시간이 지나면서 습득되는 것이다. [9]신생아들은 반사 행동을 행하며 반복을 통해 천천히 그것에 대한 통제권을 갖는다. 생후 첫 몇 개월 동안, 그들은 엄지손가락을 빠는 것과 같은 행동을 수행하는 법을 반복해서 배우는데, 이것은 그들에게 어떤 종류의 기쁨이나 만 족감을 가져다 준다. 이 단계에서, 그는, 그들이 아직 사건에 대해 충분히 예상하거나 예측할 수 없다고 주장했다. 4개월에서 8개월 정 도부터, 영아는 Piaget가 이차순환반응이라고 부르는 것을 사용하기 시작한다. 이것들은 예를 들어 딸랑이를 흔드는 것과 그것이 내는 소리를 듣는 것과 같이 한 가지 과정 이상을 결합하는 것을 포함하기 때문에 이차적이다.

그러한 행동을 통해, 영아는 원인과 결과를 배우고 자신의 행동이 그 다음 반응을 만들어낼 수 있다는 것을 깨닫기 시작한다. Piaget에 게, 이것들은 새로 습득된 행동들과 이 행동들이 대상에 미치는 영향 사이의 연관성에 대한 조건부 반응일 뿐이었으며, 이 행동들이 구 분되지 않기 때문에, 그는 그것들이 목표 지향적인 활동이 아니며, 따라서 계획된 것이 아니라고 믿었다. 그러므로, [10]아기들은 단지 천천히 대상이 자신의 자각 밖의 독립된 존재를 가지고 있다는 것을 깨닫기 시작한다. Piaget는 영아들이 9개월 정도의 나이가 될 때까지 극도로 한정된 인지 능력을 가진다고 주장했지만, 그때쯤이면, 보통 대상 영속성을 알아보는 능력을 습득했다고 판단했다.

Piaget는 이 습득을 보여주기 위해 대상 감추기 과제를 이용했다. 예를 들어, 그는 아기들에게 대상을 보여준 뒤 천이나 컵 아래 감추고 영아가 대상이 사라졌는지 아니면 그저 시야로부터 감춰진 것인지 인지했는지를 분석했다. [2]Piaget는 결론의 근거를 영아가 감춰진 물건을 찾기 위해 천이나 컵을 치움으로써 반응했는지 아닌지에 두었다. 만약 영아들이 그렇게 했다면, 그는 대상 영속성에 대해 적어도 한정된 이해력을 가지고 있는 것이라고 추정했다. 하지만, 그는 또한 만약 대상이 다른 위치로 이동되었다면, 영아는 여전히 그것을 가렸던 원래 물건을 치움으로써 찾으려 할 것이기 때문에 이 능력이 미숙하고 한정되어 있다고 시사했다. 그럼에도 불구하고, Piaget에 따르면, 이 단계는 인간 인지 발달에서 처음으로 진정한 지적 행동을 나타낸 것이었고, 그는 그것이 모든 미래의 문제 해결에 대한 근간이라고 믿었다.

그럼에도 불구하고, 모든 사람들이 Piaget의 분석이 완전히 옳다고 생각한 것은 아니었다. 캐나다 출신 심리학자 Renée Baillargeon의 영아 인지 발달에 대한 연구는 Piaget의 생각에 이의를 제기했다. [3]그녀는 어린 영아들의 한정된 운동 기능이 인지 능력의 부재로 여겨지는 원인일지도 모른다고 주장하며, 영아의 발달 정도에 적합한 실험과 시험을 수행하는 것의 중요성을 지적했다. 다시 말해서, [4]Baillargeon은 Piaget와 의견이 달랐고 그가 운동 기능 한계와 인지 한계를 혼동한 것을 비판했다. 이 가설을 시험해 보기 위해, 그녀는 손으로 하는 과제보다는 시각적 과제에 연구를 초점을 맞췄다.

[5]한 실험에서, Baillargeon은 생후 3개월인 영아에게 장난감 트럭이 스크린 뒤로 가려지기 전 트랙을 따라 굴러 내려가는 것을 보여주었으며, 영아가 이것에 익숙해질 때까지 이 과정에 여러 번 집중하게 했다. [11]그 다음에 Baillargeon은 트랙 아래로의 트럭의 이동을 막는 것처럼 보이도록 놓은 상자를 투입했다. 그러나, 트럭이 다시 아래로 보내졌을 때, 그것은 분명히 방해받지 않고 상자를 지나쳤다. Baillargeon은 영아들이 상자가 트랙 위에 놓이기 전 트럭의 정상적인 진행을 바라보는 것보다 이 예상치 못한 일을 훨씬 더 오래 바라본다는 것을 발견했다. Baillargeon은 이것으로부터 그들이 트럭이 지나가지 못하도록 막혔어야 했다는 걸 알았으며, 그렇지 않았을 때 혼란스러워했다는 결론을 내렸다. [12]그러므로 그녀는 그들이 움직이고 있을 때 영속성과 궤도를 포함하여 대상의 속성을 이해했다고 믿었다. 이것은 Piaget와 모순되었는데, Piaget는 이러한 능력들이 오직 생후 9개월에서 12개월 정도에만 발달한다고 믿었다.

그녀의 연구 결과는 현재 다양한 연구에서 널리 받아들여지고 지지받고 있는, 익숙한 일은 더 짧은 기간 동안 관심을 사로잡는 반면, 영아가 새롭거나 놀라운 일에는 더 오랫동안 집중한다는 가설에 기초한다. 이 가정은 기대 위반(VOE) 전형으로 알려지게 되었다. 그녀는 영아에게 새로운 일은 놀랍고 심지어 '불가능하다'고 판단했다. [13]Baillargeon에 따르면, 이것은 매우 어린 아이들에게 가능한 일과 가능하지 않은 일을 구분할 능력이 있다는 것을 의미하고, 이는 그들이 Piaget가 생각했던 것보다 훨씬 더 타고난 인지 능력을 가진다는 것을 암시한다.

[6]그렇지만 영아가 물리적 세계에서 성인이 하는 것과 똑같은 방법으로 대상을 이해할 수 있다는 것이 항상 성인과 같은 방식으로 판단한다는 것을 의미하지는 않는다. 그러므로, 인간 두뇌의 타고난 '사전에 습관 들이기'는 유아기와 청소년기 내내 발달을 계속해야만 한다. 이런 의미에서, [8]경험, 또는 양육은, 인간 인지 발달에서 중요한 요소로 남는다는 것은 말할 것도 없다. 그럼에도 불구하고, [7]Baillargeon과 다른 유아 발달심리학자들의 실험은 Piaget의 연구를 기반으로 했으며 노암 촘스키의 언어 습득 연구가 언어학에 혁신을 일으켰던 것과 거의 마찬가지로 이 분야에 다시 활기를 주었다.

어휘   cognition n. 인지   genetics n. 유전적 특징, 유전학   phenomenal adj. 인지할 수 있는, 감각적인   reflex behaviour phr. 반사 행동
secondary circular reaction phr. 이차순환반응   rattle n. 딸랑이(장난감)   subsequent adj. 그 다음의
undifferentiated adj. 구분되지 않는, 획일적인   goal-directed adj. 목표 지향적인   object permanence phr. 대상 영속성
surmise v. 추정하다, 추측하다   apprehension n. 이해(력)   obscure v. 가리다, 덮다   motor skill phr. 운동 기능
habituate v. 익숙하게 하다, ~을 길들이다   unimpeded adj. 방해받지 않는, 가로막는 것이 없는   property n. 속성, 특성
trajectory n. 궤도, 궤적   presumption n. 가정, 추정   violation n. 위반, 방해   paradigm n. 전형, 예   revolutionise v. 혁신을 일으키다

[1-8]

1 Piaget에 따르면, 영아들은 오직 −을 통해서만 지식을 얻는다.

   A   주변의 세계를 관찰하는 것

   B   가까이 있는 물체들과 상호교류하는 것

   C   행동을 반복하는 것을 학습하는 것

   D   다른 사람들과 소통하는 것

정답·해석·해설   HACKERS **IELTS** READING

해설 문제의 핵심어구(Piaget ~ infants gain knowledge)와 관련된 지문 내용 중 'According to Jean Piaget's famous theory ~ infants acquire intelligence only through the physical actions they perform with objects around them.'에서 Jean Piaget의 유명한 이론에 따르면 영아들은 주위에 있는 대상을 가지고 행하는 물리적 행동을 통해서만 지식을 습득한다고 하였으므로, 보기 B interacting with things close to them이 정답이다. 'actions they perform with objects around them'이 'interacting with things close to them'으로 paraphrasing되었다.

2 Piaget는 왜 영아들이 대상 영속성을 약간이나마 이해할 수 있다고 믿었는가?
   A 무엇이 대상을 감추고 있는지 알아내는 데 어려움을 느끼지 않았다.
   B 대상이 다른 위치로 옮겨졌을 때 이를 알아보았다.
   C 대상이 다른 것으로 대체되었을 때 속지 않았다.
   D 숨겨진 대상을 찾아냈다.

해설 문제의 핵심어구(Piaget believe infants have some understanding)와 관련된 지문 내용 중 'Piaget based his conclusions on whether the infants responded by removing the cloth or cup to find the concealed item. If they did, he surmised that they had at least a limited apprehension of object permanence'에서 Piaget는 결론의 근거를 영아가 감춰진 물건을 찾기 위해 천이나 컵을 치움으로써 반응했는지 아닌지에 두었으며 만약 영아들이 그렇게 했다면 그들이 대상 영속성에 대해 적어도 한정된 이해력을 가지고 있는 것이라고 추정했다고 하였으므로, 보기 D They uncovered the object that had been hidden이 정답이다. 'have at least a limited apprehension'이 'have some understanding'으로, 'find the concealed item'이 'uncovered the object ~ hidden'으로 paraphrasing되었다.

🔍 오답 확인하기
B는 지문 내용 중 'if the object was moved to another location, the infant would still try to find it by removing the original item that obscured it'에서 대상이 다른 위치로 이동되었다면 영아는 여전히 그것을 가렸던 원래 물건을 치움으로써 찾으려 할 것이라고 하였으므로 지문의 내용과 반대되는 오답이다.

3 Baillargeon에 따르면, –한 실험을 수행하는 것이 중요하다.
   A 쉽게 반복할 수 있으며 객관적인 실험
   B 습득된 능력보다는 타고난 능력에 집중된 실험
   C 영아의 발달 단계에 적합한 실험
   D 다양한 연령의 영아들을 데리고 수행된 실험

해설 문제의 핵심어구(Baillargeon ~ carry out experiments)와 관련된 지문 내용 중 'She pointed out the importance of conducting experiments ~ appropriate for the developmental level of infants'에서 Baillargeon은 영아의 발달 정도에 적합한 실험을 수행하는 것의 중요성을 지적했다고 하였으므로, 보기 C suitable for infants' stage of development가 정답이다. 'appropriate for the development level'이 'suitable for ~ stage of development'로 paraphrasing되었다.

4 Piaget에 대한 Baillargeon의 비판은 무엇이었는가?
   A 그의 가정은 불충분한 조사에 근거했다.
   B 그의 조사는 실험 증거로 뒷받침되지 않았다.
   C 그는 연구에서 시각적 과제를 너무 심하게 강조했다.
   D 그는 운동 기능의 부족을 인지 능력의 부족으로 혼동했다.

해설 문제의 핵심어구(Baillargeon's criticism)와 관련된 지문 내용 중 'Baillargeon ~ accused him of confusing motor skill limitations with cognitive limitations'에서 Baillargeon은 Piaget가 운동 기능 한계와 인지 한계를 혼동한 것을 비판했다고 하였으므로, 보기 D He mistook a lack of motor skills with a lack of cognitive ones가 정답이다. 'confusing motor skill limitations with cognitive limitations'가 'mistook a lack of motor skills with a lack of cognitive ones'로 paraphrasing되었다.

5 트럭과 관련된 실험에서, Baillargeon은

A 영아들에게 같은 과정을 여러 번 보여주었다.

B 영아들의 앞으로 스크린을 옮겼다.

C 장난감 트럭을 가지고 노는 영아들을 관찰했다.

D 영아들의 운동 기능을 시험했다.

해설 문제의 핵심어구(experiment involving a truck ~ Baillargeon)와 관련된 지문 내용 중 'In one experiment, Baillargeon showed ~ a toy truck rolling down a track ~ letting the infants focus on this process several times' 에서 한 실험에서 Baillargeon은 장난감 트럭이 트랙을 따라 굴러 내려가는 것을 보여주었으며 영아가 이 과정에 여러 번 집중하게 했다고 하였으므로, 보기 **A** showed infants the same process numerous times가 정답이다. 'letting the infants focus on this process several times'가 'showed infants the same process numerous times'로 paraphrasing되었다.

6 마지막 단락에서, 글쓴이는 대상을 이해하는 영아의 능력은 −하다고 제시한다.

A 어떻게 인간 두뇌가 어린 시절을 거쳐 발달되는지 보여준다

B 그들이 성인과 같은 수준으로 판단할 수 있다는 것을 보여준다

C 그들의 인지 능력이 타고난 것이 아니라는 것을 입증한다

D 그들이 성인처럼 판단할 수 있다는 의미가 아니다

해설 문제의 핵심어구(infants' ability to conceive of objects)와 관련된 마지막 단락의 내용 'Yet to say that infants can conceive of objects ~ in the same way that adults do does not mean that they always reason in the same manner as adults.'에서 영아가 성인이 하는 것과 똑같은 방법으로 대상을 이해할 수 있다는 것이 항상 성인과 같은 방식으로 판단한다는 것을 의미하지는 않는다고 하였으므로, 보기 **D** does not mean they are able to reason like adults가 정답이다. 'they always reason in the same manner as adults'가 'they are able to reason like adults'로 paraphrasing되었다.

🔍 오답 확인하기

B는 지문 내용 중 'does not mean that they always reason in the same manner as adults'에서 영아들이 항상 성인과 같은 수준으로 판단할 수 있다는 것은 아니라고 하였으므로 지문의 내용과 반대되는 오답이다.

7 글쓴이는 −을 비교하기 위해 노암 촘스키를 언급한다.

A 언어학 연구의 가치와 심리학 연구의 가치

B Baillargeon과 주요한 학문적 공헌을 한 다른 사람

C Baillargeon의 작업과 다른 유아 발달심리학자의 업적

D 서로 다른 학문적 목표 간 차이

해설 문제의 핵심어구(Noam Chomsky)와 관련된 지문 내용 중 'the experiments of Baillargeon ~ reenergised the field in much the same way that Noam Chomsky's studies of language acquisition revolutionised linguistics'에서 Baillargeon의 실험은 노암 촘스키의 언어 습득 연구가 언어학에 혁신을 일으켰던 것과 거의 마찬가지로 이 분야에 다시 활기를 주었다고 하였으므로, 글쓴이는 Baillargeon을 주요한 학문적 공헌을 한 노암 촘스키와 비교하기 위해 노암 촘스키를 언급했음을 알 수 있다. 따라서 보기 **B** Baillargeon with someone else who made a major academic contribution이 정답이다.

8 이 글을 쓴 글쓴이의 전반적인 목적은 무엇인가?

A 영아 발달은 본성과 양육 모두를 필요로 한다는 것을 보여주기 위해

B 인지 능력은 출생 이전에 발달한다는 것을 증명하기 위해

C 인지 능력이 영아 발달에 어떻게 영향을 미치는지 설명하기 위해

D 발달에 있어 본성이 양육보다 더 중요하다는 것을 증명하기 위해

해설 이 지문에는 목적을 나타내는 문장이 없으므로 지문 전체를 읽고 목적을 파악한다. 지문의 첫 번째 문장 'Throughout history, psychologists have debated whether people are more strongly influenced by genetics (nature) or their environment (nurture).'에서 역사를 통틀어 심리학자들은 사람이 유전적 특징(본성)에 의해 더 크게 영향을 받는지 아니면

환경(양육)에 의해 더 크게 영향을 받는지에 대해 논쟁해왔다고 하며, 영아의 인지 능력이 습득을 통해 발달한다는 이론과 영아가 인지 능력을 타고난다는 이론 두 가지를 언급하였다. 그 뒤 마지막 문단의 'it goes without saying that experience, or nurture, remains a crucial factor in human cognitive development'에서 경험 또는 양육이 인간 인지 발달에서 중요한 요소로 남는다는 것은 말할 것도 없다고 하였으므로, 지문의 목적은 영아 발달이 본성과 양육 모두를 필요로 한다는 것을 보여주기 위함임을 알 수 있다. 따라서 보기 **A** To show that infant development relies on both nature and nurture가 정답이다.

[9-11]

9 태어난 지 얼마 안 된 아기들은 ....을 통해 그들의 움직임을 익히려고 할 것이다.

해설 문제의 핵심어구(Recently born babies ~ master their movement)와 관련된 지문 내용 중 'Newborns practise reflex behaviours and slowly gain control over them through repetition.'에서 신생아들은 반사 행동을 행하며 반복을 통해 천천히 그것에 대한 통제권을 갖는다고 하였으므로, **repetition**이 정답이다. 'Newborns ~ gain control over'가 'Recently born babies ~ master'로, 'reflex behaviours'가 'movement'로 paraphrasing되었다.

10 영아들은 천천히 ....의 독립적인 존재를 이해한다.

해설 문제의 핵심어구(Infants ~ understand the independent existence)와 관련된 지문 내용 중 'only gradually do babies begin to realise that objects have an independent existence outside of their own perception'에서 아기들은 단지 천천히 대상이 자신의 자각 밖의 독립된 존재를 가지고 있다는 것을 깨닫기 시작한다고 하였으므로, **objects**가 정답이다.

11 실험에서, Baillargeon은 자동차를 방해하는 것처럼 보이는 ....을 두었다.

해설 문제의 핵심어구(In the experiment, Baillargeon)와 관련된 지문 내용 중 'Baillargeon then introduced a box which was positioned so that it looked like it would block the truck's journey down the track.'에서 그 다음에 Baillargeon은 트랙 아래로의 트럭의 이동을 막는 것처럼 보이도록 놓인 상자를 투입했다고 하였으므로, **box**가 정답이다.

[12-13] Baillargeon과 Piaget는 어떤 점에 대해 동의하지 않는가?

A 인지 발달에 있어 교육의 중요성
B 영아들이 대상 영속성을 알게 되는 나이
C 영아들이 대상들을 구별하는 것을 학습하는 방법
D 영아 인지가 선천적인 정도
E 영아 인지가 성인의 인지와 같아지는 시기

해설 문제의 핵심어구(Baillargeon and Piaget disagree)와 관련된 지문 내용 중 'She thus believed that they had an understanding of the properties of objects ~. This contradicted Piaget, who believed these abilities only developed at around nine to twelve months.'와 'According to Baillargeon ~ they have far more inborn cognitive ability than Piaget thought.'에서 대상의 속성을 이해하는 능력들이 오직 생후 9개월에서 12개월 정도에만 발달한다고 믿은 Piaget와 달리 Baillargeon은 생후 3개월인 영아들이 대상의 속성을 이해했다고 믿었으며, Baillargeon에 따르면 그들이 Piaget가 생각했던 것보다 훨씬 더 타고난 인지 능력을 가진다고 하였으므로, 보기 **B** the age that infants become aware of object permanence와 보기 **D** the extent to which infant cognition is inborn이 정답이다.

CHAPTER 02 T/F/NG (True / False / Not Given)

* 각 문제에 대한 정답의 단서는 지문에 문제 번호와 함께 별도의 색으로 표시되어 있습니다.

EXAMPLE
p.64

사회심리학자인 Robert Zajonc에 따르면, 첫째로 태어난 아이들은 어느 정도 더 지능이 뛰어난 경향이 있다. 사실, 노르웨이 연구원들에 의한 연구들은 [1]첫째로 태어난 아이들이 둘째 아이들보다 IQ 등급에서 3점을 더 기록한다는 것을 보여주었다. 이러한 종류의 차이는 또한, 보다 적은 정도로, 둘째와 셋째 아이들 사이에서도 발견되었다.

그러나, [2]지능은 출생 순서가 원인인 유일한 차이점은 아니다. 첫째로 태어난 아이들은 또한 학교에서 더 잘하며, 성인이 되었을 때 더 높은 임금을 받고, 가족에 대한 더 많은 책임을 지는 경향이 있다. [3]막내로 태어난 아이들은, 반면에, 더 재미있고, 통제가 덜 되며, 덜 위험회피적이고, 나이가 많은 형제자매들보다 더 외향적인 경향이 있다.

HACKERS PRACTICE
p.66

1	True	2	False	3	True	4	Not given
5	True	6	Not given	7	True	8	False
9	Not given	10	False	11	True	12	Not given
13	True	14	Not given	15	False	16	True
17	Not given	18	False	19	False	20	False
21	True	22	Not given	23	False	24	True
25	Not given	26	False	27	True	28	False
29	Not given	30	True	31	True		

1

푸에블로 인디언들은 천 년 넘게 미국 포 코너스 지역의 주요한 문화적 세력이었다. 초기에, 그 문명은 콜로라도 고원의 고지에 있는 개개의 농가들에 기반을 두었는데, 그곳에서 그 구성원들은 농사를 지었고 도자기와 담요 같은 다양한 수공예품들을 발달시켰다. 하지만, 11세기와 12세기 동안에 푸에블로족은 인근의 협곡으로 이동했고 [1]그들의 이름이 유래된 거대한 다가구 주거지를 지었다. 고고학자인 Kristen Kuckelman은 이것이 끊임없이 지속되는 가뭄이 고원 지대에서 농사를 짓는 것을 불가능하게 만든 이후에 발생했다고 믿는다. 그녀는 가뭄의 영향을 덜 받았기 때문에 그 지역의 주민들이 계곡으로 이동했다고 믿는다. [2]이주한 후에, 그들은 더 적은 땅에서 더 효율적으로 식량을 생산하는 방법을 배워야 했고, 따라서 궁극적으로 전문화로 이어진 농업 협력 시스템을 도입했다. 일단 협곡에 정착한 뒤, 그 문명은 노동력에 대한 수익을 극대화하기 위해 더욱 공동 사회가 되었다.

1 푸에블로족은 그들의 이름을 주택 방식에서 얻었다.

> 해설 문제의 핵심어구(their names)와 관련된 지문 내용 중 'massive multifamily dwellings from which their names are derived'에서 그들의 이름이 유래된 거대한 다가구 주거지라고 하였으므로, 주어진 문장은 지문의 내용과 일치함을 알 수 있다. 따라서 정답은 **True**이다. 'dwellings from which their names are derived'가 'got their names from their style of housing'으로 paraphrasing되었다.

2 푸에블로족은 농작지가 더 많은 인근의 지역 사회로 이동했다.

> **해설** 문제의 핵심어구(more farmland)와 관련된 지문 내용 중 'After they migrated, they had to learn how to produce food more effectively on less land'에서 이주한 후에 푸에블로족은 더 적은 땅에서 더 효율적으로 식량을 생산하는 방법을 배워야 했다고 하였으므로, 주어진 문장은 지문의 내용과 일치하지 않음을 알 수 있다. 따라서 정답은 **False**이다.

2

우리는 이제 나무와 다른 식물이 도시에서 대기 오염을 감소시키는 데 매우 귀중한 역할을 한다는 것을 알고 있다. 그렇게 오래되지 않은, 1980년대 초기에, 화학자들은 나무들이 배출물을 생산한다는 것을 발견했다. ³이것은 그 당시 미국 대통령인 로널드 레이건이 "나무들은 자동차가 야기하는 것보다 더 많은 오염을 야기한다."고 잘못 공표하도록 했다. 이것은, 물론, '배출'과 '오염'이라는 단어들이 동의어가 아니며 대통령의 발언이 정확하지 않았다는 사실에도 불구하고, 사람들로 하여금 나무들이 해롭다고 추측하게 했다. 다른 모든 생물과 마찬가지로, 나무와 식물이 신진대사의 부산물로 화학 물질을 배출하는 것이 사실이기는 하지만, 이런 배출물은 위협이 아니며, 대신에 우리가 들이마시는 산소와 꽃과 관목에 신선하고 향긋한 향기를 주는 다양한 화학적 혼합물을 포함한다. 자동차의 배출물에 의해 야기된 것과 같은, 인간이 만든 오염 물질의 상당량이 있을 때에만, 식물과 나무는 휘발성의 유기 탄화수소를 방출한다. 하지만 그렇게 할 때에는, ⁴그것들은 광화학 스모그와 같은 지표면 오존 오염 형성에 있어 관련 요소가 될 수 있다.

3 1980년대의 한 정치가는 공기 오염을 식물의 책임으로 잘못 보았다.

> **해설** 문제의 핵심어구(A politician in the 1980s)와 관련된 지문 내용 중 'This prompted the then U.S. President Ronald Reagan to falsely declare, 'Trees cause more pollution than automobiles do.''에서 이것은 1980년대 미국 대통령인 로널드 레이건이 "나무들은 자동차가 야기하는 것보다 더 많은 오염을 야기한다."고 잘못 공표하도록 했다고 하였으므로, 주어진 문장은 지문의 내용과 일치함을 알 수 있다. 따라서 정답은 **True**이다. 'falsely declare'가 'incorrectly blamed'으로 paraphrasing되었다.

4 식물은 자동차만큼 광화학 스모그에 기여한다.

> **해설** 문제의 핵심어구(photochemical smog)와 관련된 지문 내용 중 'they can become participants in the formation of such ground-level ozone pollution as photochemical smog'에서 그것들은 광화학 스모그와 같은 지표면 오존 오염 형성에 있어 관련 요소가 될 수 있다고는 하였지만, 주어진 문장의 내용은 확인할 수 없다. 따라서 정답은 **Not given**이다.

3

⁵19세기 후반 산업화와 기업의 성장은 업무상 서신이 엄청나게 증가한 환경을 조성했는데, 이는 손으로 쓴 원고보다 더 빠르고 읽기 쉽게 메시지를 기록하는 방법을 필요로 하게 했다. 이 요구를 충족시킬 수 있었던 첫 번째 기기는 Sholes and Glidden 타자기였다. 그러나, 상업적인 성공을 거두기 전에, 일부 문제들이 개선될 필요가 있었다. 예를 들어, ⁶초기 타자기의 타이프바는 매우 느리게 움직였고, 키와 다른 구성 요소들이 자주 엉키는 경향이 있었다. 이 문제를 해결하기 위해, 디자이너인 Sholes는 기계의 다음 버전에서 글자가 더 이상 알파벳 순으로 나타나지 않도록 키보드의 배치를 바꾸었다. 대신에, 그는 ST와 TH처럼, 영어에서 가장 흔히 사용되는 글자 조합들이 서로 멀리 떨어져 펼쳐지게 하려는 의도로 키를 배치했다. 이 변경은 ⁷새로운 배열이 사용자들이 글자를 찾는 데 걸리는 시간을 늘어나게 했기 때문에 기계적 엉킴과 오타의 극적인 감소를 가져왔다. 그렇게 함으로써 그것은 각각의 키가 다음 것을 치기 전에 자신의 위치로 다시 떨어지기에 충분한 시간이 있는 것을 확실하게 했다. 겉보기에는 작은 이러한 변화들이 타자기를 유용한 표기와 서신 장치로 만든 비결이었다.

5 산업화는 더 가독성 좋은 문서를 만들어 내는 기록 방법이 필요하게 했다.

> **해설** 문제의 핵심어구(Industrialisation created a need)와 관련된 지문 내용 중 'Industrialisation and corporate growth in the late 19th century ~ calling for a way to transcribe messages more quickly and legibly than handwritten script.'에서 19세기 후반 산업화와 기업의 성장은 손으로 쓴 원고보다 더 빠르고 읽기 쉽게 메시지를 기록하는 방법을 필요로 하게 했다고 하였으므로, 주어진 문장은 지문의 내용과 일치함을 알 수 있다. 따라서 정답은 **True**이다. 'calling for'가 'created a need'로, 'a way to transcribe messages'가 'a writing method'로, 'legibly'가 'readable'로 paraphrasing되었다.

6 초기 타자기들의 타입바들은 자주 교체되어야 했다.

> **해설** 문제의 핵심어구(type bars on early typewriters)와 관련된 지문 내용 중 'the type bars in their earliest typewriters moved very sluggishly'에서 초기 타자기의 타입바가 매우 느리게 움직였다고는 하였지만, 주어진 문장의 내용은 확인할 수 없다. 따라서 정답은 **Not given**이다.

7 재설계는 글자를 찾는 데 더 많은 시간이 걸리게 했다.

> **해설** 문제의 핵심어구(redesign)와 관련된 지문 내용 중 'the new arrangement increased the time it took for users to locate letters'에서 새로운 배열이 사용자들이 글자를 찾는 데 걸리는 시간을 늘어나게 했다고 하였으므로, 주어진 문장은 지문의 내용과 일치함을 알 수 있다. 따라서 정답은 **True**이다. 'new arrangement'가 'redesign'으로, 'increased the time it took'이 'more time-consuming'으로 paraphrasing되었다.

4

필기도구들은 고대부터 있어왔지만, 우리가 알고 있는 오늘날의 연필은 1560년대 큰 흑연 매장층의 발견 이후에야 나타났다. 이야기에 따르면, 몇몇 영국인 양치기들이 쓰러진 나무의 뿌리에 붙어 있는 알려지지 않은 검은색 물질을 우연히 발견했고, 그것을 만져보다가, 그것이 검은 자국을 남긴다는 것을 알게 되었다. 처음에, 그들은 그것을 누구의 양이 누구의 것인지 더 쉽게 구별할 수 있도록 가축에 낙인을 그리는 데 사용했지만, 곧 그들이 '석묵'이라고 불렀던 흑연이 매우 쉽게 막대로 만들어질 수 있으며 글자를 쓰고 그림을 그리는 데 사용될 수 있다는 것을 깨달았다. 깨지기 쉬운 성질을 줄이기 위해 그것을 끈이나 잔 나뭇가지로 감싸게 됨에 따라, [8]흑연 막대는 그 당시에 쓰이고 있던 금속 합금 철필보다 사용자가 더 적은 힘을 주도록 했을 뿐만 아니라, 훨씬 더 짙은 선을 만들어냈다. 게다가, [9]소량의 부드러운 빵을 이용해서 흑연 자국을 지우는 것과 잉크로 그 위에 그리는 것이 가능했는데 그 중 어떤 것도 납이나 목탄으로는 할 수 없었다. 머지 않아 사람들은 흑연 조각들을 잘린 나무 조각 홈 안에 붙이기 시작했고, 그렇게 함으로써 오늘날 우리에게 익숙한 훨씬 더 튼튼한 나무 연필을 만들었다.

8 흑연 막대로 글자를 쓰는 것은 다른 필기도구보다 더 많은 힘을 필요로 했다.

> **해설** 문제의 핵심어구(required more pressure)와 관련된 지문 내용 중 'a stick of graphite ~ required the user to apply less pressure than the metal alloy styluses then in use'에서 흑연 막대는 그 당시에 쓰이고 있던 금속 합금 철필보다 사용자가 더 적은 힘을 주도록 했다고 하였으므로, 주어진 문장은 지문의 내용과 일치하지 않음을 알 수 있다. 따라서 정답은 **False**이다.

9 사용자들은 흑연 자국들이 잉크로 덮인 뒤에는 그것들을 볼 수 없었다.

> **해설** 문제의 핵심어구(graphite marks after ~ inked over)와 관련된 지문 내용 중 'it was possible to erase graphite marks ~ and to draw on top of them with ink'에서 흑연 자국을 지우는 것과 잉크로 그 위에 그리는 것이 가능했다고는 하였지만, 주어진 문장의 내용은 확인할 수 없다. 따라서 정답은 **Not given**이다.

5

인간은 다른 사람들과 이어지고자 하는 욕구에 의해 행동하도록 만들어지는 선천적으로 사회적인 동물이기 때문에 사람들에게 좋은 인상을 주는 능력은 우리 중 많은 이들에게 아주 중요하다. 그러나, 때로 다른 사람들이 우리에 대해 정확히 어떻게 생각하는지를 이해하는 것은 어려울 수 있다. 그들 모두가 단순히 우리가 보이려고 노력하는 방식으로 우리를 바라본다면 쉬울 것이다. 불행히도, 우리가 마주치는 모든 사람은 그 또는 그녀 특유의 렌즈로 세상을 바라보며, [10]사람들은 그들이 신뢰하는 그들만의 사회 집단 속 사적 영역 내에서가 아니면 다른 사람들에 대해 어떻게 느끼는지에 관해 아주 솔직하지는 않은 경향이 있다. 이 때문에, 다른 사람들이 우리를 어떻게 바라보는지 알아내기 위해, 때로 우리의 상위 인지에 의존해야 할 필요가 있다.

상위 인지란 개인이 그 또는 그녀 자신에 대한 다른 사람들의 인식을 바라보는 방식이다. [11]상위 인지는 대개 강한 자의식을 가진 개인들에게는 상당히 정확한데, 그런 종류의 사람들이 그들의 언어나 행위에 다른 사람들이 어떻게 반응하는지를 쉽게 알아차리기 때문이다. 이는 그들이 사랑받는지 아닌지를 알 수 있게 해준다. 자신이 누구인지에 대해 상당한 분별력을 가진 개인들은 상황에 더 잘 맞추기 위해 자신들의 행동을 조정하는 데 아무런 어려움도 겪지 않는 경향이 있다. 즉, 만약 사랑받는 것이 그들의 궁극적인 목표라면 말이다. [12]약한 자의식을 가진 사람들은, 반면에, 다른 사람들이 그들을 보는 방식에 대해 종종 잘못된 생각을 가진다. 이는 종종 그들에게 애초에 자신감이 결여되어 있으며 그러므로 여러 개인적인 편견들을 가지고 있기 때문이다. 그들은, 예를 들어, 많은 이유로 자기 자신을 그다지 좋아하지 않을 수 있으며 그러므로 이것이 사실이 아닐 때에도, 다른 모든 사람들 또한 그들을 싫어할 것이라고 생각한다. 반대로, 다른 사람들은 사실 그들이 무례하고 부담이 되는 것일 때에도 자신들이 재치 있고 어울리기에 재미있는 사람이라고 생각할 수도 있다. 불행하게도 이러한 사람들에게는, 때로 그 결과로서 사회적인 배제와 그것과 연관되는 모든 부정적인 결과들이 발생한다.

10 사람들은 일반적으로 그들이 다른 사람들을 어떻게 인식하는지에 대해 솔직하다.

> 해설 문제의 핵심어구(People are generally honest)와 관련된 지문 내용 중 'people tend to not be very direct about how they feel about others'에서 사람들은 다른 사람들에 대해 어떻게 느끼는지에 관해 아주 솔직하지는 않은 경향이 있다고 하였으므로, 주어진 문장은 지문의 내용과 일치하지 않음을 알 수 있다. 따라서 정답은 **False**이다.

11 자의식이 강한 사람들은 대개 다른 사람들이 그들을 어떻게 바라보는지 알고 있다.

> 해설 문제의 핵심어구(Those with a strong sense of self)와 관련된 지문 내용 중 'Metaperceptions are usually fairly accurate in individuals who have a strong sense of self because these sorts of people are easily able to pick up on how others respond to their words or actions.'에서 상위 인지는 대개 강한 자의식을 가진 개인들에게는 상당히 정확한데, 그런 종류의 사람들이 그들의 언어나 행위에 다른 사람들이 어떻게 반응하는지를 쉽게 알아차리기 때문이라고 하였으므로, 주어진 문장은 지문의 내용과 일치함을 알 수 있다. 따라서 정답은 **True**이다. 'Metaperceptions are usually fairly accurate in individuals'가 'Those ~ usually know how others see them'으로 paraphrasing되었다.

12 약한 자아 인식을 가진 개인들은 그들의 행동을 조정하려고 노력할 때 실패한다.

> 해설 문제의 핵심어구(Individuals with weak self-perception)와 관련된 지문 내용 중 'People with a weak sense of self ~ are often wrong about how others see them.'에서 약한 자의식을 가진 사람들은 다른 사람들이 그들을 보는 방식에 대해 종종 잘못된 생각을 가진다고는 하였지만, 주어진 문장의 내용은 확인할 수 없다. 따라서 정답은 **Not given**이다.

6

동물들은 서로 의사소통을 하기 위해 다양한 신호를 사용한다. [13]동물 신호를 생각할 때 모두가 떠올리는 개 짖는 소리와 고양이 울음 소리 같은 청각 신호뿐 아니라, 우리는 그들이 화학적, 시각적, 그리고 촉각을 이용한 신호들도 활용한다는 것을 알고 있다. 이러한 다양한 신호 체계나 그것들의 조합을 사용하여, 몇몇 종들은 서로에게 정보를 전달하는 고도로 발전된 방법들을 발달시켜왔다. 이것의 한 가지 좋은 예시는 동물 행동학자인 카를 폰 프리슈에 의해 꿀벌에서 발견되었다. 폰 프리슈 박사는 먹이를 찾는 꿀벌이 벌집으로 돌아갈 때 추는 둥그런 8자 춤을 해석한 첫 번째 인물이었다. 그의 연구에서, 그는 이것들이 벌에게 신호 전달의 한 형태라는 것을 발견했다. 춤을 이용해서, 벌들은 질 좋은 꽃가루 공급원의 거리와 위치를 전달할 수 있었다. 그는 또한 가까이 접촉하여 춤을 춤으로써, 벌들이 냄새를 통해 먹이의 종류에 대한 신호를 보낼 수도 있다는 것에 주목했다.

그러나, 신호 전달은 먹이 수집을 위해서만 사용되지는 않는다. 많은 동물들은 그들의 영역에 대한 소유권과 경계를 신호로 알리기 위해 다양한 수단을 사용한다. 아마 가장 흔한 것은 냄새 표시일 것이다. [14]이 체계에서, 동물들은 다른 동물들에게 경고하기 위해 그들의 영역 내에서 물건에 대고 문지르거나 소변과 대변을 봄으로써 영역을 표시한다. 이것은 또한 다른 동물들을 향한 시각적 신호로 이어질 수 있다. 예를 들어, 불곰들은 나무에 그들의 냄새를 문질러 묻히고, 종종 나무껍질 안에 털 뭉치를 남긴다. 이 털 무더기들은 냄새가 흩어져 사라지고 난 후에도 곰이 그곳에 있었다는 신호를 전달할 수 있다.

동물들이 신호를 사용하여 의사소통을 할 수 있다는 많은 양의 정보는 또 다른 중요한 의문을 제기한다. 신호 전달도 언어로 여겨지는가? 19세기 동식물학자로 잘 알려진 찰스 다윈은 그의 책 '인간의 유래'(1871)를 위해 이 주제에 대한 기초 연구를 수행했다. 책에서, 다윈은 동물들의 청각 신호와 인간의 의사소통 사이의 유사성에 대해 논했다. [15]그는 궁극적으로 언어가 인간과 더 작은 동물들을 구별했다고 생각하긴 했지만, 인간처럼 새끼 새들이 부모에 의해 신호를 전달하는 것을 배운다는 것과 몇몇 긴팔원숭이들이 구애와 경쟁 상대와의 경쟁을 위해 음악적인 소리들을 활용한다는 것에 주목하지 않을 수 없었다.

13 소리는 동물들에 의해 이용되는 많은 의사소통 방법 중 하나이다.

> 해설 문제의 핵심어구(Sounds ~ communication mechanisms)와 관련된 지문 내용 중 'In addition to the auditory cues ~ that everyone thinks of when considering animal signals, we know that they also utilise chemical, visual, and tactile signals.'에서 동물 신호를 생각할 때 모두가 떠올리는 청각 신호뿐 아니라, 우리는 동물들이 화학적, 시각적, 그리고 촉각을 이용한 신호들도 활용한다는 것을 알고 있다고 하였으므로, 주어진 문장은 지문의 내용과 일치함을 알 수 있다. 따라서 정답은 **True**이다. 'the auditory cues'가 'Sounds'로 paraphrasing되었다.

14 냄새 표시는 다른 형태의 동물의 신호 전달보다 더 적은 정보를 전달한다.

> 해설 문제의 핵심어구(Scent marking)와 관련된 지문 내용 중 'In this system, animals mark their territories by rubbing on items or urinating and defecating within their territories'에서 냄새 표시 체계에서 동물들은 그들의 영역 내에서 물건에 대고 문지르거나 소변과 배변을 봄으로써 영역을 표시한다고는 하였지만, 주어진 문장의 내용은 확인할 수 없다. 따라서 정답은 **Not given**이다.

15 동물의 신호 전달과 인간의 의사소통 사이의 유사성은 다윈이 그것을 기초적인 언어라고 생각하도록 했다.

> 해설 문제의 핵심어구(Darwin to believe ~ a basic language)와 관련된 지문 내용 중 'he ultimately felt that language distinguished humans from lesser animals'에서 다윈은 궁극적으로 언어가 인간과 더 작은 동물들을 구별했다고 생각했다고 하였으므로, 주어진 문장은 지문의 내용과 일치하지 않음을 알 수 있다. 따라서 정답은 **False**이다.

7

찰스 아이브스

1874년에 태어난 현대 작곡가 찰스 아이브스는 어릴 때 음악을 공부했고 청년 시절 동안 교회 오르간 연주자로 일했다. 군악단의 리더였던 아버지의 영향을 받아, 그는 나아가 예일 대학에서 종교적인 합창곡을 작곡하기도 했다. 그러나 재능과 음악에 대한 애호에도 불구하고, 아이브스는 그의 인생 대부분에서 사업가였다.

아이브스는 1899년에 보험 회사 Charles H. Raymond & Co.에 들어갔으나 1907년에 그의 동료 중 하나였던, Julian Myrick과 함께 그 자신의 보험 회사를 설립하기 위해 그만두었다. 아이브스는 돈을 버는 데 능숙했던 영리한 사업가로 그의 동료들 사이에서 빠르게 명성을 얻었다. 하지만, 보험이 다른 무엇보다도 대중에게 도움이 되는 수단이라고 믿었기 때문에, 그는 업계의 인도주의적인 이상을 유지했고 [16]그의 시대 동안 업계 내에 널리 퍼져 있던 부패 스캔들에 연루되지 않았다. 1930년에 그가 은퇴했을 때, 아이브스와 Myrick의 회사는 미국에 있는 동종업체 중 가장 큰 회사였다.

아이브스의 사업적 성공은 그의 친구들 중 일부는 그가 작곡가였다는 것을 전혀 알지 못했을 정도로 그의 음악적인 노력을 무색하게 했다. 자비로 작품을 발표하고 거의 알려지지 않은 음악가들에게 외진 곳에서 연주하게 하면서, [17]아이브스는 주류 음악 사회와 거리를 두었다. 그렇게 한 것은 그에게 실험을 할 자신감을 주었는데, 그는 다양한 음악 장르에서 요소들을 차용했다. 예를 들어, 그는 대중음악과 십 대와 대학 시절의 종교적인 합창곡을 유럽의 연주 음악과 통합했다. 음악 평론가들 사이에서 궁극적으로 그에게 명성을 가져다 준 것은 그의 창조성과 장르를 혼합하는 능력이었다.

그의 통합에 대한 재능을 가장 전형적으로 보여주는 작품은 콩코드 소나타로 더 흔히 알려져 있는 피아노 소나타 제2번이다. 그 작품은 19세기 미국 초월주의 작가들에 의해 영감을 받은 것이었는데, 그들은 매사추세츠 주의 콩코드 부근에서 활발히 활동했다. 초월주의의 중심 교리 중 하나는, 사회와 그것의 다양한 관습보다는, 개인의 직관이 창작력으로 가는 관문을 열었다는 것이었다. [18]베토벤으로부터의 인용과, 대중음악과 종교음악으로부터의 발췌, 기차와 같은 일상생활의 소리를 활용하여, 아이브스는 그의 소나타에 이 정신을 담아내려고 했다. 그 작품의 공연 또한 실험적인 요소를 포함했다. 4악장 각각이 시작하기 전에, 아이브스는 작품에 영감을 주었던 에머슨, 호손, 올콧 가문, 소로와 같은 작가들의 작품을 낭독했다. 완성된 지 20년이 더 지난 후인 1938년에 소나타의 초연은 성공적이었으며 그의 작품에 대한 소식은 곧 널리 퍼졌다.

9년 후, 1947년에, 교향곡 제3번으로 퓰리처상을 받았을 때 아이브스는 고전 음악의 선두에 올랐다. [19]그의 생애 동안 음악적 공헌에 대한 이러한 인정을 얻었음에도 불구하고, 그는 많은 작품들이 실황으로 공연되는 것을 볼 정도로 오래 살지는 못했으며, 대중 사이에서의 아이브스의 명성은 주로 사후의 것이었다. 오늘날, 아이브스는 미국 음악사의 선구자로 여겨지고 있고, 그의 명성은 계속해서 커지고 있다. 20세기의 마지막 15년 동안에만, 그의 생애와 작품에 대해 적어도 20권의 책이 출간되었다.

16 찰스 아이브스의 생전에 보험 회사들 사이에서는 부정부패가 널리 퍼져 있었다.

> **해설** 문제의 핵심어구(Corruption was widespread)와 관련된 지문 내용 중 'the corruption scandals prevalent within it during his time'에서 그의 시대 동안 업계 내에 널리 퍼져 있던 부패 스캔들이라고 하였으므로, 주어진 문장은 지문의 내용과 일치함을 알 수 있다. 따라서 정답은 **True**이다. 'the corruption scandals prevalent'가 'Corruption was widespread'로 paraphrasing되었다.

17 주류 음악 사회는 엄격히 실험에 반대했다.

> **해설** 문제의 핵심어구(mainstream musical community)와 관련된 지문 내용 중 'Ives kept his distance from the mainstream musical community. His doing so gave him the confidence to experiment'에서 아이브스는 주류 음악 사회와 거리를 두었고 그렇게 한 것은 그에게 실험을 할 자신감을 주었다고는 하였지만, 주어진 문장의 내용은 확인할 수 없다. 따라서 정답은 **Not given**이다.

18 아이브스는 대중음악과 종교음악을 그의 소나타에 이용하지 않았다.

> **해설** 문제의 핵심어구(use popular and religious music)와 관련된 지문 내용 중 'Utilising ~ excerpts from popular and religious music ~ Ives attempted to capture this spirit in his sonata.'에서 대중음악과 종교음악으로부터의 발췌를 활용하여 아이브스는 그의 소나타에 이 정신을 담아내려고 했다고 하였으므로, 주어진 문장은 지문의 내용과 일치하지 않음을 알 수 있다. 따라서 정답은 **False**이다.

19 찰스 아이브스는 그가 사망한 이후까지 그의 작품에 대해 인정을 받지 못했다.

> **해설** 문제의 핵심어구(Charles Ives received no recognition)와 관련된 지문 내용 중 'gaining this acknowledgement for his musical contribution during his lifetime'에서 그의 생애 동안 음악적 공헌에 대한 이러한 인정을 얻었다고 하였으므로, 주어진 문장은 지문의 내용과 일치하지 않음을 알 수 있다. 따라서 정답은 **False**이다.

8

멀티태스킹의 위험

우리는 빠른 속도로 돌아가는 세상에 살고 있으며, 요즘 많은 사람들은 따라가기 위해 최대한 많은 과제들을 동시에 완료하는 것이 불가피하다고 느끼는 것처럼 보인다. 이러한 행위로 알려진 멀티태스킹은, 몇몇 사람들에게 효율적인 시간 사용을 하고 있다는 느낌을 줄 수도 있지만, 이것은 사실과 거리가 멀다. 더욱이, 처리할 수 있는 것 이상의 일을 곡예하듯 하는 것은 한 사람의 육체적 건강과 정신적인 행복에 해로운 영향을 미칠 수 있다.

일반적인 믿음과는 반대로, [20]인간의 뇌는 다양한 형태의 정보들을 동시에 처리하기 위한 준비를 제대로 갖추고 있지 않다. 너무도 준비되어 있지 않아서 우리가 멀티태스킹이라고 믿는 것은 심지어 가능하지 않을 수도 있을 정도이다. 사람들이 동시에 다양한 활동에 참여하려고 시도할 때, 뇌가 실제로 하는 것은 과제들 사이에서 정신없이 방향을 바꾸는 것이다. 하나의 활동에 완전한 주의를 하기보다는, 멀티태스킹에 참여한 사람들은 자신이 하려고 하는 각각의 것들에 한 번에 오직 몇 초 동안만 집중할 수 있다. [21]계속적으로 과제 사이를 이동하는 것은, 놀랄 것도 없이, 소모적이며 정보를 거르고 후에 그것을 기억해 내는 것을 극도로 어렵게 한다. 결국, 멀티태스킹은 우리의 속도를 늦춘다는 점에서 역효과를 낳는다. 뇌가 왔다 갔다 하며 이동하고 이전에 참여했던 활동에 초점을 다시 맞추는 데 걸리는 시간이 낭비이기 때문에, 또 다른 것을 시작하기 전에 한 과제를 끝까지 해내어 완료하는 것이 훨씬 더 효율적이다.

그것이 충분히 나쁘지 않다 하더라도, 멀티태스킹은 좋지 못한 건강으로 이어질 수 있다. 신체의 신경계를 위한 통제 시스템인 뇌가 동시에 여러 과제를 수행하려고 시도할 때, 그것은 거의 항상 스트레스 호르몬과 아드레날린을 분비한다. 이것이 발생할 때, [22]아드레날린은 일시적인 에너지 증가를 제공하고, 그 결과 종종 신체는 아무리 비능률적일지라도, 하도록 할당받은 일을 완수하게 된다. 그러나 동시에, 스트레스 호르몬의 분비는 혈압이 오르는 것을 야기하는데, 대부분의 사람들이 알고 있듯이 이는 심장이 더 힘들게 기능하도록 하기 때문에 위험할 수 있다. [23]가끔 스트레스를 받는 것은 예상되는 일이지만, 우리 중 점점 더 많은 수의 사람들이 그렇듯이, 그것을 항상 경험하는 것은 우리를 아프게 만들 수 있다. 사실, [23]만성적으로 스트레스를 받는 사람들은 정기적으로 두통, 소화 문제, 그리고 전반적인 불안감을 경험할 뿐만 아니라, 탈진, 우울증, 바이러스에도 취약하며, 심장병과 같이 잠재적으로 치명적인 질환을 앓게 될 가능성이 더 높다. 대체로, 멀티태스킹이 자극들로 가득한 세계에 대처하는 유일한 방법으로 보일 수도 있는 반면에, 우리의 건강과 생산성 모두를 손상시킬 가능성은 그것을 피할 충분한 이유가 된다.

20 뇌는 장기간에 걸친 시간 동안 여러 개의 일에 동시에 집중할 수 있다.

> **해설** 문제의 핵심어구(the brain can focus on several things)와 관련된 지문 내용 중 'the human brain is ill-equipped to process multiple forms of information simultaneously'에서 인간의 뇌는 다양한 형태의 정보들을 동시에 처리하기 위한 준비를 제대로 갖추고 있지 않다고 하였으므로, 주어진 문장은 지문의 내용과 일치하지 않음을 알 수 있다. 따라서 정답은 **False** 이다.

21 과제들 사이에서 방향을 바꾸는 것은 정보를 기억하는 것을 어렵게 한다.

> **해설** 문제의 핵심어구(remember information)와 관련된 지문 내용 중 'Repeatedly moving between tasks ~ makes it extremely difficult to filter information and recall it afterwards.'에서 계속적으로 과제 사이를 이동하는 것은 정보를 거르고 후에 그것을 기억해 내는 것을 극도로 어렵게 한다고 하였으므로, 주어진 문장은 지문의 내용과 일치함을 알 수 있다. 따라서 정답은 **True**이다. 'filter information and recall it'이 'remember information'으로 paraphrasing되었다.

22 아드레날린이 제공하는 힘은 개인의 전반적인 능률을 증가시키는 것을 돕는다.

> **해설** 문제의 핵심어구(boost that adrenaline provides)와 관련된 지문 내용 중 'the adrenaline provides a temporary energy boost'에서 아드레날린은 일시적인 에너지 증가를 제공한다고는 하였지만, 주어진 문장의 내용은 확인할 수 없다. 따라서 정답은 **Not given**이다.

23 때때로 스트레스를 경험하는 사람들은 심각한 질환이 생길 가능성이 가장 높다.

> **해설** 문제의 핵심어구(People who experience stress from time to time)와 관련된 지문 내용 중 'being stressed from time to time is to be expected'와 'the chronically stressed ~ are more likely to develop potentially fatal conditions'에서 가끔 스트레스를 받는 것은 예상되는 일이며, 만성적으로 스트레스를 받는 사람들은 잠재적으로 치명적인 질환을 앓게 될 가능성이 더 높다고 하였으므로, 주어진 문장은 지문의 내용과 일치하지 않음을 알 수 있다. 따라서 정답은 **False** 이다.

9

중세의 책
중세 시대의 그늘에서 어떻게 문자 언어가 나왔는지에 관한 이야기

중세 유럽의 초기에, 책은 매우 희귀했다. 존재했던 것들은 온전히 손으로 제작되었고 매우 비쌌는데, 이는 그것을 제작했던 가톨릭 교회 외에는, 부유한 사람들만이 소유하는 것은 고사하고 그것을 구경만 할 수 있었다는 것을 의미했다. 더욱이, 교육은 성직자들과 가장 부유한 사회 구성원들에게만 가능했다. 이것은 인구의 막대한 다수가 계속 완전히 문맹으로 있으면서 들에서 노동을 하며 일생을 보냈다는 것을 의미했고, [24]역사와 신화에 대해 그들이 아는 모든 것은 당시의 음유 시인, 음악가, 그리고 시인들에 의해 그들에게 전달된 구어로 된 이야기와 노래들에만 한정되었다. 유럽 사회에 전환점을 가져오고 후대에 정보가 전달된 방식을 변화시킨 인쇄된 책이 소개될 때까지, 이 시기의 수백 년 동안 사회는 이런 방식으로 기능했다.

그렇게 적은 책이 존재했던 주된 이유는 한 권을 만드는 것이 완성하는 데 몇 년이 걸리는 고된 작업이었다는 사실과 관련이 있었다. 속지를 생산하기 위해 동물 가죽이 보존 처리되어야 했으며, 그 다음에는 다양한 재료에서 얻은 안료를 배합하여 잉크가 만들어져야 했다. 그 다음에는 글자를 적을 깃펜을 준비하는 것과 원고가 배치되어야 하는 위치를 안내하기 위해 각각의 페이지에 선을 긋는 것이 뒤따랐다. 이러한 모든 준비가 완료되었을 때에만 서기가 실제로 책을 쓸 수 있었는데, 이것은 손으로 모든 단어를 기록하는 것을 포함했다. 그 이후에, 삽화가 추가될 수 있었고, 속지가 금, 은, 그리고 구리로 된 나뭇잎으로 만들어진 테두리로 장식될 수 있었으며, 모든 것이 제본되었다. 근본적으로, 한 권의 책을 완성하는 데 수반되는 노동의 집약도는 아주 적은 수의 책이 만들어졌으며 엘리트 계층만이 구매할 수 있었다는 것을 의미했다.

의심할 여지 없이, 중세 시대에 대부분의 책에 대한 통제권을 유지했던 것은 가톨릭 교회였다. [25]일부 수도원은 심지어 도서관을 고대 그리스와 로마의 문학, 과학, 그리고 철학 작품으로 채우는 것을 그들의 임무로 삼아, 그것들을 대대로 보존했다. 수도원이 그렇게 많은 정보를 가지면서 또 그것을 엄격히 통제할 수 있었던 것은 [26]교회가 그 시대에 심지어 귀족보다도 우위에 있는 가장 중요한 사회의 일면이었고, 성직자들이 글을 쓰고 삽화를 넣을 능력이 있는 소수의 사람들에 속해 있었다는 사실 때문이었다. 이러한 과업들은 성경의 복사본을 원하는 사람들 사이에서 수요가 많아서, 14세기까지 일부 수도원들은 오로지 그것들을 생산할 목적으로 확보되었다.

1445년에, 요한 구텐베르크라는 이름을 가진 한 남자가 인쇄기 발명으로 유럽인의 삶을 완전히 바꾸어버렸고, 궁극적으로는 전 세계인의 삶을 바꿨다. [27]구텐베르크의 인쇄기는 책을 빠르고 값싸게 생산할 수 있었는데, 이것은 유럽 사회에서 두 가지 큰 변화를 가져왔다. 첫 번째는 교황의 권한이 더 이상 문학과 정보를 통제할 수 없게 되었다는 것이었다. 책은 수도원 밖에서도 인쇄될 수 있게 되었을 뿐만 아니라, 또한 아주 저렴한 가격으로 구할 수 있어 서민들도 구입할 수 있었다. 두 번째는 문자로 된 작품들이 대중들에게 도달할 수 있게 된 것이었다. 이것은 더 많은 사람들이 읽고 쓰는 것을 배우도록 고무시켰고, 이는 식자율을 상당히 증가시켰다.

24 중세 초기에 구전 이야기는 역사적 지식을 제공했다.

> 해설 문제의 핵심어구(Oral accounts provided historical knowledge)와 관련된 지문 내용 중 'everything they knew about history ~ limited to the spoken-word stories and songs'에서 역사에 대해 그들이 아는 모든 것은 구어로 된 이야기와 노래들에만 한정되었다고 하였으므로, 주어진 문장은 지문의 내용과 일치함을 알 수 있다. 따라서 정답은 **True**이다. 'the spoken-word stories and songs'가 'Oral accounts'로 paraphrasing되었다.

25 수도원에서 사용된 특수 기법은 책들을 보존되도록 유지했다.

> 해설 문제의 핵심어구(A special technique used in monasteries)와 관련된 지문 내용 중 'Some monasteries even made it their mission to keep libraries full of ~ works of the ancient Greeks and Romans, preserving them through the ages.'에서 일부 수도원은 도서관을 고대 그리스와 로마의 작품으로 채우는 것을 그들의 임무로 삼아 그것들을 대대로 보존했다고는 하였지만, 주어진 문장의 내용은 확인할 수 없다. 따라서 정답은 **Not given**이다.

26 가톨릭 교회의 권력은 귀족의 것과 동등했다.

> 해설 문제의 핵심어구(equal to ~ the nobility)와 관련된 지문 내용 중 'the Church was the most important facet of society at the time, above even the nobility'에서 교회가 그 시대에 심지어 귀족보다도 우위에 있는 가장 중요한 사회의 일면이었다고 하였으므로, 주어진 문장은 지문의 내용과 일치하지 않음을 알 수 있다. 따라서 정답은 **False**이다.

27 인쇄기는 교회가 정보에 대해 가졌던 통제권을 완화했다.

> 해설 문제의 핵심어구(The printing press)와 관련된 지문 내용 중 'Gutenberg's press ~ resulted in two major changes in European society. The first was that papal authorities were no longer able to control literature and information'에서 구텐베르크의 인쇄기는 유럽 사회에서 두 가지 큰 변화를 가져왔는데 첫 번째는 교황의 권한이 더 이상 문학과 정보를 통제할 수 없게 되었다는 것이었다고 하였으므로, 주어진 문장은 지문의 내용과 일치함을 알 수 있다. 따라서 정답은 **True**이다. 'no longer to control'이 'loosened the control'로 paraphrasing되었다.

10

유럽의 상업 혁명
국제 무역과 식민지화의 사회 경제적 영향

유럽인들은 이슬람교도들을 그 지역에서 몰아내는 것을 목표로 했던 일련의 성전인 십자군 전쟁 동안에 중동으로부터 향신료, 비단, 그리고 다른 상품들을 접하게 되었다. 거의 200년이 넘는 전쟁 기간 동안, 많은 중동 상품들이 매우 인기 있어져서, [28]1291년에 십자군 전쟁이 마침내 끝났을 때, 유럽과 중동의 무역은 끝나지 않았다. 두 지역 간의 거래는 1453년까지 자유롭게 행해졌는데, 이때 콘스탄티노플이 정복되었다. 이는 육로로 접근할 수 없게 만들었고, 유럽인들이 중동과, 더 나아가, 아시아에 도달하는 새로운 길을 찾도록 동기를 부여했다. 유럽 열강으로서 영국, 포르투갈, 그리고 스페인의 번영과 결합된 이러한 발전은, 수익성이 좋은 무역망이 형성되고 새로운 대륙이 식민지화된 시대의 도래를 알렸다.

1492년 크리스토퍼 콜럼버스의 신세계 항해와 6년 후 바스코 다 가마의 아프리카 일주는 유럽의 첫 번째 성공들에 속했다. 오래지 않아, 아메리카 대륙에 식민지가 세워졌고, 유럽과 세계의 다른 지역을 연결하는 무역로가 개설되었다. 중동과 아시아에서 난 향신료와 비단 외에도, 유럽인들은 아프리카와 아메리카 대륙으로부터 국내와 해외 모두에서 판매될 상품의 생산에 사용하기 위해 원자재를 수입하기 시작했다. 상업 혁명으로 알려진, 16세기와 18세기 사이 유럽의 이 경제 팽창의 시기는 광범위한 결과를 낳았다.

가장 즉각적인 영향 중 하나는 인플레이션이었다. 상업 혁명 이전에, 유럽의 금과 은의 대부분이 중동과의 무역에 사용되었다. 금과 은 광산이 고갈되고 유통되는 통화가 적어지자, 가격 하락세가 발생했다. 하지만, 신세계에서 귀금속이 발견되자마자 금과 은은 유럽으로 쏟아져 들어오기 시작했다. ²⁹스페인 단독으로만 1500년과 1650년 사이에 식민지로부터 180톤 이상의 금과 16,000톤 이상의 은을 수입했고, 이 새로운 통화가 유통에 합류하면서, 가격이 극적으로 상승했다. 인플레이션은 흑사병으로부터 회복하던 인구의 상품에 대한 수요 증가에 의해 더욱 심화되었다.

상업 혁명은 사회에도 깊이 영향을 미쳤다. 통화 과잉은 더 높은 임금을 요구할 수 있었던 노동자들에게는 유리했지만, 또한 귀족들에게는 그들을 고용하는 것이 비용이 더 들게 되었다는 것을 의미했다. 그 결과, 많은 귀족 계층 구성원들은 그들의 생활 방식을 유지하기 위해 땅을 조금씩 팔아 넘겨야만 했다. 구매자들은 귀족의 다른 구성원이 아니라 새로 부유해진 상인들이었는데, 그들 중 많은 이들이 땅을 울타리로 구분했으며, ³⁰귀족들이 소작농들로 하여금 그것을 경작하도록 허가하던 전통을 깨버렸다. 돌볼 밭이 없어지자, 농부들은 도시로 이동했고 궁극적으로 새로운 도시 노동력이 되었다.

비록 상업 혁명 동안의 무역이 수익성은 좋았지만, 전쟁, 날씨, 그리고 해적 행위는 큰 손실을 초래할 수 있었다. 결과적으로, 이러한 위험을 완화하기 위해 주식 회사라고 불리는 조직들이 설립되었다. 현대적인 기업의 전신으로 여겨지는 이 회사들은, 수익의 분배를 위해 투자자들에게 주식을 매매했던 개인 소유의 회사들이었다. 주식을 팔아 번 돈은 사업의 자금을 대고 무역품을 얻는 데 사용되었다. 그리고 여전히 수송품이 망가지거나, 도둑맞거나, 혹은 분실될 가능성은 있었지만, ³¹일반적으로 다수의 투자자들이 있었다는 사실을 고려할 때, 회사와 각 주주들의 위험 부담은 아주 적었다.

28 중동과 유럽의 무역은 십자군 전쟁이 끝났을 때 중단되었다.

> 해설 문제의 핵심어구(the Crusades ended)와 관련된 지문 내용 중 'so when the Crusades finally came to an end in 1291, trade between Europe and the Middle East did not'에서 1291년에 십자군 전쟁이 마침내 끝났을 때 유럽과 중동의 무역은 끝나지 않았다고 하였으므로, 주어진 문장은 지문의 내용과 일치하지 않음을 알 수 있다. 따라서 정답은 **False**이다.

29 스페인은 아메리카 대륙으로부터 다른 어떤 유럽 국가보다도 많은 금과 은을 수입했다.

> 해설 문제의 핵심어구(Spain imported more gold and silver)와 관련된 지문 내용 중 'Spain alone imported more than 180 tonnes of gold and more than 16,000 tonnes of silver from its colonies'에서 스페인 단독으로만 식민지로부터 180톤 이상의 금과 16,000톤 이상의 은을 수입했다고는 하였지만, 주어진 문장의 내용은 확인할 수 없다. 따라서 정답은 **Not given**이다.

30 귀족들은 한때 가난한 농부들이 농업 목적으로 그들의 땅을 사용하는 것을 허락했다.

> 해설 문제의 핵심어구(The aristocracy once allowed poor farmers)와 관련된 지문 내용 중 'the tradition of the aristocracy permitting the peasants to cultivate it'에서 귀족들이 소작농들로 하여금 그것을 경작하도록 허가하던 전통이라고 하였으므로, 주어진 문장은 지문의 내용과 일치함을 알 수 있다. 따라서 정답은 **True**이다. 'permitting the peasants to cultivate it'이 'allowed poor farmers to use their land for agricultural purposes'로 paraphrasing되었다.

31 주식 회사들은 다수의 사람들이 돈을 투자했기 때문에 재정적인 위험 부담을 최소화했다.

> **해설** 문제의 핵심어구(Joint-stock companies)와 관련된 지문 내용 중 'given the fact there were generally numerous investors, the risk borne by the company and each stockholder was minimal'에서 일반적으로 다수의 투자자들이 있었다는 사실을 고려할 때 회사와 각 주주들의 위험 부담은 아주 적었다고 하였으므로, 주어진 문장은 지문의 내용과 일치함을 알 수 있다. 따라서 정답은 **True**이다. 'risk ~ was minimal'이 'minimised ~ risk'로 paraphrasing되었다.

HACKERS TEST

p.80

1 True		**2** Not given		**3** True		**4** Not given
5 True		**6** False		**7** Not given		**8** False
9 True		**10** D		**11** D		**12** developed regions
13 vehicle						

전 세계 도시화의 영향: 비용과 편익

농촌이 도시로 발전하는 과정이나 시골에서 도시 지역으로의 사람들의 이주를 나타낼 수 있는 도시화는, 고대 인류 역사에 뿌리를 두고 있다. 역사학자들은 고대 메소포타미아에서 도시화가 처음 발생했는데, 이는 최초의 진정한 도시인 우루크와 함께 기원전 4500년경에 시작되었으며, 그 후 기원전 3800년경에 우르의 설립과 함께 계속되었다는 것에 널리 동의한다.

하지만 [10]이러한 현상은 보통 현대와 더 관련이 있다. [1]유럽에서, 19세기에 산업혁명의 결과로 더 전반적이며 더 광범위한 도시화가 발생했다. 영국에서는, 도시의 인구가 1801년 17퍼센트에서 1891년 믿기 힘든 72퍼센트까지 증가했는데, 주로 공장들이 전통적으로 자급 농업에 의존했던 빈곤한 소작농들에게 유망한 일자리들을 제공한 런던, 맨체스터, 뉴캐슬, 그리고 버밍엄시로 모여들었다. 풍부한 일자리, 오락 거리, 그리고 사회복지 서비스와 함께, 도시에서의 삶은 농장 생활의 노역에 대한 훨씬 더 유망한 대안처럼 보였다.

그리고 그 매력은 계속되어 왔다. 2008년에, 세계의 도시 인구는 처음으로 시골 인구를 넘어섰다. 하지만 현대의 도시화 사례들은 1950년대 이전의 경우 그랬던 것처럼 산업화된 국가들로 분류되지 않는다. [12]그때부터, 도시화는 주로 덜 개발된 지역에서 발생해왔고, 2030년까지 사실상 모든 개발 도상 지역들에서 시골 지역보다 도시 환경에 거주하는 더 많은 사람들이 있을 것으로 추산된다. 이것에는 몇 가지 이유가 있다. 하나는 계속 확대되고 있는 세계 인구를 수용하기 위한 시골 지역의 자원 부족이다. 두 번째는 사람들이 도시와 연관 짓는 고용 기회의 매력이다. 세 번째는 대부분의 시골 지역사회가 제공할 수 있는 것보다 더 높은 품질의 의료 서비스와 교육에 대한 욕구이다.

그러나, 인구 통계에서의 이러한 변화가 많은 기회를 약속하는 반면, 난관이 없는 것은 아니라는 점을 기억하는 것이 중요하다. 종종, 취업 시장은 도시의 성장 속도를 따라가지 못한다. 이것은 [3]도시로 이주하는 많은 가난한 사람들이 경제 상황의 개선 없이 이동한 것을 깨닫게 될 것임을 의미한다. 그리고 [4]사람들의 고향에서 종종 나타나는 가족과 지역사회의 지원 없이, 도시 이주민들은 고향에 있을 때보다 자신들이 심지어 훨씬 더 궁색한 처지임을 깨달을 수 있다. 이것은 부분적으로 오늘날 우리 도시에 있는 도시 빈민가의 만연을 설명한다.

현대 도시화의 또 다른 충격적인 측면은 많은 주요 도시들을 괴롭히는 특정 범죄 유형의 높은 비율이다. Decker, Sichor, 그리고 O'Brien (1982)은 인구 밀도가 범죄에 어떻게 영향을 미치는지에 대한 상세한 연구를 수행했고 도시화와 강도 및 대면접촉 절도 같은 범죄 사이에 직접적인 상관관계가 있다는 것을 알아냈다. 그들은 또한 [13]차량 절도가 시골 지역보다 도시 지역에서 훨씬 더 높은 비율로 발생했다는 것을 발견했는데, 이는 자동차에 의존하며 대중교통이 없는 경향이 있는 인구가 더 적은 지역들보다 도시들에서 1인당 자동차 보유율이 상당히 더 적기 때문에 놀라운 결과이다. [5]도시 지역의 범죄 문제는 1960년대 후반 미국에서 정치적으로 불안했던 시기와 같이, 사회 불안의 시기에는 특히 심각하며, 법 집행 기관들에게는 미국 도시들에 만연하는 범죄를 어떻게 다룰 것인지에 대한 해답을 모색하는 것이 맡겨진다. [6]시카고 거리에 순찰을 도는 법 집행 담당자 수의 증가에도 불구하고, 그곳의 총 살인 건수는 최근에 극적으로 증가해왔다.

하지만 아마도 도시 주민들과 도시 계획가들 모두의 마음을 가장 압박하는 것은 이 엄청난 수의 사람들을 가장 잘 먹여 살리는 방법일 것이다. 지난 1세기 동안 농업의 효율성과 생산성에서 극적인 진보를 경험하긴 했지만, 수많은 도시 거주자들은 계속해서 영양 결핍으로 고통받고 있다. 이 문제는 세계 수요를 충족시킬 수 있는 것 이상인 농업 생산량 자체와는 직접적으로 관련되어 있지 않다. 오히려, 이것은 예를 들어 [7]빈곤으로 인한 식량에 대한 접근 부족과 [8]자연식품을 포장식품과 가공식품으로 대체하는 증가하는 경향의 결합이며 (de Haen, 2003), 이는 많은 도시들에서 비만과 건강 관련 문제들의 급속한 확산으로 비난받아 왔다.

더욱이, [11]슈퍼마켓에 대한 도시의 더 커진 의존도와 함께, 식량 실행 계획의 경제학은 소매업자들이 공급망을 간소화하는 것이 훨씬 더 비용 효율이 높기 때문에, 더 적은 농업 공급자를 장려한다. 이것은 수입품에 대한 훨씬 더 심한 의존으로 이어졌는데, 이는 많은 소규모 지역 농장의 배제를 야기한 추세이다. 북아메리카와 유럽의 많은 도시들에서 시험되고 있는 한 가지 해결책은 [9]도시의 정원과 온실로의 시골 농장들의 이식이다. 이것은 현지 생산 농산물을 가능하게 하는데, 이는 많은 고객들에게 매력적일 수 있다. 몇몇 대규모의 도시 농업 계획은 이미 진행 중이며 지금까지는 유망한 결과를 보여주고 있다.

어휘 urbanisation n. 도시화 cost and benefit phr. 비용과 편익 migration n. 이주, 이동 congregate v. 모이다
impoverished adj. 빈곤한 peasant n. 소작농 subsistence agriculture phr. 자급 농업 toil n. 노력, 고역 lure n. 매력, 유혹
contemporary adj. 현대의, 동시대의 relegate v. (어떤 종류·등급 등에) 분류하다, 소속시키다 demographics n. 인구 통계
prevalence n. 만연, 유행 slum n. 빈민가, 슬럼 plague v. 괴롭히다 larceny n. 절도(죄), 도둑질 per capita phr. 1인당
dire adj. 심각한, 엄청난 unrest n. 불안, 불만 volatile adj. 불안정한 tackle v. (문제 등을) 다루다 rampant adj. 만연하는
patrol v. 순찰을 돌다 undernutrition n. 영양 결핍 propensity n. 경향 substitute v. 대체하다 epidemic n. 급속한 확산, 유행
logistics n. 실행 계획 streamline v. 간소화하다 produce n. 농산물

[1-9]

1 영국의 19세기 도시 인구의 급격한 증가는 네 개의 도시에 집중되었다.

> 해설 문제의 핵심어구(England's 19th century urban population)와 관련된 지문 내용 중 'In Europe, a much broader and more extensive urbanisation occurred in the 19th century'와 'In England, the urban population increased ~ primarily congregating in the cities of London, Manchester, Newcastle, and Birmingham'에서 유럽에서 19세기에 더 전반적이며 더 광범위한 도시화가 발생했는데, 영국에서는 도시의 인구가 주로 런던, 맨체스터, 뉴캐슬, 그리고 버밍엄시로 모여들며 증가했다고 하였으므로, 주어진 문장은 지문의 내용과 일치함을 알 수 있다. 따라서 정답은 **True**이다. 'primarily congregating in the cities of London, Manchester, Newcastle, and Birmingham'이 'was focused on four cities'로 paraphrasing되었다.

2 도시 이주의 증가는 도시에서의 심각한 주택 부족으로 이어졌다.

> 해설 문제의 핵심어구(housing shortages in cities)와 관련된 내용은 지문에서 찾을 수 없다. 따라서 정답은 **Not given**이다.

3 많은 이주민들은 그들의 경제적인 상황에서 어떤 개선도 발견하지 못한다.

> 해설 문제의 핵심어구(improvement in their economic circumstances)와 관련된 지문 내용 중 'many of the poor who migrate to cities will find themselves relocated without improving their economic situations'에서 도시로 이주하는 많은 가난한 사람들이 경제 상황의 개선없이 이동한 것을 깨닫게 될 것이라고 하였으므로, 주어진 문장은 지문의 내용과 일치함을 알 수 있다. 따라서 정답은 **True**이다. 'improving their economic situations'가 'improvement in their economic circumstances'로 paraphrasing되었다.

4 도시에서의 가족 지원의 부재는 사람들을 범죄로 이끌 수 있다.

> 해설 문제의 핵심어구(a lack of family support)와 관련된 지문 내용 중 'without the family and community support ~ urban migrants can find themselves even worse off'에서 가족과 지역사회의 지원 없이 도시 이주민들은 자신들이 심지어 훨씬 더 궁색한 처지임을 깨달을 수 있다고는 하였지만, 주어진 문장의 내용은 확인할 수 없다. 따라서 정답은 **Not given**이다.

5 사회 불안은 도시에서의 범죄 증가를 야기한다.

해설 문제의 핵심어구(Social instability)와 관련된 지문 내용 중 'The problem of crime in urban areas is particularly dire in times of social unrest'에서 도시 지역의 범죄 문제는 사회 불안의 시기에는 특히 심각하다고 하였으므로, 주어진 문장은 지문의 내용과 일치함을 알 수 있다. 따라서 정답은 **True**이다. 'in times of social unrest'가 'Social instability'로 paraphrasing되었다.

6 시카고의 경찰력 증대는 살인률을 감소시켰다.

해설 문제의 핵심어구(Chicago police)와 관련된 지문 내용 중 'Despite increases in the number of law enforcement officers patrolling Chicago's streets, the total number of murders there has risen'에서 시카고 거리에 순찰을 도는 법 집행 담당자 수의 증가에도 불구하고 그곳의 총 살인 건수는 증가해왔다고 하였으므로, 주어진 문장은 지문의 내용과 일치하지 않음을 알 수 있다. 따라서 정답은 **False**이다.

7 빈곤은 그들이 신선한 야채를 살 형편이 못 되기 때문에 사람들이 식단을 제한하도록 한다.

해설 문제의 핵심어구(Poverty)와 관련된 지문 내용 중 'lack of access to foodstuffs — e.g. due to poverty'에서 빈곤으로 인한 식량에 대한 접근 부족이라고는 하였지만, 주어진 문장의 내용은 확인할 수 없다. 따라서 정답은 **Not given**이다.

8 공장 생산 식품의 이용 가능성은 비만이 감소하도록 한다.

해설 문제의 핵심어구(factory produced foods)와 관련된 지문 내용 중 'the growing propensity to substitute whole foods with packaged and processed foods ~, which has been blamed for the epidemic of obesity'에서 자연식품을 포장식품과 가공식품으로 대체하는 증가하는 경향은 비만의 급속한 확산으로 비난받아 왔다고 하였으므로, 주어진 문장은 지문의 내용과 일치하지 않음을 알 수 있다. 따라서 정답은 **False**이다.

9 도시 농장은 현지 농산물을 더 매력적으로 만들 가능성을 가지고 있다.

해설 문제의 핵심어구(Urban farms)와 관련된 지문 내용 중 'the transplantation of rural farms to urban gardens and greenhouses. This allows for locally grown produce, which might be attractive to many consumers.'에서 도시의 정원과 온실로의 시골 농장들의 이식은 현지 생산 농산물을 가능하게 하며 이는 많은 고객들에게 매력적일 수 있다고 하였으므로, 주어진 문장은 지문의 내용과 일치함을 알 수 있다. 따라서 정답은 **True**이다. 'urban gardens and greenhouses'가 'Urban farms'로 paraphrasing되었다.

[10-11]

10 두 번째 단락에서, 글쓴이는 −라고 주장한다.
   A 농업의 실패는 사람들이 어쩔 수 없이 도시로 이주하도록 했다
   B 도시화는 새로운 산업적인 관행을 가능하게 했다
   C 산업화는 도시 생활에 유익한 영향을 미칠 수 있다
   D 도시화는 현대적 동향으로 널리 여겨진다

해설 두 번째 단락의 'this phenomenon is usually associated more with modern times'에서 도시화는 보통 현대와 더 관련이 있다고 하였으므로, 보기 **D** urbanisation is widely considered a modern trend가 정답이다. 'is ~ associated more with modern times'가 'is ~ considered a modern trend'로 paraphrasing되었다.

11 글쓴이에 따르면, 슈퍼마켓에 대한 더 커진 의존도는
   A 도시 지역의 많은 소규모 식료품 잡화점의 폐점을 초래했다.
   B 도시 농업 옹호자들의 극심한 반대를 야기했다.

C   더욱 다양한 공급망의 발달을 일으켰다.
D   다른 국가들로부터의 상품에 대한 더 강한 필요를 가져왔다.

해설 문제의 핵심어구(a greater dependence on supermarkets)와 관련된 지문 내용 중 'with cities' greater dependence on supermarkets, the economics of food logistics promotes fewer agricultural sources ~. This has led to a much heavier reliance on imported goods'에서 슈퍼마켓에 대한 도시의 더 커진 의존도와 함께, 식량 실행 계획의 경제학은 더 적은 농업 공급자를 장려하며 이것은 수입품에 대한 훨씬 더 심한 의존으로 이어졌다고 하였으므로, 보기 D brought about a stronger need for goods from other countries가 정답이다. 'a much heavier reliance on imported goods'가 'a stronger need for goods from other countries'로 paraphrasing되었다.

🔍 오답 확인하기
C는 지문 내용 중 'the economics of food logistics promotes fewer agricultural sources, as it is far more cost effective for retailers to streamline their supply chains'에서 소매업자들이 공급망을 간소화하는 것이 훨씬 더 비용 효율이 높기 때문에 식량 실행 계획의 경제학은 더 적은 농업 공급자를 장려한다고 하였으므로 지문의 내용과 반대되는 오답이다.

[12-13]

12 지난 60년 간, 도시화는 부유한 국가들에서보다 덜 ....에서 주로 발생해왔다.

해설 문제의 핵심어구(urbanisation has mainly happened)와 관련된 지문 내용 중 'Since then, urbanisation has primarily occurred in less developed regions'에서 1950년대부터 도시화는 주로 덜 개발된 지역에서 발생해왔다고 하였으므로, **developed regions**가 정답이다. 'primarily occurred'가 'mainly happened'로 paraphrasing되었다.

13 시골 지역에서보다 도시에서 훨씬 더 많이 발생하는 범죄는 .... 절도이다.

해설 문제의 핵심어구(A crime that occurs far more in cities)와 관련된 지문 내용 중 'vehicle theft occurred at a much higher rate in urban areas than in rural areas'에서 차량 절도가 시골 지역보다 도시 지역에서 훨씬 더 높은 비율로 발생했다고 하였으므로, **vehicle**이 정답이다. 'at a much higher rate'가 'far more'로 paraphrasing되었다.

* 각 문제에 대한 정답의 단서는 지문에 문제 번호와 함께 별도의 색으로 표시되어 있습니다.

EXAMPLE   p.88

출생 순서의 영향을 떨쳐버릴 수 있는 여러 다른 요소들 또한 확인되었다. 이들 중 가장 중요한 것 한 가지는 성별이다. 조지아 대학의 Alan Stewart 박사는 [1]반대 성별의 다른 아이가 첫째 아이를 따라 태어나면, 둘째 아이는 첫째 아이에게 그렇게 많은 영향을 받지는 않으며 종종 자신이 첫째로 태어난 아이인 것처럼 행동한다는 것에 주목했다. 출생 간 시간의 범위 또한 출생 순서의 영향을 왜곡시킬 수 있다. [2]비교적 더 적은 기간 차이로 태어난 아이들은 정반대의 역할을 맡을 수 있다. 이것들과 전반적인 기질, 신체 크기의 차이, 그리고 독특성과 같은 다른 요소들을 고려할 때, [3]출생 순서의 영향은 성격 유형을 결정하는 데 매우 믿을 만한 것처럼 보이지는 않는다. 사실, 한 보고서는 오직 15퍼센트의 남자와 23퍼센트의 여자만이 출생 순서와 일치하는 성격을 가졌다는 것을 보여준다.

HACKERS PRACTICE   p.90

1	No	2	Yes	3	No	4	Not given
5	No	6	Yes	7	No	8	Not given
9	Yes	10	No	11	Not given	12	Yes
13	Yes	14	Yes	15	Not given	16	No
17	No	18	Yes	19	Not given	20	No
21	Yes	22	Yes	23	Not given	24	No
25	Yes	26	Not given	27	No	28	No
29	Not given	30	Yes	31	Not given		

1

몇몇 언어학자들은 언어 이해가 학습된 능력이며 그렇기 때문에, 성인은 낯선 언어조차도 어린이보다 더 잘 이해할 수 있다고 믿는다. 이 이론은 시간이 지나면서 우리가 의사소통을 할 때 언어적인 그리고 비언어적인 단서들 모두를 이해하는 능력을 개발시킨다는 개념에 기초한다. 이것은 학습 과정이기 때문에, [1]어린이들이 맥락으로부터 의미를 파악하는 것에 덜 숙련되어 있을 것이라는 사실은 타당하게만 보인다. 하지만, 이것은 사실일 가능성이 낮다. 사실, 독일 빌레펠트 대학의 언어학자들에 의한 최근의 연구는 비록 어린이들이 이야기를 듣는 동안에 시각적 단서를 정확하게 예상하지 못할지라도, 전반적인 언어 이해를 돕기 위해 빠르게 시각적 단서를 이해할 수 있다는 것을 보여주었다. 이것은 그들의 능력이 시간이 지나면서 향상되지 않을 것이라는 것을 의미하는 게 아니라, [2]비청각적 단서로부터 맥락을 결정하는 것이 언어 이해의 기본 요소라는 것을 보여준다.

> **1** 아이들은 맥락으로부터 의미를 알아낼 수 없다.

>> 해설 문제의 핵심어구(Children ~ determine meaning)와 관련된 지문 내용 중 'it seems only logical that children would be less skilled at discerning meaning from context. However, this is unlikely to be true.'에서 어린이들이 맥락으로부터 의미를 파악하는 것에 덜 숙련되어 있을 것이라는 사실은 타당하게만 보이지만 이것은 사실일 가능성이 낮다고 하였으므로, 주어진 문장은 글쓴이의 견해와 일치하지 않음을 알 수 있다. 따라서 정답은 **No**이다.

2 무언의 신호들을 이해하는 것은 인간 언어의 기본적인 측면이다.

> **해설** 문제의 핵심어구(Understanding unspoken signals)와 관련된 지문 내용 중 'determining context from non-auditory clues is a basic element of language comprehension'에서 비청각적 단서로부터 맥락을 결정하는 것이 언어 이해의 기본 요소라고 하였으므로, 주어진 문장은 글쓴이의 견해와 일치함을 알 수 있다. 따라서 정답은 **Yes**이다. 'determining context from non-auditory clues'가 'Understanding unspoken signals'로, 'a basic element'가 'a fundamental aspect'로 paraphrasing되었다.

2

처음 도입되었을 때, 동전은 '상품 화폐'로 알려졌다. 이는 [3]만들어진 재료 때문에 실제 동전이 고유한 금전적인 가치를 가지고 있었다는 것을 의미한다. 현재의 터키인 아나톨리아와 고대 그리스에서 나온 최초의 동전에서는, 이것이 호박금이라는 이름의 금과 은의 자연 합금이었다. 7세기에 이르러, 동전은 중동에서 순금과 순은으로 제조되기 시작했다. 하지만, 이는 결국 바뀌었고 동전은 고유한 가치가 없는 더 저렴한 금속으로 만들어지기 시작했다. 이러한 종류의 동전들은 정부가 가치를 단독으로 정하고 보증했기 때문에 '신용 화폐'라고 불렸다. 이것은 비논리적으로 보일 수도 있기는 하지만, 실제로 여러 가지 이점이 있었다. 아마 이들 중 가장 분명한 것은 귀금속의 가격에 따라 변화하지 않았기 때문에, 통화 가치가 더 안정적으로 남아있었다는 것이다. 뿐만 아니라, 그것은 이 값비싼 자원들을 보존했다. [4]금과 은이 값비쌌던 이유는 희귀함 때문이었고, 따라서 동전을 주조하는 데 그것들을 이용하는 것은 세계의 공급량을 줄였다. 마지막으로, 신용 화폐 체계에서는 그것들을 이루는 금속이 그렇게 값비싼 게 아니었기 때문에, 동전은 속임수에 덜 취약했다. 예를 들어, 동전이 금이나 은으로 만들어졌을 때는, 사람들은 가끔 동전의 가장자리를 깎아냈고 그 값비싼 금속을 가지고 있었다.

3 동전은 만들어진 재료 때문에 본래 고유의 금전적 가치가 없었다.

> **해설** 문제의 핵심어구(no value ~ due to the materials)와 관련된 지문 내용 중 'the actual coin had an inherent monetary value because of the materials of which it was made'에서 만들어진 재료 때문에 실제 동전이 고유한 금전적인 가치를 가지고 있었다고 하였으므로, 주어진 문장은 글쓴이의 견해와 일치하지 않음을 알 수 있다. 따라서 정답은 **No**이다.

4 귀금속은 현재 화폐가 되기에는 너무 희귀하다.

> **해설** 문제의 핵심어구(Precious metals ~ too rare)와 관련된 지문 내용 중 'The reason that gold and silver were valuable was because of their scarcity, so using them for minting coins reduced the world's supply of them.'에서 금과 은이 값비쌌던 이유는 희귀함 때문이었고 따라서 동전을 주조하는 데 그것들을 이용하는 것은 세계의 공급량을 줄였다고 하였지만, 주어진 문장의 내용은 확인할 수 없다. 따라서 정답은 **Not given**이다.

3

오늘날, 지표면의 약 30퍼센트는 삼림지로 덮여 있다. 그러나, 삼림 파괴가 매년 이 비율을 극적으로 감소시키고 있다. 현재, 인간 활동은 매년 그리스의 면적과 거의 동일한 면적인 1,370만 헥타르 이상의 삼림지를 빼앗는다. [5]우리가 목재 수요에 맞추기 위해 벌목을 하고 있다고 추정될 수도 있지만, 더 큰 원인은 사실 농업이다. 지구의 증가하는 인구는 농작물에 대한 수요를 늘려왔고 농부들은 농작물을 심을 수 있는 농지로 개조하기 위해 삼림지를 개벌하기 시작했다.

이는 브라질과 인도네시아와 같은 나라들에서 특히 그러한데, 이곳들에서는 삼림지의 넓은 면적이 콩과 기름 야자 같은 환금 작물을 위한 농지를 목적으로 개간되어 왔다. 이러한 농작물을 위해 사용되는 강도 높은 농법들은 그 문제를 더 악화시킨다. 계속되는 농작물 생산은 토양이 한때 유지할 수 있었던 것처럼 생물의 다양성을 더 이상 유지할 수 없도록 토양으로부터 영양분을 고갈시키는데, 이는 미래에 그것을 삼림지로 되돌리는 것을 거의 불가능하게 만든다. 계속되는 이러한 삼림 소멸은 우리의 환경에 심각한 영향을 미칠 것이다. 나무는 공기 중의 이산화탄소를 제거하고 대기에 물을 되돌려주는 중요한 역할을 한다. [6]만약 숲이 더 악화되도록 용납된다면, 식물과 동물의 생활 주기를 방해하고, 심지어 전 생태계를 사라지게 할 수도 있다. 이런 결과를 피하기 위해서, 우리는 삼림지를 보존하고 우리가 매년 없애는 나무를 대체할 방법을 찾아야만 한다.

5 목재는 벌목을 하는 가장 흔한 이유이다.

> 해설 문제의 핵심어구(Timber ~ most common reason)와 관련된 지문 내용 중 'While it may be assumed that we are cutting down trees to meet our timber needs, the bigger culprit is actually agriculture.'에서 우리가 목재 수요에 맞추기 위해 벌목을 하고 있다고 추정될 수도 있지만 더 큰 원인은 사실 농업이라고 하였으므로, 주어진 문장은 글쓴이의 견해와 일치하지 않음을 알 수 있다. 따라서 정답은 **No**이다.

6 삼림을 개벌하는 것은 생태계를 파괴할 위협이 있다.

> 해설 문제의 핵심어구(destroy ecological systems)와 관련된 지문 내용 중 'If the forests are allowed to further deteriorate, it could ~ eliminate entire ecosystems.'에서 만약 숲이 더 악화되도록 용납된다면 전 생태계를 사라지게 할 수도 있다고 하였으므로, 주어진 문장은 글쓴이의 견해와 일치함을 알 수 있다. 따라서 정답은 **Yes**이다. 'eliminate entire ecosystems'가 'destroy ecological systems'로 paraphrasing되었다.

4

시간이 지나면서, 사람속의 구성원들은 현대 인류의 신체적 특성을 가진 호모 사피엔스 인류의 구성원들인 해부학상 현대 인류로 변하기 위해 많은 진화적 변화를 겪었다. 오늘날, 흔히 과학계에서는 약 20만년 전에 동아프리카에서 초기 호모 사피엔스 인류가 진화했다고 믿는다. 사실, 최초의 해부학상 현대 인류의 화석은 약 19만 5천년 전으로 추정되는 시기에 그곳에서 발견되었다. [7]이 인류의 구성원들은 아프리카 고국 밖으로 서서히 이동했고 6만년 전쯤에는 한 집단이 유라시아와 중동에 정착했다. 이는 그들이 이전에 아프리카를 떠난 또 다른 초기 인류인 네안데르탈인과 접촉하게 했다. 몇몇 과학자들은 이 상호 작용이 두 집단 사이에 폭력적인 충돌을 가져왔는데, 이것이 결국 네안데르탈인의 멸종으로 이어졌다고 믿는다.

그러나, 분리된 진화가 그들의 소멸에 대한 아마 좀더 그럴듯한 설명이다. 공유 유산에도 불구하고, [8]이 두 초기 인류 집단들은 신체적 그리고 지적 양면으로 꽤 다르게 진화했다. 더 북쪽으로부터의 기후에서 보낸 시간 동안, 네안데르탈인은 초기의 해부학상 현대 인류보다 더 크고, 더 강하고, 그리고 추위에 더 익숙해지게 되었다. 다시 말해서, 그들은 신체적으로 새로 도착한 호모 사피엔스보다 우세했을 것이었다. 그러나, 뇌 구조의 차이가 두 인류에 더 큰 영향을 준 것으로 보였다. 고인류학자인 Chris Stringer는 호모 사피엔스가 네안데르탈인보다 추상적이고 창의적인 생각을 만들어내는 뇌의 영역인 전두엽이 더 컸다고 말한다. 이것은 에너지를 절약했던 식품 가공 기술뿐만 아니라 더 효율적인 수렵과 채집 방법을 개발하게 했을 것이다. [9]이러한 더 진보된 기술은 그들에게 네안데르탈인보다 장기적으로 우세하기에 충분한 이점을 주었을 것이고, 그것이 실제로 일어난 일인 것처럼 보인다.

7 근대 인류는 중동으로부터 아프리카로 이주했다.

> 해설 문제의 핵심어구(to Africa from the Middle East)와 관련된 지문 내용 중 'Members of this species gradually migrated out of their African homeland and ~ one group had settled in Eurasia and the Middle East.'에서 이 인류의 구성원들은 아프리카 고국 밖으로 서서히 이동했고 한 집단이 유라시아와 중동에 정착했다고 하였으므로, 주어진 문장은 글쓴이의 견해와 일치하지 않음을 알 수 있다. 따라서 정답은 **No**이다.

8 호모 사피엔스는 그들의 진화상 조상보다 지적으로 우월하다.

> 해설 문제의 핵심어구(intellectually superior)와 관련된 지문 내용 중 'these two groups of early humans had evolved quite differently, both physically and intellectually'에서 네안데르탈인과 호모 사피엔스가 신체적 그리고 지적 양면으로 꽤 다르게 진화했다고는 하였지만, 주어진 문장의 내용은 확인할 수 없다. 따라서 정답은 **Not given**이다.

9 네안데르탈인은 호모 사피엔스보다 기술이 좋지 않았다.

> 해설 문제의 핵심어구(Neanderthals were less skilled)와 관련된 지문 내용 중 'These more advanced skills would have given them enough of an advantage over the Neanderthals to prevail in the long term'에서 이러한 더 진보된 기술은 호모 사피엔스에게 네안데르탈인보다 장기적으로 우세하기에 충분한 이점을 주었을 것이라고 하였으므로, 주어진 문장은

글쓴이의 견해와 일치함을 알 수 있다. 따라서 정답은 **Yes**이다. 'more advanced skills would have given ~ an advantage over the Neanderthals'가 'The Neanderthals were less skilled'로 paraphrasing되었다.

5

표현학은 형태학상의, 혹은 구조상의 유사성에 근거한 생물의 체계적 분류법이다. [10]표면상으로, 표현학은 타당한 분류 방법으로 보이지만, 그것과 관련하여 몇 가지 문제가 있다. 아마 이들 중 가장 중요한 것은 [10]표현적인 분류가 때때로 종들 간의 부정확한 진화 관계를 보여준다는 것이다. 고생물학자들은 표현적인 분류가 실제로는 존재하지 않는 관계를 나타낼 수 있다는 것을 발견했다. 이것은 비슷해 보이는 종들이 밀접하게 관련이 되어 있지는 않지만, 실제로는 유사한 진화 단계에 있을 때 발생할 가능성이 가장 높다. 이런 부정확성은 표현학자들로 하여금 한 생물을 그것의 진화 집단으로부터 분리하게 할 수 있는데, 이는 그 생물이 독특한 진화 적응을 가지기 때문이다. 그것은 또한 유사한 초기 특성을 가진 생물 간의 관계를 잘못 보여주는 것으로 이어질 수 있다. 공룡의 분류는 이 문제들의 좋은 예이다. 우리는 이제 [11]중생대의 새들과 쥐라기와 백악기의 몇몇 공룡들이 매우 유사한 골격 구조를 가지고 있다는 것을 알고 있는데, 이는 그들이 진화의 연결 고리를 공유한다는 것을 나타낸다. 하지만, [11]공룡은 일반적으로 더 멀리 관련되어 있는 종들인 도마뱀과 악어와 함께 파충류로 일괄하여 다뤄진다. 이것에 대한 이유들 중 하나는 새의 독특한 진화 적응인 깃털의 존재이다. 우리가 전통적으로 공룡이 깃털을 가지고 있었다고 믿지 않았기 때문에, 표현학자들은 다른 신체적 특성을 근거로 하여 그것들을 부정확하게 분류했다. 이 모든 것은 표현적인 분류의 가장 고유한 문제들을 보여주는데 그것이 전적으로 표현학자들의 주관적인 관찰을 통해서만 행해진다는 것이다. 형태학상의 유사성에는 계층에 따른 분류가 없기 때문에, [12]연구원들은 주관적인 관찰에 근거하여 최종적인 결론을 내려야만 한다.

10 표현학은 현재 진화를 연구하는 데 있어 가장 신뢰받는 방법이다.

해설 문제의 핵심어구(Phenetics ~ the most trusted method)와 관련된 지문 내용 중 'Although, on its surface, phenetics seems to be a valid classification method, there are some problems with it.'과 'phenetic classifications sometimes show inaccurate evolutionary relationships between species'에서 표면상으로 표현학은 타당한 분류 방법으로 보이지만 그것과 관련하여 몇 가지 문제가 있으며, 표현적인 분류가 때때로 종들 간의 부정확한 진화 관계를 보여준다고 하였으므로, 주어진 문장은 글쓴이의 견해와 일치하지 않음을 알 수 있다. 따라서 정답은 **No**이다.

11 공룡들은 파충류와 조류 모두로 분류되어야 한다.

해설 문제의 핵심어구(classified as both reptiles and birds)와 관련된 지문 내용 중 'birds ~ and some dinosaurs ~ have very similar skeletal structures'와 'dinosaurs are generally lumped in with lizards and alligators ~ as reptiles'에서 새들과 몇몇 공룡들이 매우 유사한 골격 구조를 가지고 있으나 공룡은 일반적으로 도마뱀과 악어와 함께 파충류로 일괄하여 다뤄진다고는 하였지만, 주어진 문장의 내용은 확인할 수 없다. 따라서 정답은 **Not given**이다.

12 연구자들은 동일한 증거에 대해 서로 다른 결론을 내릴 수 있다.

해설 문제의 핵심어구(Researchers can come to different conclusions)와 관련된 지문 내용 중 'researchers must make the ultimate decision based on their subjective observations'에서 연구원들은 주관적인 관찰에 근거하여 최종적인 결론을 내려야만 한다고 하였으므로, 주어진 문장은 글쓴이의 견해와 일치함을 알 수 있다. 따라서 정답은 **Yes**이다. 'make ~ decision'이 'come to ~ conclusions'로 paraphrasing되었다.

6

오늘날, 고령자 3명당 1명이 여러 가지 형태의 치매로 고통받고 있다. 심신을 쇠약하게 하는 이 건강 문제를 해결하기 위해, 많은 환자들과 그들의 가족들이 대체 치료에 의지하고 있다. 이들 중 하나는 음악 치료이다. 본질적으로, 음악 치료는 노래하는 것, 연주하는 것, 또는 음악을 듣는 것을 토대 전통적인 치료로서 기능한다.

[13]이러한 치료 유형이 치매 사례들을 고칠 수는 없겠지만, 환자들이 기억을 떠올리고 그들이 자주 느끼는 불안을 덜도록 도와줄 수 있다. 신경학자 Oliver Sacks는 [14]음악을 듣는 것이 기억을 자극하고 인지 능력을 증가시키는 감정을 불러일으키기 때문에 이것이 발생한다고 믿는다. 이에 대한 주요 이유들 중 하나는 음악이 우리 삶의 모든 시기에서 큰 역할을 한다는 것이다. 의식적으로 그것에 대해 생각

하지는 않을 수 있지만, 우리는 자주 음악을 특정 활동이나 사건과 연관 짓는다. [15]그 환자의 삶의 한 부분에서 중요했던 음악을 연주함으로써, 오랫동안 잊혀졌던 기억들이 떠오를 수 있다. 이것은 영화에서 들었던 재즈 노래나 환자의 결혼식에서의 노래와 같이 특정 시기 동안 유명했거나 특별한 행사에서 연주되었던 음악을 연주할 때 발생할 수 있다. 음악 치료는 또한 환자들이 더 오랫동안 자립하도록 도울 수 있다. 음악과 일상적인 활동들을 짝지음으로써, 환자들은 음악과 그것의 패턴을 활동과 연관 짓는 것을 학습할 수 있다. 이것은 그들이 그 활동을 훨씬 더 오랫동안 기억할 수 있도록 돕는다.

아마 음악 치료에 대한 가장 흥미로운 발견은 [16]그것이 감정을 통제하는 능력을 잃어버린, 말을 하지 않는 말기 환자들에게도 효과가 있다는 것이다. 이 환자들은 그들 자신을 표현하지 못하기 때문에, 다른 사람들과는 매우 다른 요구를 가지고 있다. 이는 그들이 갇혀 있다고 느끼거나 좌절하는 것을 야기할 수 있다. 종종, 이는 불안과 분열성 행동으로 이어질 수 있다. 노래하기, 춤추기 또는 리듬 연주와 같은 음악 치료 활동을 도입함으로써, 환자들의 관심의 방향이 바뀔 수 있으며 그들은 음악을 통해 자신을 표현할 방법을 찾을 수 있게 될 것인데, 이는 그들을 진정시킬 수 있다. 놀랍게도, 이러한 효과는 거의 즉각적으로 나타나며 음악 치료 시간이 끝난 후에도 계속된다. 음악 치료사이자 연구원인 Linda A. Gerdner 박사에 의한 연구는 치료 시간의 적어도 한 시간 후에도 효과가 관찰될 수 있다는 것을 보여주었다.

13 음악 치료는 치매를 치유할 수 없다.

> 해설 문제의 핵심어구(curing dementia)와 관련된 지문 내용 중 'While this type of treatment will not cure cases of dementia'에서 음악 치료 유형이 치매 사례들을 고칠 수는 없다고 하였으므로, 주어진 문장은 글쓴이의 견해와 일치함을 알 수 있다. 따라서 정답은 **Yes**이다. 'will not cure'가 'incapable of curing'으로 paraphrasing되었다.

14 음악을 듣는 것은 환자들의 두뇌 활동을 증가시킬 수 있다.

> 해설 문제의 핵심어구(increase brain activity)와 관련된 지문 내용 중 'listening to music evokes emotions that ~ increase cognitive ability'에서 음악을 듣는 것이 인지 능력을 증가시키는 감정을 불러일으킨다고 하였으므로, 주어진 문장은 글쓴이의 견해와 일치함을 알 수 있다. 따라서 정답은 **Yes**이다. 'evoke emotions that ~ increase cognitive ability'가 'increase brain activity'로 paraphrasing되었다.

15 재즈 음악은 환자들이 과거를 기억하는 데 있어 특히 효과적이다.

> 해설 문제의 핵심어구(Jazz music)와 관련된 지문 내용 중 'By playing music that was important ~ long forgotten memories maybe recalled. This could occur when playing music that was popular during a certain time period ~ like a jazz song heard in a movie'에서 중요했던 음악을 연주함으로써 오랫동안 잊혀졌던 기억들이 떠오를 수 있는데, 이것이 영화에서 들었던 재즈 노래와 같이 특정 시기 동안 유명했던 음악을 연주할 때 발생할 수 있다고는 하였지만, 주어진 문장의 내용은 확인할 수 없다. 따라서 정답은 **Not given**이다.

16 말을 하지 못하는 환자들은 음악 치료의 도움을 받지 못한다.

> 해설 문제의 핵심어구(Patients who cannot speak)와 관련된 지문 내용 중 'it even works with non-verbal, late-stage patients who have lost the ability to control their emotions'에서 음악 치료가 감정을 통제하는 능력을 잃어버린, 말을 하지 않는 말기 환자들에게도 효과가 있다고 하였으므로, 주어진 문장은 글쓴이의 견해와 일치하지 않음을 알 수 있다. 따라서 정답은 **No**이다.

7

문자의 출현

문자의 기원을 이해하기 위해서는, 한때 유명했던 언어와 문화에 대한 두 가지 이론이 틀렸음을 밝힐 필요가 있다. 첫째로, [17]언어는 많은 학자들이 제시해온 것처럼 하나의 원형에서 유래된 것이 아니다. 그러한 견해는 주로 언어의 기원에 대한 성경의 해석에서 비롯되었으며 문자 체계가 고대 메소포타미아에서 생겨났고, 그 다음에 전 세계로 퍼져나가 발전했다고 주장했다. 더욱이, [18]진화의 생물학적 이론을 언어 발달에도 적용한 19세기 사회학자들은 문자에 공통된 조상이 있을 뿐 아니라 문자가 진화적인 계층 구조를 나타낸다고 보았는데, 이것은 알파벳 문자들을 표의 문자나 음절 문자 체계보다 우위에 두었다. 고대 세계의 언어학적 역사의 맥락에서, 그러한 관점은 유럽과 근동의 문화가 아시아, 아프리카, 혹은 중앙아메리카의 문화보다 더 많이 발전된 것으로 묘사했다. 장대한 건축, 예술, 법률, 그리고 사회 기반 시설을 갖춘, 문화적 탁월함이 풍부한 제국들이 알파벳이 아닌 문자를 쓰는 문명에 의해 건설되었다는 사실을 고려할 때, [18]이보다 더 진실에서 거리가 먼 이야기는 없다.

이제 학자들은 문자의 출현이 유목 생활 방식에서 더 지속적인 농업 방식으로의 변화와 동시에 일어난 것으로 보인다는 것에 동의한다. 사람들이 식량을 재배하고 가축을 돌보고 있었기 때문에, 재고와 소유물을 기록하는 방법을 개발하는 것이 필요해졌다. [19]또한 비옥한 초승달 지대에서뿐만 아니라, 아시아와 중앙아메리카의 고대 사회 안에서도 서로 다른 문자 형태가 발달했다는 것과 이 문명들 중 어떤 것도 그 당시에 서로 접촉하지 않았다는 것에도 동의한다. 이런 지리적 지역들 중, 아마도 이미 기원전 8000년경에, 최초의 문자가 수메르의 비옥한 초승달 지대에서 발생했을 가능성이 가장 높다. 고대 수메르인들은 본래 양, 곡식의 수량, 기름 단지, 그리고 다른 상품들을 나타내기 위해 점토로 만든 작은 삼각형, 구체, 그리고 원뿔과 같은 상징물들을 사용했다. 기본적으로, 상징물의 모양이 표현되고 있는 단어의 뜻을 전달했다. 마침내, 수메르인들은 거래를 기록하기 위해, 도장을 사용하는 것처럼, 상징물을 부드러운 점토 판에 찍기 시작했다. 훨씬 이후인, 기원전 3100년경에, [20]수메르인들은 숫자를 발명했는데, 이는 물체의 상징을 물체의 개수로부터 분리해낸 것이었고, 이는 문자와 수학이 함께 발전했을 것이라는 사실을 보여준다. 한때 고대 세계에서 가장 큰 도시였던 우루크 지방의 고고학적 발굴은 수메르의 문자가 상형 문자에서 표의 문자로 서서히 발전했음을 보여주는데, 이는 몇몇 상징들이 상징 그 자체보다는 개념을 나타냈음을 의미한다. 이 시점에, 문자는 이미 단순히 정보를 전송하는 것을 넘어서는 도구로 발전하고 있었다. 그것은 생각을 전달하고, 지식을 공유하고, 역사를 기록하는 수단이 되고 있었다.

17 언어의 기원에 관한 성경의 설명은 정확하다.

> **해설** 문제의 핵심어구(The Bible's account)와 관련된 지문 내용 중 'languages are not descended from a single prototype, as many scholars have suggested. That view largely derived from a Biblical interpretation of the origin of language'에서 언어는 많은 학자들이 제시해온 것처럼 하나의 원형에서 유래된 것이 아니며 그러한 견해는 주로 언어의 기원에 대한 성경의 해석에서 비롯되었다고 하였으므로, 주어진 문장은 글쓴이의 견해와 일치하지 않음을 알 수 있다. 따라서 정답은 **No**이다.

18 알파벳을 가진 문화들이 다른 문화들보다 더 발달한 것은 아니었다.

> **해설** 문제의 핵심어구(Cultures with alphabets)와 관련된 지문 내용 중 '19th century sociologists ~ viewed writing as ~ exhibiting an evolutionary hierarchy, which placed alphabetical scripts above ideographic or syllabic writing systems'와 'Nothing could be further from the truth'에서 19세기 사회학자들은 문자가 진화적인 계층 구조를 나타낸다고 보았으며 이것은 알파벳 문자들을 표의 문자나 음절 문자 체계보다 우위에 두었는데, 이보다 더 진실에서 거리가 먼 이야기는 없다고 하였으므로, 주어진 문장은 글쓴이의 견해와 일치함을 알 수 있다. 따라서 정답은 **Yes**이다. 'placed ~ above'가 'more advanced'로 paraphrasing되었다.

19 아시아의 문자 체계는 중동의 것들보다 덜 기술적이었다.

> **해설** 문제의 핵심어구(Asian writing systems)와 관련된 지문 내용 중 'It is also agreed that different forms of writing developed not only in the Fertile Crescent, but also within the ancient societies of Asia'에서 또한 비옥한 초승달 지대에서뿐만 아니라 아시아의 고대 사회 안에서도 서로 다른 문자 형태가 발달했다고는 하였지만, 주어진 문장의 내용은 확인할 수 없다. 따라서 정답은 **Not given**이다.

20 수메르에서, 문자는 수학과 별도로 발달했다.

> **해설** 문제의 핵심어구(In Sumer, mathematics developed)와 관련된 지문 내용 중 'the Sumerians invented numerals ~ suggesting that writing and mathematics could have evolved together'에서 수메르인들은 숫자를 발명했는데 이는 문자와 수학이 함께 발전했을 것이라는 사실을 보여준다고 하였으므로, 주어진 문장은 글쓴이의 견해와 일치하지 않음을 알 수 있다. 따라서 정답은 **No**이다.

본성과 양육: 어떤 것이 우리를 더 많이 형성하는가?

인간 감정 연구로 향하는 두 가지 주요 주제는 본성과 양육이다. 생물학적 결정론자들은 감정이 본성에 의해 결정되며 내재적으로 발달한다고 믿는다. 이 관점에 따르면, 개인의 유전자는 시간이 지나면서 개인이 어떻게 행동하고 변화할지에 영향을 미친다. 한편, 사회적 결정론자들은 감정이 양육에 의해 형성된다고 믿는데, 이는 환경이 감정 발달에서 주요한 역할을 한다는 것을 의미한다. 그들에게는, 육아, 가난, 교육, 그리고 폭력에 대한 노출과 같은 변수들은 아이의 정서 상태에 영구적으로 영향을 줄 수 있다. 그렇다면, 어떤 것이 더 큰 역할을 하는가?

사회적 결정론자들의 주요 주장은 경험에 의한 요소들로만 설명될 수 있는 중요한 차이들이 성장하는 아이들의 심리적 그리고 행동적 패턴에서 발생할 수 있고 실제로 발생한다는 것이다. 그들은, 어떤 사람이 특정한 방식으로 태어난다는 가정이 부적절한 행동에 대한 즉각적인 방어를 제공하며 인간의 행동으로부터 인간의 책임을 분리한다고 주장한다. ²¹아이의 가정 환경, 그 또는 그녀에게 주어진 기회, 그리고 그 아이가 어떻게 길러졌는지가 성장하여 어떤 성인이 될 것인지에 대해 어느 정도 요인으로 포함된다고 받아들이는 것은 타당하다. 그러나, 사회적 결정론자들의 관점은 ²²만약 그 또는 그녀의 환경적 상황이 변한다면 근본적인 기질도 변할 것임을 암시하는데, 이는 항상 사실인 것은 아니다. 결국, 연구 결과들은 많은 환경적 상황에 대한 우리의 정서적 반응을 좌우하는 근본적인 특성에 관한 한, 유전자가 주목을 받는다는 것을 시사한다.

생물학적 접근에 대한 증거는 서로 다른 문화에서 자란 사람들의 공유되는 감정 반응에서 발견될 수 있다. 1976년 저서 '언마스크, 얼굴 표정 읽는 기술'을 위해, 신경심리학자 폴 에크만과 웰레스 프리센은 표정에 관한 광범위한 비교 문화 연구를 수행했다. 에크만과 프리센은 파푸아뉴기니의 고립된 부족을 취재했고 그들에게 세계 다른 지역 사람들의 사진을 보여주었다. 심리학자들은 참여자들이 분명하게 특정한 감정의 표정을 구별할 수 있었을 뿐만 아니라 그 표정이 나타날 수 있는 상황을 묘사할 수도 있었다는 것을 알아냈다. 이것은 저자들이 ²³그 감정들의 신체적 표현뿐만 아니라, 여섯 가지 기본적인 인간 감정(분노, 혐오, 공포, 행복, 슬픔, 놀라움)들이 어떤 환경에서 성장하는지와 관계없이 사람들 사이에 보편적이라는 결론을 내리게 했다.

쌍둥이에 대한 연구에서의 최근 증거는 또한 본성이 우리의 감정 발달에 영향을 미치는 데 있어 양육보다 더 큰 역할을 한다고 시사했다. Timothy Bates 교수에 의한 에든버러 대학의 연구에서, 이란성 쌍둥이와 일란성 쌍둥이 800쌍 이상이 그들의 성격 특성을 평가하기 위해 일련의 질문을 받았다. 마침내, 정확히 똑같은 유전 정보를 공유하는 일란성 쌍둥이들이 유전 정보가 공유되지 않는 이란성 쌍둥이보다 같은 성격 특성을 지닐 가능성이 두 배 이상이라는 것이 밝혀졌다. 형제자매의 각 쌍이 같은 가정 환경과 부모를 공유했다는 것을 고려할 때, 연구원들은 사람들이 어떻게 행동하는지에 대해 DNA가 환경적 요인보다 더 큰 영향을 미쳤다는 결론을 내렸다. 이러한 생각을 더 나아가 입증한 것은 다른 형제자매들과 함께 입양된 아이들에 대한 수많은 연구이다. 대부분은, ²⁴그 아이가 입양되었을 때 유아였다고 할지라도, 그 또는 그녀의 성격에 대한 가족의 영향은 종종 사실상 무시해도 될 정도라는 것을 시사한다.

---

21 개인 환경의 특정한 측면들은 개인이 어떻게 성장하는지에 영향을 미친다.

> 해설 문제의 핵심어구(Certain aspects of one's environment)와 관련된 지문 내용 중 'It is reasonable to accept that a child's home environment, the opportunities he or she is given, and how the child is raised factor into the sort of adult that child grows up to be to some degree.'에서 아이의 가정 환경, 그 또는 그녀에게 주어진 기회, 그리고 그 아이가 어떻게 길러졌는지가 성장하여 어떤 성인이 될 것인지에 대해 어느 정도 요인으로 포함된다고 받아들이는 것은 타당하다고 하였으므로, 주어진 문장은 글쓴이의 견해와 일치함을 알 수 있다. 따라서 정답은 **Yes**이다. 'factor into the sort of adult that child grows up to be'가 'affect how one grows up'으로 paraphrasing되었다.

22 익숙하지 않은 환경이 항상 아이의 성격을 바꾸지는 않을 것이다.

> 해설 문제의 핵심어구(An unfamiliar environment)와 관련된 지문 내용 중 'the underlying character of a child will change if his or her environmental circumstances do, which is not always the case'에서 만약 그 또는 그녀의 환경적 상황이 변한다면 근본적인 기질도 변할 것이라는 것은 항상 사실인 것은 아니라고 하였으므로, 주어진 문장은 글쓴이의 견해와 일치함을 알 수 있다. 따라서 정답은 **Yes**이다. 'environmental circumstances'가 'environment'로, 'underlying character of a child'가 'child's character'로 paraphrasing되었다.

23 아이가 성장할 때 감정 표현들은 여전히 같은 상태로 남는다.

> 해설 문제의 핵심어구(Emotional expressions remain the same)와 관련된 지문 내용 중 'six basic human emotions ~ are universal among people no matter which environment they grow up in'에서 여섯 가지 기본적인 인간 감정들이 어떤 환경에서 성장하는지와 관계없이 사람들 사이에 보편적이라고는 하였지만, 주어진 문장의 내용은 확인할 수 없다. 따라서 정답은 **Not given**이다.

24 가족과의 교류는 아이의 성격에 엄청난 변화를 야기할 것이다.

> 해설 문제의 핵심어구(Family interactions)와 관련된 지문 내용 중 'even if the child is an infant when he or she is adopted, the family's effect on his or her personality is often practically negligible'에서 그 아이가 입양되었을 때 유아였다고 할지라도 그 또는 그녀의 성격에 대한 가족의 영향은 종종 사실상 무시해도 될 정도라고 하였으므로, 주어진 문장은 글쓴이의 견해와 일치하지 않음을 알 수 있다. 따라서 정답은 **No**이다.

9

조수의 엄청난 에너지를 이용하는 것

증가하고 있는 인구 통계학적 압박과 기후 변화에 대한 환경적 우려는 실현 가능한 대체 에너지원의 전 세계적 연구에 대한 자극이 되어왔다. 깨끗하고, 풍부하고, 재생 가능한 수력은 의지할 수 있는 확실한 자원이다. 그러나, [25]과거에도 그래왔던 것처럼, 대규모의 수력 발전 댐을 짓는 것은 현재 사용 중인 수력 발전력 시설이 다수의 대단히 파괴적인 생태적 사회적 문제들을 야기하는 것으로 알려져 있기 때문에 더 이상 이상적인 해결책이 아니다. 하지만 오늘날 연구가 최소한의 영향으로 깨끗한 에너지를 발생시키기 위해 조류의 놀라운 힘을 이용하는 것에 주력하고 있기 때문에 수력에 대한 모든 희망을 잃은 것은 아니다.

사실, 근본적인 기술은 오늘날 가동되고 있는 조력 발전소에서 분명히 나타나는 것처럼 이미 이용 가능하다. 한 가지 좋은 예는 세계 최초 조력 발전소인 프랑스의 La Rance이다. La Rance는 보인데, 이는 근본적으로 하구에 지어진 매우 큰 댐이라는 것을 의미한다. 수력 발전 시설처럼 물을 필요할 때까지 저장해두기보다는, La Rance의 물은 댐을 통하여 흐르고 밀물 때마다 유역에 모인다. 그 후에, 썰물이 되자마자, 유역에 있는 물은 방출되고 터빈을 통과해 빠져나가 전기를 발생시킨다. La Rance에 있는 댐이 여전히 현지 생태계에 잠재적 위협이 되고 있기는 하지만, 이 방식에 의한 전력 생산은 대단히 믿을 만하다. 조력이 중력과 계속 진행 중인 지구의 움직임, 즉 바뀔 가능성이 없는 힘에 의해 발생된다는 점에서 조수의 간만과 더 나아가, 언제 전기가 생산될 수 있는지를 정확하게 예측하는 것이 가능하다.

그런 기술의 환경적 영향이 줄어들지 않는 한 절대 실현될 수 없을지도 모르는 엄청난 가능성을 조류가 가지고 있다는 것을 인식하고 있기 때문에, 오늘날 기술자들은 댐을 사용하지 않는 수력 발전 기술을 개발하기 위해 작업하고 있다. 그들이 찾아낸 한 가지 해결책은 수중 조류를 이용하기 위해 비교적 해안에서 가까운 해저에 터빈을 설치하는 것이다. 에너지를 생산하기 위해, 수중 터빈은 파도가 오르내림에 따라 회전할 것이고, 전선을 통해 육지의 발전소에 전기를 보낼 것이다. 이 방법은 그것이 얼마 되지 않는 환경 피해를 야기할 것임을 증거들이 암시하기 때문에 매우 유망하다. 예를 들어, 이 기술은 댐에 의해 자주 야기되는 수생 생물체에 대한 피해를 일으키지 않을 것이다. 더욱이, [26]조류 발전 지역이 수중에 있을 것이기 때문에, 풍력 발전 지역의 흔한 불만 사항인 보기 흉하다는 것이나 소음 방해를 야기하지 않을 것이다.

조류 발전 지역을 위한 적절한 기반 시설을 건설하는 초기 비용이 높은 것은 사실이다. 그러나, [27]연구는 설비의 유지와 교체가 드물게 필요할 것이라는 것을 시사하며, 이는 이 대단히 효율적인 에너지원에 장기적으로 투자할 가치가 있게 만든다. 궁극적으로, 조력의 미래가 무엇일지 알 수 있는 방법은 없지만, 한 가지는 분명하다. 우리의 가장 풍부하고 무궁무진한 자원인 바다는 엄청난 가능성을 가지고 있다.

25 수력 발전 댐들은 심각한 환경 문제들을 야기할 수 있다.

> 해설 문제의 핵심어구(Hydroelectric dams)와 관련된 지문 내용 중 'building large-scale hydroelectric dams ~ is no longer an ideal solution as the hydropower facilities currently in use are known to cause a number of devastating ecological and social issues'에서 대규모의 수력 발전 댐을 짓는 것은 현재 사용 중인 수력 발전력 시설이 다수의 대단히 파괴적인 생태적 사회적 문제들을 야기하는 것으로 알려져 있기 때문에 더 이상 이상적인 해결책이 아니라고

하였으므로, 주어진 문장은 글쓴이의 견해와 일치함을 알 수 있다. 따라서 정답은 **Yes**이다. 'devastating ecological ~ issues'가 'serious environmental problems'로 paraphrasing되었다.

26 과학자들은 에너지 생산의 수단으로 바람보다 조력이 더 효과적일 것이라고 예상한다.

> 해설 문제의 핵심어구(more effective than wind)와 관련된 지문 내용 중 'because tidal farms would be located underwater, they would not be an eyesore or cause a noise disturbance – both common complaints about wind farms'에서 조류 발전 지역이 수중에 있을 것이기 때문에 풍력 발전 지역의 흔한 불만 사항인 보기 흉하다는 것이나 소음 방해를 야기하지 않을 것이라고는 하였지만, 주어진 문장의 내용은 확인할 수 없다. 따라서 정답은 **Not given**이다.

27 유지보수 비용은 조력을 비효율적으로 만든다.

> 해설 문제의 핵심어구(cost of maintenance)와 관련된 지문 내용 중 'research suggests that the maintenance and the replacement of equipment would be required infrequently, making it worthwhile in the long run to invest in this extremely efficient energy source'에서 연구는 설비의 유지와 교체가 드물게 필요할 것이라는 것을 시사하며, 이는 이 대단히 효율적인 에너지원에 장기적으로 투자할 가치가 있게 만든다고 하였으므로, 주어진 문장은 글쓴이의 견해와 일치하지 않음을 알 수 있다. 따라서 정답은 **No**이다.

🔟

내향적인 사람과 외향적인 사람: 서로 다른 성격 설명하기
인간 성격 이론의 기본 개념 뒤의 과학

1923년 저서 '심리유형'에서, 분석심리학자 카를 융은 내향적인 사람과 외향적인 사람, 두 가지의 인간 유형을 구별했다. 전자는 수줍음을 많이 타고, 세심하고, 사회적으로 염려하는 사람으로 서술된 반면 후자는 대부분의 시간을 다른 사람들과 함께 보내는 것을 즐기는 사교적인 부류로 묘사되었다. ²⁸두 성격 유형에 대한 융의 초기 분류가 전반적으로 정확했고 오랜 세월에도 불구하고 건재해왔지만, 내향성과 외향성에 대한 근본적인 원인은 한 번도 과학적으로 분석되지 않았다. 최근에서야 현대 심리학 연구자들이 외향-내향 범위에 대한 더 미묘하며 사실에 기반을 둔 해석을 제시하기 시작했다.

현대의 연구자들은 외향적인 사람의 뇌가 실제로 사회적 상호 작용 동안에 뇌의 쾌락 중추를 통제하는 신경 전달 물질인 도파민을 상당량 분비한다는 것을 발견했다. 따라서, 외향적인 사람의 뇌 활동은 예를 들어, 그 사람에게 미소가 지어질 때 눈에 띄게 증가한다. 그리고 사회적 참여로 보상을 받기 때문에, 외향적인 사람은 미소 짓는 것, 농담하는 것, 그리고 친절히 대하는 것과 같은 매력적인 행동을 계속해서 보여줌으로써 그것을 찾아내야 한다고 느낀다. 근본적으로, 우리는 이제 한때 외향적인 사람의 특성으로 여겨지던 것들이, 실제로는, 외향적인 사람들이 받고 싶어 하는 화학적 보상을 얻기 위해 사용하는 수단이라는 것을 알고 있다.

이 수단들은 표면상으로는 긍정적인 것처럼 보일 수도 있지만, 단점이 없는 것은 아니다. 사회적 보상을 얻기 위해서는 시간과 에너지에 대한 높은 투자가 필요한데, 이는 덜 사회 지향적인 일에는 거의 에너지를 남겨주지 않는다. 몇몇 연구는 외향성이 환경을 탐구하려는 더 높은 경향과 관련 있기 때문에 외향적인 사람은 내향적인 사람보다 심지어 신체 활동으로부터 다칠 가능성이 더 높다는 것을 보여주었다. 다른 연구들은 특히 그것이 사회적 보상을 초래할 것이라면 ³⁰내향적인 상대보다 충동적으로 소비하려는 의향이 훨씬 더 강하기 때문에 외향적인 사람들이 형편없는 금융설계사라는 것을 보여준다.

그러므로, 내향적인 사람이 외향적인 사람으로부터 범위의 반대쪽에 있다는 것을 고려하면, 그것은 그들이 어떤 사회적 보상도 경험하지 않으며 그러므로 다른 사람들과 교류하고 싶은 욕구가 없다는 것을 의미하는가? 그렇지는 않지만, 사회적 경험들에서 오는 보상 가치가 내향적인 사람들에게 현저히 더 적기 때문에, 왜 그들이 종종 다른 사람들을 찾고자 하는 충동이 없는지는 이해하기 쉽다. 과학은 아직 왜 그들의 사회적 보상이 적은지에 대한 만족스러운 설명을 찾지 못했지만, 몇몇 전문가들은 인류의 진화가 그것과 관련이 있다고 믿는다. 한 이론은 복잡한 사회 생활을 갖는 것이 살아남기 위해 본질적으로 외향적이어야 했던 우리의 초기 조상들 사이에서 지능, 창의력, 언어, 그리고 심지어 의식의 진화를 일으켰다고 가정한다. 내향적인 사람의 출현은 일단 생존이 더 이상 다른 사람의 관심과 도움을 얻는 것에 의존하지 않게 되고, 더 많은 시간을 지적인 활동에 쓰는 것이 선택 사항이 되었을 때 가능해졌다.

비록 내향적인 사람이 사회적 상황에서 상당량의 도파민 분비를 겪지 않기는 하지만, 지적이고 창의적인 일에 에너지를 쏟아부을 때는 그 반대가 사실이다. ³¹그렇다면, 세계의 많은 천재들과 위대한 발명가들이 내향적인 사람들이었다는 것은 놀라운 일은 아니다. 결국 복잡한 수학, 과학, 또는 철학의 어려운 문제를 연구하는 데는 상당한 혼자만의 시간이 든다. 그러므로 외향적인 사람이 지금까지 우리 인류의 진화에서 중요한 역할을 해왔을지도 모르지만, 내향적인 사람의 기여는 분명히 간과되어서는 안 된다.

28 내향적인 사람과 외향적인 사람의 초기 분류는 상당히 바뀌었다.

> **해설** 문제의 핵심어구(original categorisation)와 관련된 지문 내용 중 'Jung's early classification of the two personality types ~ has stood the test of time'에서 두 성격 유형에 대한 융의 초기 분류가 오랜 세월에도 불구하고 건재해왔다고 하였으므로, 주어진 문장은 글쓴이의 견해와 일치하지 않음을 알 수 있다. 따라서 정답은 **No**이다.

29 융의 동료 심리학자들은 내향성과 외향성에 대한 그의 이론을 한 번도 반박하지 않았다.

> **해설** 문제의 핵심어구(Jung's fellow psychologists)와 관련된 내용은 지문에서 찾을 수 없다. 따라서 정답은 **Not given**이다.

30 외향적인 사람들은 때로 부주의한 행동에 참여한다.

> **해설** 문제의 핵심어구(careless behaviour)와 관련된 지문 내용 중 'extroverts are poor financial planners since they are far more willing than their introvert counterparts to spend impulsively'에서 내향적인 상대보다 충동적으로 소비하려는 의향이 훨씬 더 강하기 때문에 외향적인 사람들이 형편없는 금융설계사라고 하였으므로, 주어진 문장은 글쓴이의 견해와 일치함을 알 수 있다. 따라서 정답은 **Yes**이다. 'to spend impulsively'가 'careless behaviour'로 paraphrasing 되었다.

31 내향적인 사람들은 일반적으로 외향적인 사람들보다 분석적인 사고에 더 강하다.

> **해설** 문제의 핵심어구(Introverts are ~ better at analytical thinking)와 관련된 지문 내용 중 'It's no surprise ~ that many of the world's geniuses and great inventors have been introverts. It takes significant time in solitude to work through complex mathematical, scientific, or philosophical puzzles'에서 세계의 많은 천재들과 위대한 발명가들이 내향적인 사람들이었다는 것은 놀라운 일이 아니며 복잡한 수학, 과학, 또는 철학의 어려운 문제들을 연구하는 데는 상당한 혼자만의 시간이 든다고는 하였지만, 주어진 문장의 내용은 확인할 수 없다. 따라서 정답은 **Not given**이다.

HACKERS TEST

p.104

1 No	**2** No	**3** Yes	**4** Not given
5 Yes	**6** Not given	**7** No	**8** Yes
9 Yes	**10** D	**11** C	**12** target language
13 linguistic ability			

다섯 번째 언어 능력
문화는 흔히 언어 강좌들에서 배제되지만, 일부는 그것이 새로운 언어를 익히는 것의 가장 중요한 측면이라고 주장한다

언어 학습자들과 강사들은 어떤 언어로든 의사소통하기 위해서는 말하기, 듣기, 읽기와 쓰기 네 가지 능력이 필요하다는 것을 알고 있다. 언어에 대한 이러한 '의사소통 중심 교수법'은 오랫동안 제2언어 학습 환경의 주요 기반이 되어 왔다. [1]이 교수법에서, 문화에 대한 몇몇 정보가 언어 학습자들에게 제공될 수 있으나, 네 가지 능력과 기초적인, 대체로 문자상의, 의사소통을 압도적으로 강조한다. 그러나, 최근에, 점점 더 많은 전문가들이 언어와 관련된 문화를 완전히 이해하는 것의 중요성을 강조함에 따라, 문화적 의사소통이라는 다섯 번째 언어 능력이 더욱 강조되고 있다. 사실, 이 '상호문화적 교수법'은 이제 너무 필수적인 것으로 간주되어서 학습자가 어떤 언어이든 진정한 구사력을 얻기를 바란다면 피할 수 없다.

언어에 대한 상호문화적 교수법은 Louise Damen의 '문화 학습: 언어 교실의 다섯 번째 관점'의 출간 이후 처음으로 언어 전문가들의 관심을 끌었다. 그 출판물에서, 그녀는 상호문화적 인식과 상호문화적 능력 개발 둘 다의 필요성에 대해 약술했고, 이 두 가지 목표를 포괄적 용어인 '실용 민족지학'에 포함시켰다. [10]Damen의 상호문화적 교수법이 암시하는 것은 모국어 능력과 목표어의 능숙도는 가르침에 있어 불충분하다는 것과 교육자들이 숙달된 관찰자이면서 효과적인 상호문화적 의사소통을 촉진할 수 있는 숙련된 문화 가이드 같은 역할을 더 수행해야만 한다는 것이다.

제2언어 학습의 문화적 맥락에서, 유용한 학습을 돕는 전형은 이해 정도를 관광객, 생존자, 이민자, 그리고 시민의 네 가지 수준으로 분류하는 4단계의 언어 습득 모델이다 (Acton and Walker de Felix, 1995). [2]이 모델에서는, 어떤 사람이든 만약 언어의 무수한 문화적 측면에 대한 철저한 이해를 하고 있지 않다면 시민 수준의 의사소통 능력을 얻는 것은 불가능하며, [12]그러한 성취는 기꺼이 다른 문화에 성공적으로 동화되고자 하고 목표어의 문화로부터의 '사회적 거리'가 극단적이지 않은 문화에서 온 의욕적인 학생들에게만 가능할 것으로 예상된다 (Schumann, 1978).

따라서, [3]'큰 네 가지' 언어 능력만으로는 외국인 화자가 제2언어를 완전히 익히거나 원어민들의 사회로 받아들여지는 데 항상 충분하지 않다는 것은 말할 것도 없다. 문화적 감성과 인식, 그리고 자신의 가치, 기준, 태도에 대한 주의 깊은 성찰 없이, [13]한 사람의 언어적 능력만으로는 그들이 '외부인'이라는 인식을 막을 수 없을지도 모른다. '내부인'의 지위를 얻기 위해서, 그 또는 그녀는 문화적 차이를 식별하고 수용하는 것뿐만 아니라 그것들을 인정하고 소중하게 여기는 것도 배워야 한다.

하지만 교실에서 어떤 문화를 가르쳐야 하는가? 단순함과 편리함을 위해서, [4]연구원들은 덜 공식적인, 일상에서 접할 수 있는 문화 요소들로부터 더 공식적인 문화 요소들을 구별하기 위해 'Big C'와 'little c' 문화를 언급한다. Big C 문화는 그 사회의 예술, 문학, 그리고 과학적 업적에 공헌한 위대한 역사적 인물뿐만 아니라 그 사회의 사회적, 정치적, 그리고 경제적 관습에 해당하는 반면 (외국어 교육 프로젝트 국가 표준, 1996), little c 문화는 그 문화의 구성원들이 의복, 주택, 음식, 교통 등을 포함하여 일상생활에 필요하다고 생각하는 행동 양식의 전부를 나타낸다.

그것을 바라보는 또 다른 방법은 [5]전자는 상류 사회의 '엘리트' 문화를 나타내지만, 후자는 평범한 사람들의 관심사와 행동에 해당한다는 것이다. 그러나 시민들이 사람들과 인사를 하고, 일을 하거나, 쇼핑하는 것과 같은 일상적인 일들에 시간을 쓴다고 할지라도, [6]그럼에도 불구하고 그들의 삶에 직접적으로 영향을 미치는 사회적 계층화와 경제 정책과 같은 더 큰 사안들에도 관심이 있기 때문에, [5]이것은 공통 부분이 전혀 없다는 것을 의미하지는 않는다. [7]일반적으로 little c 문화는 계속해서 변화하는 성질 때문에 언어 교육과정에서 가장 결여되어 있고 가장 포함시키기 어려운 경우이다.

그러나 [8]문제가 있는 사안이 통칭 '다섯 번째 능력' 그 자체에도 존재하는데, 이것은 문화가 언어 학습에 필수적인 것이라기보다는 '추가된' 요소라는 것을 시사한다. Kramsch (1993)는 문화가 가장 예상치 못했을 때 우수한 언어 학습자들을 불안하게 할 준비가 된 채 바로 처음부터 항상 배경에 있다고 주장하는데, 이는 그들이 어렵게 얻은 의사소통 능력의 한계를 분명하게 하며, 주변 세상을 이해하는 그들의 능력에 이의를 제기한다. 의사소통의 필수적이고 피할 수 없는 부분으로서 문화에 대한 이 자명한 교수법은 언어 교육의 중요성과, 언어 교육에 내재하는 도전을 강조한다.

따라서, 몇몇 교육자들은 문화를 다섯 번째 능력보다는 첫 번째 능력으로 보아야 한다고 생각한다 (Tomlinson 1999). 문화를 제1위로 두는 것이 고귀한 목표이긴 하지만, [9]그렇더라도 이것이 교육과정에서 쉽게 우선순위가 되거나 교사들이 일반적으로 이행할 수 있는 것이라고 가정하는 것은 희망에 찬 생각이다. 언어 교육과정은 현 상황에서 이미 꽉 차 있으며, 언어 교사들은 보통 어느 학생이나 학생 집단과도 매우 한정된 교육 시간을 가지고 있다. 많은 교육자들이 이 부담을 처리하도록 교육받지 않았고, 그러므로, [11]문화를 언어 교육과정의 중심에 두기 위해 현직 교육연수와 능력 개발이 필요할 것이다. 핵심은 교실에서 어떤 '다섯 번째 능력' 시간이든 '현실 세계 속' 목표어의 문화에서 학생들이 스스로를 몰두시키면서 보내는 대단히 더 많은 시간에 의해 보충되어야 할 것이라는 사실이다.

어휘 **communicative approach** phr. 의사소통 중심 교수법 **assimilate** v. 완전히 이해하다, 동화되다 **intercultural** adj. 상호문화적, 문화 간의 **command** n. 구사력 **umbrella term** phr. 포괄적 용어 **ethnography** n. 민족지학 **target language** phr. 목표어 **heuristic** adj. 학습을 돕는 **myriad** adj. 무수한 **acculturate** v. 다른 문화에 성공적으로 동화되다 **correspond** v. 해당하다, 부합하다 **mundane** adj. 일상적인 **stratification** n. 계층화 **epithet** n. 통칭, 별칭 **hard-won** adj. 어렵게 얻은 **axiomatic** adj. 자명한 **primacy** n. 제1위, 최고 **prioritise** v. 우선순위를 결정하다 **as it is** phr. 현 상황에서 **in-service training** phr. 현직 교육연수 **immerse** v. 몰두시키다, 열중시키다

1 의사소통 중심 교수법은 언어의 문화적 요소를 무시해왔다.

해설 문제의 핵심어구(The communicative approach ~ ignored the cultural component)와 관련된 지문 내용 중 'In this approach, some information about culture may be provided to language learners'에서 의사소통 중심 교수법에서 문화에 대한 몇몇 정보가 언어 학습자들에게 제공될 수 있다고 하였으므로, 주어진 문장은 글쓴이의 견해와 일치하지 않음을 알 수 있다. 따라서 정답은 **No**이다.

2 4단계 모델에서, 개인은 문화적 지식 없이도 언어 실력이 유창해질 수 있다.

해설 문제의 핵심어구(the four-stage model)와 관련된 지문 내용 중 'Under this model, it is impossible for any person to acquire a citizen level of communicative competence if they do not have a thorough understanding of the myriad cultural aspects of language'에서 4단계 모델에서는 어떤 사람이든 만약 언어의 무수한 문화적 측면에 대한 철저한 이해를 하고 있지 않다면 시민 수준의 의사소통 능력을 얻는 것은 불가능하다고 하였으므로, 주어진 문장은 글쓴이의 견해와 일치하지 않음을 알 수 있다. 따라서 정답은 **No**이다.

3 네 가지 언어 능력을 학습하는 것은 유창한 의사소통을 위해 충분하지 않다.

해설 문제의 핵심어구(the four language skills ~ not sufficient)와 관련된 지문 내용 중 'the 'big four' language skills alone are not always enough for a foreign speaker to fully master a second language'에서 '큰 네 가지' 언어 능력만으로는 외국인 화자가 제2언어를 완전히 익히는 데 항상 충분하지 않다고 하였으므로, 주어진 문장은 글쓴이의 견해와 일치함을 알 수 있다. 따라서 정답은 **Yes**이다. 'not enough ~ to fully master a second language'가 'not sufficient for fluent communication'으로 paraphrasing되었다.

4 Big C 문화와 little c 문화의 분류는 세계의 국가들에서 서로 다르다.

해설 문제의 핵심어구(categorisation of Big C and little c culture)와 관련된 지문 내용 중 'researchers refer to 'Big C' and 'little c' culture to distinguish the more formal elements of a culture from those that are encountered in less formal, everyday situations'에서 연구원들은 덜 공식적인, 일상에서 접할 수 있는 문화 요소들로부터 더 공식적인 문화 요소들을 구별하기 위해 'Big C'와 'little c' 문화를 언급한다고는 하였지만, 주어진 문장의 내용은 확인할 수 없다. 따라서 정답은 **Not given**이다.

5 Big C 문화와 little c 문화는 서로 다른 개념을 대표함에도 불구하고 관련이 없는 것은 아니다.

해설 문제의 핵심어구(Big C and little c culture are not unconnected)와 관련된 지문 내용 중 'the former represents the 'elite' culture of high society, whereas the latter corresponds to the interests and activities of ordinary people. This does not mean there is no overlap at all'에서 전자는 상류 사회의 '엘리트' 문화를 나타내고 후자는 평범한 사람들의 관심사와 행동에 해당하지만 이것은 공통 부분이 전혀 없다는 것을 의미하지는 않는다고 하였으므로, 주어진 문장은 글쓴이의 견해와 일치함을 알 수 있다. 따라서 정답은 **Yes**이다. 'there is no overlap'이 'unconnected'로 paraphrasing 되었다.

6 언어를 공부하는 학생들은 정치적인 문제에 관심을 더 가져야 한다.

해설 문제의 핵심어구(more interested in political issues)와 관련된 지문 내용 중 'they are ~ interested in bigger issues, such as social stratification and economic policy'에서 시민들이 사회적 계층화와 경제 정책과 같은 더 큰 사안들에도 관심이 있다고는 하였지만, 주어진 문장의 내용은 확인할 수 없다. 따라서 정답은 **Not given**이다.

7 Big C 문화는 교육과정에 포함하는 것이 가장 어렵다.

> 해설 문제의 핵심어구(hardest to include in curricula)와 관련된 지문 내용 중 'It is generally the case that little c culture is the most absent in language curricula and the most difficult to include'에서 일반적으로 little c 문화는 언어 교육과정에서 가장 결여되어 있고 가장 포함시키기 어려운 경우라고 하였으므로, 주어진 문장은 글쓴이의 견해와 일치하지 않음을 알 수 있다. 따라서 정답은 **No**이다.

8 문화를 '다섯 번째 능력'으로 분류하는 것은 그것이 교육에 있어 덜 중요하다는 것을 암시한다.

> 해설 문제의 핵심어구(Labelling culture a 'fifth skill')와 관련된 지문 내용 중 'a problematic issue exists with the epithet 'fifth skill' itself, which suggests that culture is an 'added on' element to language learning rather than a fundamental one'에서 문제가 있는 사안이 통칭 '다섯 번째 능력' 그 자체에도 존재하는데, 이것은 문화가 언어 학습에 필수적인 것이라기보다는 '추가된' 요소라는 것을 시사한다고 하였으므로, 주어진 문장은 글쓴이의 견해와 일치함을 알 수 있다. 따라서 정답은 **Yes**이다. 'added on element ~ rather than a fundamental one'이 'less important'로 paraphrasing되었다.

9 언어 강의에서 문화를 우선순위로 두는 것은 항상 가능한 것은 아니다.

> 해설 문제의 핵심어구(Prioritising culture in a language course)와 관련된 지문 내용 중 'it is ~ hopeful thinking to assume that it can be easily prioritised in a curriculum'에서 문화가 교육과정에서 쉽게 우선순위가 될 수 있다고 가정하는 것은 희망에 찬 생각이라고 하였으므로, 주어진 문장은 글쓴이의 견해와 일치함을 알 수 있다. 따라서 정답은 **Yes**이다. 'curriculum'이 'language course'로, 'hopeful thinking'이 'not always possible'로 paraphrasing되었다.

[10-11]

10 Louise Damen의 상호문화적 교수법에 대한 관점은 −라고 암시한다.
    A 대부분의 언어 프로그램에서 상호문화적 의사소통이 부재한다
    B 대부분의 모국어 사용자들은 그들 자신의 문화를 가르칠 능력이 없다
    C 문화와 언어는 똑같이 중요하지만 개별적으로 가르쳐야 한다
    D 언어 교사들은 언어 자체를 넘어서는 전문성을 가져야 한다

> 해설 문제의 핵심어구(Louise Damen)와 관련된 지문 내용 중 'The implication of Damen's intercultural approach is that native language skills and competence in the target language are insufficient for instruction and that educators must function more like experienced cultural guides'에서 Damen의 상호문화적 교수법이 암시하는 것은 모국어 능력과 목표어의 능숙도는 가르침에 있어 불충분하다는 것과 교육자들이 숙련된 문화 가이드 같은 역할을 더 수행해야만 한다는 것이라고 하였으므로, 보기 **D** language teachers must have expertise beyond the language itself가 정답이다. 'function ~ like experienced cultural guides'가 'have expertise beyond the language itself'로 paraphrasing 되었다.

11 글쓴이에 따르면, 교실에서 문화를 우선순위로 두기 위해 무엇이 필요한가?
    A 더 적은 학생 대 교사 간 비율
    B 교사들의 더 긴 근무 시간
    C 교육자들을 위한 추가적인 연수
    D 새로운 교육 자료의 개발

> 해설 문제의 핵심어구(making culture a priority)와 관련된 지문 내용 중 'in-service training ~ would be necessary to put culture at the centre of the language curriculum'에서 문화를 언어 교육과정의 중심에 두기 위해 현직 교육연수가 필요할 것이라고 하였으므로, 보기 **C** additional training for educators가 정답이다. 'in-service training'이 'training for educators'로 paraphrasing되었다.

[12-13]

12 ....와 비슷한 문화에서 온 학생들은 성공할 수 있는 가장 좋은 기회를 가진다.

> **해설** 문제의 핵심어구(Students from a similar culture)와 관련된 지문 내용 중 'such an achievement is likely only for highly motivated students who are ~ from a culture that is not extreme in its 'social distance' from the culture of the target language'에서 그러한 성취는 목표어의 문화로부터의 '사회적 거리'가 극단적이지 않은 문화에서 온 의욕적인 학생들에게만 가능할 것으로 예상된다고 하였으므로, **target language**가 정답이다. 'culture that is not extreme in its 'social distance''가 'a similar culture'로 paraphrasing되었다.

13 제2외국어 사용자들은 오로지 ....에만 기반해서는 내부자로 여겨질 수 없다.

> **해설** 문제의 핵심어구(to be an insider)와 관련된 지문 내용 중 'a person's linguistic ability alone may not prevent the perception that they are an 'outsider''에서 한 사람의 언어적 능력만으로는 그들이 '외부인'이라는 인식을 막을 수 없을지도 모른다고 하였으므로, **linguistic ability**가 정답이다. 'linguistic ability alone may not prevent the perception that they are an 'outsider''가 'can not appear to be an insider based solely on linguistic ability'로 paraphrasing되었다.

* 각 문제에 대한 정답의 단서는 지문에 문제 번호와 함께 별도의 색으로 표시되어 있습니다.

EXAMPLE
p.114

출생 순서의 영향에 대한 수년 간의 연구와 그것을 뒷받침하는 것처럼 보이는 많은 가족 일화에도 불구하고, 그것은 일반적으로 받아들여지지 않는다. 몇몇 과학자들은 그 영향을 '증명한' 연구들의 유효함을 부인한다. [1]그들은 연구에 활용할 표준 가족을 찾는 것은 거의 불가능하다고 지적한다. 사회경제적, 민족적, 종교적 그리고 다른 차이들로 인해, 그러한 실험에 적절한 자료를 제공할 가족을 찾는 것은 불가능하다. 게다가, 출생 순서에 대한 기존의 관점을 반박하는 사례들이 매우 많다. 예를 들어, 첫째로 태어난 아이들은 '타고난 지도자'라고 알려져 있지만, 세계 정치 지도자들에 대한 연구는 많은 지도자들이 중간에 태어났거나 마지막으로 태어난 사람들이었다는 것을 증명했다 (Hudson, 1990).

HACKERS PRACTICE
p.116

1 timber	2 4,000 tonnes	3 larvae	4 mangroves
5 gallery	6 vents	7 solar radiation	8 epidermal layer
9 daytime	10 spoked	11 axle	12 landmarks
13 50 years	14 destination	15 yaw drive	16 data
17 rotational speed	18 power station	19 floating platforms	20 depth
21 surface	22 hydrocarbons	23 steps	24 prescription
25 attitude	26 experts	27 interests	28 worse
29 research	30 infrastructure	31 (extreme) weather	32 (strictly) controlled
33 (direct) sunlight	34 local	35 precipitation (rates)	

1

역사적 건물을 연구할 때, 사람들은 건축 자재의 명확한 발전을 확인할 수 있다. [1]중세 시대 이전에, 목재는 유럽에서 가장 널리 사용되는 건축 자재였지만, 대부분의 주요 건물들에서 후에 석재로 대체되었다. 산업 시대 이전에 구조 건축에서는 금속의 사용조차 제한적이었다. 그 당시, 금속은 심미적인 매력이 한정적이어서 주로 다리와 온실에 사용되었다. 하지만, 인공 자재에 대한 대중의 인식은 바뀌었고 기술의 진보는 금속 가공 비용을 낮추었는데, 이는 그것이 더 많이 사용되는 결과를 가져왔다. 건축에서 처음 일반적으로 사용된 금속은 주철이었는데, 이것은 석재와 같이 장식 모양으로 만들어질 수 있었다. 건축가들은 심지어 주철을 건물의 골조를 짓는 데 사용하기 시작했다. 유감스럽게도, 이 특정한 금속은 장력이 낮아서 이 건물들 중 일부는 붕괴되었다. 이 문제를 해결하기 위해, 건축업자들은 연철에 의지했고 마침내는 강철에 의지했다. 19세기에 인공 자재에 대한 대중의 의견이 계속 변화함에 따라, 콘크리트 사용이 용인되었다. 강철과 콘크리트의 조합은 믿기지 않을 정도로 견고했으며 도시의 풍경을 완전히 바꾼 더 높은 건물의 건축이 가능하도록 했다. [2]세계에서 가장 높은 건물인 두바이의 부르즈 칼리파 건설은 4천 톤의 강철을 33만 입방미터의 콘크리트 그리고 5만 5천 톤의 보강 강철 철근과 결합하여 사용했다.

건축 자재의 역사

- 유럽에 있는 대부분의 중세 이전의 건물은 건설에 1 ....을 이용했다.
- 석재 건설은 중세 시기에 인기가 있어졌다.
- 인공 자재는 산업 시대 이전에 널리 이용되지 않았다.
- 세계에서 가장 높은 건물을 건설하는 것은 33만 입방미터의 콘크리트와 2 ....의 강철을 이용했다.

---

1 해설 문제의 핵심어구(pre-medieval buildings)와 관련된 지문 내용 중 'Before the medieval period, timber was the most widely used building material in Europe'에서 중세 시대 이전에 목재는 유럽에서 가장 널리 사용되는 건축 자재였다고 하였으므로, **timber**가 정답이다. 'Before the medieval period'가 'pre-medieval'로 paraphrasing되었다.

2 해설 문제의 핵심어구(world's highest skyscraper)와 관련된 지문 내용 중 'Construction of the tallest building in the world ~ used 4,000 tonnes of steel'에서 세계에서 가장 높은 건물의 건설은 4천 톤의 강철을 사용했다고 하였으므로, **4,000 tonnes**가 정답이다. 'tallest building in the world'가 'world's highest skyscraper'로 paraphrasing되었다.

2

만약 당신이 열대 산호초를 따라 스노클링을 하거나 다이빙을 한 적이 있다면, 그때 당신은 아마 수면 아래에 있는 동안 규칙적으로 오도독하는 소리를 들었을 것이다. 이것은 형형색색의 비늘돔들이 앵무새와 같은 부리로 암초 표면의 조류를 물어 뜯고 긁어서 제거할 때 만들어진다. 이 흥미로운 물고기들의 생활 주기는 알을 낳기 위해 외해로 이동할 때 시작되는데, 그곳에서 알들은 부화한다. 이후에 ³그들은 어린 시절을 바다의 플랑크톤들 속에서 유충으로 보낸다. ⁴그 후 청소년기에 그들은 맹그로브로 이동하고 그 다음 포식자들로부터 숨고 청소할 암초로 이동한다. 흥미롭게도, 이 성장 과정 내내, 모든 비늘돔은 담갈색의 암컷이다. 이것은 비늘돔이 인접적 자웅동체이기 때문인데, 이는 그들이 나이가 들면서 성별이 바뀐다는 것을 의미한다. 삶의 말기에 접어들면, 어린 암컷 비늘돔은 더 색이 다채로운 수컷으로 바뀐다. 그 다음에 이러한 수컷들은 이제 더 어린 암컷 비늘돔 무리를 모아서 모두가 암컷인 또 다른 비늘돔 유충 집단을 낳기 위해 산란한다. 비늘돔의 더욱 흥미로운 측면은 암초의 생태에 있어 그것의 중요성이다. 세계자연보전연맹의 연구원들에 따르면, 비늘돔의 청소 활동이 없다면, 암초들은 곧 조류로 들끓어서 죽게 될 것이다.

비늘돔 생활 주기

산란
어른 비늘돔은 알을 낳기 위해 외해로 이동한다.

처음 단계
비늘돔은 바다의 플랑크톤 산지에 3 ....로서 들어간다.

청소년 단계
청소년기의 비늘돔은 암초로 이동하기 전에 4 ....에서 시간을 보낸다.

말기 단계
어른 비늘돔은 암컷 무리와 함께 암초에 산다.

---

3 해설 문제의 핵심어구(ocean's plankton fields)와 관련된 지문 내용 중 'their early life is spent as larvae in the ocean's plankton population'에서 비늘돔은 어린 시절을 바다의 플랑크톤들 속에서 유충으로 보낸다고 하였으므로, **larvae**가 정답이다. 'early life is spent as larvae in the ocean's plankton population'이 'enter the ocean's plankton fields as larvae'로 paraphrasing되었다.

정답·해석·해설 HACKERS **IELTS** READING

3

짐바브웨의 Eastgate 센터는 현대 중층 상업 건축물의 모범 사례일 것이다. 그것은 기계적으로 작동되는 에어컨이 없도록 건축되었는데, 이는 그 복합 건물의 소유주들에게 약 3백만 파운드의 절약을 가져왔다. 놀랍게도, 이 건물은 불편할 만큼 덥거나 춥지 않다. 이것은 건축가가 설계할 때 생체 모방 공정을 사용했기 때문이다. 생체 모방은 자연 과정에 대한 인간의 연구와 복잡한 인간의 문제를 해결하기 위해 그것을 모방하는 것을 포함한다. 이 경우, 디자이너 Mick Pearce는 흰개미의 언덕에서 영감을 받았다. 나무를 먹이로 삼는 이 해충은 높이 25미터에 달할 수 있는 거대한 언덕을 짓는다. 하지만, 대부분의 흰개미들은 언덕의 위쪽에 살지 않으며, [5]언덕 밑부분의 좁고 긴 방에 산다. 위쪽의 높은 구조물은 기본적으로 큰 굴뚝이다. 그것은 따뜻한 공기를 위쪽으로 이동시키는 중심 통로를 포함한다. 그리고 나서 이 따뜻한 공기는 언덕 꼭대기 근처의 구멍을 통해 빠져나간다. [6]밑부분의 방사 통풍구는 바람을 끌어들이고 언덕의 밑부분에서 공기를 식힘으로써 이 작용을 강화하는데, 이는 구조물 내에서 대류 순환을 발생시킨다. 이 과정을 이해한 후에, Pearce는 Eastgate 센터의 건물들을 중심 통로를 둘러싼 일련의 방들로 설계했다. 각 방에는 흰개미의 언덕에서와 같이 열기 방출을 야기하는 통로를 향한 그리고 건물 외벽을 향한 배관이 있다. 지속적인 공기 흐름을 만들며 중앙 통로로 공기를 끌어들이는 환풍구는 이 시스템을 돕는다. 이 시스템을 통해서, Eastgate 센터의 사무실들은 바깥 온도와 상관없이 약 섭씨 23도의 안정적인 내부 온도를 가진다.

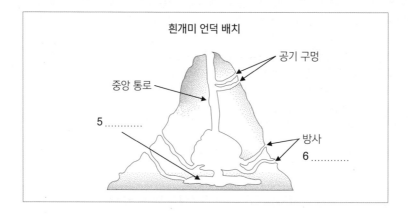

흰개미 언덕 배치

공기 구멍

중앙 통로

5 ....

방사

6 ....

5 해설 문제의 위치와 관련된 지문 내용 중 'they live in a gallery at the base of it'에서 흰개미들은 언덕 밑부분의 좁고 긴 방에 산다고 하였으므로, **gallery**가 정답이다.

6 해설 문제 주변의 핵심 내용(radial)과 관련된 지문 내용 중 'Radial vents at the base intensify this action by capturing the wind and cooling the air at the base of the mound'에서 밑부분의 방사 통풍구는 바람을 끌어들이고 언덕의 밑부분에서 공기를 식힘으로써 이 작용을 강화한다고 하였으므로, **vents**가 정답이다.

4

초원 생태계는 평평한 지대나 부드럽게 경사진 굽이치는 산, 그리고 초본 식물의 지배로 특징지어진다. 나무, 관목, 그리고 다른 목본은 사실상 초원에는 없고, [7]태양 복사열과 거친 바람으로부터의 피난처가 거의 없다. 초원은 대체적으로 적당한 연평균 강수량을 갖지만, 여름에는 때때로 심각한 가뭄이 나타난다. 따라서, 식물이 초원 생태계에서 번성하기 위해서는, 계절적으로 건조한 조건을 견뎌야 한다. 이러한 생태계에서 살아남기에 적당한 초본 중에는 초원 잔디가 있는데, 이들은 생존을 위한 몇 가지의 적응기전을 가지고 있다.

초원 잔디의 잎은 폭이 다양하지만, 대부분 길고, 얇은 잎이다. [8]잎의 상피층에는 기공이라고 불리는 작은 구멍이 있는데, 그것은 이산화탄소를 들여보내고 산소를 내보내기 위해 열리거나, 수분을 보유하기 위해 닫힐 수 있다. 이산화탄소는 식물 광합성에 필수적이기 때문에, 기공은 가스 교환을 위해 넓혀진 상태로 있어야 한다. 그러나, 잎 내부의 기실은 수증기로 가득 차 있는데, 이는 구멍이 닫혀있지 않으면 증발하며 건조한 환경에서 위기를 야기한다. 이 문제를 극복하기 위해, 초원 잔디는 낮과 밤을 구별하도록 진화했다. [9]낮 동안, 잔디는 수분 손실을 최소화하기 위해 기공을 닫은 상태로 유지한다. 그리고 공기가 더 차가운 저녁에는 호흡을 위해 기공을 확장한다.

초원 잔디의 생존 방법

혹독한 초원 환경
- 몇 개의 작은 언덕이 있는 평평한 땅
- 7 ....과 거친 바람으로부터 제한된 보호
- 매년 약간의 강수, 그러나 여름은 가뭄을 야기함

초원 잔디의 진화적 적응
- 기공:
  - 잎의 8 ....에 있는 작은 구멍
- 이산화탄소를 들이고 산소를 내보내기 위해 열려 있거나, 혹은 수분을 보존하기 위해 닫혀 있음
- 기공은 수분 손실을 줄이기 위해 9 .... 동안에 닫혀 있음
- 식물 기공은 더 시원한 밤 공기에는 열림

---

7 해설 문제의 핵심어구(high winds)와 관련된 지문 내용 중 'there is very little shelter from the solar radiation and harsh breezes'에서 태양 복사열과 거친 바람으로부터의 피난처가 거의 없다고 하였으므로, **solar radiation**이 정답이다. 'very little shelter'가 'limited amount of protection'으로, 'harsh breezes'가 'high winds'로 paraphrasing되었다.

8 해설 문제의 핵심어구(Tiny holes)와 관련된 지문 내용 중 'On the epidermal layer of the leaves are small holes'에서 잎의 상피층에는 작은 구멍이 있다고 하였으므로, **epidermal layer**가 정답이다. 'small holes'가 'tiny holes'로 paraphrasing 되었다.

9 해설 문제의 핵심어구(The stomata remain closed)와 관련된 지문 내용 중 'In the daytime, the grasses keep their stomata shut'에서 낮 동안 잔디는 기공을 닫은 상태로 유지한다고 하였으므로, **daytime**이 정답이다. 'keep their stomata shut'이 'The stomata remain closed'로 paraphrasing되었다.

5

기원전 2000년경, 당대의 전투를 바꾼 새로운 발명품인, 말이 끄는 전차가 출현했다. 이 가벼운 마차는 기마 궁사들에게 그들의 적을 공격할 수 있는 평평한 단을 제공했다. 이 시기 전에는 빨리 전진하고자 했던 군대들은 말을 탔지만, 이는 안장과 등자가 발명되지 않았기 때문에 번거로웠다. 이것은 말을 모는 것과, 말 위에 매달리는 것, 그리고 화살을 쏘는 것을 동시에 하는 것을 어렵게 했다. 전차들은 이것을 훨씬 용이하게 해주었다. 가장 기본적으로, 전차는 한 필 또는 그 이상의 말의 뒤에서 끌어지는 바퀴가 달린 단이었다. 아마도 이러한 전투차량 중 가장 유명한 것은 고대 이집트인들에 의해 사용되었을 것이다. 전차를 발명하지는 않았지만, 이집트인들은 유용성을 향상시키기 위해 그것들을 개조했다. 가장 큰 변화는 [10]기존의 원판 바퀴 대신 새롭게 발명된 살이 있는 바퀴를 사용하여 전차의 전체적인 무게를 줄인 것이었다. 이것은 말들이 전차를 더 빠르게 끄는 것을 용이하게 했다. 하지만, 속도는 이집트인들에 의해 시행된 변화들 중 유일한 장점은 아니었다. 그들은 또한 굴레가 있는 안장의 사용과 기본적인 설계의 변경을 통해 전차를 훨씬 더 쉽게 제어할 수 있도록 만들었다. 굴레가 있는 안장은 미끄러지는 것을 방지하고 통제력을 증가시키기 위해 말의 가슴과 배를 가로지르는 가죽 조각과 함께 말 등에 놓은 안장과 같은 안장 받침이었다. 굴레가 있는 안장에 긴 나무 막대로 연결된 기수의 받침 또한 다시 설계되었다. 기수를 전차의 차축에 더 가깝게 옮김으로써, 기수들에게 더 안정적으로 되었는데, 이는 적들을 더 쉽게 조준하고 쏠 수 있도록 만들었다. 마지막으로, [11]이집트인들은 전차의 단에 대한 마찰을 방지하기 위해 차축을 금속으로 감쌌다. 이것은 차량의 움직임을 향상시켰을 뿐 아니라, 더 견실하게 만듦으로써 차량에 대한 손상 또한 줄였다. 유감스럽게도, 이것들 중 어느 개선도 전차의 설계에 내재된 다른 문제점들을 수정하지는 못했으며, 기원전 1500년경 말을 탄 기병 부대가 대부분의 군사 기지에서 그것들을 대체했다. 하지만, 그것들은 추후 몇백 년 간 경주 차량으로 사용되며 남았다.

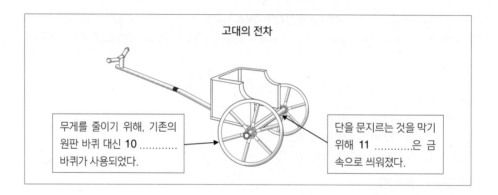

고대의 전차

무게를 줄이기 위해, 기존의 원판 바퀴 대신 10 .... 바퀴가 사용되었다.

단을 문지르는 것을 막기 위해 11 ....은 금속으로 씌워졌다.

10 해설 문제의 핵심어구(instead of ~ disk wheels)와 관련된 지문 내용 중 'lightening the overall weight of the chariot by utilising newly invented spoked wheels rather than the traditional disk wheel'에서 기존의 원판 바퀴 대신 새롭게 발명된 살이 있는 바퀴를 사용하여 전차의 전체적인 무게를 줄인 것이라고 하였으므로, **spoked**가 정답이다. 'lightening the overall weight'가 'to reduce weight'로 paraphrasing되었다.

11 해설 문제의 핵심어구(covered with metal)와 관련된 지문 내용 중 'the Egyptians covered the axle with metal to prevent friction against the chariot's platform'에서 이집트인들은 전차의 단에 대한 마찰을 방지하기 위해 차축을 금속으로 감쌌다고 하였으므로, **axle**이 정답이다. 'prevent friction against'가 'stop ~ rubbing'으로 paraphrasing되었다.

6

매년, 수백만 마리의 새들이 날씨의 변화로 인해 먹이를 찾는 것이 어려워지거나 잠재적 짝짓기 상대를 찾아야 하는 시기에 한 지역에서 다른 지역으로 옮기는 연례 이동을 한다. 이 여정들 중 일부는 상당히 단순하며 근처 지역으로 이동하는 것만을 포함하지만, 다른 여정들은 10,000킬로미터 이상에 걸칠 수 있다. 이렇게 먼 거리를 이동하기 위해, 새들은 항해하기 위한 강한 능력을 갖춰야만 한다. 오늘날, 새들은 항해를 위한 세 가지 방법을 가지고 있다고 여겨진다. 조종, 방위 측정, 그리고 정확한 항해이다. 조종은 우리가 가장 흔히 길을 찾는 방법이기 때문에, 이것들 중 가장 이해하기 쉽다. 간단히 말하자면, 그들은 쉽게 알아볼 수 있는 하나의 눈에 띄는 지형지물에서 다음 것으로 이동한다. ¹²우리가 슈퍼마켓에서 집으로 갈 때 특정한 지형 다음에 왼쪽으로 돌아야 한다는 것을 아는 것과 매우 유사하게, 새들은 호수와 같은 다음 지형에 도착할 때까지 남북으로 흐르는 강과 같은 지형지물을 따라가야 한다는 것을 안다. 하지만, 이것은 문제를 일으킬 수 있다. 새가 강을 바라볼 때, 어느 방향을 향해야 하는가? 이 문제에 대응하기 위해, 새들은 방위 측정이라는 두 번째 방법을 사용할 수 있는데, 이는 방향을 알아내기 위한 단서를 활용하는 것을 수반한다. ¹³지난 50년 동안, 과학자들은 방향을 확인하기 위해 태양과 별들을 나침반처럼 사용하는 새들을 관측해왔다. 심지어 일부 새들은 자신의 위치를 알기 위해 지구의 자기장을 감지하고 활용할 수 있는 것으로 밝혀졌다. 마지막 방법은 ¹⁴정확한 항해인데, 이는 새들이 최종 목적지를 정하고 그들의 현재 위치에서 그곳으로 가는 길을 찾도록 한다. 과학자들에게, 이것은 조류 항해의 가장 매력적인 면인데, 그 이유는 그것이 다른 두 가지 방법과 같이 간단히 설명될 수 없기 때문이다. 가장 기본적으로, 정확한 항해는 새들이 다른 두 가지 시스템의 문제점을 보완할 수 있는 방법이다. 예를 들어, 새가 정남쪽으로 날아가는 법이나 특정한 지리적 지형지물을 따라가는 법만 안다면 길을 잃기 매우 쉬울 것이다. 만일 폭풍우가 새를 서쪽 먼 곳으로 밀어 붙였다면, 남쪽으로 날아가는 것은 새를 올바른 목적지로 데려다주지는 않을 것이다. 또한, 만일 지형지물이 마지막 이동 후에 파괴되었다면 새는 무엇을 해야 할 것인가? 정확한 항해에 사용되는 방법이 발견되지는 않았지만, Thomas Collett 교수와 같은 몇몇 연구자들은 새들이 '인지 지도'를 가지고 있다고 생각한다. 그들은 새들이 길을 찾기 위해서 조종과 방위 측정 그리고 그들의 생체 시계로부터 얻은 단서들과 함께, 이 지도를 사용할 수 있다고 생각한다.

조류의 항해 방법

조종	방위 측정	정확한 항해
새들은 마치 인간이 일상 심부름을 하는 것과 같이 그들이 항해하기 위해 알아보는 12 ....을 찾는다.	지난 13 .... 간 새들이 태양이나 별의 위치 같은 단서를 이용한다는 것이 밝혀졌다.	새들은 현재의 위치와 최종 14 .... 사이에 항로를 정한다.

12 해설 문제의 첫 행(Piloting)을 통해 문제가 조종에 대한 내용임을 알 수 있다. 문제의 핵심어구(Birds look for ~ they recognise to navigate by)와 관련된 지문 내용 중 'Much like we know to turn left after a certain feature ~ birds know to follow landmarks'에서 우리가 특정한 지형 다음에 왼쪽으로 돌아야 한다는 것을 아는 것과 매우 유사하게 새들은 지형지물을 따라가야 한다는 것을 안다고 하였으므로, **landmarks**가 정답이다. 'birds know to follow'가 'Birds look for'로 paraphrasing되었다.

13 해설 문제의 첫 행(Orientation)을 통해 문제가 방위 측정에 대한 내용임을 알 수 있다. 문제의 핵심어구(the location of the sun or stars)와 관련된 지문 내용 중 'Over the course of the last 50 years, scientists have observed birds using the sun and stars as compasses to check their direction.'에서 지난 50년 동안 과학자들은 방향을 확인하기 위해 태양과 별들을 나침반처럼 사용하는 새들을 관찰해왔다고 하였으므로, **50 years**가 정답이다. 'using the sun and stars as compasses'가 'using cues such as the location of the sun or stars'로 paraphrasing되었다.

14 해설 문제의 첫 행(True Navigation)을 통해 문제가 정확한 항해에 대한 내용임을 알 수 있다. 문제의 핵심어구(Birds set a course)와 관련된 지문 내용 중 'true navigation, which requires the bird to determine its final destination and find a way to it from their current location'에서 정확한 항해가 새들이 최종 목적지를 정하고 그들의 현재 위치에서 그곳으로 가는 길을 찾도록 한다고 하였으므로, **destination**이 정답이다. 'determine ~ and find a way'가 'set a course'로 paraphrasing 되었다.

7

풍력

풍력은 대개 곡물을 빻거나 물을 퍼 올렸던 풍차의 형태로 거의 이천 년 동안 인류에 의해 사용되어 왔다. 수평축 풍차는 중동 전역으로 퍼져나가 그 후 중앙아시아, 중국 그리고 인도로 수출되기 전에 고대 페르시아에 처음 도입되었다. 유럽 농업에서의 전형적인 수직축 풍차는 처음에 영국, 프랑스 북부와 플랜더스에서 중세 시대에 사용되기 시작했다. 정점이었던 1850년에, 유럽 전역에 약 20만 개의 풍차가 있었다고 생각되지만, 이 숫자는 산업 혁명이 뿌리를 내리며 급격히 감소했다.

이제 풍력은 신재생 에너지의 형태로 극적인 재기를 하고 있으며, 선진국 도처에서 우뚝 솟은 풍력 발전용 터빈으로 가득 찬 들판의 독특한 광경은 점점 더 흔해지고 있다. 풍력은 풍부한 에너지원인데, 이는 가스를 배출하지 않고 적은 토지만을 사용한다. 건설에 상당한 투자가 필요하지만, 풍력 발전 지역은 다른 에너지원들보다 운영하는 데 훨씬 비용이 적게 들고, 환경에 대한 영향이 제한적이다. 덴마크는 현재 전기 에너지의 40퍼센트를 바람으로부터 발생시키며 전 세계에서 80개 이상의 다른 국가들이 전기를 생산하기 위해 풍력을 사용하고 있다. 중국에서는 특히 풍력에 상당한 투자가 이루어지는데, 중국은 이미 서쪽의 간쑤 지방에 위치한, 세계에서 가장 큰 풍력 발전소를 보유하고 있다.

풍력은 전력을 생산하는 에너지 발전기에 동력을 공급하기 위해 바람에 의해 발생되는 운동 에너지를 사용함으로써 아주 간단하게 작동한다. 각 풍력 발전 터빈은 튜브형 강철로 만들어진 탑으로 이루어져 있는데, 그 꼭대기에는 날개와 축으로 구성된 회전 날개와, 안에 변속기와 발전기가 있는 엔진실이 있다. 바람이 풍력 발전용 터빈을 향해 불 때, 날개를 추진하는데, 이는 회전 날개가 최적량의 바람을 끌어 모으도록 조절하는 상하 요동 시스템에 의해 최적화된 시스템이다. 이것은 [15]탑 내부의 요 전동 장치에 의해 보충되는데, 이는 날개가 바람을 똑바로 마주하도록 하기 위해 엔진실을 회전시킨다. [16]터빈 뒤쪽에 있는 풍속계는 풍속과 방향 정보를 수집해서 요 전동 장치와 상하 요동 시스템이 터빈을 알맞게 조절할 수 있도록 한다. 너무 강한 바람은 날개를 손상시킬 수 있으므로, 바람이 너무 강해서는 안 되며 따라서 풍력 발전용 터빈의 컴퓨터 시스템은 강풍을 피하는 것을 확실히 한다. 비상시 회전 날개는 또한 브레이크에 연결되며, 이것은 회전 날개를 언제든지 멈추게 할 수 있다.

날개는 낮은 속도로 움직이는 기둥에 연결되어 있어서, 바람이 날개를 돌릴 때 이 기둥 또한 돌기 시작한다. [17]이것은 결과적으로 변속기 안의 톱니들이 회전하도록 하는데, 이는 낮은 속도로 도는 기둥의 회전을 빠른 속도로 도는 기둥으로 전달하여, 에너지를 발생시키기 위해 필요한 정도로 회전 속도를 증가시킨다. 그리고 나서 높은 속도로 회전하는 기둥은 60사이클의 교류 발전기를 작동시키는데, 이는 [18]탑을 타고 내려가 집, 직장 그리고 공장에서 사용되기 위해 알맞은 전압으로 전환될 발전소로 이동하는 전력으로 에너지를 변환한다.

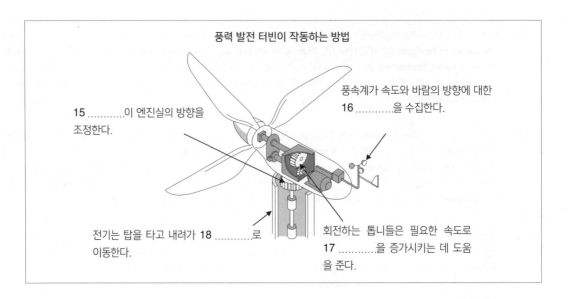

풍력 발전 터빈이 작동하는 방법

15 ....이 엔진실의 방향을 조정한다.

풍속계가 속도와 바람의 방향에 대한 16 ....을 수집한다.

전기는 탑을 타고 내려가 18 ....로 이동한다.

회전하는 톱니들은 필요한 속도로 17 ....을 증가시키는 데 도움을 준다.

15 해설 문제의 핵심어구(controls the direction of the nacelle)와 관련된 지문 내용 중 'a yaw drive inside the tower, which turns the nacelle'에서 엔진실을 회전시키는 탑 내부의 요 전동 장치라고 하였으므로, **yaw drive**가 정답이다. 'turns the nacelle'이 'controls the direction of the nacelle'로 paraphrasing되었다.

16 해설 문제의 핵심어구(anemometre)와 관련된 지문 내용 중 'An anemometre ~ collects wind speed and direction data'에서 풍속계는 풍속과 방향 정보를 수집한다고 하였으므로, **data**가 정답이다. 'wind speed and direction data'가 'data about the speed and direction of the wind'로 paraphrasing되었다.

17 해설 문제의 핵심어구(Spinning cogs)와 관련된 지문 내용 중 'the cogs in the gear box spin ~ increasing the rotational speed to the rate required to generate energy'에서 변속기 안의 톱니들이 회전하며 에너지를 발생시키기 위해 필요한 정도로 회전 속도를 증가시킨다고 하였으므로, **rotational speed**가 정답이다. 'rate required to generate energy'가 'required rate'로 paraphrasing되었다.

18 해설 문제의 핵심어구(electricity goes down the tower to)와 관련된 지문 내용 중 'electricity which travels down the tower and into a power station'에서 탑을 타고 내려가 발전소로 이동하는 전력이라고 하였으므로, **power station**이 정답이다. 'travels down the tower and into a power station'이 'goes down the tower to a power station'으로 paraphrasing되었다.

8

천연가스: 땅으로부터 당신의 집까지

최근 석유에 대한 수요의 감소와 석탄에서 오염 물질을 덜 배출하는 에너지원으로의 이행을 고려할 때, 천연가스는 향후 몇년 간 화석 연료의 생산량을 넘어설 것으로 예상된다. 세계 에너지 수요가 사상 최고치이기 때문에, 천연가스는 매우 효율적이며 세계 특정 지역에서 풍부하게 구할 수 있으므로 해결책이 될 수 있다. 하지만 소비자들에게 이 다용도의 에너지원을 공급하는 것은 복잡하고 다면적인 절차이다.

첫째로, 가스는 지표면으로 끌어올려져야 하고 가스전에 구멍을 뚫음으로써 추출되어야 하는데, 이는 육지와 해저 아래 모두에서 발견될 수 있다. 내륙에서 가스를 추출하는 것이 가스전을 향해 아래쪽으로 시추하는 것을 수반하는 반면, [19]앞바다 해저 매장량에 접근하는 것은 먼저 기술자들이 작업을 할 수 있는 물에 뜨는 플랫폼을 만드는 것을 필요로 한다. 그리고 나서, 가스전이 해수면 아래로 얼마나 깊이 위치해 있느냐에 따라, 알맞은 추출 기술이 사용된다. 만일 천연가스 공급원이 얕은 물에 있다면, 케이블 시추, 또는 충격식 시추라고 불리는 기술이 사용된다. 이것은 천연가스층이 뚫리고 가스가 방출될 때까지 반복적으로 케이블을 그것에 붙어 있는 금속 비트와 함께 해저에 떨어뜨리는 것을 수반한다. 하지만, [20]더 깊이 위치한 매장층에 도달하는 일반적인 방법은, 필요할 경우 금속 시추 비트를 땅 속 수천 피트 아래로 회전시킬 수 있는 거대한 회전 드릴을 사용하는 것이다. 매장층에 구멍이 뚫리면, [21]강력한 펌프가 가스를 지표면으로 끌어당긴다.

다음 단계는 추출 장소에서 근처의 가공 처리 공장으로 가공되지 않은 가스를 퍼 올리는 것인데, 여기에서 [22]작업자들이 그것을 주요 성분인 메탄으로 환원시킨다. [22]천연가스는 단일 가스가 아닌 원유, 메탄, 프로판, 에탄, 그리고 부탄을 포함하는 다양한 탄화 수소로 구성되어 있다. 수증기, 헬륨, 질소, 그리고 이산화탄소 또한 때때로 나타날 수 있다. [23]메탄을 분리시키고 다른 성분들을 제거하는 과정은 여러 단계를 수반하는데, 이것은 천연가스 생산 비용이 전반적으로 상당히 높아지도록 할 수 있다. 하지만, [23]프로판, 원유, 그리고 부탄과 같은 일부 부산물들은 그것들 자체의 가치를 가지고 있으며 그 다양한 단계들의 비용을 상쇄하기 위해 판매될 수 있다.

가공 처리 후에, 가스는 그 자원을 한 장소에서 다른 곳으로 끌어올릴 수 있는 거대한 지하 배관 시스템을 통해 겨냥하는 고객 시장으로 운송되어야 한다. 대부분의 경우, 가스는 최종 사용 장소로 주, 도, 그리고 심지어 국가 경계를 건너 먼 거리를 이동한다. 계량 센터가 가스가 측정되고 관리될 수 있도록 배관의 구간을 따라 지어지고, 동시에 밸브가 약 10킬로미터마다 발견된다. 이 밸브들은 보수 정비 필요가 발생할 경우 파이프 내부로 들어가는 작업자들에게 안전한 접근을 제공하기 위해 가스가 차단될 수 있도록 열리고 닫히며 배관을 통과하는 가스의 흐름을 통제할 수 있다. 절차의 마지막 단계는 배전선으로 가스의 방향을 바꾸는 것인데, 이는 무엇보다도, 난방과 전기 그리고 자동차의 전력 공급원으로서 사용될 수 있는 지역으로 가스를 운반한다.

천연 가스를 추출하고 정제하는 과정

> 가스 매장층이 해수면의 아래에 있다면, 19 ....이 지어진다.
> 결과: 기술자들이 작업을 할 공간이 있다.

↓

> 기술자들은 해양 바닥에 무거운 금속 비트를 반복해서 떨어뜨리거나, 가스 매장층의 20 ....가 훨씬 깊은 경우 땅에 구멍을 뚫는다.
> 결과: 천연가스가 방출되고 펌프를 이용해 21 ....로 끌어올려질 수 있다.

↓

> 가스는 가공 처리 공장으로 수송된다.
> 결과: 메탄이 22 ....과 존재할 수 있는 다른 성분들로부터 분리된다.

↓

> 천연가스의 부산물이 판매된다.
> 결과: 수익은 메탄을 분리시키는 것과 관련된 다양한 23 ....의 비용을 지불하는 데 도움이 될 수 있다.

19   해설   문제의 핵심어구(Engineers ~ work from)와 관련된 지문 내용 중 'accessing an offshore reserve necessitates first constructing floating platforms'에서 앞바다 해저 매장량에 접근하는 것은 먼저 물에 뜨는 플랫폼을 만드는 것을 필요로 한다고 하였으므로, **floating platforms**가 정답이다. 'offshore'가 'beneath the water's surface'로 paraphrasing되었다.

20   해설   문제의 핵심어구(drill a hole in the soil)와 관련된 지문 내용 중 'The usual method of reaching a reservoir located at a greater depth ~ is to use a large rotary drill capable of spinning a metal drill bit thousands of feet into the soil'에서 더 깊이 위치한 매장층에 도달하는 일반적인 방법은 금속 시추 비트를 땅 속 수천 피트 아래로 회전시킬 수 있는 거대한 회전 드릴을 사용하는 것이라고 하였으므로, **depth**가 정답이다. 'use a large rotary drill capable of spinning ~ into the soil'이 'drill a hole in the soil'로 paraphrasing되었다.

21   해설   문제의 핵심어구(natural gas ~ using pumps)와 관련된 지문 내용 중 'powerful pumps draw the gas toward the surface'에서 강력한 펌프가 가스를 지표면으로 끌어당긴다고 하였으므로, **surface**가 정답이다. 'draw the gas toward the surface'가 'Natural gas ~ can be brought to the surface'로 paraphrasing되었다.

22 해설 문제의 핵심어구(Methane is separated)와 관련된 지문 내용 중 'operators reduce it to its principal component – methane. Natural gas is ~ made up of various hydrocarbons'와 'Water vapour, helium, nitrogen, and carbon dioxide are also sometimes present'에서 작업자들이 천연가스를 주요 성분인 메탄으로 환원시키며 천연가스는 다양한 탄화수소로 구성되어 있다고 하였으므로, **hydrocarbons**가 정답이다. 'reduce it to ~ methane'이 'Methane is separated'로, 'Water vapour, helium, nitrogen, and carbon dioxide'가 'other elements'로, 'sometimes present'가 'might be present'로 paraphrasing되었다.

23 해설 문제의 핵심어구(Byproducts)와 관련된 지문 내용 중 'The process of isolating methane and disposing of the other parts involves multiple steps'와 'some byproducts ~ can be sold to offset the expenses of those various steps'에서 메탄을 분리시키고 다른 성분들을 제거하는 과정은 여러 단계를 수반하며 일부 부산물들은 그 다양한 단계들의 비용을 상쇄하기 위해 판매될 수 있다고 하였으므로, **steps**가 정답이다. 'offset the expenses of those various steps'가 'help pay for the various steps'로 paraphrasing되었다.

9

위약은 의약품의 지위를 차지할까?

위약은 의사들이 때때로 환자들에게 투여하는 가짜 약이다. 약물학적 물질을 포함하지는 않지만, 위약을 받는 환자들은 종종 이 설탕 알약이 증상을 완화하거나 심지어는 병을 치료할 수 있는 능력을 가지고 있다고 확신한다. 가장 주목할 만한 것은 때때로, 위약이 실제로 그렇게 한다는 것이다. 이 이해할 수 없는 정신적 의학적 현상은 플라시보 효과라고 알려져 있다.

²⁴일부 의료 전문가들은 위약의 명백한 효험이 처방전을 작성하는 단순한 행위에 있다고 믿는다. 기본적으로, 환자들은 그들에게 약을 처방하는 것이 가능하다면 질병을 극복할 수 있을 것이라고 생각한다고 여겨진다. 이 견해는 의학적 치료를 추구하는 사람들 중 높은 비율의 사람들이 몸이 스스로 치유할 수 있는 병을 앓고 있다는 것을 보여주는 연구들에 의해 입증된다. 하지만, 환자들은 전혀 다르게 생각하며, ²⁵이러한 사고방식은 결국 병세가 나아지면, 호전되는 것을 오직 처방받은 약 덕분으로 돌리게 한다. 이것은 그들을 치료하는 의사의 능력에 대한 믿음과 함께, 몇몇 사람들이 위약의 긍정적인 성능의 이유라고 말하는 것이다.

그럼에도 불구하고, ²⁶대부분의 전문가들은 그런 관행이 의사와 환자 간의 관계에 위반된다고 제시하며 환자들에게 위약을 투여하는 것을 강력하게 반대한다. 의료 윤리 규범은 신뢰가 가장 중요하며 의사들은 솔직해야 한다고 주장한다. 하지만, ²⁷일부 의사들은 그렇게 하는 것이 환자들을 위한 최선이라고 믿기 때문에 잘못된 정보를 제공하거나 사실을 얼버무리고 넘어가고자 하는 유혹을 받는다. 예를 들면, 한 의사는 그렇게 하지 않았다면 거부할 수도 있는 치료를 받도록 환자들을 설득하기 위해 가능한 결과의 더 낙관적인 그림을 제시하는 것을 선택할 수 있다. 결국 모든 것을 바꿀 수 있는 것은 여전히 치료가 가능하다는 믿음으로부터 나오는 희망이다.

더 나아간 연구들은 ²⁸진짜 약 대신 위약을 받았다는 것을 안 일부 환자들에 대해 알려준다. 많은 사례에서, 이것은 악화된 증상과 건강이 나빠지는 결과를 낳으며 환자들이 그들의 의사에 대한 신뢰를 잃도록 한다. 의료 과실에 대한 소송의 가능성으로 인해, 임상에서의 위약 사용은 점점 흔치 않은 일이 되었다. ²⁹요즘, 위약은 거의 실험 대상들에게 그들이 위약을 받거나 받지 않을 수 있다는 것을 미리 알려주며 모든 가능한 위험성에 대해 사전에 이야기해주는 연구 상황에서만 투여된다. 또한, 고지에 입각한 동의가 준수되도록 보장하는 정책이 시행되는데, 이는 의학 연구와 관행을 위한 기준을 플라시보 효과라고 불리는 것의 추후 연구의 필요성과 보조를 맞추도록 한 것이다.

플라시보 효과

위약이 기능하는 방식

• 일부 전문가들은 위약의 유효성이 의사가 24 ....을 만드는 것 때문일 수 있다고 생각한다.

• 연구 결과는 약을 요구하는 많은 환자들이 그것 없이 치유될 것이라는 사실을 보여준다.

• 환자의 25 ....은 그들이 느끼는 그 어떠한 호전도 약 때문이라고 생각하게 한다.

의사들의 의견

• 대부분의 26 ....은 환자에게 위약을 주는 것에 반대한다.

• 의사들의 정직함은 윤리적으로 중요하다고 간주된다.

• 의사들은 가끔 사실을 말하지 않는 것이 환자의 27 ....을 위한 것이라고 생각한다.

• 그들이 위약을 받았다는 것을 알게 된 환자의 건강은 28 ....하게 될 수 있다.

현재의 사용법

• 오늘날, 위약은 대부분 29 ....을 위해 이용된다.

24 해설 문제의 핵심어구(A placebo's effectiveness)와 관련된 지문 내용 중 'Some medical practitioners believe that the apparent efficacy of placebos lies in the simple act of writing a prescription.'에서 일부 의료 전문가들은 위약의 명백한 효험이 처방전을 작성하는 단순한 행위에 있다고 믿는다고 하였으므로, **prescription**이 정답이다. 'apparent efficacy ~ lies in'이 'effectiveness could be due to'로 paraphrasing되었다.

25 해설 문제의 핵심어구(improvement ~ due to medicine)와 관련된 지문 내용 중 'this attitude makes them attribute getting better ~ solely to the medication they were prescribed'에서 이러한 사고방식은 호전되는 것을 오직 처방받은 약 덕분으로 돌리게 한다고 하였으므로, **attitude**가 정답이다. 'attribute getting better'가 'think any improvement ~ due to'로 paraphrasing되었다.

26 해설 문제의 핵심어구(against giving patients placebos)와 관련된 지문 내용 중 'most experts strongly oppose medicating patients with placebos'에서 대부분의 전문가들은 환자들에게 위약을 투여하는 것을 강력하게 반대한다고 하였으므로, **experts**가 정답이다. 'strongly oppose'가 'be against'로 paraphrasing되었다.

27 해설 문제의 핵심어구(not to tell the truth)와 관련된 지문 내용 중 'some physicians are tempted to ~ gloss over the truth because they believe doing so is in the patient's best interests'에서 일부 의사들은 그렇게 하는 것이 환자들을 위한 최선이라고 믿기 때문에 사실을 얼버무리고 넘어가고자 한다고 하였으므로, **interests**가 정답이다. 'gloss over the truth'가 'not to tell the truth'로 paraphrasing되었다.

28 해설 문제의 핵심어구(find out they've been given placebos)와 관련된 지문 내용 중 'patients learning they have been given placebos ~ their health taking a turn for the worse'에서 위약을 받았다는 것을 안 환자들의 건강이 나빠지는 결과를 낳는다고 하였으므로, **worse**가 정답이다. 'their health taking a turn for the worse'가 'the health of patients ~ can become worse'로 paraphrasing되었다.

29 해설 문제의 핵심어구(Today ~ mostly used for)와 관련된 지문 내용 중 'These days, placebos are almost exclusively administered in research situations'에서 요즘 위약은 거의 연구 상황에서만 투여된다고 하였으므로, research situations가 답이 될 수 있다. 지시문에서 한 단어로만 답을 작성하라고 하였으므로, **research**가 정답이다. 'almost exclusively administered in research situations'가 'mostly used for research'로 paraphrasing되었다.

🔟

도시 농업

지난 한 세기 동안, 농업은 작은 규모의 생계를 기반으로 한 활동에서 산업화된 세계적인 사업으로 변화했다. 그러나, 그 산업은 현재 경작 가능한 토지의 부족으로 극심한 부담을 겪고 있다. 게다가, 연구 결과들은 도시에서의 더 확실한 일거리를 위해 사람들이 점점 농업을 포기할 것임을 보여주었다. 이것은 이미 부담을 겪고 있는 세계적인 식량 공급에 더욱 압박을 가할 것이다. 사회는 생계를 위한 주민들의 기본적인 욕구가 계속해서 충족될 수 있도록 보장하는 획기적이고 새로운 방법들을 고안해내야 한다.

³⁰세계의 도시 계획자들이 증가하는 농경지 부족에 관한 문제를 해결하기 위해 받아들이고 있는 한 가지 추세는 도시 농업인데, 이것은 작물을 기르기 위해 건물, 공터, 그리고 뒤뜰과 같이 도시에서 볼 수 있는 기반 시설을 이용한다. 이것을 실행하는 것의 한 가지 장점은 재배자와 구매자에게 농업 생산품에 대한 빠른 접근이 제공됨에 따라 식품을 운송하는 데 자원이 더 적게 사용된다는 것이다. 또한, 많은 도시 농업 사업에서 영양분이 풍부한 물에서 식물을 재배하는 방식인 수경 재배를 활용하기 때문에, 유해한 농업 방식으로 인해 계속해서 미네랄 저하를 직면하고 있는 토양이 보존된다. 마지막으로, ³²도시의 건물들은 식물들을 엄격히 통제되는 환경에서 재배하는 것을 더 쉽게 해주기 때문에, 도시 농업은 ³¹극단적인 날씨로 인해 때때로 작물을 잃는 문제를 해결한다.

도시 농업의 본보기가 되는 사례는 일본 도쿄에 있는 Pasona 본사 아래에 위치한 농지인데, 이곳에는 200가지 이상의 식물 종들이 43,000제곱피트의 공간에서 자란다. 식물들은 수경과 토양 기반 농법 모두를 사용하여 재배되며, 지능형 실내 온도 조절 시스템이 습도, 온도 그리고 미풍을 관리한다. ³³Pasona에 있는 농지는 지하에 위치해서 식물들이 살아남기 위해 필요로 하는 직사광선을 받을 수 없기 때문에, 인공 조명이 그곳에서 길러지는 작물의 생명을 유지하게 한다. 지구의 저 반대편인 뉴욕시에서는, 사람들이 옥상 온실 재배로 전향하고 있다. 이러한 작업들 중 하나는, BrightFarms라는 것으로, 조명, 선풍기, 차양 커튼, 그리고 발열 담요를 작동시키기 위한 자동 센서를 자랑한다. 그것은 또한 빗물을 받아서 저장할 수 있는 탱크를 가지고 있다. ³⁴지역 슈퍼마켓과 음식점에 매일 거의 500파운드의 농작물을 판매하는 BrightFarms는, 탄소 발자국을 최소한으로 하면서 배달 차량에 드는 비용을 쓰지 않을 수 있다.

도시 농업이 지금까지 도쿄와 뉴욕과 같은 장소에서 경험한 성공에도 불구하고, 극복되어야 할 큰 장애물들이 남아있다는 것에 주목하는 것이 중요하다. 한 가지 과제는 도심 지역이나 근처에 있는 토양이 인체에 유해한 많은 양의 납을 함유하고 있기 때문에 농장으로 오염되지 않은 충분한 양의 토양을 공급하는 것에 있다. 토양을 전혀 사용하지 않고 대신 수경 재배 시스템에 의존하는 것은 특히 ³⁵강수량에 부정적인 영향을 미치는 세계 기후 변화로 인해 세계의 많은 지역에 믿을 수 있고 안전한 담수의 수원이 부족하기 때문에 아직까지는 모든 곳에서 선택 사항은 아니다. 하지만, 수경 재배 시스템에서 안전하게 사용할 수 있도록 바닷물로부터 소금을 분리하는 능력과 오염된 토양을 처리하기 위한 방법의 고안과 같은 새로운 발전은 이러한 문제들을 곧 해결할 수 있도록 도울 것이다.

문제	해결 방안
더 많은 사람들이 농업을 포기하고 도시로 이동할 것이다.	사회는 사람들에게 식량을 공급할 새로운 방법을 개발하는 것을 시작해야 한다.
농작물을 재배할 땅이 부족하다.	도시의 30 ....을 이용하여 식물을 재배한다.
가끔 31 .... 때문에 작물을 잃는다.	식물을 32 .... 환경에서 간수한다.
Pasona 본사 아래의 농지는 33 ....을 받지 않는다.	인공 조명을 이용해 식물을 살아 있도록 유지한다.
배달 차량을 구매하고 이용하는 것은 추가 비용이 든다.	상품을 34 .... 고객에게 판매한다.
기후 변화로 인해 35 ....에 부정적인 영향이 있어왔다.	바닷물에서 소금을 제거해 작물에 이용하기에 안전하도록 한다.

30 해설 왼쪽 열의 핵심 내용(lack of land ~ to grow agricultural crops)과 관련된 지문 내용 중 'One trend that city planners ~ are embracing to address concerns about the growing lack of agricultural land is urban farming, which utilises infrastructure found in cities ~ to grow crops.'에서 도시 계획자들이 증가하는 농경지 부족에 관한 문제를 해결하기 위해 받아들이고 있는 한 가지 추세는 도시 농업인데, 이것은 작물을 기르기 위해 도시에서 볼 수 있는 기반 시설을 이용한다고 하였으므로, **infrastructure**가 정답이다. 'utilises infrastructure found in cities ~ to grow crops'가 'Grow plants using urban infrastructure'로 paraphrasing되었다.

31 해설 문제의 핵심어구(Crops ~ lost)와 관련된 지문 내용 중 'sometimes losing crops to extreme weather'에서 극단적인 날씨로 인해 때때로 작물을 잃는다고 하였으므로, **(extreme) weather**가 정답이다. 'losing crops to'가 'Crops are ~ lost because of'로 paraphrasing되었다.

32 해설 왼쪽 열의 핵심 내용(Crops are ~ lost)과 관련된 지문 내용 중 'city structures make it easier to cultivate plants in a strictly controlled environment'에서 도시의 건물들은 식물들을 엄격히 통제되는 환경에서 재배하는 것을 더 쉽게 해준다고 하였으므로, **(strictly) controlled**가 정답이다. 'cultivate'가 'Take care of'로 paraphrasing되었다.

33 해설 문제의 핵심어구(Pasona headquarters)와 관련된 지문 내용 중 'the farm at Pasona is located underground and has no direct sunlight'에서 Pasona에 있는 농지는 지하에 위치해서 직사광선을 받을 수 없다고 하였으므로, **(direct) sunlight**가 정답이다. 'the farm ~ located underground'가 'The farm beneath'로 paraphrasing되었다.

34 해설 왼쪽 열의 핵심 내용(delivery vehicles)과 관련된 지문 내용 중 'Selling ~ to local supermarkets and restaurants, BrightFarms is able to avoid the expense of investing in delivery vehicles'에서 지역 슈퍼마켓과 음식점에 판매하는

BrightFarms는 배달 차량에 드는 비용을 쓰지 않을 수 있다고 하였으므로, **local**이 정답이다. 'supermarkets and restaurants'가 'clients'로 paraphrasing되었다.

35 해설 문제의 핵심어구(climate change)와 관련된 지문 내용 중 'with global climate change negatively affecting precipitation rates'에서 강수량에 부정적인 영향을 미치는 세계 기후 변화라고 하였으므로, **precipitation (rates)**가 정답이다. 'negatively affecting'이 'a negative effect on'으로 paraphrasing되었다.

HACKERS TEST

p.130

1	model	**2**	monopoly	**3**	equipment	**4**	styles
5	dominant	**6**	21,000 workers	**7**	Yes	**8**	No
9	No	**10**	Yes	**11**	Not given	**12**	Yes
13	No	**14**	Not given				

포드사 대 제너럴 모터스사: 거대 자동차 조직들의 경쟁

현대 자동차 산업은 미국에서부터 시작되었는데, 이곳에서 두 개의 거대 자동차 조직인 포드 자동차사와 제너럴 모터스사가, 경제 역사상 가장 엄청난 기업 경쟁들 중 하나의 주요 참여자들이 되었다. [2]헨리 포드의 포드 자동차사는 빠르게 시작했고 자동차 제조에 있어 초기 독점을 누렸다. 그것은 생산, 경제 규모에서 주도적인 리더가 되었고, 전 세계적인 중개망을 누렸다. 하지만 머지 않아, 제너럴 모터스사는 스스로 어마어마한 세력으로 성장했다. 1910년대 초반에는, 이 두 회사들이 세계 자동차 산업의 반 이상을 구성했고 세계에서 가장 큰 몇몇 공장단지를 운영하고 있었다. 생산과 규모에 대한 공통적인 기반에도 불구하고, [7]두 회사는 사업 모델이나 전략에서 상당한 차이가 있었다.

포드사의 경우, 생산 시설에 대한 막대한 투자는 유명한 T형 자동차라는 [1]하나의 모델 제조에만 전념했으므로 초점이 단일했다. [8]회사의 표준화된 디자인은 대중 시장을 목표로 했고 '보통 사람'을 위한 보편적인 자동차를 만들기 위해 생산 가격을 낮게 유지하도록 해주었다. 이 전략은 단기적으로는 훌륭하다고 증명되었음에도 불구하고, [8]장기적으로는 엄청나게 비용이 드는 것으로 판명되었다. 치열해진 경쟁과 T형 자동차의 뒤쳐지는 유행이 1920년대 후반에 포드사로 하여금 이들의 상품을 바꾸는 것을 불가피하게 만들었을 때, 시설들은 충분히 장비가 갖춰져 있지 않았다. 다른 모델의 생산을 가능하게 하기 위해 사실상 [3]모든 장비가 해체되고 다시 만들어지거나 교체되어야 했다. 설상가상으로, [9]포드는 그의 제조 전략을 바꾸지 않았다. 그는 T형 자동차를 대체하기 위한 새로운 모델인 A형 자동차를 생산하기 위해 그저 그것을 복제했다. 요컨대, 포드는 기업가로서는 뛰어났지만, 변화하는 시장 현실들에 적응할 의향이 없는 것으로 명성을 쌓았다.

제너럴 모터스사는 20세기 초반에 전혀 다른 경험을 했다. 제너럴 모터스사가 비록 1920년에 시장 점유율은 2위였지만, 총 판매 수량은 포드사의 25퍼센트도 되지 않았다. [10]하지만 제너럴 모터스사는 라이벌사 창립자의 시야 밖이었던 것 같은 이점을 지니고 있었다. 제너럴 모터스사 경영 간부들은 과점적 경쟁을 이해했다. 회사의 첫 CEO인 [11]윌리엄 듀런트는 자동차들이나 자동차 부품들을 생산하는 많은 작은 회사들을 장악하여 큰 자동차 회사를 만드는 것에 착수했다. 듀런트는 자동차 시장이 변할 수 있다는 것을 이해했다. 그래서, [4]제너럴 모터스사는 여러 본체 스타일과 자동차 크기의 생산이 가능하지만 차대와 같은 표준화된, 그리고 교체 가능한 부품들을 활용하는 공장들을 세웠다. 회사는 또한 더 개성 있고 더 우아한 무언가를 원하며 또 구매할 여유가 있는 다른 계층의 사람들에게 관심을 끌 수 있는 럭셔리 브랜드들을 소개했다. 마지막으로, 획기적인 마케팅 돌파구로서, [12]제너럴 모터스사는 매년 기종 전환을 선보였고, 이러한 연례 상품 다양성은 고객들의 예전 자동차들이 아직 완전히 기능하더라도 새로운 모델로 업그레이드하도록 설득하는 데 매우 영향력이 있었다.

듀런트의 계승자인 앨프리드 P. 슬론은 기존의 모델을 기반으로 했고 전체적인 운영이 투자 수익률을 최대화하는 것을 확실히 하기 위해 모든 부서로부터 구체화된 재정과 성과 정보를 전달하는 절차를 시행했다. 그는 또한 모델들에 교차해서 교체 가능한 부분들을 이용하는 것을 강조하고자 노력했고, 이에 더해 고객 동향과 시장 조건들을 알아내기 위해 자원들을 투자했다. [13]이는 그들이 과거의 경기

순환에 비추어 경제 동향의 예상 지표를 만들 수 있도록 수요에 있어서의 계절별 그리고 장기적 변동, 구매자 소득 수준, 물가 전망 등과 같은 온갖 종류의 고객 수요 정보를 수집하는 것을 포함했다. ¹³이 방책은 효과적이었음이 증명되었고, ⁵이는 그 후 몇 년 간 제너럴 모터스사가 포드사를 서서히 추월할 것임을 의미했으며, 제너럴 모터스사가 반 세기 동안 경쟁 구도에서 우월한 지위를 유지하게 했다.

하지만, 70년대와 80년대에는, 제너럴 모터스사가 소유하던 시장 점유율은 저렴한 제품군에서는 일본 그리고 고급 제품군에서는 독일과의 해외 경쟁에 직면하여 약화되기 시작했고 이것은, 안전과 환경의 질과 관련해 커져가는 우려에 대한 제너럴 모터스사의 적대감과 결합하여, 1990년대까지 포드사가 다시 우위로 돌아올 수 있는 기회를 주었다. 1975년에서 2000년 사이에, 제너럴 모터스사의 시장 점유율은 55퍼센트에서 27퍼센트로 급락했다. 비록 시장점유율이 완전히 따라잡지는 못했지만, 마찬가지로 도전과 차질을 경험했음에도 불구하고 포드사는 전체적으로 호전되었다. 중반에 들어 다시 재기하기 이전까지 1980년대 초반에 포드사는 33억 달러의 손실을 겪었다. 포드사는 생산 비용을 크게 줄이기 시작했고, ¹⁴이들의 1985년의 신제품인, 기체 역학으로 설계된 토러스는 시장에서 매우 호평을 받았다. 이러한 변화들은, 안전 및 환경과 관련해 커가는 우려에 대한 적응과 결합하여, 회사가 성공적으로 유지되도록 했다.

그 후 2008년 경제 위기에 따른 압도적인 자동차 산업 침체기가 왔고, 이는 두 거대 기업들의 역경을 더 복잡하게 만들었다. 위기의 서곡에 해당하는 몇 년 동안에, 포드사는 회사가 부도를 피하도록 도와준 안전한 결정들을 내렸다. 예를 들어, 포드사는 연료를 많이 소비하는 스포츠 실용차의 줄어드는 수요를 예상하여, 그들의 거대한 자동차들 중 하나인, 익스커션을 제거했다. 그들은 그것의 생산을 휘발유 가격이 치솟음에 따라 더욱 시장성이 높아진 중간 크기 자동차들의 더 많은 생산으로 대체했다. 제너럴 모터스사는 이런 통찰력을 가지고 있지 않았고 트럭과 스포츠 실용차의 생산에 계속해서 크게 의지했다. 그들은 또한 멕시코의 전체 국채와 동등한 채무를 축적했다. 결과적으로, ⁶최대 21,000명의 직원들을 해고하고 오직 뷰익, 캐딜락, GMC 그리고 시보레만을 남기고 3개의 브랜드를 제거한 것조차 그 회사가 부도를 선언하는 것을 막지 못했는데, 2009년 6월에 그들은 실제로 그렇게 했다. 막대한, 그리고 악명 높은 정부의 긴급구제가 아니었다면, 제너럴 모터스사가 사라졌을 것임은 의심할 여지가 없다.

어휘   giant n. 거대 조직 monopoly n. 독점 scale n. 규모 in one's own right phr. 스스로 ground n. 기반 standardised adj. 표준화된 mass n. 대중 lagging adj. 뒤쳐지는 replicate v. 복제하다 excel v. 뛰어나다 entrepreneur n. 기업가 oligopolistic adj. 과점적 chassis n. 차대 successor n. 계승자 variation n. 변동 commodity price phr. 물가 erode v. 약화되다 antagonism n. 적대감 prominence n. 우위 plummet v. 급락하다 setback n. 차질 plight n. 역경 bankruptcy n. 부도 dwindle v. 줄어들다 gas-guzzling adj. 연료를 많이 소비하는 foresight n. 통찰력 amass v. 축적하다 liability n. 채무 on par phr. ~와 동등한

[1-6]

기업	기존 전략	성과	실패
포드사	단 한 가지 1 ....을 만드는 데 완전히 전념했음	빠르게 시작했고 자동차 산업에서 2 ....을 자랑했음	한때 모든 3 ....을 다시 만들거나 대체해야 했음
제너럴 모터스사	다양한 자동차 크기와 본체 4 ....을 생산할 수 있음	50년 동안 경쟁 구도에서 5 .... 지위를 유지했음	부도를 선언하기 전 6 ....만큼을 해고했음

1 해설 문제의 첫 열(Ford)과 첫 행(Original Strategy)을 통해 문제가 포드사의 기존 전략에 대한 내용임을 알 수 있다. 문제의 핵심어구(totally dedicated to making)와 관련된 지문 내용 중 'it was entirely dedicated to the manufacture of a single model'에서 포드사는 하나의 모델 제조에만 전념했다고 하였으므로, **model**이 정답이다. 'entirely dedicated to the manufacture'가 'totally dedicated to making'으로 paraphrasing되었다.

2 해설 문제의 첫 열(Ford)과 첫 행(Achievements)을 통해 문제가 포드사의 성과에 대한 내용임을 알 수 있다. 문제의 핵심어구(began rapidly and boasted)와 관련된 지문 내용 중 'Henry Ford's Ford Motor Company started out quickly and enjoyed an early monopoly in car making.'에서 헨리 포드의 포드 자동차사는 빠르게 시작했고 자동차 제조에 있어 초기 독점을 누렸다고 하였으므로, **monopoly**가 정답이다. 'started out quickly and enjoyed an early monopoly in car making'이 'began rapidly and boasted a monopoly in the automobile industry'로 paraphrasing되었다.

3 해설 문제의 첫 열(Ford)과 첫 행(Failures)을 통해 문제가 포드사의 실패에 대한 내용임을 알 수 있다. 문제의 핵심어구(had to rebuild or replace)와 관련된 지문 내용 중 'every piece of equipment had to be torn down and rebuilt or replaced'에서 모든 장비가 해체되고 다시 만들어지거나 교체되어야 했다고 하였으므로, **equipment**가 정답이다. 'every piece of equipment'가 'all equipment'로 paraphrasing되었다.

4 해설 문제의 첫 열(General Motors)과 첫 행(Original Strategy)을 통해 문제가 제너럴 모터스사의 기존 전략에 대한 내용임을 알 수 있다. 문제의 핵심어구(a range of car sizes and body)와 관련된 지문 내용 중 'GM created factories that made use of standardised and interchangeable parts ~ but which allowed for the production of various body styles and car sizes'에서 제너럴 모터스사는 여러 본체 스타일과 자동차 크기의 생산이 가능하지만 표준화된, 그리고 교체 가능한 부품들을 활용하는 공장들을 세웠다고 하였으므로, **styles**가 정답이다. 'allowed for the production of various body styles and car sizes'가 'capable of producing a range of car sizes and body styles'로 paraphrasing되었다.

5 해설 문제의 첫 열(General Motors)과 첫 행(Achievements)을 통해 문제가 제너럴 모터스사의 성과에 대한 내용임을 알 수 있다. 문제의 핵심어구(rivalry for 50 years)와 관련된 지문 내용 중 'it meant GM would gradually overtake Ford ~ allowing it to maintain a dominant position in the rivalry for half a century'에서 이는 그 후 몇 년 간 제너럴 모터스사가 포드사를 서서히 추월할 것임을 의미했으며 제너럴 모터스사가 반 세기 동안 경쟁 구도에서 우월한 지위를 유지하게 했다고 하였으므로, **dominant**가 정답이다. 'maintain a dominant position ~ for half a century'가 'held a dominant position ~ for 50 years'로 paraphrasing되었다.

6 해설 문제의 첫 열(General Motors)과 첫 행(Failures)을 통해 문제가 제너럴 모터스사의 실패에 대한 내용임을 알 수 있다. 문제의 핵심어구(before declaring bankruptcy)와 관련된 지문 내용 중 'even laying off up to 21,000 workers ~ could not keep it from declaring bankruptcy'에서 최대 21,000명의 직원들을 해고한 것조차 제너럴 모터스사가 부도를 선언하는 것을 막지 못했다고 하였으므로, **21,000 workers**가 정답이다.

[7-14]

7 제너럴 모터스사와 포드사는 그들의 사업 계획에 있어 크게 달랐다.

8 포드사의 공통된 디자인 사용은 장기적으로 돈을 절약하게 했다.

9 포드사는 A형 자동차를 생산하기 위해 그의 제조 계획을 바꿨다.

10 제너럴 모터스사의 지도자들은 헨리 포드에게는 부족했던 경쟁에 대한 이해를 하고 있었다.

11 듀런트는 포드사가 소유한 회사의 통제권을 쥐려 시도했다.

12 제너럴 모터스사에 의해 소개된 연례 기종 전환은 매우 성공적이었다.

13 소비자 정보를 수집하는 것에 대한 제너럴 모터스사의 투자는 결국 비효과적이었다.

14 1985년 토러스는 포드사 자동차 중 가장 매력적인 디자인이었다.

7 해설 문제의 핵심어구(differed ~ in their business planning)와 관련된 지문 내용 중 'the two firms nonetheless had significant differences in their business models and strategies'에서 두 회사는 사업 모델이나 전략에서 상당한 차이가 있었다고 하였으므로, 주어진 문장은 글쓴이의 견해와 일치함을 알 수 있다. 따라서 정답은 **Yes**이다. 'had significant differences in their business models and strategies'가 'differed greatly in their business planning'으로 paraphrasing되었다.

8 해설 문제의 핵심어구(Ford's use of a universal design)와 관련된 지문 내용 중 'The company's standardised design ~ allowed them to keep production costs down'과 'it turned out to be extremely costly in the long term'에서 회사의 표준화된 디자인은 생산 가격을 낮게 유지하도록 했지만 장기적으로는 엄청나게 비용이 드는 것으로 판명되었다고 하였으므로, 주어진 문장은 글쓴이의 견해와 일치하지 않음을 알 수 있다. 따라서 정답은 **No**이다.

9 해설 문제의 핵심어구(produce the Model A)와 관련된 지문 내용 중 'Ford did not alter his manufacturing strategy'와 'He merely replicated it to produce a new model, the Model A'에서 포드는 그의 제조 전략을 바꾸지 않았고 새로운 모델인 A형 자동차를 생산하기 위해 그저 그것을 복제했다고 하였으므로, 주어진 문장은 글쓴이의 견해와 일치하지 않음을 알 수 있다. 따라서 정답은 **No**이다.

10 해설 문제의 핵심어구(GM leaders had an understanding)와 관련된 지문 내용 중 'Yet GM had an advantage that seemingly was outside the scope of the rival's founder: GM executives understood oligopolistic competition.' 에서 하지만 제너럴 모터스사는 라이벌사 창립자의 시야 밖이었던 것 같은 이점을 지니고 있었으며 제너럴 모터스사 경영 간부들은 과점적 경쟁을 이해했다고 하였으므로, 주어진 문장은 글쓴이의 견해와 일치함을 알 수 있다. 따라서 정답은 **Yes** 이다. 'GM executives understood ~ competition'이 'GM leaders had an understanding about competition'으로 paraphrasing되었다.

11 해설 문제의 핵심어구(Durant attempted to gain control)와 관련된 지문 내용 중 'William Durant, set out to create a large automobile company by gaining control of numerous small companies'에서 윌리엄 듀런트는 많은 작은 회사들을 장악하여 큰 자동차 회사를 만드는 것에 착수했다고는 하였지만, 주어진 문장의 내용은 확인할 수 없다. 따라서 정답은 **Not given**이다.

12 해설 문제의 핵심어구(The yearly model changes)와 관련된 지문 내용 중 'GM introduced annual model changes, and this annual product variety was influential in convincing customers'에서 제너럴 모터스사는 매년 기종 전환을 선보였고 이러한 연례 상품 다양성은 고객들을 설득하는 데 매우 영향력이 있었다고 하였으므로, 주어진 문장은 글쓴이의 견해와 일치함을 알 수 있다. 따라서 정답은 **Yes**이다. 'influential in convincing customers'가 'highly successful'로 paraphrasing되었다.

13 해설 문제의 핵심어구(gathering consumer information)와 관련된 지문 내용 중 'This included the collecting of all manner of consumer-demand information'과 'This plan proved effective'에서 온갖 종류의 고객 수요 정보를 수집하는 것을 포함했던 방책은 효과적이었음이 증명되었다고 하였으므로, 주어진 문장은 글쓴이의 견해와 일치하지 않음을 알 수 있다. 따라서 정답은 **No**이다.

14 해설 문제의 핵심어구(The 1985 Taurus)와 관련된 지문 내용 중 'its new introduction for 1985, the aerodynamic Taurus, was very well received in the market'에서 포드사의 1985년의 신제품인 기체 역학으로 설계된 토러스는 시장에서 매우 호평을 받았다고는 하였지만, 주어진 문장의 내용은 확인할 수 없다. 따라서 정답은 **Not given**이다.

CHAPTER 05 Sentence Completion

* 각 문제에 대한 정답의 단서는 지문에 문제 번호와 함께 별도의 색으로 표시되어 있습니다.

EXAMPLE
p.138

나중에 태어난 형제자매들의 경우, 그들의 성격은 출생 순서에 따라 크게 영향을 받을 수 있다. 그들보다 나이가 많은 형제자매에게 명백하게 더 유리한 가족 체계에서 혜택을 받을 가능성이 낮기 때문에, 그들은 경쟁의 장을 균등하게 할 방법을 찾아야 한다. 이것이 이루어지는 한 가지 방법은 [1]유머의 사용을 통한 것인데, 이는 다른 가족 구성원들과 문제가 생기거나 언쟁하는 것을 피하기 위해 막내로 태어난 아이들이 종종 의존하는 것이다. 이는 막내로 태어난 아이들 사이에서 더 재미있고 별난 성격으로 이어질 수 있다. 반면에, 첫째로 태어난 아이들은, 더 어린 형제자매들에게 모범을 보이도록 기대되기 때문에, 어린 나이에도 더 책임감이 강하고 성숙한 경향이 있다.

HACKERS PRACTICE
p.140

1	D	2	B	3	B
4	C	5	G	6	A
7	E	8	queen	9	chain
10	silk	11	oral tradition	12	versions
13	title	14	adult themes	15	societal contributions
16	cultural differences	17	(uniform) standards/(uniform) education standards		
18	sprawl	19	pollution	20	electricity
21	generations	22	D	23	A
24	E	25	mental	26	sense organs
27	anxiety	28	B	29	E
30	G	31	C		

1

세계에서 가장 유명한 극작가인 셰익스피어의 조각상은, 런던의 웨스트 엔드에 있는 레스터 광장에 세워져 있다. 웨스트 엔드는 세계의 몇몇 최고급 연극들을 보여주는 40곳의 장소들을 자랑하는 주요 관광지이기 때문에, 이는 또한 꽤 잘 어울린다. Theatreland라고도 알려진 이 지역은 빅토리아 시대와 에드워드 시대까지 거슬러 올라가는 많은 극장들을 포함하는, 다채로운 역사를 가지고 있다. [1]이 역사적인 건물들은 현재 런던의 가장 바쁜 지구들 중 한 곳에 최신식 상점들 및 사무실들과 공존한다. 웨스트 엔드의 극장들 중 가장 오래된 것은 화재로 인해 여러 번 재건축되었음에도 불구하고 1663년에 문을 연 드루어리레인 극장이다. 웨스트 엔드 극장들은 현대의 작품들, 고전의 재공연, 그리고, 가장 유명한, 뮤지컬을 포함하는 다수의 공연들을 계속해서 무대에 올리고 있다. [2]후자는 가장 많은 청중을 끌어 모으며, 몇십 년 동안 계속 공연되고 있는 것으로 알려졌다. '레미제라블'과 '오페라의 유령'이 그러한데, 모두 1980년대 중반에 시작해 모든 웨스트 엔드의 상연 작품들 중 가장 수익을 많이 올리는 작품들에 속한다.

1 웨스트 엔드에 있는 많은 극장들은 −하다.

2 웨스트 엔드의 가장 인기 있는 연극들은 −하다.

1 해설 문제의 핵심어구(theatres in the West End)와 관련된 지문 내용 중 'These historical buildings now coexist with contemporary shops and offices'에서 이 역사적인 건물들은 현재 최신식 상점들 및 사무실들과 공존한다고 하였으므로, 보기 D are located alongside modern structures가 정답이다. 'coexist with contemporary shops and offices'가 'are located alongside modern structures'로 paraphrasing되었다.

2 해설 문제의 핵심어구(most popular)와 관련된 지문 내용 중 'The latter draw the most viewers, and have been known to run for decades.'에서 뮤지컬은 가장 많은 청중을 끌어 모으며 몇십 년 동안 계속 공연되고 있는 것으로 알려졌다고 하였으므로, 보기 B have been running for decades가 정답이다. 'draw the most viewers'가 'The most popular'로 paraphrasing되었다.

2

³반려동물의 주인들은 오랫동안 그들의 반려동물이 공감, 질투, 그리고 죄책감과 같은 감정을 보여준다고 믿어왔지만, 역사적으로 과학자들은 이것이 불가능하다고 주장해왔다. 그들은 오로지 인간만이 감정을 느끼며 우리들이 다른 종에게서 감정을 인식하는 것은 인격화, 또는 동물에게 인간의 특성을 귀속시키는 것 때문이라고 생각했다. 하지만, 최근의 연구는 이것이 사실이 아닐 수도 있다는 것을 보여주었다. 대개 말을 할 수 없는 영아들에게 사용되는 실험 방법을 활용함으로써, 샌디에이고의 캘리포니아 대학 연구원인 Christine Harris와 Caroline Prouvost는 주인이 다른 개들에게 애정을 보여주었을 때 개들이 질투하는 행동을 드러냈다는 것을 발견했다. ⁴또 다른 사회적 종의 입증할 수 있는 질투에 대한 발견은 감정이 온전히 인간의 특성일 가능성이 낮다는 것을 보여준다. Laurel Braitman과 Elizabeth Marshall Thomas와 같은 역사 인류학자들은 이보다 더 나아간다. 그들은 감정이 진화적 의의를 가지고 있으며 우리가 동물에게서 인간의 감정을 발견할 때, 우리가 오래 전 우리의 공유된 과거에서 획득한 공통된 특징을 알아보는 것이라고 제시한다.

3   과학자들은 전통적으로 동물들이 –하다고 느꼈다.

4   부러움을 보이는 개들은 감정이 –하다는 것을 증명한다.

3 해설 문제의 핵심어구(Scientists traditionally felt)와 관련된 지문 내용 중 'While pet owners have long believed that their animal companions display feelings ~ scientists have historically said that this was impossible. They held that only humans felt emotions'에서 반려동물의 주인들은 오랫동안 그들의 반려동물이 감정을 보여준다고 믿어왔지만, 역사적으로 과학자들은 이것이 불가능하다고 주장해왔으며 그들은 오로지 인간만이 감정을 느낀다고 생각했다고 하였으므로, 보기 B lack the emotions가 정답이다. 'only humans felt emotions'가 'animals lack the emotions'로 paraphrasing되었다.

4 해설 문제의 핵심어구(Dogs showing envy)와 관련된 지문 내용 중 'The discovery of demonstrable jealousy in another social species indicates that emotions are not likely a strictly human trait.'에서 또 다른 사회적 종의 입증할

수 있는 질투에 대한 발견은 감정이 온전히 인간의 특성일 가능성이 낮다는 것을 보여준다고 하였으므로, 보기 **C** are present in more than one species가 정답이다. 'demonstrable jealousy in another social species indicates'가 'Dogs showing envy proves'로, 'not likely a strictly human trait'가 'present in more than one species'로 paraphrasing 되었다.

3

기업들은 이윤을 위해 제품을 생산하거나 서비스를 수행하고자 설립되었지만, 그들이 또한 지역 사회에 환원해야 한다는 보편적인 합의가 있다. [5]많은 기업 소유주들과 경영자들이 이 신념을 공유하며 그들이 사회적 약자들을 위해 환경을 개선할 책임을 지고 있다고 느낀다. 탐스 슈즈사와 같은 이들 중 일부는 실제로 이것을 염두에 두고 설립되었다. 창사 이래로, 탐스사는 한 켤레가 팔릴 때마다 어려움에 처한 사람에게 신발 한 켤레를 기부해왔다. 지금까지, 이것은 5천만 켤레 이상의 신발을 기부하는 결과를 낳았다. 화장품 회사인 뉴스킨사는 사회적 책임을 지고 있는 기업의 또 다른 사례이다. 그들은 'Nourish the Children'이라는 기획을 마련했는데, 이것은 고객이 구매를 할 때 빈곤한 아이들에게 건강한 식사를 기부할 수 있도록 한다. 이러한 프로그램들은 가난에 대한 그들의 영향력에 대해 칭찬받을 만하지만, 또한 그것에 착수하는 회사들의 순익에도 도움을 준다. [6]사회적으로 책임을 지는 이러한 종류의 프로그램을 광고함으로써, 회사들은 이윤을 증대시킨다. 이것은 [7]그 프로그램들이 사회적 문제들에 대해 염려하는 고객들로 하여금 그 기업을 애용함으로써 세상에 좋은 일을 하고 있다고 느끼도록 하기 때문이다. 전반적으로, 이러한 종류의 기업 프로그램들은 관련된 모든 사람들에게 긍정적인 영향을 미치며 다른 기업들이 따라야 할 본보기가 되어야 한다.

5 일부 기업 대표들은 -하는 것이 중요하다고 생각한다.

6 기업의 베푸는 프로그램들은 -할 수 있다.

7 많은 소비자들은 그들이 -할 때 기분이 좋아진다.

A 회사들을 더 성공적으로 만든다
B 경제 불황기 동안 무료 물품을 제공한다
C 직원들에게 수익을 분배한다
D 회사 정책의 변화를 광고한다
E 자선 프로그램을 가진 사업체들을 지지한다
F 소비자 구매의 영향을 줄인다
G 어려움에 처한 사람들을 위해 더 좋은 환경을 만든다

5 해설 문제의 핵심어구(corporate leaders)와 관련된 지문 내용 중 'Many corporate owners and managers ~ feel that they have a responsibility to improve conditions for the disadvantaged.'에서 많은 기업 소유주들과 경영자들이 그들이 사회적 약자들을 위해 환경을 개선할 책임을 지고 있다고 느낀다고 하였으므로, 보기 **G** make better conditions for people in need가 정답이다. 'improve conditions for the disadvantaged'가 'make better conditions for people in need'로 paraphrasing되었다.

6 해설 문제의 핵심어구(Corporate giving programmes)와 관련된 지문 내용 중 'By advertising these types of socially responsible programmes, companies boost profits.'에서 사회적으로 책임을 지는 이러한 종류의 프로그램을 광고함으로써 회사들은 이윤을 증대시킨다고 하였으므로, 보기 **A** make companies more successful이 정답이다. 'boost profits'가 'make more successful'로 paraphrasing되었다.

7 해설 문제의 핵심어구(Many consumers feel better)와 관련된 지문 내용 중 'the programmes make customers ~ feel that they are doing good in the world by patronising the company'에서 그 프로그램들이 고객들로 하여금 그 기업을 애용함으로써 세상에 좋은 일을 하고 있다고 느끼도록 한다고 하였으므로, 보기 **E** support businesses with charitable programmes가 정답이다. 'patronising the company'가 'support businesses'로 paraphrasing되었다.

동남아시아와 호주에서 발견되는 베짜기개미들은 나무 꼭대기 높이 위치한 살아있는 잎으로부터 보금자리를 짓는 그들의 재능으로 가장 유명하다. 대부분의 개미 종들처럼, 베짜기개미의 삶은 여왕개미를 부양하는 것을 중심으로 돌아간다. 사실, 그들이 보금자리를 짓는 것이 애초에 그녀의 시중을 들기 위함이다. ⁸모든 것은 여왕개미가 잎에 한 배의 알을 낳고 그들이 성충 일개미가 될 때까지 유충들을 키움으로써 군집을 이루는 것으로부터 시작한다. 군집의 크기를 늘리기 위해, 여왕개미는 알을 더 낳아야 하지만, 이것은 이미 성충이 된 개미들을 위한 추가적인 생활 공간이 필요하게 할 것이다. 따라서, 보금자리가 지어져야 하는데 이는 상당한 협력을 필요로 하는 과제이다. 먼저, 개미 한 마리가 멀리 떨어져 있는 잎을 향해 몸을 뻗는다. ⁹혼자서는 그것에 닿을 수 없기 때문에, 다른 개미들이 잎이 마침내 붙잡힐 때까지 띠를 형성하며 첫 번째 개미에 매달린다. 일단 잎을 잡으면, 그들은 두 잎이 한데 모일 때까지 다 함께 잡아당긴다. 잎들을 그 자리에 유지시키며, 그들은 다른 일개미들이 유충을 들고 오기를 기다리는데, 이들은 실을 생산할 수 있다. ¹⁰유충은 그들의 침샘으로부터 실을 내보내도록 유도되고, 일개미들은 기본적으로 그것들을 묶으면서, 그 끈적이는 물질을 하나의 잎에서 다른 나뭇잎에 바른다. 궁극적으로, 이 과정은 군집의 증가하는 개체 수를 수용하기에 충분히 큰 보금자리가 지어질 때까지 반복되고, 이 주기는 여왕개미가 알을 더 낳을 때마다 마찬가지로 반복된다.

8   …………은 알을 낳고 새끼를 키움으로써 군집을 세운다.

9   개미들은 잎을 모으기 위해 …………을 형성하려고 결합한다.

10   유충의 …………은 보금자리의 잎에 붙는다.

8   해설 문제의 핵심어구(establishes a colony)와 관련된 지문 내용 중 'It all starts with a queen founding a colony by laying a clutch of eggs ~ and raising the larvae'에서 모든 것은 여왕개미가 한 배의 알을 낳고 유충들을 키움으로써 군집을 이루는 것으로부터 시작한다고 하였으므로, **queen**이 정답이다. 'laying a clutch of eggs ~ and raising the larvae'가 'laying eggs and raising young'으로 paraphrasing되었다.

9   해설 문제의 핵심어구(collect leaves)와 관련된 지문 내용 중 'Unable to get to it alone, the other ants hold onto the first ant, forming a chain until the leaf is finally grasped.'에서 혼자서는 그것에 닿을 수 없기 때문에 다른 개미들이 잎이 마침내 붙잡힐 때까지 띠를 형성하며 첫 번째 개미에 매달린다고 하였으므로, **chain**이 정답이다. 'the other ants hold onto the first ant'가 'The ants connect'로 paraphrasing되었다.

10   해설 문제의 핵심어구(sticks to the leaves)와 관련된 지문 내용 중 'The larvae are prompted to release the silk ~ and the worker ants dab the sticky substance from one leaf to another'에서 유충은 실을 내보내도록 유도되고 일개미들은 그 끈적이는 물질을 하나의 잎에서 다른 나뭇잎에 바른다고 하였으므로, **silk**가 정답이다. 'dab the sticky substance from one leaf to another'가 'sticks to the leaves of a nest'로 paraphrasing되었다.

'신데렐라', '백설 공주', 그리고 '잠자는 숲 속의 공주'는 모두 고전 애니메이션으로 간주되지만, 세 가지 모두 사실 흔히 그림 형제로 알려진 두 명의 독일 작가들에 의해 출판된 이야기를 기반으로 한 것이다. 야코프 그림과 빌헬름 그림이 종종 이러한 동화들의 작가로써 거론되지만, 그들은 사실 스스로 그 이야기들을 생각해내지는 않았다. ¹¹그 이야기들은 그림 형제보다 훨씬 이전에 독일과 근처 지역들에서 한 세대로부터 다음 세대로 구전으로 전해 내려왔다. 하지만, 그 형제는, 이야기들이 잊혀질 위험에 처했다고 생각하여, 그것들을 기록하기 시작했다. 이렇게 하기 위해, 그들은 그 문화권의 이야기들을 알아내고자 친구들, 친척들, 작가들 그리고 귀족들을 취재했다. 이야기들을 수집한 후에, 그림 형제는 그것들을 문서로 만드는 것에 착수했다. 글을 쓰고 편집하는 과정 동안, ¹²그들은 같은 이야기의 다른 버전들을 결합했으며 문체의 일관성을 부여하고 기본적인 줄거리를 개선하기 위해 그것들을 편집했는데, 그렇게 함으로써 그 이야기들을 그들의 것으로 만들었다. ¹³마침내 출간되었을 때, 그들의 책 '아이들과 가정의 민화'는 베스트셀러였다. 그것은 계속해서 여러 차례 재인쇄되었으며 마침내 책의 제목이 '그림 동화'로 변경되었다. 이것이 우리가 그 책에 대해 여전히 사용하는 이름임에도 불구하고, 그것이 포함했던 이야기들은 오늘날 우리가 알고 있는 것들과 완전히 같지는 않았다. ¹⁴그 형제의 원작 이야기들의 대부분은 아이들을 위해 쓰여진 것이 아니었기 때문에, 어른을 위한 주제들을 더 많이 가지고 있었다. 시간이 지나면서, 이야기들은 어린 독자들에게 더 적합하게 하기 위해 편집되었고 전 세계 어린이 도서관의 주요 품목이 되었다. 실제로, 그들의 작품은 100개 이상의 언어로 번역되었다.

11 형제가 이용한 이야기들은 ....에 의해 전해졌다.

12 형제는 같은 이야기의 많은 다양한 ....을 취합했다.

13 책 '아이들과 가정의 민화'의 본래의 ....은 첫 출판 후에 바뀌었다.

14 형제의 작품에 있는 ....은 그것들이 어린 독자를 위한 것이 아니었다는 것을 보여준다.

11 해설 문제의 핵심어구(The stories ~ handed down)와 관련된 지문 내용 중 'The stories had been passed down through the oral tradition'에서 그 이야기들은 구전으로 전해 내려왔다고 하였으므로, **oral tradition**이 정답이다. 'passed down through'가 'handed down by'로 paraphrasing되었다.

12 해설 문제의 핵심어구(put together many different ~ of the same story)와 관련된 지문 내용 중 'they combined differing versions of the same tales'에서 그들은 같은 이야기의 다른 버전들을 결합했다고 하였으므로, **versions**가 정답이다. 'combined differing versions of the same tales'가 'put together many different versions of the same story'로 paraphrasing되었다.

13 해설 문제의 핵심어구(The book *Nursery and Household Tales*)와 관련된 지문 내용 중 'When it was finally published, their book *Nursery and Household Tales* was a blockbuster. It ~ had its title altered'에서 마침내 출간되었을 때, 그들의 책 '아이들과 가정의 민화'는 베스트셀러였고 책의 제목이 변경되었다고 하였으므로, **title**이 정답이다. 'had its title altered'가 'title was changed'로 paraphrasing되었다.

14 해설 문제의 핵심어구(not for young readers)와 관련된 지문 내용 중 'Most of the brothers' original stories had more adult themes, as they had not been written for children.'에서 그 형제의 원작 이야기들의 대부분은 아이들을 위해 쓰여진 것이 아니었기 때문에 어른을 위한 주제들을 더 많이 가지고 있었다고 하였으므로, **adult themes**가 정답이다. 'had not been written for children'이 'were not for young readers'로 paraphrasing되었다.

6

교육은 사회에 의해 다루어지는 가장 중요한 사안들 중 하나이다. [15]그것은 사람들에게 세상에서 살아남는 데 필요한 기본적인 기술을 제공하지만, 또한 그들에게 사회적 기여를 할 수 있도록 한다. 실제로, 미국의 전 영부인이었던 엘리너 루스벨트는 교육이 훌륭한 시민의 자질을 위해 필수적이라고 주장했다. 유감스럽게도, 미국과 같은 거대한 다문화 사회에서, 대중들을 교육하는 것은 어려울 수 있다. M. S. Rosenberg 박사에 따르면, 이것은 교육에 대한 뚜렷이 다른 문화적 접근법 때문이다. 예를 들어, 동양계 미국인 학생들의 부모는 때때로 그들에게 얌전히 앉고, 귀를 기울여 들으며, 교사들과 눈을 마주치는 것을 피하라고 할 수 있는데, 이는 이것들이 그들 문화권의 교육적인 가치였기 때문이다. 이것은 대부분의 유럽과 미국 학생들에게 주입된 토론 수업 그리고 시선을 마주치는 것의 중요성과 매우 대조적이다. 이 문제는 문화권들이 교실에서의 교사의 역할을 바라보는 다양한 방식에 의해 심화될 수 있다. 유럽과 미국의 부모들은 흔히 교사를 그들의 아이들을 교육하는 데 있어서 함께 일하는 참여자로 생각한다. 대부분의 히스패닉 문화권은, 반면에, 교사들을 전문가라고 여기며 교육과 관련된 의사 결정의 거의 모든 측면에서 그들의 의견에 따른다. 유감스럽게도, [16]이러한 문화적 차이를 이해하지 못하는 것은 학생들에게 심각한 부정적 영향을 미칠 수 있다. 유럽과 미국의 교육 방식으로 훈련된 교사들은 그 문화권 학생들의 적극적인 참여를 다른 학생들의 참여보다 우수하다고 생각할 수 있다. 그들은 또한 유럽과 미국의 부모들의 관여를 아이들의 교육에 대한 더 큰 관심의 신호로 여길 수 있다. 하지만, 그들은 문화적 규범을 단순히 잘못 이해하는 것일 수 있다. 이러한 문제들을 피하고 다문화적 환경에서 더 효율적으로 가르치기 위해, 교사들은 문화적 차이를 인식하고 그것들을 반영하기 위해 그들의 교육과 평가 방식을 조정하도록 교육받는다. 다시 말해서, [17]그들은 문화적 다양성을 고려하는 균등한 교육 기준을 시행하려고 노력한다.

15 교육은 필수적인 지식과 ....을 할 기회를 제공한다.

16 ....을 이해하는 데 실패하는 것은 학생들에게 상당한 부정적인 영향을 미칠 수 있다.

17 교사들은 서로 다른 배경을 존중하는 ....을 실시하려고 노력한다.

15 해설 문제의 핵심어구(Education provides ~ opportunity)와 관련된 지문 내용 중 'it also allows them to make societal contributions'에서 교육은 또한 그들에게 사회적 기여를 할 수 있도록 한다고 하였으므로, **societal contributions**가 정답이다. 'allows them to'가 'provide the opportunity to'로 paraphrasing되었다.

16 해설 문제의 핵심어구(a significant negative effect on students)와 관련된 지문 내용 중 'not understanding these cultural differences can have a major negative impact on students'에서 이러한 문화적 차이를 이해하지 못하는 것은 학생들에게 심각한 부정적 영향을 미칠 수 있다고 하였으므로, **cultural differences**가 정답이다. 'major negative impact'가 'significant negative effect'로 paraphrasing되었다.

17 해설 문제의 핵심어구(Teachers ~ put in place)와 관련된 지문 내용 중 'they attempt to implement uniform education standards which allow for cultural diversity'에서 교사들은 문화적 다양성을 고려하는 균등한 교육 기준을 시행하려고 노력한다고 하였으므로, **(uniform) standards/(uniform) education standards**가 정답이다. 'attempt to implement'가 'trying to put in place'로, 'allow for cultural diversity'가 'respect different backgrounds'로 paraphrasing되었다.

7

도시 밀도를 통한 자연 보호

환경적 지속 가능성을 생각할 때 머리에 떠오르는 첫 이미지는 대개 빽빽하게 사람들로 가득 찬 도시의 풍경은 아니다. 하지만, 1974년 저자 조지 단치그와 토마스 사티의 '조밀한 도시: 살기 좋은 도시 환경을 위한 계획'이 발행된 이래로, 대부분의 도시 계획자들은 지구를 푸르게 지키기 위한 가장 효율적인 방법이 꽉 찬 도시에 가능한 한 많은 사람들을 가득 채우는 것이라는 사실에 동의한다. 그들은, ¹⁸사람들을 도시에 수용해야 하는 가장 중요한 이유는 주변 지역으로의 도시 지역의 확장인 도시 스프롤 현상을 줄이기 위함이라고 말한다. 개발되지 않은 지역으로의 인구의 침해는 경작할 수 있는 땅과 생태계를 파괴할 뿐만 아니라, 또한 에너지 비효율적이고 자동차 의존적인 교외를 조성한다. 바깥으로 향하도록 도시를 건설하는 것보다는 위쪽으로 향하도록 건설하는 것이 이것을 피하기 위한 가장 좋은 방법이다.

만일 모든 사람들이 도시에 거주한다면, ¹⁹자동차의 필요성은 매우 줄어들 것인데, 이는 그것들이 유발하는 오염을 최소화하고 작동하는 데 필요한 화석 연료를 보존할 것이다. 연구들은 뉴욕과 같이 조밀하게 인구가 몰려 있는 도시에 사는 사람들은, 대중교통이 즉시 이용 가능하고 걷는 것이나 자전거를 타는 것이 종종 선택 가능한 사항이기 때문에 차를 소유할 가능성이 40퍼센트 더 낮으며 휘발유를 훨씬 더 적게 사용한다는 것을 보여준다. 도시에서 운전을 하는 것이 더욱더 어려워졌다는 것 또한 사람들이 그것을 포기하는 데 기여한다. 애석하게도 도로에 머물러 있는 다른 차량들의 공급 과잉은 말할 필요도 없이, 주차 제한 그리고 비싼 통행료와 씨름해야 하기 때문에, 많은 도시 거주자들은 훨씬 더 매력적인 이용 가능한 대체 교통이 있을 때 그저 운전을 하지 않는 것을 선택한다.

하지만 도시의 환경적 지속 가능성은 단순한 교통 이상의 것과 관련이 있다. 그것은 또한 주거에 대한 것이다. 고밀도 도시에 사는 사람들의 대다수는 아파트 건물에 거주하는데, 이것은 세계에서 가장 에너지 효율적인 주거 건축물이다. 아파트 건물의 공유되는 벽은 더 적은 열이 손실된다는 것을 의미하며 따라서, 열을 생산하기 위해 더 적은 연료가 사용된다는 것을 의미한다. 게다가, ²⁰대개 아파트는, 말하자면, 교외의 전형적인 단독 주택보다 작기 때문에, 한 가구당 훨씬 더 적은 전기가 소비되는데, 이는 인구가 드문드문 분포되어 있는 지역보다 사실상 50퍼센트만큼 더 적다. 그러므로 가장 밀도가 높은 도시 거주자들의 탄소 발자국이 세계 평균보다 약 30퍼센트 정도 더 적다는 것은 놀라운 일이 아니다.

궁극적으로, ²¹수백만 명의 다른 사람들과 어깨를 맞대고 있는 것이 불쾌해 보일 수도 있겠지만, 이는 다음 세대들이 살아가는 데 필요할 자원을 보존하면서 우리의 끝없이 증가하는 인구를 제어할 가장 좋은 방법이다. 오늘날 존재하는 도시들은 완벽한 것과는 거리가 멀지만, 그것은 도시 공동체를 더 지속 가능할 뿐 아니라 살기에 더 좋은 장소로 만들기 위해 디젤 자동차 무리를 하이브리드와 전기 자동차로 교체하는 것에서부터 낡고, 비효율적인 사회 기반 시설을 새롭게 하는 것까지 아직도 할 수 있는 일이 많이 있음을 의미한다.

18 사람들을 도시에 수용하는 주요한 이유는 ....을 제한하기 위함이다.

19 차에 대한 필요성의 큰 하락은 ....을 줄이고 화석 연료를 절약할 것이다.

20 더 작은 크기 때문에, 도시의 아파트들은 교외의 주택들보다 ....을 덜 사용한다.

21 인구가 조밀하게 몰려있는 도시에서 사는 것은 미래의 ....을 위해 자원을 보호하는 가장 좋은 방법이다.

정답·해설·해설

HACKERS IELTS READING

18 해설 문제의 핵심어구(containing people in cities is to limit)와 관련된 지문 내용 중 'The most important reason to contain people in cities ~ is to decrease sprawl'에서 사람들을 도시에 수용해야 하는 가장 중요한 이유는 도시 스프롤 현상을 줄이기 위함이라고 하였으므로, **sprawl**이 정답이다. 'most important reason ~ is to decrease'가 'primary reason ~ is to limit'으로 paraphrasing되었다.

19 해설 문제의 핵심어구(decrease in the need for cars)와 관련된 지문 내용 중 'the need for automobiles would be greatly reduced, which would minimise the pollution they cause'에서 자동차의 필요성은 매우 줄어들 것인데 이는 그것들이 유발하는 오염을 최소화할 것이라고 하였으므로, **pollution**이 정답이다. 'minimise the pollution'이 'reduce pollution'으로 paraphrasing되었다.

20 해설 문제의 핵심어구(their smaller size, urban apartments)와 관련된 지문 내용 중 'because apartments are usually smaller than ~ home in the suburbs, far less electricity is consumed'에서 대개 아파트는 교외의 주택보다 작기 때문에 훨씬 더 적은 전기가 소비된다고 하였으므로, **electricity**가 정답이다. 'because apartments are usually smaller'가 'due to their smaller size'로 paraphrasing되었다.

21 해설 문제의 핵심어구(protect resources for future)와 관련된 지문 내용 중 'while being shoulder-to-shoulder with millions of other people may seem unpleasant, it is the best way ~ preserving the resources that subsequent generations will need to survive'에서 수백만 명의 다른 사람들과 어깨를 맞대고 있는 것이 불쾌해 보일 수도 있겠지만 이는 다음 세대들이 살아가는 데 필요할 자원을 보존할 가장 좋은 방법이라고 하였으므로, **generations**가 정답이다. 'being shoulder-to-shoulder with millions of other people'이 'Living in densely populated cities'로 paraphrasing되었다.

8

유전자 치료
획기적인 치료법

의학 연구에 매년 수백만 달러의 비용이 쓰이고, 전례 없는 속도로 새로운 기술이 개발되고 있으며 중요한 발견들이 이루어지고 있음에도 불구하고, 암과 에이즈와 같은 많은 치명적인 질병들에 대한 치료법은 여전히 과학자들에게 발견되지 않고 있다. 하지만 유전자 치료로 알려진 치료 유형에 희망이 있을 수 있는데, 이것은 환자의 세포를 조작하기 위해 유전 형질을 이용하는 것을 수반한다. 이 개념은 1972년에 '인류의 유전 질병을 위한 유전자 치료?'에서 Theodore Friedmann과 Richard Roblin에 의해 처음으로 제안되었다. 이 논문은 건강한 DNA가 유전 질병을 앓고 있는 사람들의 결함이 있는 DNA를 대체하는 데 사용될 수 있다는 미국의 의사 Stanfield Roger의 초기 개념을 인용했다. Roger의 개념을 확장하여, Friedmann과 Roblin은 제대로 기능을 하도록 결함이 있는 유전자를 고치고, 대체하고, 혹은 보완하는 데 건강한 DNA가 사용될 수 있는 방법들을 제안했다. 연구자들은 빠르게 이 획기적인 새로운 개념에 착수했으며, 1990년 9월 미국에서 첫 번째 유전자 치료의 사례가 승인되었다.

유전자 치료가 그 이후로 몇 년 간 백혈병, 혈우병, 그리고 파킨슨병과 같은 병을 앓는 환자들을 성공적으로 치료했음에도 불구하고, 그것에 문제들이 없는 것은 아니다. 환자에게 건강한 DNA를 주는 것의 가장 어려운 부분은 건강하지 않은 세포가 그것을 받아들이도록 하는 것이다. 수용 세포에 건강한 DNA를 직접 주입하는 것을 포함하는 기술들이 약간의 성공을 보여주었지만, 더 흔히 사용되는 방법은 외부의 유전 형질을 다른 세포로 옮기는 운송 수단으로서 기능하는 DNA 분자인 매개체의 사용을 통한 것이다.

²²바이러스는 자연적으로 세포에 침투하기 때문에 가장 흔히 사용되는 매개체이다. ²²그것들이 사용될 때, 일부 바이러스의 DNA는 제거되며 치료 DNA로 대체되지만, 바이러스의 구조적인 순서는 그대로 유지되며 매개체의 '중추'로서 기능한다. 이것은 환자의 세포에 그것이 들어오는 것을 허용하도록 속이지만, 항상 기대했던 것처럼 작동하지는 않는다. 이것은 ²³동시에 치료 유전자를 죽이면서, 환자의 면역 체계가 기능을 발휘하여 바이러스와 싸워 이길 가능성이 언제나 존재한다는 사실 때문이다. 이 과정은 환자 내부에서 염증 반응을 일으킬 수 있으며, 어떤 경우에는, 장기부전으로 이어질 수 있다.

그렇지 않으면, 바이러스성 매개체는 환자의 내부에 들어가 질병을 유발할 가능성이 있으며 건강한 것들을 포함하여 의도했던 것보다 더 많은 세포를 표적으로 삼을 수도 있다. ²⁴이러한 위험들로 인해, 유전자 치료는 아직도 실험적인 것으로 간주되며 그것을 받을 수 있는 유일한 방법은 임상 시험의 참여를 통해서이다. 의사들은 그들이 유전자 치료가 인체에 미칠 수 있는 모든 가능한 영향에 대해 이해하기까지 아직도 갈 길이 멀고, 따라서 추후 발전이 이루어지고 식품 의약국과 국립 보건원 모두가 그 치료법이 주류 의술에 들어가기에 충분히 안전하다고 간주할 때까지 연구는 계속될 것이다.

22 바이러스가 매개체로 사용될 때, 그것의 구조는 -하다.

23 면역 체계가 바이러스와 싸울 때, 그것은 또한 -하다.

24 특정 위험들 때문에, 유전자 치료는 -하다.

A 질병을 치료하기로 되어 있는 유전 형질도 파괴한다
B 생명을 위협하는 질병을 치료할 수 있다
C 추가된 건강한 DNA를 받아들인다
D 그것의 기본 형태를 유지한다
E 지금으로서는 시험적인 상태로 남아 있다
F 환자의 세포에 침입한다
G 병든 요소를 제거한다

22 해설 문제의 핵심어구(used as a vector, its structure)와 관련된 지문 내용 중 'Viruses are the most commonly used vectors'와 'When they are used ~ the virus's structural sequence stays intact'에서 바이러스는 가장 흔히 사용되는 매개체이며 그것들이 사용될 때 바이러스의 구조적인 순서는 그대로 유지된다고 하였으므로, 보기 **D** retains its basic form 이 정답이다. 'virus's structural sequence stays intact'가 'its structure retains its basic form'으로 paraphrasing되었다.

23 해설 문제의 핵심어구(immune system fights viruses)와 관련된 지문 내용 중 'the patient's immune system will kick in and fight off the virus, killing the therapeutic gene at the same time'에서 동시에 치료 유전자를 죽이면서 환자의 면역 체계가 기능을 발휘하여 바이러스와 싸워 이길 것이라고 하였으므로, 보기 **A** destroys any genetic material that is meant to cure disease가 정답이다. 'killing the therapeutic gene'이 'destroys genetic material that is meant to cure disease'로 paraphrasing되었다.

24 해설 문제의 핵심어구(Due to certain dangers)와 관련된 지문 내용 중 'Because of these risks, gene therapy is still considered experimental'에서 이러한 위험들로 인해 유전자 치료는 아직도 실험적인 것으로 간주된다고 하였으므로, 보기 **E** remains experimental for now가 정답이다. 'Because of these risks'가 'Due to certain dangers'로 paraphrasing 되었다.

9

감정의 심리학

그것들이 인간 행동의 너무나 넓은 범위를 아우르기 때문에, 감정은 항상 심리학적 연구의 중심적 위치였다. 감정 이론을 처음으로 소개한 인물 중 하나는 그리스의 철학자 아리스토텔레스였는데, 그는 그것들이 식욕과 관련이 있다고 생각했다. 이 생각은 찰스 다윈이 감정의 진화론적 개념을 만들어낼 때까지 수세기 동안 지배했다. 다윈은 감정이 자연 도태를 통해 진화했고 그러므로 목적을 가지고 있는 것이 틀림없다고 제안했다. 그러나, 그의 생각들은 심리학이라는 분야가 더 중요해지면서 대체되었다.

감정이 어떻게 작용하는지에 대한 매우 영향력 있는 이론은 William James와 Carl Lange 두 학자들에 의해 19세기 후반에 독립적으로 발전되었다. James-Lange설로 알려지게 된 이 이론은 생리적인 자극이 감정의 경험으로 이어진다고 제안했다. [25]이는 감정이 주로 정신적인 성격인 것이라는 전통적인 개념의 반전이었다. James와 Lange의 개념에서는 신체가 감정적 반응의 원천이었다. [26]James는 감각 기관이 외부 물체의 자극을 최초로 경험하는 신체의 부분이고, 이것들로부터의 정보는 그 다음에 뇌로 전달된다고 제안했다.

James-Lange설이 20세기 초에 지배적인 감정의 개념적인 해석이 되면서, 그것은 다른 연구자들에게 비판을 부추겼다. 한 비판적인 반응은 1920년대에 하버드 대학 생리학자 Walter Bradford Cannon과 그의 학생 Philip Bard로부터 왔다. Cannon과 Bard는 시상의 부위가 감정적 반응의 중심으로, 감정적 반응은 뇌의 시상하부 구조 내의 인지 반응의 결과라고 믿었다. Cannon과 Bard에 따르면, 감정에 대한 신체적 반응은 정신적 반응과 분리되어 고려될 수 있으며 언제나 그것들을 앞서지는 않는다.

James-Lange이론이 신체를 특히 중시하고 Cannon-Bard이론이 뇌를 우선시한 반면, 감정의 2요인 이론은 더 균형 잡힌 접근을 제공했다. 1960년대에 Stanley Schachter와 Jerome E. Singer에 의해 내세워진 이 이론은 감정적 반응이 신체적 자극과 정신적 표지의 두 가지 요인에 근거한다고 제안했다. 따라서, 어떤 사람이 감정을 경험할 때, 그들은 처음에 어떠한 형태의 생리적인 자극을 느끼고 그 다음에 그들의 환경에서 이것을 감정이라고 부르는 데 사용할 수 있는 것들을 찾는다. [27]누군가가 불안감의 신체적 증상을 느끼지만 그것들이 애정의 자극과 관련되어 있다고 믿을 때와 같이, 이는 때때로 오귀인을 야기할 수 있다. 심리학 집단 내에서의 분명한 의견 일치 없이, 감정이 마음에서 형성되는지 신체에서 형성되는지에 대한 논란은 계속될 것으로 보인다.

25 James-Lange 이론은 ....한 경험으로서의 감정이라는 전통적인 생각을 반박했다.

26 James는 ....이 뇌보다 자극을 먼저 경험한다고 믿었다.

27 ....의 징후는 때때로 애정의 감각과 혼동될 수 있다.

25 해설 문제의 핵심어구(James-Lange theory countered)와 관련된 지문 내용 중 'This was a reversal of the conventional conception that emotion was primarily mental in character.'에서 이는 감정이 주로 정신적인 성격인 것이라는 전통적인 개념의 반전이었다고 하였으므로, **mental**이 정답이다. 'reversal'이 'countered'로, 'conventional'이 'traditional'로 paraphrasing되었다.

26 해설 문제의 핵심어구(experience a stimulus before the brain)와 관련된 지문 내용 중 'James suggested that the sense organs are the first part of the body to experience the stimulus of an outside object, and that the information from these is then passed to the brain.'에서 James는 감각 기관이 외부 물체의 자극을 최초로 경험하는 신체의 부분이고, 이것들로부터의 정보는 그 다음에 뇌로 전달된다고 제안했다고 하였으므로, **sense organs**가 정답이다. 'sense organs are the first part of the body to experience the stimulus'가 'sense organs experience a stimulus before'로 paraphrasing되었다.

27 해설 문제의 핵심어구(confused with romantic sensations)와 관련된 지문 내용 중 'This can occasionally result in misattribution, as when someone feels the physical symptoms of anxiety, but believes them to be related to romantic arousal.'에서 누군가가 불안감의 신체적 증상을 느끼지만 그것들이 애정의 자극과 관련되어 있다고 믿을 때와 같이, 이는 때때로 오귀인을 야기할 수 있다고 하였으므로, **anxiety**가 정답이다. 'symptoms'가 'signs'로, 'arousal'이 'sensations'로 paraphrasing되었다.

10

피진어 말하기

'필요는 발명의 어머니이다'라는 말은 오랫동안 쓰여 왔으며, 언어학적 맥락에서 이 생각이 피진어보다 더 해당되는 것은 어디에도 없다. 아프리카, 카리브 해, 하와이, 그리고 동남아시아의 일부 지역 도처에서 발견되는 피진어는 둘 혹은 그 이상의 집단이 오랜 기간 동안 의사소통해야 하지만 구성원들이 공통의 언어를 공유하지 않을 때 발달하는 단순한 방언이다.

역사적으로, 피진어는 17세기와 18세기 동안 유럽 열강들의 신세계로의 식민 침략으로 인해 생겨났다. [28]영국, 프랑스, 포르투갈, 스페인, 그리고 네덜란드인들이 아메리카의 여러 지역을 식민화하면서, 그들이 말로 의사소통을 할 수 없는 원주민 부족들과 접촉하게 될 것은 불가피했다. 처음에, 그들은 이야기의 요지를 이해시키기 위해 몇 가지 손동작을 사용했을지도 모르지만, 인간은 선천적으로 언어 습득의 경향이 있으며 결국, 물물 교환과 같은 활동을 용이하게 하기 위해 단어를 배우고 사용하게 되었다.

수백만 명의 아프리카인들이 아메리카의 대규모 농장으로 보내졌던 노예 무역은, 특히 피진어의 더 큰 발전의 원인이다. 상당히 많은 방언이 아프리카 전역에서 사용되었고 사람들이 그 대륙의 다양한 지역에서 붙잡혔기 때문에, 새로운 노예들은 종종 그들의 포획자와 동료 노예들의 말을 이해할 수 없었다. [29]어쨌든 의사소통을 하기 위해, 그들은 한 언어로부터 한 단어를 가져오고 또 다른 언어로부터 한 단어를 가져오며 적응해야 했다. 결국, 이 방법을 통해, 가장 기본적인 정보를 전달하는 것이 가능해졌으며 사람들은 그들이 가장 많이 사용하는 언어로 이 체계가 없는 방언에 의존하기 시작했다.

피진어는 집단에 따라 각기 다르지만, 특정한 특성을 공유한다. 19세기 미국의 민속학자인 Charles Leland에 따르면, 모든 피진어들은 아주 어린 아이가 의사소통하는 것과 비슷하게 들린다. 특히, 단어의 발음만이 대체로 거의 정확하며 품사는 매우 유연한데, 이는 종종 즉흥적으로 변경된다. ³⁰그는 또한 피진어의 구사자들이 언어의 관습을 무시하는 경향이 있다는 것을 발견했다. 예를 들어, 대명사와 전치사 같은 기능어들을 말에 포함하지 않고, 그들은 거의 오로지 내용어에만 의존한다. 기본적으로, 가장 필수적인 어휘에 대한 얕은 지식을 가지고 문법을 염두에 두지 않는 피진어의 구사자들은, 그들의 요지는 전달할 수 있지만 그 이상은 할 수 없다.

물론, 피진어는 대개 오래 지속되지 않는다. 일반적으로, 몇 십 년 이내에, 아이들이 피진어 구사자들의 가정에서 태어날 때, 한 집단이 다른 집단의 언어를 배웠거나 두 집단 모두 새로운 공통의 언어를 배웠을 것이다. 때때로, 피진어 구사의 필요성은 한 집단이 지역을 떠날 때 사라진다. 예를 들어, 프랑스의 베트남 점령 기간 동안, 많은 베트남인들이 자신들의 제국주의 통치자들과 피진 프랑스어로 의사소통하는 법을 습득했다. ³¹베트남이 1954년 독립을 선언하고 프랑스인들이 떠났을 때, 이 방언은 더 이상 필요하지 않았고, 따라서 사람들은 대부분 그들의 주 언어를 다시 말하기 시작했다. 다음 세대의 아이들이 피진어를 모국어로 삼는 것을 의미하는, 피진어가 부활하는 드문 사례들에서, 피진어는 언제나 완전히 발달된 어휘와 문법 체계와 함께 점점 표준화되며 구조화되도록 발달한다. 결국, 그것은 크리올어로 알려진 구어체 언어의 한 형태가 된다.

28 원주민과 소통하기 위해, 유럽인들은 처음에 -에 의존했을지도 모른다.

29 노예들은 -을 위해 다양한 방언의 단어들을 결합했다.

30 Charles Leland에 따르면, 피진어 구사자는 -을 고수하지 않는다.

31 베트남의 피진 프랑스어는 -의 전형적인 예를 들기 위해 언급되었다.

A 피진어에 구조를 제공하는 과정
B 몸짓 언어의 사용
C 결국 불필요해진 방언
D 피진어의 다음 세대로의 전달
E 아메리카에서 사람들과의 소통
F 억압받은 사람들에게 지속되는 식민주의의 영향
G 일반적으로 언어 표현을 형성하는 기준들

28 해설 문제의 핵심어구(To communicate with natives)와 관련된 지문 내용 중 'As the British, French, Portuguese, Spanish, and Dutch colonised various areas of the Americas, it was inevitable that they would come into contact with native peoples with whom they were unable to communicate verbally. Initially, they may have used a few hand gestures'에서 영국, 프랑스, 포르투갈, 스페인, 그리고 네덜란드인들이 아메리카의 여러 지역을 식민화하면서 그들이 말로 의사소통을 할 수 없는 원주민 부족들과 접촉하게 될 것은 불가피했으며 처음에 그들은 몇 가지 손동작을 사용했을지도 모른다고 하였으므로, 보기 B the use of body language가 정답이다. 'used a few hand gestures'가 'relied on the use of body language'로 paraphrasing되었다.

29 해설 문제의 핵심어구(Slaves combined words)와 관련된 지문 내용 중 'In order to communicate at all, they were forced to adapt, picking up a word from one language here and a word from another language there.'에서 어쨌든 의사소통을 하기 위해 그들은 한 언어로부터 한 단어를 가져오고 또 다른 언어로부터 한 단어를 가져오며 적응해야 했다고 하였으므로, 보기 E communication with people in the Americas가 정답이다. 'picking up a word from one language here and a word from another language there'가 'combine words from various dialects'로 paraphrasing되었다.

30 해설 문제의 핵심어구(Charles Leland)와 관련된 지문 내용 중 'He also found that speakers of pidgin languages tend to ignore the conventions of language.'에서 그는 또한 피진어의 구사자들이 언어의 관습을 무시하는 경향이 있다는 것을 발견했다고 하였으므로, 보기 G the standards that generally shape verbal expression이 정답이다. 'tend to ignore the conventions'가 'not stick to the standards'로 paraphrasing되었다.

해설 문제의 핵심어구(Pidgin French in Vietnam)와 관련된 지문 내용 중 'When Vietnam declared its independence in 1954 and the French left, there was no longer a need for this dialect'에서 베트남이 1954년 독립을 선언하고 프랑스인들이 떠났을 때 피진 프랑스어는 더 이상 필요하지 않았다고 하였으므로, 보기 C a dialect that eventually became unnecessary가 정답이다. 'there was no longer a need'가 'eventually became unnecessary'로 paraphrasing되었다.

HACKERS TEST

p.154

1	E	2	D	3	F	4	B
5	G	6	digital model	7	(horizontal) layers	8	function
9	kidney	10	toxicity	11	False	12	True
13	Not given	14	True				

3D 프린터와 인체 조직
3D 인쇄가 의학의 미래인가?

3D 프린터를 위한 기술이 1980년대부터 있어왔음에도 불구하고, 3D 프린터가 상업적으로 널리 이용 가능해진 것은 그리 오래되지 않았다. [6]디지털 모델로부터 거의 모든 모양의 3차원 입체 물건을 생산하는 일은 그 이후 이 획기적인 기술의 발견을 적용할 방법을 열렬히 찾는 경제의 거의 모든 분야들과 함께, 기하급수적으로 시작되었다. 대부분의 사람들이 3D 인쇄가 건축, 공사, 산업 디자인, 그리고 항공우주산업과 같은 분야에 유용할 것이라고 예상하는 반면, [11]생명공학과 의학 연구에 대한 이 기술의 영향을 고려하는 사람들은 거의 없다. 하지만, 사실, 살아있는 인체 조직, 그리고 잠재적으로는 심지어 온전한 장기를 만들어내는 능력은 의학계를 매우 흥분하게 만든 것이었다.

지난 20년 동안, [1]의학 연구자들은 의학적인 목적으로 3차원의 생물학적 구조를 만들어내기 위해 이 기술을 활용하는 방법들을 실험해왔다. 이것이 어떻게 가능한지 이해하기 위해서는, 3D 인쇄가 어떻게 작동하는지 아는 것이 중요하다. 첫 번째 단계는 컴퓨터 이용 설계 소프트웨어 프로그램을 사용하여 원하는 물건의 3D 이미지를 만드는 것이다. [7]그러면 그 프로그램은 디지털 물체를 인쇄 단계를 위한 설계도가 되는 수백 또는 심지어 수천 개의 수평인 층들로 자른다. 인쇄 자체는 추가적인 과정을 이용하여 완성되는데, 이 과정에서 프린터가 일련의 횡단면들로부터 모델을 만들어내기 위해 바닥으로부터 위로 액체, 가루, 종이 또는 다른 물질의 연속적인 층들을 쌓는다. 그 후 그것은 최종적인 형태를 만들어내기 위해 이 층들을 결합한다.

그 기술이 알려지자마자, 의학 연구원들은 "다른 물질을 가지고 하듯이 살아있는 세포를 겹겹이 쌓고, 그렇게 함으로써 조직과 같은 생물학적 구조를 제작하는 것이 어떨까?"라고 생각했다. 2000년대 중반 이래로, 생명공학 회사들은 이 질문을 계속해 왔다. [8]몇 년 만에, 그들은 세포 기능과 생존 능력을 보존하는 인체 조직들을 생산하는 데 있어 상당한 성공을 거두었다. 지금까지 이와 같이 성공적으로 생산된 인체 조직의 종류들은 판막뿐 아니라 폐와 심장 근육의 일부, 그리고 심지어 인간의 귀까지 포함한다. [12]이 조직들을 실험실 동물들에게 이식하는 실험들은 굉장히 긍정적인 결과를 낳았다. 외과 전문의들 또한 피부와 근육을 포함하여 바이오프린트된* 몇몇 조직들을 인간 환자들에게 이식할 수 있었다.

이러한 발전들이 유망하기는 하지만, [2]가장 중요한 목표는 이식이 필요한 사람들을 위해 내부 장기들을 인쇄하는 데 있다. [3]복잡한 장기 기관을 만드는 것은 특히 그것이 인체와 융합될 때까지 생존하기에 충분한 산소를 가지고 있는 것을 만들어내는 것과 관련하여 커다란 도전이다. 하버드 대학 Jennifer Lewis 연구실의 최근의 한 획기적인 발견은 최초로 3D 인쇄된 신장 조직을 만들어냄으로써 이것을 현실에 더 가깝게 했다. [4]연구실의 연구원들은 신장 조직이 만들어지는 복잡한 구조와, 조직을 살아있는 상태로 유지하는 데 필수적인 혈관계 모두를 인쇄할 수 있도록 하는 혁신적인 바이오프린팅 시스템을 고안해냈다. 이 시스템을 이용하여 그들은 신장의 기본적인 부분이자 혈액을 여과시키는 것을 맡고 있는 요소인 근위 세뇨관을 생산할 수 있게 되었다. [9]Jennifer Lewis 팀은 수년 안에 온전한 신장을 생산할 수 있기를 희망한다. 세계 인구의 약 10퍼센트가 만성 신장 질환을 앓고 있고, 이식을 받기 전까지 많은 사람들이 기계에 의존하고 있기 때문에, 이것은 몇 백만 명의 사람들에게 인생을 바꾸는 의학적인 진보가 될 수 있을 것이다. [13]과학자들은 이제 3D 인쇄된 다른 장기들 또한 십 년이 채 지나기 전에 이용 가능해질 것이라고 믿는다.

장기 교체 이외에, 바이오프린트된 조직은 또한 의학 연구와 의약품 개발에도 사용될 수 있다. 예를 들어, 과학자들은 [14]매우 작을지라도, 바이오프린트된 간의 조각들이 다 자란 인간의 간과 매우 비슷한 방식으로 의약품에 반응한다는 것을 알아냈다. [10]이것은 연구자들이 비용이 많이 드는 환자들과의 임상 시험을 승인하기 전에 새로운 의약품의 독성을 시험하는 것을 가능하게 했다. 매년 임상 시험에서 수십억 달러를 절약할 수 있는 가능성은 투자자들의 관심을 끌었다. 곧 일어날 듯한 다른 가능성들도 있다. 몇몇 실험실들은 현재 피부 세포들을 상처에 직접 적용할 수 있는 바이오프린터들을 개발하고 있다. [5]레이저와 함께 작동하는 이 프린터는 상처의 크기와 깊이를 스캔하고 그 후 상처 부위에 제재를 얼마나 놓을지를 결정하는 데 사용될 상처의 3D 위상 지도를 생산할 것이다. 같은 기술이 신체가 잘 치유되지 않는 노인들이나 당뇨가 있는 사람들의 상처를 낫게 하는 데 사용될 수 있다. 그것은 궁극적으로 큰 상처를 꿰매는 것과 같은 간단한 수술의 해결책이 될 수도 있다. 조직들을 바이오프린팅하는 것이 유용할 수 있는 모든 방식들을 생각하면, 이것이 의학계를 강타하고 있는 것이 놀라운 일은 아니다.

*바이오프린트하다: 바이오프린터를 사용하여 생물학적인 구조(조직, 장기 등)를 3D 인쇄하는 것

어휘 tissue n. 조직 solid adj. 입체의 exponentially adv. 기하급수적으로 aerospace n. 항공우주산업 horizontal adj. 수평의 blueprint n. 설계도, 청사진 cross section phr. 횡단면, 단면도 viability n. 생존 능력 valve n. 판막 transplant v. 이식하다 integrate v. 융합하다, 통합하다 kidney n. 신장 vascular system phr. 혈관계 proximal tubule phr. 근위 세뇨관 sliver n. (깨지거나 잘라낸) 조각 toxicity n. 독성 on the horizon phr. 곧 일어날 듯한 topological adj. 위상의 deposit v. (특정한 곳에) 놓다, 두다 diabetes n. 당뇨 take ~ by storm phr. 강타하다, 단숨에 사로잡다

[1-5]

1 의학 연구원들은 -하기 위해 실험을 수행해왔다.

2 바이오 프린팅 기술의 최종 목적은 -하는 것이다.

3 어려운 과제는 그것들이 -할 때까지 충분한 산소를 가진 장기를 만드는 것이다.

4 하버드 연구원들은 -할 수 있는 구조를 만드는 과정을 개발했다.

5 레이저와 프린터는 상처를 스캔한 후에 -할 수 있다.

A 의료 기기를 만든다
B 조직을 살아있는 상태로 유지한다
C 도움 없이 수술을 진행한다
D 인간의 이식을 위해 장기를 제공한다
E 의학에서의 사용을 위해 3D 생물 구조를 만든다
F 인체와 융합한다
G 상처의 3D 지도를 만든다

---

1 해설 문제의 핵심어구(Medical researchers ~ conducting tests)와 관련된 지문 내용 중 'medical researchers have been experimenting with ways to use the technology to create three-dimensional biological structures for medical purposes'에서 의학 연구자들은 의학적인 목적으로 3차원의 생물학적 구조를 만들어내기 위해 이 기술을 활용하는 방법들을 실험해왔다고 하였으므로, 보기 **E** make 3D biological structures for use in medicine이 정답이다. 'create three-dimensional biological structures for medical purposes'가 'make 3D biological structures for use in medicine'으로 paraphrasing되었다.

2 해설 문제의 핵심어구(The eventual goal)와 관련된 지문 내용 중 'the ultimate goal remains printing internal organs for humans in need of a transplant'에서 가장 중요한 목표는 이식이 필요한 사람들을 위해 내부 장기들을 인쇄하는 데 있다고 하였으므로, 보기 **D** provide organs for transplants in humans가 정답이다. 'printing internal organs for humans in need of a transplant'가 'provide organs for transplants in humans'로 paraphrasing되었다.

3 해설 문제의 핵심어구(organs with sufficient oxygen)와 관련된 지문 내용 중 'Developing complex organs is a major challenge, especially in regard to creating one that has enough oxygen to survive until it can integrate with the body.'에서 복잡한 장기 기관을 만드는 것은 특히 그것이 인체와 융합될 때까지 생존하기에 충분한 산소를 가지고 있는 것을 만들어내는 것과 관련하여 커다란 도전이라고 하였으므로, 보기 **F** fuse with the body가 정답이다. 'integrate with the body'가 'fuse with the body'로 paraphrasing되었다.

4 해설 문제의 핵심어구(Harvard researchers developed)와 관련된 지문 내용 중 'Researchers at the lab came up with an innovative bioprinting process that allows them to print ~ the vascular systems which are necessary to keep the tissue alive.'에서 연구실의 연구원들은 조직을 살아있는 상태로 유지하는 데 필수적인 혈관계를 인쇄할 수 있도록 하는 혁신적인 바이오프린팅 시스템을 고안해냈다고 하였으므로, 보기 **B** keep tissues alive가 정답이다. 'came up with'가 'developed'로 paraphrasing되었다.

5 해설 문제의 핵심어구(scan an injury)와 관련된 지문 내용 중 'Working in conjunction with a laser, the printer would scan the size and depth of an injury and then produce a topological 3D map of the wound'에서 레이저와 함께 작동하는 이 프린터는 상처의 크기와 깊이를 스캔하고 그 후 상처의 3D 위상 지도를 생산할 것이라고 하였으므로, 보기 **G** create a 3D map of the wound가 정답이다. 'Working in conjunction with a laser, the printer would scan the size and depth of an injury'가 'A laser and printer could ~ scan an injury'로 paraphrasing되었다.

[6-10]

6 최근 몇 년 간, ...에 기반을 둔 다양한 3D 물체들을 만드는 일이 폭발적으로 증가했다.

7 인쇄 이전에, 컴퓨터 프로그램은 3D 이미지를 많은 ....으로 잘라 설계도를 만든다.

8 짧은 시간 안에, 생명공학 회사들은 세포의 ....과 생존 능력을 유지하는 인체 조직을 만들었다.

9 하버드 대학의 한 팀은 가까운 미래에 완전한 ....을 생산하는 것을 목표로 한다.

10 연구자들은 이제 인체 시험 전에 약물의 ....을 시험할 수 있다.

6 해설 문제의 핵심어구(creating various 3D objects ~ has exploded)와 관련된 지문 내용 중 'The practice of producing three-dimensional solid objects of almost any shape from a digital model has since taken off exponentially'에서 디지털 모델로부터 거의 모든 모양의 3차원 입체 물건을 생산하는 일은 그 이후 기하급수적으로 시작되었다고 하였으므로, **digital model**이 정답이다. 'producing three-dimensional solid objects of almost any shape ~ has since taken off exponentially'가 'creating various 3D objects ~ has exploded'로 paraphrasing되었다.

7 해설 문제의 핵심어구(cutting a 3D image into)와 관련된 지문 내용 중 'The program then slices the digital object into hundreds or even thousands of horizontal layers that become the blueprint'에서 그러면 그 프로그램은 디지털 물체를 설계도가 되는 수백 또는 심지어 수천 개의 수평적인 층들로 자른다고 하였으므로, **(horizontal) layers**가 정답이다. 'slices the digital object into'가 'cutting a 3D image into'로 paraphrasing되었다.

8 해설 문제의 핵심어구(biotech firms)와 관련된 지문 내용 중 'In only a few years, they achieved significant success in producing human tissues that preserve cell function and viability.'에서 몇 년 만에 생명공학 회사들은 세포 기능과 생존 능력을 보존하는 인체 조직들을 생산하는 데 있어 상당한 성공을 거두었다고 하였으므로, **function**이 정답이다. 'preserve cell function and viability'가 'maintained the function and viability of cells'으로 paraphrasing되었다.

9 해설 문제의 핵심어구(A team at Harvard)와 관련된 지문 내용 중 'The Jennifer Lewis team hopes to be able to manufacture a kidney in its entirety in a matter of years.'에서 Jennifer Lewis 팀은 수년 안에 온전한 신장을 생산할 수 있기를 희망한다고 하였으므로, **kidney**가 정답이다. 'hopes to be able to manufacture'가 'aims to produce'로 paraphrasing되었다.

10 해설 문제의 핵심어구(prior to human trials)와 관련된 지문 내용 중 'This has allowed researchers to test the toxicity of new drugs before approving expensive clinical trials with patients.'에서 이것은 연구자들이 비용이 많이 드는 환자들과의 임상 시험을 승인하기 전에 새로운 의약품의 독성을 시험하는 것을 가능하게 했다고 하였으므로, **toxicity**가 정답이다. 'before approving ~ clinical trials with patients'가 'prior to human trials'로 paraphrasing되었다.

[11-14]

11 대부분의 사람들은 의학적 연구에서의 3D 인쇄의 유용성을 이해한다.

해설 문제의 핵심어구(usefulness of 3D printing for medical research)와 관련된 지문 내용 중 'few consider the implications of this technology for ~ medical research'에서 의학 연구에 대한 이 기술의 영향을 고려하는 사람들은 거의 없다고 하였으므로, 주어진 문장은 지문의 내용과 일치하지 않음을 알 수 있다. 따라서 정답은 **False**이다.

12 동물에 대한 바이오프린트된 조직의 시험들은 유망한 결과를 보였다.

해설 문제의 핵심어구(Tests of bioprinted tissue in animals)와 관련된 지문 내용 중 'Experiments transplanting these tissues into laboratory animals have produced overwhelmingly positive results.'에서 이 조직들을 실험실 동물들에게 이식하는 실험들은 굉장히 긍정적인 결과를 낳았다고 하였으므로, 주어진 문장은 지문의 내용과 일치함을 알 수 있다. 따라서 정답은 **True**이다. 'produced overwhelmingly positive results'가 'have shown promising results'로 paraphrasing 되었다.

13 3D 인쇄된 장기를 이용하는 것은 10년 내에 이식의 비용을 낮출 수 있다.

해설 문제의 핵심어구(3D printed organs ~ 10 years)와 관련된 지문 내용 중 'Scientists now believe that other 3D printed organs could also be available in less than a decade.'에서 과학자들은 이제 3D 인쇄된 다른 장기들 또한 십 년이 채 지나기 전에 이용 가능해질 것이라고 믿는다고는 하였지만, 주어진 문장의 내용은 확인할 수 없다. 따라서 정답은 **Not given**이다.

14 의약품은 온전한 간에 하는 것과 마찬가지로 바이오프린트된 작은 간의 조각들에 영향을 미친다.

해설 문제의 핵심어구(Drugs affect small bioprinted pieces)와 관련된 지문 내용 중 'bioprinted slivers of liver, although extremely tiny, respond to drugs in ways that are very similar to the full-grown human liver'에서 매우 작을지라도 바이오프린트된 간의 조각들이 다 자란 인간의 간과 매우 비슷한 방식으로 의약품에 반응한다고 하였으므로, 주어진 문장은 지문의 내용과 일치함을 알 수 있다. 따라서 정답은 **True**이다. 'slivers of liver'가 'pieces of liver'로, 'full-grown human liver'가 'whole liver'로 paraphrasing되었다.

CHAPTER 06 Summary Completion

* 각 문제에 대한 정답의 단서는 지문에 문제 번호와 함께 별도의 색으로 표시되어 있습니다.

EXAMPLE
p.162

낙타와 비슷한 라마는 한때 북아메리카에 서식했지만, 마지막 빙하기 때 사라졌다. 그러나, 남아메리카에서는 생존했는데, 그 곳에서 잉카족이 그것을 다양한 목적으로 사용했다. 그들은 이르면 6,000년 전에 라마를 사육했고 그 동물과 친밀한 관계를 형성했다. 서기 600년에 이르러, [1]그 동물들은 농부들과 주민들에게 식료품과 건축 자재를 운송하는 짐 운반용 동물로서 매우 중요해졌다. 큰 수컷 동물은 약 30킬로그램의 화물을 하루에 20킬로미터 운반할 수 있었다. 속도가 대단하지는 않았지만, 그들의 훈련 가능성은 다른 어떤 동물들보다도 더 그 일에 그들을 적합하게 했다. 라마들은 엄청난 거리에 걸쳐 사람이 자재를 운반하거나 끄는 부담을 크게 완화해주었다.

HACKERS PRACTICE
p.164

1	security	2	techniques	3	fabric
4	warriors	5	muscles	6	false statement
7	gestures	8	C	9	G
10	D	11	F	12	E
13	D	14	A	15	D
16	G	17	H	18	E
19	factories	20	cities	21	lifestyle
22	E	23	D	24	B
25	C	26	natural resources	27	horse-drawn wagons
28	barrier	29	ships/boats	30	G
31	C	32	E	33	A
34	F				

1

1879년에, 캐나다 정부는 캐나다의 제조업체들을 보호하고 서부 국경 지역의 정착을 촉진하는 것을 추구했던 경제 계획인 내셔널폴리시를 제정했다. 계획의 주요 지지자인 존 맥도널드 수상의 주 목표는 수입 제품에 대한 캐나다의 의존성을 줄이는 것이었다. 이것을 이루기 위해, 그는 수입되었던 모든 제품에 높은 관세를 도입했다. 그는 [1]관세가 캐나다인들을 위한 더 높은 생활 수준과 더 나은 고용 보장으로 이어질 것이라고 주장했고, 이는 동부의 제조업 분야의 사람들에게 실제로 그러했는데, 그곳에서 캐나다는 즉각적으로 증가된 생산과 수익을 경험했다.

그러나 서부 정착의 포부는 실현이 지체되었다. 무료 혹은 저렴한 땅으로 해외의 농부들을 불러들이는 것을 시도했던 적극적인 이민 캠페인에도 불구하고, 캐나다는 1880년대에 이민자 수의 하락을 목격했다. 경제학자 Ken Norrie에 따르면, 이것은 내셔널폴리시의 영향력이 서부의 정착에는 썩 좋지 않았다는 것을 보여준다. 실제로, [2]향상된 농업 기술과 전 세계적으로 순조로운 경제 상황과 같은 외부적 요인들이 주로 원인들이었다. 예를 들어, 밀의 가격은 1891년과 1921년 사이에 네 배가 되었고, 이것은 이윤을 추구하는 농업 종사자들을 캐나다의 비옥한 밀 생산 지역으로 떼지어 몰려오게 했다.

내셔널폴리시는 제조 산업을 보호하고 경제 성장과 서부의 정착을 장려하기 위해 계획되었다. 높은 관세를 이용하여, 수상은 국가의 동부 지역의 생활 수준과 고용 1 ....을 증가시켰다. 그러나 서부 정착의 목표는 빨리 이루어지지 않았다. 실제로, 내셔널폴리시는 이에 대해 그리 크지 않은 영향을 미쳤다. 농업에서의 더 나은 2 ....과 순조로운 세계 경제가 더 중요했다.

1 해설 문제의 핵심어구(high tariff)와 관련된 지문 내용 중 'the tariff would lead to a higher standard of living and greater employment security ~ and it did for those in the manufacturing sectors of the East'에서 관세는 더 높은 생활 수준과 더 나은 고용 보장으로 이어질 것이었고 이는 동부의 제조업 분야의 사람들에게 실제로 그러했다고 하였으므로, 정답은 **security**이다. 'employment security'가 'job security'로 paraphrasing되었다.

2 해설 문제의 핵심어구(in agriculture)와 관련된 지문 내용 중 'the development of improved agricultural techniques, and favourable economic conditions globally, were largely responsible'에서 향상된 농업 기술과 전 세계적으로 순조로운 경제 상황이 주로 원인이었다고 하였으므로, 정답은 **techniques**이다. 'improved agricultural techniques'가 'Better techniques in agriculture'로, 'favourable economic conditions'가 'good world economy'로 paraphrasing되었다.

2

오늘날 옷에 금속 단추나 징을 붙이는 것은 1980년대의 펑크 그리고 메탈 하위 문화와 관련되어 있지만, 이 관행은 새로운 것이 아니다. 사실, 금속 단추나 징은 자기 자신을 보호하고 공격의 태도를 드러내는 것이 필요했던 시간만큼 계속 존재해 왔다. ³에를 들어, 중세의 미늘 갑옷은 천 위의 강판으로 구성된 갑옷의 형태였고, 이 판들은 현대 패션에서 사용되는 금속 단추와 유사한 금속 기구로 천 위에 고정되었다. 하지만 강판이 붙어 있도록 유지하는 것 외에도, 그것들은 무겁고 뭉툭한 무기의 충격을 흡수하는 것을 돕고 칼날이 뚫고 들어오는 것을 어렵게 했다. 이와 같은 방안은 동물들에게 입혔던 보호 장구에도 적용되었다. 특히, 사냥개들은, 고대 로마의 주인들이 사자나 곰과 같이 위험한 사냥감을 잡기 위해 그들을 데리고 나갈 때 주로 징으로 된 목걸이가 채워졌다. 이렇게 하면, 개가 목을 물려도, 징이 개를 보호해주고 그 과정에서 더 사나운 맹수를 다치게 할 수도 있었다. 그리고 ⁴애초에 금속이나 징이 박힌 의복을 입은 유일한 사람들은 전사였다는 것이 상당히 명백했기 때문에, 위협 또한 이유들 중 하나였다. 사람들은 자연히 그러한 옷을 입은 사람 근처에는 가지 않았다. 본질적으로, 요즘은 금속이나 징이 실질적으로 이용되지는 않지만, 그것들은 포악성의 상징이자 거리를 두라는 다른 사람들에 대한 경고로서 존속하고 있다.

금속 단추의 역사

금속 단추와 징은 역사를 통틀어 보호를 위해 사용되었다. 미늘 갑옷으로 알려진 중세 갑옷의 한 종류에서는 그것들이 강판을 3 ....에 고정해, 사람들을 부상으로부터 안전하게 했다. 그것들은 또한 위협을 위해 사용되었다. 금속 단추와 징이 박힌 옷을 입은 사람들은 그들이 4 ....였기 때문에 위험하다고 알려졌으며, 따라서 다른 사람들은 그들을 피했다.

3 해설 문제의 핵심어구(medieval armour known as the brigandine)와 관련된 지문 내용 중 'The medieval brigandine ~ was a form of armour that consisted of steel plates on top of fabric, and the plates were riveted there by fasteners that resembled the studs'에서 중세의 미늘 갑옷은 천 위의 강판으로 구성된 갑옷의 형태였고 이 판들은 금속 단추와 유사한 금속 기구로 천 위에 고정되었다고 하였으므로, **fabric**이 정답이다. 'the plates were riveted ~ by fasteners'가 'they fastened steel plates to'로 paraphrasing되었다.

4 해설 문제의 핵심어구(people in spiked or studded clothes)와 관련된 지문 내용 중 'the only individuals who wore studded or spiked garments ~ were warriors'에서 금속이나 징이 박힌 의복을 입은 유일한 사람들은 전사였다고 하였으므로, **warriors**가 정답이다. 'individuals who wore studded or spiked garments'가 'people in spiked or studded clothes'로 paraphrasing되었다.

3

가끔은 가면을 쓰거나 사실을 과장하고 싶을 때가 있겠지만, 우리 중에 가장 설득력 있는 사람도 단 한 명의 의심도 사지 않는 사기 행위를 해낼 수는 없는 것으로 보인다. 이는 [5]인간의 얼굴에 있는 근육이 무의식 중에 감정에 반응하기 때문이다. 거짓말을 하는 사람이 실제로 어떻게 느끼는지 드러내는 노려봄, 능글맞은 웃음, 그리고 찡그림은 그 혹은 그녀의 얼굴에 아주 짧은 순간 동안 확 나타나는데, 사실 이는 너무 짧아서 연구 심리학자 폴 에크만은 이러한 감정 표현을 '미세 표정'이라고 지칭했지만, 이는 실제로 발생하며, 탐지할 수 있다. 에크만에 따르면, 7가지의 보편적인 미세 표정에는 혐오, 분노, 두려움, 슬픔, 기쁨, 놀람, 그리고 경멸이 있다. 우리가 이 감정 중 어느 한 가지를 느낄 때, 그것들은 적어도 20분의 1초 동안 우리의 통제를 넘어선다. [6]허위 진술을 하는 사람을 녹화하고, 테이프를 한 장면 한 장면 살펴보는 것은 실제로 매우 진실되어 보이는 사람들에게서도 이러한 표정들을 적발해낼 수 있다. 물론, 이것이 항상 선택 가능한 사항인 것은 아니다. 그런 경우에는, [7]얼굴을 가리는 손 동작을 지켜보는 것이 바람직하다. 얼굴에서 가장 감정을 많이 보여주는 부분인 눈과 입 가까이에 손을 가져가는 사람들은 미세 표정이 발생하는 그 짧은 순간을 들키는 것을 피하고자 노력하고 있을 수도 있다.

> 우리가 특정 감정을 느낄 때 우리의 얼굴 5 ....의 자동적인 반응 때문에, 완벽한 거짓말은 가능하지 않을 수 있다. 미세 표정이라고 불리는 이러한 반응들은, 6 ....을 하는 어떤 사람을 찍은 비디오테이프의 각 장면을 분석함으로써 밝혀질 수 있다. 이것이 가능하지 않은 경우에는, 얼굴을 가리는 손 7 ....을 지켜보는 것이 좋은 방안이다.

5 해설 문제의 핵심어구(automatic reactions)와 관련된 지문 내용 중 'muscles in the human face react involuntarily to emotions'에서 인간의 얼굴에 있는 근육이 무의식 중에 감정에 반응한다고 하였으므로, **muscles**가 정답이다. 'muscles in the human face react involuntarily'가 'automatic reactions of our facial muscles'로 paraphrasing되었다.

6 해설 문제의 핵심어구(frames of a videotape)와 관련된 지문 내용 중 'Videotaping a person who is providing a false statement and then going through the tape frame by frame can reveal these expressions'에서 허위 진술을 하는 사람을 녹화하고 테이프를 한 장면 한 장면 살펴보는 것은 이러한 표정들을 적발해낼 수 있다고 하였으므로, **false statement**가 정답이다. 'going through the tape frame by frame'이 'analysing the individual frames of a videotape'으로 paraphrasing되었다.

7 해설 문제의 핵심어구(hide the face)와 관련된 지문 내용 중 'keeping an eye out for hand gestures that obscure the face is advisable'에서 얼굴을 가리는 손 동작을 지켜보는 것이 바람직하다고 하였으므로, **gestures**가 정답이다. 'keeping an eye out for'가 'watch for'로, 'obscure the face'가 'hide the face'로 paraphrasing되었다.

4

블루길은 남아메리카에서 가장 유명한 낚시용 물고기 중 하나이며 민물 호수나 연못에서 자주 발견된다. 상대적으로 작은 이 물고기는 그들의 특이한 짝짓기 습성 때문에 야생 생물학자들의 집중적인 연구 대상이 되어왔다. 수컷이 새끼들을 돌본다는 점에서는 다른 어류와 유사하지만, 블루길은 몇몇 수컷이 다른 더 큰 수컷을 위한 알을 수정시키기 위해 속임수와 모방을 이용한다는 점이 특이하다. 수컷 블루길의 약 20퍼센트는 그들이 완전히 자라기 전에 속임수를 써서 짝짓기 과정에 진입하는 것을 시도한다. [8]cuckold 혹은 sneaker로 알려진 이 물고기들은 수컷 성어를 찾아내, 그 수컷의 구역 근처 수초에 숨어, 암컷 물고기 떼가 그곳을 지나기를 기다린다. 암컷은 짝을 고르면, 몸을 기울여 대략 30개의 알을 방출한다. 보통은, 그곳에 거주하는 수컷 성어가 자신의 정자를 이 알들에 뿌리겠지만, 그 수컷이 그것들에 도달할 기회를 얻기 전에, 작은 cuckold가 직접 그 알들을 수정시키기 위해 안전 지대에서 나와 더 큰 수컷의 둥지로 쏜살같이 돌진할 것이고, 잡히지 않은 채 재빨리 원래 있던 곳으로 돌아올 것이다.

이 전략으로, [9]cuckold는 가능한 한 많은 알을 그것들이 구덩이에 자리잡기 전에 수정시킬 수 있으며, 그 후에 들키지 않고 탈출하기 위해 그의 작은 몸집을 이용한다. 하지만, 이 기술은 어린 블루길만 사용할 수 있는데, 다 자란 블루길의 크기는 이 작업을 위해 필요한 민첩성을 불가능하게 하기 때문이다. 그렇더라도, 더 성숙한 cuckold는 그들의 목표를 달성하기 위해 다른 방법을 취하기도 한다. 다 자란 cuckold는 여전히 대부분의 수컷 블루길보다 작아서 암컷으로 오인되기 쉽다. 그들이 자라면서, [10]cuckold는 암컷의 몸에 있는 것과 비슷한 명암이 있는 부분과 줄무늬를 몸에 가지게 되는데, 이는 다른 수컷들로부터 완벽하게 자신을 위장시켜 눈에 띄지 않고 쉽게 암컷의 무리 속으로 끼어들 수 있게 한다. 이런 식으로, 그들은 급강하하여 가라앉은 알을 수정시키기 전에 근처의 암컷이 알을 방출하기로 결정할 때까지 기다린다. 최적의 알들이 수정된다면, cuckold는 자신의 생식 임무를 완수한 것이다.

블루길 cuckold는 그들을 위한 것이 아닌 알을 수정시키는 데 속임수를 쓴다. 그들은 다른 수컷의 8 .... 가까이에 숨어 알맞은 순간에 뛰어듦으로써 이를 수행한다. cuckold는 대부분의 수컷들보다 훨씬 작은 9 ....을 가지고 있기 때문에, 쉽고 빠르게 위험에서 벗어날 수 있다. 더 성숙한 cuckold는 다른 방법을 가지고 있다. 여전히 대부분의 수컷들만큼 크지 않기 때문에, 그들은 암컷 블루길들과 헤엄치며 한 암컷이 알을 낳을 때까지 기다린다. 그들은 암컷에게 있는 것과 같은 10 ....을 띠고 있기 때문에 들키는 것을 피할 수 있다.

A 구덩이	B 색깔	C 둥지	D 무늬
E 정자	F 꼬리	G 몸	

8 해설 문제의 핵심어구(hiding near another male's)와 관련된 지문 내용 중 'these fish ~ will seek out a large parental male, hide in the weeds adjacent to the male's grounds'에서 이 물고기들은 수컷 성어를 찾아내 그 수컷의 구역 근처 수초에 숨는다고 하였으므로, **C** nest가 정답이다. 'adjacent to the male's grounds'가 'near another male's nest'로 paraphrasing되었다.

9 해설 문제의 핵심어구(a much smaller ~ than most males)와 관련된 지문 내용 중 'the cuckold can ~ use his undersized body to escape undetected'에서 cuckold는 들키지 않고 탈출하기 위해 그의 작은 몸집을 이용한다고 하였으므로, **G** body가 정답이다. 'Undersized'가 'much smaller'로 paraphrasing되었다.

10 해설 문제의 핵심어구(looks like the one on females)와 관련된 지문 내용 중 'the cuckold will acquire a set of shaded areas and stripes on its body that is similar to that on females'에서 cuckold는 암컷의 몸에 있는 것과 비슷한 명암이 있는 부분과 줄무늬를 몸에 가지게 된다고 하였으므로, **D** pattern이 정답이다. 'acquire a set of shaded areas and stripes on its body that is similar to that'이 'take on a pattern that looks like the one'으로 paraphrasing되었다.

5

종종 현대의 창안물이라고 여겨지기는 하지만, 동물원은 사실 수천 년에 걸친 동물 감금의 역사에 깊이 새겨져 있다. [11]이집트 히에라콘폴리스 근처의 발굴 작업 중 발견된 것은 도시의 묘지에 묻힌 하마, 코끼리, 개코원숭이 그리고 살쾡이의 잔존물을 보여주었다. 기원전 약 3500년까지 거슬러 올라가는 이 잔존물은 [12]권력을 보여주고, 적을 위협하고, 통치자나 손님을 접대하고, 심지어 사냥을 하기 위해 사회의 가장 부유한 구성원에 의해 유지된 개인 동물 수집품인, 동물 사육소의 존재를 암시한다. 동물 사육소는 이집트와 다른 곳들에서 상당한 기간 동안 인기가 있었다. 기원전 약 1500년경에 통치했던 이집트의 해트세프수트 여왕은, 현재의 소말리아인 푼트까지의 원정 동안 획득했던 동물들의 사육소를 보유하고 있었다. 비슷한 시기에 중국에서는, Wen Wang 황제가 Garden of Intelligence를 설립했는데, 이는 1,500에이커의 부지에서 길러진 거대한 동물 무리를 포함했다.

동물 사육소는 14세기에서 16세기 사이에 멕시코 중부 아즈텍 문화의 중심이기도 했다. 스페인 탐험가 에르난 코르테스가 1520년에 신세계에 도착했을 때, 그는 아즈텍 통치자 몬테수마의 수도인 테노치티틀란에서의 엄청난 동물 무리의 발견에 대해 기록했다. 300명이 넘는 사람들이 역사상 가장 큰 동물 모음이라고 알려진 대규모 왕족 동물 사육소를 돌보도록 배정받았다. 동물들이 수용되었던 단지는 2개의 주요 건물, 식물원 그리고 수족관이 있어 그것 자체로 매우 장엄했다. 유감스럽게도, 이 시설들과 그곳에서 길러졌던 동물들은 이후 스페인인들에 의한 습격 중에 소실되었다. 18세기에 유럽에서는 동물원이 동물 사육소를 대체하기 시작했는데, [13]이 계몽주의 시대는 과학과 이성에 대한 새로운 신념이 시작되게 했으며, 이는 생물학 분야까지 확장되었다. 그 결과 [14]동물원은 자연 서식지와 비슷한 것에서 동물들의 과학적 관측을 용이하게 하고자 창설되었다. 그것들은 필요한 자금을 확보하는 것을 보장하기 위해 입장료를 받고 대중에게 공개되었다. 이러한 현대 동물원 중의 최초는, 동물학의 새로운 시대의 막을 열고 동물 사육소를 오래된 역사 속에 둔, 오스트리아의 빈에서 1752년에 개방된 쇤브룬 동물원이었다.

이집트의 도시 히에라콘폴리스의 고고학적 발굴은 많은 동물 종들의 11 ....을 보여주었는데, 이는 수천 년 전에 도시의 묘지 내에 묻힌 것들이었다. 이것은 이국적인 생물들의 개인 수집품인 동물 사육소의 증거였다. 12 ....은 그들의 권위를 보여주거나 적을 겁주기 위해 그러한 소장품을 이용했다.

우리가 오늘날 알고 있는 동물원은 유럽 전역에 계몽주의가, 13 ....을 포함하는 과학에 대한 관심을 퍼트린 18세기에 등장하기 시작했다. 이러한 동물원들은 동물들이 연구될 수 있도록, 동물들을 위한 자연적인 14 ....과 같은 것을 만들려고 노력했다.

| A 환경 | B 군대 | C 정원 | D 생물학 |
| E 상류층 | F 유해 | G 건축학 | |

11 해설 문제의 핵심어구(archaeological dig in the Egyptian city)와 관련된 지문 내용 중 'A discovery during excavations near Hierakonpolis, Egypt, uncovered the remnants of hippos, elephants, baboons and wildcats buried in the city's cemetery.'에서 이집트 히에라콘폴리스 근처의 발굴 작업 중 발견된 것은 도시의 묘지에 묻힌 하마, 코끼리, 개코원숭이 그리고 살쾡이의 잔존물을 보여주었다고 하였으므로, **F** remains가 정답이다. 'uncovered the remnants of hippos, elephants, baboons and wildcats'가 'revealed the remains of many species of animal'로 paraphrasing되었다.

12 해설 문제의 핵심어구(to show their authority and scare enemies)와 관련된 지문 내용 중 'a menagerie, a private collection of animals kept by the wealthiest members of society to demonstrate power, to intimidate enemies'에서 권력을 보여주고 적을 위협하기 위해 사회의 가장 부유한 구성원에 의해 유지된 개인 동물 수집품인 동물 사육소라고 하였으므로, **E** elite가 정답이다. 'to demonstrate power, to intimidate enemies'가 'to show their authority and scare enemies'로 paraphrasing되었다.

13 해설 문제의 핵심어구(Enlightenment spread an interest in science)와 관련된 지문 내용 중 'the Age of Enlightenment ushered in a new belief in science and reason, which extended to the field of biology'에서 이 계몽주의 시대는 과학과 이성에 대한 새로운 신념이 시작되게 했으며 이는 생물학 분야로까지 확장되었다고 하였으므로, **D** biology가 정답이다. 'new belief in science and reason, which extended to the field of biology'가 'interest in science throughout Europe, which included biology'로 paraphrasing되었다.

14 해설 문제의 핵심어구(zoos tried to create)와 관련된 지문 내용 중 'zoos were created to facilitate the scientific observation of animals in something similar to their natural habitat'에서 동물원은 자연 서식지와 비슷한 것에서 동물들의 과학적 관측을 용이하게 하고자 창설되었다고 하였으므로, **A** environment가 정답이다. 'similar to their natural habitat'이 'like a natural environment'로 paraphrasing되었다.

6

수달에는 13종이 있으며, 모두 강과 같은 물과 관련이 있거나 해달의 경우, 바다의 해안 지역과 관련이 있다. [16]수달은 가늘고 긴 몸, 짤막한 팔과 다리, 그리고 물갈퀴가 있는 발로 식별되는데, 이는 그들이 상당한 민첩성으로 물을 가로지르게 해준다. 그들은 또한 물속에서 긴 시간 동안 숨을 참을 수 있으며, 몇몇 수달은 최대 5분 동안 수면 아래에 있는 것이 관측되기도 했다. 그들은 [15]털로도 식별될 수 있는데, 이는 매우 촘촘하며 안타깝게도 역사를 통틀어 그들을 인간의 표적으로 만들었다. 북태평양의 해안 지역에 사는 해달은, 동물 중 가장 굵은 털을 가지고 있다. 역사적으로, 이는 그것이 사냥꾼에게 가장 수익성이 좋은 동물이 되도록 했으며 해달의 전 세계적 개체 수의 급격한 하락으로 이어졌는데, 이는 이제서야 완화되기 시작하고 있다. 털의 가치가 높아짐에 따라, 그 털에 붙여진 이름인 이 '부드러운 금'에 대한 수요 또한 증가했으며 'Great Hunt'라고 불리는 시대를 초래했다. [17]약 1741년부터 1911년까지 이어진 이 시기 동안, 러시아와 다른 지역에서 온 사냥꾼들은 엄청난 강도로 야생 해달 개체 수를 파괴했다.

해달 사냥은 많은 개체군의 소멸이 상업성 사냥을 불가능하게 한 뒤에야 줄어들기 시작했다. 결국 1911년에 해달 사냥을 금지한 국제 협약이 체결되었다. 그 시점에 이르러, 해달은 약 2천 마리만이 야생에 남아 있다고 추산되었으며, 대부분의 전문가들은 이 종이 결국 멸종될 것이라고 생각했다. 하지만, 20세기 동안의 보호 노력은 해달 개체 수의 상당한 증가와, 그들이 거의 완전히 사라졌던 태평양 해안 서식지로의 귀환에 기여했다. 그럼에도 불구하고, 해달은 여전히 멸종 위기 동물로 간주되며, 밀렵뿐만 아니라 낚시, 질병, 그리고 오염에 의해 위협받고 있다. [18]해달은 해양 보존의 훌륭한 성공담 중 하나를 보여주지만, 그들의 회복은 여전히 인간 활동으로 위협받고 있으며, 그 성공을 유지하는 것은 새로워진 경각심을 필요로 한다.

수달을 구하는 것

긴 시간 동안 물속에서 숨을 참을 수 있는 능력으로 잘 알려져 있는 수달은, 불행히도 그것의 15 ....한 털 때문에 사냥꾼들의 표적이 되어 왔다. 그들의 털과 함께, 이 수달들은 짧은 팔과 16 ....한 몸을 가 진 것으로 유명하다.

17 ....한 수달 개체군은 그들의 털이 세계에서 가장 수익성이 높은 상품 중 하나였던 기간인 18세기 동안에 극심하게 사냥을 당했다. 그러나 20세기 초에 금지법이 도입되었고 개체군은 성공적인 18 ....의 보존 활동의 드문 사례로 회복되었다.

A 윤이 나는	B 튼튼한	C 현지의	D 숱이 많은
E 해양의	F 전 세계적인	G 긴	H 야생의

---

15 해설 문제의 핵심어구(the target of hunters)와 관련된 지문 내용 중 'their fur, which is very dense and has unfortunately made them the target of humans throughout history'에서 수달의 털은 매우 촘촘하며 안타깝게도 역사를 통틀어 그들을 인간의 표적으로 만들었다고 하였으므로, **D** thick이 정답이다. 'their fur, which is very dense'가 'its thick fur'로 paraphrasing되었다.

16 해설 문제의 핵심어구(having short arms and)와 관련된 지문 내용 중 'Otters can be distinguished by their elongated body, their stubby arms and legs'에서 수달은 가늘고 긴 몸, 짤막한 팔과 다리로 식별된다고 하였으므로, **G** long이 정답이다. 'elongated body'가 'long bodies'로 paraphrasing되었다.

17 해설 문제의 핵심어구(hunted intensely during the 18th century)와 관련된 지문 내용 중 'During this period, which lasted from approximately 1741 to 1911, hunters from Russia and other regions ravaged wild sea otter populations with great intensity.'에서 약 1741년부터 1911년까지 이어진 이 시기 동안, 러시아와 다른 지역에서 온 사냥꾼들은 엄청난 강도로 야생 해달 개체 수를 파괴했다고 하였으므로, **H** wild가 정답이다. 'ravaged wild sea otter populations'가 'The wild otter population was hunted intensely'로 paraphrasing되었다.

18 해설 문제의 핵심어구(a successful ~ conservation effort)와 관련된 지문 내용 중 'Sea otters may represent one of the great success stories of marine conservation'에서 해달은 해양 보존의 훌륭한 성공담 중 하나를 보여준다고 하였으므로, **E** marine이 정답이다. 'success stories of marine conservation'이 'a successful marine conservation effort'로 paraphrasing되었다.

7

증기 동력이 산업 혁명을 이끈 방법

19세기 동안에 영국 경제의 극적인 성장을 야기한 산업화와 도시화 이전에는, 대부분의 노동은 육체 노동이나 동물에 의해 행해졌으며, 열은 유기 물질을 태움으로써 공급되었고, 에너지 수요는 물레방아로 충족되었다. 수력이 풍부하고 값싼 에너지를 공급해주긴 했지만, 지리적 제한은 그것을 불편하게 했다. 하지만, 증기 기관은 이와 같은 한계를 직면하지 않았다. 이것이 산업 혁명의 상징이자 모든 서부 문명이 결국 겪게 될 근본적인 변화의 원동력이 되기까지는 오래 걸리지 않았다.

영리 기업들이 증기 동력 기기들로 장비를 갖추기 시작하면서, 제조 산업은 완전히 바뀌었다. 예를 들어, 증기 동력으로 작동하는 직물 기계들은, 한 바퀴의 회전에 여러 가닥의 실을 자아낼 수 있었고 레버, 캠, 그리고 톱니바퀴를 사용하여 정밀한 움직임을 조정할 수 있었다. 이런 장비가 효율적으로 기계 동력을 생산하기 위해서는, 보일러로 물을 데웠어야 했는데, 이는 싸고 믿음직한 연료인 석탄을 필요로 했기 때문에, 채광 산업도 득을 보았다.

운송업에서는, 높은 마력의 증기 기관이 선박과 기관차에 생기를 불어넣어 주었는데, 그것들의 안전성, 정밀성, 그리고 속도를 상당히 개선시켰다. 그 결과, 도시의 공장 경영주들은 전에는 갈 수 없었던 지역에 상대적으로 적은 시간 안에 다수의 완제품을 운송할 수 있었고, 동시에 ¹⁹멀리 떨어진 영국 식민지들에서 오는 원자재들은 더 작은 생산 시설을 대체한 거대하고 비용 효율적인 공장으로 빠르게 이동되었다. ²⁰이 대형 공장들은, 처음에는 주거 지역의 변두리에 지어졌지만, 제조업자들이 제공하는 일자리에 매료된 영국 인구의 절반 이상이 시골에서 도시로 이동하면서, 도시로 확장해 나갔다. ²¹도시의 삶에 적응하는 것은 대부분의 영국인에게 놀랄 만한 생활 방식의 변화를 야기했다.

그중에는 치솟는 식자율과 함께, 사람들이 읽을 줄 알게 되었다는 것이 있었다. 이전에 책은 생산하기에 시간이 많이 들고 값비쌌기 때문에 희귀하고 엄격히 통제되는 자원이었지만, 이러한 새로운 장비의 효율성 덕분에 하루에도 수백만 장의 글이 책으로 대량 생산될 수 있게 되었다. 인쇄기와 글을 읽고 쓸 줄 아는 능력으로 인해, 정치, 철학, 그리고 과학 분야에서 새로운 사고 형식이 사람들 사이에 퍼지기 시작했다.

결국, 증기 기관의 시대는 19세기 말에 이르러 끝에 가까워졌는데, 이때 그것은 전기라고 불리는 새로운 형태의 동력으로 교체되었다. 전기가 현대 생활의 필수적인 부분이긴 하지만, 증기 동력이라는 기술의 획기적 발견과 그것이 원동력이 된 사회적, 지적, 문화적 발달 없이 이것이 가능했을지는 의심스럽다.

도시화와 증기 기관

증기 기관은 제조업자들이 전 세계로부터 그들의 19 ....로 자원을 가져올 수 있게 해주었다. 처음에, 그것들은 거주 지역들의 변두리에 지어졌지만, 머지않아 20 ....에 문을 열기 시작했다. 사람들은 공장 노동이 제공하는 새로운 기회를 쫓아 시골에서의 노동을 그만두었다. 이것은 대부분의 영국인 인구의 21 ....에 많은 변화로 이어졌다.

---

19 해설 문제의 핵심어구(bring resources ~ into their)와 관련된 지문 내용 중 'raw materials from distant British colonies zoomed into the massive and more cost-effective factories'에서 멀리 떨어진 영국 식민지들에서 오는 원자재들은 거대하고 비용 효율적인 공장으로 빠르게 이동되었다고 하였으므로, **factories**가 정답이다. 'raw materials from distant British colonies zoomed into'가 'bring resources from all around the world'로 paraphrasing되었다.

20 해설 문제의 핵심어구(built on the edges of populated areas)와 관련된 지문 내용 중 'These mega factories, although initially built on the outskirts of residential areas, expanded into cities'에서 이 대형 공장들은 처음에는 주거 지역의 변두리에 지어졌지만 도시로 확장해 나갔다고 하였으므로, **cities**가 정답이다. 'initially built on the outskirts of residential areas'가 'At first, they were built on the edges of populated areas'로, 'expanded into'가 'began opening in'으로 paraphrasing되었다.

21 해설 문제의 핵심어구(many changes ~ of the British population)와 관련된 지문 내용 중 'Adjusting to life in cities would prompt eye-opening lifestyle shifts for the majority of British people.'에서 도시의 삶에 적응하는 것은 대부분의 영국인에게 놀랄 만한 생활 방식의 변화를 야기했다고 하였으므로, 정답은 **lifestyle**이다. 'eye-opening lifestyle shifts for the majority of British people'이 'many changes in the lifestyle of most of the British population'으로 paraphrasing되었다.

8

사라지는 우리의 열대 우림

라틴 아메리카에서 주로 발견되지만 또한 아시아와 아프리카에도 존재하는 전 세계의 열대 우림은 매년 4만 6천에서 5만 8천 제곱마일을 잃어가며 포위당한 상태이다. 세계의 이러한 지역들은 그곳에 사는 수많은 식물군과 동물군을 위해서뿐만 아니라, 지구 자체에도 없어서는 안 되는 곳이다. 이는 인간이 지속해서 화석 연료를 태우며 대기 중에 내뿜는 대량의 이산화탄소를 초목이 흡수하여 환경 오염 수준을 조절하기 때문이다. 지구의 열대 우림에 있는 나무가 급속도로 사라지고 있기 때문에, 그들은 이 생태학적 임무를 수행하는 것이 덜 가능해졌고, 그로 인해 기후 변화를 가속시키고 있으며 이와 관련된 전 지구적 영향이 불가피한 현실이 되게 한다.

산림 벌채로 인한 세계 열대 우림의 광범위한 파괴의 요인은 다양하지만 모두 산업 발전과 인구 증가와 관련이 있다. ²²열대 우림의 자원이 착취되는 한 가지 방식은 지속 불가능한 상업적 벌목 관행에 의한 것이다. ²³벌목꾼은 다 자란 나무만을 베도록 허용되며, 그렇게 할 때 과도한 손상을 야기하는 것을 피해야 한다. 하지만, ²⁴거대한 나무들은 쓰러지면서 다른 형태의 많은 초목을 파괴할 수밖에 없게 된다. 나무를 베는 것은 또한 우거진 숲의 지붕에 구멍을 만들기도 한다. 자연적으로 회복되려면 수천 년이 걸리는 이 구멍들은 숲을 가로지르기 위해 사용되는 중장비들이 흙에 되돌릴 수 없는 해를 끼치기 때문에 영구적으로 채워지지 않을 가능성이 있다. 한편, 높은 육류 제품의 수요는 가축 먹이의 재료인 콩을 기르기 위해 숲의 광대한 지역을 태우는 것으로 이어졌다. 이는 흙으로부터 영양분을 서서히 빼앗는데, 작물 수확량이 하락하고 더 많은 지역을 개간하도록 하는 것은 시간 문제일 뿐이다.

흙의 부식과, 더 나아가 나무의 손실을 일으키는 것은 광산업과 석유 프로젝트이다. 예를 들어, 아마존에서의 금 채취는 고농도의 수은을 필요로 하는데, 이는 흙에 침투하여 땅을 메마르게 한다. 또한, 이 지역에서의 석유 매장층의 발견 이래로, 수많은 석유 유출 사고가 있어왔다. ²⁵석유 오염은 토양의 성질을 바꾸는 것으로 널리 알려져 있는데, 이는 영향을 받은 지역에서 무언가 다시 자라날 가능성이 낮다는 것을 의미한다. 게다가, 채광과 석유 추출과 같은 활동이 가능하기 위해서는, 도로를 건설하기 위해 나무가 베어져야 한다. 건설되는 도로의 약 40미터마다 개발업체들은 600 제곱킬로미터의 열대우림을 희생시킨다고 추정된다. 설상가상으로, 도로들은 열대 우림을 불법 벌목꾼, 정착민들, 땅 투기꾼들에게 개방하는데, 그들의 활동 역시 초목의 큰 면적이 사라지는 결과를 낳는 경향이 있다.

불행하게도, 열대 우림이 주로 발견되는 나라들은 나무를 보존하는 것보다, 증가하는 빚과 가난과 같은 더 직접적인 문제에 직면해 있다. 부유한 나라들로부터 자금을 후원받는 것이 도움이 되긴 하지만, 그것은 임시 처방의 해결책일 뿐이다. 지구의 미래가 가장 중요하다는 것을 공동으로 인정해야만 우리는 남아 있는 열대 우림을 지키기 시작할 수 있을 것이다.

삼림 파괴의 원인

삼림 파괴가 지속되는 원인들 중 하나는 상업적으로 이행될 때 벌목이 22 ....하다는 것이다. 벌목 회사들은 23 ....한 것들만 베도록 허용된다. 하지만 이것은 주변의 24 ....에 연쇄적인 영향을 미칠 수 있으며, 이는 나무들이 넘어질 때 훼손될 수 있다.

한층 더 한 삼림의 위협은 귀금속이나 화석 연료의 채굴인데, 이는 예를 들어 해로운 화학 약품이 금을 채굴하기 위해 사용될 때 주변의 토양에 부정적인 영향을 미칠 수 있다. 비슷하게, 토양의 25 ....은 석유 유출로 인한 오염에 의해 완전히 바뀔 수 있다.

A	불법의	B	식물	C	특성
D	다 자란	E	지속 불가능한	F	균형
G	흔한	H	농도	I	흙

---

22 해설 문제의 핵심어구(logging ~ commercially)와 관련된 지문 내용 중 'One way rainforest resources are exploited is through unsustainable commercial logging practices.'에서 열대 우림의 자원이 착취되는 한 가지 방식은 지속 불가능한 상업적 벌목 관행에 의한 것이라고 하였으므로, **E** unsustainable이 정답이다. 'rainforest resources are exploited'가 'deforestation persists'로 paraphrasing되었다.

23 해설 문제의 핵심어구(logging companies are only allowed to remove)와 관련된 지문 내용 중 'Loggers are only permitted to cut down trees that are fully grown'에서 벌목꾼은 다 자란 나무만을 베도록 허용된다고 하였으므로, **D** mature가 정답이다. 'permitted to cut down'이 'allowed to remove'로 paraphrasing되었다.

24 해설 문제의 핵심어구(damaged as trees collapse)와 관련된 지문 내용 중 'massive trees cannot help but tear down numerous other forms of vegetation in the process of collapsing'에서 거대한 나무들은 쓰러지면서 다른 형태의 많은 초목을 파괴할 수밖에 없게 된다고 하였으므로, **B** plants가 정답이다. 'in the process of collapsing'이 'as trees collapse'로 paraphrasing되었다.

25 해설 문제의 핵심어구(transformed by contamination from oil spills)와 관련된 지문 내용 중 'It is well known that oil contamination changes the properties of earth'에서 석유 오염은 토양의 성질을 바꾸는 것으로 널리 알려져 있다고 하였으므로, **C qualities**가 정답이다. 'changes the properties of earth'가 'the qualities of soil can be completely transformed'로 paraphrasing되었다.

9

미국을 만드는 것: 이리 운하

뉴욕의 허드슨 강을 통해 오대호와 대서양을 연결하는 이리 운하는, 그 시대의 가장 영향력 있는 공공사업 중 하나였다. 8년의 공사 뒤에 1825년에 처음 개통된 그것은, 무역을 극적으로 증가시킨 것, 뉴욕을 번창하는 국제적 항구로 만든 것, 그리고 서부로의 개척에 원동력이 된 것에 공이 있다고 여겨진다.

²⁶오대호를 둘러싼 주들은 천연자원이 풍부한 곳인데, 이는 19세기 초에 미국 동해안에 살고 있던 식민지 개척자들이 접근하기 매우 어려웠다. 마찬가지로, 뉴욕과 같은 도시에서 이용 가능한 유럽의 물품들은 국가의 내륙에서는 사실상 알려지지 않았다. 아직 철도가 설립되지 않았기 때문에, ²⁷물자를 이리저리 옮길 수 있는 유일한 수단은 한정된 용량의 무역품을 수용하는 운송 수단인 수레 마차뿐이었다. 게다가, ²⁸대부분의 여정은 애팔래치아 산맥으로 인한 장벽은 물론이고, 좋지 않은 도로 상태 때문에 몇 주씩 지속되었으며, 각 여정이 수반한 시간과 노동을 고려하면 상당한 양의 돈이 들었다. 그러나, ²⁹이리 운하가 개통된 이후, 선박이 최대 50톤의 화물을 한 곳에서 다른 곳으로 며칠 만에 운반할 수 있었다. 그것들이 정말 많은 것들을 옮길 수 있었기 때문에, 운송되는 물품량이 급증했으며, 어떤 상품의 가격은 최대 95퍼센트까지 하락했다. 머지않아 매일 수백 척의 배가 뉴욕시를 드나들었고, 그곳을 미국에서 가장 분주한 항구로 만들었다.

뉴욕시에 많은 물품이 유입됨에 따라, 정부가 동해안을 따라, 서인도에, 그리고 대서양을 건너 유럽에까지 물품을 운송하기 시작하는 것이 타당했다. 그렇게 하는 것은 매우 이익이 되었지만, 세입은 거기서 그치지 않았다. 배달되는 여러 화물들 각각에 운송료가 징수되었으며, 이는 정부가 곧 금고를 가득 채울 수 있도록 했다. 다른 것 중에서도, 돈은 운하를 건설하기 위해 사용되었던 7백만 달러를 지불하고, 워싱턴의 국정 운영에 자금을 대는 것을 돕고, 나이아가라 폭포와 같이 운하 노선을 따라 있는 인기 있는 지역을 광고하기 위해 사용되었다. 결과적으로, 매년 운하를 이용하기 위해 뉴욕으로 모여드는 수천 명의 사람들과 함께, 뉴욕은 빠르게 미국인과 해외 여행객들 모두가 찾는 최고의 목적지가 되었다.

뉴욕으로 가는 것이 더는 어렵지 않다는 사실과 함께, 뉴욕의 계속되는 번영은, 운하 사용의 첫 몇 년 만에 12만 4천 명에서 거의 80만 명으로의 인구 증가를 경험했다. 상당히 많은 사람이 뉴욕시로 이주했지만, 몇몇은 운하 노선 중 다른 착륙장에 내리기도 했는데, 이곳에는 다수의 신흥 도시가 설립되어 있었다. 이는 뉴욕의 로체스터나 버펄로와 같은 지역에 인구를 형성하는 데 이바지했다. 그뿐만 아니라, 운하가 애팔래치아 산맥을 넘어 서부로도 이어졌기 때문에, 사람들로 하여금 오대호 인근 주인 미시간, 오하이오, 인디애나, 그리고 일리노이를 향해 더 멀리 가도록 고무했다. 이 지역들에 정착한 사람 중 다수는 값싼 경작지의 이용 가능성에 매력을 느껴 미국으로 온 새로운 유럽 이민자들이었다. 몇십 년 안에, 이 지역은 국가에 밀을 공급하는 곡창 지대로서 미국 농업의 심장부로 자리를 확고히 했다.

이리 운하 이전의 삶

오대호 지역에는 많은 26 ....이 있었다. 그러나, 그것들을 뉴욕의 식민지 주민에게 수송할 유일한 방법은 27 ....의 이용을 통해서뿐이었다. 이러한 여정은 오래 걸렸고 매우 힘들었다. 주된 28 ....은 애팔래치아 산맥이었고, 그것을 지나는 것은 시간 소모가 컸고 비용이 많이 들었다. 오대호 지역에 도달하는 어려움 때문에, 그곳의 주민은 해안에서 구할 수 있는 외국 물품을 구매할 수 없었다. 운하가 지어진 후에, 29 ....은 매우 짧은 시간 안에 그들의 목적지로 많은 양의 화물을 운송할 수 있었다.

---

26 해설 문제의 핵심어구(many ~ in the Great Lakes region)와 관련된 지문 내용 중 'The states surrounding the Great Lakes are home to a wealth of natural resources'에서 오대호를 둘러싼 주들은 천연자원이 풍부한 곳이라고 하였으므로, **natural resources**가 정답이다. 'The states surrounding the Great Lakes'가 'in the Great Lakes region'으로 paraphrasing되었다.

27 해설 문제의 핵심어구(only way to transport)와 관련된 지문 내용 중 'the only way of moving supplies back and forth was by horse-drawn wagons'에서 물자를 이리저리 옮길 수 있는 유일한 수단은 수레 마차뿐이었다고 하였으므로, **horse-drawn wagons**가 정답이다. 'moving ~ back and forth'가 'transport ~ to'로 paraphrasing되었다.

28 해설 문제의 핵심어구(Appalachian Mountains)와 관련된 지문 내용 중 'most journeys lasted weeks due to ~ the barrier created by the Appalachian Mountains, and cost a significant amount of money'에서 대부분의 여정은 애팔래치아 산맥으로 인한 장벽 때문에 몇 주씩 지속되었으며 상당한 양의 돈이 들었다고 하였으므로, **barrier**가 정답이다. 'barrier created by the Appalachian Mountains'가 'barrier was the Appalachian Mountains'로 paraphrasing 되었다.

29 해설 문제의 핵심어구(carry ~ to their destinations in a very short time)와 관련된 지문 내용 중 'once the Erie Canal opened, ships were able to haul up to 50 tonnes of freight from point to point in a matter of days'에서, 이리 운하가 개통된 이후 선박이 최대 50톤의 화물을 한 곳에서 다른 곳으로 며칠 만에 운반할 수 있었다고 하였으므로, **ships/boats**가 정답이다. 'haul up to 50 tonnes of freight ~ in a matter of days'가 'carry a great amount of cargo ~ in a very short time'으로 paraphrasing되었다.

10

암흑 물질

신기한 관측

우주의 보이지 않는 물질의 존재는 네덜란드 천문학자인 얀 헨드릭 오르트가 은하계의 바깥쪽에 있는 별들이 은하계 가장자리의 약한 중력을 고려했을 때 그들이 움직여야 하는 것보다 훨씬 더 빠르게 움직이는 것을 관측했던 1932년에 그에 의해 처음 제시되었다. 오르트는 그들의 속도가 강한 중력을 가진 물질에 의해 영향을 받고 있다고 생각했는데, 그는 이것이 보이지 않았기 때문에 '암흑 물질'이라고 불렀다. 1년 뒤에 이 발견을 입증한 것은 스위스 천문학자인 프리츠 츠비키였는데, 그는 비슷한 관측을 한 후, 보이지 않는 것들 사이에 숨겨진 질량이 있다고 주장했다. 그러나, 질량이 있는 물질이 보이지 않는다는 것은 알려지지 않았었기 때문에 어느 주장도 과학계에 받아들여지지 않았다.

보이지 않는 망

1950년대에 이르러, 외딴 별들이 실제로 은하계의 중심에 있는 별들과 같은 속도를 가졌다는 것을 확인할 만큼 기술이 충분히 발달했다. 과학자들은 이것이 가능하기 위해서는 은하계가 상당한 양의 암흑 물질을 포함하고 있어야 한다고 추정했고, 따라서 이 찾기 힘든 물질에 대해 그들이 알아낼 수 있는 만큼 최대한 알아내는 것에 착수했다. 컴퓨터 생성 모형의 도움을 받아, 그들은 우주 전체 질량의 최대 85퍼센트를 구성하는 암흑 물질의 가는 실이 망을 형성하고 있으며 이 망 안에 엮여 있는 것들이 우주에서 보이는 모든 물질이라고 추측했다. 몇몇은 암흑 물질의 명백한 기능이 우주에 있는 다양한 구성 요소를 하나로 묶는 것이라는 점에서 암흑 물질을 결합 조직에 비유했다. 다시 말해서, 그것 없이는, 은하계는 그야말로 따로 떨어져 나가 떠내려가게 될 것이었다.

암흑 물질의 구성 요소에 관한 이론들

하지만 ³⁰암흑 물질은 도대체 무엇으로 만들어졌는가? 많은 우주론자들은 ³⁰이것이 아직 밝혀지지 않은 아원자 입자로 구성되었을 것이라고 믿는다. 반면, 몇몇 천문학자는 거대하고 촘촘한 광륜 물질, 혹은 마초를 가능성으로 여긴다. 마초는 은하계의 광륜 속에 존재하지만 낮은 광명으로 인해 발견이 불가능하다고 여겨진다. 다른 천문학자들은 윔프, 혹은 약하게 반응하는 거대한 입자들이 유력한 후보라고 생각한다. 윔프는 현재로써는 가설이지만 ³¹과학자들은 그것들이 빅뱅 직후에 생성되었다고 믿기 때문에 인기 있는 대안이다. 거대하고, 천천히 움직이며, 빛을 낼 수 없다는 점에서, 이 입자들이 함께 모여서 우주의 구조를 형성했다는 이론이 제시된다. 놀랄 것도 없이, ³²그것들의 존재를 증명하기 위한 시도가 결정되었으며, 강입자충돌기와 같은 최신 기술이 결과를 내기 위해 현재 사용되고 있다.

암흑 물질 발견하기

여전히 확실한 증거가 부족하긴 하지만, 암흑 물질 이론에 대한 지지는 광범위하게 증가했다. ³³이것이 실제로 존재한다는 것과, 빛을 생산할 수 없음에도 불구하고, 이것이 탐지될 수 있다는 것이 현재 과학자들 사이에서의 일치된 의견이다. 이는 이것이 은하계로부터 오는 빛이 일그러지도록 만들어, 선명한 착시를 만들어낸다는 사실 때문이다. ³⁴이 현상들을 관측하는 과학자들은 암흑 물질의 대략적인 위치를 알아내기 위해 빛의 이동을 측정한다. 그들은 그 다음 이 위치를 지도에 기록한다. 암흑 물질을 찾는 데 착수한 과학자들이 종종 아무런 성과를 내지 못하기는 하지만, 그들은 낙관적인 상태를 유지하며 27억 광년이나 떨어진 은하계의 성단에서 암흑 물질을 탐지하고 발견하는 것이 가능했다는 독일 뮌헨의 한 팀에 의한 것과 같은 발견들에서 동기를 부여받는다.

암흑 물질은 무엇인가?

무엇이 암흑 물질을 구성하는지에 대해 많은 이론들이 있다. 일부는 그것이 발견되지 않은 30 ....으로 만들어졌다고 말하며, 반면 다른 사람들은 촘촘한 광륜 물체가 더 가능성 있는 후보라고 생각한다. 윔프 또한 또 다른 가능성이다. 이는 그들의 31 ....이 빅뱅 직후에 시작되었을 수 있기 때문이다. 이 입자들의 32 ....은 과학자들이 현재 강입자충돌기를 이용해 증명하려는 것이다. 이제 과학자들은 암흑 물질이 33 ....을 생산할 수 없음에도 불구하고, 어떻게든 그것을 탐지할 수 있다고 믿는다. 그들은 그것의 34 ....을 판별하고 지도에 기록하기 위해 은하계에 의해 내뿜어지는 빛에 대한 암흑 물질의 영향을 조사하고 있다.

A 빛	B 힘	C 생성
D 속도	E 존재	F 위치
G 입자	H 착각	

---

30 해설 문제의 핵심어구(what comprises, made up of an undiscovered)와 관련된 지문 내용 중 'what is dark matter made of?'와 'it may be composed of a subatomic particle that has not yet been identified'에서 암흑 물질이 아직 밝혀지지 않은 아원자 입자로 구성되었을 것이라고 하였으므로, **G** particle이 정답이다. 'composed of a subatomic particle that has not yet been identified'가 'made up of an undiscovered particle'로 paraphrasing되었다.

31 해설 문제의 핵심어구(immediately following the Big Bang)와 관련된 지문 내용 중 'scientists believe that they formed shortly after the Big Bang'에서 과학자들은 윔프가 빅뱅 직후에 생성되었다고 믿는다고 하였으므로, **C** formation이 정답이다. 'formed shortly after'가 'their formation may have begun immediately following'으로 paraphrasing되었다.

32 해설 문제의 핵심어구(prove using the Large Hadron Collider)와 관련된 지문 내용 중 'attempts to prove their existence have been determined, and state-of-the-art technologies, such as the Large Hadron Collider, are currently being used to try to produce them'에서 입자들의 존재를 증명하기 위한 시도가 결정되었으며 강입자충돌기와 같은 최신 기술이 결과를 내기 위해 현재 사용되고 있다고 하였으므로, **E** presence가 정답이다. 'attempts to prove ~ have been determined'가 'trying to prove'로 paraphrasing되었다.

33 해설 문제의 핵심어구(dark matter produces no)와 관련된 지문 내용 중 'It is now the consensus among scientists that it does exist and that, despite its inability to produce light, it can be detected.'에서 암흑 물질이 실제로 존재한다는 것과 빛을 생산할 수 없음에도 불구하고 이것이 탐지될 수 있다는 것이 현재 과학자들 사이에서의 일치된 의견이라고 하였으므로, **A** light가 정답이다. 'despite its inability to produce light'가 'even though dark matter produces no light'로 paraphrasing되었다.

34 해설 문제의 핵심어구(chart it on a map)와 관련된 지문 내용 중 'Scientists observing these phenomena measure the displacement of light to determine the approximate location of the dark matter. They then chart these positions on maps.'에서 이 현상들을 관측하는 과학자들은 암흑 물질의 대략적인 위치를 알아내기 위해 빛의 이동을 측정한 다음 이 위치를 지도에 기록한다고 하였으므로, **F** position이 정답이다. 'determine the approximate location'이 'judge its position'으로 paraphrasing되었다.

1	I	2	G	3	B
4	E	5	D	6	F
7	A	8	F	9	D
10	E	11	motor nerves	12	sound waves
13	feedback link				

언어 연쇄 과정
의사소통을 가능하게 하는 과정의 개요

인간 언어 체계의 복잡성과 융통성이 우리를 다른 동물과 구별하는 것이라고 주장할 수 있다. 하지만 언어는 진화적으로 말하자면 겨우 지난 20만 년 동안 발생한 최근 현상이며, 그것은 기본적인 생물학에 기반을 둔 것이다. 이 생물학적 원리는 대체로 인지에 관한 것인데, [8]영장류 연구는 영장류와 인간 사이에 언어 능력을 위한 해부학상의 역량에 있어 의미 있는 차이는 없다는 것을 보여준다. 그러므로 인류를 구분짓는 것은, 말하고 듣는 것을 위해 신체 기관과 결합하여 작용하는 언어에 대한 우리의 인지 능력이다.

말하고 이해하는 것을 위한 신경생리학적 과정은 복잡하며 인지 능력과 함께 다수의 기관이 결합하여 작용하는 것을 필요로 한다. 이 과정은 '언어 연쇄 과정'이라고 명명되었으며 이것이 어떻게 작동하는지 이해하기 위해서는 언어학, 인지 과학, 생물학 그리고 의사소통하기 위해 언어가 어떻게 사용되는지에 대한 학문인 화용론의 연합이 필요하다. 언어 연쇄 과정은 화자에게서 청자에게 말의 한 부분이 전달되는 과정을 설명하는데, [9]이는 관련된 신체와 인지 과정의 복잡한 상호 작용을 보여주는 여러 개의 단계로 나뉜다.

언어 연쇄 과정은 [1]뇌, 감각 신경과 음파와 더불어 성대와 귀 사이의 반응이 어떻게 의미에 영향을 미치며 완전한 이해를 가능하게 하거나 혹은 방해하는지 알고자 하는 연구자들에게 유용하다. 의사소통의 실험적 학문인 담화 과학은, 언어가 정신보다는 신체적 과정인 순간에 중점을 둔다. [2]그러므로 이 분야에 관련된 연구자들은 청각적 소리들과 발화가 어떻게 연관되어 있는지 그리고 음성이 어조와 감정에 따라 어떻게 달라지는지를 알아내기 위해 언어 연쇄 과정을 연구한다.

언어 연쇄 과정 자체는 화자의 생각으로부터 청자의 생각으로 메시지가 이동할 때 발생하는 과정을 설명한다. 이 과정은 많은 단계로 나누어질 수 있으며, 각각 화자 혹은 청자의 머리의 다른 부위에서 발생한다. [3]이는 연쇄 과정에 포함된 언어학적이며 생물학적인 절차들의 복잡한 조합을 반영하는 단계들이 연속하는 중에 발생한다. 이 단계들은 언어학적 단계, 생리학적 단계 그리고 음향학적 단계를 포함하며, 발성은 성공적으로 소통되기 위해 이 세 가지를 모두 사용해야 한다.

언어 연쇄 과정의 첫 번째 단계는 메시지를 언어학상의 개념으로 부호화하는 것인데, 이는 뇌에서 발생한다. 이 단계에서 메시지는 언어학적 형태로 표현되어야 하며 일관성이 있을 수 있도록 발음 요소가 정확하게 설정되어야 한다. 이 부호화 다음에는 [11]뇌의 적합한 명령이 발성 기관에 도달하기까지 자극의 형태로 운동 신경을 따라 이동할 것인데, 발성 기관은 폐, 성대, 혀 그리고 입술을 포함한다. 그 다음 이들은 집합적으로 음파를 만들어냄으로써 발화의 과정을 행할 것이다. 연쇄 과정에서 소리를 발생시키는 이 부분은 공력 소음학 과정이라고도 알려져 있다.

[12]음파는 공기를 통해 청자에게로 이동하며, 그곳에서 청자의 귀의 청각 구조에 의해 청취되고 뇌로 이동되는 신경 자극으로 변환된다. 여기서 그들은 의미를 수립하기 위해 해독된다. 이때의 뇌 활동은 화자의 말에 대한 인식과 이러한 청각적인 감각들의 발음과 의미로서의 해석, 즉 메시지가 이해되었는지를 보여준다. [4]이는 화자의 뇌와 청자의 뇌 사이에 연결을 성립시키는데, 이는 언어 연쇄 과정의 궁극적인 목표이며 의사소통을 가능하게 하는 것이다.

연쇄 과정에는 한 단계가 더 있는데, 이는 [5]화자의 발성 기관에서부터 그 혹은 그녀의 귀까지의 음파의 동시 전송이다. [13]이것은 화자가 자신의 말의 일관성이나 정확성을 확인할 수 있도록 하는 반응 연결을 만든다. 이 단계는 [6]이것이 화자가 자신이 의도했던 것과 자신의 표현의 질을 비교하고 이 반응에 근거하여 조정을 할 수 있도록 하기 때문에 소통의 과정에 필수적이다. 난청에 의한 이 반응 고리의 붕괴는 조리 있게 말할 수 있는 능력에 상당히 해로운 영향을 미칠 수 있다.

전반적으로 [7]이 언어 연쇄 과정은 말의 원리를 밝히며 의사소통 연구의 뼈대를 수립한다. 연구자들은 발화 과정에 대한 반응의 역할뿐 아니라, 뇌가 정확히 어떻게 의미를 부호화하는지, 발성 기관이 어떻게 음파를 만들어낼 수 있는지를 계속해서 철저하게 조사하고 있다. 이 과정이 의사소통의 인지적 그리고 청각적 원리를 설명하긴 하지만, [10]시각적 요소들 역시 매우 중요한데, 표정이나 신체의 동작은 의미 생성에 핵심적 역할을 한다는 것은 주목할 만하다. 언어 연쇄 과정에서 보여지는 과정이 거의 동시에, 혹은 적어도 음속으로 일어난다는 것 또한 기억할 만한데, 이 사실은 인체의 경이로운 복잡성과 역량을 분명히 보여준다.

어휘   **versatility** n. 융통성, 다재 다능   **anatomical** adj. 해부학상의, 해부의   **apparatus** n. 기관   **cognitive science** phr. 인지 과학
       pragmatics n. 화용론   **interplay** n. 상호 작용   **sensory nerve** phr. 감각 신경   **sound wave** phr. 음파   **vocal cords** phr. 성대
       articulation n. 발화, 발음   **style** n. 어조, 방식   **utterance** n. 발성, 말   **coherent** adj. 일관성 있는, 분명히 말할 수 있는
       motor nerve phr. 운동 신경   **impulse** n. 자극   **enact** v. 행하다, (법을) 제정하다   **aeroacoustic** adj. 공력 소음학의   **decode** v. 해독하다
       expression n. 표현, 음조   **disruption** n. 붕괴, 두절   **loop** n. 고리   **deafness** n. 난청, 귀먹음   **detrimental** adj. 해로운
       delve into phr. 철저하게 조사하다   **staggering** adj. 경이로운, 믿기 어려운

[1-7]

언어 연쇄 과정 연구하기

전문가들은 뇌와 다른 청각 요소 사이의 반응에 대해 알기 위해 언어 연쇄 과정을 이용할 수 있다. 이 반응은 완전한 1 ....에 도움이 될 수도 있고 지장을 줄 수도 있다. 그들은 또한 청각음과 2 ....의 관계에 대해 지식을 얻을 수 있다. 언어 연쇄 과정의 다양한 단계들은 다른 과정들의 복잡한 3 ....을 나타내는 서로 다른 단계에서 발생한다. 언어 연쇄 과정의 마지막 4 ....은 화자와 청자의 뇌 사이의 연결을 성립시키는 것이다. 부가적인 단계는 화자의 성대와 귀 사이의 음파의 5 ....을 수반한다. 그 후에 반응은 그 또는 그녀의 6 ....이 화자가 의도한 질과 부합하는지를 확인하게 해준다. 전반적으로, 언어 연쇄 과정은 인류를 사회적이며, 소통적인 종으로 발달하게 한 기본적인 측면이다. 발화의 기반에 있는 것은 이 연쇄 과정이며, 그것은 의사소통 연구에 7 ....을 세운다.

A 뼈대	B 조합	C 감각
D 전송	E 목표	F 표현
G 발화	H 지각	I 이해

---

1   해설   문제의 핵심어구(feedback can be supportive of or disruptive to)와 관련된 지문 내용 중 'the feedback ~ either enable or disrupt full understanding'에서 반응이 완전한 이해를 가능하게 하거나 혹은 방해한다고 하였으므로, **I** understanding이 정답이다. 'enable or disrupt'가 'be supportive of or disruptive to'로 paraphrasing되었다.

2   해설   문제의 핵심어구(relationship of acoustic sounds to)와 관련된 지문 내용 중 'Researchers ~ study the speech chain to determine how acoustic sounds relate to articulation'에서 연구자들은 청각적 소리들과 발화가 어떻게 연관되어 있는지 알아내기 위해 언어 연쇄 과정을 연구한다고 하였으므로, **G** articulation이 정답이다. 'how acoustic sounds relate to articulation'이 'relationship of acoustic sounds to articulation'으로 paraphrasing되었다.

3   해설   문제의 핵심어구(happen on different levels)와 관련된 지문 내용 중 'It also occurs on a succession of levels which reflect the complex coordination of linguistic and biological processes'에서 이는 언어학적이며 생물학적 절차들의 복잡한 조합을 반영하는 단계들이 연속하는 중에 발생한다고 하였으므로, **B** coordination이 정답이다. 'complex coordination of linguistic and biological processes'가 'complicated coordination of different processes'로 paraphrasing되었다.

4   해설   문제의 핵심어구(a connection between the brain of a speaker and listener)와 관련된 지문 내용 중 'This establishes a connection between the speaker's brain and the listener's brain, which is the ultimate aim of the speech chain'에서 이는 화자의 뇌와 청자의 뇌 사이에 연결을 성립시키는데, 이는 언어 연쇄 과정의 궁극적인 목표라고 하였으므로, **E** aim이 정답이다. 'the speaker's brain and the listener's brain'이 'brain of a speaker and listener'로 paraphrasing되었다.

5   해설   문제의 핵심어구(sound between the speaker's vocal cords and ears)와 관련된 지문 내용 중 'the simultaneous transmission of sound waves to the speaker's ears from his or her vocal organs'에서 화자의 발성 기관에서부터 그

혹은 그녀의 귀까지의 음파의 동시 전송이라고 하였으므로, **D** transmission이 정답이다. 'to the speaker's ears from his or her vocal organs'가 'between the speaker's vocal cords and ears'로 paraphrasing되었다.

6 해설 문제의 핵심어구(feedback ~ lets the speaker make sure)와 관련된 지문 내용 중 'it allows the speaker to compare the quality of their expression with what they intended'에서 반응 연결은 화자가 자신이 의도했던 것과 자신의 표현의 질을 비교할 수 있도록 한다고 하였으므로, **F** expression이 정답이다. 'compare the quality of their expression'이 'make sure that his or her expression meets the intended quality'로 paraphrasing되었다.

7 해설 문제의 핵심어구(chain ~ sets up)와 관련된 지문 내용 중 'this speech chain ~ establishes a framework for the study of communication'에서 이 언어 연쇄 과정은 의사소통 연구의 뼈대를 수립한다고 하였으므로, **A** framework가 정답이다. 'establishes a framework for the study of communication'이 'sets up the framework for communication research'로 paraphrasing되었다.

[8-10]

8 인간은 -하기 때문에 다른 영장류와 다르다.

9 발화를 단계로 나누는 것은 -하다.

10 의미 생산에 있어 시각적 요소는 -하다.

> A 의사소통의 반응에 크게 의존한다
> B 의사소통을 할 때 감각 신경만을 사용한다
> C 독특한 해부학적 발성 기관을 이용한다
> D 인지와 신체적 과정의 상호 작용을 보여준다
> E 몸의 움직임과 얼굴의 표정을 포함한다
> F 발화를 위한 신체적 능력 이상을 갖는다
> G 언어적 신호를 시각적 상징으로 변환한다

8 해설 문제의 핵심어구(differs from other primates)와 관련된 지문 내용 중 'studies of primates show no significant difference between them and humans in their anatomical capacity for speech. It is our cognitive capacity for language, ~ therefore distinguishes humanity.'에서 영장류 연구는 영장류와 인간 사이에 언어 능력을 위한 해부학상의 역량에 있어 의미 있는 차이는 없다는 것을 보여주었으며 인류를 구분짓는 것은 언어에 대한 우리의 인지 능력이라고 하였으므로, 보기 **F** has more than just a physical capacity for speech가 정답이다. 'distinguishes humanity'가 'humans differ from'으로 paraphrasing되었다.

9 해설 문제의 핵심어구(speech into stages)와 관련된 지문 내용 중 'breaking it down into multiple stages which reveal the complex interplay of physical and cognitive processes involved'에서 언어 연쇄 과정은 관련된 신체와 인지 과정의 복잡한 상호 작용을 보여주는 여러 개의 단계로 나뉜다고 하였으므로, 보기 **D** shows the interaction of cognitive and physical processes가 정답이다. 'reveal the ~ interplay'가 'shows the interaction'으로 paraphrasing되었다.

10 해설 문제의 핵심어구(visual component)와 관련된 지문 내용 중 'there is also a very important visual element: facial gestures and bodily motions play a key part in the production of meaning'에서 시각적 요소들 역시 매우 중요한데 표정이나 신체의 동작은 의미 생성에 핵심적 역할을 한다고 하였으므로, 보기 **E** includes body movements and facial expressions가 정답이다. 'facial gestures and bodily motions'가 'body movements and facial expressions'로 paraphrasing되었다.

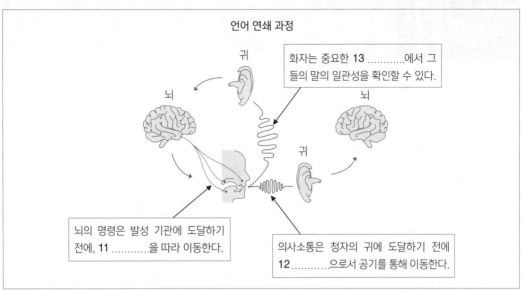

언어 연쇄 과정

귀

뇌

뇌

화자는 중요한 13 ....에서 그들의 말의 일관성을 확인할 수 있다.

귀

뇌의 명령은 발성 기관에 도달하기 전에, 11 ....을 따라 이동한다.

의사소통은 청자의 귀에 도달하기 전에 12 ....으로서 공기를 통해 이동한다.

11 해설 문제의 핵심어구(instructions from the brain)와 관련된 지문 내용 중 'the appropriate instructions of the brain will travel along the motor nerves'에서 뇌의 적합한 명령이 운동 신경을 따라 이동한다고 하였으므로, **motor nerves**가 정답이다. 'appropriate instructions of the brain'이 'instructions from the brain'으로 paraphrasing되었다.

12 해설 문제의 핵심어구(travels through the air)와 관련된 지문 내용 중 'The sound waves travel through the air, toward the listener'에서 음파는 공기를 통해 청자에게로 이동한다고 하였으므로, **sound waves**가 정답이다. 'The sound waves travel ~ toward the listener'가 'The communication travels ~ as sound waves before reaching the listener's ear'로 paraphrasing되었다.

13 해설 문제의 핵심어구(check their statement's coherence)와 관련된 지문 내용 중 'This creates a feedback link which allows the speaker to check the coherence or accuracy of their own statement.'에서 이것은 화자가 자신의 말의 일관성이나 정확성을 확인할 수 있도록 하는 반응 연결을 만든다고 하였으므로, **feedback link**가 정답이다. 'coherence or accuracy of their own statement'가 'their statement's coherence'로 paraphrasing되었다.

* 각 문제에 대한 정답의 단서는 지문에 문제 번호와 함께 별도의 색으로 표시되어 있습니다.

EXAMPLE
p.186

심리학자 Tom Gilovich에 따르면, 직관에 근거한 결정들은 주로 순간적으로 내려지고, 이러한 결정은 항상 잘 알고 있는 것이거나 이성적 사고의 결과물인 것은 아니다. 직관적 의사 결정의 문제점을 알아보는 가장 쉬운 방법 중 하나는 사람들이 게임을 하는 동안 행동하는 방식을 살펴보는 것이다. 모든 사람이 대부분의 게임이 순전히 운에 의한 것임을 이해하고 있음에도 불구하고, 게임을 하는 사람들은 종종 비이성적인 감정에 따라 내기를 한다.

경영 컨설턴트 [1]Lyndsay Swinton은 이성적이고 의도적인 의사 결정은, 반면에, 더 적절한 결과가 보장될 수 있도록 결정이 규율에 의해 접근되게 한다고 지적한다. 이것은 의도적인 의사 결정 절차가 단지 그 순간에 어떻게 느껴지는지보다는 결정의 더 큰 영향을 고려하는 것을 요구하기 때문이다. 결국, 그것은 더 적은 부정적인 영향을 가진 더 적절한 선택을 낳는다.

HACKERS PRACTICE
p.188

1 B	2 A	3 A	4 A	5 B
6 C	7 C	8 B	9 C	10 A
11 B	12 B	13 C	14 A	15 B
16 A	17 B	18 C	19 A	20 B
21 B	22 A	23 B	24 C	25 C
26 B	27 D	28 A	29 C	30 B
31 C	32 A	33 D	34 E	

1

주로 꿀 생산으로 알려져 있기는 하지만, 벌은 사실 우리의 식단을 이루는 주요 곡물의 꽃가루 매개자로써 인간의 안녕에 더 중요하다. 실제로, 미국 환경보호국은 꽃가루 매개자들이 우리가 먹는 음식의 세 입 중 약 한 입에 대해 책임을 지고 있다고 말한다. 만약 이것이 사실이라면, 꿀벌 수가 점점 줄어들고 있다는 사실은 그들의 생존뿐만 아니라, 우리의 생존에 대한 우려의 주된 원인일 것이다. 코넬 대학의 곤충학과 부교수인 Nicholas Calderone에 의해 수행된 연구는, 꿀벌과 다른 곤충들에 의해 수분된 농작물이 미국에서 290억 달러의 연간 농가 소득에 기여했음을 보여주었으며, 이는 농업적으로 그리고 경제적으로 그들의 중요성의 정도를 보여주었다. [1]이 요점은 상파울루 대학의 수석 교수인 Vera Lucia Imperatriz-Fonseca에 의해 강조되었는데, 그녀는 국제연합 보고서에서 꽃가루 매개자의 건강이 우리 자신의 건강과 직결되어 있다고 기술했다. 실제로, [2]영국의 Simon Potts 교수에 의한 연구는 꿀벌 군집의 엄청난 감소가 어떻게 농업을 마찬가지로 다수가 위기에 처해있는 야생 벌 종의 수분에 의존하게 만들었는지 보여주었다.

1   벌과 같이 작물을 수분하는 생물체들의 번영은 인간의 건강과 직접적 연관이 있다.

2   농업은 수분을 위해 특정 종류의 벌에 의존하게 되었다.

1 해설 문제의 핵심어구(connection to human health)와 관련된 지문 내용 중 'This point was emphasised by Vera Lucia Imperatriz-Fonseca ~ who stated ~ pollinator's health is directly linked to our own well-being.'에서 이 요점은 Vera Lucia Imperatriz-Fonseca에 의해 강조되었는데 그녀는 꽃가루 매개자의 건강이 우리 자신의 건강과 직결되어 있다고 기술했다고 하였으므로, 보기 **B** Vera Lucia Imperatriz-Fonseca가 정답이다. 'directly linked to our own well-being'이 'has a direct connection to human health'로 paraphrasing되었다.

2 해설 문제의 핵심어구(Agriculture has become dependent)와 관련된 지문 내용 중 'a study by Professor Simon Potts in the UK revealed how a massive decline in honeybee colonies has made agriculture reliant upon pollination by wild bee species'에서 영국의 Simon Potts 교수에 의한 연구는 꿀벌 군집의 엄청난 감소가 어떻게 농업을 야생 벌 종의 수분에 의존하게 만들었는지 보여주었다고 하였으므로, 보기 **A** Simon Potts가 정답이다. 'reliant upon pollination by wild bee species'가 'dependent on a certain kind of bee for pollination'으로 paraphrasing되었다.

2

250년보다 더 역사가 짧은데도 불구하고, 미국은 세계 경제 강국 중 하나가 되었다. 이 나라의 위치, 큰 면적, 풍부한 천연자원이 성공에 주요한 역할을 했을지라도, 운송 산업의 발전 없이는 이러한 요인들이 큰 영향을 발휘하지 못했을 것이다. 약 1800년까지는, 이 나라는 화물 요구를 위해 선박과 배와 같은 수상 운송에 주로 의존했다. [6]나라가 다소 작았고 대부분의 초기 도시들은 동해안에 위치했기 때문에, 초기의 미국인들은 이러한 형태의 운송을 이용하여 서로 그리고 유럽 무역 상대국과 쉽게 무역을 할 수 있었다. 그러나, 19세기를 겪으면서, 루이지애나 구입지가 나라의 크기를 두 배로 늘렸고 결국 서해안까지 이르게 되었다. 이는 배로 닿을 수 없는 거대한 내륙 지역을 낳았고 그 결과 수상 교통 시대의 끝을 맞았다. 그 문제는 대륙 횡단의 철도 체계를 건설함으로써 해결되었는데, 이것은 미국에 지상 교통의 시대를 가져왔다. 새로운 철도는 최초로 한 해안에서 다른 해안으로의 대형 물품들의 대규모 운송을 가능하게 했다. 나중에, [5]자동차 발명 이후로, 고속도로가 이러한 대륙 간 시스템을 모방했고 사람들은 쉽게 스스로 운전하여 국토를 횡단할 수 있었다. 이런 지상 체계들은 1900년대 중반부터 후반까지 미국의 교통을 지배했다. [4]그 이후의 시기는 비행기 여행과 정보 통신 기술의 동시 출현을 경험했다. [3]항공 교통 시대가 시작되면서, 사람들은 며칠이나 몇 주가 아니라 수 시간에 걸쳐 여행하거나 소포를 전국에 보낼 수 있었고, 정보를 전송하는 것도 즉각적으로 할 수 있게 되었다.

3   우편 서비스의 속도는 하루 이하로 줄어들었다.

4   새로운 종류의 여행이 새로운 기술과 같은 시기에 나타났다.

5   새로운 체계가 혼자서 전국을 여행하는 방법을 제공했다.

6   한 해안의 도시들의 위치는 무역을 쉽게 했다.

3 해설 문제의 핵심어구(speed of the postal service)와 관련된 지문 내용 중 'As the air-based transportation era began, people could ~ send parcels across the country in a matter of hours rather than days or weeks'에서 항공 교통 시대가 시작되면서 사람들은 며칠이나 몇 주가 아니라 수 시간에 걸쳐 소포를 전국에 보낼 수 있었다고 하였으므로, 보기 **A** Air-based transportation era가 정답이다. 'in a matter of hours'가 'less than a day'로 paraphrasing되었다.

4 해설 문제의 핵심어구(at the same time as a new technology)와 관련된 지문 내용 중 'The following period saw the simultaneous rise of air travel and information technology.'에서 그 이후의 시기는 비행기 여행과 정보 통신 기술의 동시의 출현을 경험했다고 하였으므로, 보기 **A** Air-based transportation era가 정답이다. 'simultaneous rise'가 'emerged at the same time as'로 paraphrasing되었다.

5 해설 문제의 핵심어구(travelling alone across the country)와 관련된 지문 내용 중 'after the invention of the automobile ~ people could easily drive across the country on their own'에서 자동차 발명 이후로 사람들은 쉽게 스스로 운전하여 국토를 횡단할 수 있었다고 하였으므로, 보기 **B** Land-based transportation era가 정답이다. 'drive ~ on their own'이 'travelling alone'으로 paraphrasing되었다.

6 해설 문제의 핵심어구(made trade easy)와 관련된 지문 내용 중 'Since ~ most early cities were on the East Coast, early Americans could easily trade ~ using this form of transportation.'에서 대부분의 초기 도시들은 동해안에 위치했기 때문에 초기의 미국인들은 수상 운송을 이용하여 쉽게 무역을 할 수 있었다고 하였으므로, 보기 **C** Water-based transportation era가 정답이다. 'most early cities ~ on the East Coast'가 'location of cities on one coast'로 paraphrasing되었다.

3

수면은 모든 동물들에게 필수적인 것이고, 일부 과학자들에 따르면, 우리의 공통된 진화 계보에 대해 무언가를 드러낼 수 있다. 수면의 보편성 때문에, 많은 초기 수면 연구자들은 수면이 동물 진화에서 매우 일찍 시작되었을 것이라고 생각했다. 하지만, 이러한 견해는 캘리포니아 대학의 Jerry Siegel과 같은 몇몇 과학자들에 의해 이의가 제기되는데, 그는 수면의 필요는 각각의 종에서 따로 발달했을 수 있다고 제안했다. [7]그는, "그것은 오히려 융합 진화의 사례일 수 있다"고 말하며, 수면이 공통적인 진화의 선조로부터 물려받은 특성이라기보다는 '동물의 환경에 적응하는 것'이라고 제안했다. Siegel의 이론은 하루에 최대 18시간을 잘 수 있는 주머니쥐부터, 매일 수백 번의 짧은 낮잠을 자는 새들까지 다양한 종에 걸친 수면 패턴에 있어서의 큰 차이에 의해 뒷받침된다. 또한 그는 한 번에 한 쪽의 뇌를 재울 수 있는 능력으로 잘 알려진 돌고래들이, 또 하나의 독특한 수면 패턴을 가지고 있다는 것을 알아냈다. 어른 돌고래가 출산을 한 후, 그녀와 그녀의 새끼 둘 다 오랫동안 잠을 자지 않는다. 육상 포유류에게 일어나는 것과는 반대인 이런 행동은, 보편적인 수면 방식을 이어받는다기보다는 동물들이 자신의 수면 방식에 적응한다는 것을 시사한다. 그럼에도 불구하고 많은 과학자들은 왜 모든 동물들에게 수면이 필요한지에 대한 중요한 이론을 발견하고 싶어 한다. [8]세인트루이스에 있는 워싱턴 대학의 연구원 Paul Shaw는, 다른 동물들로부터의 매복 공격에 취약하다는 점에서 '수면은 대가가 크기' 때문에 그것의 보편성에 대한 근본적인 진화적 이유가 있는 것이 틀림없다고 주장한다. Shaw는 수면 연구의 선구자 Alan Rechtschaffen을 인용하는데, 그는, "만약 수면이 전적으로 중요한 기능을 하지 않는다면, 그것은 진화가 만든 가장 큰 실수이다"라고 말했다.

7 동물들은 보편적인 특성을 이어받았다기보다는, 그들의 특정한 주변 환경에 맞추기 위해 독특한 수면 습관을 발달시켰다.

8 잠자고 있는 동물이 포식자로부터의 공격에 훨씬 더 노출되어 있다는 것을 생각하면 수면의 중요성은 분명하다.

과학자 리스트

A Alan Rechtschaffen
B Paul Shaw
C Jerry Siegel

---

7 해설 문제의 핵심어구(specific surroundings, rather than ~ a general trait)와 관련된 지문 내용 중 'he states, suggesting that sleep is 'an adaptation to an animal's environment' rather than a trait inherited from a common evolutionary ancestor'에서 Jerry Siegel은 수면이 공통적인 진화의 선조로부터 물려받은 특성이라기보다는 '동물의 환경에 적응하는 것'이라고 제안했다고 하였으므로, 보기 **C** Jerry Siegel이 정답이다. 'adaptation to an animals' environment'가 'match their specific surroundings'로, 'inherited from a common evolutionary ancestor'가 'inheriting a general trait'로 paraphrasing되었다.

8 해설 문제의 핵심어구(open to attack from a predator)와 관련된 지문 내용 중 'Paul Shaw ~ claims that because 'sleep is costly' in terms of vulnerability to ambush from other animals, there must be an underlying evolutionary reason for its universality.'에서 Paul Shaw는 다른 동물들로부터의 매복 공격에 취약하다는 점에서 '수면은 대가가 크기' 때문에 그것의 보편성에 대한 근본적인 진화적 이유가 있는 것이 틀림없다고 주장한다고 하였으므로, 보기 **B** Paul Shaw가 정답이다. 'vulnerability to ambush from other animals'가 'much more open to attack from a predator'로 paraphrasing되었다.

4

[10]자연에서, 대부분의 동물들은 쓴맛을 가진 것을 먹는 것을 피한다. 옥스포드 연구원 J. Zhang에 따르면, 이것은 쓴맛이 흔히 독성을 암시하기 때문에 발생한다. 그러므로, 동물들은 쓴 음식을 피함으로써 생명을 연장할 수 있다. 이러한 지식을 활용하여, 일부 제조업자들은 쓴맛을 동물 퇴치제에 사용하기 시작했다. 실제로, [11]연구원 A. L. Riley는 그의 연구에서 물체에 쓴맛의 화합물을 바르는 것이 그것들을 피하도록 새들을 훈련시킬 수 있다는 것을 보여주었다. 흥미롭게도, 인간은 다른 동물들이 보여주는 쓴맛에 대한 반감을 상실한 것처럼 보인다. 이는 상업적 식료품 생산에서의 우리의 쓴맛 사용을 통해 보여질 수 있다. 식료품 제조업자들은 특정 음식에 이러한 맛을 더하기 위해 특별히 '쓴맛이 나게 하는 물질'을 개발해왔다.

쓴맛이 나게 하는 이러한 물질을 사용하는 하나의 좋은 예는 맥주를 양조할 때 나타난다. 양조업자들이 그들의 제품에 더하는 홉은 맥아 속에서 발효되는 설탕의 단맛과 균형을 이루도록 쓴맛을 첨가하기 위한 것이다. 이것은 카페인이 콜라에 첨가되는 이유이기도 하다. 카페인이 제거되면, 콜라는 그저 질릴 정도로 탄산이 많은 물에 불과하며 반드시 쓴맛이 나게 하는 다른 물질과 균형이 이루어져야 한다. 이것들 중 하나는 향이 좋은 허브와 다른 식물 원료들로부터 만들어진 액체 '고미약'이다. 상업적으로 이용 가능한 이 액체들은 음식 및 칵테일 조제에 있어 현재 널리 사용되고 있으나, 그것들은 한때 굉장히 다른 용도로 사용되었다. 그것들은 자양 강장제로 간주되었다. House of Angostura에 의해 만들어진 유명한 '고미약'의 경우가 바로 그러했다. [9]Johann Gottlieb Benjamin Siegert 박사는 뱃멀미를 완화하기 위한 혼합물을 만들었고 선원들에게 상품을 광고했다. 시간이 흐르면서, 그의 상품은 레모네이드나 사제라크 칵테일과 같은 음료의 단맛을 줄이기 위해 사용되었다.

9 질환을 완화시키는 상품을 개발했다

10 동물들이 특정 맛을 가진 음식을 왜 피하는지에 대해 설명했다

11 쓴맛이 나는 물품들을 사용하여 동물들을 훈련시키는 것에 대한 연구를 했다

> **사람들 리스트**
>
> **A** Zhang
> **B** Riley
> **C** Siegert

9 해설 문제의 핵심어구(relieve a medical condition)와 관련된 지문 내용 중 'Dr Johann Gottlieb Benjamin Siegert developed the concoction to ease seasickness'에서 Johann Gottlieb Benjamin Siegert 박사는 뱃멀미를 완화하기 위한 혼합물을 만들었다고 하였으므로, 보기 **C** Siegert가 정답이다. 'ease seasickness'가 'relieve a medical condition'으로 paraphrasing되었다.

10 해설 문제의 핵심어구(animals avoid ~ certain taste)와 관련된 지문 내용 중 'In nature, most animals avoid eating things that have a bitter taste. This occurs, according to Oxford researcher J. Zhang, because bitterness often indicates toxicity.'에서 자연에서 대부분의 동물들은 쓴맛을 가진 것을 먹는 것을 피하는데, 옥스포드 연구원 J. Zhang에 따르면 이것은 쓴맛이 흔히 독성을 암시하기 때문에 발생한다고 하였으므로, 보기 **A** Zhang이 정답이다. 'avoid eating things that have a bitter taste'가 'avoid food with a certain taste'로 paraphrasing되었다.

11 해설 문제의 핵심어구(train animals)와 관련된 지문 내용 중 'researcher A. L. Riley showed in his research that applying bitter compounds to objects could train birds to avoid them'에서 연구원 A. L. Riley는 그의 연구에서 물체에 쓴맛의 화합물을 바르는 것이 그것들을 피하도록 새들을 훈련시킬 수 있다는 것을 보여주었다고 하였으므로, 보기 **B** Riley가 정답이다. 'applying bitter compounds to objects'가 'using bitter items'로 paraphrasing되었다.

5

중동에 있는 티그리스와 유프라테스 강 사이의 지역에는 상주인구의 성장 이전 수백 혹은 수천 년 전부터 원시인들이 거주해온 것으로 알려져 있다. ¹⁴지역의 비옥함으로 인해 19세기 초 고고학자 James Breasted에 의해 '비옥한 초승달 지대'라고 명명된 이 지역은 초기 거주민들이 그들 스스로와 가족을 먹여 살릴 수 있게 해주었던 토지, 강, 그리고 야생 동물들로부터의 풍부한 생산물들을 제공했다. 결국, 이것은 최초의 활발한 식료품 생산을 발생시켰으며, 마침내, 최초의 진정한 정착 문명을 초래했다. 시간이 지나면서, 식료품을 정기적으로 생산할 수 있는 이러한 문명의 능력은 이 지역의 인구수 증가로 이어졌으며, 기원전 4500년경에는, 흥미로운 일이 일어났다. 사람들은 우루크라 불리는 대규모의, 밀집된 영구 정착지를 세웠는데, 이것은 우리가 현재 최초의 도시로 알고 있는 곳이다.

¹²새 도시 우루크에는 전부 일건 벽돌로 지어진 커다란 사원, 주택, 그리고 다른 건물들이 있었다. 역사학자 Stephen Bertman에 따르면, 이것은 다른 곳에서 건축에 흔히 이용되는 목재와 석재의 부족 때문이었다. 우리는 이러한 벽돌의 이용으로 그들이 기둥, 아치, 그리고 방어 장벽과 같은 대규모의 구조물을 최초로 만들어낼 수 있었다는 것을 알고 있지만, 이것은 왜 이러한 정착지가 발달되었는가를 설명하지는 못한다. '길가메시의 서사시'와 같은 전통적인 개작된 이야기에서는, 이 문명의 지도자가 도시와 요새들을 짓는 것을 명령했다. 그러나, 인류학자 Jason Ur에 의한 연구는 이것에 이의를 제기한다. ¹³Ur 박사의 연구에 따르면, 초기 도시화는 정치적인 지도자 때문이 아니라, 자연스럽게 발생했을 가능성이 크다. 그는 중앙 언덕 주변에 이 지역의 서로 다른 문명들이 정착했다는 것을 보여주었다. 이러한 무리들은 서로 다른 문명들이 가까이 살 수 있도록 해주었으나, 적절한 사회적인 거리는 유지했다. 시간이 지남에 따라, 그들은 합쳐져 하나의 지도자를 가진 상호 연결된 도시를 형성했다.

12 그는 초기 사회가 일건 벽돌을 사용한 이유를 알아냈다.

13 그는 최초 도시들의 성장이 자연스럽게 일어났다는 것을 밝혔다.

14 그는 한 지역의 농업적 강점을 대표하는 용어를 만들었다.

연구원 리스트

A James Breasted
B Stephen Bertman
C Jason Ur

---

12 해설 문제의 핵심어구(sun-dried bricks)와 관련된 지문 내용 중 'The new city of Uruk had ~ buildings created entirely with sun-dried bricks.'와 'This, according to historian Stephen Bertman, was due to the lack of timber and stone commonly used in construction elsewhere.'에서 새 도시 우루크에는 전부 일건 벽돌로 지어진 건물들이 있었으며 역사학자 Stephen Bertman에 따르면 이것은 다른 곳에서 건축에 흔히 이용되는 목재와 석재의 부족 때문이었다고 하였으므로, 보기 **B** Stephen Bertman이 정답이다.

13 해설 문제의 핵심어구(first cities happened naturally)와 관련된 지문 내용 중 'According to Dr Ur's research, early urbanisation likely occurred organically'에서 Ur 박사의 연구에 따르면 초기 도시화는 자연스럽게 발생했을 가능성이 크다고 하였으므로, 보기 **C** Jason Ur가 정답이다. 'early urbanisation likely occurred organically'가 'growth of the first cities happened naturally'로 paraphrasing되었다.

14 해설 문제의 핵심어구(coined a term)와 관련된 지문 내용 중 'This area, which was named the 'Fertile Crescent' by early 19th-century archaeologist James Breasted for its fertility'에서 지역의 비옥함으로 인해 19세기 초 고고학자

James Breasted에 의해 '비옥한 초승달 지대'라고 명명된 이 지역이라고 하였으므로, 보기 **A James Breasted**가 정답이다. 'fertility'가 'agricultural strength'로 paraphrasing되었다.

6

많은 부모들은 그들의 아이들이 더 이상 이전과 같은 사람이 아니라며 불평한다. 사춘기 이전의 단계에서, 이 아이들은 대개 유순하고 순종적이었다. 그들은 매우 다정했으며 그들과 교감하는 데 아마 아무런 문제가 없었을 그들의 부모들에게 애착을 가졌다. [16]이 시기에, 많은 부모들은 그들이 자녀와 절대로 약해지지 않을 강한 유대를 가지고 있다고 믿는다. 그들에게 유감스럽게도, 이러한 시기는 약 10~13살까지만 지속된다. 자녀들은 사춘기에 접어들면서, 그들을 다루기 매우 어렵게 하는 변화들을 겪는다. [17]부모님과의 증가한 갈등, 급격한 감정 변화, 그리고 점점 더 위험해지는 행동의 이 시기는 초기 심리학자 G. S. Hall로 하여금 이러한 초기 십대 시기를 '질풍노도'의 시기라고 부르게 했다.

이 십대 시기와 관련된 바람직하지 않은 행동의 한 가지 원인은 이 시기에 몸이 겪는 급격한 변화 때문이다. 청소년의 신체는 급격히 발달하며 그들은 어린아이 같은 충동과 정서적 불안을 가진 채 행동하는 어른처럼 보일 수도 있다. 이것은 부모를 실망시킬 수 있지만, 이는 단지 이러한 행동을 통제하는 부분인 뇌의 전두엽이 아직 완전히 발달하지 않았다는 신호이다. 실제로, Donald Stuss는 때로는 전두엽이 20대 초기에서 중반에 이르기까지 완전히 성장하지 않는다는 사실을 알아냈다. 이러한 신체적 변화 이외에도, 청소년의 사회적 교류도 큰 변화를 겪는다. [15]대부분의 청소년들은 성인으로서 그들 스스로 사회에 들어갈 준비를 하며 부모에게서 거리를 두게 되고 외부의 관계에 중점을 둔다. 이 거리는 1950년대에 나타났던 것보다 현재 더 두드러지게 나타난다. 오늘날, 더욱더 상호 연결된 세계가 우리가 가정 밖에서 만들어가는 사회적인 관계의 수를 급격히 늘어나게 했다. 청소년들은 더 큰 도시에서 살아가며 현실 세계 상황과 온라인 상호 작용 그리고 소셜 미디어 속에서 더 많은 사람들과 교류하면서 자신이 누군지 알아내야만 한다. 이는 과거보다 더 큰 정체성의 혼란으로 이어질 수 있으며 청소년들의 '질풍노도'의 시기를 다뤄야 하는 부모의 스트레스를 증가시킬 수 있다.

15 가족과의 관계는 다른 사람들과 어울리는 것보다 덜 중요하다.

16 아이들과 부모님 사이에 깊은 친밀감이 존재한다.

17 더 많은 안전하지 않은 행동들이 있다.

A	사춘기 이전
B	십대 시기

15 해설 문제의 핵심어구(socialising with others)와 관련된 지문 내용 중 'Most adolescents will become distant from their parents and focus on external relationships'에서 대부분의 청소년들은 부모에게서 거리를 두게 되고 외부의 관계에 중점을 둔다고 하였으므로, 보기 **B Teenage period**가 정답이다. 'focus on external relationships'가 'socialising with others'로 paraphrasing되었다.

16 해설 문제의 핵심어구(connection ~ between children and parents)와 관련된 지문 내용 중 'At this point, many parents believe that they have a strong bond with their children'에서 이 시기에 많은 부모들은 그들이 자녀와 강한 유대를 가지고 있다고 믿는다고 하였으므로, 보기 **A Preadolescence**가 정답이다. 'a strong bond'가 'A deep connection'으로 paraphrasing되었다.

17 해설 문제의 핵심어구(unsafe activities)와 관련된 지문 내용 중 'This period of ~ increasingly risky behaviour caused early psychologist G. S. Hall to refer to this early teenage period as the 'storm and stress' stage.'에서 점점 더 위험해지는 행동의 이 시기는 초기 심리학자 G. S. Hall로 하여금 이러한 초기 십대 시기를 '질풍노도'의 시기라고 부르게 했다고 하였으므로, 보기 **B Teenage period**가 정답이다. 'increasingly risky behaviour'가 'more unsafe activities'로 paraphrasing되었다.

하품은 기능을 가지고 있는가?

우리가 하품을 하는 이유에 대한 이론은 2,000년 전보다도 이전인 히포크라테스 시대로 거슬러 올라가는데, 그는 하품을 하는 것을 호흡기관이 폐로부터 '나쁜 공기'를 제거하는 방법이라고 생각했다. 수 세기 이후, 과학자들은 하품이 뇌의 산소 부족을 나타낸다고 주장했다. 오늘날, 우리는 이들 중 어떤 것도 확실한 과학적 가치를 가지지 못한다는 것을 알고 있는데, 이는 현대의 연구자들로 하여금 우리의 가장 흔한 반사 작용 중 하나인 하품의 신비를 풀기 위해 계속해서 노력하도록 했다.

메릴랜드 대학의 신경과학자인 Robert Provine은, 사람들이 지루하거나, 배고프거나, 피로할 때 가장 많이 하품을 하는 경향이 있다는 명백한 것을 지적한다. 이러한 모든 상태들은 눈앞에 있는 어떤 과업에도 집중하지 못하는 무능으로 쉽게 이어지기 때문에, 그는 하품이란 우리의 신체가 우리에게 기운을 차려야 한다는 것을 알리는 방법이라고 생각한다. 이 이론이 시험을 거쳤을 때, 연구 대상들이 실제로 하품 직후에 어떤 종류의 신체적인 활동에 참여하려는 경향이 있다는 것이 발견되었으며, 이는 연구 대상들의 하품이 그들을 깨우고 자극을 찾아 나서도록 이끌었다는 것을 시사한다. 본질적으로, [20]Provine은 하품이 자극의 부재로 인해 일어나며 단순히 우리의 신체가 초점을 다시 맞추는 방식이라고 주장한다.

한편, 너무 많은 것들이 사람들이 하품하도록 유발하는 것처럼 보이기 때문에 단순히 자극의 부족을 탓하는 것은 거의 만족스럽지 못하다. 아마 우리들 중 많은 이에게 친숙한 하나의 상황은 바로 [18]다른 누군가가 하품하는 것을 본 다음 스스로 하품하는 것을 조절할 수 없다는 것이다. Catriona Morrison이 이끄는 리즈 대학의 연구원 팀은 이것이 우리가 다른 사람에게 공감을 보이려는 경향과 관련 있다고 믿는다. 다시 말해서, 누군가가 피로감에 하품을 하고, 같은 방의 다른 사람들도 이를 따라 한다면, 이것은 아마도 그들이 원래 하품을 한 사람과 그들을 동일시하고 그에게 동정심을 느끼기 때문이다. 이러한 주장은 하품이 같은 가족이나 사회집단의 구성원들 사이에서 가장 전염성이 높으며 공감할 수 있는 능력의 결여와 관련된 질환인 자폐와 정신 이상을 앓는 사람들 사이에서 가장 낮다는 것을 증명하는 연구들에 의해 입증된다.

한편, 올버니 대학의 진화심리학자 Gordon Gallup은 [19]하품이 잠재적인 위협에 대해 집단 구성원에게 경고하는 방법으로서 발달했다는 그의 가설의 기반을 Provine과 Morrison의 이론 모두에 둔다. 증진된 경각심이 하품을 뒤따르고 그것이 전염성이 있다는 점에 동의하면서, 그는 초기의 인간이 공격에 대비해야 한다는 메시지를 다른 사람에게 재빠르게 전달하기 위해 이러한 효과를 활용했다고 생각한다. 본질적으로, 만약 모두가 하품을 하고 이것으로 인해 더욱 경각심을 느꼈다면, 포식자의 먹이로 전락할 가능성은 훨씬 낮았다.

18 하품은 우리 주변에 있는 사람들과 같은 감정을 경험하는 능력과 관련되어 있을 수도 있다.

19 하품의 전염성은 한 집단 내 구성원들의 각성을 증진하는 데 도움이 되었다.

20 하품은 자극 부족의 결과이고 우리의 신체가 다시 집중하려는 시도이다.

연구원 리스트

A Gordon Gallup
B Robert Provine
C Catriona Morrison

---

18 해설 문제의 핵심어구(same emotions as the people around us)와 관련된 지문 내용 중 'being unable to control ouselves from yawning after seeing someone else yawn'과 'A team of researchers ~ headed by Catriona Morrison believe that this has to do with our inclination to show empathy for other people.'에서 Catriona Morrison이 이끄는 연구원 팀은 다른 누군가가 하품하는 것을 본 다음 스스로 하품하는 것을 조절할 수 없다는 것이 우리가 다른 사람에게 공감을 보이려는 경향과 관련 있다고 믿는다고 하였으므로, 보기 **C** Catriona Morrison이 정답이다. 'empathy for other people'이 'same emotions as the people around us'로 paraphrasing되었다.

19 해설 문제의 핵심어구(yawning ~ to promote alertness)와 관련된 지문 내용 중 'his hypothesis that yawning developed as a way to alert group members to potential threats'에서 하품이 잠재적인 위협에 대해 집단 구성원에게 경고하는 방법으로서 발달했다는 Gordon Gallup의 가설이라고 하였으므로, 보기 **A** Gordon Gallup이 정답이다. 'alert group members'가 'promote alertness among members of a group'으로 paraphrasing되었다.

해설 문제의 핵심어구(lack of stimuli ~ refocus)와 관련된 지문 내용 중 'Provine contends that yawning occurs due to an absence of stimuli and is simply how our bodies try to regain focus.'에서 Provine은 하품이 자극의 부재로 인해 일어나며 단순히 우리의 신체가 초점을 다시 맞추는 방식이라고 주장한다고 하였으므로, 보기 **B** Robert Provine이 정답이다. 'try to regain focus'가 'attempt ~ to refocus'로 paraphrasing되었다.

8

몸짓의 중요성

몸짓은 필수적이며 종종 간과되는 의사소통의 한 요소이다. 이것은 구어에 대한 보완이거나 그 자체로 자율적인 언어 체계일 수 있다. [24]인지과학자 Philip Lieberman은 몸짓이 사실상 가장 오래된 형태의 언어이고 인류 진화의 언어 이전 단계에 기원을 둔다고 제시했다. [25]Lieberman은 그의 이론을 뒷받침하기 위해 영장류와 유아들 모두의 몸짓 사용에 대한 연구를 실행했다. Lieberman은 언어에서 몸짓이 형성되었다기보다, 비언어적인 몸짓으로부터 언어가 형성되었고, 현재 우리의 몸짓 사용은 언어 이전의 의사소통에 기인한다고 주장했다.

Natasha Abner, Kensy Cooperrider 그리고 Susan Goldin-Meadow가 '언어학자들을 위한 몸짓: 유용한 입문서'라는 그들의 글에서 언급하듯이, 몸짓은 크게 의사소통적인 것과 정보를 제공하는 것이라는 두 가지 범주로 나뉜다. 전자는 강조를 제공하기 위한 것이든, 혹은 문자 그대로의 의미를 변형하는 것을 통한 것이든, 언어적 의사소통에 더해 의식적으로 사용되는 의도적으로 만들어지는 의사소통적인 몸짓을 포함한다. 반면, 정보를 제공하는 의사소통은 반드시 의사소통적 행위의 일부인 것은 아니지만, 그럼에도 불구하고 그러한 행동의 의미를 바꿀 수 있는 수동적이거나 비자발적인 몸짓을 말한다. [22]'Gesture'지의 공동 편집자이자 이 주제에 관해 세계적 권위자인 Adam Kendon은, 다양한 몸짓을 구별하는 분류 체계를 만들었다. 이것들은 수반되는 말을 반영하는 몸짓인 '손짓', 문장의 일부를 대체하는 '말에 끼워넣어진 몸짓', 언어적 의사소통 바깥에서 일어나는, 검지와 엄지를 맞닿게 함으로써 만들어지는 'OK' 상징과 같은 관습화된 신호들인 '상징', 수화 체계에서 어휘적 의미를 가지는 몸짓인 '수화의 몸짓'을 포함한다. Kendon은 서구 문화에서 몸짓에 대해 가져온 오랜 세월 동안의 관심을 의사소통에 대한 그것의 중요성의 증거로 인용한다. 로마 철학자이자 정치가인 키케로가 그의 작품 '변론가론'에서 강조하듯이, 몸짓이 효과적인 수사에 있어서 매우 중요한 부분으로 여겨졌던 고전주의 시대에 이러한 관심은 명백히 드러났다. 또한 그것은 천주교에서 불교에 이르기까지, 종교의 독특한 몸짓 체계에서 분명히 나타나는데, 이를 통해 신자들은 다양한 복잡한 뜻을 전달할 수 있다.

몸짓에 대한 현대의 학구적인 관심은 몸짓이 의사소통의 보편적인 형태라는 것을 시사하는 인류의 언어 이전 시기와, 많은 비언어적인 몸짓 신호들을 수집하는 것을 가능하게 하는 대면 의사소통의 철저한 심리학적 이해에 대한 최근의 관심이라는 두 가지 뿌리에서 비롯된다. 개인적인 의사소통 체계로서의 몸짓의 복잡함은 서로 다른 의미를 표현할 수 있는 몸짓의 다양한 변형에서 뚜렷하게 나타난다. [21]Geneviève Calbris는 몸짓 변형들이 '어떻게 몸짓이 어휘를 설명하는 수단이 아니라 발화 과정 동안 형성되고 표현되는 기저에 있는 생각을 나타내는가'를 보여준다고 제시한다. [23]이는 시간과 관련된 몸짓들에 대한 Calbris의 분석에서 명백히 드러나는데, 이것은 기간에 대한 복잡하고 다양한 의미를 언어적 의사소통 없이 표현할 수 있다. Calbris에 따르면, 매우 다양한 이러한 몸짓 변형들은 이 의사소통 체계의 복잡성을 드러내는데, 이는 언어적 의사소통의 의미를 강조하거나 바꾸는 것 모두를 할 수 있다.

21 몸짓이 어휘의 기저에 있는 생각을 상징한다고 제안했다

22 다른 종류의 몸짓을 구분짓는 접근법을 만들었다

23 어떻게 몸짓들이 시간에 대한 많은 것들을 말할 수 있는지에 대한 분석을 진행했다

24 몸짓이 언어에 앞선다는 이론을 성립했다

25 유인원의 몸짓 사용에 대한 연구를 진행했다

사람들 리스트

A Adam Kendon
B Geneviève Calbris
C Philip Lieberman
D Natasha Abner
E Susan Goldin-Meadow

21 해설 문제의 핵심어구(idea lying beneath words)와 관련된 지문 내용 중 'Geneviève Calbris suggests that gesture variants reveal how 'gesture is not a word illustrator but represents an underlying thought'에서 Geneviève Calbris는 몸짓 변형들이 '어떻게 몸짓이 어휘를 설명하는 수단이 아니라 기저에 있는 생각을 나타내는가'를 보여준다고 제시한다고 하였으므로, 보기 **B Geneviève Calbris**가 정답이다. 'represents an underlying thought'이 'stood for an idea lying beneath words'로 paraphrasing되었다.

22 해설 문제의 핵심어구(distinguish different types of gestures)와 관련된 지문 내용 중 'Adam Kendon ~ has developed a categorisation system for differentiating various gestures.'에서 Adam Kendon은 다양한 몸짓을 구별하는 분류 체계를 만들었다고 하였으므로, 보기 **A Adam Kendon**이 정답이다. 'differentiating various gestures'가 'distinguish different types of gestures'로 paraphrasing되었다.

23 해설 문제의 핵심어구(say ~ things about time)와 관련된 지문 내용 중 'This is apparent in Calbris's analysis of gestures related to time, which can express ~ meanings about duration without the use of verbal communication.'에서 이는 시간과 관련된 몸짓들에 대한 Calbris의 분석에서 명백히 드러나는데, 이것은 기간에 대한 의미를 언어적 의사소통 없이 표현할 수 있다고 하였으므로, 보기 **B Geneviève Calbris**가 정답이다. 'express ~ meanings about duration'이 'say many different things about time'으로 paraphrasing되었다.

24 해설 문제의 핵심어구(gesture preceded language)와 관련된 지문 내용 중 'Cognitive scientist Philip Lieberman has suggested that ~ it originated in the pre-linguistic stage of human evolution.'에서 인지과학자 Philip Lieberman은 몸짓이 인류 진화의 언어 이전 단계에 기원을 둔다고 제시했다고 하였으므로, 보기 **C Philip Lieberman**이 정답이다. 'originated in the pre-linguistic stage'가 'preceded language'로 paraphrasing되었다.

25 해설 문제의 핵심어구(gestures by apes)와 관련된 지문 내용 중 'Lieberman has carried out research into the use of gesture by both primates and infants'에서 Lieberman은 영장류와 유아들 모두의 몸짓 사용에 대한 연구를 실행했다고 하였으므로, 보기 **C Philip Lieberman**이 정답이다. 'primates'가 'apes'로 paraphrasing되었다.

9

추리 소설은 문학 장르인가?

에드가 앨런 포가 1814년 소설 '모르그 가의 살인'에서 오귀스트 뒤팽을 소개했을 때, '탐정'이라는 단어는 없었다. 하지만, 한 명석한 아마추어가 경찰들보다 더 뛰어나게 추적한다는 발상은 많은 작가들의 흥미를 불러일으켰으며, 그들은 그들만의 범죄소설을 창작하기 시작했다. 그러나, 이러한 초기 이야기들에서의 줄거리와 등장 인물들의 예측 가능성을 고려할 때, 독자들은 추리 소설이 독립적인 장르이기는 한 것인지에 대한 의문을 제기하기 시작했다.

오늘날, 범죄소설은 이전보다 더욱 복잡하다는 점은 부정할 수 없다. 추리 소설 작가 Simon Brett는 현대 이야기들의 범죄는 더 이상 이분법적이지 않으며 탐정들은 도덕적으로 잘못이 전혀 없는 것처럼 그려지지 않는다고 지적한다. [28]그는 또한 사건이 마지막에 이르러 깔끔하게 마무리되지 않으므로 추리 소설들이 공식을 따른다는 주장을 반박하는데, 이는 줄거리를 예측하기 힘들게 할 수 있다는 것을 보여준다. 그럼 무엇이 범죄소설을 만드는가? 적어도, 모든 소설에 수수께끼가 있다는 점이다.

그러나 추리 소설가 Nicholas Blincoe는 추리 소설의 유사성은 더 멀리 확대되며, 이는 이 장르를 쉽게 구별할 수 있는 것으로 만든다고 믿는다. 모든 이야기에는 범죄와 그 해결법 (혹은 미해결), 범죄가 행해진 공동체, 그리고 중심인물들이 있다. [27]Blincoe는 이 특징들은 장르의 정의를 내리는 데 필요하지만 장르를 한정짓지는 않는다고 주장하는데, 이는 작가들이 그들의 작업에 있어 많은 측면에서 어느 정도의 자유가 있다는 것을 암시한다. 그에 따르면, 범죄소설은 "가장 폭넓은 전형 그리고 줄거리 또는 등장인물에 있어 가장 창의적인 즉흥 요소를 제공했다".

주류 작가들이 본인의 작품에 범죄소설 양식의 요소들을 포함하는 것으로 알려져 있다는 사실은 이 장르가 뚜렷이 구별된다는 생각에 무게를 더한다. 26추리 소설가 Phyllis Dorothy James에 따르면, 때때로 탐정 소설의 줄거리들은 다른 장르의 소설의 훨씬 더 광대한 줄거리에 엮여 있는 것이 발견된다. 그녀는 존 르 카레의 1974년 소설 'Tinker, Tailor, Soldier, Spy'의 사례를 인용한다. 엄밀히 말해 간첩 소설인 이 이야기에서는, 주인공이 범법자를 찾기 위한 시간 싸움이라는 범죄소설의 흔한 주제를 포함하는 사건을 맡기 위해 은퇴에서 다시 돌아온다.

29범죄소설 마니아인 George Demko에 따르면, 범죄소설을 나타내는 또 다른 특징은 배경이 활용되는 방식이다. 구체적으로, 추리 수수께끼들은 실제 장소와 시간에서 일어나며, 이는 사건에 상당한 영향을 미친다. 그는 1940년대 멕시코를 배경으로 한 범죄소설들에서 만연하게 퍼져 있던 부정부패가 어떻게 부각되었는지를 예로 제공하며, 논문에서 이에 대해 다룬다. 범죄자의 환경이 부분적으로 범죄를 저지른 이유라는 것을 설명함으로써, 독자들은 개인의 끔찍한 행위에 대해 사회 전체가 책임이 있는지 생각하게 된다.

아마 추리 소설이 자신만의 장르를 누릴 가치가 있다는 것에 대한 가장 간단한 주장은 모든 계층의 사람들이 그것을 읽는다는 점이다. 그것이 매력적이고 긴장감이 넘친다는 것은 틀림없이 많은 헌신적인 팬들을 위한 마음을 끄는 요소이지만, 범죄소설의 인기는 더 깊이 들어가며, 진실을 알고자 하는 사람들의 본질적 욕구를 이용한다. 현대 시인인 T. S. 엘리엇은 추리 소설의 엄청난 팬으로써, 그것들의 매력은 미스터리의 수학적 미학에 있다고 믿었다. 궁극적으로, 최고들만 풀 수 있는 수수께끼를 선사함으로써, 추리 소설은 우리의 내적 본질에 매력을 뽐내는 것이다.

26 추리 소설의 특징인 서술 기법은 때때로 다른 종류의 소설에서도 찾을 수 있다.

27 추리 소설은 특정한 규칙을 따라야 하지만 작가들은 다른 모든 측면에서는 자유롭게 독창적일 수 있다.

28 추리 소설이 항상 마지막에 해결되는 것은 아니라는 점은 그것들이 예측 불가하다는 것을 증명한다.

29 작가가 실제 사회적 또는 역사적 시점을 배경으로 이용하는 것은 범죄소설을 하나의 장르로 구별짓는다.

사람들 리스트

A Simon Brett
B Phyllis Dorothy James
C George Demko
D Nicholas Blincoe
E T. S. Eliot

---

26 해설 문제의 핵심어구(Narratives ~ found in other types of fiction)와 관련된 지문 내용 중 'According to the detective novelist Phyllis Dorothy James, sometimes detective story plots are found weaved into the much broader plots of other genres of fiction.'에서 추리 소설가 Phyllis Dorothy James에 따르면 때때로 탐정 소설의 줄거리들은 다른 장르의 소설의 훨씬 더 광대한 줄거리에 엮여 있는 것이 발견된다고 하였으므로, 보기 **B** Phyllis Dorothy James가 정답이다. 'detective story plots'가 'narratives that are characteristic of detective stories'로 paraphrasing되었다.

27 해설 문제의 핵심어구(follow certain rules but writers are free)와 관련된 지문 내용 중 'These characteristics are necessary to define the genre but do not, argues Blincoe, limit it, suggesting that writers have a degree of freedom in many facets of their work.'에서 Blincoe는 이 특징들은 장르의 정의를 내리는 데 필요하지만 장르를 한정짓지는 않는다고 주장하는데, 이는 작가들이 그들의 작업에 있어 많은 측면에서 어느 정도의 자유가 있다는 것을 암시한다고 하였으므로, 보기 **D** Nicholas Blincoe가 정답이다. 'freedom in many facets'가 'free ~ in all other aspects'로 paraphrasing되었다.

해설 문제의 핵심어구(not always solved in the end)와 관련된 지문 내용 중 'He also refutes claims that detective stories follow a formula as cases are not always neatly resolved by the end, which shows that plotlines can be hard to predict.'에서 Simon Brett는 또한 사건이 마지막에 이르러 깔끔하게 마무리되지 않으므로 추리 소설들이 공식을 따른다는 주장을 반박하는데 이는 줄거리를 예측하기 힘들게 할 수 있다는 것을 보여준다고 하였으므로, 보기 A Simon Brett가 정답이다. 'neatly resolved'가 'solved'로, 'hard to predict'가 'unpredictable'로 paraphrasing되었다.

29 해설 문제의 핵심어구(actual social or historical period)와 관련된 지문 내용 중 'According to crime fiction aficionado George Demko, another characteristic that sets crime fiction apart is how the setting is used. Specifically, detective mysteries often take place in a real place and time, and this has a significant impact on the case.'에서 범죄소설 마니아인 Geroge Demko에 따르면 범죄 소설을 나타내는 또 다른 특징은 배경이 활용되는 방식인데, 구체적으로 추리 수수께끼들은 실제 장소와 시간에서 일어나며 이는 사건에 상당한 영향을 미친다고 하였으므로, 보기 C George Demko가 정답이다. 'sets ~ apart'가 'distinguishes'로 paraphrasing되었다.

10

기후 변화와 인간 갈등

학계가 기후 변화를 연구해오는 동안, 날씨 변화가 강우량 부족과 토양 악화를 야기한다는 이론이 제시되어 왔다. 우리 중 많은 이들이 생태학적인 반향에 대해 즉각적으로 생각하게 되는 데 반해, 우리 중 더 적은 사람들만이 경작 가능한 토지의 상실과 이에 뒤따르는 형편없는 곡물 수확량이 더 높은 비율의 빈곤, 정치적 불안정, 기근, 전쟁, 그리고 마침내 인류의 많은 이들의 죽음으로 이어진다는 것을 자각한다.

물론, 이것이 실제로 발생할지를 알아내기 위해 한 지역의 기후를 바꾸는 것은 연구자들의 능력 밖이다. 그러나, 역사를 통틀어 기후 이상 그리고 인간 갈등에 대한 그것의 연관성에 관한 현존하는 문서들을 연구함으로써, 연구자들은 어떤 결론을 이끌어낼 수 있으며 미래에 어떤 일이 발생할지에 대해 추측할 수 있다. 버클리에 있는 캘리포니아 대학의 Solomon Hsiang이 이끄는 한 팀이 아마 기후 변화가 인간의 행동에 어떻게 영향을 미칠 것인지를 예측하는 데 가장 가까이 왔을 것이다.

그들의 연구에 따르면, 극단적인 날씨는 실제로 인간 갈등의 증가에 있어 강한 연관성을 보여준다. 구체적으로, 더 따뜻한 기온 또는 더 극심한 강우량으로의 기후의 각 표준편차의 변화에 대해, 대인 간 그리고 대 집단 간 폭력성은 각각 4퍼센트와 14퍼센트 증가했다. Hsiang 박사의 결론은 놀랍다. [30]그는 인간이 거주하고 있는 세계의 도처에 있는 장소들이 2050년까지 상당히 따뜻해질 것으로 예상되기 때문에, 향후 30년 내에 이 기후 변화는 인간 갈등의 증가를 야기할 것이라고 주장한다.

Hsiang의 결론을 지지하는 최근의 상황들이 있는가? 애석하게도, 그렇다. 다르푸르가 아마 가장 좋은 예시일 것이다. 2007년에, [31]국제 연합 환경계획의 상임 이사 Achim Steiner는 다르푸르를 '최초의 기후 변화 전쟁'이라고 부른 연구 결과 보고서를 발행했다. 그 국가는 지난 40년 동안 강우량의 30퍼센트 감소를 경험했고, 2000년대 초반에, 국가의 북부에서의 강우량 부족은 농업 생산을 급격히 감소하도록 했다. 그들의 삶을 유지하게 할 음식이나 물이 없이, 200만 명이 넘는 사람들이 남부의 난민 캠프로 이주했는데, 이곳에서 긴장이 고조되기 시작했고, 마침내 2003년 충돌이 발발했다. 최대 500,000명의 민간인이 사망한 것으로 추정되며, 이것은 기아로 사망한 사람들은 포함하지 않는다.

[32]캘리포니아 대학의 농업 경제학자인 Marshall Burke와 같은 다른 교수들은, 다르푸르가 최초의 기후 변화 전쟁은 아니라고 주장한다. 그는 더 따뜻해진 기온으로 인한 내전의 역사를 가진 것으로 사하라 사막 이남 아프리카를 지적한다. 예를 들어, 소말리아는 현재까지 20년이 넘도록 교전 중이다. 그리고 사우스캐롤라이나 대학의 Edward Carr 교수와 같은 몇몇 교수들은 Hsiang의 연구를 비판했다. [34]Carr는 갈등의 원인으로 오로지 기후에 초점을 맞추는 것은 환원주의적이고 위험하다고 강조하며 그것이 비생산적이거나 심지어 문제가 있는 방향으로 정책 결정에 불균형적으로 영향을 미칠 수 있다고 제시했다.

[33]포츠담 기후 영향 연구소의 Carl Schleussner 박사에 따르면, "치명적인 기후 관련 자연 재해들은 민족적으로 분열된 사회에서 특히 비극적인 방식으로 나타나는 것처럼 보이는 파괴적인 잠재력을 가지고 있다". 본질적으로, 국가 전체가 기후 변화로 인한 기근에 직면해 있고 명백한 다수 집단이 없으므로, 사람들의 헌신은 그들 각각의 집단에 있다. 그리고 각각의 집단이 생존을 가능하게 하는 더 많은 토지를 얻는다는 동일한 목표를 가지고 있기 때문에 집단 간 폭력적인 분쟁이 피할 수 없게 되었던 것이다.

30 향후 몇십 년 안에 인간 갈등의 비율은 크게 증가할 것이다.

31 다르푸르는 기후 변화로 인해 갈등이 발생한 최초의 장소이다.

32 다르푸르에서의 전쟁 이전에 아프리카에서의 다른 전쟁들은 기온 상승으로 인해 발생했다.

33 기후 변화와 관련된 갈등은 다양한 민족이 있는 국가들에서 발생할 가능성이 더 높다.

34 갈등의 한 가지 원인에 집중하는 것은 정책 입안자들에게 문제가 있는 결과를 낳을 수 있다.

연구원 리스트

A Marshall Burke
B Solomon Hsiang
C Achim Steiner
D Carl Schleussner
E Edward Carr

---

30 해설 문제의 핵심어구(human conflict will increase ~ next few decades)와 관련된 지문 내용 중 'He argues that ~ this climate change will result in an increase in human conflicts in the next 30 years.'에서 Hsiang 박사는 향후 30년 내에 이 기후 변화는 인간 갈등의 증가를 야기할 것이라고 주장한다고 하였으므로, 보기 **B** Solomon Hsiang이 정답이다. 'result in an increase'가 'increase significantly'로, '30 years'가 'few decades'로 paraphrasing되었다.

31 해설 문제의 핵심어구(Darfur is the first location)와 관련된 지문 내용 중 'Achim Steiner ~ published a research report calling Darfur 'the first climate change war''에서 Achim Steiner는 다르푸르를 '최초의 기후 변화 전쟁'이라고 부른 연구 결과 보고서를 발행했다고 하였으므로, 보기 **C** Achim Steiner가 정답이다. 'climate change war'가 'conflict has erupted due to climate change'로 paraphrasing되었다.

32 해설 문제의 핵심어구(wars in Africa before the one in Darfur)와 관련된 지문 내용 중 'Marshall Burke ~ contend that Darfur is hardly the first climate change war. He points to sub-Saharan Africa as having a history of civil wars due to warmer temperatures.'에서 Marshall Burke는 다르푸르가 최초의 기후 변화 전쟁은 아니라고 주장하며 그는 더 따뜻해진 기온으로 인한 내전의 역사를 가진 것으로 사하라 사막 이남 아프리카를 지적한다고 하였으므로, 보기 **A** Marshall Burke가 정답이다. 'warmer temperatures'가 'increases in temperature'로 paraphrasing되었다.

33 해설 문제의 핵심어구(multiple ethnicities)와 관련된 지문 내용 중 'According to Dr Carl Schleussner ~ 'Devastating climate-related natural disasters have a disruptive potential that seems to play out in ethnically fractionalised societies in a particularly tragic way'.'에서 Carl Schleussner 박사에 따르면 "치명적인 기후 관련 자연 재해들은 민족적으로 분열된 사회에서 특히 비극적인 방식으로 나타나는 것처럼 보이는 파괴적인 잠재력을 가지고 있다"고 하였으므로, 보기 **D** Carl Schleussner가 정답이다. 'ethnically fractionalised societies'가 'countries with multiple ethnicities'로 paraphrasing되었다.

34 해설 문제의 핵심어구(policy makers)와 관련된 지문 내용 중 'Carr emphasised that focusing solely on climate as a conflict cause is both reductive and dangerous, suggesting that it might disproportionately influence policy decisions in unproductive or even problematic directions.'에서 Carr는 갈등의 원인으로 오로지 기후에 초점을 맞추는 것은 환원주의적이고 위험하다고 강조하며 그것이 비생산적이거나 심지어 문제가 있는 방향으로 정책 결정에 불균형적으로 영향을 미칠 수 있다고 제시했다고 하였으므로, 보기 **E** Edward Carr가 정답이다. 'focusing solely on climate as a conflict cause'가 'Concentrating on one cause for conflicts'로 paraphrasing되었다.

1 E	2 A	3 B	4 D	5 C
6 B	7 D	8 I	9 E	10 H
11 True	12 True	13 False		

식물에 지능이 있는가?

1973년 저서 '식물의 비밀스러운 삶'에서, Peter Tompkins와 Christopher Bird는 식물이 감정을 가졌으며, 인간의 감정과 생각을 읽을 수 있고, 고전 음악을 매우 좋아한다고 전했다. [11]그들의 주장은 과학계의 구성원들에게 엄청난 논란을 가져왔는데, 많은 사람들이 생각하고 감정을 느끼는 것은 뇌의 존재를 필요로 하며 식물에는 내부이든 외부이든, 간접적으로라도 그것과 유사한 것은 없다고 주장했다. 하지만, [12]그들의 식물이 다정하게 다루어지면 더 잘 자란다고 믿은 독서계의 구성원들은 재빨리 그들의 지지를 보냈다. Tompkins와 Bird의 책 속의 많은 증거가 그 후로 신용받지는 못했지만, 그 후 식물이 감정이 없는 유기체 이상이라고 주장하는 많은 기사와 연구 결과들이 발표되었다.

웨스턴 오스트레일리아 대학에서 Monica Gagliano의 팀에 의해 시행되었으며 '생태학'지에 실린 유명한 실험은 언급할 만하다. 이 실험을 위해, [7]과학자들은 미모사를 선택했는데, 이것은 위험을 감지할 때 자연적인 보호 적응으로 잎을 반사적으로 오므린다. [8]그들은 수직 난간이 있는 장치를 고안했는데, 이는 화분에 심어진 미모사가 고무 바닥에 안착하기 전 미끄러져 내려갈 수 있는 것이었으며, 그 후 다수의 식물들이 약 15센티미터 높이에서 떨어지는 충격을 겪게 했다. 화분이 푹신한 표면 위로 겨우 짧은 거리만 떨어지기 때문에 식물들은 아무런 손상을 입지 않았지만, 충격은 식물의 잎이 오므라들게 하기에는 충분할 만큼 상당했다. 하지만 Gagliano의 팀은 지능을 실험하고 있었기 때문에, [9]그들은 식물에서 반사적인 반응 이상을 찾고 있었다. [10]그들은 식물이 그들의 경험을 기억해내고 심지어 그것으로부터 학습하는 것까지도 할 수 있는지 알아내고 싶어 했다.

그들의 가설을 시험하기 위해, 그들은 몇 초의 간격을 두고 식물을 60번 떨어뜨렸는데, 일련의 60번의 낙하가 총 7번 반복되었다. 팀은 끝날 무렵에, 식물의 잎이 오므리는 것을 멈춘 것을 관측했다. 이것은 그들이 경험에 '적응'했으며 더 이상 떨어지는 것을 위협으로 감지하지 않았다는 것을 나타냈다. 그리고 식물은 다시 실험을 겪기 전까지 거의 한 주 동안 손대지 않은 채로 남아 있었다. 이번에는, 몇몇 미모사는 낙하에 대한 반응으로 전혀 잎을 오므리지 않았고, 반면 다른 것들은 한두 번 떨어진 뒤에 잎을 오므리는 것을 중단했다. [4]Gagliano는 식물이 이전 실험에서 어떤 일이 일어났는지에 대한 기억을 가지고 있다고 판단했으며, 그들이 기억과 유사한 무언가를 가졌다고 주장했다. [1]널리 알려진 Gagliano의 연구는, '배우는 것'을 '적응하는 것'과 혼합했다는 것으로 비판받았다. 브리티시컬럼비아 대학의 식물학자 Fred Sack은, 구별이 매우 명확하다고 제안했다. 식물들은 진화하며, 동물들은 학습한다.

식물이 '생각할' 수 있다는 견해를 제기하는 또 다른 연구는 나무가 스스로를 조직화할 수 있는 방식에 중점을 두었다. [2]브리티시컬럼비아 대학의 산림생태학자 Suzanne Simard는, 자원을 공유하고 동료 나무들을 보호하는 방식으로 숲의 나무들이 널리 분포된 네트워크 안에서 어떻게 자신들을 배열하는지를 알아냈다. 그들은 나무에 방사성 탄소를 주입하고 가이거 계수관을 가지고 군락을 거쳐 영양소와 화학 신호의 이동을 따라갔다. 이 이동을 이용하여 그들이 만든 도표는 가장 오래된 나무들이 중추 역할을 했고 많게는 47개의 관계를 다른 나무들과 맺고 있음을 보여주었다. 그들은, 도표가 마치 항공 노선도처럼 보였다고 말했다. 네트워크를 통해, 나무는 중력, 습도, 빛, 압력, 부피, 가스, 소금, 미생물 그리고 잠재적 위험에 대한 정보를 공유할 수 있을 것이며, 정보를 받는 식물은 그들이 자라는 방향을 변경하거나, 성장을 억제하거나, 혹은 다른 식물들에게 경고를 전달할 수 있을 것이다.

하지만, 식물의 지능에 대한 회의론자들은 높이 평가되는 식물학자이자 생물학자인 Jagandish Chandra Bose 경에 의해 실험대에 묶인 당근에 수행된 실험과 같은 많은 이상한 유사과학적 실험들에서 공격 수단을 찾는다. Bose는, 당근에 연결된 장치가 '경련, 놀라움 그리고 떨림'을 기록하는 것을 본 후, '그러므로 과학은 당근과 같이 둔감한 채소의 감정까지도 밝혀낼 수 있다'고 주장했다. 더욱 도발적인 것은 거짓말 탐지기 교관이 된 전 CIA 요원인 Cleve Backster의 실험이었는데, 그는 자신의 사무실에 있는 [13]분재 화초의 잎에 다음도 기록계를 연결했다. Backster는 그가 의도적으로 식물을 불태우는 생각을 했을 때, 기기가 활동력의 급상승을 기록했다는 것을 발견했다. [6]이는 식물이 생각할 수 있을 뿐만 아니라, 생각을 읽을 수도 있다는 결론으로 그를 이끌었다. 또 다른 실험에서, 그는 5명의 지원자를 모집하여 그 중 한 명에게 방 안에 있는 두 식물 중 하나를 뿌리째 뽑고, 짓밟고, 그리고 훼손하도록 했다. 그 다음, [3]Backster는 지원자들을 한 명씩 방에 들어가게 했고, 가해자가 방에 들어왔을 때, 다음도 기록계의 계량기가 '격노했다'고 주장했는데, 이는 그가 살아남은 식물이 살인자를 알아보았다고 선언하도록 했다.

식물이 통찰력이 있는 것이든 혹은 단지 더 원시적인 방식으로 환경의 자극에 반응하는 것이든, 실험적 증거는 식물이, 동물과 유사하게, 습관화가 가능하다는 견해를 뒷받침한다. 하지만 이것이 식물들이 뇌를 갖고 있다는 뜻일까? '느끼다', '인지하다', '배우다' 그리고 '기억하다'와 같은와 같은 단어들은 주로 뇌가 있는 생물에게 사용되며, 지지자들은 뉴런과 시냅스를 포함하여, 지식을 위해 뇌가 필수적이지 않음을 증명해야 한다. [5]'식물 신경생물학' 분야의 선두 주자인 Stefano Mancuso는, "만약 당신이 식물이라면, 뇌를 가지고 있는 것은 장점이 아니다"라고 말하며, 그러므로 식물들의 지능에 대해 말할 때 우리들은 뇌의 반응 관점에서 생각하는 것을 멈춰야 한다고 말한다. 그러므로, Mancuso와 같은 지지자들은 특별한 세포들과 세포망, 그리고 전기 혹은 화학적 신호들을 가지고 하는 것과 같은 자극과 정보를 처리하는 다른 방법들이 식물의 어떠한 형태의 지능에 대한 명확한 지표라는 것을 언젠가 결정적으로 증명할 것이라는 희망으로 연구를 계속하고 있다.

어휘 predilection n. 매우 좋아함 uproar n. 엄청난 논란, 대소동 reading public phr. 독서계 discredit v. 신용하지 않다
 insentient adj. 감정이 없는 mimosa n. 미모사 apparatus n. 장치, 기구 knee-jerk adj. 반사적인 interval n. 간격
 postulate v. 주장하다 akin adj. ~과 유사한 conflate v. 혼합하다, 융합하다 botanist n. 식물학자
 Geiger counter phr. 가이거 계수관(방사능 측정기) hub n. 중추, 중심지 microbe n. 미생물 sceptic n. 회의론자
 ammunition n. 공격 수단, 탄약 bizarre adj. 이상한, 별난 pseudoscientific adj. 유사과학적인 abound v. 많이 있다, 풍부하다
 twitch n. 경련 start n. 놀라움, 움찔함 tremor n. 떨림 stolid adj. 둔감한 provocative adj. 도발적인, 화나게 하는
 polygraph n. 다용도 기록계, 거짓말 탐지기 surge n. 급상승, 동요 root up phr. 뿌리째 뽑다 stomp on phr. 짓밟다
 habituation n. 습관화

[1-6]

1 식물 적응은 학습과 혼동되어서는 안 된다.

2 나무들은 공유와 보호를 촉진하기 위해 자신들을 배치한다.

3 식물들은 폭력적인 행동을 한 사람을 알아볼 수 있다.

4 이전 실험의 사건에 대한 식물의 회상 능력은 어떠한 종류의 기억력을 암시한다.

5 식물 지능을 뇌와 관련해 생각하는 것은 오해의 소지가 있다.

6 식물은 인간의 생각을 이해할 수 있다.

연구원 리스트

A Suzanne Simard
B Cleve Backster
C Stefano Mancuso
D Monica Gagliano
E Fred Sack

---

1 해설 문제의 핵심어구(not be confused with learning)와 관련된 지문 내용 중 'Gagliano's research ~ was criticised for conflating 'learning' with 'adapting'. Fred Sack ~ suggested that the distinction was very clear; plants evolve, animals learn.'에서 Gagliano의 연구는 '배우는 것'을 '적응하는 것'과 혼합했다는 것으로 비판받았고 Fred Sack은 구별이 매우 명확하다고 제안하며 식물들은 진화하고 동물들은 학습한다고 했다고 하였으므로, 보기 E Fred Sack이 정답이다. 'distinction was very clear'가 'should not be confused'로 paraphrasing되었다.

2 해설 문제의 핵심어구(Trees ~ sharing and protection)와 관련된 지문 내용 중 'Suzanne Simard ~ discovered how trees in a forest arrange themselves in widely distributed networks in a manner that allows the trees to share resources and protect fellow trees.'에서 Suzanne Simard는 자원을 공유하고 동료 나무들을 보호하는 방식으로 숲의 나무들이 널리 분포된 네트워크 안에서 어떻게 자신들을 배열하는지를 알아냈다고 하였으므로, 보기 A Suzanne Simard가 정답이다. 'allows the trees to share resources and protect fellow trees'가 'promote sharing and protection'으로 paraphrasing되었다.

3 해설 문제의 핵심어구(Plants can identify ~ violent act)와 관련된 지문 내용 중 'Backster ~ claimed that polygraph metre 'went wild' when the perpetrator entered the room, leading him to declare that the surviving plant had identified the killer'에서 Backster는 가해자가 방에 들어왔을 때 다음도 기록계의 계량기가 '격노했다'고 주장했는데 이는 그가 살아남은 식물이 살인자를 알아보았다고 선언하도록 했다고 하였으므로, 보기 **B Cleve Backster**가 정답이다. 'killer'가 'who had done a violent act'로 paraphrasing되었다.

4 해설 문제의 핵심어구(recall of events in a previous experiment)와 관련된 지문 내용 중 'Gagliano reasoned that the plants had a recollection of what had happened in the prior experiment, and postulated they had something akin to memory.'에서 Gagliano는 식물이 이전 실험에서 어떤 일이 일어났는지에 대한 기억을 가지고 있다고 판단했으며 그들이 기억과 유사한 무언가를 가졌다고 주장했다고 하였으므로, 보기 **D Monica Gagliano**가 정답이다. 'a recollection of what had happened in the prior experiment'가 'recall of events in a previous experiment'로, 'something akin to memory'가 'some form of memory'로 paraphrasing되었다.

5 해설 문제의 핵심어구(misleading ~ in terms of brains)와 관련된 지문 내용 중 'Stefano Mancuso ~ states that ~ we should stop thinking in terms of brain responses when it comes to plant intelligence.'에서 Stefano Mancuso는 식물들의 지능에 대해 말할 때 우리들은 뇌의 반응 관점에서 생각하는 것을 멈춰야 한다고 말한다고 하였으므로, 보기 **C Stefano Mancuso**가 정답이다. 'we should stop thinking'이 'it is misleading to think'로 paraphrasing되었다.

6 해설 문제의 핵심어구(understand people's thoughts)와 관련된 지문 내용 중 'This led him to the conclusion that not only can plants think, but they can also read minds.'에서 식물이 생각할 수 있을 뿐만 아니라 생각을 읽을 수도 있다는 결론으로 Backster를 이끌었다고 하였으므로, 보기 **B Cleve Backster**가 정답이다. 'read minds'가 'understand people's thoughts'로 paraphrasing되었다.

[7-10]

식물의 지능을 시험하는 것

Monica Gagliano의 팀은 위험에 대한 반응을 통해 식물의 지능을 시험하려고 착수했다. 그들은 잎을 오므림으로써 위협에 대응하는 **7** ....을 발달시켰기 때문에 미모사 식물을 선정했다. 팀은 식물들을 **8** .... 아래로 밀어 떨어뜨림으로써 이를 시험했다. 낙하는 해롭지는 않았지만, 식물들은 떨어졌을 때 잎을 오므렸다.

그러나, Gagliano의 팀은 지능의 문제에 집중했고, 단순히 식물의 즉각적인 **9** ....을 시험하는 것을 바라지 않았다. 그러므로 이 활동은 식물들이 그들의 **10** ....을 기억해내고 그것이 해롭지 않았다는 것을 이해할지 확인하기 위해 반복되었다. 결국 식물의 잎은 닫는 것을 멈췄고, 이는 Gagliano로 하여금 식물들이 이것이 위험이 아니라는 것을 학습했다고 결론짓게 했다.

A 계단	B 부상	C 기억
D 적응	E 반응	F 채용
G 고무	H 경험	I 난간

---

7 해설 문제의 핵심어구(developed ~ through which it counters threats by folding its leaves)와 관련된 지문 내용 중 'the scientists selected the mimosa plant, which reactively folds its leaves as a natural protective adaptation when the plant perceives danger'에서 과학자들은 미모사를 선택했는데 이것은 위험을 감지할 때 자연적인 보호 적응으로 잎을 반사적으로 오므린다고 하였으므로, **D adaptation**이 정답이다. 'reactively folds its leaves as a natural protective adaptation'이 'an adaptation through which it counters threats by folding its leaves'로 paraphrasing되었다.

8 해설 문제의 핵심어구(pushing the plants down)와 관련된 지문 내용 중 'They came up with an apparatus with a vertical rail, which potted mimosa plants could slide down'에서 그들은 수직 난간이 있는 장치를 고안했는데 이는 화분에 심어진 미모사가 미끄러져 내려갈 수 있는 것이었다고 하였으므로, **I** rail이 정답이다. 'plants could slide down'이 'pushing the plants down'으로 paraphrasing되었다.

9 해설 문제의 핵심어구(did not want to simply test the plant's immediate)와 관련된 지문 내용 중 'they were seeking more than a knee-jerk reaction from the plants'에서 그들은 식물에서 반사적인 반응 이상을 찾고 있었다고 하였으므로, **E** reaction이 정답이다. 'seeking more than a knee-jerk reaction from the plants'가 'did not want to simply test the plant's immediate reaction'으로 paraphrasing되었다.

10 해설 문제의 핵심어구(if the plants would recollect their)와 관련된 지문 내용 중 'they wanted to determine if the plants would be able to recall their experience'에서 그들은 식물이 그들의 경험을 기억해낼 수 있는지 알아내고 싶어 했다고 하였으므로, **H** experience가 정답이다. 'determine if the plants would be able to recall'이 'see if the plants would recollect'로 paraphrasing되었다.

[11-13]

11 Tompkins와 Bird의 주장은 과학자들 사이에서 논쟁을 일으켰다.

12 식물을 소유한 몇몇 독자들은 Tompkins와 Bird의 저서 속 생각에 동의했다.

13 다용도 기록계에 연결되었을 때, 식물은 주어진 자극에 반응을 하지 않았다.

11 해설 문제의 핵심어구(claims of Tompkins and Bird)와 관련된 지문 내용 중 'Their assertions generated an uproar among members of the scientific community'에서 그들의 주장은 과학계의 구성원에게 엄청난 논란을 가져왔다고 하였으므로, 주어진 문장은 지문의 내용과 일치함을 알 수 있다. 따라서 정답은 **True**이다. 'generated an uproar among members of the scientific community'가 'caused controversy among scientists'로 paraphrasing되었다.

12 해설 문제의 핵심어구(Some readers who owned plants)와 관련된 지문 내용 중 'members of the reading public who believed that their plants thrived when dealt with affectionately were quick to give their support'에서 그들의 식물이 다정하게 다루어지면 더 잘 자란다고 믿은 독서계의 구성원들은 재빨리 그들의 지지를 보냈다고 하였으므로, 주어진 문장은 지문의 내용과 일치함을 알 수 있다. 따라서 정답은 **True**이다. 'members of the reading public'이 'Some readers'로, 'give their support'가 'agreed with the ideas'로 paraphrasing되었다.

13 해설 문제의 핵심어구(connected to a polygraph machine)와 관련된 지문 내용 중 'connected a polygraph machine to a leaf of the houseplant in his office'와 'Backster found out that ~ the machine registered a surge of activity.'에서 분재 화초의 잎에 다용도 기록계를 연결했을 때 Backster는 기기가 활동력의 급상승을 기록했다는 것을 발견했다고 하였으므로, 주어진 문장은 지문의 내용과 일치하지 않음을 알 수 있다. 따라서 정답은 **False**이다.

* 각 문제에 대한 정답의 단서는 지문에 문제 번호와 함께 별도의 색으로 표시되어 있습니다.

EXAMPLE

p.210

A 돌연변이 동물들이 자연에서 전례가 없는 것은 아니지만, 최근에 발견된 두 개의 머리를 가진 상어의 숫자는 예상했던 것보다 훨씬 높다. 지난 10년간 적어도 5마리가 발견되었다. 게다가, 연구원 Valentin Sans-Coma는 심지어 산란 상어 종에서 최초로 한 마리를 발견했다. 이 발견들은 과학자들을 당황하게 했다.

B 그들은 아직 비교적 희귀하기 때문에, 하나의 확정적인 돌연변이의 원인을 정확히 찾아내기는 어렵다. 그러나, [1]한 가지 특이한 설명은 남획을 돌연변이 상어의 증가하는 숫자에 대한 책임으로 본다. 해양 과학자 Nicolas Ehemann에 따르면, 인간의 어업 활동은 바다에 있는 상어 수의 극적인 감소로 이어졌고, 따라서 더 작은 유전자 공급원으로 이어졌다. 그는 이것이 더 많은 유전적 기형을 낳는 더 잦은 근친 교배로 이어졌다고 주장한다.

HACKERS PRACTICE

p.212

1 C	2 B	3 B	4 C	5 C
6 B	7 A	8 D	9 C	10 D
11 A	12 D	13 C	14 D	15 A
16 A	17 C	18 B	19 D	20 C
21 D	22 E	23 B	24 B	25 D
26 B	27 E	28 C	29 A	30 E
31 B	32 F	33 D	34 A	

1

A 오늘날, 350종 이상의 현존하는 앵무새 종이 있다. 이 똑똑한 새들은 다양한 크기와 선명한 색깔들로 나타난다. 그들은 말을 따라 할 수 있는 능력으로 전 세계에서 애완동물로 소중하게 여겨지지만, 자신들의 고향에서 언제나 사랑받지는 않는다.

B 이에 대한 하나의 좋은 예시는 호주인데, 이곳은 머리에 선명한 노란색 깃털이 있는 커다란 앵무새인 큰유황앵무의 고향이다. 이 새들은 거대한 무리로 이동을 하며 지역 주민들에게 골칫거리가 되었다. [2]그들의 재잘거림과 동트기 전의 울음소리가 사람들을 방해할 뿐만 아니라, 그들은 또한 매우 파괴적이다. 지역 농민들과 집주인들은 종종 그들이 물어뜯음으로써 작물들을 죽이고 주택 건설에 쓰이는 목재를 훼손한다고 불평한다. 그들은 또한 영역을 넓히고 있는데, 이는 다른 토종 새들을 쫓아낸다.

C 이러한 문제를 해결하기 위해서, 큰유황앵무는 일부 지역에서 유해 동물 종으로 지정되었다. [1]이것은 그들이 새로운 지역으로 수입되는 것을 막고 그들의 소유권에 규제를 둔다. 어떤 지역에서는, 개체 수를 억제하고 현지 생태계를 파괴하는 것을 방지하기 위해 정기적으로 실시되는 추려내기도 있다. 이러한 정책들이 영향을 미칠 수도 있지만, 문제를 해결할 수 있을지는 불확실하다.

  1 특정 지역에서 한 조류 종을 금지하는 것에 대한 언급

  2 소음과 관련해 앵무새가 어떻게 인간에게 영향을 주는지에 대한 세부 설명

1   **해설** 문제의 핵심어구(banning a bird species)와 관련된 지문 내용 중 단락 C의 'This prevents them from being imported into new areas and puts regulations on their ownership.'에서 이것은 큰유황앵무가 새로운 지역으로 수입되는 것을 막고 그들의 소유권에 규제를 둔다고 하였으므로, 단락 C가 정답이다.

2   **해설** 문제의 핵심어구(in terms of noise)와 관련된 지문 내용 중 단락 B의 'their chatter and pre-dawn calls disturb humans'에서 그들의 재잘거림과 동트기 전의 울음소리가 사람들을 방해한다고 하였으므로, 단락 B가 정답이다.

2

A 1600년대 중반에 독일의 연금술사인 헤닝 브란트는 중요한 발견을 해냈다. 그는 소변을 증발시키고 남은 잔여물을 데움으로써, 새로운 기화 물질을 증류시켰는데, 그는 그것이 비금속을 금으로 바꿀 수 있는 물질인 현자의 돌이라고 생각했다. 브란트에게는 유감스럽게도, 현자의 돌은 그저 미신에 불과했고 그가 사실상 발견한 것은 원소 인의 한 형태였다.

B 이후의 실험을 통해, 과학자들은 브란트의 광물의 다른 형태들에 대해 추가적인 발견을 했다. 예를 들어, 가장 순수한 상태인 흰색 인일 때, ³그 광물은 가연성이 매우 높아서 공기와 접촉하게 되면 확 타오르기 때문에, 수중에 보관되어야 한다. 또한, 그것은 독성이 있고 심각한 화상을 야기할 수 있으므로 도구를 가지고 다루어져야만 한다. 이러한 속성들은 흰색 인을 쓸모 없는 것으로 보이게 할 수 있지만, 사실 군수품이라는 한 분야에서 그것을 중요하게 만든다. 많은 방화 무기들이 이 원소의 이러한 형태를 활용하여 개발되었다.

C 대부분의 다른 용도를 위해서는, 흰색 인은 가열을 통해 더 안정적인 붉은 형태로 변환되어야 한다. 붉은 인은 흰색 형태처럼 저절로 불이 붙지는 않을 것이지만, 가열되었을 때 독성이 있는 증기를 생산하는 것과 같이 위험이 없는 것은 아니다. 그럼에도 불구하고, 그것의 사용은 꽤 흔하다. 우리는 이것을 우리의 집에서 볼 수 있다. 성냥 머리의 빨간 물질은 붉은 인의 한 형태이다. ⁴붉은 인은 또한 가루로 갈아 비료로도 사용될 수 있다.

    3   화학물을 공기와 결합하는 것의 위험에 대한 설명

    4   인의 한 형태의 농업적인 사용에 대한 언급

3   **해설** 문제의 핵심어구(dangers of combining ~ with air)와 관련된 지문 내용 중 단락 B의 'the mineral is so combustible that it will burst into flames if it comes into contact with air'에서 그 광물은 가연성이 매우 높아서 공기와 접촉하게 되면 확 타오른다고 하였으므로, 단락 B가 정답이다. 'comes into contact'가 'combining ~ with'로 paraphrasing되었다.

4   **해설** 문제의 핵심어구(agricultural uses)와 관련된 지문 내용 중 단락 C의 'Red phosphorous can also be ~ used as a fertiliser.'에서 붉은 인은 또한 비료로도 사용될 수 있다고 하였으므로, 단락 C가 정답이다.

3

A 탄소는 오늘날 공기, 땅, 그리고 살아있는 모든 생물과 같이 우리 주변의 모든 곳에서 발견되지만 그것은 만들어지지도 파괴되지도 않는다. 이는 탄소 순환이라고 불리는 과정 때문이다. 지구 탄소의 99퍼센트는 지각의 암석들 안에 갇혀있지만, 이 과정을 통해, 그것은 서서히 대기로 방출된다. 그렇게 되면 식물들은 광합성을 하기 위해 탄소를 이산화탄소로 흡수하고, 그것이 소비된 뒤 동물들에게 그것을 전달한다. 결국, ⁷이 동물들이 죽어 그들의 몸이 분해될 때, 탄소는 토양으로 돌아간다.

B ⁶탄소 주기의 자주 간과되는 측면은 대기 중 탄소의 농도를 결정하는 데 바다가 매우 중요한 요인이라는 점이다. 우리의 바다는 큰 이산화탄소 흡수계, 혹은 저장고의 역할을 한다. 이는 이산화탄소가 대기에서 바다로 진입하고, 화학 작용을 거쳐, 그곳에 갇혀버리기 때문에 발생한다. 불행히도, 산업혁명 이래로, 바다가 이산화탄소를 흡수할 수 있는 능력은 동일하게 유지되어 온 반면, 화석 연료의 연소는 우리가 대기 중으로 방출하는 이산화탄소의 양을 매우 증가시켰다. 이는 대기 중 이산화탄소의 축적을 야기하고 있으며 더 높은 지구의 기온으로 이어지고 있다.

C 산업혁명 이후부터의 증가된 바닷속 이산화탄소 농도는 또한 해양 생물들의 문제로 이어지고 있다. 이산화탄소가 바닷물에 용해되며 발생하는 화학 반응은 해수면의 피에이치 수치를 감소시킨다. 이러한 산성화는 플랑크톤이나 산호와 같은 미세한 해양 생물의

성장을 늦춘다. ⁵이런 작은 생물들은 해양 먹이그물의 토대를 형성하기 때문에, 산성화는 전 생태계에 부정적인 영향을 미칠 수 있다. 그리고, 우리 또한 해양 먹이그물에 의존하고 있기 때문에, 우리의 식량 공급도 위협을 받는다.

5 하나의 절차가 전체 체계에 영향을 주는 이유

6 탄소 주기에 있어 바다의 역할

7 탄소가 어떻게 흙으로 다시 돌아오게 되는지

5 해설 문제의 핵심어구(influence a whole system)와 관련된 지문 내용 중 단락 C의 'These tiny organisms form the base of the marine food web, so the acidification can have a negative impact on the entire system.'에서 이런 작은 생물들은 해양 먹이그물의 토대를 형성하기 때문에 산성화가 전 생태계에 부정적인 영향을 미칠 수 있다고 하였으므로, 단락 **C**가 정답이다.

6 해설 문제의 핵심어구(oceans ~ carbon-cycle)와 관련된 지문 내용 중 단락 B의 'An often overlooked aspect of the carbon cycle is that oceans are a highly significant factor in determining the level of carbon in the atmosphere. Our oceans act as large carbon sinks'에서 탄소 주기의 자주 간과되는 측면은 대기 중 탄소의 정도를 결정하는 데 바다가 매우 중요한 요인이라는 점이며 우리의 바다는 큰 이산화탄소 흡수계의 역할을 한다고 하였으므로, 단락 **B**가 정답이다.

7 해설 문제의 핵심어구(carbon ~ back into the earth)와 관련된 지문 내용 중 단락 A의 'as these animals die and their bodies decompose, the carbon is returned to the soil'에서 이 동물들이 죽어 그들의 몸이 분해될 때 탄소는 토양으로 돌아간다고 하였으므로, 단락 **A**가 정답이다. 'is returned to the soil'이 'gets put back into earth'로 paraphrasing되었다.

4

A 오늘날의 노령화 인구로 인하여, 노동 인구의 고령층에 대한 토론이 가열되기 시작했다. 어떤 사람들은 노동 인구 내 그들의 장기적인 자리가 사회에 해로울 수 있다고 믿는다. 다른 사람들은 고령자 고용이 사회적 결속력과 경제 성장을 위해 긍정적인 결과를 낳을 수 있다고 생각한다.

B 현재의 퇴직 연령을 넘어선 고령자들을 고용하는 것을 반대하는 사람들은 일반적으로 건강 문제와 기술적 능력의 부족이 특정한 직무를 수행하는 노년층의 능력을 제한하기 때문에, 고령 노동력은 덜 생산적이라는 주장을 인용한다. 이것은 심한 노년층에는 해당하는 사항일 수 있지만, 미국에서 60대 이상의 현 세대는 특히 이전 세대들과 비교했을 때 고학력자이며 상대적으로 건강하다.

C 다른 사람들은 고령자를 교육하는 것이 너무 어렵다고 불평한다. 그들은, "늙은 개에게는 새로운 재주를 가르칠 수 없다"고 말한다. 그러나, 이 또한 오해의 소지가 있는 주장이다. 고령층은 풍부한 경험을 가지고 있는데, 이는 올바른 관리와 함께, 적절한 상황에서 매우 효과적일 수 있다. ⁹많은 이들이 이미 직업 시장에서 유용할 수 있는 적절한 기술을 보유하고 있으며 업계의 활동에 있어 조예가 깊은데, 이는 교육의 필요성을 완전히 제거한다.

D 약간의 타당성이 있는 고령자 고용에 반대하는 한 가지 주장은 그들이 취업 시장에서 이용 가능한 일자리의 수를 줄인다는 것이다. 고령자에게 주어지는 일자리 하나당, 더 젊은 사람에게는 하나의 일자리가 이용 불가능해진다. 이것은 사실이지만, 고령층과 더 젊은 사람들이 일반적으로 구하는 직업은 상당히 다르다. 일자리를 차지한다기보다는, 그들은 대개 다른 누구도 원하지 않는 일자리를 채우고 있으므로, 고령층을 고용하는 것을 피할 이유가 거의 없다는 것은 분명하다. 사실, ⁸이것은 고령자와 고용주 모두에게 긍정적인 영향을 미칠 것이다. ¹⁰그것은 또한 고령층이 사회 보장 제도 또는 연금에 의존할 필요성을 줄임으로써, 사회 전체의 재산을 절약할 것이다.

8 고용주와 직원에 대한 잠재적인 이익에 대한 주장

9 훈련이 필요하지 않을 수도 있는 이유

10 사회 복지에 대한 고령자 고용의 한 가지 영향

8 해설 문제의 핵심어구(benefits to employers and workers)와 관련된 지문 내용 중 단락 **D**의 'it will likely have a positive impact on both the senior and the employer'에서 이것은 고령자와 고용주 모두에게 긍정적인 영향을 미칠 것이라고 하였으므로, 단락 **D**가 정답이다. 'positive impact'가 'possible benefits'로 paraphrasing되었다.

9 해설 문제의 핵심어구(training ~ not be needed)와 관련된 지문 내용 중 단락 **C**의 'Many already have applicable skills that can be useful in the job market and are well-versed in the activities of the business world, eliminating the need for training altogether.'에서 많은 이들이 이미 직업 시장에서 유용할 수 있는 적절한 기술을 보유하고 있으며 업계의 활동에 있어 조예가 깊은데 이는 교육의 필요성을 완전히 제거한다고 하였으므로, 단락 **C**가 정답이다. 'eliminating the need for training'이 'training may not be needed'로 paraphrasing되었다.

10 해설 문제의 핵심어구(senior employment on welfare)와 관련된 지문 내용 중 단락 **D**의 'It will also reduce the need for seniors to rely upon social security programs or pensions, thereby saving money for the entire society.'에서 그것은 또한 고령층이 사회 보장 제도 또는 연금에 의존할 필요성을 줄임으로써 사회 전체의 재산을 절약할 것이라고 하였으므로, 단락 **D**가 정답이다.

5

A 모든 교사들이 알고 있듯이, 같은 나이의 학생들이 속하는 집단의 능력은 대개 크게 다르지 않다. 그러나 가끔, [11]어떤 학생은 너무나도 뛰어나서 많은 과목에 있어 그 또는 그녀는 급우들과 상당히 보조가 맞지 않으며, 이것은 그 학생과 학급 모두의 진도에 있어 지장을 주는 영향을 미칠 수 있다. 이러한 상황에서 명백한 전략은 그러한 학생이 한 학년을 선행하는 것을 허용하는 것이다. 그러나, 이것이 반드시 최선책인 것은 아니며, 어떤 사람들은 영재 학생들을 그들의 학년 군 속에서 도전시킬 것을 지지한다. 무엇이 최상의 접근법인가에 대한 논쟁은 교육 전문가들 사이에서 '월반 대 심화학습'이라고 알려져 있다.

B 더 높은 학년으로의 월반은, 표면적으로는 영재 학생을 다루는 것에 관하여 가장 간단한 해결책인 반면, 사실 주어진 학년에서 그들이 배웠을 능력들을 불가피하게 놓치게 될 것이므로 그들을 지체시킬 수 있다. 논의가 되고 있는 학생들은 또한 새로운 또래 집단과 일련의 기대치에 적응하기 위해 고군분투하며 월반으로 인한 막중한 압박감으로 고통받을 수 있다. 그들의 사회 집단과, 그것이 제공하는 정서적인 지지로부터의 분리는, 또 하나의 주요 문제점이다.

C 다른 한편으로 심화학습은 학생들이 그들이 원래의 학급 속에서 스스로 능력을 발휘할 기회를 제공하는 것을 포함하기 때문에, 더욱 시행하기 어려울 수 있다. [13]그러므로 교사들은 영재 학생들의 강점 및 능력과 일치하는 심화학습 프로그램을 만들어 내는 것과, 그들이 같은 나이의 다른 학생들과 계속해서 사회적으로 관계를 맺을 수 있도록 또래 집단과의 관계를 유지하는 동시에 심화학습을 할 수 있게 해주는 것이 기대된다.

D 연구들은 영재 학생들을 다루는 가장 효과적인 전략은 특정 과목에 있어서의 어느 정도의 월반과 다른 부분에 있어서의 심화학습을 결합하는 것이라는 것을 보여주었다. 이것은 논의가 되고 있는 학생들에게 맞춰진, 그 또는 그녀의 강점과 약점을 여러모로 활용할 수 있는 프로그램을 필요하게 만든다. 사실상, 영국을 포함하여, 많은 나라들에서 영재 학생을 다루는 데 있어서의 근본적인 문제는, 월반과 심화학습 중 어느 접근법을 택할 것인가가 아니라 [12]둘 중의 어느 것도 가능하지 않으며 학생들은 교육 연구가 Maureen Marron이 경직된 '융통성이 없는 방식'이라고 부르는 것 속에서 또래집단과 공부할 것을 강요받는다는 것이다.

11 영재 학생이 그들의 급우에게 미칠 수 있는 영향에 대한 언급

12 영재 학생의 선택권 부족에 대한 언급

13 교사들이 어떻게 영재 학생이 그들의 또래 집단 속에서 성공하도록 도울 수 있는지

11 해설 문제의 핵심어구(effect gifted students can have on their classmates)와 관련된 지문 내용 중 단락 **A**의 'a student will be so talented that he or she is dramatically out of step with his or her classmates ~, and this can have a disruptive effect on both the student's progress and that of the class'에서 어떤 학생은 너무나도 뛰어나서 그 또는 그녀는 급우들과 상당히 보조가 맞지 않으며 이것은 그 학생과 학급 모두의 진도에 있어 지장을 주는 영향을 미칠 수 있다고 하였으므로, 단락 **A**가 정답이다.

12 해설 문제의 핵심어구(shortage of options)와 관련된 지문 내용 중 단락 D의 'neither is available, and students are forced to learn ~ with their age group'에서 둘 중의 어느 것도 가능하지 않으며 학생들은 또래집단과 공부할 것을 강요받는다고 하였으므로, 단락 **D**가 정답이다. 'neither is available'이 'shortage of options'로 paraphrasing되었다.

13 해설 문제의 핵심어구(teachers can help talented students)와 관련된 지문 내용 중 단락 C의 'Teachers are therefore expected to generate an enrichment programme ~, and allow them to take on advanced work while maintaining a connection with their peer group'에서 그러므로 교사들은 심화학습 프로그램을 만들어 내는 것과 영재 학생들이 또래 집단과의 관계를 유지하는 동시에 심화학습을 할 수 있게 해주는 것이 기대된다고 하였으므로, 단락 **C**가 정답이다.

6

A 미국 태평양 연안 북서부 토착 공동체들은 물질의 소유에서 초래되는 정신적인 부담을 스스로에게서 없애기 위해 포틀래치라고 알려진, 재산의 의식적인 분배를 행했다. ¹⁵이 공동 행사들은 대개 사냥철의 풍성함을 나타내기 위해 성대한 잔치를 중심으로 진행되었다. ¹⁶이 잔치들은 다른 음식들과 함께, 많은 양의 연어 혹은 물개 고기를 특별히 포함하였으며, 사회 원로들, 기도 치료사들, 그리고 먼 곳에서 온 방문객들이 주로 참석했다. 이러한 존경받는 손님들에게 경의를 표하기 위해, 주최자들은 일상적인 상황들에서 사용되는 것들보다 훨씬 더 화려하게 장식된, 손으로 조각되고 색칠된 특별한 접시에 음식을 차렸다.

B 포틀래치는 노래와 춤으로도 축하되었다. 이 활동들은 조상들을 기리고, 연애를 축하하고 풍요에 대한 감사를 표하기 위한 것이었다. 춤들은 개별 가족들에 의해 각각 행해졌으므로, 또한 그들만의 독특한 유산을 보여줄 수 있는 기회를 제공했다. 또한, 일부 가수들과 무용수들은 포틀래치 내내 초자연적인 존재들을 묘사하는 가면을 썼다. 이것들은 특정 가문에게 노래와 춤을 부여한 존재들을 기리기 위한 것이었다.

C 하지만, 아마도 포틀래치의 가장 중요한 측면은 선물을 주는 것이었을 것이다. 이 행위는 너그러움을 보여주었을 뿐만 아니라, 부족 구성원들이 물질적인 소유물들을 내주도록 했다. 이렇게 함으로써, 그들은 빚을 갚고, 도움에 대한 고마움을 표현하고, 지속되는 관계를 보장할 수 있었다. 이러한 모든 행위들은 사회의 공동 가치들을 강화했다. 부족 구성원들은, 그러므로, 카누, 담요, 그리고 다른 물건들을 교환했을 것이다. 옮기기에 너무 크거나 귀중해 보이면, 그것들은 그저 파괴되었다.

D 이러한 행사들의 큰 문화적 중요성에도 불구하고, 아메리카 식민지의 유럽 정부들은 그것을 인정하지 않았다. 부족 구성원들이 자신들의 새로운 사회에 동화하도록 강제하기 위해서, 정부는 이 관습을 금지했다. 이것은, 물론, 의식을 근절시키지 못했다. ¹⁴그것들은 1900년대 중반에 금지령이 해제될 때까지 그저 비밀스럽게 행해졌다.

14 토착민들이 그들의 관습에 대한 제재를 어떻게 다루었는지

15 사냥철의 수확량을 축하하는 방법의 예시

16 먼 곳에서부터 이동한 방문객들에 대한 언급

14 해설 문제의 핵심어구(handled restrictions)와 관련된 지문 내용 중 단락 D의 'They were simply performed in secret until the ban was lifted in the mid-1900s.'에서 의식들은 1900년대 중반에 금지령이 해제될 때까지 그저 비밀스럽게 행해졌다고 하였으므로, 단락 **D**가 정답이다.

15 해설 문제의 핵심어구(the hunting season's yield)와 관련된 지문 내용 중 단락 A의 'These communal events usually centred on a large feast to reflect the bounty of the hunting season.'에서 이 공동 행사들은 대개 사냥철의 풍성함을 나타내기 위해 성대한 잔치를 중심으로 진행되었다고 하였으므로, 단락 **A**가 정답이다.

16 해설 문제의 핵심어구(visitors travelling from far away)와 관련된 지문 내용 중 단락 A의 'These feasts ~ were usually attended by ~ visitors from great distances.'에서 이 잔치들은 먼 곳에서 온 방문객들이 주로 참석했다고 하였으므로, 단락 **A**가 정답이다. 'great distances'가 'far away'로 paraphrasing되었다.

7

사라지는 사자들

A 한때 유럽의 넓게 트인 큰 지역을 거닐었던 사자들은, 기후 변화가 지형을 바꿨던 마지막 빙하기 동안에 수가 줄어들기 시작했다. 이전에, 평평한 초원 지역이었던 광대한 스텝 지대는 대륙을 덮고 있었는데, 이는 사자들이 먹이를 찾고 잡는 것을 쉽게 해주었다. 하지만 환경이 따뜻해지고 높은 숲이 자라면서, 다른 동물들은 사냥하기가 훨씬 더 어려워졌다. 먹이를 구하기 어려워지면서, 사자들이 이전의 수를 유지하는 것은 불가능해졌다.

B 하지만, 유사 시대 동안 남유럽에서 가끔 사자의 목격이 있었다. 고대 그리스 역사학자 헤로도토스에 따르면, 이 대형 고양이과 동물들이 아켈로스강과 네스토스강 사이에서 발견되었을 수 있다. 이 곳이 비교적 작은 지리적 지역이기 때문에, 이 종은 아마 이때 그 지역에서 이미 사라지는 중이었을 것인데, [18]그것의 종말은 틀림없이 그리스인들의 사냥 스포츠에 대한 사랑과 경기장에서 싸울 짐승에 대한 로마인들의 욕구로 인해 앞당겨졌을 것이다.

C [17]아프리카에 대해서 말하자면, 사자들은 19세기까지 상당수가 살아남았는데, 이때 그들은 인구 증가로 인해 사라지기 시작했다. 기계는 사람들이 황무지에 접근하게 해주었기 때문에, 인간의 사자와의 접촉은 극적으로 증가했고 총에 맞거나 화학적 살충제로 독살되는 사자의 수도 증가했다. 사실, 사자의 수는 200년도 안 되는 기간 동안 약 95퍼센트가 감소했다. [20]현재 대륙에 남아있는 약 3만 마리 중 거의 모두가 사하라 이남 지역에 있고 많은 수가 서식지 용도 변경, 농부들과의 충돌, 인간들 사이의 야생 동물 고기 거래로 인한 먹이 상실에 직면해 있다. 2050년까지 이 지역의 인구가 두 배가 될 것을 고려하면, 사자의 미래는 암울해 보인다.

D 아시아에서의 사자의 상황은 더 심각하다. 유일하게 살아남은 아시아의 사자 집단은 현재 인도의 기르 국립 공원에 살고 있다. 보호받는 상태임에도 불구하고, 그곳에 살고 있는 수백 마리는 단지 약 열두 마리의 사자들의 자손으로 상당히 근친 교배되었기 때문에, 심각한 위험에 처해 있다. 이것은 그들을 유전적으로 약하게 하고 질병에 취약하게 한다. [19]만약 전염성 질병이 퍼지면, 많은 사자들이 죽을 것이고, 그들의 수는 회복이 불가능한 수준으로 감소할 수 있다.

E 아시아의 사자들은 공식적으로 멸종 위험이 아주 높고 아프리카 사자들은 미국 어류 및 야생동물관리국에 의해 최근 멸종 위기에 처한 종으로 목록에 올라 있기 때문에, 환경 보호 활동가 집단이 이 대형 고양이과 동물들을 멸종으로부터 보호하고 싶어 한다는 것은 확실하다. 그들의 노력은 칭찬받아야 하지만, 현실은 사자의 미래와 지금까지 그들의 종말을 이끈 패턴의 잠재적인 전환이 국제적인 수준의 사자 보호에 대한 약속에 의존할 것이라는 것이다.

17 아프리카에서 사자의 수가 감소하기 시작한 시기에 대한 언급

18 인간의 오락 목적을 위한 사자 사용에 대한 언급

19 한 종류의 사자를 전멸시킬 수 있는 것의 예시

20 오늘날 사자의 먹이 공급 부족의 이유

---

17 해설 문제의 핵심어구(began to fall in Africa)와 관련된 지문 내용 중 단락 C의 'As for Africa, lions survived in significant numbers until the 19th century, when they began to vanish due to human population growth.'에서 아프리카에 대해서 말하자면 사자들은 19세기까지 상당수가 살아남았는데 이때 그들은 인구 증가로 인해 사라지기 시작했다고 하였으므로, 단락 **C**가 정답이다.

18 해설 문제의 핵심어구(human entertainment)와 관련된 지문 내용 중 단락 B의 'its demise no doubt hastened by the Greeks' love of sport hunting and the Romans' demand for beasts to fight in their arenas'에서 사자의 종말은 틀림없이 그리스인들의 사냥 스포츠에 대한 사랑과 경기장에서 싸울 짐승에 대한 로마인들의 욕구로 인해 앞당겨졌을 것이라고 하였으므로, 단락 **B**가 정답이다.

19 해설 문제의 핵심어구(might wipe out)와 관련된 지문 내용 중 단락 D의 'if a contagious illness were to spread, many of the lions would perish, and their numbers might fall to unrecoverable levels.'에서 만약 전염성 질병이 퍼지면 많은 사자들이 죽을 것이고 그들의 수는 회복이 불가능한 수준으로 감소할 수 있다고 하였으므로, 단락 **D**가 정답이다. 'perish'가 'wipe out'으로 paraphrasing되었다.

8

언어와 방언

A 만약 두 화자가 서로 다른 표현, 속어, 그리고 억양을 사용하는데도 불구하고 서로를 이해할 수 있다면, 그들은 같은 언어를 말하는 것일까? 그것은 사회언어학자들을 오랫동안 괴롭혀 온 질문인데, 그들은 더 공식적으로 인정받는 유형과 동족 관계에 있는 지역 특유의 말 유형인 방언으로부터 정확히 무엇이 언어를 구별되게 하는지를 정의하기 위해 분투한다. 물론, 하나가 다른 하나로부터 어떻게 구별되는지 그리고 언어 종류들이 어떻게 연관되어 있는지에 대해 여러 가지 견해들이 있다.

B [24]몇몇 언어학자들은 역사적인 기원이 중요하다고 믿는데, 그들은 더 오래된 의사소통의 종류로부터 파생된 모든 말의 형태를 방언으로 본다. 이런 개념에 의하면, 프랑스어와 이탈리아어와 같은 근대 로망스어는, 라틴어에서 파생된 방언일 것이다. 그러나 이러한 견해는 이 언어들이 같은 언어에서 왔을지도 모르지만, 그들이 이제 서로 꽤 떨어져 있으며 반드시 서로 이해할 수 있는 것은 아니기 때문에 다소 결함이 있다. 다시 말해서, 이탈리아어 화자들과 프랑스어 화자들은 그들 각자의 말에 유사성이 거의 없기 때문에 서로를 이해할 수 없을 것이다. 마찬가지로, 그들은 언어 사용 문제를 해결하기 위해 동일한 언어 권위자와 상의하는 것이 유용하지 않다는 것을 알게 될 것이다. 이것은 [23]로망스어들이 다양한 유사성을 공유했던 라틴어의 초기 방언들이긴 했지만, 유럽 전역의 다양한 집단들의 이주로 인해 시간이 지나면서 진화해왔고 이제 방언이라기보다는 독립된 공식 언어들로 여겨진다는 것을 의미한다.

C 한편, 말의 유형을 언어로 지정하는 더 적절한 방법은 그것이 공식적으로 인정받는지를 보는 것인데, 이것은 그것이 공식적인 정부 서신에 사용되는지, 고유한 문법을 가졌는지, 그리고 학교에서 학습되는지를 의미한다. 하지만 이 '공식적인' 인정이 정말로 언어들과 방언들을 구분하는가? 사실 지리적으로 떨어져 있는 지역들에서 사용되는 언어들과의 명백한 유사점들을 고려해 볼 때 몇몇 인정된 언어들은 방언들과 상당히 유사해 보인다. 하지만 별개의 언어들이 대개 속어와 관용 표현에서 나타나는 단 몇 가지 예외와 함께, 거의 같은 어휘와 문법을 공유하게 될 때, 그것들은 지역 특유의 방언이라기보다는 '표준 형식'이라고 불린다.

D 이것에 해당하는 한 언어는 [21]영어인데, 영어에는 영국식, 미국식, 캐나다식, 그리고 호주식을 포함한 다양한 표준 형식이 있다. 각 언어들 간에 어휘, 발화 양식, 그리고 심지어 철자법까지 서로 다르다. 예를 들어, 영국인이 'I've got a new car'라고 말하는 반면, 캐나다인은 'I have a new car'라고 말한다. 한편, 비록 서로가 서로를 이해할지라도 호주인의 말은 미국인의 것과 매우 다르다. 전 세계에서 사용되고 있는 다양한 형태의 영어는 사실 그 자체가 게르만어족의 뿌리를 가지는 영국식 영어까지 거슬러 올라가기 때문에, 모든 영어 사용자들이 서로를 거의 이해할 수 있다는 것을 고려하면 영어의 모든 형태가 방언이 아닐까? 그럴 것 같지 않다. 그것들은 그들 각각의 나라의 정부에 의해 인정받고 있으며 그들 고유의 표준화된 표기 체계를 가지고 있기 때문에, 각각의 지위는 '언어'의 그것으로 승격된다.

E 궁극적으로, 그것들 모두가 보편적인 의사소통을 가능하게 하기 때문에, 언어와 방언의 만족스러운 구분을 찾으려고 노력하는 것은 도전이다. [22]우리가 오늘날 사용하는 언어와 방언은 그것들 이전의 모든 말의 형태가 그러했던 것처럼 시간이 지나면서 바뀔 것이고, 다른 것들이 다수의 인구에게 채택된 동안, 몇몇은 쓰이지 않게 될 것이다. 현재로는, 7천 개 이상의 언어가 있는 이 세계의 서로 다른 지역 출신인 두 사람이 서로를 꽤 잘 이해할 수 있다면, 그들이 의사소통을 잘 할 수 있는 것이라는 사실에 동의하는 것이 그저 최선일 것이다.

21 다양한 형태를 가진 현대 언어의 예시

22 언어와 방언의 잠재적 미래에 대한 진술

23 하나의 언어가 어떻게 다양한 언어들로 발달했는지에 대한 설명

24 역사가 어떻게 방언을 정의하는 데에 도움을 주는지

21 해설 문제의 핵심어구(a modern language with various forms)와 관련된 지문 내용 중 단락 D의 'English, for which there are various standard forms, including British, American, Canadian, and Australian'에서 영어에는 영국식, 미국식, 캐나다식, 그리고 호주식을 포함한 다양한 표준 형식이 있다고 하였으므로, 단락 **D**가 정답이다.

22 해설 문제의 핵심어구(potential future)와 관련된 지문 내용 중 단락 E의 'The languages and dialects we use today will change over time ~ and some will fall out of use while others will be adopted by large portions of the population.'에서 우리가 오늘날 사용하는 언어와 방언은 시간이 지나면서 바뀔 것이고 다른 것들이 다수의 인구에게 채택될 동안 몇몇은 쓰이지 않게 될 것이라고 하였으므로, 단락 **E**가 정답이다.

23 해설 문제의 핵심어구(a language developed into various languages)와 관련된 지문 내용 중 단락 B의 'though the Romance languages were initially dialects of Latin that shared various similarities, they have evolved over time ~ and are now considered separate official languages rather than dialects'에서 로망스어들이 다양한 유사성을 공유했던 라틴어의 초기 방언들이긴 했지만 시간이 지나면서 진화해왔고 이제 방언이라기보다는 독립된 공식 언어들로 여겨진다고 하였으므로, 단락 **B**가 정답이다.

24 해설 문제의 핵심어구(history could help)와 관련된 지문 내용 중 단락 B의 'Some linguists believe historical origins are significant, viewing any speech form that is derived from an older variety of communication as being a dialect.'에서 몇몇 언어학자들은 역사적인 기원이 중요하다고 믿는데 그들은 더 오래된 의사소통의 종류로부터 파생된 모든 말의 형태를 방언으로 본다고 하였으므로, 단락 **B**가 정답이다.

9

증가하는 항생 물질에 대한 내성

A 수십 년간의 남용의 유산으로, 항생 물질에 대한 내성은 전 세계에 퍼지고 있으며 전문가들에 의해 세계인의 건강과 발전에 가장 위험한 위협 중 하나로 인정되었다. 항생 물질에 대한 내성은 유전적 돌연변이를 통해 또는 점진적인 내성의 증가를 통해 박테리아가 변형되고 항생 물질의 영향을 받지 않게 될 때 발생한다. 나타나는 박테리아는 다루기가 극도로 어렵고, 어떤 경우에는 그들에 대응하기 위한 약이 존재하지 않는다. 이것은 너무도 긴급한 문제가 되고 있어서 [29]세계보건기구는 이것을 '세계 건강에 대한 가장 큰 위협 중 하나'로 묘사했으며, 그것에 대응하려는 시도로서 세계적인 시행 계획을 도입했다.

B 항생 물질에 대한 내성은 광범위한 효용으로 인한 수십 년간의 남용과 이 약들의 효능에 대한 교육의 부족으로 인해 나타났다. 이 것은 [26]의사의 처방전 없이 살 수 있는 규제되지 않는 항생제의 판매로 인해 악화되었다. 항생제 사용의 약 절반이 불필요한 것으로 추정된다. 예를 들어, 바이러스에 영향을 미치지 않는데도 불구하고 많은 사람들이 일반 감기에 항생제를 복용한다. 항생제의 남용은 항생제가 더 강한 변종이 증식하도록 하고 그것들을 치료하도록 고안된 약에 대한 면역력이 생기도록 하기 때문에, 더 강한 박테리아의 성장을 야기한다.

C 이러한 박테리아 변종은 다중약물에 내성이 있는 것으로, 또는 슈퍼버그로 알려져 있고, 세계 전역에서 건강상의 주요 위험이다. 매년 수백만 명이 약물에 내성이 있는 이러한 박테리아로 인해 사망하는 것으로 추정되며, 치료할 수 없는 감염의 수는 증가하고 있다. 폐렴, 대장균, 그리고 임질을 포함한 몇 가지 흔한 박테리아 감염들은, 이제 항생제에 대한 면역을 발달시키고 있으며 연구원들은 대체 치료를 찾기 위해 애쓰고 있다. [28]만약 방치된다면, 항생 물질에 내성이 있는 박테리아는 2050년까지 최대 3억 명의 사람들을 사망하게 할 것으로 예측되었다.

D 항생 물질에 대한 내성의 원인이 되는 것은 인간의 남용뿐 아니라 또한 동물에 대한 과도한 처방이다. 미국에서 판매되는 항생제의 80퍼센트가 동물들에게 제공되는 것으로 추산되며, 그것들은 대개 아픈 동물들에게 제공되지 않는다. 실제로, 동물의 건강과 번성을 향상시키기 위해 항생제를 일반 먹이에 섞는 것은 큰 농장에서는 종종 있는 흔한 일이다. 인간과 마찬가지로, 이것은 [25]약물에 내성이 있는 박테리아의 성장을 위한 촉매제로 작용하는데, 이것은 식료품으로 퍼질 수 있고 인간을 감염시킬 수 있다.

E 항생 물질에 대한 내성과의 싸움은 세계적인 건강 관련 우선 순위이고, 세계의 연구소들은 그 문제에 대한 해결에 애쓰고 있다. 약물에 내성이 있는 박테리아의 변종들이 그들에게 새로운 항생제로 직접적으로 대응하는 것이 불가능할 정도로 높은 속도로 나타나고 있기 때문에, 새로운 유형의 항생제를 개발하는 것은 더 이상 실현 가능한 선택권이 아니다. 그러나, [27]주목할 만한 최근의 큰 발전이 있었다. 과학자들은 다수의 박테리아 변종에서 항생 물질에 대한 내성을 뒤바꾸는 분자를 발견했다. 이것은 의사들이 현재 쓸

정답·해석·해설

HACKERS **IELTS** READING

모 없다고 생각되는 약을 사용하도록 할 수 있다. 이 분자는 아직 인간에게 시험되지는 않았기 때문에, 아직 개발 초기 단계에 있다. 그렇더라도 그것은 증가하는 세계 건강의 위협에 맞서는 최선의 희망일 것이다.

25 음식이 어떻게 약물에 내성이 있는 박테리아에 의해 오염될 수 있는지에 대한 설명

26 의사와 상의하지 않고 약을 구매하는 것에 대한 언급

27 가능한 새로운 치료에 대한 언급

28 생명이 위협에 처한 사람 수에 대한 언급

29 이 문제에 대해 한 세계적인 단체가 어떻게 대응했는지에 대한 설명

25 해설 문제의 핵심어구(food could be infected)와 관련된 지문 내용 중 단락 D의 'the development of drug resistant bacteria, which can spread into food products and infect humans'에서 약물에 내성이 있는 박테리아의 성장은 식료품으로 퍼질 수 있고 인간을 감염시킬 수 있다고 하였으므로, 단락 **D**가 정답이다.

26 해설 문제의 핵심어구(without consulting a doctor)와 관련된 지문 내용 중 단락 B의 'the unregulated sale of antibiotic drugs over the counter, without a doctor's prescription'에서 의사의 처방전 없이 살 수 있는 규제되지 않는 항생제의 판매라고 하였으므로, 단락 **B**가 정답이다. 'doctor's prescription'이 'consulting a doctor'로 paraphrasing되었다.

27 해설 문제의 핵심어구(new treatment)와 관련된 지문 내용 중 단락 E의 'there has been a recent breakthrough that could be significant; scientists have discovered a molecule that reverses antibiotic resistance in multiple strains of bacteria'에서 주목할 만한 최근의 큰 발전이 있었는데 과학자들은 다수의 박테리아 변종에서 항생 물질에 대한 내성을 뒤바꾸는 분자를 발견했다고 하였으므로, 단락 **E**가 정답이다.

28 해설 문제의 핵심어구(the number of people)와 관련된 지문 내용 중 단락 C의 'It has been predicted that ~ antibiotic resistant bacteria will kill up to 300 million people'에서 항생 물질에 내성이 있는 박테리아는 최대 3억 명의 사람들을 사망하게 할 것으로 예측되었다고 하였으므로, 단락 **C**가 정답이다. 'kill'이 'lives might be at risk'로 paraphrasing되었다.

29 해설 문제의 핵심어구(a global body has responded)와 관련된 지문 내용 중 단락 A의 'World Health Organisation ~ has introduced a global action plan'에서 세계보건기구는 세계적인 시행 계획을 도입했다고 하였으므로, 단락 **A**가 정답이다.

🔟

산호초의 생존

A 태평양, 대서양 그리고 인도양 이 세 주요 바다의 열대 지역과 아열대 지역에는 다양한 크기의 풍부한 산호초가 있다. ³⁴산호는 잘 자라기 위해 충분한 햇빛, 깨끗한 물, 황록공생조류 또는 조류의 존재, 그리고 섭씨 17도에서 34도 범위 내 온도를 필요로 하기 때문에, 그들은 해수면 아래 200피트보다 얕은 곳에 위치해 있다. 이러한 특정한 생태상의 요건들 때문에, 산호초는 대개 지구의 남반구의 얕은 해저 대지가 나타나는 지역에서 발견된다.

B 필요한 조건들이 충족될 때, 산호는 거대한 구조로 성장할 수 있다. 살아 있는 유기체, 특히 산호충은, 산호의 단단한 외골격을 만들기 위해 탄산칼슘을 분비한다. 이윽고, 산호 군체는 고도로 상호 연결된 다양한 생태계인 암초를 형성한다. 암초가 자라면서, ³¹산호에 서식하는 많은 유기체들 사이에 상호간의 협동과 공생의 복잡한 체계가 발달한다. 산호가 많은 해양 생물들의 생존에 대단히 중요하다고 말하는 것은 과장이 아니다. 사실, 많은 사람들은 산호초를 '바다의 우림'이라고 묘사하며, 우림처럼, 만약 파괴된다면, 그것들에 의존하는 유기체들은 멸종될 위기에 처하거나 사라진다.

C 지난 몇십 년 동안, 과학자들은 산호가 인간에게도 여러모로 중요하다는 것을 발견했다. 그들은 해양생물들에게 대단히 중요한 생태계를 제공할 뿐만 아니라, 대기 중의 이산화탄소를 제거하고 바다 폭풍으로부터 육지를 보호하기도 한다. 더욱이, 산호초는 관광객들을 끌어 모으는데, 이는 매년 약 3,750억 달러 가치의 일자리를 제공한다. 인류에 대한 산호의 가치와 바다의 건강을 유지하는 데 있어서의 그들의 중요성에도 불구하고, 그들은 점점 더 인간의 활동으로 인한 파괴의 위험에 처해 있다.

D 조사 연구는 산호초의 주요 위험이 모두 인간 활동에 관련되어 있음을 나타낸다. 예를 들어, 지구 온난화 때문에, 바닷물이 너무 따뜻해지면, 산호는 그들의 조직에 살고 있는 황록공생조류를 방출한다. ³³이것은 산호가 흰색으로 변하게 하는, 산호 탈색으로 알려진 현상을 야기한다. 이때 산호가 죽은 것은 아니긴 하지만, 건강은 심각한 위기에 처한 것이다. 살충제와 비료의 사용, 화학적 오염, 퇴적 작용, 삼림 벌채, 그리고 유막은, 또한 모두 산호에 큰 피해를 주었다.

E 이 위협은 해마다 커지고 있고, 이것은 산호의 건강에 대해 극적인 영향을 미치고 있다. 한 연구는 세계 산호초의 약 70퍼센트가 인간 활동에 의해 위협을 받고 있거나 파괴되었다는 결론을 내렸다. 몇몇 암초는 회복 가능성이 있긴 하지만, 약 20퍼센트는 재생의 가망이 없다. ³⁰자메이카의 암초는 가장 심한 피해를 입었고, 약 95퍼센트가 이제 완전히 파괴되었다.

F 호주의 대보초에 관한 보고서는 수질의 저하가 산호의 건강 악화를 야기하고 있었다는 결론을 내렸다. 이에 대응하여, ³²호주 정부는 암초를 보호하기 위해 몹시 애써왔고, 그 결과로 그곳의 생태계는 다른 지역에 위치한 암초들보다 생존할 가능성이 더 많다. 세계의 정치인들에게 너무 늦기 전에 이를 따르고 산호초의 감소를 중단시키려는 의지, 혹은, 방법이 있는지는 지켜봐야 한다.

30 산호초가 넓은 손상을 입은 나라의 예시

31 산호초에 사는 생물체 사이에서 발달하는 관계에 대한 설명

32 성공적인 보존 노력에 대한 언급

33 산호의 외관 변화에 대한 언급

34 산호가 번성하기 위해 필요한 조건에 대한 세부 설명

---

30 해설 문제의 핵심어구(a country ~ widespread damage)와 관련된 지문 내용 중 단락 E의 'Jamaica's reefs have been hit the hardest, and about 95 per cent of them have now been completely destroyed.'에서 자메이카의 암초는 가장 심한 피해를 입었고 약 95퍼센트가 이제 완전히 파괴되었다고 하였으므로, 단락 **E**가 정답이다. 'completely destroyed' 가 'widespread damage'로 paraphrasing되었다.

31 해설 문제의 핵심어구(the relationship ~ develops among creatures)와 관련된 지문 내용 중 단락 B의 'a complex system of mutual cooperation and symbiosis develops among many of the organisms that inhabit the corals' 에서 산호에 서식하는 많은 유기체들 사이에 상호간의 협동과 공생의 복잡한 체계가 발달한다고 하였으므로, 단락 **B**가 정답이다.

32 해설 문제의 핵심어구(a successful conservation effort)와 관련된 지문 내용 중 단락 F의 'the Australian government has made a great effort to protect the reef, with the result that its ecosystem is more likely to survive than reefs located in other areas'에서 호주 정부는 암초를 보호하기 위해 몹시 애써왔고 그 결과로 그곳의 생태계는 다른 지역에 위치한 암초들보다 생존할 가능성이 더 많다고 하였으므로, 단락 **F**가 정답이다. 'effort to protect'가 'conservation effort'로 paraphrasing되었다.

33 해설 문제의 핵심어구(change in coral appearance)와 관련된 지문 내용 중 단락 D의 'This causes the corals to turn white in colour, a phenomenon known as coral bleaching.'에서 이것은 산호가 흰색으로 변하게 하는, 산호 탈색으로 알려진 현상을 야기한다고 하였으므로, 단락 **D**가 정답이다.

34 해설 문제의 핵심어구(conditions corals need)와 관련된 지문 내용 중 단락 A의 'corals require sufficient sunlight, clear water, the presence of zooxanthellae or algae, and a temperature range of 17 to 34 degrees Celsius in order to thrive'에서 산호는 잘 자라기 위해 충분한 햇빛, 깨끗한 물, 황록공생조류 또는 조류의 존재, 그리고 섭씨 17도에서 34도 범위 내 온도를 필요로 한다고 하였으므로, 단락 **A**가 정답이다.

1	D	2	A	3	F
4	C	5	G	6	E
7	F	8	B	9	portability
10	mechanisation/mechanization	11	(skilled) artisans	12	jewellers/jewelers
13	water-powered mills	14	apprentices		

시간 기록하기: 영국, 스위스, 그리고 미국에서의 시계 제조

A 고대부터 다양한 종류의 시계들이 유통되었지만, 현대적인 개념의 시계 산업의 역사는 18세기부터 시작된다. 그 전에는, [2]시계와 손목시계는 취미에 열심인 부유한 사람들의 영역에만 제한되었고, 대강 시간을 알리는 용도로만 사용되었지만, 산업혁명으로 초래된 교통의 변화는 시간 엄수를 필수적인 사항으로 만들었으며 대중들의 사고 속에 시간 개념을 굳게 하도록 도왔다.

B 디자인, 생산, 그리고 무역에 있어, 영국은 현대 시계 산업의 선두주자였다. [9]정확함과 휴대성으로 알려진 시계를 생산하는 영국인들의 경향은 증가하는 이동 인구의 필요에 완벽하게 적합했으며, 영국에서의 초기 철도 발달은 19세기 상반기에 시장 패권에 대한 기폭제를 제공했다. 철도의 안전하고 예측 가능한 작동은 시간 엄수에 크게 의존했기 때문에, 기술자들이 그들의 크로노미터를 맞추게 하기 위해 시계가 철도망 전역에 간격을 두고 설치되었으며, [8]시계들이 지속적으로 정확하게 조정될 수 있도록 전보 서비스가 기차역들에 주기적으로 시간을 전송했다.

C 이것은 사고를 방지하는 것을 돕고 철도 회사들이 더 빠듯한 일정을 유지하도록 허용하는 동시에, [4]또한 여행객들이 더 정확하게 도착, 출발, 그리고 연결편을 예측할 수 있도록 도왔다. 이러한 발전은 충분한 재력이 있는 사람들이 회중시계를 구입하도록 유도하며, 사회 전역에 걸쳐 시간의 중요성에 대한 급증하는 인식의 토대가 되었다. 그러므로, 기차 여행은 시계의 수요를 증가시켰으며 영국의 전반적인 시계 산업을 강화시켰다.

D 하지만, 영국의 시스템에는 경쟁자들에 의해 이용될 결점이 있었다. 다시 말해, 영국 시장은 오로지 수작업 시계에 집중되어 있었으며, [10]비밀스러운 기술로 수입을 얻던 탐욕스러운 장인들은 기계화를 위협으로 여겼고 '가짜 시계'를 만들기 위한 기계의 사용에 대해 적극적으로 반대 활동을 펼쳤다. 그로 인해, 영국의 시계 제품들은 생산하는 데 매우 비용이 많이 들도록 유지되었다. 그러나 [1]영국이 기계화에 대해 적대적이었던 반면, 이것은 스위스에서는 해당되지 않았는데, 그곳에서 기업들은 판과 바퀴와 같은 개별적인 부품의 자동화 생산을 실험을 하기 시작했다. 몇몇 부분들을 만들기 위해 기계를 사용함으로써, 스위스의 시계들은 영국의 시계들보다 더 빠르고 저렴하게 생산될 수 있었다.

E 하지만 스위스는 완전히 기계화된 생산의 유혹에 굴복하지는 않았다. 대신, [11]그들은 제품 생산의 초기 단계에서 반쯤 완성된 제품을 생산하기 위해 기계가 사용되고, 고도로 숙련된 장인들에게 마지막 마무리에 대한 책임이 있는 탄력적인 시스템을 차용했다. 스위스 시계는 수작업 세공의 다양성과 품질을 희생시키지 않고 효율적으로 생산될 수 있었기 때문에, 이런 접근법은 각각의 장점을 제공했다. [6]최첨단 기계와 전문가 및 적응력 있는 노동력은 스위스 회사들로 하여금 시장 수요의 변동과 소비자 기호에 빠르게 반응할 수 있도록 했고, 스위스의 시계들, 특히 손목시계는, 점차 구매자들의 마음 속에 '최고 품질'과 동의어가 되었다. [12]'스위스 제품'이라는 이름 아래 만들어진 시계들은 국내와 국외 모두의 보석상과 고급 상점에서 높은 가격에 팔렸으며, 마침내 스위스인들은 인정받는 시계 산업의 대표로서 영국인들을 추월했고 오랜 시간 동안 그 자리를 유지했다. 스위스에서 만들어진 많은 시계들은 결국 미국 시장에 진출하게 되었는데, 미국의 시계 제조공들은 품질을 희생하여 수량에 초점을 맞추었다.

F 비록 미국이 그들의 유럽 상대에 비해 숙련된 장인들의 순전한 숫자 자체는 부족했지만, [7]미국 장인들은 대량 생산의 기술을 완성하며 값싼 시계의 장을 열었다. 1815년에 이르러, [13]코네티컷 주의 기술자 Eli Terry는, 숙련된 노동자에 의한 어떤 조작이나 미세 조정 없이 바로 조립될 수 있는 완벽히 균일하며 교체 가능한 부품들을 제작하기 위해 수력으로 돌아가는 물방아를 사용하고 있었다. 결과적으로, [14]그의 시계들은 장인들에 대한 필요 없이 견습생들에 의해 빠르게 생산될 수 있었다. 그의 사업의 상업적 가치를 이해하여, [3]Terry는 특허를 통해 그의 방식을 보호하려 했지만, 그의 법적 조치는 경쟁자들의 형세를 오래 저지시키지는 않았다. 다른 기업들은 그를 따라 했고 1800년대 후반에 이르러, 미국인들은 시계를 대규모로 빠르고 값싸게 생산하고 있었다. 1899년에, 잉거솔 시계 회사의 '양키' 회중 시계는 1달러에 팔렸고, 이러한 1달러짜리 시계들은 매일 약 8000개씩 조립 라인에서 완성되고 있었다.

G 미국이 거의 누구라도 장만할 수 있는 시계를 생산할 수 있었다는 사실은 큰 장점을 가지고 있었다. 미국의 시계와 손목시계는 세계 시장을 휩쓸었고, 결국 판매량뿐 아니라 수익에서도 스위스 상표들을 추월하게 되었다. 1945년과 1970년 사이에, [5]세계 시계 시장에서의 스위스의 점유율은 80퍼센트에서 42퍼센트로 급락했으며, 1970년에 이르러, 미국의 두 시계 회사인 타이멕스사와 부로바사가, 각각 세계 판매량과 총 수익에서 1위를 했다.

어휘 timepiece n. 시계 in circulation phr. 유통되는 realm n. 영역, 범위 crude adj. 대강의; 거친 cement v. 굳게 하다, 접합하다
mass n. (일반) 대중 penchant n. 경향, 애호 portability n. 휴대성 catalyst n. 기폭제, 촉매제 synchronise v. (시간을) 맞추다
chronometer n. 크로노미터(정밀한 경도 측정용 시계) wire v. 전송하다, 전보를 보내다 underpin v. 토대가 되다 burgeoning adj. 급증하는
bolster v. 강화시키다, 북돋다 exploit v. 이용하다, 착취하다 namely adv. 다시 말해, 즉 avaricious adj. 탐욕스러운
craftsman n. 장인, 공예가 esoteric adj. 비밀스러운 lobby against phr. 반대 활동을 펼치다, ~에 반대하는 운동을 하다 fashion v. 만들다
artisan n. 장인 best of both worlds phr. 각각의 장점 moniker n. 이름, 별명 fetch v. 팔리다, 가져오다
fabricate v. 제작하다, 날조하다 journeyman n. 장인 undertaking n. 사업, 일 safeguard v. 보호하다 on the order of phr. 약, 대략
plummet v. 급락하다

[1-8]

1 기계화에 대한 영국과 스위스의 태도 차이

2 사회의 한 계층으로 시계가 한정되는 것에 대한 언급

3 한 개인이 어떻게 법적으로 그의 제조 과정을 보호하려고 시도했는지에 대한 언급

4 시간을 엄수하는 것이 기차 여행자에게 제공한 이점에 대한 예시

5 세계 회사들 간 세계 시장 점유율의 변화에 대한 설명

6 특정 시계들이 솜씨로 인정받았던 이유

7 어떻게 미국의 대량 생산이 저렴한 시계를 위한 토대를 놓았는지에 대한 진술

8 시간을 엄수하는 것이 초기 철도망에서 어떻게 유지되었는지

1 해설 문제의 핵심어구(British and Swiss attitudes)와 관련된 지문 내용 중 단락 D의 'while the British were antagonistic toward mechanisation, this was not the case in Switzerland'에서 영국이 기계화에 대해 적대적이었던 반면, 이것은 스위스에서는 해당되지 않았다고 하였으므로, 단락 D가 정답이다.

2 해설 문제의 핵심어구(watches being restricted)와 관련된 지문 내용 중 단락 A의 'clocks and watches were largely confined to the realms of wealthy hobbyists'에서 시계와 손목시계는 취미에 열심인 부유한 사람들의 영역에만 제한되었다고 하였으므로, 단락 A가 정답이다. 'clocks and watches ~ confined'가 'watches ~ restricted'로 paraphrasing되었다.

3 해설 문제의 핵심어구(legally protect)와 관련된 지문 내용 중 단락 F의 'Terry attempted to safeguard his methods with patents'에서 Terry는 특허를 통해 그의 방식을 보호하려 했다고 하였으므로, 단락 F가 정답이다.

4 해설 문제의 핵심어구(benefits that timekeeping provided for rail travellers)와 관련된 지문 내용 중 단락 C의 'it also helped travellers to anticipate arrivals, departures, and connections with greater precision'에서 또한 여행객들이 더 정확하게 도착, 출발, 그리고 연결편을 예측할 수 있도록 도왔다고 하였으므로, 단락 C가 정답이다.

5 해설 문제의 핵심어구(global market shares)와 관련된 지문 내용 중 단락 G의 'the Swiss share of the global watch market plummeted from 80 to 42 per cent, and by 1970, two US watch companies ~ ranked first in worldwide sales and total revenues'에서 세계 시계 시장에서의 스위스의 점유율은 80퍼센트에서 42퍼센트로 급락했으며 1970년에 이르러 미국의 두 시계 회사가 세계 판매량과 총 수익에서 1위를 했다고 하였으므로, 단락 G가 정답이다.

6 해설 문제의 핵심어구(recognised for their craftsmanship)와 관련된 지문 내용 중 단락 E의 'State-of-the-art machinery and an expert and adaptable workforce allowed Swiss companies to respond quickly to fluctuations in market demand and consumer preferences, and Swiss timepieces ~ gradually became synonymous with 'top quality' in the minds of buyers.'에서 최첨단 기계와 전문가 및 적응력 있는 노동력은 스위스 회사들로 하여금 시장 수요의 변동과 소비자 기호에 빠르게 반응할 수 있도록 했고 스위스의 시계들은 점차 구매자들의 마음 속에 '최고 품질'과 동의어가 되었다고 하였으므로, 단락 E가 정답이다.

7 해설 문제의 핵심어구(American mass production)와 관련된 지문 내용 중 단락 F의 'American artisans paved the way for inexpensive timepieces through perfecting the art of mass production'에서 미국 장인들은 대량 생산의 기술을 완성하며 값싼 시계의 장을 열었다고 하였으므로, 단락 F가 정답이다. 'paved the way'가 'laid the foundation'로 paraphrasing되었다.

8 해설 문제의 핵심어구(timekeeping was maintained on early railway networks)와 관련된 지문 내용 중 단락 B의 'telegraph services would periodically wire times to stations throughout the railway system so that clocks could be continually adjusted for accuracy'에서 시계들이 지속적으로 정확하게 조정될 수 있도록 전보 서비스가 기차역들에 주기적으로 시간을 전송했다고 하였으므로, 단락 B가 정답이다.

[9-14]

세 나라의 이야기: 영국, 스위스, 그리고 미국에서의 시계 산업

- 영국 시계들은 그들의 정확성뿐 아니라 9 ....으로 유명했다.
- 영국 장인들은 10 ....을 그들의 산업에 대한 위험으로 보았다.
- 스위스 시계들은 부분적으로는 기계에 의해 만들어졌지만 11 ....이 마지막 마무리를 제공했다.
- 스위스 시계들은 비쌌고 고급 상점과 12 ....에서 찾을 수 있었다.
- 미국에서, 13 ....은 교체 가능한 일반 부품을 만드는 데 사용되었다.
- Eli Terry는 그의 시계가 14 ....에 의해 빠르게 조립되었기 때문에, 장인이 필요하지 않았다.

---

9 해설 문제의 핵심어구(British clocks ~ renowned for ~ accuracy)와 관련된 지문 내용 중 'The British penchant for producing clocks known for their accuracy and portability'에서 정확함과 휴대성으로 알려진 시계를 생산하는 영국인들의 경향이라고 하였으므로, **portability**가 정답이다. 'The British penchant for producing clocks known'이 'British clocks were renowned'로 paraphrasing되었다.

10 해설 문제의 핵심어구(danger to their industry)와 관련된 지문 내용 중 'avaricious craftsmen who profited from their esoteric skills viewed mechanisation as a threat'에서 비밀스러운 기술로 수입을 얻던 탐욕스러운 장인들은 기계화를 위협으로 여겼다고 하였으므로, **mechanisation/mechanization**이 정답이다. 'viewed as a threat'이 'saw as a danger'로 paraphrasing되었다.

11 해설 문제의 핵심어구(supplied the final touches)와 관련된 지문 내용 중 'they adopted a flexible system whereby machines were used in the first stage of production ~ and highly skilled artisans were responsible for the final touches'에서 스위스는 제품 생산의 초기 단계에서 기계가 사용되고 고도로 숙련된 장인들에게 마지막 마무리에 대한 책임이 있는 탄력적인 시스템을 차용했다고 하였으므로, 'highly skilled artisans'가 답이 될 수 있다. 지시문에서 두 단어 이내로 답을 작성하라고 하였으므로, **(skilled) artisans**가 정답다. 'highly skilled artisans were responsible for'가 '(skilled) artisans supplied'로 paraphrasing되었다.

12 해설 문제의 핵심어구(found in high-end shops)와 관련된 지문 내용 중 'Watches under the moniker 'Swiss made' fetched handsome prices in jewellers and other high-end shops both at home and abroad'에서 '스위스 제품' 이라는 이름 아래 만들어진 시계들은 보석상과 고급 상점에서 높은 가격에 팔렸다고 하였으므로, **jewellers/jewelers**가 정답이다. 'Watches ~ fetched handsome prices'가 'Swiss watches were costly'로 paraphrasing되었다.

13 해설 문제의 핵심어구(parts that were interchangeable)와 관련된 지문 내용 중 'Eli Terry, an engineer in Connecticut, was using water-powered mills to fabricate completely uniform and interchangeable parts'에서 코네티컷 주의 기술자 Eli Terry는 완벽히 균일하며 교체 가능한 부품들을 제작하기 위해 수력으로 돌아가는 물방아를 사용하고 있었다고 하였으므로, **water-powered mills**가 정답이다. 'fabricate ~ uniform and interchangeable parts'가 'make regular parts that were interchangeable'로 paraphrasing되었다.

14 해설 문제의 핵심어구(not require journeymen)와 관련된 지문 내용 중 'his clocks could be produced quickly by apprentices without the need for journeymen'에서 Eli Terry의 시계들은 장인들에 대한 필요 없이 견습생에 의해 빠르게 생산될 수 있었다고 하였으므로, **apprentices**가 정답이다. 'without the need for journeymen'이 'did not require journeymen'으로, 'clocks could be produced quickly'가 'clocks were rapidly put together'로 paraphrasing되었다.

* 각 문제에 대한 정답의 단서는 지문에 문제 번호와 함께 별도의 색으로 표시되어 있습니다.

EXAMPLE
p.233

[1]라마는 잉카 사회의 필수적인 요소였다. 고대 아메리카에서 유일하게 사육된 큰 동물인 라마는 잉카 사람들에게 음식과 직물의 재료를 제공했다. 한 마리의 다 자란 수컷은 100킬로그램의 고기를 내주었는데, 이는 보관을 위해 건조될 수 있었다. 가볍고 영양가가 높은 말린 라마 고기는 잉카의 군인들과 여행자들의 주식이었다. 그 동물들의 가죽은 날씨를 잘 견디는 의복을 위한 가죽으로 변형되었다. 예를 들어, 잉카 사람들의 가죽신 밑창은 라마 가죽으로 만들어졌다. 게다가, 털은 천으로 바뀌었는데, 이는 평민들이 입던 의복을 위해 사용되었다.

HACKERS PRACTICE
p.236

1	iii	2	i	3	iv	4	i	5	vi
6	iv	7	ii	8	ii	9	v	10	i
11	iv	12	iii	13	ii	14	iii	15	v
16	iv	17	ii	18	iv	19	vii	20	ii
21	i	22	vi	23	iv	24	viii	25	ii
26	ii	27	viii	28	iv	29	iii	30	viii
31	iv	32	vii	33	v	34	vi		

1

제목 리스트

i   극세사에 관한 대립되는 견해
ii 극세사의 활용을 확장할 필요성
iii 새로운 인조 물질의 개발
iv 새로운 제품의 향후 응용

1 단락 A

2 단락 B

A 20세기에, [1]일본의 한 선구자가 부드럽고, 극도로 얇은 합성 섬유의 생산에 있어 기술의 획기적 발전을 이루었다. 이 극세사는 비단실보다 더 가늘고, 인간의 머리카락보다 100배 더 얇다. 기업가인 미요시 오카모토는 폴리에스테르와 나일론이라는 두 가지의 합성섬유가 서로 엮이도록 작은 관에 넣어 압박하고 열을 가함으로써 이 섬유를 처음으로 생산했다. 그 후, 극세사 기술은 미국과 스웨덴을 장악했는데, 그곳에서 지속적으로 개선이 이루어져, 그것의 잠재적 용도를 확장했다. 오늘날에는, 레이온 섬유와 아크릴 섬유를 포함한 다양한 재료가 극세사를 만들기 위해 사용되었는데, 이것들은 의류, 세척용 천, 그리고 차량용 커버와 같은 수많은 응용에 있어 활용된다.

B 하지만, [2]이 합성 기술은 또한 엄청난 논란의 원인이 되기도 했다. 한편으로는, 많은 사람이 그것의 장점들을 높이 평가했다. 예를 들어, 이 섬유들을 엮어 만든 세척용 천은 그것의 무게의 7배에 달하는 액체를 흡수할 수 있으며, 대부분은 세척용 화학 약품을 필

요로 하지도 않는다. 동물 보호 운동가들은 그것이 비단과 모직에 대한 의존을 제한하기 때문에 극세사를 수용하기도 했다. 다른 한편으로, 몇몇 사람들은 극세사가 환경을 훼손하고 있으며 금지되어야 한다고 생각한다. 이는 가는 섬유가 대량으로 우리의 상수도에 유입되고 있기 때문이다. 실제로, 미시간 호에서 발견된 합성수지의 16퍼센트 가량이 이러한 석유를 원료로 한 합성섬유의 형태였다.

1 해설 단락 A의 중심 문장 'a pioneer in Japan made a technological breakthrough in the production of soft, and extremely thin, synthetic fibres'에서 일본의 한 선구자가 부드럽고 극도로 얇은 합성 섬유의 생산에 있어 기술의 획기적 발전을 이루었다고 하였으므로, 보기 **iii** The development of a new manmade material이 정답이다. 'synthetic fibres' 가 'manmade material'로 paraphrasing되었다.

2 해설 단락 B의 중심 문장 'this synthetic technology has also become the source of tremendous controversy'에서 이 합성 기술은 또한 엄청난 논란의 원인이 되기도 했다고 하였으므로, 보기 **i** Opposing views on microfibres가 정답이다. 'controversy'가 'Opposing views'로 paraphrasing되었다.

2

제목 리스트

i   고대의 거대동물이 멸종한 이유에 대한 서로 다른 견해
ii   왜 호주에 유대목 동물이 많은지
iii   어떻게 유대목 동물들이 멸종을 피했는지
iv   왜 호주 포유동물들이 독특한지

---

3 섹션 A

4 섹션 B

A 호주에 있는 포유동물들의 독특한 특징 한 가지는 모두 유대목 동물이라는 것이다. 총 159종의 호주 유대목 동물들이 현재 확인되는데, 이는 세계에서 유일한 압도적인 수이다. 또 다른 뚜렷한 특징은 호주의 포유류 유대목 동물들이 세계의 다른 거대 포유동물들보다 작은 경향이 있다는 것이다. 흔히, '거대동물'이라는 용어는 100 킬로그램 이상의 무게가 나가는 동물들을 가리킨다. 하지만 호주의 포유동물들은 더 작기 때문에, 생물학자들은 45킬로그램 이상의 몸무게를 가진 호주 동물군을 포함시키기 위해 그 기준을 수정했다.

B 그러나, 이런 작은 크기는 항상 그러했던 것은 아니었다. 화석 기록은 호주의 거대동물이 한때 번성했지만, 가장 거대한 동물들은 약 4만 5천 년 전 멸종했다는 것을 보여준다. 수년 간, ⁴주요 이론은 인간이 남획을 함으로써 거대동물을 대대적으로 살상했다는 것이었다. 이런 가설은 기퍼드 밀러 교수에 의해 받아들여지는데, 그는 침전물 중심부 견본 연구에 참여했다. 그의 팀은 거대 초식동물들의 대변에 있는 균류 포자의 존재에 초점을 맞췄고 멸종 이전 몇 천 년 동안 급락하기 전에는 포자가 아주 많았다는 사실을 발견했다. 이 지역이 또한 5만년 전쯤의 인류 거주 흔적을 보여주기 때문에, 연구원들은 인류의 정착과 거대동물 사망 사이의 인과 관계를 추론했다.

⁴더 최근의 주장들은 기후 변화에 책임을 돌린다. 밴더빌트 대학의 Larisa Desantis는 기후 변화가 거대동물의 사망을 야기했다고 주장한다. 그녀와 그녀의 팀은 거대 초식 동물들의 화석 치아의 변화하는 패턴을 연구했다. 치아 에나멜에 축적되어 있는 탄소와 산소의 동위 원소를 비교함으로써, 그들은 치아가 형성되었을 때 환경의 평균 온도를 추론했다. 그녀는 그 결과 멸종 이전에 기후가 변화하면서 그들의 식단이 갑작스럽게 변하기 시작했다는 것을 알아낼 수 있었는데, 이는 훨씬 건조한 기후가 적절한 먹이를 사라지게 했다는 것을 암시한다.

3 해설 이 섹션에는 중심 문장이 없으므로, 섹션 전체를 읽고 중심 내용을 파악한다. 섹션 A는 호주에 있는 포유동물들은 유대목 동물이며 다른 거대 포유동물들보다 작기 때문에 독특하다는 내용에 대해 주로 언급하고 있다. 따라서 이를 '왜 호주 포유동물들이 독특한지'로 요약한 보기 **iv** Why Australian mammals are unique가 정답이다.

3

> **제목 리스트**
>
> i 자동차 판매 증가의 이유
> ii 미국에서의 자동차 사용의 변화
> iii 미국의 교통 수단의 역사
> iv 차량 소유의 문제점
> v 교통 문제의 해결책을 찾는 것
> vi 미국에 대한 자동차의 영향

5 단락 A

6 단락 B

7 단락 C

A ⁵미국 역사에서, 개인 차량 소유의 증가만큼 미국인의 생활 양식에 엄청난 영향을 끼친 것은 아마 없을 것이다. 자동차는 미국인들이 그들의 거대한 국가를 쉽게 이동할 수 있도록 했고 자유를 상징하게 되었다. 차량 소유는 통과 의례가 되었고 점점 더 많은 미국인들이 차량을 구매하면서, 이는 국가의 인구 통계에 큰 변화를 야기했다. 증가한 기동력 덕분에, 미국인들은 도시에서 교외로 이사할 수 있었다. 많은 이들에게, 마당과 하얀 말뚝 울타리가 있는 교외에 있는 집을 소유하는 것은 '아메리칸 드림'을 상징하게 되었다.

B 하지만, 몇몇 사람들은 자동차를 자유의 위대한 상징으로 보지 않는다. 사실, ⁶그들은 자동차에 대한 우리의 의존성을 짐이라고 여긴다. 대부분의 사람들에게, 끝없이 인상되는 자동차의 가격은 자동차를 큰 투자로 만든다. 게다가, 연료, 보험, 그리고 유지 비용은 자동차를 더욱 감당하기 어렵게 만든다. 이것은 개인적인 문제로 보일 수 있지만, 이는 사회 전체에 심각한 부정적인 영향을 미쳐 왔다. 앞서 언급한 교외로의 도피가 개인 차량을 구매할 형편이 되는 중산층 및 상류층 시민들을 도시로부터 유출시켰을 때, 도시의 전반적인 소득 수준은 감소했다. 이는 세입 감소와 광범위한 도시의 쇠퇴로 이어졌다.

C 흥미롭게도, 현재 2억 5천만 대의 차가 미국의 도로 위에 있는데도, 몇몇 사람들은 국가가 Phil Goodwin 교수가 'peak car'라고 부르는 것에 도달했다고 믿는다. 이는 기본적으로 미국인들이 그들이 이전에 했던 것보다 차로 덜 이동하고 있다는 것을 의미한다. 이것에 대해 가장 흔하게 인용되는 이유 중 하나는 사람들이 다시 도시로 돌아오고 있다는 것이다. 이 재도시화와 함께, 시민들은 이용할 수 있는 대중교통에 대한 증가된 접근권을 가지고 있다. 차량을 구매하고 유지하는 비용과 이러한 대중교통을 비교한 뒤, 많은 미국인들은 차량 소유를 완전히 포기하기 시작했다.

7 해설 이 단락에는 중심 문장이 없으므로, 단락 전체를 읽고 중심 내용을 파악한다. 단락 C는 재도시화로 인한 대중교통 접근권의 증가로 미국인들이 이전에 비해 차를 덜 사용하고 있다는 내용에 대해 주로 언급하고 있다. 따라서 이를 '미국에서의 자동차 사용의 변화'로 요약한 보기 **ii** Changes in automobile use in the United States가 정답이다.

4

제목 리스트

i   기업 관리 방식에 관한 최근 견해

ii   새로운 경영 방식 개발의 필요성

iii   기업 경영에 있어 성공하기 위해 필요한 조건들

iv   상업에 대한 산업혁명의 기여

v   직장 조직을 위한 새로운 운영 계획의 개발

vi   초기 노동 운동에 관한 한 가지 설명

8   단락 A

9   단락 B

10   단락 C

A   산업혁명은 18세기 후반에서 19세기 초반까지 제조업에 거대한 변화를 야기했다. 이 시기 동안, 제조업은 작은 자택 기반 기업에서 기계를 가지고 작업하는 많은 직원들이 있는 큰 공장으로 이동했다. 안타깝게도, 이 변화에는 새로운 체계의 효율성을 극대화하기 위한 경영 방식에 있어서의 변화는 동반되지 않았다. 잘못된 경영이 증가한 생산량으로 인한 이득을 감소시키는 재정 손실을 야기하고 있다는 것은 이내 명백해졌다. [8]그러므로, 새로운 경영 방식에 대한 절실한 필요성이 있었다.

B   이 문제를 처음으로 제기한 사람 중 한 명은 미국의 기술자인 [9]프레드릭 윈슬로 테일러였는데, 그의 실험들은 '과학적 경영'이라는 노동 인구를 지휘하는 새로운 방식을 가져왔다. 이 새로운 경영 방식은 기업을 더 효율적이고 합리적인 방법으로 조직하고자 했다. 그의 연구를 통해, 테일러는 그 시대의 경영 방식의 몇 가지 문제점을 알아냈다. 전체 생산 공정에 대한 지식의 부족이 이들 중 가장 기본적인 것이었다. 경영자들에게 더 많은 지식을 제공함으로써, 테일러는 경영자들이 업무의 모든 측면들을 더 잘 이해하고 일부 제조 공정의 비능률을 발견할 수 있을 것이라고 믿었다. 그는 또한 관리자의 근본적인 역할이 잘못되었다고 여겼다. 그는 사무직의 경영 방식을 선호했는데, 이 방식에서 관리자들은 직원들의 역할, 행동 양식, 그리고 시간을 통제했다. 나아가, 그는 업무들을 검토하고 업무를 수행하는 가장 효율적인 방식을 산출함으로써 최대 직원 효율을 알아내기 위한 공식을 개발했다. 이는 가장 이상적인 한 삽 분량의 흙의 양과 손수레를 밀 때 직원이 움직여야 하는 속도를 알아내는 것을 포함했다.

C   테일러의 연구는 세부 사항까지 통제되는 권력 체계로 이어졌지만, [10]현대의 여론은 이것이 긍정적인 결과였다고 말하지 않는다. 그들은 테일러의 경영 방식이 인간성이 말살되고 불만스러워 하는 근로자들을 초래한다고 주장한다. 그리고 그들은 또한 1900년대 초반의 노동 운동을 초래하고 첫 노동조합을 야기한 것이 바로 이러한 감정들임을 지적한다.

8 해설 단락 A의 중심 문장 'Therefore, there was a pressing need for a new way of management.'에서 그러므로 새로운 경영 방식에 대한 절실한 필요성이 있었다고 하였으므로, 보기 **ii** The need to develop new management styles가 정답이다. 'a new way of management'가 'new management styles'로 paraphrasing되었다.

9 해설 단락 B의 중심 문장 'Frederick Winslow Taylor, whose experiments brought about a new way to direct the workforce ~. This new management style sought to organise companies in a more efficient and rational way.' 에서 프레드릭 윈슬로 테일러의 실험들이 노동 인구를 지휘하는 새로운 방식을 가져왔으며 이 새로운 경영 방식은 기업을 더 효율적이고 합리적인 방법으로 조직하고자 했다고 하였으므로, 보기 **v** The development of a new scheme for workplace organisation이 정답이다. 'a new way to direct the workforce'가 'a new scheme for workplace organisation'으로 paraphrasing되었다.

정답·해석·해설

HACKERS **IELTS** READING

10 해설 단락 C의 중심 문장 'contemporary opinions do not suggest that this was a positive outcome'에서 현대의 여론은 이것이 긍정적인 결과였다고 말하지 않는다고 하였으므로, 보기 **i** Current views about a style of business administration이 정답이다. 'contemporary opinions'가 'Current views'로 paraphrasing되었다.

제목 리스트

i   인간 언어의 독특한 측면에 관한 설명
ii   덜 일반적인 언어 발달 이론에 관한 설명
iii   언어 기원의 한 개념에 기반한 다양한 이론들
iv   언어의 기원을 알아내는 것의 어려움
v   초기 인류 의사소통에 대한 물리적 증거의 발견
vi   언어를 사용하지 않는 종과 소통하기 위해 사용되는 방법

11   단락 A

12   단락 B

13   단락 C

A   [11]연구원들은 천 년 동안 인간 언어의 기원을 이해하기 위해 노력해왔다. 하지만, 이 일은 연구될 수 있는 물질적 증거가 적기 때문에 상당히 어렵다. 이 때문에, 언어학자들은 인간의 언어적 의사소통이 어떻게, 언제, 그리고 왜 시작되었는지에 관한 정보를 추론하기 위해 현대 언어, 언어 습득 이론 그리고 언어 체계 연구를 이용해야 한다. 이 기술들을 사용하여, 두 가지 주요 이론이 발달했다. 이것들은 언어가 의사소통의 이전 형태에서 진화된 것이고 시간이 흐르면서 점차 등장한 것이라고 말하는 연속성 이론과, 인간 언어는 독특한 형태의 의사소통이며 아마도 갑작스럽게 등장했을 것이라는 비연속 이론이다.

B   [12]연속성 이론들은 종종 발성, 몸짓, 그리고 사회적 기원 이론들로 나뉜다. 발성 이론에 따르면, 언어는 자연의 소리를 흉내 내고 물건을 식별하기 위해 소리들을 사용하던 영장류로부터 비롯되었다. 한편, 몸짓 이론은 인간이 두 발로 걷게 되면서 수화의 형태를 개발했지만, 시간이 지나면서 이는 소리들로 대체되었다고 가정한다. 두 이론 모두 각자의 가치가 있지만, 많은 사회언어학자들은 사회의 복잡성과 함께 언어가 생존 수단으로써 발달했다고 믿는다. 다른 사회 구성원들에 대한 정보를 퍼뜨림으로써, 초기 인류는 동맹을 조직하고 친구와 적을 식별할 수 있었다.

C   반대로, [13]상대적으로 수가 더 적은 비연속 이론들은 갑작스러운 언어의 발달을 지적한다. 이는 주로 신의 개입의 결과라고 여겨진다. 많은 전통적인 이야기들은 언어가 어떻게 신이나 다른 초자연적인 신적 존재들로부터 인간에게 주어졌는지에 대해 설명한다. 하지만, 유전적 비연속 이론의 다른 지지자들은 인간이 언어에 대한 선천적인 능력을 갖추고 있다고 믿게 되었다. 이는, 노암 촘스키에 따르면, 언어가 진화적 변화로 의해 즉각적으로 등장했을 가능성이 있다는 것을 뜻한다. 많은 언어학자들은 처음에 이 이론을 묵살했지만, 언어들 간 관계에 대한 증가하는 증거는 이 이론의 인기를 높이고 있다.

11   해설 단락 A의 중심 문장 'Researchers have tried to understand the origin of human language for millennia. However, this job is quite difficult'에서 연구원들은 천 년 동안 인간 언어의 기원을 이해하기 위해 노력해왔지만 이 일은 상당히 어렵다고 하였으므로, 보기 **iv** Difficulty in determining the birth of language가 정답이다. 'the origin of human language'가 'the birth of language'로 paraphrasing되었다.

12   해설 단락 B의 중심 문장 'Continuity theories are often divided into vocal, gestural, and social origin theories.'에서 연속성 이론들은 종종 발성, 몸짓, 그리고 사회적 기원 이론들로 나뉜다고 하였으므로, 보기 **iii** Various theories based on one idea of language origin이 정답이다.

13   해설 단락 C의 중심 문장 'the relatively fewer discontinuity theories point to a sudden development of language'에서 상대적으로 수가 더 적은 비연속 이론들은 갑작스러운 언어의 발달을 지적한다고 하였으므로, 보기 **ii** A description of less common language development theories가 정답이다. 'relatively fewer'가 'less common'으로 paraphrasing 되었다.

6

제목 리스트

i   지리적 위치가 동물 무리에게 미치는 영향

ii   기후 변화가 큰도마뱀에게 미친 영향

iii   종 번식의 증거

iv   인간 개입의 결과

v   큰도마뱀의 생존으로 이어진 두 가지 요소

vi   낮은 번식률에 관한 설명

14   단락 A

15   단락 B

16   단락 C

17   단락 D

A   최근에, 오타고 대학 연구진은 놀라운 발견을 했다. [14]그들은 뉴질랜드의 남섬에서 큰도마뱀의 알의 잔해를 발견했다. 큰도마뱀은 100년이 넘도록 뉴질랜드의 주요 섬 두 곳 중 어느 곳에서도 번식하지 않았기 때문에 이는 매우 중요했다. 이 새로운 발견은 환경 보호 활동가들을 들뜨게 했는데 그것이 본토에 번식 집단을 다시 들여오고자 했던 노력이 성공적이었음을 보여주기 때문이다.

B   이 작은 파충류는 등에 세모 모양의 피부주름 벗이 있으며 약 75센티미터까지 자랄 수 있다. 이들은 2억년 전에 번성했던 훼두목 중 유일하게 살아있는 종이다. 이는 거대한 포식자들이 없는 고립된 군도에 거주한 것이 원인일 수 있다. 이런 군도들은 조분석을 만들어내는 많은 바닷새 개체군들이 있는데, 이것은 큰도마뱀이 먹는 기생충들을 끌어들인다. [15]이 두 가지 요인 모두가 그들이 수억 년 동안 번성하도록 했다.

C   안타깝게도, [16]인간 활동은 큰도마뱀 개체 수에 크게 영향을 끼쳤다. 이는 인간이 섬에 도달했을 때 큰도마뱀의 알을 먹어치웠던 토종이 아닌 동물들, 이를테면 쥐 같은 것들이 유입되었기 때문이다. 이는 낮은 번식률로 인해 개체군을 완전히 파괴했다. 약 25퍼센트의 큰도마뱀들이 이 쥐들로 인해 사망한 것으로 추정된다.

D   놀랍게도, [17]기후 변화 또한 큰도마뱀의 개체 수에 큰 영향을 미친다. 큰도마뱀의 성별은, 다른 일부 파충류들의 성별과 같이, 둥지 온도에 영향을 받는다. 둥지의 온도가 섭씨 21도 이하일 때, 부화한 새끼는 암컷일 것이지만 단 1도의 온도 상승만으로도 수컷이 태어난다. 상승하는 기온은 현재 새로 부화하는 새끼들이 암컷일 가능성을 낮추고 있다. 이 때문에, 연구원들은 이 고대의 종을 구할 혁신적인 보호 방법을 찾아내야 한다.

14   해설   단락 A의 중심 문장 'They found the remains of eggs from the tuatara on New Zealand's South Island. This was important because tuatara had not reproduced ~ in over a century.'에서 연구진이 뉴질랜드의 남섬에서 큰도마뱀의 알의 잔해를 발견했으며 큰도마뱀은 100년이 넘도록 번식하지 않았기 때문에 이는 매우 중요했다고 하였으므로, 보기 **iii** Evidence of the reproduction of a species가 정답이다. 'remains of eggs'가 'Evidence of the reproduction'으로 paraphrasing되었다.

15   해설   단락 B의 중심 문장 'Both of these factors allowed them to flourish for hundreds of millions of years.'에서 이 두 가지 요인 모두가 큰도마뱀들이 수억 년 동안 번성하도록 했다고 하였으므로, 보기 **v** Two keys that have led to the tuatara's survival이 정답이다. 'Both of these factors'가 'Two keys'로 paraphrasing되었다.

16 해설 단락 C의 중심 문장 'human activity greatly affected the tuatara populations'에서 인간 활동은 큰도마뱀 개체 수에 크게 영향을 끼쳤다고 하였으므로, 보기 **iv** The consequences of human intervention이 정답이다. 'human activity'가 'human intervention'으로 paraphrasing되었다.

17 해설 단락 D의 중심 문장 'climate change also has a strong influence on the numbers of the tuatara'에서 기후 변화 또한 큰도마뱀의 개체 수에 큰 영향을 미친다고 하였으므로, 보기 **ii** The impact of climate change on the tuatara가 정답이다. 'a strong influence on the numbers of tuatara'가 'impact ~ on the tuatara'로 paraphrasing되었다.

7

제목 리스트

i   외상 후 스트레스 장애 환자들을 위한 다양한 치료 유형
ii   외상 후 스트레스 장애의 몇 가지 증상들
iii   외상 후 스트레스 장애를 발견하는 것의 어려움
iv   외상 후 스트레스 장애라는 용어의 의미와 기원
v   가족에게 미치는 영향
vi   명상이 외상 후 스트레스 장애에 도움이 되는 이유
vii   외상 후 스트레스 장애로 이어지는 정신적 외상의 원인

---

18 단락 A

19 단락 B

20 단락 C

21 단락 D

외상 후 스트레스 장애

A   외상 후 스트레스 장애는 참전 용사들에게서 처음으로 관찰되었던 임상 정신 질환이다. 이 질환은 생명을 위협하거나, 심각한 부상의 원인이거나, 혹은 영향을 받은 사람이 극심한 두려움, 무력함 또는 공포로 반응한 무언가인 정신적 외상으로부터 발생한다. 1970년대에, 베트남 전쟁의 여파로, 복귀한 많은 미국 군인들에게서 한 가지 행동 패턴이 관측될 수 있었다. 그들은 감정적으로 냉담하고, 짜증을 잘 내고, 잠을 자는 데 어려움을 겪었으며 쉽게 분노하는 경향이 있었다. 힘들어하는 참전 용사들을 변호하던 베트남 전쟁 반대 운동가들은 그들의 여러 가지 심각한 심리적 증상을 설명하기 위해 '월남전 후 증후군'이라는 용어를 만들었다.

B   외상 후 스트레스 장애를 야기하는 정신적 외상의 종류는 거의 언제나 예측되지 않으며, 관련된 사람에게 정신적 외상을 초래한 사건을 중단시킬 수 없다는 무력함을 느끼도록 만든다. 그러한 정신적 외상을 야기하는 경향이 있는 상황들은 다양하다. 사고, 심각한 범죄, 전투 경험, 그리고 사랑하는 사람의 갑작스러운 죽음은 모두 외상 후 스트레스 장애로 이어질 수 있다. 하지만, 정신적 외상을 겪는 모든 사람들에게 외상 후 스트레스 장애가 발생하지는 않으며, 연구원들은 여전히 왜 어떤 사람들은 이 질환에 더욱 쉽게 영향을 받는지 알아내기 위해 노력하고 있다.

C   외상 후 스트레스 장애의 증상은 정신적 외상을 초래한 사건에 대한 반복되는 기억이나 악몽, 주변 세상으로부터의 분리, 정신적 외상과 관련된 모든 것으로부터의 회피 그리고 더 커진 불안감 또는 '과다각성'을 포함할 수 있다. 외상 후 스트레스 장애를 겪고 있는 사람들은 그들이 당면한 환경에 아무런 위협의 조짐이 없을 때에도 끊임없이 경계한다. 이 고조된 상태의 불안과 과민성은 분노 표출이나 난폭한 공격성의 경향이 있는 것, 집중하는 데 어려움을 느끼는 것, 그리고 잠을 자는 데 어려움을 겪는 것과 같은 다른 결과를 낳기도 한다.

D   일반적인 믿음과 반대로, 외상 후 스트레스 장애는 치료할 수 있는 질환이며, [21]외상 후 스트레스 장애를 겪는 사람들이 이용할 수 있는 다양한 치료법이 있다. 환자가 외상 후 스트레스 장애를 진단받으면, 그들은 거의 항상 항불안제나 항우울증 유형의 약을 지급받는데, 이는 주로 다른 형태의 치료와 함께 사용된다. 외상 후 스트레스 장애 환자를 위한 가장 효율적인 치료 모델은 노출 치료, 안구운동 민감 소실 및 재처리 요법(EMDR), 그리고 일지적 행동 치료(CBT)이다. 이름이 암시하듯이, 노출 치료는 그들을 둔감해

지도록 만들기 위해 안전한 환경에서 환자를 정신적 외상에 노출시키는 것을 포함한다. EMDR는 사람들이 정신적 외상의 기억을 처리할 수 있도록 돕기 위해 노출 치료와 안내를 받으며 눈을 움직이는 것을 결합한다. 한편, CBT는 정신적 외상의 기억을 더 효과적으로 다룰 수 있도록 돕는 이완 기법이나 명상 기법과 같은 기술을 환자들에게 가르친다. 이런 치료법들이 매우 효과적일 수 있긴 하지만, 많은 외상 후 스트레스 장애 환자들은 그들이 살아가는 동안 고통스러운 재발을 경험할 것이다. 그러므로 장기적인 보살핌과 지지가 가능하도록 보장하는 것이 다른 무엇보다도 중요하다.

18 **해설** 이 단락에는 중심 문장이 없으므로, 단락 전체를 읽고 중심 내용을 파악한다. 단락 A는 외상 후 스트레스 장애의 정의와 그 용어가 만들어진 배경에 대해 주로 언급하고 있다. 따라서 이를 '외상 후 스트레스 장애라는 용어의 의미와 기원'으로 요약한 보기 **iv** The meaning and origin of the term PTSD가 정답이다.

19 **해설** 이 단락에는 중심 문장이 없으므로, 단락 전체를 읽고 중심 내용을 파악한다. 단락 B는 외상 후 스트레스 장애를 유발하는 정신적 외상의 원인들에 대해 주로 언급하고 있다. 따라서 이를 '외상 후 스트레스 장애로 이어지는 정신적 외상의 원인'으로 요약한 **vii** Causes of trauma that can lead to PTSD가 정답이다.

20 **해설** 이 단락에는 중심 문장이 없으므로, 단락 전체를 읽고 중심 내용을 파악한다. 단락 C는 외상 후 스트레스 장애의 증상 및 환자들에게서 나타나는 행동에 대해 주로 언급하고 있다. 따라서 이를 '외상 후 스트레스 장애의 몇 가지 증상들'로 요약한 보기 **ii** Some symptoms of PTSD가 정답이다.

21 **해설** 단락 D의 중심 문장 'there is a range of treatments available to PTSD sufferers'에서 외상 후 스트레스 장애를 겪는 사람들이 이용할 수 있는 다양한 치료법이 있다고 한 뒤, 여러 가지 치료 유형들에 대해 언급하고 있으므로, 보기 **i** Various types of care for PTSD patients가 정답이다. 'a range of treatments'가 'Various types of care'로 paraphrasing 되었다.

8

제목 리스트

i 눈 화장이 연인의 마음을 끌 수 있다는 증거
ii 의식이 아닌 미용을 위한 눈 화장
iii 이집트 상형문자에 나타난 눈 화장
iv 악마를 쫓아내기 위한 그리스의 눈 화장 사용
v 마스카라의 발달
vi 미신과 눈 화장의 기원에 대한 그것의 연관성
vii 화장품을 위해 사용되는 색소 종류의 변화
viii 극장으로부터 주류 사회로 옮겨간 화장품

22 단락 A

23 단락 B

24 단락 C

25 단락 D

눈 화장의 민속적 뿌리

A '악마의 눈'은 세계 도처에서 많은 민속 전통의 요소이며, 그 의미의 정확한 본질은 각 문화마다 다르지만, 일반적으로 탐욕이나, 혹은 질투라는 죄를 상징한다고 여겨진다. 많은 전설에 따르면, 시기심이 강한 사람은 갈망을 가지고 그 또는 그녀를 바라봄으로써 의도치 않게 다른 사람을 해칠 수 있다. 고고학자들은 이런 미신이 보호법으로서의 눈 화장의 기원과 연결되어 있다고 믿는다. 예를 들어, 고대 이집트에서는, 악마의 눈에 대한 보호법은 눈에 검댕과 광물의 혼합물인 콜을 바르는 것을 수반했다. 전형적인 혼합물은 구리, 재, 납, 그리고 산화철에서 나오는 황갈색 색소인 황토의 몇 가지 조합을 포함했다.

B ²³고대 그리스에서는, 기원전 1세기에 눈 주변의 화장품 사용이 악마를 막기 위한 의례적 의식인 액막이 주술의 한 형태로서 독립적으로 발달했다. 남성과 여성 모두 얇은 팬에 기름을 태움으로써 만들어진 검은 색소인 유연으로 눈에 선을 그렸으며 미신적 행위로서 가끔 그들의 눈썹을 진하게 했다. 그리스의 고고학자들은 액막이 눈이 그려진 흑회식 음료 용기를 발견했는데, 그들은 이것이 독으로부터 용기를 사용하는 사람을 보호하기 위해 그려졌다고 믿는다. 그러므로, 위협에 대한 이런 종류의 방어적인 대응을 발달시킨 문명은 이집트인뿐만이 아니었다.

C ²⁴지중해에서 화장품의 사용은 매우 흔하여 초기에는 연극의 장치로서, 그리고 이후에는 패션으로서 사회의 다른 측면에서 자리잡았다. 예를 들어, 무대 위에서, 배우들은 특유의 인물을 상징하기 위해 가면을 사용했고, 이 가면들은 원하는 특징을 강조하기 위해 색이 칠해졌다. 이는 부분적으로, 많은 관중에게 얼굴이 잘 보일 수 있도록 해야 할 필요가 있었기 때문이었지만, 동시에, 실제 얼굴 모습에서 벗어나 환상의 느낌을 전달하기 위한 수단이었다. 결국 극장에서 얼굴에 직접 눈 화장을 하는 풍습은 특히 사교 모임에서 상류 사회의 몇몇 일원에 의해 그대로 되풀이되었다. 덧붙여, 색소의 종류와 화장품의 형태도 많아졌으며, 점차 화려한 물감, 반짝이, 광택이 연기자와 대중들 모두의 눈을 돋보이게 하기 시작했다.

D 현대에서는, ²⁵눈 화장을 하는 것이 전 세계적으로 많은 여성들에게 일상적인 일이 되었는데, 그들 중 대부분은 무언가를 기념하기 위해서라기보다는 아름다움을 강조하기 위해 눈 화장을 한다. 아이섀도나 마스카라와 같은 현대의 화장품들은 이제 거대한 세계 화장품 산업의 일부이며 세계적으로 일상적인 상황에서 눈을 강조하는 수단으로 사용된다. 많은 사회에서, 남자들의 눈 화장도 점점 더 보편화되고 있으며, 미신적인 이유보다는 미용을 위한 것이긴 하지만, 이는 고대의 남녀 공용이었던 눈 화장의 기원을 부활시키는 현상이다. 그러므로 눈 화장은 현대 사회에서 여느 때보다 인기 있으며, 사용에 있어서 계급과 성별 모두의 경계를 넘어서 확장하고 있다.

22 해설 이 단락에는 중심 문장이 없으므로, 단락 전체를 읽고 중심 내용을 파악한다. 단락 A는 '악마의 눈'과 관련된 미신과 그 미신이 어떻게 눈 화장의 기원과 관련되어 있는지에 대해 주로 언급하고 있다. 따라서 이를 '미신과 눈 화장의 기원에 대한 그것의 연관성'으로 요약한 보기 **vi** A superstition and its connection to the origins of eye makeup이 정답이다.

23 해설 단락 B의 중심 문장 'In Ancient Greece, the use of cosmetics around the eye developed independently in the first century B.C. as a form of apotropaic magic, a ritual observance that was intended to ward off evil.'에서 고대 그리스에서는 기원전 1세기에 눈 주변의 화장품 사용이 악마를 막기 위한 의례적 의식인 액막이 주술의 한 형태로서 독립적으로 발달했다고 하였으므로, 보기 **iv** The use of eye makeup in Greece to keep evil away가 정답이다. 'ward off evil'이 'keep evil away'로 paraphrasing되었다.

24 해설 단락 C의 중심 문장 'The use of cosmetics was so common ~ that they found their way into other facets of society, initially as a theatrical device, and later as fashion.'에서 화장품의 사용은 매우 흔하여 초기에는 연극의 장치로서 그리고 이후에는 패션으로서 사회의 다른 측면에서 자리잡았다고 한 뒤, 극장에서의 눈 화장 풍습과 눈 화장이 상류 사회를 거쳐 대중들에게로 옮겨간 과정에 대해 언급하고 있으므로, 보기 **viii** Cosmetics from the theatre to mainstream society가 정답이다.

25 해설 단락 D의 중심 문장 'applying eye makeup has become a mundane daily ritual across the globe for many women, most of whom wear it to highlight beauty, rather than for any celebratory reason'에서 눈 화장을 하는 것이 전 세계적으로 많은 여성들에게 일상적인 일이 되었는데, 그들 중 대부분은 무언가를 기념하기 위해서라기보다는 아름다움을 강조하기 위해 그것을 한다고 하였으므로, 보기 **ii** Eye makeup for beauty rather than celebration이 정답이다. 'to highlight beauty, rather than for any celebratory reason'이 'for beauty rather than celebration'으로 paraphrasing되었다.

9

제목 리스트

i   보편적인 투표권의 발달
ii 영국의 영향력으로부터 모습을 드러낸 미국
iii 지방 정부에 초점을 맞추는 것
iv 비민주적 선거 제도
v   대영제국의 종말
vi 영국 군주제의 발달
vii 미국 민주주의의 부패
viii 영국 민주주의의 왕실 기원

26 단락 A

27 단락 B

28 단락 C

29 단락 D

영국과 미국의 민주주의

A 유럽인들이 처음으로 대륙에 도착한 이후 다양한 민족적 배경을 가진 수많은 사람들이 북아메리카로 이주했다. 하지만, 식민지 시대에는, 영국인들의 미국으로의 이민이 압도적이었고 그들 고국의 정치적 그리고 법적 가치를 가지고 왔다. 식민지가 발전하고 미국이 독립을 위한 투쟁을 시작하면서, 새로운 형태의 민주주의를 도입하려는 미국 헌법 제정자들의 바람뿐 아니라 국토의 지형과 사회 구조 때문에 차이점들이 드러났다. 이 차이점들은 미국 민주주의가 기존의 식민지 시대 통치자들로부터 어떻게 갈라져서 발전했는지를 밝힐 것이었다. 미국의 독특한 대의 제도 체계는 부분적으로는 영국의 방식에서 영감을 받았지만, 좀 더 지역에 중점을 두기 위해 귀족과 왕족의 기원은 소거되었다.

B ²⁷영국의 대의 정치 형태는 중세의 영국 왕들이 '백성들의 소원'과 관련하여 소수의 믿을 만한 사람들에게서 조언을 얻었던 관습에서 기원했다. 영국 군주들은 사람들로부터 지지를 얻고, 결과적으로, 복종을 얻는 것에 있어 자문의 역할을 알고 있었다. 그 후에 발전된 의회 제도는 상원과 하원, 즉 각각 귀족 의회와 평민 의회로 구성되었다. 귀족 의회는 성직자들과 귀족을 위한 세습 조직으로서 설립되었고, 평민 의회는 자치구라고 불리는 행정 구역들에서 선출된 의원들로 구성되었다.

C ²⁸영국의 의회 제도가 각 계층의 이해를 대표한다고 주장하는 서로 다른 두 개의 분리된 의회를 가지고 있었음에도 불구하고, 선거는 민주적인 것과는 거리가 멀었다. 총선거는 인구의 극히 적은 일부로 구성된 유권자 집단을 야기한 체계인 엄격한 선거구에 기반을 두었다. 결과적으로, 인구가 흩어져 없어진 정치적으로 영향력이 있는 자치구들은 인구가 많은 도시와 같은 숫자인 두 명의 의원을 선출할 수 있었다. 이런 불균형적인 대의권을 가진 선거구 중 일부는 유권자가 10명도 되지 않았다. 관련된 문제 한 가지는 이런 지구들이 한 명의 부유한 귀족에 의해 효과적으로 통제될 수 있다는 사실이었다. 뇌물 수수가 종종 만연했고, 희망에 찬 의원들은 뇌물을 주거나 표를 위해 지지자들에게 공약을 제의하고, 혹은 간단히 그 자치구를 구매해버리기도 했다. 이런 관행들은 민주주의라기보다는 이미 내정된 합의와 유사한 투표 절차를 야기했다.

D 대서양 건너편에서는 상황이 매우 달랐다. ²⁹식민지에서 입법 의회가 생긴 방식은 사회 계층의 영향에 의해서라기보다는, 지역 및 현지 사회 공동체의 특수한 요구에 의해 좌우되었다. 식민지 헌장은 대의 정치를 허가하기는 했지만, 요구하지는 않았기 때문에, 개별 식민지 의회는 상대적 이질성이라는 환경 아래 발달했다. 따라서 입법 기관들은 나라 전체의 관심사를 다루기 위해서가 아니라, 개별 집단의 관심사를 다루기 위해 발생했는데, 이는 어떤 면에서 우리가 오늘날 알고 있는 미국의 민주주의의 기초를 닦은 다수와 다양성을 강조했다.

> **26** **해설** 이 단락에는 중심 문장이 없으므로, 단락 전체를 읽고 중심 내용을 파악한다. 단락 A는 초기에 영국의 가치를 가지고 왔던 미국에서 어떻게 영국과는 다른 형태의 민주주의가 발전하게 되었는지에 대해 주로 언급하고 있다. 따라서 이를 '영국의 영향력으로부터 모습을 드러낸 미국'으로 요약한 보기 **ii** America emerging from Britain's influence가 정답이다.

27 해설 단락 B의 중심 문장 'Britain's model of representative government had its origins in the practice of medieval English kings, who enlisted the advice of a small group of confidants'에서 영국의 대의 정치 형태는 중세의 영국 왕들이 소수의 믿을 만한 사람들에게서 조언을 얻었던 관습에서 기원했다고 하였으므로, 보기 **viii** The royal roots of British democracy가 정답이다. 'origins in the practice of medieval English kings'가 'royal roots'로 paraphrasing되었다.

28 해설 단락 C의 중심 문장 'Even though the British parliamentary system had two separate houses ~, elections were far from democratic.'에서 영국의 의회 제도가 서로 다른 두 개의 분리된 의회를 가지고 있었음에도 불구하고 선거는 민주적인 것과는 거리가 멀었다고 한 뒤, 선거 제도가 어떻게 비민주적으로 운영되었는지에 대해 언급하고 있으므로, 보기 **iv** An undemocratic electoral system이 정답이다. 'far from democratic'이 'undemocratic'으로 paraphrasing되었다.

29 해설 단락 D의 중심 문장 'the manner in which the legislative assemblies arose in the colonies was not governed by the influence of a social hierarchy, but rather, the particular needs of regional and local communities.'에서 식민지에서 입법 의회가 생긴 방식은 사회 계층의 영향에 의해서라기보다는 지역 및 현지 사회 공동체의 특수한 요구에 의해 좌우되었다고 한 뒤, 입법 기관들이 개별 집단의 관심사를 다루기 위해 발생했다는 내용에 대해 언급하고 있으므로, 보기 **iii** Focusing on regional government가 정답이다.

10

	제목 리스트
i	기본 소득제를 시행하는 국가들
ii	기술이 어떻게 문화를 변화시켰는지
iii	디지털 통신의 혁명
iv	기계화의 기원
v	디지털 경제를 위해 필요한 기술
vi	실업 완화의 전망
vii	디지털화의 장단점
viii	자동화의 악영향
ix	컴퓨터화에 의한 무역의 변화

30 단락 A

31 단락 B

32 단락 C

33 단락 D

34 단락 E

기술과 노동 인구

A ³⁰산업, 서비스 분야 그리고 전통적인 사무직에서 업무 현장의 기술적 변화는 점점 더 많은 직무가 자동화됨에 따라 전 세계의 고용에 매우 부정적인 영향을 끼칠 조짐을 보이고 있다. 자동화는 불가피할 뿐만 아니라, 이미 많은 산업에서 일어나고 있으며, 세계의 정치인들과 경제학자들은 그 부정적인 영향을 완화하는 것이 가능하긴 할 것인지에 대해 고려하고 있는데, 그 중 가장 절박한 것은 대규모 실업의 가능성이다. 로봇이 사람들의 직업을 차지하는 것은 한때 공상 과학 소설의 주제였지만, 많은 사람들에게 이는 다음 10년 안에 현실이 될 것이다.

B ³¹기계화로의 이러한 이동은 디지털 시대의 전조인 산업 혁명으로 거슬러 올라갈 수 있는데, 이는 현재 일상 생활의 전 영역으로 확장된 기술과 인류의 공생 관계를 시작했다. 산업 혁명은 수공업의 기계 기반 과정으로의 대체를 인도했다. 전반적으로, 이 혁신들은 산업화된 국가들의 경제에 긍정적인 영향을 끼쳤는데, 이 국가들은 전례 없는 기간 동안 지속적인 성장을 경험했다. 하지만, 20세기 중반에 대량 생산 기술로의 광범위한 변화는 특별한 기술이 필요하지 않은 공장 일자리들이 더 이상 쓸모없도록 했는데, 이는

오늘날까지 이어지는 추세를 시작되게 했다.

C 1970년대에는, 개인 컴퓨터의 등장이 '디지털 시대'의 시작을 알렸으며, 선진국에서는 컴퓨터화에 기반을 둔 첨단 기술의 변화가 일어났다. 제조업뿐만 아니라, 서비스와 커뮤니케이션 분야도 전보다 훨씬 더 효율적이고 편리해졌다. 많은 사람들이 이러한 전례 없는 편의를 누리는 동안, 디지털화는 또한 많은 서비스 분야의 일자리를 사라지게 했다. 타자수, 전화 교환원, 그리고 생산 라인 일자리들은 대체로 사라졌으며, 한때 중산층의 영역이었던 기술을 요구하는 많은 일자리들 또한 이제는 자동화에 의해 위협받고 있다.

D 이것은 다음 십 년 동안 극적으로 증가할 것으로 보이는 동향이다. [33]현대의 취직 능력은 프로그래밍에 관한 것이든 다른 컴퓨터 관련 역량에 관한 것이든, 기술 역량에 매우 의존할 것이다. 많은 저명한 기술 관련 권위자들은 이미 컴퓨터 코드를 만드는 것이나 알고리즘을 만들어내는 것을 배움으로써 사람들이 '새로운 기술을 배워야' 한다는 것을 권장하기 위해 나섰고, 젊은 층에게 그런 기술을 가르치는 것은 이미 매우 강조되고 있다. 그러나, 특히 컴퓨터가 스스로 코딩 작업을 할 수 있기 때문에, 자동화로 인해 사라질 엄청난 양의 일자리를 대체할 충분한 코딩 직업이 있을지는 지켜봐야 한다.

E 대규모 실업을 완화하는 방법으로 제안된 한 가지 해결책은 보편적 기본 소득을 도입하는 것인데, 이는 국가의 모든 시민이 매달 무조건적으로 돈을 받는 것이다. 이 급진적인 방안은 경제학자들 사이에서 많은 지지를 얻었지만, 그런 극단적인 조치를 정치인들이 실행할 의향이 있는지는 의심스럽다. 특히 낮아진 취업률로 인해 세입이 감소할 것이기 때문에, 그러한 지불금의 자금을 어떻게 댈 것인지에 대한 문제는 복잡한 일이다. 그러나, 자동화로 인해 점점 더 많은 사람들이 실직 상태가 되고 있기 때문에, 전 세계의 정부들은 행동을 취할 수밖에 없을 것이다.

30 **해설** 단락 A의 중심 문장 'The technological transformation of the workplace ~ threatens to have a largely negative impact on global employment as more and more jobs are automated.'에서 업무 현장의 기술적 변화는 점점 더 많은 직무가 자동화됨에 따라 전 세계의 고용에 매우 부정적인 영향을 끼칠 조짐을 보이고 있다고 하였으므로, 보기 **viii** The damaging impact of automation이 정답이다. 'largely negative impact'가 'damaging impact'로 paraphrasing 되었다.

31 **해설** 단락 B의 중심 문장 'This shift towards mechanisation can be traced back to the Industrial Revolution'에서 기계화로의 이러한 이동은 디지털 시대의 전조인 산업 혁명으로 거슬러 올라갈 수 있다고 한 뒤, 산업 혁명에 의한 기계 기반 과정으로의 이동에 대해 언급하고 있으므로, 보기 **iv** The origins of mechanisation이 정답이다.

32 **해설** 이 단락에는 중심 문장이 없으므로, 단락 전체를 읽고 중심 내용을 파악한다. 단락 C는 디지털화에 따른 효율성과 편의라는 장점과 일자리 상실이라는 단점에 대해 주로 언급하고 있다. 따라서 이를 '디지털화의 장단점'으로 요약한 보기 **vii** Pros and cons of digitisation이 정답이다.

33 **해설** 단락 D의 중심 문장 'Employability in the modern age will be very much contingent on technical ability'에서 현대의 취직 능력은 기술 역량에 매우 의존할 것이라고 한 뒤, 컴퓨터 코드를 만드는 것이나 알고리즘을 만들어내는 것과 같은 새로운 기술을 배우는 것의 필요성에 대해 언급하고 있으므로, 보기 **v** Necessary skills for the digital economy가 정답이다.

34 **해설** 이 단락에는 중심 문장이 없으므로, 단락 전체를 읽고 중심 내용을 파악한다. 단락 E는 대규모 실업을 완화하기 위한 해결책과 그 해결책의 실행 전망에 대해 주로 언급하고 있다. 따라서 이를 '실업 완화의 전망'으로 요약한 보기 **vi** The prospects for alleviating unemployment가 정답이다.

정답·해석·해설

HACKERS **IELTS** READING

1	v	2	ii	3	viii	4	vii	5	iv
6	i	7	True	8	False	9	True	10	True
11	Not given	12	False	13	Not given				

[1-6]

제목 리스트

i 산림 붕괴와 가능한 해결책에 대한 연구

ii 세계 특정 지역의 산림 파괴

iii 토지 이용 형태의 역사와 그것이 산림에 끼치는 영향

iv 산림 붕괴의 토종 동물 몰살에 대한 연구

v 우주에서 본 산림 파괴의 규모

vi 산림 파괴가 어떻게 시작되었는가에 대한 한가지 설명

vii 생태계 전반에 대한 산림 붕괴의 영향

viii 무손상 산림의 소실과 산림 파괴 문제를 다룰 필요성

---

1 단락 A

2 단락 B

3 단락 C

4 단락 D

5 단락 E

6 단락 F

산림 붕괴: 커져가는 우려
숲이 붕괴되면, 지역 생태계에 대한 결과는 대개 심각하다

A 산림 파괴는 최근 몇 년 간 증가하는 비율로 발생해왔으며, 이런 경향은 생태계에 대한 잠재적으로 치명적인 영향 때문에 생태학자들에게 걱정스러운 일이다. 산림 파괴의 전체 규모는 원격 탐사 과학자인 Matthew Hansen이 이끄는 팀에 의해 시행된 연구로 인해 분명해졌는데, 그는 미국 지질연구소에 의해 생성된 60만 장 이상의 지구 위성 사진을 검토했다. 팀은 [7]13년의 기간 동안 세계적으로 약 2백 3십만 제곱킬로미터에 해당하는 땅의 산림이 파괴되었다고 추산했다. 연구원들은 나무가 어디에서 자라고 사라지고 있는지를 분명하게 보여주는 세계 최초의 고해상도 지도를 제작하기도 했으며, 이 지도는 몇 가지 명백한 패턴을 보여주었다.

B 예를 들어, 정확한 위치가 주기적으로 변하긴 했지만, 자료는 대부분의 산림 파괴가 아열대 지역과 열대 지역에서 일어났음을 입증했다. 최근에 전 세계의 모든 습윤 열대 우림 상실의 거의 절반이 브라질에서만 나타났다고 보고되었다. 놀랍게도, [8]아마존 숲의 막대한 90퍼센트가 농작물, 방목지, 그리고 도시 개발을 위해 개간되었다. 하지만 규제와 환경 운동가들의 활동에 의해 최근 수년 간 브라질의 삼림 파괴율은 줄어들었고, 인도네시아가 이제 가장 높은 산림 파괴율을 가진 국가로 브라질을 넘어섰다. 자료는 [9]나무가 비탈 지대에서보다 저지대의 지역에서 더 급격히 사라지고 있다는 것도 보여주었는데, 이는 이 지역들이 더 접근하기 쉽고 벌목과 개발에 더 적합하기 때문이다. 게다가, 연구는 인구가 거의 없는 지역에서만 연구원들이 거의 훼손되지 않은 숲의 지속적인 확산을 발견한다는 것을 알아냈다.

C 항속림이나 무손상 산림은 적어도 500제곱킬로미터 크기의, 인간 활동이 아주 조금 일어나거나 아예 없는 손상되지 않은 넓은 산림 생태로 정의된다. 이런 생태계는 다양한 종류의 동물과 식물 종을 부양할 수 있다. 그것은 또한 탄소를 저장하는 중요한 역할을 하기도 하는데, 이는 지구 온난화를 억제하는 데 도움이 되며, 물 순환을 조절하는 것도 돕는다. 오늘날, [10]지구에 존재하는 숲

의 23.5퍼센트만이 손상되지 않은 상태인데, 이는 총 토지의 8.8퍼센트일 뿐이다. 최근에, 단지 10년 동안에 지구의 무손상 산림은 7퍼센트 이상 줄어들었고, 반면 이 숲들 중 오직 12퍼센트만이 보호되었다고 추산되었다. 게다가, 가장 최근의 상실률은 10년 전 상실률의 3배였다. [3]이러한 무손상 산림들의 빠른 소실은 산림 파괴 문제에 정면으로 맞서야 할 심각한 필요성을 입증한다.

D 하지만 인간 활동이 집중된 지역에서는, 대부분의 숲은 단절로 특징지어진다. 이는 나무가 다른 목적을 위해 벌목될 때 고립된 부분, 혹은 파편만이 남기 때문이다. [4]이러한 산림 벌채의 결과는 산림 붕괴로 알려져 있으며, 이는 전체 생태계의 지속가능성에 극적으로 충격을 줄 수 있는 영향을 미친다. [11]대부분의 나무가 베어지고 나면, 이것은 초원과 같이 전혀 다른 환경으로 둘러싸인 산림지대의 고립된 부분만을 남긴다. 나무들의 부재로 인해, 땅은 강한 바람과 폭풍우에 노출되게 된다. [12]햇빛에 그대로 노출되면서, 이 지역은 온도 상승을 경험한다. 이런 새로운 환경은 산림지대의 초본 식물에게 치명적인데, 이 식물들은 이러한 가혹한 환경에서 살아갈 수 없다. 산림 조류는 알을 품기에 적절한 서식지를 잃게 되며, 밀림에 의존하는 포식 동물에게는 먹이를 사냥할 때 더 이상 그들의 몸을 숨겨줄 곳이 없다. 이 동물들은 적절한 서식지를 찾아 떠나야 하며 그렇지 않으면 죽게 될 것이다. 광활했던 숲은 빽빽한 숲의 윗부분과 숲의 중심부의 관목에 의존했던 종들에게 도움이 되지 않는 잡동사니에 불과하게 된다.

E 동물에게 미치는 이 부정적인 영향은 수력 발전 저수지가 건설된 태국의 토착종을 관찰하고 있던 연구원들에 의해 목격되었다. 샌디에이고에 있는 캘리포니아 대학의 과학자들은 댐 건설이 국립 공원을 침수시켜 새로 생긴 호수에 숲으로 된 섬 약 90곳을 남긴 이후인 1990년에, 생쥐, 쥐, 그리고 나무 두더지를 포함한 12종의 작은 토착 포유류들을 연구하기 시작했다. 25년 만에, 거의 모든 동물들이 사라졌는데, 이는 연구원들이 예상했던 것보다 2배에서 3배 더 빨랐다. 대학원생인 Luke Wilson은 "그것은 생태학적 대전쟁 같았다."고 말했다. 분열된 숲은 그야말로 동물들을 부양하기 위한 자원이 부족했다. 그러므로 붕괴된 숲은 토종 생물의 다양성에 급격한 감소를 야기한다고 볼 수 있다.

F 현재, 산림 붕괴에 대한 연구는 존재하는 숲의 패턴들과, 이 패턴들이 어떻게 변해왔는지, 그리고 이 패턴들이 산림 생태계의 생물의 다양성에 어떤 영향을 미치는지에 중점을 두고 있다. 하지만, 일부 전문가들은 분열을 야기하는 요인들의 분석과 어떻게 인간 활동이 산업과 자연을 이롭게 하도록 변할 수 있을지에 대한 재평가를 제안한다. [13]베넹에 있는 티크 재배지의 분석에 기반을 둔 한 가지 제안은, 고립된 자연 산림 사이의 정연한 회랑 지대에 상업적으로 가치 있는 나무를 심는 것이다. 이는 목재 생산을 제공하고 붕괴된 산림 환경을 연결하도록 돕는 생태학적 기능을 수행할 것이다.

어휘 fragmentation n. 붕괴, 분열 deforestation n. 산림 파괴(벌채) devastating adj. 치명적인, 엄청난 remote sensing phr. 원격 탐사 high-resolution adj. 고해상도의 whopping adj. 막대한 grazing n. 방목지 overtake v. 넘어서다, 능가하다 lowland adj. 저지대의 terrain n. 지대, 지형 scant adj. 거의 없는 intact adj. 무손상의, 온전한 dire adj. 심각한 repercussion n. 영향 windswept adj. 강한 바람에 노출되어 있는 elements n. 폭풍우, 악천후 herbaceous adj. 초본의 predatory adj. 포식의 prey n. 먹이 perish v. 죽다, 사라지다 patchwork n. 잡동사니, 긁어 모은 것 conducive adj. 도움이 되는 undergrowth n. 관목 tree shrew phr. 나무 두더지 Armageddon n. (지구 종말을 초래할 듯한) 대전쟁, 아마겟돈 biodiversity n. (생물의) 다양성 teak n. 티크(특히 가구의 재료로 많이 쓰이는 단단한 재목)

1 해설 이 단락에는 중심 문장이 없으므로, 단락 전체를 읽고 중심 내용을 파악한다. 단락 A는 지구 위성 사진을 분석함으로써 원격 탐사 과학 팀이 확인한 산림 파괴의 규모에 대해 주로 언급하고 있다. 따라서 이를 '우주에서 본 산림 파괴의 규모'로 요약한 보기 **v The scale of deforestation seen from space**가 정답이다.

2 해설 이 단락에는 중심 문장이 없으므로, 단락 전체를 읽고 중심 내용을 파악한다. 단락 B는 산림 파괴가 중점적으로 일어나고 있는 브라질과 인도네시아의 상황에 대해 주로 언급하고 있다. 따라서 이를 '세계 특정 지역의 산림 파괴'로 요약한 보기 **ii Deforestation in certain areas of the world**가 정답이다.

3 해설 단락 C의 중심 문장 'The rapid vanishing of these intact forests demonstrates the dire necessity of confronting the issue of deforestation.'에서 이러한 무손상 산림들의 빠른 소실은 산림 파괴 문제에 정면으로 맞서야 할 심각한 필요성을 입증한다고 하였으므로, 보기 **viii Loss of intact forests and the need to address deforestation**이 정답이다. 'necessity of confronting the issue of deforestation'이 'need to address deforestation'으로 paraphrasing되었다.

4 해설 단락 D의 중심 문장 'This consequence of deforestation is known as forest fragmentation, and it has repercussions that can dramatically impact the sustainability of the whole ecosystems.'에서 이러한 산림 벌채의 결과는 산림 붕괴로 알려져 있으며 이는 전체 생태계의 지속가능성에 극적으로 충격을 줄 수 있는 영향을 미친다고 하였으므로, 보기 **vii Forest fragmentation's impact on entire ecosystems**가 정답이다. 'repercussions that can dramatically

impact the sustainability of the whole ecosystems'가 'impact on entire ecosystems'로 paraphrasing되었다.

5 해설 이 단락에는 중심 문장이 없으므로, 단락 전체를 읽고 중심 내용을 파악한다. 단락 E는 태국에서 수력 발전 저수지가 건설된 이후 토착 포유류들을 거의 사라지게 만들었던 분열된 숲의 부정적 영향에 대한 연구를 주로 언급하고 있다. 따라서 이를 '산림 붕괴의 토종 동물 몰살에 대한 연구'로 요약한 보기 **iv** A study of forest fragmentation's destruction of native animals 가 정답이다.

6 해설 이 단락에는 중심 문장이 없으므로, 단락 전체를 읽고 중심 내용을 파악한다. 단락 F는 현재 산림 붕괴 연구의 동향과 인간 활동이 산업과 자연 모두를 이롭게 할 수 있는 해결책에 대해 주로 언급하고 있다. 따라서 이를 '산림 붕괴와 가능한 해결책에 대한 연구'로 요약한 **i** Research into forest fragmentation and possible solutions가 정답이다.

[7-13]

7 단 십 년이 넘는 기간 동안 2백만 제곱킬로미터 이상의 산림이 파괴되었다.

8 산림 파괴에도 불구하고 아마존에는 90퍼센트의 숲이 유지되었다.

9 구릉 지대보다 평지에서 더 빠르게 산림 파괴가 일어나고 있다.

10 지구 육지의 10퍼센트 미만이 무손상 산림으로 덮여있다.

11 산림 파괴는 숲의 야생 동물을 해치지만 초원의 종에게는 득이 된다.

12 초본 식물은 나무가 잘려 나간 뒤 더 많은 햇빛 속에서 번성한다.

13 최근에, 베넹은 산림 생태계를 보호하기 위해 규제를 시작했다.

7 해설 문제의 핵심어구(Over two million square kilometres of forest)와 관련된 지문 내용 중 'approximately 2.3 million km² of land was deforested worldwide during a 13-year period'에서 13년의 기간 동안 세계적으로 약 2백 3십만 제곱킬로미터에 해당하는 땅의 산림이 파괴되었다고 하였으므로, 주어진 문장은 지문의 내용과 일치함을 알 수 있다. 따라서 정답은 **True**이다. 'deforested'가 'forest was lost'로 paraphrasing되었다.

8 해설 문제의 핵심어구(The Amazon)와 관련된 지문 내용 중 'a whopping 90 per cent of the forest cover in the Amazon has been cleared for crops, grazing, and urban development'에서 아마존 숲의 막대한 90퍼센트가 농작물, 방목지, 그리고 도시 개발을 위해 개간되었다고 하였으므로, 주어진 문장은 지문의 내용과 일치하지 않음을 알 수 있다. 따라서 정답은 **False**이다.

9 해설 문제의 핵심어구(Flat land is experiencing more rapid deforestation)와 관련된 지문 내용 중 'trees are disappearing more rapidly in lowland areas than on sloped terrain'에서 나무가 비탈 지대에서보다 저지대의 지역에서 더 급격히 사라지고 있다고 하였으므로, 주어진 문장은 지문의 내용과 일치함을 알 수 있다. 따라서 정답은 **True**이다. 'lowland areas'가 'Flat land'로, 'sloped terrain'이 'areas with hills'로 paraphrasing되었다.

10 해설 문제의 핵심어구(intact forest)와 관련된 지문 내용 중 'only 23.5 per cent of existing forest on Earth is intact; this is a mere 8.8 per cent of total land area'에서 지구에 존재하는 숲의 23.5퍼센트만이 손상되지 않은 상태인데, 이는 총 토지의 8.8퍼센트일 뿐이라고 하였으므로, 주어진 문장은 지문의 내용과 일치함을 알 수 있다. 따라서 정답은 **True**이다. 'existing forest on Earth is intact'가 'intact forest'로 paraphrasing되었다.

11 해설 문제의 핵심어구(species fit for grassland)와 관련된 지문 내용 중 'When the majority of trees are cut down, this leaves isolated patches of wooded land bound by completely different habitats, such as grassland.'에서 대부분의 나무가 베어지고 나면 이것은 초원과 같이 전혀 다른 환경으로 둘러싸인 산림 지대의 고립된 부분만을 남긴다고는 하였지만, 주어진 문장의 내용은 확인할 수 없다. 따라서 정답은 **Not given**이다.

12 해설 문제의 핵심어구(Herbaceous plants do well)와 관련된 지문의 내용 'Laid bare to sunlight, these areas experience a rise in temperatures. These new conditions are devastating to herbaceous woodland plants'에서 햇빛에 그대로 노출되면서 이 지역은 온도 상승을 경험하며 이런 새로운 환경은 산림지대의 초본 식물에게 치명적인데, 이 식물들은 이러한 가혹한 환경에서 살아갈 수 없다고 하였으므로, 주어진 문장은 지문의 내용과 일치하지 않음을 알 수 있다. 따라서 정답은 **False**이다.

13 해설 문제의 핵심어구(Benin)와 관련된 지문 내용 중 'One proposal, based on analysis of teak plantations in Benin, is to plant commercially valuable trees in planned corridors between areas of isolated natural forest.'에서 베넹에 있는 티크 재배지의 분석에 기반을 둔 한 가지 제안은 고립된 자연 산림 사이의 정연한 회랑 지대에 상업적으로 가치 있는 나무를 심는 것이라고는 하였지만, 주어진 문장의 내용은 확인할 수 없다. 따라서 정답은 **Not given**이다.

* 각 문제에 대한 정답의 단서는 지문에 문제 번호와 함께 별도의 색으로 표시되어 있습니다.

EXAMPLE

p.258

유엔 인구 전망 보고서는 평균적인 전 세계의 기대수명이 70세에 도달했으며 몇몇 선진국에서는 80세 이상에 도달했다고 밝혔다. 사람들은 더 오래 살고 있을 뿐 아니라, 노년까지 더 나은 건강을 누리고 있다. 이것은 좋은 소식이기는 하지만, [1]고령 인구에게 실업이라는 새로운 문제를 가져왔다. 전통적으로, 사람들은 특정 나이에 은퇴했고 노동 인구로부터 완전히 떠났다. 그러나, 이제, 사람들은 증가한 수명으로 인해 더 길어진 은퇴 기간의 자금을 비축하기 위해 일을 계속해야 할지도 모른다. 불행히도, 이런 고령자들에게 직업을 찾는 일은 어려울 수 있다. 고용주들은 그들이 더 많은 훈련과 병가를 필요로 하거나, 그들이 덜 생산적일 것이라고 걱정할 수 있다.

HACKERS PRACTICE

p.260

1 quick disassembly	2 glossy (finish)	3 genetics
4 tide(s)	5 blink comparator	6 dwarf planet
7 balloon(s)	8 poacher(s)	9 tobacco
10 (divine) wisdom	11 upper echelon(s)	12 length
13 algae	14 gills	15 solar
16 unhealthy	17 reconnaissance	18 submersible(s)
19 tectonic plates	20 chimney(s)	21 (age of) 65
22 (severe) anxiety	23 muscle deterioration	24 muscle memory
25 linguistic (model)	26 autism	

1

벽에 물감을 바로 바르는 것을 포함하는 예술 활동인 벽화는, 최초의 그림 종류였다. 벽화는 분리될 수 없었지만, 이후에, 판넬에 그림을 그리는 기법이 개발되었다. 판넬화는 나중에 조립되었던 얇고 가느다란 나무 조각들 위에 그려졌다. 이러한 제작 과정은 또한 나중에 빠르게 해체하는 것을 가능하게 했다. [1]빠른 해체는 이 그림들을 휴대하기 매우 쉽게 만든 특징이었다. 14세기에, 화가들은 천으로 된 캔버스에 그림을 그리기 시작했는데, 이것은 가벼워서 작업하고 운반하기 쉬웠다. 캔버스의 표면은 나무보다 물감을 훨씬 잘 유지시켰고 휘거나 금이 가지 않는 경향이 있었다. 그러나, 짜여진 천은 르네상스 회기들이 좋아하지 않았던 방식으로 그림의 표면에 영향을 끼쳤다. [2]그들은 반들반들한 마감 칠 상태를 얻고자 했고, 그래서 사진의 질감과 유사하도록 그림의 질감을 매끄럽게 하기 위해 무엇이든 하고자 했다.

1 어떤 특징이 판넬화를 옮기기 쉽게 했는가?

> 해설 문제의 핵심어구(easy to move)와 관련된 지문 내용 중 'Quick disassembly was a feature which made these paintings highly portable.'에서 빠른 해체는 이 그림들을 휴대하기 매우 쉽게 만든 특징이었다고 하였으므로, **quick disassembly**가 정답이다. 'highly portable'이 'easy to move'로 paraphrasing되었다.

2 르네상스 화가들은 어떤 질감을 얻고자 했는가?

> 해설 문제의 핵심어구(Renaissance artists want)와 관련된 지문 내용 중 'They wanted to attain a glossy finish'에서 그들은 반들반들한 마감 칠 상태를 얻고자 했다고 하였으므로, **glossy (finish)**가 정답이다.

2

동물은 환경 주기에 규칙적으로 반응하는 체내 기제를 가지고 있다. 한 주기는 여러 다양한 기간에 따라 움직일 수 있지만, 그 중 가장 분명한 것은 달의 모습, 계절 패턴, 그리고 24시간 주기와 관련된 것들이다. 생체 시계라고 불리는 이 기제는 동물이 앞으로 다가올 환경적 사건들을 알아차리게 하고, 자는 시간, 짝짓기를 하는 시간, 그리고 먹이를 먹는 시간을 조절하는 기능을 한다. ³생물이 가지는 생체 시계의 종류는 일반적으로 외부 자극보다는 유전적 특징에 의존한다. ⁴게와 같은 생물들은 조수의 오르내림에 따라 선천적으로 행동을 조절한다. 한편, 날씨가 추워지면서 낮과 밤의 길이에 극적인 변화가 있는 세계의 지역들에서는, 대부분의 동물들이 계절 패턴의 영향을 받는다. 예를 들어, 불곰의 생체 시계는 겨울이 다가옴에 따라 날이 점점 짧아진다는 것을 지각할 것이고 동면 상태에 들어가기 전에 많은 양의 음식을 섭취함으로써 대응할 것이다.

3 무엇이 보통 동물들이 가지는 생체 시계의 종류를 결정하는가?

> 해설 문제의 핵심어구(determines the sort of biological clock)와 관련된 지문 내용 중 'The kind of biological clock an organism has generally depends on its genetics'에서 생물이 가지는 생체 시계의 종류는 일반적으로 유전적 특징에 의존한다고 하였으므로, **genetics**가 정답이다. 'generally depends on'이 'commonly determines'로 paraphrasing 되었다.

4 무엇이 높이에 따라 몇몇 해양 생물들이 다르게 행동하도록 하는가?

> 해설 문제의 핵심어구(according to its height)와 관련된 지문 내용 중 'Creatures such as crabs innately regulate their behaviours according to the rise and fall of the tides.'에서 게와 같은 생물들은 조수의 오르내림에 따라 선천적으로 행동을 조절한다고 하였으므로, **tide(s)**가 정답이다. 'regulate ~ behaviours'가 'act differently'로, 'according to the rise and fall'이 'according to its height'로 paraphrasing되었다.

3

1900년대 초반에, 천문학자들은 알려지지 않은 물체의 인력이 해왕성과 천왕성의 궤도에 영향을 주고 있다는 것을 알아차렸다. 그들은 그것이 무엇이든 간에 그 원인이었던 것을 'Planet X'라고 잠정적으로 명명했고 그것을 찾기 시작했다. 관련된 과학자들 중 한 명은 퍼시벌 로웰이었고, 끊임없는 계산과 관측을 통해, 결국 이 찾기 힘든 천체가 발견될 상공의 구역을 알아낸 사람이 그였다. 1916년에 그가 사망했을 때, 다른 천문학자들이 그의 작업을 계속했다. 그들 중 하나인, ⁵클라이드 톰보는, 체계적으로 며칠에 한 번씩 상공의 다양한 구역들의 사진을 찍었고 그런 다음 블링크 콤퍼레이터라는 기계를 사용해서 사진들을 분석했다. 이 기계는 한 이미지에서 다음 것으로 빠르게 교차함으로써 작동하는데, 이는 사용자들이 어떤 두 개의 사진 사이의 차이를 찾을 수 있게 해준다. 그는 이 기술이 상공에 있는 물체가 위치를 바꾸는지 볼 수 있게 해줄 것이라고 믿었다. 마침내, 1930년에, 그는 Planet X가 예측되었던 곳에서 움직이는 빛의 입자를 알아냈다. 뒤이은 몇 달 동안의 망원경 분석은 물체의 궤도를 발견했고 그 존재를 확인했다. ⁶Planet X는 나중에 명왕성으로 명명되었고, 왜소행성이라고 확인될 때까지 우리 태양계의 아홉 번째 행성으로 남아 있었다.

5 클라이드 톰보는 어떤 기기를 가지고 그의 사진들을 연구했는가?

> 해설 문제의 핵심어구(Clyde Tombaugh)와 관련된 지문 내용 중 'Clyde Tombaugh, systematically took photographs ~ and then analysed them using a machine called a blink comparator'에서 클라이드 톰보는 체계적으로 사진을 찍었고 그런 다음 블링크 콤퍼레이터라는 기계를 사용해서 사진들을 분석했다고 하였으므로, **blink comparator**가 정답이다. 'analysed them'이 'study ~ photos'로 paraphrasing되었다.

6 명왕성은 이후에 어떤 종류의 행성으로 확인되었는가?

4

가장 간단한 표현으로, 드론은 무인의, 원격으로 조종되는 항공기이다. [7]드론을 사용한다는 생각은 1850년대 이탈리아에 대한 오스트리아의 전쟁 중에 시작되었다. 이 분쟁 동안, 드론은 폭탄으로 가득 찬 풍선의 형태였다. 하지만 이제 그것들은 일반 대중들에게 이용이 가능하기 때문에, 사람들은 일상 생활의 일들을 용이하게 해줄 뿐 아니라 사회 전반을 개선하는 매우 획기적인 활용법을 발견하고 있다. 매우 효율적인 스마트폰의 구조를 갖추고 있기 때문에, 그것들은 영상을 포착하고, 사진을 찍고, 그리고 데이터를 무선으로 전송하기 위해 GPS 기능을 이용할 수 있다. 그것들의 비행할 수 있는 능력에 이러한 모든 특징을 더하는 것은 산불, 갑작스런 홍수, 그리고 교통의 흐름을 감시하고, 농업 생산을 최적화하며, 국경을 안전하게 유지하는 것을 가능하게 한다. 성능을 넓히기 위해 드론에 다른 기계를 갖추는 것도 가능하다. 예를 들어, 병원들은 약과 보급품을 접근하기 어려운 지역들로 수송하는 일이 맡겨진 드론에 성공적으로 화물 수송용 컨테이너를 부착했다. 한편, 몇몇 드론은 열 감지기를 갖추고 있다. 이런 유형의 드론의 사용은 무수히 많지만, 현재로서는 공원과 야생동물 관리 당국에 매우 유용하다는 것을 보여주고 있다. 심장 박동만큼 섬세한 생명의 징후를 알아챌 수 있기 때문에, [8]드론은 보호 구역에 들어간 밀렵꾼들을 찾아냄으로써 멸종 위기에 처한 종을 안전하게 보호하는 것을 돕는다.

매일같이 발전하는 기술과 더불어, 드론의 장래성은 무한해 보이지만, 좋은 일에만 쓰일 것이라고 예상하는 것은 낙관적이다. 그러므로 미국연방항공국(FAA)이 드론을 관리하는 새로운 법률을 엄중히 시행하는 것이 필수적이다. 이것은 인구 밀도가 높거나 보안인 구역에서의 사용 금지 규정과 구매 후 각 드론의 등록이 완료되어야 한다는 요건을 포함한다.

7 초기의 드론은 무엇과 유사했는가?

8 드론들은 동물을 보호하기 위해 무엇을 발견하는 것을 돕는가?

5

카카오 열매는 아즈텍 사람들에게 막대한 중요성을 지녔다. 오늘날 우리가 그것으로 만드는 초콜릿과는 다르게, 아즈텍 시대 동안에 카카오 열매는 대부분 고추나 바닐라와 결합되었고 향긋한 음료를 만드는 데 사용되었다. 그러나, 이것은 후식이 아니었다. 역사적 기록들은 [9]종종 연회 마지막에 마셨으며 담배와 함께 제공되었던 그 음료가, 엄청나게 취하게 만들 수 있다는 것에 주목해왔다. 이것은 몇몇 학자들이 그 음료가 와인과 혼합되었거나 술로 바꾸기 위해 내용물이 발효 작용을 거쳤다고 추측하도록 했다. 아마 그 음료를 용인될 수 있는 형태의 통화로 여겨지기에 충분히 가치 있도록 만들었던 것은 이 효과였을 것이다. 하지만 그것은 [10]아즈텍 사람들이 카카오 나무가 천국과 이승을 잇는 다리이며 카카오 열매를 먹는 것이 사람에게 신성한 지혜를 서서히 주입시킨다고 믿었던 것과 더 관련이 있었다. 이러한 이유로, [11]카카오 분말로 만든 음료는 흔히 신에게 드리는 의식의 제물로 포함되었고, 특별한 행사를 기념하는 데 사용되었으며, 주로 사회의 상류 계급 구성원에 한정되었다. 하지만 한 가지 문제가 있었다. 카카오 나무는 아즈텍 테노치티틀란의 궁전에서는 자라지 않았는데, 이곳의 기후는 너무 차갑고 건조했다. 아즈텍 사람들에게는 다행스럽게도, 그것은 정복한 나라들에서 얻을 수 있었다. 아즈텍 사람들의 통치 하에, 이 나라들은 조공이라고 불린, 상품과 노동의 형태로 세금을 내야 했다. 이 지역들에서 자원을 징수할 때가 되면, 카카오 열매는 확실히 최우선 순위였다.

9 아즈텍 문화에서 정찬의 마지막에 향긋한 음료와 함께 무엇이 종종 제공되었는가?

해설 문제의 핵심어구(at the end of a formal meal)와 관련된 지문 내용 중 'the beverage, often drunk at the end of a banquet and served with tobacco'에서 종종 연회 마지막에 마셨으며 담배와 함께 제공되었던 그 음료라고 하였으므로, **tobacco**가 정답이다. 'at the end of a banquet'이 'at the end of a formal meal'로 paraphrasing되었다.

10 아즈텍 사람들은 코코아를 먹음으로써 무엇이 얻어질 수 있다고 믿었는가?

해설 문제의 핵심어구(gained by eating cocoa)와 관련된 지문 내용 중 'the Aztecs believed that ~ consuming cocoa beans instilled one with divine wisdom'에서 아즈텍 사람들이 카카오 열매를 먹는 것이 사람에게 신성한 지혜를 서서히 주입시킨다고 믿었다고 하였으므로, **(divine) wisdom**이 정답이다. 'consuming cocoa beans'가 'eating cocoa'로 paraphrasing되었다.

11 아즈텍 사회의 어떤 집단이 코코아 음료와 관련되었는가?

해설 문제의 핵심어구(section of Aztec society ~ cocoa drinks)와 관련된 지문 내용 중 'drinks made of cocoa were ~ mostly limited to members of the upper echelons of society'에서 카카오 분말로 만든 음료는 주로 사회의 상류 계급 구성원에 한정되었다고 하였으므로, **upper echelon(s)**가 정답이다. 'were ~ limited to'가 'were ~ associated with'로 paraphrasing되었다.

6

이른 봄에, 개구리는 동면에서 깨어나 수생 번식지로 나아간다. 수컷이 먼저 도착하여 암컷에게 자신들의 존재를 알리기 위해 짝짓기 울음소리를 내기 시작하는데, [12]암컷은 울음소리의 길이에 근거하여 짝을 선택한다. 울음소리는 또한 자신들의 공간을 침해하는 것으로부터 잠재적인 경쟁자들을 막으려는 희망으로, 다른 수컷들에 대한 경고의 역할을 한다. 성공한 수컷은 암컷과 포접이라고 알려진 짝짓기를 하는데, 이것의 목표는 암컷이 얕고 흐르지 않는 물속에 알을 낳으면 수컷이 동시에 정자로 그 알을 수정시키는 것이다. 수천 개가 될 수 있는 이러한 알들은 물속에서 부푸는 두껍고, 영양분이 풍부한 젤리와 같은 물질로 싸여있다. 이때 부모는 보통 알을 떠나버리기 때문에, 이 물질은 연약한 배아를 위한 보호 수단으로서의 역할을 한다. 배아가 자라면서, 올챙이가 되고, 운이 좋다면, 그들은 부드러운 포장으로부터 모습을 드러낸다. 최대 95퍼센트에 이르는, 높은 비율의 개구리 알들은 포식이나 갑작스런 혹한 또는 가뭄과 같은 환경 피해로 인해 부화하는 데 실패한다. [13]생의 초기 동안, 올챙이들은 주로 조류로 이루어진 식사를 한다. 이 시기에 그들은 변태를 완료하기 위해 많은 양의 에너지가 필요하기 때문에 왕성하게 먹어야만 한다. 물고기처럼, 올챙이는 물속에서 숨을 쉴 수 있게 하는 아가미와 수영을 할 수 있게 하는 꼬리를 가지고 있다. 하지만, 몇 주 내에, [14]피부가 아가미 위로 자라기 시작하는데, 이것은 그 자리에 폐가 자라면서 결국 사라진다. 약 6주에서 9주 후에, 올챙이는 곤충을 먹기 시작하며 식물은 더 적게 먹는다. 이 시기에, 팔과 다리도 생기기 시작하며, 꼬리는 마침내 커지는 신체에 완전히 흡수되기 전에 점점 작아지게 된다. 그들은 이제 작은 성체와 유사하며 물을 떠날 수 있다. 먹이를 얼마나 입수할 수 있느냐에 따라, 개구리는 12주에서 16주의 나이 사이에 완전히 성장하고 짝짓기를 할 준비가 될 것이며, 모든 주기를 다시 한번 시작하게 될 것이다.

12 수컷 개구리 울음의 어떤 측면이 짝을 찾을 수 있을지를 결정하는가?

해설 문제의 핵심어구(male frog's call)와 관련된 지문 내용 중 'females, who select mates based on the length of their songs'에서 암컷은 울음소리의 길이에 근거하여 짝을 선택한다고 하였으므로, **length**가 정답이다. 'based on'이 'determines'로 paraphrasing되었다.

13 생애 초기에 올챙이에 의해 섭취되는 먹이의 주된 종류는 무엇인가?

해설 문제의 핵심어구(food eaten ~ in its early life)와 관련된 지문 내용 중 'During the early part of their lives, tadpoles have a diet that is made up primarily of algae.'에서 생의 초기 동안 올챙이들은 주로 조류로 이루어진 식사를 한다고

하였으므로, **algae**가 정답이다. 'diet that is made up primarily of'가 'main type of food eaten'으로 paraphrasing 되었다.

14 올챙이가 개구리가 될 때 폐는 무엇을 대체하는가?

> 해설 문제의 핵심어구(lungs replace)와 관련된 지문 내용 중 'skin starts to grow over their gills, which eventually disappear, with lungs developing in their place'에서 피부가 아가미 위로 자라기 시작하는데 이것은 그 자리에 폐가 자라면서 결국 사라진다고 하였으므로, **gills**가 정답이다. 'lungs developing in their place'가 'lungs replace'로 paraphrasing되었다.

7

GPS는 무엇인가?

GPS, 혹은 지구위치파악시스템은, 지구상의 거의 어떤 지역에서든 대상의 상세한 위치를 알아내거나 아주 정확한 시간 정보를 제공하는 데 사용되는 항법 및 추적 시스템이다. 미국방부에 의해 설계되어 통제되는 GPS는, 원래 군사적 사용을 목적으로 했으나, 오늘날에는 자동차 운행 시스템 등의 다양한 민간 기기에서도 흔히 사용되고 있다.

이것은 우주, 제어, 그리고 사용자의 세 부분으로 나뉜다. 우주 부분은 GPS 위성의 네트워크로 구성되어 있는데, GPS 위성은 하루에 두 번 정확히 같은 궤도로 지구 주위를 돌면서 신호 정보를 전송한다. [15]태양에너지로 움직이는 GPS 위성은, 일식에도 계속 작동하도록 하기 위한 예비 전지를 갖추고 있다. 각각의 위성에 달린 작은 추진 로켓은 위성이 계속 올바른 경로로 비행하게 한다.

통제 부분은 GPS 위성의 항로를 감시하고, 위성에 탑재된 원자 시계들의 시간을 일치시키며 위성에 의한 전송을 위해 자료를 수집하고 전송하는 것을 맡고 있는 세계 각지의 지상 기지들로 구성된다. 이 지상 관제소들은 그들이 정확한 GPS 자료를 전송하기에 충분히 정밀하다는 것을 확실하게 하기 위해 위성의 궤도를 측정하는 데 자동화된 절차를 이용한다. [16]위성의 궤도가 항로를 이탈하면, 지상 관제소는 그것을 '비정상'이라고 표시하는데, 이것은 다시 '이상 없음'이라고 표시될 시점인 궤도를 수정하는 시점까지는 그것이 사용될 수 없다는 것을 의미한다.

사용자 부분은 GPS 수신기들로 구성되는데, 이는 다수의 위성들로부터 얻은 거리 측정치를 이용해서 사용자의 정확한 위치를 파악하는 장치이다. GPS 수신기는 위도와 경도를 보여주는 2차원적 위치를 산출하고 움직임을 추적하기 위해 최소한 3개 위성으로부터의 신호를 따라가야 한다. 4대 이상의 위성이 있는 지역에서는, 수신기가 사용자의 3차원적 위치, 즉 위도, 경도, 그리고 고도를 파악할 수 있다. 사용자의 위치가 결정되면, GPS 장치는 속도, 방위, 그리고 이동거리 등의 다른 정보도 산출할 수 있다.

GPS가 오늘날 개인 항법을 위한 수단으로서 널리 알려져 있긴 하지만, GPS의 적용은 훨씬 더 광범위하다. 그것들은 국제 무역, 농업, 재난 구호, 구조 지질학, 로봇 공학, 그리고 그보다 더 많은 것을 포함한다. [17]세계의 군대들은 또한 항법과 정찰을 위해 GPS를 사용하지만, 그 기술은 미국에 의해 소유되고 관리되기 때문에, 1999년 인도와 파키스탄 간의 카르길 전쟁에서 발생했던 것처럼, 다른 나라들이 사용하는 것을 거부할 수 있다. 가장 일반적인 사용은 아마도 휴대 전화에서인데, 여기서 GPS는 지상 위치뿐만 아니라, 시계 동기화와 긴급 호출에도 사용된다.

15 GPS 위성들에 동력을 공급하는 에너지의 종류는 무엇인가?

> 해설 문제의 핵심어구(energy powers)와 관련된 지문 내용 중 'Powered by solar energy, they'에서 태양에너지로 움직이는 GPS 위성이라고 하였으므로, 'solar energy'가 답이 될 수 있다. 지시문에서 한 단어로만 답을 작성하라고 하였으므로, **solar**가 정답이다.

16 만약 위성들이 지구 주위의 잘못된 항로 위에 있다고 여겨진다면 무엇이라고 명명되는가?

> 해설 문제의 핵심어구(on an incorrect path)와 관련된 지문 내용 중 'If the orbit of a satellite veers off course, the ground stations mark it 'unhealthy''에서 위성의 궤도가 항로를 이탈하면 지상 관제소는 그것을 '비정상'이라고 표시한다고 하였으므로, **unhealthy**가 정답이다. 'the orbit of a satellite veers off course'가 'be on an incorrect path'로 paraphrasing되었다.

17 GPS는 항법과 더불어 군대에 어떤 능력을 제공하는가?

> 해설 문제의 핵심어구(GPS offer armies)와 관련된 지문 내용 중 'Militaries around the world also use GPS for navigation and reconnaissance'에서 세계의 군대들은 또한 항법과 정찰을 위해 GPS를 사용한다고 하였으므로, **reconnaissance**가 정답이다.

8

열수 분출공

1970년대 이전에, 과학자들은 해저의 혹독한 환경에서 어떤 생물체도 아마 살아남을 수 없었을 것이라고 추정했는데, 주된 이유는 식물이 광합성을 위해 필요로 하는 햇빛의 부족이었다. 해저를 연구하려는 진지한 시도는 19세기 후반에 시작되었으나, 연구자들은 여러 난제에 직면했는데, 주로 그들이 타고 이동했던 배가 그 깊이에서 극한의 압력을 견디는 장비를 갖추지 못했다는 사실이었다. 이러한 여행들은 몇몇 배가 일단 물에 잠기면 해수면으로 다시 돌아오지 못했기 때문에 매우 위험했다. 그러나, 1970년대에 심해 속 극한의 환경을 견디도록 설계된 운송 수단인 [18]잠수함의 도입과 함께 이 문제들에 대한 해결책이 생기게 되었다. 이 새로운 기술 덕분에 연구원들은 광대한 생태계를 발견했는데, 이 생태계의 존재는 바닷물이 지구의 핵 안에서 흐르는 마그마와 만나게 하는 열수 분출공 때문에 가능하다.

[19]열수 분출공은 세계의 많은 바다에 존재하고, 보통 지질 구조판 사이의 갈라진 틈에서 발견된다. 이 지질 구조판들이 멀리 떨어질 때, 마그마가 솟아오르고 차가워져 새로운 지각을 형성한다. 바다의 지각이 팽창하면서, 지각은 얇아지고 이 띠들에 큰 틈들이 생겨난다. 이 틈들은 바닷물이 지구 지각의 깊은 부분까지 관통할 수 있는 이상적인 조건을 만들었다.

물이 지각 속으로 깊이 들어가면 그것은 마그마와 만나 극한의 고온에 도달한다. 지각 내 압력이 커지면서, 바닷물은 따뜻해지고 그 후 대양저로 솟아오르는데, 도중에 지구의 지각 내에 있는 미네랄을 용해시킨다. 물이 분출구에서 밖으로 뿜어져 나오기 전에, 결국 바다의 얼어붙을 듯한 기온과 합쳐지면서 비교적 빠르게 차가워지게 되긴 하지만, 물의 온도는 섭씨 400도까지도 도달할 수 있다. 뜨거운 물과 차가운 물이 만날 때, 뜨거운 물에 떠 있던 미네랄은 분출구에서 나오면서 굳어지고 대양저로 떨어진다. [20]이것은 분출구 주변의 미네랄 퇴적을 야기하는데, 이는 분화구로 알려져 있는 큰 구조를 만든다.

대양저 위 분출구 주변 미네랄의 존재는 주변 지역이 생물체들로 번성하는 생태계를 지속시키는 것을 가능하게 한다. 박테리아는 미네랄을 에너지로 전환시키고, 이렇게 하여 주변 종들에게 영양분을 제공한다. 과학자들은 화학 합성이라고 알려져 있는, 이런 방식으로 미네랄을 에너지로 전환시키는 과정에 매료되어 있는데, 그것이 에너지가 햇빛 없이 발달하는 몇 안 되는 사례 중 하나이기 때문이다. 그들은 또한 이 분출구에서 에너지로 전환되는 주요 미네랄 중 하나가 대부분의 식물성 생물체에게 매우 유독한 미네랄인 황화수소이기 때문에 이 과정에 관심이 있다. 열수 분출공을 연구하는 과학자들은 수백만 년 전에 산소도 별로 없이 생물들이 어떻게 살아남았는지 드러낼 수 있을지도 모르기 때문에, 이 유독한 미네랄이 지구에 있는 생물체의 기원을 밝혀줄 수 있을 것이라고 추측해오고 있다.

18 어떤 기술이 과학자들이 심해 탐험의 문제를 극복하게 했는가?

> 해설 문제의 핵심어구(overcome the challenges of deep sea exploration)와 관련된 지문 내용 중 'A solution to these problems came ~ with the introduction of submersibles'에서 잠수함의 도입과 함께 이 문제들에 대한 해결책이 생기게 되었다고 하였으므로, **submersible(s)**가 정답이다. 'A solution came to ~ problems'가 'overcome the challenges'로 paraphrasing되었다.

19 열수 분출공은 대개 어떤 지질학적인 지형 사이에서 발견되는가?

> 해설 문제의 핵심어구(hydrothermal vents usually found in between)와 관련된 지문 내용 중 'Hydrothermal vents ~ are typically found in the gaps between tectonic plates.'에서 열수 분출공은 보통 지질 구조판 사이의 갈라진 틈에서 발견된다고 하였으므로, **tectonic plates**가 정답이다.

20 열수 분출공 주변에서 발달하는 거대한 구조를 묘사하기 위해 어떤 용어가 사용되는가?

> 해설 문제의 핵심어구(large structures which develop near hydrothermal vents)와 관련된 지문 내용 중 'This causes an accumulation of minerals around the vent, which results in large formations known as chimneys.'에서 이것은 분출구 주변의 미네랄 퇴적을 야기하는데 이는 분화구로 알려져 있는 큰 구조를 만든다고 하였으므로, **chimney(s)**가 정답이다. 'results in large formations'가 'large structures ~ develop'으로 paraphrasing되었다.

9

치매의 비극

통계 자료는 전 세계적으로 약 3천 560만 명의 사람들이 점진적인 인지 능력 상실과, 결국에는, 죽음을 야기하는 뇌 장애인 치매를 앓고 있다는 것을 나타낸다. ²¹65세 이후부터는 질환이 발생할 위험이 5년마다 두 배가 되기 때문에, 사회는 빠르게 노화하고 있는 인구를 우리가 어떻게 보살필 것인지에 대해 점점 더 우려하게 되고 있다.

치매는 시간이 갈수록 뇌의 신경 세포가 악화되도록 하며, 따라서 치매를 앓는 사람들은 배우고, 판단하고, 말하고, 과거의 경험을 기억해 내고, 그들의 정서반응을 통제하는 데 어려움을 겪는다. 심지어 치매를 앓는 사람들이 그들의 가족 구성원을 알아보지 못하는 것은 매우 흔하다. 이것은 분명히 아들, 딸, 혹은 배우자에게 속상한 경험인 동시에, 익숙한 얼굴이 누구인지 알아보지 못하는 것은 치매 환자들을 가장 혼란스럽게 하며 좌절감을 준다. 그러므로 ²²심각한 불안이 치매와 관련되어 있다는 것과 이 수반되는 질환이 정신병과 공격성 발작을 야기함으로써 흔히 이 장애를 악화시킨다는 것은 놀랍지 않다.

치매 환자들이 자신들의 생각과 기분을 이해하는 능력을 잃기 때문에, 그들의 행동은 예측할 수 없게 된다. 그들은 '파국반응'으로 알려진 것을 겪을 수 있는데, 이것은 스스로 통제할 수 없는 상황에 처한 것을 발견함에 따른 눈물 또는 분노로의 갑작스러운 감정 변화를 포함한다. 목적 없이 돌아다니고, 차량을 운전하려고 시도하고, 혹은 식사하는 것을 잊어버리는 것을 막기 위해, 그들은 보통 전임 보호와 관리를 필요로 할 것이다. 이것은 ²³치매 말기에 있는 사람들에게는 불가피한 일이 되는데, 이때 그들은 근육 퇴화 때문에 움직임을 통제하거나 심지어 음식을 소화하는 능력을 잃을 수 있다. 허약하며 현실과의 접촉 없이, 치매 환자들은 이 시점에 질병에 감염되기 매우 쉬워지고 자주 사고나 흔한 감기로 쓰러진다.

그들의 가족과 돌보는 사람들이 받는 치매 환자들에 대한 부담은 꽤 심각하다. 가족 구성원이나 배우자를 천천히 잃는 감정적 희생은 말할 것도 없이, 돌보는 사람들은 흔히 혼란, 불합리함, 그리고 가끔 그들이 사랑하는 사람들의 모욕적인 행동에 대처하는 것으로부터 극도의 피로를 경험한다. 치매 환자들에게 돌봄을 제공하기 위해 필요한 시간과 자원의 양을 고려할 때 경제적 악영향은 똑같이 파괴적일 수 있다. 자택 돌봄을 실행하기 위해 전임 간호사를 고용하는 것이나 환자를 요양 시설이나 양로원으로 옮기도록 준비하는 것은 인구의 다수가 감당할 수 없는 큰 비용이다.

우리가 아직 치매의 난제를 다룰 능력을 갖추지 않은 것은 분명하다. 환자와 그들의 가족을 위해 더 많은 공공 의료 및 사회 복지 서비스를 개발하는 것에 더하여, 정부가 적극적으로 그 질환에 대한 대중의 인식을 높이는 것이 권장된다. 이렇게 함으로써, 사람들은 나이가 들면서 그 증상들을 더 자각하게 될 것이고 언제 도움을 구해야 하는지 알게 될 것이다. 조기 진단과 더불어, 증상은 초기부터 관리될 수 있는데, 이것은 삶을 크게 연장시킬 수 있다. 조기 진단은 또한 환자들에게 그들 자신의 장기적인 치료를 계획하고 자신들의 일을 정리할 기회를 준다. 이 끔찍한 고통의 치료법을 찾을 때까지, 환자들의 일상 생활을 개선하고 마지막 날들을 품위 있게 살 수 있도록 도와주는 자원이 필수적이다.

21 몇 세 이후에 5년마다 치매가 발병할 가능성이 두 배가 되는가?

> 해설 문제의 핵심어구(chance of developing dementia double)와 관련된 지문 내용 중 'the risk of developing the condition doubles every half decade after the age of 65'에서 65세 이후부터는 질환이 발생할 위험이 5년마다 두 배가 된다고 하였으므로, **(age of) 65**가 정답이다. 'every half decade'가 'every five years'로 paraphrasing되었다.

22 어떤 개별적인 질환이 치매의 증상을 악화시킬 수 있는가?

> 해설 문제의 핵심어구(make the symptoms of dementia worse)와 관련된 지문 내용 중 'severe anxiety goes hand in hand with dementia and that this accompanying condition often exacerbates the disorder'에서 심각한

불안이 치매와 관련되어 있으며 이 수반되는 질환이 흔히 이 장애를 악화시킨다고 하였으므로, **(severe) anxiety**가 정답이다. 'exacerbates the disorder'가 'make the symptoms ~ worse'로 paraphrasing되었다.

23 무엇이 치매 말기에 움직임과 음식 소화에 문제를 일으키는가?

해설 문제의 핵심어구(in the final stages of dementia)와 관련된 지문 내용 중 'people in the final stages of dementia, when they may also lose the ability to control their movements or even digest food due to muscle deterioration'에서 치매 말기에 있는 사람들은 이때 근육 퇴화 때문에 움직임을 통제하거나 심지어 음식을 소화하는 능력을 잃을 수 있다고 하였으므로, **muscle deterioration**이 정답이다. 'lose the ability to control their movements or even digest food'가 'causes problems with motion and food digestion'으로 paraphrasing되었다.

10

유아 교육과 수화

다른 사람들과 의사소통하는 능력은 모든 개개인의 정서 발달과 행복에 필수적인데, 이는 수화가 청각 장애가 있는 사람들과 귀가 잘 안 들리는 사람들을 위한 매우 유용한 수단인 이유이다. 수화를 배우는 것이 들을 수 있는 사람들, 특히 매우 어린아이들에게 많은 혜택을 제공한다는 것 또한 점점 더 분명해지고 있다.

가장 기본적인 수준에서, 어린이들에게 수화를 가르치는 것은 그들에게 청각 장애인에 대한 관심과 세심함을 서서히 주입시킨다. 하지만, 그것은 또한 어린이들이 제2언어를 습득하게 하는데, 이것은 일반적으로 2개 국어를 말하는 능력이 인지 능력을 향상시킨다고 받아들여지기 때문에 유익하다. 구술 능력이 제한되어 있는 유아와 아기들이 움직임에 강한 반응을 하기 때문에 이것은 특히 수화의 경우에 해당하는 것처럼 보인다. 모든 교육자와 부모가 아는 것처럼, 노래나 이야기에 동작이 들어가면, ²⁴아이들은 그 움직임을 계속해서 반복하려는 경향이 있다. 이런 방식으로 근육 기억을 발달시킴으로써, 아이들은 특정 움직임과 관련시켜 생각하기 때문에 단어들을 더 잘 잊지 않을 수 있다.

이러한 반응은 다중 지능 이론과 관련이 있는데, 이것은 사람들이 언어적, 논리-수학적, 신체-운동 감각적, 음악적, 시각적, 대인적, 그리고 개인적 등 서로 다른 다양한 방법으로 배우고, 기억하고, 이해한다고 제시한다. 이 이론의 개발자인 하버드 대학 인지와 교육 교수 Howard Gardner에 따르면, ²⁵대부분의 교육 과정은 언어 모델을 기초로 하고, 이것은 언어적으로 지능이 덜 발달한 학생들을 방해한다. 모든 다양한 지능들이 포용될 때, 아이들은 더 높은 성공의 가능성과 더 균형이 잡힌 교육을 제공받는다. 들을 수 있는 아이들에게 수화를 가르치는 것은 많은 지능들을 적용하는 훌륭한 방법으로 밝혀졌다.

예를 들어, 수화를 하든 혹은 아이의 손바닥에 단어를 그리든, 말하거나 노래할 때 손을 사용함으로써 교육자들은 신체-운동 감각적 그리고 시각적 학습자들뿐만 아니라 언어적 그리고 음악적 학습자들도 만족시킬 수 있다. 이것은 학생들이 피부로 느끼거나 수화로 보는 것에 더하여 말해지거나 노래로 불러지는 단어를 들을 수 있기 때문이다. 마찬가지로, 수화는 이런 유형의 학습자들이 문법을 이해하기 더 쉽도록 만드는 패턴으로 가득 차 있기 때문에 논리-수학적 학습자들을 도울 수 있다. 한편, 대인적 학습자와 개인적 학습자는 각각 다른 아이들과 함께 그리고 그들 스스로 수화를 연습할 수 있다.

하지만 아마 매우 어린 아이들을 더 나은 학습자로 만드는 것만큼 중요한 것은 수화가 성인이 이해할 수 있는 방식으로 아이들의 기본적인 욕구와 필요를 표현하는 쉬운 방법을 제공한다는 것이다. 알래스카에 있는 조기 교육 자원 센터인 Thread의 전문성 개발 담당자 Cassie Hulse는 "아이들은 규칙적으로 수화를 사용하고 있고, 그들이 효과적으로 우리와 의사소통하는 것을 보는 것은 매우 보람 있고 신나는 일이다. 이점들 중 하나는 우리 보육 센터에 있는 아이들은 원하는 것을 '우리에게 말할' 수 있기 때문에 덜 좌절한다는 것이다."라고 말한다. 이것은 ²⁶말할 수는 있으나 생각과 기분을 전달하는 것이 어려운 일이라고 느끼는 자폐증과 같은 질환을 가진 아이들에게도 마찬가지로 적용된다.

궁극적으로, 아이에게 수화를 가르치는 것은 득이 될 뿐 손해를 볼 것은 없다. 배우도록 격려하는 것에서부터, 의사소통할 수 있도록 하는 것까지, 수화는 아이들이 삶에서 앞으로 한 발짝 나아가게 해준다.

24 동작 반복을 통하여 아이들은 무엇을 개발시키는가?

> 해설 문제의 핵심어구(through the repetition of motions)와 관련된 지문 내용 중 'children tend to repeat the movements over and over. By developing muscle memory in this way'에서 아이들은 움직임을 계속해서 반복하려는 경향이 있고 이런 방식으로 근육 기억을 발달시킨다고 하였으므로, **muscle memory**가 정답이다. 'repeat the movements over and over'가 'the repetition of motions'로 paraphrasing되었다.

25 어떤 교육 모델이 몇몇 학생들을 성공하는 것으로부터 방해할 수 있는가?

> 해설 문제의 핵심어구(prevent some students from succeeding)와 관련된 지문 내용 중 'most educational curricula are based on the linguistic model, and this holds less verbally intelligent students back'에서 대부분의 교육 과정은 언어 모델을 기초로 하고 이것은 언어적으로 지능이 덜 발달한 학생들을 방해한다고 하였으므로, **linguistic (model)**이 정답이다. 'holds ~ students back'이 'prevent some students from succeeding'으로 paraphrasing되었다.

26 어떤 장애가 감정을 말로 옮기는 아이들의 능력을 저해하는가?

> 해설 문제의 핵심어구(ability to translate their emotions into speech)와 관련된 지문 내용 중 'children with conditions like autism who may be able to speak but find conveying their thoughts and feelings a challenge'에서 말할 수는 있으나 생각과 기분을 전달하는 것이 어려운 일이라고 느끼는 자폐증과 같은 질환을 가진 아이들이라고 하였으므로, **autism**이 정답이다. 'conveying feelings'가 'translate their emotions into speech'로 paraphrasing되었다.

HACKERS TEST

p.274

1	11 (males)	2	Scottish nobles	3	thatched (roofs/roof)
4	saltwater	5	10 hectares	6	Avalon Marshes
7	A	8	E	9	F
10	B	11	C	12-13	C, D

영국의 알락해오라기: 우려 앞에서의 희망에 대한 이유

A 현대에, 수많은 종들이 영구적으로 지구에서 사라졌다. 유사하게, 많은 종들이 현지에서 희귀해지거나 없어지게 되었고, 이런 경우들 또한 환경 보호 활동가들의 근심거리이다. 한 가지 예는 유럽, 아시아, 그리고 아프리카 일부 지역들의 도처에 매우 광범위한 분포를 가지고 있는 조류 종인 왜가리과의 알락해오라기이다. 전 세계적으로 수없이 많음에도 불구하고, 그것은 개체 수가 지난 두 세기 동안 급락한 영국과 같은 몇몇 지역에서는 분투해왔다. 이것은 정기적인 겨울 철새들은 영국의 일부 지역들에서 주기적으로 나타나기 때문에 이주하지 않는 번식 쌍들에 특히 해당된다. [7]영국에서, 알락해오라기는 1911년에 다시 나타나기 이전 1880년대 후반까지 멸종되었다. 그 후 알락해오라기의 개체 수는 1960년대까지 점차 증가했는데, 이때 다시 한 번 극적으로 감소하기 시작했다. [1]1990년대 초반까지, 알락해오라기는 11마리의 수컷만이 남은 채, 수백 년만에 두 번째로 영국에서 사라질 지경에 놓였다.

B [2]그 새들이 매 사냥을 행했던 스코틀랜드의 귀족들에게 수월한 표적이었고, 매우 맛있는 고기로 인해 일반적으로 사람들 사이에서 매우 가치가 있었기 때문에, 1800년대 초기에는 사냥이 알락해오라기에 대한 가장 큰 위협이었을 것이다. 하지만 19세기 후반기의 알락해오라기의 죽음과, 1960년대부터 1990년대까지의 기간을 포함하는 좀 더 최근의 감소는, 환경의 잘못된 관리 때문이었다. 이것의 많은 부분이 인간에 의해 유발된 서식지 상실 또는 파괴의 결과였는데, [10]주로 농업적인 목적을 위한 습지의 배수를 통한 것이었다. 알락해오라기들은 담수 습지를 필요로 하며, 영국에서 이 새들은 특히 갈대밭과 관련이 있다. 실제로, 이 갈대 습지들은 이 취약한 종의 생명선이다. 많게는 이 서식지의 40퍼센트가 1945년과 1990년 사이에 인간의 개발로 인해 사라진 것으로 추산된다.

C   그러나, 몇몇 서식지의 상실은 식물과 나무의 침해로 인한 습지 배수 때문이었다. 흥미롭게도, 이 또한 인간의 행동 양식 때문이었다. ³역사적으로 영국에서는, 초가 지붕 산업에서의 사용을 위해 갈대들이 베어지고, 건조되고, 꾸러미로 묶였는데, 이는 아직까지도 몇몇 영국 마을에서 발견되는 전통적인 초가 지붕을 공급했다. 하지만 현대에, ¹¹건물 양식의 변화는 알락해오라기들에게 유리한 것처럼 보이는 갈대 단일 재배를 전통적으로 유지해왔던 이러한 관습의 부재로 이어졌다. 그러므로, 습지를 자연에 맡기는 것은 역설적이게도 알락해오라기 감소의 원인이 되었다.

D   계속되는 난제는 ⁴이런 종류의 가장 큰 습지들이 영국의 동해안 지역에 있는데, 이곳에서는 그 습지들이 가끔이기는 하지만 되풀이하여 발생하는 해수의 침투에 취약하다는 것이다. 이러한 갈대 습지들이 알락해오라기 개체 수를 부양하기는 하지만, 그것들 또한 전적으로 의지하기에는 자연적인 조수의 영향을 받을 위험이 있다. 또한, ¹²이 새들의 식습관은 크게 장어와 러드 두 물고기를 바탕으로 하는데, 이 물고기들 또한 갈대밭의 빈번한 방문객들이다. 역류된 음식에 대한 연구들이 새끼 알락해오라기의 식단이 거의 전적으로 이 물고기들로 이루어져 있다는 것을 시사하기 때문에, ¹³이런 의존성은 특히 번식기에 해당한다.

E   그렇다면, 문제에 대한 답은, 알락해오라기의 거주에 적절한 완전히 새로운 습지의 조성인데, 이는 현존하는 것들의 확장과 함께 진행되어야만 하며, 이 난제는 최근 환경 보호 활동가들에 의해 착수되었다. 아발론 습지에서는, 역사를 통틀어 많은 경우에 개발로 인해 개간되었던 전통적인 습지를 되찾기 위한 환경 프로젝트들이 실행되었다. 이런 사업은 그 결과 작은, 조망 규모의 새로운 갈대밭을 만들어냈으며, 그것들이 스스로 거대한 알락해오라기 개체 수를 유지하기에는 불충분하긴 해도, 영국의 전반적인 알락해오라기 개체 수는 상당히 증가시킨다. ⁸이러한 노력은 근본적으로 광물과 토탄이 상업 목적으로 추출되고 난 이후의 습지 재생 이용 프로젝트였다. 유사하게, 왕립 애조 협회(RSPB)와 같은 단체들이 '이전에는 상상할 수 없었던 규모로 새로운 습지를 만들기 위해' 동원되었다.

F   ⁹환경론자들은 100만 헥타르 이상이 새로운 갈대밭의 조성에 적절하다고 결론을 내렸고, 초가 지붕 산업의 부활에서 협력자를 찾았다. ⁵10헥타르의 공간이 한 계절 내내 한 명의 갈대 베는 사람을 부양할 수 있으며, 추가적인 1000헥타르마다 알락해오라기를 50마리씩 더 부양할 수 있다는 것을 고려할 때, 성공적인 알락해오라기의 회복에 방해가 되는 것은 정부 기관들과, 민간 기업계와, 그리고 토지 소유주들의 집단적 의지뿐이다.

G   보호 노력 덕분에, 1997년 이후 알락해오라기의 개체 수는 증가하기 시작했고, 영국에서 알락해오라기의 미래가 불투명하긴 하지만, 최근의 동향을 기반으로 했을 때 아마도 희망적이다. 이 새들이 매우 비밀스럽고 관찰하기 어렵기 때문에, 숫자가 수컷의 울음소리('굵은 울리는 소리')에서 추산되어야 하므로 총계가 정확하지는 않지만 구체적인 연구들이 유망한 결과들을 보여준다. 400곳에 이르는 부지의 종합적인 평가는 최소한 600마리의 알락해오라기가 2009년~2010년 겨울 영국에 있었다는 것을 알아냈다. 이들 중, 연구자들은 약 3분의 2가 겨울 철새들이었으며, 아마도 200마리 가량은 1년 내내 상주하는 텃새들이라고 추산했다. 최근에, RSPB의 후속 부분 조사는 최소한 132마리의 수컷 텃새들이 있었다는 것을 나타냈으며, ⁶현지 개체 수 증가의 예시로, 아발론 습지는 알락해오라기의 개체 수가 지난 몇 계절 동안 상당히 증가했다는 것을 전했다.

어휘   Eurasian bittern n. 알락해오라기   heron n. 왜가리   plummet v. 급락하다, 곤두박질치다   falconry n. 매 사냥(훈련)
palatable adj. 맛있는, 맛좋은   demise n. 죽음, 종말   encompass v. 포함하다, 아우르다   wetland n. 습지   reed n. 갈대
marsh n. 습지   encroachment n. 침해, 잠식   thatched roof n. 초가 지붕   monoculture n. 단일 재배   susceptible n. 취약한, 민감한
infiltration n. 침투   regurgitate v. 역류시키다   undertaking n. 사업   reclamation n. 재생 (이용), 개간   mobilise v. 동원되다, 조직되다
resurgence n. 부활, 재기   collective adj. 집합적인

[1-6]

1 1990년대 초기에 몇 마리의 알락해오라기가 남았는가?

해설 문제의 핵심어구(in the early 1990s)와 관련된 지문 내용 중 'By the early 1990s, the bittern was on the verge of vanishing in the UK ~ with as few as 11 males remaining.'에서 1990년대 초반까지 알락해오라기는 11마리의 수컷만이 남은 채 영국에서 사라질 지경에 놓였다고 하였으므로, **11 (males)**이 정답이다.

2 알락해오라기의 사냥과 관련하여 누가 언급되었는가?

해설 문제의 핵심어구(hunting of bitterns)와 관련된 지문 내용 중 'Hunting was probably the greatest threat to the bittern ~ as the birds were easy targets for Scottish nobles who practised falconry'에서 그 새들이 매 사냥을 행했던 스코틀랜드의 귀족들에게 수월한 표적이었기 때문에 사냥이 알락해오라기에 대한 가장 큰 위협이었을 것이라고 하였으므로, **Scottish nobles**가 정답이다. 'easy targets for'가 'in relation to the hunting'으로 paraphrasing되었다.

3 영국의 주택에서 전통적으로 어떤 종류의 지붕이 사용되었는가?

해설 문제의 핵심어구(roofs ~ on houses in Great Britain)와 관련된 지문 내용 중 'Historically in Great Britain, reeds were cut, dried, and bundled for use in the thatching industry, which supplied the traditional thatched roofs'

에서 역사적으로 영국에서는 초가 지붕 산업에서의 사용을 위해 갈대들이 베어지고, 건조되고, 꾸러미로 묶였는데, 이는 전통적인 초가 지붕을 공급했다고 하였으므로, **thatched (roofs/roof)**가 정답이다.

4 영국의 동부에서 때때로 무엇이 갈대 습지로 흘러 들어오는가?

해설 문제의 핵심어구(in the east of England)와 관련된 지문 내용 중 'the largest remaining marshes of this type are in the eastern coastal areas of England, where they are susceptible to occasional but recurring infiltration by saltwater'에서 이런 종류의 가장 큰 습지들이 영국의 동해안 지역에 있는데 이곳에서는 그 습지들이 가끔이기는 하지만 되풀이하여 발생하는 해수의 침투에 취약하다고 하였으므로, **saltwater**가 정답이다. 'infiltration by'가 'flows onto'로 paraphrasing되었다.

5 얼만큼의 땅이 한 계절 동안 갈대 베는 사람 한 명을 부양하기 위해 필요한가?

해설 문제의 핵심어구(support a reed cutter)와 관련된 지문 내용 중 'A space of 10 hectares can sustain one reed cutter for a whole season'에서 10헥타르의 공간이 한 계절 내내 한 명의 갈대 베는 사람을 부양할 수 있다고 하였으므로, **10 hectares**가 정답이다.

6 어떤 현지 지역이 알락해오라기 개체 수 증가를 겪었는가?

해설 문제의 핵심어구(local area ~ increase in bittern population)와 관련된 지문 내용 중 'in an example of localised population growth, Avalon Marshes reported that their population of bitterns had grown considerably over the past few seasons'에서 현지 개체 수 증가의 예시로 아발론 습지는 알락해오라기의 개체 수가 지난 몇 계절 동안 상당히 증가했다는 것을 전했다고 하였으므로, **Avalon Marshes**가 정답이다. 'grown considerably'가 'saw an increase'로 paraphrasing되었다.

[7-11]

7 영국에서 알락해오라기의 이전의 멸종에 대한 언급

해설 문제의 핵심어구(prior extinction of bitterns in the United Kingdom)와 관련된 지문 내용 중 단락 A의 'In the UK, the bittern became extinct by the late 1880s before reappearing in 1911.'에서 영국에서 알락해오라기는 1911년에 다시 나타나기 이전 1880년대 후반까지 멸종되었다고 하였으므로, 단락 **A**가 정답이다.

8 습지가 상업적인 사용 이후 어떻게 구제되었는지

해설 문제의 핵심어구(a wetland was rescued)와 관련된 지문 내용 중 단락 E의 'This effort was essentially a wetland reclamation project after minerals and peat had been extracted for commercial purposes.'에서 이러한 노력은 근본적으로 광물과 토탄이 상업 목적으로 추출되고 난 이후의 습지 재생 이용 프로젝트였다고 하였으므로, 단락 **E**가 정답이다. 'reclamation'이 'was rescued'로 paraphrasing되었다.

9 새로운 갈대밭을 조성하기에 적절한 양의 토지에 대한 설명

해설 문제의 핵심어구(creating new reeds)와 관련된 지문 내용 중 단락 F의 'Environmentalists have determined that upwards of 1 million hectares are suitable for the creation of new reed beds'에서 환경론자들은 100만 헥타르 이상이 새로운 갈대밭의 조성에 적절하다고 결론을 내렸다고 하였으므로, 단락 **F**가 정답이다.

10 농업을 지원하기 위해 배수되는 습지에 대한 진술

해설 문제의 핵심어구(drained to support agriculture)와 관련된 지문 내용 중 단락 B의 'primarily through the draining of wetlands for agricultural purposes'에서 주로 농업적인 목적을 위한 습지의 배수를 통한 것이었다고 하였으므로, 단락 **B**가 정답이다.

11 갈대를 베는 것의 감소가 알락해오라기 개체 수에 부정적인 영향을 미친 방식

해설 문제의 핵심어구(decline in reed cutting)와 관련된 지문 내용 중 단락 C의 'changes in building patterns led to the decline of this practice, which had traditionally maintained the reed monoculture that bitterns seem to favour. Thus, leaving the wetlands to nature ironically contributed to the bittern's demise.'에서 건물 양식의 변화는 알락해오라기들에게 유리한 것처럼 보이는 갈대 단일 재배를 전통적으로 유지해왔던 이러한 관습의 부재로 이어졌으며, 그러므로 습지를 자연에 맡기는 것은 역설적이게도 알락해오라기 감소의 원인이 되었다고 하였으므로, 단락 **C**가 정답이다.

[12-13] 알락해오라기들이 먹이로 의존하는 물고기의 어떤 **두 가지** 특징들이 언급되었는가?

A 주로 조수 지역에서 발견된다.
B 과거보다 훨씬 더 수가 많다.
C 종종 갈대밭에서 시간을 보낸다.
D 특히 번식기에 중요하다.
E 곧 멸종할 위기에 처해 있다.

해설 문제의 핵심어구(the fish that bitterns rely on for food)와 관련된 지문 내용 중 'the diet of these birds is based heavily on two fish, eels and rudd, which are also frequent visitors to reed beds'와 'This dependence is particularly true in the breeding season'에서 이 새들의 식습관은 크게 장어와 러드 두 물고기를 바탕으로 하는데 이 물고기들 또한 갈대밭의 빈번한 방문객들이며 이런 의존성은 특히 번식기에 해당한다고 하였으므로, 보기 **C** They often spend time in reed beds와 보기 **D** They are especially important in the breeding season이 정답이다. 'frequent visitors to'가 'often spend time in'으로, 'dependence is particularly true'가 'especially important'로 paraphrasing되었다.

* 각 문제에 대한 정답의 단서는 지문에 문제 번호와 함께 별도의 색으로 표시되어 있습니다.

1 False	2 Not given	3 True	4 False
5 Not given	6 False	7 True	8 scroll
9 varnish	10 replica	11 oxidiser/oxidizer	12 earthquake
13 cable(s)	14 D	15 C	16 A
17 G	18 F	19 E	20 cue(s)
21 episode	22 experiences	23 cognitive	24 False
25 Not given	26 True	27 C	28 A
29 G	30 B	31 E	32 No
33 Yes	34 Not given	35 Yes	36 D
37 C	38 A	39 B	40 D

READING PASSAGE 1

약속의 구름: 2008년 올림픽 성화와 봉송

이탈리아 토리노에서의 2006년 동계 올림픽 전에, 중국에 본사를 둔 국제 컴퓨터 회사인 레노버사는, 2006년 대회뿐만 아니라 2008년 중국 베이징 하계 올림픽의 올림픽 후원업체가 되기로 계약을 맺었다. 또한, 레노버사는 2008년 올림픽의 성화를 디자인할 기회도 얻어냈다. 회사의 디자인인 '약속의 구름'은, 300개가 넘는 경쟁업체들의 디자인들 중에서 가장 인기를 얻었다. '약속의 구름'은 현대 기술 디자인과 중국의 전통적인 미의식 및 문화 요소들을 결합하고자 했다. [8]이 디자인은 중국의 상서로운 색인 빨간색뿐 아니라 고대 중국의 네 가지 위대한 발명에 속하는 종이의 발명을 의미하는 중국의 전통적인 두루마리, 그리고 시각적으로 오륜에 대한 생각을 떠올리게 하는 소용돌이치는 '행운의 구름'의 형태를 본떴다.

그러나 이것은 그저 보기에만 아름다운 것이 아니었다. 성화를 제작하기 위해 사용되었던 최첨단 기술은 부분적으로는 그래픽 디자인이었고 부분적으로는 로켓 공학이었다. 윤이 나는 가벼운 알루미늄과 마그네슘 합금으로 만들어진 성화는, 높이 72센티미터에 단 985그램이었다. 그 국제 디자이너 팀은 '보는 사람에게는 매력적이고, 나르는 사람에게는 가벼운' 성화를 제작하고자 했다. [9]성화의 들기 쉬운 특징에 마찬가지로 기여한 것은 잡는 것과 쉽게 다루는 것을 용이하게 한 손잡이 위의 얇은 고무 기반 광택제의 존재였다.

[1]성화의 내부에 대해서는, 레노버사는 중국 항공과학산업단체에 의지했다. 실제로, 민간 및 국가 지원을 받는 중국의 기술적 감각이 완전히 발휘되었다. 단연 중요한 것은 [10]운동선수들이 히말라야 산맥의 정상으로 복제품을 운반하는 널리 홍보되는 부가적인 여정을 포함하여 성화 봉송의 긴 여정 내내 불꽃이 켜져 있는 상태를 유지하게 하는 것이었다. [2]올림픽 성화의 손잡이 안에는 순수 액상 프로판이 들어있는 작은 금속 용기가 있었는데, 이는 추위에 대한 프로판의 강한 내성으로 인해 혼합 가스를 사용하던 전통적인 관례를 대신하여 선택되었을 것이다. [3]점화 장치가 켜지면, 그것은 압력이 급격히 낮아지게 했는데, 이는 가스가 기화되어 성화의 위쪽에 있는 작은 구멍들을 통해 흘러가, '영영 꺼지지 않는' 올림픽 불꽃에 연료를 공급하도록 했다.

설계자들은 또한 불꽃이 꺼지는 것에 대해 한층 더 나아간 안전을 제공했던 압력 안정 장치와 열 회수 장치를 고안해냈으며, 이 불꽃이 매우 낮은 기압, 극한의 온도, 그리고 강풍에 견뎌야 하는 [11]에베레스트산과 같이 산소가 낮은 환경적 조건에서도 프로판이 연소할 수 있도록 필요한 공기를 공급하기 위해 복제품에 특별한 산화제를 포함하는 통찰력도 지니고 있었다. 대체로, 이 올림픽 성화는 영하 40도까지의 온도, 시간당 5센티미터의 강우량, 그리고 시속 65킬로미터의 풍속을 견딜 수 있다는 소문이 퍼졌으며, 이런 철저한 준비는 5월 8일 산악인 팀이 세계에서 가장 유명한 산의 정상에 오르는 것이 텔레비전 생방송으로 전 세계에 방영되었을 때 결실을 얻었다. 이 부가적인 여정은 그때 중국 본토에서 행해지고 있었던 주요 봉송과는 별개로 진행되었다.

물론, 성화 봉송 주자들은 명성 있는 올림픽 성화 봉송에서 그것을 지닐 수 있도록 선택된 사람들이었으며, 21,800명의 참가자가 주요

성화 봉송에서 뛸 수 있는 기회를 얻었다. ⁴이 봉송은 올림픽 역사상 가장 길었으며, 그리스의 올림피아에서 2008년 3월에 시작하여 개막식에서의 성화대 점화와 함께 중국 베이징에서 8월에 종료되었다. 성화 주자들은 6개 대륙, 21개 국가, 113개의 중국 도시를 포함하여 13만 7천 킬로미터의 길을 횡단했으며, 그러므로 이는 진정한 의미의 세계 일주였다. 이 성화 봉송은 규모 면에서 전례가 없었지만, 그것의 훌륭함은 이례적이고 유감스러운 상황들에 의해 때로 빛을 잃기도 했다. 예를 들어, ¹²청두 지방을 거치는 것으로 계획되어 있던 6월의 여정은 2008년 5월에 그곳에서 발생한 충격적인 규모 7.9의 지진으로 인해 8월까지 연기되었다.

게다가, 성화 봉송은 티베트에 대한 중국의 태도를 바꾸기를 요구하고 전반적으로 논란이 많은 중국의 인권 기록을 비난하는 활동가들의 광범위한 정치적 집회와 시위를 견뎌야 했다. 그 결과, ⁵성화 봉송은 안전 면에서 이례적으로 비용이 많이 들었다. 런던에서는, 올림픽 성화의 불꽃을 꺼뜨리고 후원업체들이 성화 봉송과 올림픽 대회를 거부하는 것을 장려하고자 한 수천 명의 시위자들에 맞서기 위해 거의 2,000명의 경관들이 고용되었는데, 이는 75만 파운드가 들었다. 그리고 프랑스에서는, ⁶파리를 지날 때 3,000대 이상의 경찰 오토바이가 성화 및 성화 주자들과 동행했다. 어떤 의미에서는, 친선과 올림픽의 상징을 대표하는 성화의 감동적이고 상징적인 효과가 논쟁과 ⁶주변의 보안으로 인해 약화되었는데, 그것은 성화에 대한 대중의 접근을 저해했다. 전 세계로의 '조화의 여정'은 결국 그렇게 조화롭지 못했으며, ⁷외신은 '웃음거리의 여정'이나 '성화의 여정 혼돈 속으로 떨어지다'와 같은 제목을 사용하며 봉송에 대해 험담하는 말들을 쏟아낼 기회에 달려들었다.

그러나, 마침내, 성화는 8월 6일 베이징에 도착하여 3일 동안 수도 주위를 행진하며 제자리를 찾았다. 마지막 봉송은 일곱 명의 유명한 중국 선수들에 의해 진행되었는데, 각각 교대로 경기장까지 성화를 들었고, 그곳에서 성화는 올림픽 체조 6관왕인 Ning Li에게 전달되었다. ¹³극적인 마무리로, Li가 마치 날아오른 것처럼 와이어로프에 의해 공중으로 들어올려지는 것으로 봉송은 끝이 났고, 그는 눈부시고 의기양양한 모습으로 마침내 성화대에 도달하여 점화하기 전에 경기장 한 바퀴를 완전히 '비행했다'.

어휘   upstage v. (~보다) 인기를 얻다, 앞지르다   wed v. 결합하다   auspicious adj. 상서로운   evoke v. 떠올리게 하다, 환기하다
cutting-edge adj. 최첨단의   fashion from phr. ~으로 만들다   alloy n. 합금   wield v. 들다, 휘두르다   varnish n. 광택제, 니스
Aerospace Science and Industry Group phr. 항공과학산업단체   acumen n. 감각   canister n. 금속 용기, 통   precedent n. 관례
vaporise v. 기화하다   fuel v. 연료를 공급하다   oxidiser n. 산화제   combust v. 연소하다   rigorous adj. 철저한   scale v. 오르다
traverse v. 횡단하다, 가로지르다   magnitude n. 규모   demonstration n. 집회, 시위   condemn v. 비난하다
law enforcement officer phr. 경관, 법 집행자   mute v. 약화하다, 완화하다   pounce v. 달려들다, 덮치다
disparaging adj. 험담하는, 비난하는   farce n. 웃음거리   lap n. 한 바퀴   dazzling adj. 눈부신

[1-7]

1   성화에 사용된 디자인과 기술은 오로지 레노버사에 의해 개발되었다.

2   레노버사의 2008년 성화는 히말라야 산맥으로 운반되었을 때 다른 종류의 프로판을 필요로 했다.

3   성화의 점화 장치를 켜는 것은 압력의 즉각적인 하락을 야기했다.

4   2008년 성화 봉송이 중대한 프로젝트이긴 했지만, 역사상 가장 긴 것은 아니었다.

5   런던에서의 봉송을 위한 보안 비용은 전체 노선에서 가장 높았다.

6   파리에서는, 더 적은 보안으로 인해 성화에 대한 대중의 접근이 컸다.

7   일부 언론 매체는 성화 봉송에 대해 부정적인 논평을 했다.

1   해설 문제의 핵심어구(solely developed by Lenovo)와 관련된 지문 내용 중 'For the internal portion of the torch, Lenovo turned to the China Aerospace Science and Industry Group.'에서 성화의 내부에 대해서는 레노버사는 중국 항공과학산업단체에 의지했다고 하였으므로, 주어진 문장은 지문의 내용과 일치하지 않음을 알 수 있다. 따라서 정답은 **False**이다.

2   해설 문제의 핵심어구(a different type of propane)와 관련된 지문 내용 중 'Inside the handle of the Olympic torch was a small canister of pure liquid propane, which was presumably chosen over the conventional precedent of using mixed gases'에서 올림픽 성화의 손잡이 안에는 순수 액상 프로판이 들어있는 작은 금속 용기가 있었는데 이는 혼합 가스를 사용하던 전통적인 관례를 대신하여 선택되었을 것이라고는 하였지만, 주어진 문장의 내용은 확인할 수 없다. 따라서 정답은 **Not given**이다.

정답·해석·해설 HACKERS IELTS READING

3 해설 문제의 핵심어구(Turning the torch's ignition switch on)와 관련된 지문 내용 중 'When the ignition switch was turned on, it created a sudden drop in pressure'에서 점화 장치가 켜지면 그것은 압력이 급격히 낮아지게 했다고 하였으므로, 주어진 문장은 지문의 내용과 일치함을 알 수 있다. 따라서 정답은 **True**이다. 'a sudden drop'이 'an instantaneous decrease'로 paraphrasing되었다.

4 해설 문제의 핵심어구(the longest in history)와 관련된 지문 내용 중 'The relay was the longest in Olympic history'에서 이 봉송은 올림픽 역사상 가장 길었다고 하였으므로, 주어진 문장은 지문의 내용과 일치하지 않음을 알 수 있다. 따라서 정답은 **False**이다.

5 해설 문제의 핵심어구(The security cost for the London)와 관련된 지문 내용 중 'the torch relay was unusually costly in terms of security: in London, nearly 2,000 law enforcement officers were employed'에서 성화 봉송은 안전 면에서 이례적으로 비용이 많이 들었으며 런던에서는 거의 2,000명의 경관들이 고용되었다고는 하였지만, 주어진 문장의 내용은 확인할 수 없다. 따라서 정답은 **Not given**이다.

6 해설 문제의 핵심어구(In Paris, the public access)와 관련된 지문 내용 중 'over 3,000 motorcycle police accompanied the torch and torch bearers as they travelled through Paris'와 'surrounding security presence, which inhibited the torch's public accessibility'에서 파리를 지날 때 3,000대 이상의 경찰 오토바이가 성화 및 성화 주자들과 동행했으며 주변의 보안이 성화에 대한 대중의 접근을 저해했다고 하였으므로, 주어진 문장은 지문의 내용과 일치하지 않음을 알 수 있다. 따라서 정답은 **False**이다.

7 해설 문제의 핵심어구(Some media outlets)와 관련된 지문 내용 중 'the international press pounced on the opportunity to make disparaging statements about the relay'에서 외신은 봉송에 대해 험담하는 말들을 쏟아낼 기회에 달려들었다고 하였으므로, 주어진 문장은 지문의 내용과 일치함을 알 수 있다. 따라서 정답은 **True**이다. 'international press'가 'Some media outlets'로, 'disparaging statements'가 'negative comments'로 paraphrasing되었다.

[8-13]

8 올림픽 성화의 물리적 디자인은 어떤 전통적인 중국의 모티브에 주로 기반했는가?

9 성화를 더 들기 쉽도록 하기 위해 성화의 외부에 무엇이 추가되었는가?

10 운동선수들은 그들이 히말라야 산 정상으로 갔을 때 무엇을 옮겼는가?

11 성화의 어느 부분이 에베레스트산의 험한 환경을 불꽃이 견딜 수 있도록 했는가?

12 어떤 자연 재해가 성화 봉송 일정의 장애물로 언급되었는가?

13 봉송의 마지막 주자가 경기장 위에 떠있는 것처럼 보일 수 있도록 한 것은 무엇인가?

8 해설 문제의 핵심어구(traditional Chinese motif)와 관련된 지문 내용 중 'The design mimicked the form of a traditional Chinese scroll'에서 이 디자인은 중국의 전통적인 두루마리의 형태를 본떴다고 하였으므로, **scroll**이 정답이다. 'mimicked the form of a traditional Chinese'가 'traditional Chinese motif ~ largely based on'으로 paraphrasing되었다.

9 해설 문제의 핵심어구(make it easier to carry)와 관련된 지문 내용 중 'contributing to the item's wieldable quality was the presence of a thin rubber-based varnish on the handle'에서 성화의 들기 쉬운 특징에 기여한 것은 손잡이 위의 얇은 고무 기반 광택제의 존재였다고 하였으므로, 'rubber-based varnish'가 답이 될 수 있다. 지시문에서 한 단어로만 답을 작성하라고 하였으므로, **varnish**가 정답이다. 'wieldable'이 'easier to carry'로 paraphrasing되었다.

10 해설 문제의 핵심어구(athletes ~ the top of the Himalayas)와 관련된 지문 내용 중 'athletes lugged a modified replica to the summit of the Himalayan mountain range'에서 운동선수들이 히말라야 산맥의 정상으로 복제품을 운반했다고 하였으므로, 'modified replica'가 답이 될 수 있다. 지시문에서 한 단어로만 답을 작성하라고 하였으므로, **replica**가 정답이다.

11 해설 문제의 핵심어구(withstand harsh conditions on Mt. Everest)와 관련된 지문 내용 중 'a special oxidiser ~ to supply the necessary oxygen for propane to combust in environmental conditions of low oxygen, such as on Mt. Everest'에서 에베레스트산과 같이 산소가 낮은 환경적 조건에서도 프로판이 연소할 수 있도록 필요한 공기를 공급하기 위한 특별한 산화제라고 하였으므로, **oxidiser/oxidizer**가 정답이다.

12 해설 문제의 핵심어구(disruption to the schedule)와 관련된 지문 내용 중 'the planned June trip through the province of Sichuan was postponed until August due to the devastating 7.9 magnitude earthquake'에서 청두 지방을 거치는 것으로 계획되어 있던 6월의 여정은 충격적인 규모 7.9의 지진으로 인해 8월까지 연기되었다고 하였으므로, **earthquake**가 정답이다. 'postponed'가 'disruption to the schedule'로 paraphrasing되었다.

13 해설 문제의 핵심어구(final athlete in the relay)와 관련된 지문 내용 중 'In a dramatic finale, the relay ended with Li being lifted in the air by cables as if he had taken flight'에서 극적인 마무리로 Li가 마치 날아오른 것처럼 와이어로프에 의해 공중으로 들어올려지는 것으로 봉송은 끝이 났다고 하였으므로, **cable(s)**가 정답이다. 'as if he had taken flight'이 'appear suspended'로 paraphrasing되었다.

READING PASSAGE 2

지나간 날들의 향기: 냄새는 기억과 특별히 밀접하게 연관되어 있는가?

A [20]냄새가 기억에 대한 가장 강력한 단서라는 일반적이며 널리 퍼져 있는 주장이 존재한다. 이 옛말은 대중적인 출판물들뿐 아니라 과학 관련 출판물들에서도 공표되어 왔다. [16]'향수는 액체로 된 기억이며' '냄새는 아픔을 주는 지뢰처럼 우리의 기억 속에서 부드럽게 폭발한다'는 1990년 다이앤 애커먼의 기술을 예로 들면, 감정과 기억에 있어 후각의 역할이 문학적인 암시와 풍유에서 삶으로 생생하게 다가온다.

B 냄새를 통해, 우리는 즉각적으로 우리의 과거로부터의 변하지 않은 가상의 발췌록으로 되돌아간다. 1991년에, [21]Trygg Engen은 냄새가 삽화적인 기억을 만들어내는데, 이는 하나의 기억에서 아주 온전하게 탄생한 대단히 상세한 자전적 삽화를 제공한다고 썼다. 그는 이것을 어의적 기억과 대비했는데, 이는 단어, 범주, 지표화, 그리고 기타 비슷한 것들에 의존한다. 그의 관점에서, 냄새는 감각들 중 가장 근본적인 것이며 언어보다 앞선 원시 세계의 산물이다. 하지만 향기가 정말로 일반적인 통념이 시사하는 것과 같이 추억에 대한 그런 강력한 단서인가?

C 냄새에 의해 유발된 기억이라는 현상은 엇갈리는 결과들과 함께, 실험들로 연구되어 왔다. 듀크 대학의 David Rubin과 그의 동료들은 향기에 대한 개념 대신에, 실제 향기가 기억에 있어 특별한 기능을 가진다는 가정을 연구하고자 했다. 1984년에, 그들은 40명의 학생 참가자들을 모집했고 그들에게 무작위로 냄새 혹은 그 냄새를 뜻하는 글로 쓰여진 단어들이 제시되도록 배정했다. [15]그들은 특히 어린 시절의 기억을 불러일으킬 수 있는, 익숙할 것이라고 생각한 냄새들을 이용했다. 이것들은 존슨앤드존슨사의 베이비 파우더, 반창고, 비누, 땅콩 버터 등을 포함했다.

D 그 다음에 참가자들은 향기 혹은 기술된 것에 의해 일깨워진 모든 기억을 묘사하고 '그 기억은 얼마나 분명하거나 생생했는가?' 혹은 '그 기억의 시간 동안 감정적으로 무엇을 느꼈는가?'와 같은 질문들에 대답하도록 요청받았다. 두 번째 실험에서, [14]연구원들은 비슷한 방법을 사용했으나 실제 향기와 글로 쓰여진 단어에 더해 그 냄새를 나타내는 사진을 추가했다. 그 팀은 실제의 향기에 의해 유발된 기억이 이전에는 전혀 떠오른 적이 없거나 혹은 덜 자주 떠오른 경향이 있었으며, [24]냄새가 종종 사진과 단어보다 더 즐겁거나 감동적인 기억을 불러일으킬지도 모른다는 것과 같은 놀라운 발견을 했다.

E 뒤이은 실험들은 이 주제에 대해 보다 분명하게 설명했다. 2000년에, 영국의 심리학자인 리버풀 대학의 John Downes는 실제 향기와 기억 간 관련성이 나이와 얽혀 있는 것처럼 보인다는 것을 발견했다. 그는 60대 후반과 70대 초반의 피실험자를 모았고, 그들에게 후각적 단서 또는 언어적 단서(냄새와 관련된 단어들)들을 제시했으며, 마음 속에 떠오른 관련 있는 자전적 경험을 묘사할 것을 요청했다. 그들의 분석은 [19]실제 냄새가 언어적 단서보다 훨씬 어린 나이로부터의 기억을 유발했다는 것을 보여주었다. 전자는 6세부터 10세까지의 기억을 불러오는 경향이 있었으나, 후자는 일반적으로 11세부터 25세 나이까지의 기억을 떠오르게 했다. 이것은 [22]냄새가 아동기의 경험에 대한 맥락적인 세부 정보들의 배경을 제공하는 데 있어 중요한 요소라는 것과 언어의 의미를 이해하는 능력들은 아동기의 후반까지도 여전히 제한되어 있으며 청소년기까지 계속 형성되기 때문에 냄새가 실제로 삽화적 기억과 밀접하게 관련되어 있다는 것 모두를 시사한다.

정답·해석·해설

HACKERS IELTS READING

F [18]또 다른 흥미로운 실험은 1999년 '영국 심리학 저널'지의 기사에 기술되었다. 글쓴이인 카디프 대학의 John Aggleton은, 천재적인 방식으로 이중 신호 방법론을 적용했다. [18]그는 실험실 밖에서 냄새와 기억의 관계를 실험하고자 했고, 따라서 그는 요크시의 박물관인 조빅 바이킹 센터를 방문했는데, 이곳의 한 전시에는 다감각 효과를 위해 파이프로 전시장까지 보내지는 '바이킹 냄새'가 있었다. Aggleton은 이런 냄새들이 몇 년 후에 재방문객들이 전시의 세부 사항을 기억하는 데 도움이 될 것인지를 알고 싶어 했다. 그는 세 집단의 돌아온 박물관 방문객들에게 동일한 본래의 '바이킹 냄새', 통제 냄새, 그리고 무향이 있는 환경이라는 다양한 조건에서 설문지를 주었다. 그는 그 다음에 실험을 되풀이했으나 각 집단마다 바뀐 조건을 가지고 되풀이했다. '바이킹 냄새'가 있는 상황에서 두 번째 실험을 한 집단만이 설문에서 그 성과가 개선되었다. 그러므로, Aggleton은 냄새들이 '그 냄새들이 있던 상황에서 본래 제시된 정보의 기억을 돕는 강력한 맥락적 단서를 제공할 수 있다'고 결론지었다.

G 여전히, [26]대다수의 전문가들은 냄새에 의해 유발된 기억이 다른 어떤 자극보다도 더 정확하다는 증거가 없기 때문에 냄새가 기억에 대한 '최고의' 단서라는 생각은 매우 근거 없는 생각이라는 데 동의한다. 그러나, 냄새와 관련된 기억들이 본질적으로 더 감정적이라는 합의는 있는 것처럼 보인다. '옥스포드 사회신경학 편람'에 실린 Rachel Hertz의 논문에 따르면, [17]냄새가 기억을 유발할 때, 이것은 먼저 감정적인 느낌을 자아내는데, '그 이후에 처음 그 감정을 유발한 사건이 떠오른다. 다시 말하면, [23]냄새에 의해 유발되는 기억의 경험적인 순서는 관련되어 있는 신경학적인 경로의 시간의 순서를 따르는 것처럼 보인다.' [23]이 순서는 감각-지각으로부터 대뇌 변연계-감정으로 나아가며 그 다음에 더 높은 인지 구조로 나아간다. Hertz는 '냄새에 의해 유발된 기억의 하향식과는 대조적인 상향식 시간 전개가 다른 기억 경험들로부터 그것을 구별하는 것인지도 모른다'고 주장한다.

H 그러므로, 후각과 감정적 기억의 강한 연계는 의심할 여지 없이 인간의 생존에 있어 주요한 역할을 했기 때문에 진화적인 기반을 가졌을 가능성이 있다. 해부학적으로, 후각 중추는 뇌의 가장 기본적인 부분과 아주 인접해 있는데, 이는 감정 경험과 기억을 직접적으로 책임지고 있다. 단 두 개의 시냅스만이 감정, 감정적 행동, 그리고 동기 부여를 책임지고 있는 일련의 뉴런인 편도체로부터 후신경을 분리한다. 진화적인 용어로, 이 통합적인 감정 중추는, 사실, 전체 변연계는, 뇌의 후각 구역에서 생겨났다. 이것을 고려할 때, Michael Jawer와 같은 일부 연구자들은, 후각이 없이는, 우리가 절대로 감정을 가지도록 진화하지 못했을 것이라고 주장했다.

어휘 intertwine v. 밀접하게 연관되다 circulate v. (소문 등이) 퍼지다, 유포되다 adage n. 옛말, 속담 promulgate v. 공표하다 detonate v. 폭발하다 poignant adj. (심신에) 아픔을 주는, 가슴 아픈 land mine phr. 지뢰 olfactory adj. 후각의 allusion n. 암시 allegory n. 풍유, 상징 semantic adj. 어의의, 의미론적인 primal adj. 근본적인, 원시의 received wisdom phr. 일반적(사회적) 통념 subsequent adj. 뒤이은, 이후의 shed light on phr. 설명하다 backdrop n. 배경, 환경 double-cue n. 이중 신호 repeat visitor phr. 재방문객 temporal adj. 시간의 limbic adj. (대뇌) 변연계의, 가장자리의 anatomically adv. 해부학적으로 close proximity phr. 인접, 아주 가까움 amygdala n. 편도체

[14-19]

14 냄새를 의미하는 사진들의 사용

15 잘 알려진 향기의 예시

16 비유로 나타낸 냄새의 사용에 대한 언급

17 감정이 어떻게 기억으로부터 유발되는지에 대한 언급

18 일상적인 환경에서 수행된 연구에 대한 설명

19 서로 다른 단서들이 어떻게 서로 다른 나이 기간의 기억을 유발하는지

14 해설 문제의 핵심어구(use of photos)와 관련된 지문 내용 중 단락 D의 'the researchers ~ added photographs representative of an odour'에서 연구원들은 그 냄새를 나타내는 사진을 추가했다고 하였으므로, 단락 D가 정답이다.

15 해설 문제의 핵심어구(well-known scents)와 관련된 지문 내용 중 단락 C의 'They utilised what they thought would be familiar smells, particularly ones that might provoke an early memory; these included Johnson & Johnson's baby powder, plasters, soap, peanut butter, etc.'에서 그들은 특히 어린 시절의 기억을 불러일으킬 수 있는, 익숙할 것이라고 생각한 냄새들을 이용했으며 이것들은 존슨앤드존슨사의 베이비 파우더, 반창고, 비누, 땅콩 버터 등을 포함했다고 하였으므로, 단락 C가 정답이다. 'familiar smells'가 'well-known scents'로 paraphrasing되었다.

16 해설 문제의 핵심어구(smell in metaphor)와 관련된 지문 내용 중 단락 A의 "'Perfume is liquid memory' and 'Smells detonate softly in our memory like poignant land mines'"에서 '향수는 액체로 된 기억이다', '냄새는 아픔을 주는 지뢰처럼 우리의 기억 속에서 부드럽게 폭발한다'와 같이 냄새를 비유적으로 나타낸 표현이 제시되었으며, '~ the role of the olfactory sense in emotion and memory comes vividly to life in literary allusion and allegory'에서 후각의 역할이 문학적인 암시와 풍유에서 삶으로 생생하게 다가온다고 언급하였으므로, 단락 A가 정답이다.

17 해설 문제의 핵심어구(feelings arise from memories)와 관련된 지문 내용 중 단락 G의 'when an odour evokes a memory, this first creates emotional sensations'에서 냄새가 기억을 유발할 때 이것은 먼저 감정적인 느낌을 자아낸다고 하였으므로, 단락 G가 정답이다.

18 해설 문제의 핵심어구(study conducted in a real-life setting)와 관련된 지문 내용 중 단락 F의 'Another interesting experiment was described in a 1999 article in the *British Journal of Psychology*.'와 'he sought to test the relationship between odour and memory outside the laboratory'에서 또 다른 흥미로운 실험이 1999년 '영국 심리학 저널'지의 기사에 기술되었으며 그는 실험실 밖에서 냄새와 기억의 관계를 실험하고자 했다고 하였으므로, 단락 F가 정답이다. 'outside the laboratory'가 'in a real-life setting'으로 paraphrasing되었다.

19 해설 문제의 핵심어구(different age periods)와 관련된 지문 내용 중 단락 E의 'the actual odours triggered memories from a much younger age than the verbal cues. The former tended to revive recollections from age 6 to 10, whereas the latter generally evoked memories from between 11 and 25 years of age.'에서 실제 냄새가 언어적 단서보다 훨씬 어린 나이로부터의 기억을 유발했다는 것을 보여주었으며 전자는 6세부터 10세까지의 기억을 불러오는 경향이 있었으나, 후자는 일반적으로 11세부터 25세 나이까지의 기억을 떠오르게 했다고 하였으므로, 단락 E가 정답이다.

[20-23]

냄새와 기억
– 냄새는 기억을 불러오는 데 가장 강력한 20 ....일 수도 있다

기억의 종류
– Trygg Engen: 냄새는 하나의 기억에서 어떤 사람의 인생의 선명한 21 ....을 제공할 수 있다
– 냄새는 감각들 중 가장 근본적인 것일 수 있다

아동기의 기억을 불러일으키는 것
– John Downes: 냄새는 진술보다 기억을 더 많이 일으킨다
– 냄새는 어린 나이부터의 22 ....에 대한 배경 지식을 제공한다

냄새 기억의 순서
– Rachel Hertz: 냄새와 관련된 기억은 감각/지각으로부터 변연계/감정적인 것으로 그리고 더 상급의
  23 .... 구조로 나아간다
– 냄새는 진화에 확고한 기반을 두고 있다

20 해설 문제의 핵심어구(the most powerful)와 관련된 지문 내용 중 'claim that odours are the strongest cues to memory'에서 냄새가 기억에 대한 가장 강력한 단서라는 주장이라고 하였으므로, **cue(s)**가 정답이다. 'the strongest ~ to memory'가 'the most powerful ~ in bringing up memory'로 paraphrasing되었다.

21 해설 문제의 핵심어구(Trygg Engen)와 관련된 지문 내용 중 'Trygg Engen wrote that smell generates episodic memory, providing a richly detailed autobiographical episode'에서 Trygg Engen은 냄새가 삽화적인 기억을 만들어내는데 이는 대단히 상세한 자전적 삽화를 제공한다고 썼다고 하였으므로, 'richly detailed autobiographical episode'가 답이 될 수 있다. 지시문에서 한 단어로만 답을 작성하라고 하였으므로, **episode**가 정답이다.

22 해설 문제의 핵심어구(Smell gives background information)와 관련된 지문 내용 중 'smell is a crucial factor in providing a backdrop of contextual details for childhood experiences'에서 냄새가 아동기의 경험에 대한 맥락적인 세부 정보들의 배경을 제공하는 데 있어 중요한 요소라고 하였으므로, **experiences**가 정답이다. 'is a crucial factor in providing a backdrop of contextual details'가 'gives background information'으로 paraphrasing되었다.

23 해설 문제의 핵심어구(Rachel Hertz)와 관련된 지문 내용 중 'the experiential order of odour-evoked memory appears to follow the temporal sequence of the neurological pathways that are involved'와 'This order progresses from the sensory-perceptual, to the limbic-emotional and then on to higher cognitive structures.'에서 냄새에 의해 유발되는 기억의 경험적인 순서는 관련되어 있는 신경학적인 경로의 시간의 순서를 따르는 것처럼 보이며, 이 순서는 감각-지각으로부터 대뇌 변연계-감정으로 나아가며 그 다음에 더 높은 인지 구조로 나아간다고 하였으므로, **cognitive**가 정답이다.

[24-26]

24 사진들은 냄새들보다 더 감동적인 기억을 불러일으킨다.

25 냄새는 기억에 있어 맛보다 더 효과적이다.

26 기억에 있어 냄새의 더 나은 정확성은 증명되지 않았다.

24 해설 문제의 핵심어구(Photographs ~ more moving memories)와 관련된 지문 내용 중 'odour might often evoke a more pleasing or emotional memory than pictures or words'에서 냄새가 종종 사진과 단어보다 더 즐겁거나 감동적인 기억을 불러일으킬지도 모른다고 하였으므로, 주어진 문장은 지문의 내용과 일치하지 않음을 알 수 있다. 따라서 정답은 **False**이다.

25 해설 문제의 핵심어구(effective than taste)와 관련된 내용은 지문에서 찾을 수 없다. 따라서 정답은 **Not given**이다.

26 해설 문제의 핵심어구(better accuracy of smell)와 관련된 지문 내용 중 'the vast majority of experts agree that the notion of smell being the 'best' cue to memory is largely unfounded because there is no proof that an odour-evoked memory is more accurate'에서 대다수의 전문가들은 냄새에 의해 유발된 기억이 더 정확하다는 증거가 없기 때문에 냄새가 기억에 대한 '최고의' 단서라는 생각은 매우 근거 없는 생각이라는 데 동의한다고 하였으므로, 주어진 문장은 지문의 내용과 일치함을 알 수 있다. 따라서 정답은 **True**이다. 'smell being the 'best' cue'가 'The better accuracy'로 paraphrasing되었다.

READING PASSAGE 3

집단 행동

대부분의 사람들은 자신을 스스로 결정을 내리는 자주적인 사람으로 여긴다. 하지만, 연구들은 순응이 선천적인 인간의 충동이며, 사람들이 그저 조화를 이루기 위해 놀랄 만큼 많은 것을 할 수 있다는 것을 보여주었다.

사회학에서, 한 집단 내 구성원들의 행동의 유사성은 집단 행동으로 알려져 있으며, 집단에 속한 사람들의 특이한 측면은 그들이 다른 구성원들의 생각, 의견, 그리고 행동에 순응하는 경향이 있다는 것이다. 때때로, 사람들은 자신의 도덕적 윤리적 규범과 상충하는 행동에 참여하기도 한다. ²⁷일부는 타협하기에는 구성원 자격을 너무 가치 있다고 여기기 때문에 이러한 관습 규범을 위반한다. 그러한 경우, 양심이 동요될 수 있지만, 그럼에도 결국 그들은 집단에 동조하는 경향이 있다. 많은 연구들이 이 현상을 분석해왔으며 설명하고자 노력해왔다.

³⁶미국의 형태주의 심리학자 솔로몬 애쉬에 의해 진행된 일련의 실험들은, 구성원들의 관점이 틀렸다고 해도 집단 구성원이 동료 구성원들의 관점에 순응하고자 하는지 시험했다. 각 실험에서, 그는 한 테이블에 일곱 명의 그룹을 앉히고 한 장에는 한 줄, 나머지 한 장에는 각기 다른 길이의 세 줄이 있는 두 장의 카드를 보여주었다. 그 후 참가자들은 두 번째 카드의 세 줄 중 어떤 줄이 첫 번째 카드의 한 줄과 같은 길이인지 대답하도록 요청받았다. 하지만, 함정이 있었다. 각 실험에서, 일곱 명의 피험자 중 한 명만 '진짜'였다. 다른 사람들은 특정 방식으로 질문에 답변하도록 지시받았다. 구체적으로, ³⁷그들은 진짜 학생이 순응하도록 압박하기 위해 몇 가지 질문에 의

도적으로 틀리게 대답하도록 지시받았다. ³²애쉬는 절반 이상의 진짜 피험자들이 적어도 한 번은 틀린 답에 동의했다는 것을 발견했다.

하지만 정말 이것이 단순히 동료 집단으로부터 받는 사회적 압력이나 주류를 거스르는 것에 대한 두려움 때문인가? 신경학자 그레고리 번스는 생리학상의 설명을 추구했고 옳지 않다고 느낄 때에도 개인이 집단과 일치하는 결정을 할 때 뇌의 어떤 부분이 '활성화'되는지 알아내기 위해 MRI 스캐너를 가지고 실험을 수행했다. 그는 만약 동료 집단으로부터 받는 사회적 압력이 원인이라면, 갈등을 관리하는 것과 관련되어 있는 전뇌의 활동에서 변화를 관측할 수 있을 것이라고 추론했다. 하지만 ³⁸번스가 발견한 것은 사람들이 집단의 의견을 따를 때, 뇌의 뒤쪽 부분이 자극되었다는 것이었다. ²⁸이는 공간 지각에 변화가 일어났음을 암시했으며, 번스로 하여금 가짜 응답자들이 했던 틀린 응답이 문자 그대로 진짜 참가자들의 인지를 바꾸었다고 결론짓게 했다. 그러므로, 그는 애쉬 실험의 참가자들이 단순히 동료 집단의 압력에 굴복한 것이었다는 생각에 이의를 제기했다. 사실, 그들은 실제로 줄의 길이를 틀린 응답이 주어지지 않았다면 그들이 보았을 것과 다르게 보고 있었다.

사회심리학자 스탠리 밀그램은 1960년대 초기 예일 대학에서의 실험에서 이보다 더 나아갔다. ³⁹밀그램의 실험은 권력에 대한 극단적인 복종과 그것의 잠재적으로 부정적인 영향에 초점을 맞춘 첫 번째 대규모 실험이라는 점에서 획기적이었다. 밀그램은 피험자들에게 그들이 학습과 기억에 관한 연구에 참여하고 있다고 이야기한 뒤 학습에 대한 처벌의 역할을 결정하는 정해진 목표와 함께, 그들에게 '교사'가 되도록 지시했다. 하지만, ³³밀그램은 사실 그렇게 하도록 지시를 받았을 때 다른 사람들을 벌하기 위해 사람들이 할 수 있는 극단을 알아내고자 했다. ²⁹밀그램이 설계한 실험에서, 피험자들은 맞는 답을 하지 못했을 때마다 전기 충격을 가함으로써 사실은 배우였던 '학습자'들을 처벌하도록 지시받았다. 그의 실험은 배우들이 고통 속에서 시험을 멈추라고 비명을 지르는 상황에서도, 대부분의 '교사'가 실험자의 요구에 따라 계속해서 충격을 집행했다는 것을 증명했다.

캘리포니아 주 팔로앨토의 한 고등학교 교사에 의해 수행되었던 더 험악한 실험은 순응하는 것의 위험을 강조한다. 어떻게 한 국가의 시민들이 독재 하에 살아가는 것을 수용하도록 설득될 수 있는지 묻는 질문에 의해 중단했을 때 역사 교사 Ron Jones는 전체주의에 대해 수업을 하고 있었다. 이는 그에게 한 아이디어를 떠오르게 했다. 그 다음 주에, 그는 규율의 긍정적인 특성에 대해 강의하고 ³⁰'제3의 물결'이라는 이름 아래 새로운 규칙들을 도입했는데, 이는 학생들이 3단어 이하로 간결하게 대답할 것을 지시했다. 그는 또한 '규율을 통한 힘, 공동체를 통한 힘' 같은 구호를 도입했고 학생들이 이 새로운 좌우명을 일어나서 복창하게 했다. 게다가, ⁴⁰그는 제3의 물결 경례와 회원증도 도입했으며, 구성원들이 규율을 어기는 다른 사람들을 보고할 것을 제시했다. 그는 그들이 기꺼이 그렇게 했을 때 큰 충격을 받았다.

실험이 4일째 되던 날, Jones는 학생들에게 제3의 물결이 실제 역사의 정치 운동에 기반한 것이었으며 다음 날 운동의 지도자가 누구인지 밝히겠다고 말한 뒤, 아돌프 히틀러와 제2차 세계 대전 동안의 독일 노동수용소 장면을 담은 영상을 보여줌으로써 그렇게 했다. 학생들은 깜짝 놀랐고, 몇 명은 울기도 했다. Jones는 집단의 목적을 고려했을 때, 그들이 집단의 근거가 되는 자신의 신념과 원칙을 고찰하지 못했음을 지적했다. '제3의 물결'이라는 이름은 우연이 아니었다. 실제로, 새로운 제3 제국이 거의 탄생할 뻔했던 것이었다.

실험과 별개로, 어느 사회에서든, 집단 구성원들이 협력과 건전한 의사결정을 위해 어느 정도 순응해야 함은 말할 필요도 없다. 그러나 ³¹융통성 없는 순응의 위험은 피해야 하며, 그렇지 않으면 이것은 '집단 사고'를 낳게 되는데, 이는 비판적 사고를 희생시키며 의견, 원인, 행동, 또는 결정에 대한 과잉 충성을 야기할 수 있다. 그러므로, 어느 집단에서든, ³⁴한 가지 제안의 영향을 모든 가능한 각도에서 살펴보았다는 것을 확실히 하기 위해 어떤 형태의 일탈이 필요하다. 그러나, 극단적인 형태의 일탈은 교착 상태, 논쟁, 혹은 무질서를 초래할 수도 있다. 그러므로, ³⁵해로운 비판은 최대한 경계하여 대하는 동시에 건설적인 형태의 비판이 권장되는 것이 매우 중요하다.

어휘   autonomous adj. 자주적인 conformity n. 순응 conform v. 순응하다, 따르다 conventional adj. 관습적인
       compromise v. 타협하다, 양보하다 Gestalt psychologist phr. 형태주의 심리학자 catch n. 함정, 책략 neurologist n. 신경학자
       physiological adj. 생리학상의 forebrain n. 전뇌 posterior adj. 뒤쪽에 있는 give in phr. ~에 굴복하다, 항복하다
       groundbreaking adj. 획기적인 repercussion n. 영향 administer v. 집행하다 ominous adj. 험악한, 불길한 underscore v. 강조하다
       totalitarianism n. 전체주의 institute v. 도입하다 mandate v. 지시하다 succinctly adv. 간결하게 recite v. 복창하다
       salute n. 경례, 인사 conviction n. 신념, 의견 deviance n. 일탈 stalemate n. 교착 상태, 막다른 골목 anarchy n. 무질서
       imperative adj. 중요한, 피할 수 없는 vigilance n. 경계, 조심

[27-31]

27 집단의 구성원 자격이 매우 가치 있다고 여겨질 때, 사람들은 -하다.

28 번스에 따르면, 잘못된 대답들은 -하다.

29 밀그램의 실험에서, 피험자들은 -하도록 지시받았다.

30 제3의 물결 실험은 학생들이 -할 것을 요구했다.

31 지나친 순응은 -할 수 있기 때문에 피해야 한다.

A 참가자들의 실제 인식을 바꾸었다
B 간결한 답으로 질문에 대답한다
C 일반적으로 인정되는 규범을 어긴다
D 순응이 행동에 영향을 미친다는 것을 증명한다
E 비판적인 사고를 방해한다
F 집단의 결정에 영향을 미친다
G 잘못된 응답에 처벌을 가한다

---

27 해설 문제의 핵심어구(membership of a group)와 관련된 지문 내용 중 'Some violate these conventional codes because they perceive membership as too valuable to compromise.'에서 일부는 타협하기에는 구성원 자격을 너무 가치 있다고 여기기 때문에 이러한 관습 규범을 위반한다고 하였으므로, 보기 **C** go against the accepted code가 정답이다. 'perceive membership as too valuable'이 'membership of a group ~ considered so desirable'로, 'violate these conventional codes'가 'go against the accepted code'로 paraphrasing되었다.

28 해설 문제의 핵심어구(Berns, the false responses)와 관련된 지문 내용 중 'This ~ led Berns to conclude that the incorrect responses the false respondents had provided literally altered the perception of the true participants.'에서 이는 번스로 하여금 가짜 응답자들이 했던 틀린 응답이 문자 그대로 진짜 참가자들의 인지를 바꾸었다고 결론짓게 했다고 하였으므로, 보기 **A** have changed the participant's actual perception이 정답이다. 'literally altered the perception of the true participants'가 'changed the participant's actual perception'으로 paraphrasing되었다.

29 해설 문제의 핵심어구(Milgram's experiment)와 관련된 지문 내용 중 'In the experiment Milgram designed, the subjects were instructed to punish the 'learners' ~ each time they failed to offer the correct answer.'에서 밀그램이 설계한 실험에서 피험자들은 맞는 답을 하지 못했을 때마다 '학습자'들을 처벌하도록 지시받았다고 하였으므로, 보기 **G** impose punishment at false responses가 정답이다. 'instructed to punish the 'learners' ~ each time they failed to offer the correct answer'가 'told to impose punishment at false responses'로 paraphrasing되었다.

30 해설 문제의 핵심어구(The Third Wave experiment)와 관련된 지문 내용 중 ''Third Wave', which mandated that students answer questions succinctly, in three words or less'에서 학생들이 3단어 이하로 간결하게 대답할 것을 지시한 '제3의 물결'이라고 하였으므로, 보기 **B** respond to questions with concise answers가 정답이다. 'answer questions succinctly'가 'respond to questions with concise answers'로 paraphrasing되었다.

31 해설 문제의 핵심어구(Strict compliance should be avoided)와 관련된 지문 내용 중 'the dangers of rigid conformity must be avoided, or it can result in 'groupthink', creating excessive loyalty ~ at the expense of critical thinking'에서 융통성 없는 순응의 위험은 피해야 하며 그렇지 않으면 이것은 '집단 사고'를 낳게 되는데, 이는 비판적 사고를 희생시키며 과잉 충성을 야기할 수 있다고 하였으므로, 보기 **E** get in the way of critical thinking이 정답이다. 'at the expense of'가 'get in the way'로 paraphrasing되었다.

[32-35]

32 애쉬는 아주 적은 수의 진짜 참가자들만이 틀린 답을 선택했다는 것을 발견했다.

33 밀그램은 개인이 지시받았을 때 타인에게 얼만큼의 처벌을 가할지를 시험하고자 했다.

34 모든 형태의 일탈은 제안이 실현하기에 충분히 효율적이라는 것을 보장할 것이다.

35 이롭지 않은 비판은 가장 조심해서 살펴야 한다.

32 해설 문제의 핵심어구(Asch ~ only a few of the real participants)와 관련된 지문 내용 중 'Asch discovered that more than half of the real subjects went along with the incorrect answer at least once.'에서 애쉬는 절반 이상의 진짜 피험자들이 적어도 한 번은 틀린 답에 동의했다는 것을 발견했다고 하였으므로, 주어진 문장은 글쓴이의 견해와 일치하지 않음을 알 수 있다. 따라서 정답은 **No**이다.

33 해설 문제의 핵심어구(Milgram intended to test how much punishment)와 관련된 지문 내용 중 'what Milgram actually wanted to do was find out the extremes to which people would go to punish others when instructed to do so'에서 밀그램은 사실 그렇게 하도록 지시를 받았을 때 다른 사람들을 벌하기 위해 사람들이 할 수 있는 극단을 알아내고자 했다고 하였으므로, 주어진 문장은 글쓴이의 견해와 일치함을 알 수 있다. 따라서 정답은 **Yes**이다. 'find out the extremes to which people would go to punish others'가 'test how much punishment a person would inflict'로 paraphrasing되었다.

34 해설 문제의 핵심어구(Any form of deviance)와 관련된 지문 내용 중 'deviance in some form is necessary to guarantee that the ramifications of a proposition are explored from every possible angle'에서 한 가지 제안의 영향을 모든 가능한 각도에서 살펴보았다는 것을 확실히 하기 위해 어떤 형태의 일탈이 필요하다고는 하였지만, 주어진 문장의 내용은 확인할 수 없다. 따라서 정답은 **Not given**이다.

35 해설 문제의 핵심어구(Criticism which is not beneficial)와 관련된 지문 내용 중 'it is imperative that ~ destructive criticism is regarded with the utmost vigilance'에서 해로운 비판은 최대한 경계하여 대하는 것이 매우 중요하다고 하였으므로, 주어진 문장은 글쓴이의 의견과 일치함을 알 수 있다. 따라서 정답은 **Yes**이다. 'is regarded with the utmost vigilance'가 'viewed with the greatest caution'으로 paraphrasing되었다.

[36-40]

36 솔로몬 애쉬가 알아내고자 했던 것은 무엇인가?
A 어떤 유형의 사람들이 집단 여론에 순응하는지
B 사람들이 올바른 선택에 어떻게 반응했는지
C 사람들이 집단의 잘못된 관점을 식별할 수 있는지
D 사람들이 잘못된 의견에 순응할 것인지

해설 문제의 핵심어구(Solomon Asch)와 관련된 지문 내용 중 'A series of tests conducted by Solomon Asch ~ examined the willingness of a group member to conform to the viewpoint of fellow members even if the members' viewpoint was incorrect.'에서 솔로몬 애쉬에 의해 진행된 일련의 실험들은 구성원들의 관점이 틀렸다고 해도 집단 구성원이 동료 구성원들의 관점에 순응하고자 하는지 시험했다고 하였으므로, 보기 **D** whether people would conform to a wrong opinion이 정답이다. 'the willingness of a group member to conform ~ even if the members' viewpoint was incorrect'가 'whether people would conform to a wrong opinion'으로 paraphrasing되었다.

🔍 오답 확인하기
B는 지문 내용 중 'examined the willingness ~ to conform to the viewpoint of fellow members even if the members' viewpoint was incorrect'에서 구성원들의 관점이 틀렸다고 해도 동료 구성원들의 관점에 순응하고자 하는지 시험했다고 하였으므로, 지문의 내용과 반대되는 오답이다.
C는 지문의 'even if the members' viewpoint was incorrect'를 활용하여 혼동을 주었지만, 솔로몬 애쉬가 알아내고자 했던 것은 사람들이 집단의 잘못된 관점을 식별할 수 있는지가 아니라 집단의 잘못된 관점에 순응하고자 하는지라고 하였으므로 오답이다.

37 애쉬의 연구에서 가짜 참가자들은 -하기 위해 그곳에 있었다.

  A 진짜 참가자들의 응답에 이의를 제기하기 위해
  B 집단의 다른 구성원들의 대답에 동의하기 위해
  C 잘못된 응답을 함으로써 진짜 참가자들이 순응하도록 압박하기 위해
  D 다른 참가자들에게 순응하도록 요청하기 위해

> 해설 문제의 핵심어구(The false participants in Asch's study)와 관련된 지문 내용 중 'they were told to purposely answer some questions incorrectly to pressure the real student to conform'에서 그들은 진짜 학생이 순응하도록 압박하기 위해 몇 가지 질문에 의도적으로 틀리게 대답하도록 지시받았다고 하였으므로, 보기 **C** pressure the real participant to conform by giving wrong answers가 정답이다. 'answer some questions incorrectly'가 'giving wrong answers'로 paraphrasing되었다.

38 실험을 수행할 때, Gregory Berns는 -을 발견했다.

  A 집단의 결정을 받아들이는 것은 뇌의 뒤쪽 부분의 활동을 만들어냈다
  B 참가자들은 애쉬의 실험에 이용되었던 사람들과 같았다
  C 생리학상의 설명은 이전의 연구원들에게 대체로 무시되었다
  D 뇌의 앞부분이 사람들의 순응하는 경향의 원인이다

> 해설 문제의 핵심어구인(experiment conducted by Gregory Berns)와 관련된 지문 내용 중 'But what Berns discovered was that when people follow a group's opinion, the posterior areas of the brain were stimulated'에서 번스가 발견한 것은 사람들이 집단의 의견을 따를 때 뇌의 뒤쪽 부분이 자극되었다는 것이었다고 하였으므로, 보기 **A** accepting group decisions created activity in the posterior regions of the brain이 정답이다. 'people follow a group's opinion'이 'accepting group decisions'로, 'the posterior areas of the brain were stimulated'가 'created activity in the posterior regions of the brain'으로 paraphrasing되었다.

39 글쓴이에 따르면, 밀그램의 실험은 -했기 때문에 획기적이었다.

  A 학습과 처벌 간의 관계를 조사했다
  B 권력을 받아들이는 것의 가능한 부정적인 결과를 강조했다
  C 의심하지 않는 참가자들에게 전기 충격을 처음으로 사용했다
  D 학생의 학습 전반에 있어 기억이 수행하는 역할에 대해 회의적이었다

> 해설 문제의 핵심어구(Milgram's experiments were innovative)와 관련된 지문 내용 중 'The Milgram experiments were groundbreaking in that they were the first extensive ones carried out that focused on extreme obedience to authority and its potentially destructive repercussions.'에서 밀그램의 실험은 권력에 대한 극단적인 복종과 그것의 잠재적으로 부정적인 영향에 초점을 맞춘 첫 번째 대규모 실험이라는 점에서 획기적이었다고 하였으므로, 보기 **B** they emphasised the possible negative consequences of accepting authority가 정답이다. 'potentially destructive repercussions'가 'possible negative consequences'로 paraphrasing되었다.

40 제3의 물결 실험을 수행한 교사는 학생들이 -했을 때 충격을 받았다.

  A 위반에 대한 처벌을 제안했을 때
  B 규율에 대해 강력히 반대했을 때
  C 그에게 저항하기 위해 단체를 조직했을 때
  D 규율을 따르지 않은 동급생들을 고발했을 때

> 해설 문제의 핵심어구(The teacher ~ was shocked)와 관련된 지문 내용 중 'he ~ suggested that members report others who were breaking rules. He was astounded when they willingly did so.'에서 그는 구성원들이 규율을 어기는 다른 사람들을 보고할 것을 제시했으며 그들이 기꺼이 그렇게 했을 때 큰 충격을 받았다고 하였으므로, 보기 **D** told on classmates who didn't follow the rules가 정답이다. 'report others who were breaking rules'가 'told on classmates who didn't follow the rules'로 paraphrasing되었다.